BEING AND GOD

BEING AND GOD

A Systematic Approach in
Confrontation with Martin
Heidegger, Emmanuel Levinas,
and Jean-Luc Marion

Lorenz B. Puntel

Translated by and in collaboration with Alan White

Northwestern University Press
Evanston, Illinois

Northwestern University Press
www.nupress.northwestern.edu

Originally published in German as *Sein und Gott: Ein systematischer Ansatz in Auseinandersetzung mit M. Heidegger, É. Lévinas und J.-L. Marion* by Mohr Siebeck, Tübingen, 2010.

Printed in the United States of America

10 9 8 7 6 5 4 3 2 1

ISBN 978-0-8101-2853-8

The Library of Congress has cataloged the original, hardcover edition as follows:

Puntel, Lorenz B. (Lorenz Bruno)
  [Sein und Gott. English]
  Being and God : a systematic approach in confrontation with Martin Heidegger, Emmanuel Levinas, and Jean-Luc Marion / Lorenz B. Puntel ; translated by and in collaboration with Alan White.
     p. cm.
  "Originally published in German as Sein und Gott: Ein systematischer Ansatz in Auseinandersetzung mit M. Heidegger, É. Lévinas und J.-L. Marion by Mohr Siebeck, Tubingen, 2010"—T.p. verso.
  Includes bibliographical references and index.
  ISBN 978-0-8101-2770-8 (cloth : alk. paper)
  1. Ontology. 2. God. 3. Heidegger, Martin, 1889–1976. 4. Levinas, Emmanuel. 5. Marion, Jean-Luc, 1946– I. White, Alan, 1951– II. Title.
  BD313.B8613 2011
  110—dc22

                                                          2011009133

⊗The paper used in this publication meets the minimum requirements of the American National Standard for Information Sciences—Permanence of Paper for Printed Library Materials, ANSI Z39.48-1992.

ἡ ψθχὴ τὰ ὄντα πώς ἐστι πάντα
Anima quodammodo omnia
The mind is in a certain way all things
—Aristotle, *De anima*

L'homme passe infiniment l'homme
Man infinitely transcends man
—Pascal, *Pensées*

Overview of Contents

Detailed Table of Contents

Preface

The writing of this book is the result of the timely coincidence of two factors. The first factor was an intention of mine further to expand the structural-systematic conception of philosophy, whose general theoretical framework I presented in *Structure and Being: A Theoretical Framework for a Systematic Philosophy* (2008; *Struktur und Sein*, 2006), to cover at least some additional, central topics. One of these topics is Being and God, which is the crown of that part of this philosophy that *Structure and Being* calls comprehensive systematics.

The second factor was my conviction that I could and should work to clarify the arena within which, at present, the so-called question of God is being discussed. How this question is currently being posed, considered, and answered can drive philosophers who think systematically nearly to despair. The question "Does God exist?" is in every respect so vague, so indeterminate, so unclear, and above all so ambiguous as to rule out the possibility of its having a direct, clear, and well-reasoned answer. Having given many lectures and participated in many discussions at more than a few universities in many countries over the past few years, I had concluded that the confused state of the discussion is due primarily, even if not exclusively, to a fundamental lack of clarity concerning what it is about (no matter how that may be designated) and therefore also concerning what can, should, or must be presupposed by and demanded of articulations of it.

This conclusion led me to envisage this book in its current form. That form was shaped more precisely by two additional convictions. The first, drawn from years of philosophical investigation and reflection, is that what the question of God asks about can be clearly identified only within the framework of a comprehensive conception of reality or—in more precise philosophical terms—of Being as such and as a whole. The second is drawn from intensive analyses of works of authors involved in the current discussions of the question of God, and of the approaches to the question taken by those authors. This second conviction is that the most radical resistance to clarification of the question of God comes not from the traditional opponents and critics of so-called metaphysics, but instead from authors classified as postmodernist.

To make this last conviction more precise but also more complicated—perhaps, one might say, to make matters worse—I must add that the postmodernist authors who most radically reject approaching the question of God via frameworks including conceptions of Being are ones who accept and insistently defend conceptions of God that are putatively Jewish or Christian.

As is well known, postmodernism flows from many historical sources, especially the works of authors such as Nietzsche, Heidegger, and Wittgenstein. With respect to the subject matter of this book and the position it defends, Heidegger is doubtless the most important of those sources because the postmodernists who classify themselves as Jewish or Christian rely decisively on him. This book shows that for the most part this reliance is only apparent, because these authors' interpretations of Heidegger are distortions.

I have discovered that in discussions with postmodernist authors, particularly concerning the subject matter of this book, as a rule nothing is said beyond general characterizations and obviously superficial remarks. Scarcely any interpreter or critic gets at the heart of postmodernist positions. It is my intention to do otherwise. I attempt to accomplish two tasks: first, I seek to reveal the initial and fundamental assumptions from which the often astonishing views of postmodernists grow; second, I determine how coherent those positions are. The results of my accomplishing these tasks are themselves astonishing.

It is impossible, in a single book, to accomplish these two tasks for the entire spectrum of postmodernist thinking. For this reason I decided to subject to extremely thorough critical analysis the approaches of two of the most important postmodernist thinkers—more precisely, the two postmodernist authors who are the most important critics and opponents of systematic approaches to the question of God such as the one undertaken in this book. These are—how could it be otherwise?—two French authors: Emmanuel Levinas, whose orientation is Jewish, and Jean-Luc Marion, whose orientation is Christian. Required both by the critiques of these authors and for adequate understanding of this book's systematic conception is a thoroughgoing interpretation and evaluation of Heidegger's thinking, so the book also includes a chapter devoted to it.

The explanations given above clarify the title and subtitle of this book. Additional clarification is provided by the "Introduction."

This book often relies on my systematic work *Structure and Being*, mentioned above, both in its interpretative-critical chapters (1, 2, and 4) and—especially—in its systematic chapter (3). This reliance is unavoidable because it would be impossible fully to provide complete systematic explanations of and arguments for both the systematic conception and the critiques presented in this book. As is well known, it is rarely the case that authors, in criticizing other positions, can rely on any already articulated comprehensive positions. Almost always there is no such comprehensive position, at least not in any publicly available form. Reliance on *Structure and Being* is thus an extraordinarily valuable asset both for the presentation of my own systematic position as it relates to the subject matter of this book and for my critiques of other positions.

In developing and presenting the conception defended in this book I have been supported by many colleagues and friends from many countries. I thank them all, although I can name only a few: Christina Schneider, Karl-Heinz Uthemann, Josef Schmidt (all from Germany), Philippe Capelle (Paris), and Manfredo A. de Oliveira and Emildo Stein (both from Brazil). I am uniquely grateful to Alan White (Williams College, United States), who scrupulously read various drafts of the book's individual chapters, making important suggestions concerning both content and linguistic presentation. At the same time, he began work on this English version.

Last but not least I would like to thank Dr. Georg Siebeck for his constant interest, his tireless engagement, and his fairness and generosity.

On Citations

To simplify the references and to attain the most optimal available readability, this book uses citations of two types. Works that are cited only rarely or occasionally are identified in footnotes via provision of the author's name, brief title, publication date, and page(s). Full details for such works are provided in the list of Works Cited. Passages from frequently cited works are identified not in footnotes but in the main text, via abbreviations of various sorts. The abbreviations are clarified in entries for relevant authors in the Works Cited; in entries for authors, works cited via abbreviation appear first, followed by other works, in alphabetical order. In citations, "t.a." abbreviates "translation altered."

Numbered footnotes are translated from *Sein und Gott;* footnotes designated by letters are exclusive to *Being and God.*

A Note on "Being" and "being"

German and Latin each have two substantives for which English has only one: for both the German *Sein* and the Latin *esse,* and for the German *Seiendes* and the Latin *ens,* English has only the gerund "being." Because the distinction between *Sein/esse* and *Seiendes/ens* is of absolutely central importance to this book, it uses "Being" to translate *Sein/esse* (and "Beyng" for *Seyn,* which Heidegger sometimes uses in place of *Sein*). This capitalization is merely a typographical device; it is utterly irrelevant to the book's consideration of philosophical issues concerning Being and God.

Problems arise with verbal forms including "to be," "is," "are," etc. A first problem is that just as running is what runners do (as runners), but running is not a runner and does not run, Being is what beings do (as beings), but Being is not a being and does not be. Hence, just as "Running runs" is incorrect, so too is "Being is," if the latter is interpreted as indicating either that Being is a being, or that Being is what Being does (see 2.1[1][i], below). Further clarification of this state of affairs requires closer consideration of "is."

As is widely known, "is" is used (as is "are") in the following three ways in ordinary English:

(1) to articulate identity, as in Frege's famous sentence, "A fact is [=] a thought that is true" and in the colloquial "Two plus two is four";

(2) as copula, connecting predicate to subject, as in "Socrates is a philosopher" (although following Frege, this "is" is generally assimilated into the predicate—for example, is-a-philosopher—and so ceases to be a self-standing component of the sentence);

(3) as indicating ontological status (presence or absence), as in "God is" or—in its most common colloquial appearances—following "there," as in "There is nothing to eat in this house, but there is a lot to drink."

Because of its flexibility in ordinary English, "is" can be used in formulations about being, but also in ones about Being. An example sufficiently intelligible at this point for the purposes of this note—but one that is clarified below, particularly by chapter 3—is the following: the sentence "Aristotle is human" can be interpreted as indicating what kind of being Aristotle is—he is a human being and not (say) a rock or a tiger—or as articulating Aristotle's mode of Being—his mode of Being is Being-human. Because there are such formulations, in this book "is," "are," etc., are generally not capitalized even in formulations that concern Being rather than being. The reason is that if they were, this would suggest that formulations wherein they were not capitalized would concern being rather than Being—and, as the just-introduced example shows, that is not always the case. Whether specific instances of "is," "are," etc., concern being or Being usually must be determined by consideration of their contexts.

Particular problems arise in chapter 4, with the treatments of works of Levinas and Marion, because in many of those works, it is at best difficult to determine whether "Being" or "being" would be the appropriate translation. To make the difficulty of these cases apparent, the unusual term "B/being" is used.

BEING AND GOD

Introduction

There is at present no question so often posed, so differently formulated, so radically misunderstood, and so often wholly inadequately answered as the so-called question of God. The overall goal of this book is to overcome the inadequacies, unclarities, and biases that currently befog this question, and to do so on the philosophical level. For that reason, this book is philosophical in the strict sense of being theoretical; it therefore provides nothing like instructions concerning how clearly understanding the question of God could or should lead anyone to change his or her life. Emphasizing this is important because consideration of the question of God has now reached the grotesque point at which the voices speaking for and against God are not only those of philosophical theoreticians, but also those of media figures of all sorts and indeed those of anonymous drafters of slogans that appear on public transportation vehicles.[1]

This book is not only philosophical, it is *systematically* philosophical. Its most important and most comprehensive thesis is the following: it is philosophically reasonable, intelligible, and appropriate to raise questions about "God," effectively to deal with those questions, and to provide answers to those questions that are rational in every respect only within the framework of a comprehensive conception of reality or—better—of Being as such and as a whole. This thesis is indicated, in a nutshell, by the title of this book: *Being and God*. Any conception of "God" that is not situated within an explicitly presented or implicitly presupposed theory of Being as such and as a whole—and hence, obviously, any such conception presented in conjunction with the rejection of such theories—can only be a conception of something or other, an X, that putatively does or does not "exist" beyond the world familiar to us and somehow separately from it, but that cannot ultimately be made either intelligible or reason-

---

[1] The "Atheist Bus Campaign" began in London in October 2008 when space on buses bore the slogan "There's probably no God. Now stop worrying and enjoy your life." There followed many similar campaigns in the major cities of many other countries.

able. Expressed in the terminology of a long tradition: such a "God," such a something-or-other, such an X could be nothing but an idol.

The specific goal of this book is not the development of a theory of God that would be in any way complete; it is instead the clarification of a philosophical framework within which such a theory could be developed. "God" is a term (and *God* a concept) from the realm of religion rather than from that of philosophy. It has (or ought to have or to retain) a strict connection to religion. For this reason, Heidegger's famous question, "How does God come into philosophy?" (*ID* 55; t.a.) is a good one, although it should be more precisely formulated, as follows: when, in what way, and under what presuppositions does God in the genuine sense (and that is the religious sense) become a subject matter for philosophy? This does not first happen when in one way or another something "primordial" is brought into view (traditionally, the something is a first principle, no matter how designated: a first cause, a first or highest being, etc.). In the conception presented in this book, this primordial something-or-other is first designated as absolutely necessary Being. "God" becomes a subject matter for the book only when philosophical explication of absolutely necessary Being reaches the point at which it reveals a connection to religion. At that point, however, it is not anything that is first or highest in any of the traditional senses.

It is indispensable to emphasize the precise sense of the briefly described specific goal of this book in order that the analyses and considerations presented in the book not be misunderstood from the beginning. This strictly limited goal is made more precise by the introduction of the two most important aspects of the *comprehensive* question of God.

The first aspect is contentual: the comprehensive question asks *all* the theoretical questions that can be raised about God. These extend from such expansive questions as that of what would have to be for there to be God, and whether—and if so, how—God's Being (or, to use the traditional term, existence) could be proved, to quite specific questions— often the only kinds of questions about God treated in analytic philosophy—like that of the compatibility of the affirmation of God with the undeniable existence of evil in the world. This immense and extremely manifold subject matter is not the subject matter of this book. It is devoted to only one question, the one that for philosophy is the absolutely first and most essential question within the extraordinarily complex domain of the comprehensive question of God. That is the question of *whether, and if so, how,* philosophical theorization can reach the point at which it is reasonable or perhaps requisite to introduce the word "God," which comes from the history of religions, into that theorization.

As briefly indicated above, this book answers its whether question with "yes" and its how question by showing how. It does so by developing the following central thesis: the asked-about point can be reached only within the framework of a comprehensive conception of actuality or, in the systematic terminology of this book, of Being as such and as a whole. "Within the framework" does not here articulate a restriction, nor does it require anything like (pre)conditions and above all nothing like any sort of pre-given space or horizon within which "God" would be nothing other than one item among others; if it did articulate or require anything of any of these sorts, it could appear to be vulnerable to the charges post-modernists repeatedly raise against what they call metaphysics. Quite to the contrary, "within this framework" indicates the dimension that, fully determined and fully explicated, is appropriately designated as God. God is the end point of the structural-systematic philosophy as a philosophical theory of everything, the fully unfolded conception of Being. This is nothing like the kind of superficial or abstract identification of "Being" and "God" that many postmodernist philosophers speak of. If it is appropriate at all to introduce "identifications"—and introducing them at all is highly problematic—then the resulting formulations might include the following: God is Being-in-the-complete-sense, or Being-in-its-entire-fullness.

The second aspect of the comprehensively understood question of God, as it is formulated and often treated at present, is practical and methodological. This means the following: the extraordinarily numerous ways of treating the question of God are oriented, most typically, around perspectives that concern the contentual questions about God (if at all) only secondarily; they are primarily (and often exclusively) guided by considerations and criteria that are drawn from concrete or practical factors. Among these are the following: apologetics, which seeks to convince people that they ought to accept or affirm "God"; consideration of the concrete situation of the people to whom the treatment of the question of God is directed; the questions people find interesting, people's attitudes toward questions about God, etc.; and the rhetorical-argumentative means, acquired through exchanges with everyday people, whose use is deemed likely to persuade them, etc.

This book wholly ignores all of these practical-methodic considerations, and thus the entire second aspect of current treatments of the question of God. It does not aim to convince anyone to embrace faith in God (or anything of the sort). It takes absolutely no consideration of factors of any sort that have to do with the so-called concrete situation of human beings. The book treats its subject matter strictly and exclusively on the purely philosophical-theoretical level. "Philosophical-theoretical" is, in the author's view, pleonastic. Pointing this out, however, is neither unreasonable nor redundant, because more than a few philosophers (and theologians) do not view philosophy (or theology) as a strictly theoretical endeavor. And although all of the questions included within the first aspect of the comprehensive question of God *can* be raised within this book's strictly philosophical-theoretical framework, most are *not* raised within this book itself.[2]

At this point it is appropriate to explain a peculiarity of this book: its *critical* aspect. It is of course not exclusively critical. Chapter 3 presents a *systematic-philosophical* treatment of the question of God, but only as an approach. Because the systematic philosophy within which this treatment is situated is presented in extensive detail in *Structure and Being,* sufficient for the purposes of this book is a brief account of those aspects of that systematic philosophy that are required by the treatment of the question of God. But with this systematic account alone, the book could not achieve the specific goal introduced above, because that requires it to subject to penetrating critical analysis the currently most important counterpositions to its own systematic conception.

The book presupposes—it does not argue—that the counterpositions most important at present come neither from the domain of the empirical sciences nor from the tradition of critiques of metaphysics starting (especially) with Kant, particularly logical empiricism or positivism, but instead, surprisingly, from Jewish and Christian authors. For far and away the most part, these authors engage in what is called postmodernist philosophy (and/or theology). Postmodernism, taken as a whole, would be difficult to characterize; it appears to be a hodgepodge of works whose most fundamental common feature is the radical and total rejection of "metaphysics." What is meant by "metaphysics," however, is so superficial and distorted that countering the rejections of all who are included within the hodgepodge appears to be unreasonable because it appears to be impossible.

For this reason, this book proceeds otherwise. Instead of globally considering all of postmodernism and all of the many authors who qualify as postmodernist, it subjects to penetrating and thorough critical analysis only the most important and most influential opponents of the central thesis of the book (introduced above). The author is convinced

---

[2] A work that treats nearly all aspects of the question of God and nearly all currently defended positions relating to that question is A. Kreiner's *Das wahre Antlitz Gottes—oder was wir meinen, wenn wir Gott sagen (The True Face of God—or What We Mean When We Say "God")* (2006). Kreiner's bibliography is comprehensive (it is 29 pages long). Revealingly, Kreiner does not consider the line of questioning pursued in this book (*Being and God*).

that at present and in the recent past, the two postmodernists who most radically oppose attempts to articulate a positive relation between philosophies (or thinkings) of Being and conceptions of God—in a word, any positive relation whatsoever between Being and God—are two French authors, the Jewish Emmanuel Levinas and the Christian Jean-Luc Marion. It is for this reason that chapter 4 of this book thoroughly examines and critically evaluates the works of these authors most centrally relevant to the issue of Being and God.

Postmodernism comes to be largely due to the influence of some of the major thinkers of the nineteenth and twentieth centuries, especially (although there are others) Hegel, Nietzsche, and Husserl. But the thinker who, with respect to the specific subject matter of this book, has exerted far and away the most decisive influence on Levinas and Marion is Martin Heidegger. Heidegger's significance, moreover, is in no way exhausted by the influence he has had and continues to have on postmodernism. All of chapter 2 is devoted to Heidegger. The reason for this is that Heidegger is an absolutely central figure as far as the subject matter and goal of this book are concerned. He is central for two reasons.

First, Heidegger is the philosopher who, more than any other, both retrieved from near oblivion and sought to reformulate the most central question of philosophy, the question of Being. Heidegger made this absolutely epochal contribution in the 1920s and 1930s. To be sure, Heidegger's later development followed paths that, philosophically, are not only problematic but are indeed unacceptable. His radical rejection of formal logic and of everything characteristic of clear and rigorous philosophizing is emphatically and uncompromisingly rejected by the author of this book. It remains the case, however, that his work on the question of Being provides extraordinarily important stimuli for rigorously philosophical work on this question. In addition, the publication of his complete works has made available posthumously published writings that are particularly relevant to the subject matter of this book. Subjecting to detailed and meticulous analysis his critique of metaphysics, his attempted "retrieval [*Wiederholung*]" of the question of Being (*BT* §1, 21ff.), and his wrestling with the problem of the relation between Being and God require the devotion to him of an entire chapter.

Second: as indicated above, Heidegger is the philosopher to whom especially postmodernists chiefly appeal in their radical rejections of metaphysics and of any and every conception of the entirety of actuality, of Being as such and as a whole. To be sure, their appeals to Heidegger are as a rule extraordinarily superficial ones. These authors come nowhere near to providing adequate interpretations of or appropriations from Heidegger. To the contrary, the Heidegger who is the major source of postmodern thinking is (so to speak) a Heidegger *à la française,* but this distorted Heidegger has come to have a significant influence on thinkers in other countries as well.

That the postmodernists rely on a distorted Heidegger—indeed, a caricature of Heidegger—is shown in this book chiefly in two ways. First, what the postmodernists appropriate from Heidegger is limited to a few aspects of his misinterpretation of Western metaphysics, and indeed usually on the basis of nothing more than a few catchphrases, especially the one according to which Western metaphysics is onto-theology. No doubt, superficial reading of a few of Heidegger's works could give rise to this practice, but Heidegger's thinking as a whole is far more complex and nuanced than any such reading could reveal. The postmodernists have, however, in their own way extended their one-sidedly and distortedly appropriated version of Heidegger's critique of metaphysics in so radical—and, again, so superficial—a manner to the entire philosophical-theological tradition of Western metaphysics that what they do can scarcely be traced to Heidegger. Second, the postmodernists' reception of Heidegger is strikingly naive and uncritical. This is particularly the case with the slogan introduced above, which has become something like a *dogma postmodernisticum antimetaphysicum.* Chapter 4 of this book contains revealing examples and thereby evidence of this utterly inadequate manner of proceeding.

The state of affairs just described led the author to thoroughly consider this entire problematic. This required subjecting Heidegger's thinking to an exhaustive analysis and evaluation. Because, however, the author's own systematic approach to the question of Being and God is likewise influenced by Heidegger—although in a manner wholly different from that in which the postmodernists are influenced by him—the treatment of Heidegger's thinking is best placed before the presentation of the author's systematic conception.

From the preceding considerations emerged the architectonic in accordance with which this book is divided—as indicated by its subtitle—into its four chapters. That the three authors named in the subtitle—Heidegger, Levinas, and Marion—appear in the book's architectonic where they do is explained by the ways in which they are relevant to the book's subject matter. Heidegger comes first, because although he does not develop an identifiable and positive conception of God, he does engage in a "thinking of Being" that is of central significance to this book's subject matter. The systematic approach sketched in chapter 3 is significantly inspired by Heidegger's thinking; that approach is also more intelligible when preceded by the treatment of Heidegger. Levinas and Marion, on the other hand, are authors who present idiosyncratic conceptions of God on the basis of absolutely radical rejections of any and every comprehensive conception of Being. The critical analyses of their thought are therefore most appropriately placed after the treatment of Heidegger and the presentation of the positive systematic approach.

This introduction must present and explain one additional factor. In order for the philosophical consequentiality of the central theses of this book to be accurately assessed, they should—the author concluded—be presented, explained, and defended in contrast to positions other than postmodernist ones. For this reason, chapter 1—which is in some ways introductory—treats a number of examples of *inadequate* approaches to the question of God, some direct and unsystematic, some indirect and partially systematic, and some anti-systematic. To be emphasized is that it treats *only* a few particularly striking *examples* of such positions. Presenting even a partial critical presentation of *all* positions currently taken on the question of God is a task far beyond the scope of this book. Also to be emphasized, however, is that the examples that are considered vary enormously from one another in terms both of substance and of historical influence. Among them, the thinking of Thomas Aquinas is of outstanding significance. For this reason, his thinking is not only subjected to thoroughgoing critical analysis in chapter 1, but also referred to again and again in the other chapters in the book.[a]

---

[a] As becomes clear especially in chapter 2, chapter 1's demonstration that Aquinas's metaphysics is *not* an onto-theo-logy is centrally important to the argument undermining Heidegger's thesis that *all* of Western metaphysics is onto-theo-logy.

Chapter 1

Inadequate Approaches to the Question of God

1.1 Initial Clarifications

As is well known, the question of God has been presented and addressed in a great many ways, these ways being based in specific modes of discourse. This book concerns only *philosophical* modes (more precisely: modes that consider themselves to be or designate themselves as philosophical). With respect to the task of attaining clarity concerning these forms, a classification of them is highly desirable. But it is not clear that a classification is possible. On first consideration, it appears to be scarcely possible. The situation changes, however, if specific criteria for a classification are explicitly identified. Such criteria determine the classification in that they appear as some among various possible ones.

The criterion used here is the one most appropriate given the central thesis of this book, formulated in the "Introduction," according to which to ask *adequately* about God, to treat the questions that then arise *effectively* and to *answer* them in ways that are *rational* in every respect requires that the questioning proceed within the framework of a comprehensive philosophical conception concerning reality or Being as such and as a whole. Different approaches to the question concerning God can be classified in accordance with how they relate to this central thesis. It turns out that they relate to it in an enormous variety of ways, so even the classification that attends strictly to this criterion remains incomplete. It is, however, sufficient for the purposes of this book.

The approaches presented and criticized in this first chapter are *inadequate* in at least one (and in some cases in both) of the following two respects. The first is their total or partial failure to clarify or to explain the immense spectrum of presuppositions on which direct talk about God is based. The second respect is wholly different, because contentual: these approaches (or at least most of them) start from some individual, isolated aspect of or phenomenon in the world (somehow understood), for example, from a specific concept or phenomenon (such as motion or causality).

Approaches exhibiting the first inadequacy are philosophically secondary or dependent, and because what they are secondary to or dependent on remains unclear and unexplained, their philosophical status remains undetermined. Those suffering from the second inadequacy can yield only one-sided concepts of God, ones that are wholly inadequate to the idea of the divine because they allow God to appear only as a function of some *single* aspect of the world, not as the dimension that encompasses the world as a whole. No such "God" can ultimately be thought of legitimately or even coherently.

This chapter treats only a few inadequate approaches; they serve only as examples of such approaches.

Because the terms/concepts *unsystematic, anti-systematic, semi-systematic, direct,* and *indirect* are used in what follows to distinguish among inadequate approaches to the question of God, these terms/concepts require explanation at this point. The explanations are of them *only* as they are used in this book. *Unsystematic* approaches are ones that do not explicitly articulate the essential philosophical contexts within which their sentences, their theories, their subject matters, indeed every one of their theoretical elements and thus all of their talk of God, is unavoidably situated. *Anti-systematic* approaches are strictly distinct from *unsystematic* ones. *Anti-systematic* approaches are ones that explicitly deny the reasonability and indeed the possibility—and so, of course, the unavoidability—of making explicit the essential contexts, presuppositions, and implications of philosophical articulation. *Semi-systematic* approaches are those that articulate their contexts, presuppositions, and implications only in part and insufficiently.

Direct approaches to the question of God are ones that introduce no preliminary or intermediate stages that must be passed through before the term/concept *God* is introduced as intelligible. *God* is accepted from the outset as having a sense that, in one way or another, can simply be presupposed, in some cases on the basis of the putative familiarity of that sense. To put the point loosely: direct approaches to the question of God presuppose that those who take them know from the outset what they are talking about. There are many varieties of direct approaches, of highly divergent types. Most of them rely on some pre-understanding of the Christian God. Of particular importance is that none of them relies or recognizes—at least not explicitly—the distinction, central to this book, between absolutely necessary Being on the one hand and God on the other.

Indirect approaches are characterized by two factors. First, their talk of God is introduced and clarified by preliminary theoretical explanations and lines of argumentation; second, the results of these lines of argumentation—concretely, what enters in conclusions of so-called proofs of God's existence—is, even if first accurately characterized, then immediately designated as God. The best-known case of an indirect approach is that of the Christian metaphysical tradition, especially Thomas Aquinas's so-called proofs of God's existence (his five "ways," "*viae*"). For example, his first way (*prima via*)—his first proof—concludes that there is a first mover, but Aquinas immediately adds, "And all understand this as God."[1]

The preceding clarifications have a number of consequences. One is that fully unsystematic approaches can only be direct approaches. A second is that semi-systematic and indirect approaches can have various forms. It is generally the case, however, that semi-systematic approaches are also indirect. This book pays particular attention to the semi-systematic, indirect approach taken by Thomas Aquinas; it is considered below in section 1.3.2.

The approach defended in this book, presented below in chapter 3, is a *purely systematic* one in a strict sense. It can be qualified neither as direct nor as indirect. What prevents such qualification is the central thesis that constitutes what is original about this conception. At this point, it suffices briefly to characterize it negatively and then positively. Negatively, it takes questions like the so often posed and in the widest variety of ways answered question about the so-called existence of God to be senseless, precisely because of the wholly unexplained and unreasonable presuppositions on which they depend. In addition, semi-systematic, indirect approaches use arguments to introduce some phenomenon or other or some concept or some state of affairs in order to move from it to God. These procedures, too, are radically rejected by this book, because the "God" any one of them reaches is a quite restricted "God," in that that "God" is determined only in relation to some specific segment or aspect of the universe, not in relation to the entire universe or, better, to Being as such and as a whole.

Positively, this book's systematic approach can be characterized at this point as follows: it introduces God only by way of a comprehensive explication of the primordial, universal dimension of Being. At this point, to be sure, this formulation is at best scarcely intelligible. It is, however, thoroughly explained and presented in chapter 3. Here, it serves only as a preliminary and programmatic clarification of the book's strictly systematic approach to the question of God.

---

[1] "Et hoc omnes intelligunt Deum" (*STh* I q. 2 a. 3 c.).

1.2 Wholly Unsystematic Direct Approaches

1.2.1 Pascal's Wager

Pascal's wager is a characteristic example of a wholly unsystematic direct approach. This famous "argument" need not be thoroughly presented here, much less critically assessed. Its introduction serves only to show how wholly inadequate the approach is when considered systematically. This does not mean that there cannot or could not be people who find Pascal's line of thought persuasive. "Considered systematically" means here, as throughout this book, "considered in light of all the criteria and requirements that must be satisfied if the most complete intelligibility attainable by human beings is to be achieved."

The purposes of this section are best served by reliance on Pascal's own words, accompanied by some clarificatory remarks.[2]

Pascal accepts "that there is nothing to prevent our knowing the existence of a thing, without knowing its essence." On this basis he immediately asserts, "We know the existence of the infinite, but not its essence. . . . We know neither the existence nor the essence of God."[3] And then comes the decisive passage:

> Let us then examine this point, and say, "God is, or He is not." But to which side shall we incline? Reason can decide nothing here. There is an infinite chaos which separates us. A game is being played at the extremity of this infinite distance where heads or tails will turn up. What will you wager?[4]

> You have two things to lose, the true and the highest good; and two things to stake, your reason and your will, your knowledge and your happiness; and your nature has two things to shun, error and misery. . . . Let us weigh the gain and the loss in wagering that God is. Let us estimate these two chances. If you gain, you gain all; if you lose, you lose nothing. Wager, then, without hesitation that He is.[5]

---

[2] Blaise Pascal, *Pensées: The Provincial Letters* (New York: Random House, 1941), 80. All Pascal quotations are from *Pensées* 233.

[3] Ibid.

[4] Ibid., 81.

[5] Ibid.

Neither the specifics of Pascal's position nor his lengthy explanations need be considered here. The task instead is to ask how this approach to the question of God is to be assessed. No matter how it is to be judged from the perspective of probability- or decision-theory, considered from that of systematic philosophy it is fully inadequate. What is meant here by "God"? The comprehensive context of Pascal's works makes clear that the talk is of the *Christian* God, and indeed of the specific understanding of that God that is formulated in his famous *Mémorial*, as shown below (see 1.3.2.1[2]).

The fatal weakness of this approach is its absolute and total lack of intelligibility. The "God" of the wager is a peculiar factor concerning which the thinking human being has an extensive series of fundamental questions. Assuming that the wager is accepted in the positive sense and that a wager is made, how intelligible would be the assumption that the God in question exists? Even what that would mean remains wholly unclear. All of the presuppositions and all of the implications remain fully in the dark.

1.2.2 Hans Küng's Approach Based on "Fundamental Trust"

The Catholic theologian and philosopher Hans Küng has developed his own approach to the question of God, one that attains its orientation and inspiration from the attempt to take directly and completely into consideration as many as possible of the aspects of this question that relate to human life.[6] His conception arises from consideration of the concrete existential situation of human beings with respect to the question of God in light of the histories of the philosophical, theological, literary, and scientific treatments of the question. He ignores virtually no aspect of this complex state of affairs. The result is the presentation of a conception that exhibits, in a specific respect, a significant similarity to Pascal's direct access to God. The decisive difference is that Küng presents his conception within the context of monumental scholarship in various domains, particularly those of the histories of philosophy and theology. What results is, however, extremely simple and thin: it is a specific form of a direct and wholly unsystematic approach to the question of God.

The decisive question for Küng is the following: What would be different if God existed (*DGE* 562ff.), or what would be, if God existed (567)? With effusive rhetoric, Küng provides a thorough answer by means of such assertions as the following: "*If* God exists, then a fundamental

---

[6] Hans Küng, *Does God Exist? An Answer for Today* (1980).

solution of the riddle of persistently uncertain reality is indicated, in the sense that a fundamental answer . . . will have been found to the question of the wherefrom of reality" (566; t.a.), and "*If* God exists, then an answer *has* been found at least in principle to the riddle of my persistently uncertain human existence" (567). Küng's goal is to replace the conditional "*if* God exists" with the affirmative "God exists." He attempts to do this by taking into consideration both the phenomenon of atheism and the entire biblical background of the tradition of Judeo-Christian thinking, paying particular attention to Protestant theology. Thus, he maintains (568), "*It is possible to deny God. Atheism cannot be eliminated rationally. It is irrefutable*"—but also, at the same time, "*Affirmation of God is also possible. Atheism cannot be rationally established. It is undemonstrable*" (569).

Küng's magical incantation is the following: "God—a matter of trust." He presents this as "the knot which is decisive for the solution of the question of the existence of God," a solution that he has "prepared in extensive discussions on the natural theology of Vatican I, on the dialectical theology of Barth and Bultmann and Kant's theology of moral postulates." He summarizes as follows (569–70; t.a.):

- *If God is, he is the answer to the radical uncertainty of reality.*
- *The fact that God is, can be assumed:*
  not strictly by virtue of a proof or indication of pure reason (natural theology),
  not unconditionally by virtue of a moral postulate of practical reason (Kant),
  not exclusively by virtue of the biblical testimony (dialectical theology),
  but only in a confidence *rooted in reality itself.*

Küng terms the assumption that God exists (570) "belief in God" or "faith in God," characterizing the latter as a "trusting commitment to an ultimate ground, support and meaning of reality." His more precise explication of this "trusting commitment" or "fundamental trust" consists only of extensive literarily and apologetically brilliant assertions, in particular the following: "*Denial of God implies an* ultimately unjustified *fundamental trust in reality*" (571). Conversely, according to Küng, "*affirmation of God implies an* ultimately justified *fundamental trust in reality*" (572). The justifiedness of faith in God, according to Küng, "is not an outward rationality, *which could produce an assured security*" (574); it is instead "an inward rationality, *which can offer a fundamental certainty. In this accomplishment, by the 'practice' of boldly trusting in God's reality, man experiences the reasonableness of the trust*" (574). Again, Küng summarizes (574–75):

> *Like fundamental trust, belief in God, too, is*
> - *a matter not only of human reason but of the whole concrete, living man . . .*
> - *therefore superrational . . .*

- *but not irrational . . .*
- *not, then, a blind decision, devoid of reality, but one that is grounded in and related to reality and rationally justified in concrete life . . .*
- *realized in a concrete relationship with our fellow men . . .*
- *not grasped once and for all, but constantly to be freshly realized.*

As the preceding passage makes clear, Küng's approach is typically direct and wholly unsystematic, with an emphatically strong apologetic and indeed confessional character. Because the approach aims to persuade, it appeals to all the factors that can bring readers to agree. This approach may therefore be interesting and even appropriate for apologetic purposes, but philosophically it is wholly inadequate, as shown particularly by the introduction of two brief points.

First, from the beginning the talk is of "God" in a wholly undetermined and undifferentiated manner. One must constantly ask just what is meant by the question, "Does *God* exist?" Only after Küng has justified belief in the existence of God in the manner described above does he begin to explain what "God" is. As a theoretical procedure, this is unintelligible and unacceptable. Even later, it becomes clear that Küng's concern throughout is with the *Christian* God. Given this, however, Küng should have shown at the beginning that what he terms "fundamental trust in reality," which forms the basis of his argumentation, is grounded in God *as so understood*. This Küng does not do. The entire course of "argumentation" is ultimately a kind of sermon.

Second, Küng's approach is wholly *unsystematic* in the sense explained above. What that means here, specifically, is that *none* of the central concepts that arise in his exposition is at all clarified, including, most importantly, *faith, belief, fundamental trust,* and *reality*. "God" appears here as a peculiar X that is "determined" solely by means of wholly vague and undetermined concepts. Particularly here, it becomes clear that an adequate approach to the question of God is possible only within the framework of a clear and developed conception or theory of the entirety of Being (of actuality).

1.2.3 Alvin Plantinga: Direct and Immediately Warranted Belief in God as *Sensus Divinitatis*

Another example of a direct and in a certain respect unsystematic approach to the question of God is that of Alvin Plantinga. The approach is unsystematic with respect to ontology or metaphysics, and thus with respect to what is of decisive importance for this book. The approach is unsystematic only in a certain respect because Plantinga thoroughly anchors his approach *in a purely epistemic respect* within a systematic framework. The specific character of this approach lies precisely in the fact that it is on the one hand extremely direct, indeed simple, without in the slightest thematizing any perspective that is not purely epistemic.

Plantinga presents an ambitious epistemology in two volumes; it presumably is the most ambitious and complete treatment of this discipline currently available.[7] A third volume, titled *Warranted Christian Belief* (= *WCB*),[8] builds on the general epistemological work and presents what may be termed a systematic epistemology of Christian belief.

[1] In opposition to all internalist conceptions in epistemology, Plantinga defends a decidedly pure externalist conception of justification. The central thesis of justificational *internalism* is the following: justification is a duty of the rationally proceeding subject; it consists in the requirement that the subject be justified in affirming any sentence or conviction, whereby justifications are characterized as factors that either are or can be explicitly available to the subject. Justificational *externalism* rejects this so-understood connection of factors identified as justifications with explicit availability to the subject; it understands justification instead as purely objective in the sense that a conviction, a sentence, etc., is justified when objective factors are available, such that the objectivity holds even if the subject is unaware of these factors.

In order to make this radical distinction terminologically recognizable, Plantinga—in opposition to other analytic epistemologists—uses the term "justification" in a purely internalist sense and introduces the otherwise unusual term "warrant" to designate his version of a purely externalist position.[a]

[2] Plantinga develops an extensive and quite complicated theory of warrant. Generally considered, warrant is the factor that characterizes the distinction between true belief and knowledge. Differently stated: warrant is the factor that must be present if a true belief is to attain the status of knowledge. But how is this factor to be determined? Plantinga develops a conception that sharply diverges from what is currently mainstream epistemology, one that he traces to Aristotle and Thomas Aquinas. He presents its central thought as follows:

> [A] belief has warrant just if it is produced by cognitive processes or faculties that are functioning properly, in a cognitive environment

---

[7] Alvin Plantinga, *Warrant: The Current Debate* (1993); *Warrant and Proper Function* (1993).

[8] Oxford University Press (2000).

[a] Three sentences in *Sein und Gott* concerning German translations for Plantinga's terms are not translated here.

that is propitious for that exercise of cognitive powers, according to a design plan that is successfully aimed at the production of true belief. (*WCB* xi)

The central concept is thus *proper functioning* of the cognitive powers. This concept is both traditional and difficult to determine. With great acuity, Plantinga exerts immense efforts to clarify all aspects of this concept. The intensive discussion of his position shows that the concept is burdened with many problems, although this cannot be considered here. What is important here is characterizing Plantinga's position with respect to the question of God on the basis of his epistemological presuppositions.

[3] According to Plantinga, Christian belief can make the claim to have warrant, as is indicated by the title of the extensive third volume of his trilogy: *Warranted Christian Belief*. According to Plantinga, the attempt to show that this is so can be understood in two wholly different ways. First, such an attempt is "an exercise in apologetics and philosophy of religion, an attempt to demonstrate the failure of a range of objections to Christian belief"; second, the attempt is "an exercise in Christian philosophy [consisting] in the effort to consider and answer philosophical questions—the sort of questions philosophers ask and answer—from a Christian perspective" (*WCB* xiii). But this distinction is clear only on the abstract level. In the case of the first way it is in principle clear what it means to engage in "an exercise in . . . philosophy of religion," but introducing the philosophy of religion in conjunction with apologetics (clearly to be understood as apologetics of Christian belief) makes immediately clear how ambiguous such an exercise is. In addition, one must ask how (i.e., in accordance with what method) this "exercise in apologetics and philosophy of religion" is to proceed: from one or another Christian perspective or from a somehow neutral (hence purely philosophical) perspective?

As shown in what follows, Plantinga's position—despite its in-part magnificent insights and achievements—is not fundamentally free from ambiguities. Indeed, Plantinga simultaneously puts to work the two perspectives he purports to hold apart, i.e., the external or neutral and the immanently Christian. What is unclear is how this simultaneity or conjunction is to be understood and defended; on this issue, a hole gapes in Plantinga's otherwise admirable undertaking.

According to Plantinga, "classical Christian belief" has two components. The first, which he terms the theistic, he describes as well known from classical Christian metaphysics. The second component is the specifically Christian one, available from the tradition of Christian theology. With respect to so-understood Christian belief he distinguishes between

two fundamentally different categories of questions: de jure questions and de facto questions. De jure questions are epistemic questions, questions about whether Christian belief is rational, warranted, etc.; de facto questions concern the truth of Christian belief.

One of the central theses of his book is the following: there is no sensible or ultimately tenable de jure objection against Christian belief that would be independent of a corresponding de facto objection. On its basis he concludes: "And so the dispute as to whether theistic belief is rational (warranted) can't be settled just by attending to epistemological considerations; it is at bottom not merely an epistemological dispute, but an ontological or theological dispute" (*WCB* 190). The first point to be raised here is that it is not clear whether the "or" at the end of this sentence is to be read inclusively or exclusively. The unclarity stems from the facts that Plantinga rarely speaks of ontology, and that the few passages in which he does do not make clear just how he understands it. Despite this unclarity, however, Plantinga does, in the passage just quoted, make the point that is decisive for his approach. The consequences of this point are shown below.

[4] Plantinga presents a "model" that he terms the Aquinas/Calvin (A/C) model.[9] In doing so, he appeals to central assertions from Calvin,

---

[9] Plantinga links his model more strongly to Calvin than to Aquinas, and just how he connects it to Aquinas is far from clear. He relies particularly on the following text from *Summa contra Gentiles*, book 3, chapter 38 (which [on p. 176] he mistakenly identifies as *Summa Theologiae* I, q. 2 a. 1 ad 1):

There is a certain general and confused knowledge of God, which is in almost all men, whether from the fact that, as some think, the existence of God, like other principles of demonstration, is self-evident, as we have stated in the First Book, or, as seems nearer the truth, because by his natural reason, man is able at once to arrive at some knowledge of God. For seeing that natural things are arranged in a certain order—since there cannot be order without a cause of order—men, for the most part, perceive that there is one who arranges in order the things that we see. *But who or of what kind this cause of order may be, or whether there be but one, cannot be gathered from this general consideration: even so, when we see a man in motion, and performing other works, we perceive that in him there is a cause of these operations, which is not in other things, and we give this cause the name of* soul, *but without knowing yet what the soul is, whether it be a body, or how it brings about the operations in question.* (emphasis added)

[Est . . . quaedam communis et confusa Dei cognitio, quae quasi omnibus hominibus adest: sive hoc sit per hoc quod Deum esse sit per se notum, sicut alia demonstrationis principia, sicut quibusdam videtur . . . ; sive, quod magis verum videtur, quia naturali ratione statim homo in aliquam Dei cognitionem pervenire potest. Videntes enim homines res naturales secundum ordinem certum currere; cum ordinatio absque ordinatore non sit, percipiunt, ut in pluribus, aliquem esse ordinatoren rerum quas videmus. Quis autem, vel qualis, vel si unus tantum est ordinator naturae, nondum statim ex hac communi consideratione habetur: sicut, cum videmus hominem moveri et alia opera

especially those expressing Calvin's notion of the *sensus divinitatis,* which Plantinga interprets as follows: "The basic idea, I think, is that there is a kind of faculty or a cognitive mechanism, what Calvin calls a *sensus divinitatis* or sense of divinity, which in a wide variety of circumstances produces in us beliefs about God" (*WCB* 172). The biblical background for such a conception is, as is widely known, the following passage from Paul's *Epistle to the Romans:*

---

agere, percimus ei inesse quandam causam harum operationum quae aliis rebus non inest, et hanc causam animam nominamus; nondum utem scientes quid sit anima, si est corpus, vel qualiter operationes predictas efficiat.]

Plantinga's interpretation of this text is cautious, but nonetheless in part not wholly correct. Above all, he misses what is to Aquinas the central point. Plantinga fails to cite the passages italicized in the selection quoted above; instead, he proceeds immediately to comment on additional passages from Aquinas—ones not contained in the selection quoted above—about errors, including ones indicating that some have believed that there is no orderer except in the heavenly bodies. Plantinga then writes:

Perhaps we can understand Aquinas as follows. Consider the description *that which orders what we see.* This description in fact applies to God. One who believes that it does indeed apply to something or other can therefore have *de re* knowledge of God; for example, she can believe of *that which orders what we see* that it has one or another properties—that it exists, is powerful, and indeed orders what we see. This would be to believe *de re* of God that he exists, is powerful, and indeed orders what we see. But this knowledge also "admits of many errors": for example, the naturalist thinks that what orders what we see is, in fact, the ensemble of natural laws; she therefore believes *de re* of God that he is the ensemble of natural laws. (*WCB* 177)

Here, Plantinga commits a significant error in applying (the description) "the x that orders the things that we see" to God. How does "God" enter this account? What sense does it make to introduce "God" here? There is no way to know what "God" could mean here. For this reason, the use of the word "God" here is completely empty; it has no semantic content.

Plantinga's error is more problematic than is the error that can be found within the framework of Aquinas's "five ways," when he says of each of the conclusions of the five demonstrations, "And that (namely, the first mover, the first cause, etc.) all term *God.*" Aquinas's is a significant *methodological error,* as shown below (1.3.2.1[2]). Nevertheless, Aquinas's error is less serious than is Plantinga's, for two reasons. First, Aquinas terms "God" only such factors (the conclusions of the demonstrations) as can be brought into connection with the (Christian) concept *God,* whereas Plantinga uses this term (in conjunction with a *de re* belief) even for the totality of the laws of nature. Second, Plantinga fails to note that the passage from Aquinas cited above articulates a clear awareness of the just-described problem concerning the introduction of the term "God." As noted above, it is significant that Plantinga fails to cite precisely this passage, according to which "*who or of what kind this cause of order may be, or whether there be but one, cannot be gathered from this general consideration.*" This means that Aquinas views and conceives of this cause of order as absolutely *open:* it is above all an *explicandum* or *determinandum.* In this passage Aquinas is scrupulous in that he avoids designating the orderer arrived at in the described fashion as "God." Chapter 3 of this book provides systematic clarification for this state of affairs.

> The wrath of God is being revealed from heaven against all the godless-
> ness and wickedness of men who suppress the truth by their wickedness,
> since what may be known about God is plain to them, because God has
> made it plain to them. For since the creation of the world God's invis-
> ible qualities—his eternal power and divine nature—have been clearly
> seen, being understood from what has been made.[10]

Plantinga interprets this in just Calvin's sense. The natural understanding of God articulated in this passage is, according to Plantinga, not the
result of a deduction or of any kind of argument; instead, it is immediate. To be sure, this natural knowledge may be occasioned by the observation of nature, but it is not the conclusion of a proof or an argument.
Plantinga ascribes to this immediate knowledge of God the status of a
basic knowledge, one that is not dependent on any premises, no matter
how understood.

Plantinga explains further that *classical epistemological foundationalism* assumes "basic beliefs," such as those occasioned by memory, perception, experience, and so forth. This foundationalism does not, however,
include belief in God among such beliefs; to the contrary, it demands
that the assertion that God exists be "proved," i.e., that it be the conclusion of a sound argument. Plantinga directly opposes this last thesis of
epistemological foundationalism. The general schema of his argumentation can be briefly summarized as follows: it would be nonsensical to
say that certain beliefs that are immediately occasioned by perception,
experience, etc., are unjustified only because they are immediate, i.e.,
not proved—because they do not appear as conclusions of arguments.
According to Plantinga, it is equally nonsensical to maintain that belief
in God is unjustified or irrational unless it is affirmed on the basis of a
proof, thus as the conclusion of an argument. Belief in God is indeed immediate, and thus has a status analogous to that of the beliefs occasioned
by perception, experience, etc.

Plantinga goes significantly further than many conceptions that affirm immediate belief in God in that he adds an essential thesis, i.e., that
this belief can be warranted. He writes:

> It isn't just that the believer in God is within her epistemic rights in
> accepting theistic belief in the basic way. That is indeed so; more than
> that, however, this belief can have warrant for the person in question,
> warrant that is often sufficient for knowledge. The *sensus divinitatis* is a
> belief-producing faculty (or power, or mechanism) that under the right

---

[10] Romans 1:18–20, New International Version.

conditions produces belief that isn't evidentially based on other beliefs. On this model, our cognitive faculties have been designed and created by God; the design plan, therefore, is a design plan in the literal and paradigmatic sense. It is a blueprint or plan for our ways of functioning, and it has been developed and instituted by a conscious, intelligent agent. The purpose of the *sensus divinitatis* is to enable us to have true beliefs about God; when it functions properly, it ordinarily *does* produce true beliefs about God. These beliefs therefore meet the conditions for warrant; if the beliefs produced are strong enough, then they constitute knowledge. (179)

Plantinga emphasizes that it does not follow from this conception that theistic belief could not be warranted or justified or grounded in any other way, including through proofs or arguments that are based on other items of knowledge (premises). It also does not follow that natural or philosophical theology or some other kind of argumentative procedure is of no worth for the intellectual and spiritual life of the believer (*WCB* 179n16). But Plantinga also emphasizes—following the making of an opaque theoretical leap—that (original) sin can damage the *sensus divinitatis* and in fact in cases has damaged it.

[5] The preceding account concerns only what Plantinga identifies as the first component of Christian belief, the theistic one. It is now appropriate briefly to consider Plantinga's methodic procedure with respect to the second component, the component of Christian belief in the genuine sense. In a fundamental respect Plantinga proceeds here wholly along the lines of traditional (both Catholic and Protestant) theology. He names his specific version of this procedure "the expanded Aquinas/Calvin (A/C) model." This model contains nothing other than what are considered by the Christian churches to be the most important truths about the Trinitarian God, Jesus Christ, sin, redemption, etc.

To be noted at once is that Plantinga thinks fundamentally within the framework of the Calvinistic theological tradition, and also that he often speaks a language resembling that of the Bible or of catechisms. From the perspective of the European—and especially of the German-speaking—tradition of both Catholic and Protestant theology, much that Plantinga says is far too simple. Also to be noted is that Plantinga's project is an epistemological one (in his sense!), although he also emphasizes that all his epistemological questions have ontological or theological presuppositions (see above).

It is extremely significant that Plantinga's explanations correspond fully to a traditional conception represented in Catholic theology: that we have access to revealed truths not through the natural light of reason, but only through a supernatural light given only to the faithful. At the same

time, what is peculiar to Plantinga's conception—only sketched here—
lies in his thesis that Christian belief, so understood—thus including the
just-presented second component, the genuinely Christian one, thus
also including Christian faith—must count as justified, rational, and warranted. But how so? Plantinga's central thesis is problematic at best. What
he terms "justification" concerns the internal perspective of a subject, the
duty to legitimate maintained theses and felt convictions. If justification
is understood in this way, then it is wholly comprehensible that Christian
faith can be justified. The same holds for rationality in the internal sense
(thus, concerning the perspective of a subject). But how do matters stand
with external (objective) rationality and with warrant (i.e., external or
objective grounding or justification)? Warrant is decisive here because, if
it is present, external/objective rationality follows easily from it.

Plantinga maintains that Christian belief can also qualify as warranted. He summarily explains how he understands this in the following
passage (*WCB* 245–46):

> How can it [the extended Aquinas/Calvin model] be a model for a
> way in which Christian belief has or could have justification, rationality,
> warrant? The answer is simplicity itself. These beliefs do not come to
> the Christian just by way of memory, perception, reason, testimony, the
> *sensus divinitatis,* or any other cognitive faculties with which we human
> beings were originally created; they come instead by way of the work of
> the Holy Spirit, who gets us to accept, causes us to believe, these great
> truths of the gospel. These beliefs don't come just by way of the normal
> operation of our natural faculties; they are a supernatural gift. Still, the
> Christian who has received this gift of faith will of course be *justified*
> (in the basic sense of the term) in believing as he does; there will be
> nothing contrary to epistemic or other duty in so believing.

In conclusion, Plantinga shows how on this basis both internal and
external rationality can be given. What he finally says with respect to warrant is the following: "Finally, on the model, these beliefs will also have
warrant for believers: they will be produced in them by a belief-producing
process." To be sure, this is an utterly unique process that is completely
distinct from all "natural" processes, precisely because this "involves a
special, supernatural activity on the part of the Holy Spirit," but this in
no way means that the effects of this divine act "cannot enjoy warrant,
and warrant sufficient for knowledge" (*WCB* 246n10).

[6] Here, many critical questions press. In this subsection, only a
few are briefly formulated and clarified.

[i] What, ultimately, can the assumption of the proper functional-

ity of our cognitive faculties give us? Many fundamental problems arise here. One of the problems emerges from the fact that our cognitive faculties can operate dysfunctionally. Otherwise, every search for knowledge and thus for truth would have to succeed. That not every search does need not be demonstrated. Plantinga takes this fact into consideration in two ways. First, he says again and again that under appropriate conditions our cognitive faculties often or usually function properly, although he does not explain why this is the case. Second, however—and this is his real response to the problem—he takes recourse to the Christian doctrine of (original) sin: sin is what has brought disorder, dysfunctionality, and pathology into our cognitive faculties. But even if one basically accepts this doctrine, it is far too vague and indeterminate to be concretely helpful with respect to the epistemological problem. How can one ascertain that, in a specific, concrete case, there is no dysfunctionality in our cognitive faculties? Adequate functionality can serve at best as a wholly general, abstract, and indeterminate criterion either for justification or for warrant.

[ii] The epistemology defended in Plantinga's trilogy appears to contain an enormous circularity. Proper function is considered to be warrant. Plantinga develops an extensive—and ambitious—theory of proper function. But is this theory itself warranted? If so, then the account is viciously circular. If not, however, then it is not warranted. Can Plantinga avoid this dilemma? His trilogy contains no clear and compelling answer to this question.

Plantinga himself raises the question of circularity and attempts to answer it (*WCB* 351):

> Isn't it true that my own proposal has warrant for me (or anyone who accepts it) only if theistic belief is in fact true and, indeed, warranted? I propose the extended A/C model as a model for the way in which Christian and theistic belief can have warrant, but won't it be the case that I am warranted in proposing this model only if, in fact, the model or something like it is correct, and Christian belief does have warrant?

Plantinga's answer is "no." He explains this "no" by making his model more precise in three ways: "What I claim for the model is only that it is (1) possible, (2) subject to no philosophical objections that do not assume that Christian belief is false, and (3) such that if Christian belief is true, the model is at least close to the truth." He then adds: "But obviously it is not the case that my assertion of or belief in the truth of (1), (2), or (3) has warrant only if the model is true or Christian belief is warranted."

Plantinga himself notes that this answer or explanation does not provide complete clarity. He therefore poses the question (*WCB* 351–52): "Now suppose I proposed the model as indeed the truth (or close to the truth) about the way Christian belief has warrant: *then,* would my proposal be in some way circular?" He asks, "Well, why should we think so?" and then attempts to explain and to clarify the fundamental idea. One must attend carefully to what he says (352):

> Because central Christian beliefs are included in or entailed by the model, I am warranted in thinking the model true only if I am warranted in accepting Christian belief; those central Christian beliefs must already have warrant, for me, if my belief that the model is true is to have warrant. But then am I not involved in some kind of objectionable circle?

Plantinga's answer to his question is laconic: "I can't see how." This answer is so simple—which is *not* to say that it is satisfactory—as to raise questions concerning whether his extremely long and complicated treatment of this issue is requisite. Plantinga simply concedes that it is true that having Christian beliefs is a constituent of the extended A/C model; this has as a consequence that one's having warrant for one's Christian beliefs is presupposed by one's having warrant for one's acceptance of the extended A/C model. Surprisingly, Plantinga simply rejects this obvious line of argument, saying, "It is not the case, however, that if Christian belief has warrant for me, then the model must also have warrant for me." And he explains: "That would be true if I *argued* for Christian belief by way of an argument one premise of which was the extended A/C model." Had he done that, he would have relied on a *circulus vitiosus.* The vicious circle would be unavoidable only if the only way Christian belief could have warrant were for it to be the conclusion of such an argument. But that, he says, is not the case. Instead: "The source of warrant for Christian belief, according to the model, is not argument of any sort; in particular, its warrant does not arise from some argument about how Christian belief can have warrant."

In the end, then, Plantinga defends a kind of immediate, basic foundationalism.

[7] It is clear that Plantinga's genuine or primary goal is to show that Christian belief has warrant or is rational or is justified. Showing this would answer what he calls the de jure question. But he also holds the following: "The *de jure* question is not independent of the *de facto* question" (190). The de facto question is the truth question. Given that the truth question is essentially connected to the warrant question, the question presses: how does Plantinga answer the truth question?

[i] To the question of the truth of Christian belief Plantinga always responds with conditionals: *If* Christian belief is true. . . . How is this to be assessed?

He writes:

> What I claim for this [the *extended* Aquinas/Calvin] model is that there aren't any successful philosophical objections to it. . . . The point here is that *if* Christian belief is true, then it could very well have warrant in the way proposed here. . . . *If* (as I claim) the fact is there are no good philosophical objections to the model, given the *truth* of Christian belief, then any successful objection to the model will also have to be a successful objection to the truth of Christian belief. (*WCB* 285; emphases added)

And concerning theistic belief he poses the question, is this belief, the belief in God, a basic and warranted belief? He provides two succinct answers: "A. If false, probably not" (*WCB* 186) and "B. If true, probably so" (*WCB* 188). The two answers emerge from abstract considerations of the relation between truth and warrant/rationality. The answers are the same in the case of Christian belief.

What, however, is the status of an *explicit, non-conditional* sentence asserting that Christian belief is true? Developing an extensive conception showing that Christian belief is "probably" warranted/rational *if* it is true, while failing to address directly and clearly the question of *whether* Christian belief is true, does not qualify as a genuine "exercise in apologetics." One who is rational in the only relevant and interesting sense of "rational" both should and would say that what finally matters is truth; if possession of truth entails warrant, justification, and rationality, well and good, but if truth can be possessed without warrant, justification, and rationality, or if warrant, justification, and rationality are or can be given when truth remains in question, this would only show that warrant, justification, and rationality are not what ultimately matter.

[ii] Concerning the question whether Christian belief is true, Plantinga has two views that require brief consideration. First, he notes that in his chapter 10 he treats a number of objections to the thesis that Christian belief is true—something he indeed does, and in excellent fashion. Yet it is not clear why he only responds to such objections without responding directly to the question itself. Second, there are some (few) passages in which Plantinga to some degree explains and makes precise his conditional response to the question. Thus, he maintains with respect both to the A/C model and the expanded A/C model first that it is possible that they are true, and second that there are no decisive objections to them. He then makes a third point:

> Third, I believe that the models . . . are not only possible and beyond
> philosophical challenge but also *true,* or at least versimilitudinous, close
> to the truth. Still, I don't claim to *show* that they are true. That is be-
> cause the A/C model entails the truth of theism and the extended A/C
> model the truth of classical Christianity. To show that these models are
> true, therefore, would also be to show that theism and Christianity are
> true; and *I don't know how to do something one could sensibly call 'showing'*
> *that either of these is true.* (169–70; emphasis added)

These are peculiar contentions. The question presses: why devote
a book of over 500 pages, along with various other works, to support so
modest a thesis: he believes that his models are true, that the models
entail the truth of Christian belief, and he believes that Christian belief
is true, but he does not know how one could "show" or "demonstrate"
any of these beliefs to be true. Even of the so-called proofs of God's existence, which he deems "good arguments" (*WCB* 170), he says that they
lack the status of "showings" or "demonstrations."

Questions arise here that are, in the terminology of this book, systematic questions. Of central importance is the question of how *truth* is
to be understood. This is a question Plantinga utterly fails to consider—
not only the definitional question, but an extensive series of related questions that are central to various philosophical domains.[11] The issue of
truth also involves the question of how epistemology relates to ontology
and metaphysics. Because Plantinga does not address this question, what
he means by "prove," "demonstrate," and "show" remains unclear. His
remarks on this topic are for the most part vague and indeterminate.

[iii] There is, however, one passage wherein Plantinga provides—at
least indirectly—an indication of why he maintains that one can neither
"show" nor "demonstrate" either the truth of his models or, therefore,
that of theistic or Christian belief. Having asserted that it is relatively
easy to show that Christian belief is justified and internally rational, he
continues as follows:

> External rationality and warrant are harder. The only way I can see
> to argue that Christian belief has *these* virtues is to argue that Chris-
> tian belief is, indeed, *true. I don't propose to offer such an argument. That*
> *is because I don't know of an argument for Christian belief that seems very*
> *likely to convince one who doesn't already accept its conclusion.* That is noth-
> ing against Christian belief, however, and indeed I shall argue that if

---

[11] See *Structure and Being,* especially sections 2.5 and 3.3.

> Christian beliefs are true, then the standard and most satisfactory way to
> hold them will not be as the conclusions of argument. (*WCB* 200–201;
> emphasis added)

What is crucial in this passage concerns what it means "to convince."
Plantinga here mixes different levels that must be held apart: the psychological level and the strictly logical-objective level. The logical-objective
soundness of an argument is in no way dependent on how successful
the argument is on the psychological level, that is, the level of conviction. The psychological level provides no criteria relevant to assessing the
soundness of any argument.[12]

The passage quoted just above reveals that the central weakness of
Plantinga's purely epistemic approach lies in the wholly unsystematic
character of his treatment of the question of God. The relations of the
epistemic dimension to the dimensions of the truth concept and of ontology remain unanalyzed. Moreover, his talk of "God" is wholly indeterminate and splendidly isolated. What is centrally lacking is an ontological/metaphysical conception of the entirety of actuality, of Being.

[iv] Plantinga explicitly refers to the central task just identified.
Having asserted that the de jure question is not independent of the de
facto question, he writes the following (*WCB* 190):

> And here we see the ontological or metaphysical or ultimately religious
> roots of the question as to the rationality or warrant or lack thereof
> for belief in God. What you properly take to be rational, at least in the
> sense of warranted, depends on what sort of metaphysical and religious
> stance you adopt. It depends on what kind of beings you think human
> beings are. . . . Your view as to what sort of creature a human being is
> will determine or at any rate heavily influence your views as to whether
> theistic belief is warranted or not warranted, rational or irrational for
> human beings.

These are remarkable assertions. They indicate the importance of
an immense task, that of developing a comprehensive conception not
only of human beings in any narrow sense, but of actuality or Being as a
whole. If one undertakes this task, then the epistemological framework
is wholly displaced. As chapter 3 of this book shows, talk of "God" can
have a clear and defensible sense only within the framework of such a
comprehensive systematic conception.

---

[12] On the problematic of justification and grounding, see *Structure and Being*, section 1.5.

1.3 Semi-Systematic Indirect Approaches

Those who take approaches of this sort indirectly address and then respond to the question of God, beginning from specific starting points that are components of a specific comprehensive philosophical-theological conception: metaphysics with a Christian orientation. The starting points are specific phenomena in the world (such as motion, causality, or order). Whatever starting point is selected is then "explained" on the basis of metaphysical principles such that what explains the starting point—an explanatory X—is the conclusion of an argument (or, in the traditional and often still-used terminology, a proof). These approaches are indirect because of their reliance on these starting points, although it is also the case that the explanatory X is directly or immediately named "God" or identified with God.

These approaches are semi-systematic because the comprehensive conception on whose basis they develop does not exhibit any strict systematic unity; the comprehensive conception is usually mostly implicit, and never completely explicit.

This book does not aim to present any of these approaches in anything approaching its entirety. Instead, it presents a few positions and schools of thought that are particularly important examples of approaches of this kind.

1.3.1 The Christian Tradition of Metaphysics of Being: (At Least) Six Significations of "Metaphysics"

Metaphysics with a Christian orientation has a grand, long, and extremely complex tradition. The purposes of this book require consideration only of one specific school of thought within this tradition. This is the school that develops what is interpretable in one way or another as a comprehensive philosophical conception of Being and that has in Thomas Aquinas its most important representative. As this section shows, this comprehensive metaphysical conception has many aspects, of which its treatment of God is only one. The section presents and evaluates that aspect in light of others, above all those that concern the either purely implicitly present or presupposed or at most partially explained conception of Being.

Before this task can be undertaken, it is important—particularly given the broader purposes of this book—to consider the term/concept *metaphysics*.

[1] Scarcely any philosophical word has had so chaotic a history as the word "metaphysics": it has been understood and misunderstood in

an enormous variety of ways. This book notes many examples from the fateful history of the word. Given this background, it is at present highly problematic to use the word except either in treatments of specific authors or in conjunction with clarifications of precisely how the word is to be understood. Accounts that proceed otherwise can scarcely avoid being swallowed up in the word's chaotic history. Nevertheless, it is also difficult to avoid using the word. The word is contained in the vocabulary of the structural-systematic philosophy presented in *Structure and Being*, but is used within that philosophy only sparingly, indeed marginally, and only in conjunction with careful clarification.[13]

Clarification here can begin with the identification and brief description of six significations that, in the recent past and in the present, have been and are associated with the term "metaphysics." These six significations do not completely span the semantic spectrum constituted by contemporary uses of the term, but they are the six significations that are the most relevant to this book. Other significations cannot be considered here. For this reason, it would be a mistake to take what follows to be anything like a history or catalog of *all* of the meanings that have been or are attached to the word "metaphysics." Moreover, the six meanings that are considered are not thoroughly explained; instead, only a brief classification is provided. What follows thereafter often refers back to these classifications.

Two additional preliminary remarks are in order. First, given the chaotic history of the term it is astonishing, not to say scarcely understandable, that in the domain of analytic philosophy this term is currently used extensively and as though its use were wholly non-problematic. It must be added that analytic philosophers use the term almost exclusively to designate what since the time of Christian Wolff has been termed *metaphysica specialis*, and that in a quite specific fashion. So understood, metaphysics investigates specific domains and aspects of "the world" such as the constitution of matter, space and time, and the philosophy of mind, and specific general topics such as the problem of universals.[14] Extraordinarily rarely—and even then usually only in inchoate fashion—is the subject matter of *metaphysica generalis*, above all the fundamental structures of the world or reality or Being, even envisaged.

---

[13] See *Structure and Being*, chapter 5.

[14] See any of the recently published handbooks of and companions to metaphysics. Several contributions to current discussions on the status of what is now called metaphysics are collected and presented in a book, edited by David Chalmers, D. Manley, and R. Wasserman, whose title, which is similar to those of many other recent works, is *Metametaphysics: New Essays on the Foundations of Ontology* (2009).

Second, a different development is significantly more important for this book: as indicated above in the "Introduction," the currently strongest and most radical opposition to metaphysics stems not from the well-known traditional critics of metaphysics including Kantian criticism, positivism, pragmatism, etc., but from Jewish and Christian authors who either rely on the later works of Wittgenstein or call themselves (or are called by others) postmodernists. Chapter 4 of this book treats the two presumably most radical of these postmodernist critics of metaphysics understood as philosophy of Being, i.e., Emmanuel Levinas and Jean-Luc Marion. Given this, it is the more important to attain clarity at the outset concerning how the term "metaphysics" arises in various contexts within this book.

The purposes of this book make it appropriate to distinguish among (at least) six significations or forms of metaphysics. That the characterizations given of them are in part strikingly negative is explained by the fact that chapter 3 of this book presents a conception that is distinct from all of them. The forms of metaphysics introduced here all relate—either positively or negatively—to the tradition of *Christian* metaphysics. Those that relate to it positively either explicitly affirm it or attempt in one way or another to improve on it; those that relate to it negatively explicitly—and often radically and vehemently—reject it. Aristotelian metaphysics is not included in the classification, but is instead simply presupposed as the form of metaphysics from which Christian metaphysics developed.

[2] For reasons of historical precedence and of historical influence, the *first* form of metaphysics to be considered is that of Thomas Aquinas; it is designated as the Aquinian metaphysics of Being. Section 1.3.2, below, considers this form in significant detail. It is important to note here that over the course of the centuries, Aquinas's thinking has been subjected both to abbreviation and to utter distortion.

The *second* form of metaphysics is the position that for centuries has been termed scholastic metaphysics. In a specific respect, this version of metaphysics has been presented in a historically influential form, and in a certain sense codified, by Alexander Baumgarten and Christian Wolff. This is the version of metaphysics inherited and criticized by Kant.

The *third* form is a version that, particularly with respect to methodology, is a radically modified form of Aquinian metaphysics and scholastic metaphysics. It results from the adoption and application of Kant's transcendental method, albeit in a significantly reinterpreted form. This version of metaphysics is usually termed transcendental Thomism. It is particularly important because it is, historically, the first form of metaphysics that accords a central significance to subjectivity and anthropology.

The *fourth* form or version of metaphysics can—critically—be termed Heidegger's stereotype of metaphysics. As this book shows in many places, Heidegger understands and interprets metaphysics in general, and particularly Christian metaphysics, as what he calls onto-theo-logy—or at least this is how he is generally interpreted, particularly by Jewish and Christian authors. This book shows below that Heidegger's stereotype requires scrupulous correction.

The *fifth* form or version is misinterpreted or distorted metaphysics. This form results from a peculiar mixture of the four previously introduced forms or versions, although the fourth version, the understanding of metaphysics as onto-theo-logy, constitutes by far the most important ingredient. This factor, onto-theo-logy, is what can reasonably be termed the fundamental anti-metaphysical *dogma fidei postmodernisticum*. Postmodernist anti-metaphysical thinking is at heart anti-ontotheology. This book subjects this distorting understanding of metaphysics to a fundamental critique, particularly in chapter 4.

In order to characterize the *sixth* form or version of metaphysics, it is necessary—faute de mieux—to introduce an unusual designation. It is formed in analogy to the familiar distinction between deep structure(s) and surface structure(s). The term "deep metaphysics" is consequently used to name this sixth form. An alternative would be to rely on the historically significant designation *philosophia perennis,* transforming it into *metaphysica perennis profunda.* This is the form that fully actualizes the capability for human thinking that is utilized by all forms of the discipline named metaphysics throughout the history of philosophy, but that is not fully actualized by any of those forms. One could, following Kant, term metaphysics in this sense "metaphysics as a natural predisposition (*metaphysica naturalis*)" and as "actual" (*CPuR* B21), presupposing, however, that one does not accept Kant's negative charges against the possibility that metaphysics of this sort could attain the status of a science. There are two particularly good reasons for rejecting Kant's critique. First, they are directed not against this version of metaphysics, but against the scholastic metaphysics introduced above (the second signification or version); second, Kant's critique rests on important assumptions that do not withstand critical analysis.[15]

Nevertheless, there is a kernel of truth in Kant's distinction between metaphysics as a natural disposition and metaphysics as science; it is indeed the case that no version of metaphysics—including that of the structural-systematic philosophy—can be simply identified with deep

---

[15] The author presents his critique of Kant in various writings. See especially *Structure and Being,* chapter 2; and "Transzendentaler und absoluter Idealismus," in *SGTh,* 193–221.

metaphysics. Against Kant, however, it in no way follows from this that no metaphysics—thus, clearly, including the one presented in this book—can be a science. Ultimately, whether any deep metaphysics is a science depends on what is meant by "science," and the current understanding of science is vastly different from Kant's. The version of deep metaphysics presented here claims to be a theory that is both to be taken seriously and true. To be sure, these various terms/concepts, including *theory, true,* etc., are newly interpreted within the theoretical framework of the structural-systematic philosophy, as explained below and in *Structure and Being.*[16] When in this book the word "metaphysics" is used to name the discipline that is a component of the structural-systematic philosophy, it is always to be understood to mean *deep* metaphysics. Which significNEWLINE-ation of "metaphysics" is intended in specific cases is always clear from the context.

1.3.2 Thomas Aquinas: The Unreflectedness, Deficiency, Complexity, and Inspirational Power of His Conceptions of Being (*Esse*) and God

In the history of treatments of the question of God, the thought of the philosopher and theologian Thomas Aquinas is of absolutely central imNEWLINE-portance. As the long and extremely complex history of its interpretaNEWLINE-tion and reception shows, however, Aquinas's thought exhibits high deNEWLINE-grees of unity and originality, but also a lack of systematic reflection and indeed some incoherence. The following account considers, in appropriNEWLINE-ate brevity, points relevant to the question of God.

1.3.2.1 A Superficial, Peripheral, and Fully Inadequate Approach: The "Five Ways"

[1] The locus classicus of the metaphysically indirect, semi-systematic approach to the question of God is constituted by Thomas's famous five ways (*quinque viae*).[17] This section neither presents those ways in detail nor assesses them for their cogency. The reason it does not is that all these ways and all similar ways (or similar putative demonstrations or proofs), as they are generally and virtually unanimously understood and evaluated, are irreparably flawed. Their flaws are not, however, ones idenNEWLINE-tified in the voluminous available literature. They are of a different sort, and one that shows the long-lasting discussion of their validity or cogency

---

[16] See especially chapters 1 and 2.

[17] *STh* I q. 2 a. 3. Aquinas also treats these ways at various other places in his works.

to lack a target. Why and how this is so is specified below, following some important interpretive, commentative, and substantive clarifications.

Aquinas's first way starts with the phenomenon of motion and ends with a first mover, the unmoved mover. His path from the former to the latter is based on the principle, "Everything that is moved is moved by something else" and on the impossibility of an infinite sequence of moved movers. The second way, the one most discussed both through history and at present, concerns the phenomenon of causality within the world as we know it; Aquinas asks whether the causal sequence presupposes a first cause and answers that it does, basing this answer on an assumption that he formulates as follows: the chain of effective causes cannot regress infinitely because that would make explanation of the causal relations we witness impossible.

The third way is the most significant, albeit not in the form Aquinas provides, but because of an insight implicit to it but inadequately developed by it. Because of the importance of this insight for chapter 3 of this book—the systematic part—the third way is considered here in more extensive detail. This way is the so-called proof from contingency. On the basis of the fact that there are things that have the possibility both of being and of not being, Thomas concludes that "it is necessary to assume something that is necessary in itself and that does not have the cause of its necessity from elsewhere, but that is [instead] the cause of necessity for other [things]." The argument is as follows:

> It is . . . impossible that everything that is of this sort [i.e., everything that has the possibility both of being and of not being] always is [variant text: that everything that is is of this—contingent—sort], because that which possibly cannot be is, at some time, not. Therefore, if everything has the possibility of not being, then at one time there was nothing. If, however, this were true, then there would be nothing now, because what is not can begin to be only via something that is. Thus, if (at some time) there were no beings, then it would have been impossible that anything began to be, and there would be nothing now; but this is manifestly false. Thus, not all beings are only possible, but there must also be something necessary among the things.[18]

---

[18] Translated from the German translation used in *Sein und Gott,* which is based on *Die Gottesbeweise aus der "Summe gegen die Heiden" und der "Summe der Theologie"* (1982), 55–57. The original Latin text (*"ex recensione leonina"*) is as follows:

> Impossibile est autem omnia quae sunt talia, semper esse [variant text: . . . omnia quae sunt talia esse]: quia quod possibile est non esse, quandoque non est. Si igitur omnia

As chapter 3 shows, this way (or putative proof) contains, in a certain respect, an important intuition. But Aquinas's text does not adequately develop the intuition, for three reasons. First, the decisive premise—"It is impossible that everything that is [contingent] always is"—is ambitious, but is not adequately explained; moreover, it is insufficiently grounded. Differently stated: the insight on which the premise is based can be explained and supported only within the framework of a comprehensive conception of Being as a whole (chapter 3 presents such a framework, and then returns to the insight). Second, the argument fails because it includes time as a factor; this inclusion brings with it an array of insoluble problems.[19] Third, Aquinas begins from a specific phenomenon in the world—the fact that there are contingent entities. The inadequacy of any such starting point is shown below. Despite these three deficiencies, however, this third way does, as noted, contain an insight that is important to comprehensively systematic philosophical reflection.

The fourth way is termed the proof from stages (or from stages of Being or of perfection). Its starting point is the fact that things vary in degrees of perfection with respect to Being, truth, goodness, beauty, etc. Thomas argues as follows:

> More and less are said of different things insofar as they approach, in varying ways, a [principle] that is a maximum (a highest degree). . . . Therefore, there is something that is most true, best, and most noble and consequently that is to the highest degree.

Adding the concept *cause,* he concludes: "Therefore there is something that is the cause of Being, goodness, and of all perfections in all beings." The fifth way is the so-called teleological proof. Both the inanimate and the animate constituents of nature, including human beings, exhibit high degrees of order. All individual organisms and other things are interrelated and strive, as individuals and collectively, toward a goal (a telos), even if that goal is nothing more than self-preservation. Because non-minded things, like stones, plants, and animals, lack reason and knowledge, they cannot on their own effect this order, and cannot strive for any goal. Because, however, it is also not human beings who provide

---

sunt possibilia non esse, aliquando nihil fuit in rebus. Sed si hoc est verum, etiam nunc nihil esset: quia quod non est, non incipit esse nisi per aliquid quod est; si igitur nihil fuit ens, impossibile fuit quod aliquid inciperet esse, et sic modo nihil esset: quod patet esse falsum. Non ergo omnia entia sunt possibilia: sed oportet aliquid esse necessarium in rebus.

[19] See the treatment in *Structure and Being,* section 5.3.

or aim at the order of the world, the orderer of the world can only be the transcendent minded being "that all name God." The thought behind this fifth way is currently enjoying an astonishing renaissance under the designation "argument from design" (or "design argument").

[2] As noted above, the purposes of this book do not require that Aquinas's five ways be analyzed in detail or assessed. They are introduced only as famous (historical) examples of a specific approach to the question of God that is wholly insufficient and inadequate. Here, only two remarks concerning the briefly sketched arguments need be made.

First, one reason that these ways are wholly insufficient and inadequate is that each is based on a single phenomenon in the world; each thus concerns only a segment or part of the world (the universe, Being as a whole). The world as a whole, the universe, Being as a whole remains unthematized. For this reason, even if the arguments of the five ways were sound, their end points could not qualify as determinations even of an inchoatively meaningful concept *God*. Differently stated: if *God* is identified with a principle (or anything similar) that does not adequately encompass Being as a whole, then there is no reason for philosophy (or theology) to be concerned with it. The only one of Aquinas's ways that could avoid this fundamental problem is, as noted above, the third, which is based on an insight that concerns Being as a whole. To be sure, however, this insight can be adequately developed only if a wholly differently oriented conception of Being as a whole is developed or presupposed, and that would also change the way this way would be understood. This is shown in chapter 3.

The second remark important here concerns the end points of the five ways (and of all similar arguments). Taken strictly, these ways do nothing more than proceed from specific points or phenomena in the world to one or another first or highest point. Aquinas's text, however, also includes a kind of addition or commentary of the form, "and that [namely, the first mover, the first cause, the necessary being, etc.] all call 'God.'" The addition of these formulations is the *greatest methodological error* Aquinas ever made, although it is important to note that the error is not fatal when located within the entire context of Aquinas's thought. Also to be emphasized, however, is that these formulations have become classic and have therefore done an extraordinary amount of damage. They have been and continue to be the major source of objections to "the metaphysical God" and "the God of the philosophers," objections that have been and continue to be powerfully influential in Western intellectual history. Here, it suffices to introduce two relevant historical facts.

The first fact is that the identification of Aquinas's end points with God has been and continues to be the source of one of the deepest oppositions between Catholic and Protestant theology. This opposition is known as the question concerning natural theology, although to be noted is that "natural theology" is used, in the long history of this opposition, in a variety of different senses.[20] One point, however, has always been and remains clear: Protestant theologians have been virtually unanimous in their opposition to any God reached as the conclusion of any metaphysical argument, whereas Catholic theologians have virtually unanimously supported such arguments. As shown below, the Protestant objection is based on a deep misunderstanding, but it is also the case that the Catholic position, as presented in the form of scholastic metaphysics, is deeply one-sided. Doubtless, the historical origin of these two errors lies in formulations like Aquinas's.

The second fact to be cited is the lasting influence of a famous passage from Pascal's *Mémorial,* a passage that is intelligible only on the basis of the tradition emerging from Aquinas's formulations. In *Mémorial,* Pascal describes a deep experience whose central formulation is the following:

> The God of Abraham, the God of Isaac, the God of Jacob, not of the philosophers and the scholars. Certitude. Certitude. Sentiment, Joy, Peace. God of Jesus Christ.[21]

This famous text is often introduced in order to document a (putative) opposition between the biblical God and the "God of the philosophers." It may be that it does articulate such an opposition. But a different interpretation cannot—at least not a priori—be excluded, one according to which the sentence articulates not an opposition but a complementarity, in the following sense: Pascal turns to God not only or not primarily as "God" is articulated in philosophy (the philosophy of his time), but also as "God" to whose genuine signification the entire biblical message contributes in an absolutely decisive fashion. Briefly: this second interpretation would say that the "God of the philosophers" is wholly abstract, or largely (still) undetermined, whereas the biblical God is (so to speak) the fully determined God. However this may be, the passage shows that Pascal relates to a tradition of talk about God that has its classical expression in the formulations of Aquinas cited above.

[3] The works and doctrines of the authors of the Christian meta-

---

[20] See W. Pannenberg, *Systematische Theologie,* vol. 1 (1988), especially chapter 2.

[21] "Dieu d'Abraham, Dieu d'Isaac, Dieu de Jacob, non des philosophes et des savants. Certitude. Certitude. Sentiment, Joie, Paix. Dieu de Jésus-Christ." Blaise Pascal, *Oeuvres complètes,* La Pléiade, 544.

physical tradition, and especially those of Thomas Aquinas, are—even when they are as extensive as the *Summa Theologiae*—partial presentations of a comprehensive conception that is far from adequately articulated in those presentations. For this reason, such presentations are correctly understood and interpreted only when the comprehensive vision that they partially present is taken into consideration. This involves identifying both the strengths and the weaknesses both of the partial presentations and of the comprehensive vision.

Consideration of the summa form of presentation clarifies this unusual relation between partial presentation and comprehensive vision. A summa is not a system; it is instead an immensely complex doctrinal whole whose parts are generally only quite loosely interconnected. They must therefore be not only read and interpreted, but often also corrected, in light of the comprehensive vision that they presuppose but never adequately articulate.

This state of affairs is exemplified by what Aquinas says in the *Summa Theologiae* about God, from those most problematic statements that are found in the five ways/proofs about what "all call God" to the central clarifications of God as Holy Trinity. Do the various theses actually cohere? And if so, how? It cannot be denied that within Aquinas's works there are elements that are, in Heidegger's language, onto-theo-logical. The five ways/proofs are undeniably among them. But (as indicated above) the crucial question is that of the status of these elements within the whole of Aquinas's teachings. Differently stated: are these ways/proofs of decisive importance to Aquinas's teachings as a whole? In his work as it stands—as it is presented—Aquinas assumes, and attempts to show, that the various "highest points" with which the five ways/proofs end fit together in one way or another. In addition, he shows that all "pure perfections [*perfectiones purae*]" and especially Being and essence, *esse* and *essentia*—are identical in God (or, more precisely, *as* God). This is a weakness in his thinking, because this identity thesis is problematic, indeed somehow artificial. At the same time, however, it is the case that the onto-theo-logical elements in Aquinas's works are *not* of decisive importance for his thought as a whole.

1.3.2.2 Being (Esse) and God According to Aquinas: A Significant but One-Sided and Undeveloped Conception

[1] Aquinas's conception of Being (*esse*) constitutes his most significant point of originality, but as important as this conception is, it remains—as the following account shows—far from completely developed with respect both to its own content and to its implications. The most important reason for this is presumably that Aquinas articulates it within the frame-

work of a metaphysical conception whose central concepts derive from Aristotle; these include *essence, substance-accidents, substratum, subject, subsistence, form-matter,* and *cause.* How this conceptual framework prevents Aquinas from adequately articulating his conception of Being is shown in what follows.[22]

The second main reason Aquinas's conception of Being has remained undeveloped is that it has, over the course of the centuries, been variously interpreted and has gradually come to be largely ignored. Only toward the end of the 1930s do exegetes begin to speak of a "rediscovery of the originality" of Aquinas's conception of Being.[23] There follows an intensive discussion concerning what interpretation of this conception is correct, and defenses of this conception from Heidegger's charge that an "oblivion of Being" characterizes Western metaphysics in its entirety. This literature cannot be considered here; instead, it suffices to note that it contains nothing that contributes importantly to articulating any systematic conception of Being. As shown in what follows, it remains most common today to rely on the scarcely problematized thesis that Aquinas is a typical representative of a metaphysics of Being that is onto-theological in Heidegger's sense.

This book counters the Heidegger-inspired assessment of Aquinas's conception of Being by making two centrally important points. First: the accuracy of Heidegger's accusation that Aquinas exhibits an oblivion of Being can be assessed only if it is made clear what Heidegger understands by "Being"—and this is not easily done. Second: as noted above more than once, although a deep and highly significant conception of Being is articulated in Aquinas's works, that conception is only minimally articulated, with the consequence not only that its implications for other topics remain unexplored, but also that it itself remains one-sided and undeveloped.

The first point introduced in the preceding paragraph is thoroughly treated in chapter 2. What follows here presents the two aspects of the second point that are most important for the purposes of this book.

[2] Aquinas's initially central thesis about Being (*esse*) is the following: "Being (*ens*) is what the understanding conceives first as what is most familiar to it and into which it resolves all of its conceptions."[24] But *ens* is

---

[22] On this historical-systematic complex of problems, see Puntel, "Das Denken von Thomas von Aquin als summarisch-unreflektiertes Seins- und Analogiedenken," in *SGTh,* 35–143.

[23] See especially the works of L. B. Geiger, C. Fabro, L. de Raeymaeker, É. Gilson, and B. Welte. On the history of Thomism in the twentieth century, see B. Mondin, *La metafisica di S. Tommaso d'Aquino e i suoi interpreti* (2002).

[24] "Illud autem quod primo intellectus concipit quasi notissimum, et in quo conceptiones omnes resolvit, est ens" (*De ver.* q. 1 a. 1).

what "has" *esse;* it can therefore be understood only as the concretization of *esse.* Aquinas articulates this concretization on the basis of the schemata *recipient-received* and *bearer-form.* He also uses the following terms: *ens, essentia, actus essendi, perfectio essendi, virtus essendi, esse commune, esse ipsum, esse per se subsistens,* and others. How all these terms are to be understood cannot be shown here;[25] here, the question is only how Aquinas understands *esse,* and how that understanding is to be assessed.

Clarifying how Aquinas understands *esse* requires distinguishing between what he explicitly formulates or articulates and what remains implicitly present or presupposed. The *explicit answer* to the question of how Aquinas understands *esse* is clear: "*Esse* . . . is act,"[26] such that this act is the ultimate or deepest act in the hierarchy of all other explicitly provided or even merely thinkable acts: "What I call *esse* is the actuality of all acts and is therefore the perfection of all perfections."[27] In this respect *esse* differs from *ens*—Being differs from being(s)—and from all ontological factors such as *essentia, forma, subjectum,* etc. Because and insofar as *esse* in this sense differs from these other factors, it does not encompass them; *esse* in this sense cannot, therefore, be the all-encompassing dimension.

The famous dispute, ranging over centuries, concerning the question whether the distinction between *esse* and *essentia*—Being and essence—is a real one (*distinctio realis*) or only a conceptual one (*distinctio rationis*) results from failures to consider the complexities both of the relevant texts and of the issue at hand. If one holds that there is a real distinction, an unanswerable question arises: how is *essentia* to be understood and explained? If, on the other hand, one holds that the distinction is merely conceptual, then the following question presses: how is *esse* then to be understood in the *comprehensive sense?* The dispute itself ultimately makes little sense. If one considers only the *explicit* level of Aquinas's texts, then one cannot ascribe to *esse* a comprehensive character. It is thus clear that one cannot appeal to *esse* as so understood to maintain that Aquinas evades Heidegger's charge that he has forgotten Being. This holds, of course, only if one assumes that Heidegger understands Being in an absolutely comprehensive sense—which one could assume without presupposing that he adequately articulates that sense. Heidegger's understanding of Being is considered in chapter 2.

There are, however, texts of Aquinas that can be interpreted such that more than *actus essendi* is understood by *esse,* but this understanding,

---

[25] See the work cited in note 22, above.

[26] "Esse autem actus est" (*ScG* book 1, p. 38).

[27] "Hoc quod dico esse est actualitas omnium actuum, et propter hoc est perfectio omnium perfectionum" (*De pot.* q. 7 a. 2 ad 9).

presupposed in many passages, remains wholly unarticulated; the author shows this in the essay on Aquinas cited more than once above. The most interesting text, which is of great significance for this book, is the following passage from chapter 11 of book 4 of *Summa contra Gentiles:*

> In God is everything that belongs to the meaning of subsistence, of essence, or of Being itself. It is characteristic of him not to *Be* in anything else, insofar as he subsists. It is characteristic of him to *Be* something determinate insofar as he is essentiality. It is characteristic of him to *Be* Being-in-act on the basis of Being itself.[28]

Three times—in the case of each of the three moments—there is talk here of *esse:* "not *Being* in another," "*Being* something determinate," "*Being* in act." What *comprehensive meaning* of Being is both disclosed and concealed by these formulations? It is a *threefold* meaning. The comprehensive meaning as the unitary event of the threefold of this structure would be Being in the primordial sense, "fulfilled Being [*totum esse*]," in a term Aquinas occasionally uses.[29] The "sistence" of "subsistence" is the from which and the toward which, the primordial self that unfolds itself contentually through the moments of "*esse quid*—Being something determinate"—and "*esse in actu*—Being-in-act." This sense of Being, only implicit in the passage, is remarkable. But it is developed neither in Aquinas nor in the tradition of the interpretation and reception of his thought.[30]

[3] We come now to the point that is decisive with respect to Aqui-

---

[28] "In deo est quicquid pertinet ad rationem vel subsistentis, vel essentiae, vel ipsius esse: convenit enim ei non *esse* in aliquo, inquantam est subsistens; esse quid, inquantum est essentia; et *esse* in actu, ratione ipsius esse" (emphasis added).

[29] See, e.g., "Because God's Being . . . is not in any sort of receptacle, but is pure Being, it is not limited to a specific mode of perfection of Being; instead, it has the entire fullness of Being [Esse . . . Dei, cum non sit in aliquo receptum, sed sit esse purum, non limitatur ad aliquem modum perfectionis essendi, sed totum esse in se habet]" (*De pot.* q. 1 a. 2).

[30] Bernard Montagnes is one of the few interpreters who—at least in principle—takes a similar position:

> At bottom, the entire discussion turns on the following question: how can one at the same time accord a positive meaning or content to essence as formal act and attribute all perfection to *esse* understood in a strongly distinct fashion? Without doubt, it is necessary to recognize that the *perfectio essendi* includes the *triple determination* of essence as formal principle, of *esse* as act, and of the subject who exercises the act by means of form; the *three* are not really identical except in God alone. (Review of C. Fabro, *Participation et causalité* [1960], 20–21; emphasis added)

Montagnes does not, however, realize how consequential this triple determination is.

nas's approach to the question of God. In opposition to the absolutely and directly false Heideggerian theses attributing to Aquinas an onto-theo-logical metaphysics of Being, Aquinas's *actual* and genuine conception of God is articulated in the famous formulation according to which God is *ipsum esse per se subsistens, Being itself subsisting through itself.* God is not a being (*ens*) among other beings, thus not anything like the highest, first, or maximal being. Undeniably, Aquinas's works contain formulations that characterize God as such a being—as *ens primum, ens supremum, maxime ens*, etc. But if on the basis of such texts one ascribes to Aquinas an onto-theo-logical position, one overlooks two vital points. First, such formulations are extremely rare, particularly when compared to what is reasonably termed his standard formulation, according to which God is Being itself subsisting through itself. At the very least, one should attempt to clarify how the apparently conflicting formulations are to be understood, and one should thereby take into consideration their relative frequencies. Second, it is easily shown that the formulations characterizing God as a being—as *ens*—are used for exclusively *linguistic-stylistic* reasons and are to be understood accordingly. It suffices here to introduce two characteristic passages:

> God in the *maximal* sense is a being, but not in the sense that his Being would be determined [or delimited] in accordance with any sort of nature that receives it; instead, God is Being subsisting through itself, not determined [or delimited] by any mode.[31]

> It is manifest that the *first being*, who is God, is an infinite act, because [this being] has in itself the entire fullness of Being [*totam essendi*], and is therefore not limited to any sort of nature or genus or species. From this it follows that his Being itself cannot be understood as if it inhered, so to speak, in any nature or genus or species that would not be identical with its Being [*esse*]; for in this manner it would be confined to such a nature. For this reason we say that God is his Being itself.[32]

---

[31] "[Deus] est . . . maxime ens, inquantum est non habens aliquod esse determinatum per aliquam naturam cui adveniat, sed est ipsum esse subsistens, omnibus modis indeterminatum" (*STh* I q. 11 a. 4).

[32] "Manifestum est enim quod primum ens, quod Deus est, est actus infinitus, utpote habens in se totam essendi plenitudinem, non contractam ad aliquam naturam generis vel speciei. Unde oportet quod ipsum esse eius non sit esse quasi inditum alicui naturae quae non sit suum esse; quia sic finiretur ad illam naturam. Unde dicimus, quod Deus est ipsum suum esse" (*De spiritualibus creaturis*, q. un. a. 1).

Although, as often noted above, Aquinas does not further develop this conception of Being, that does not prevent it from being, even in its minimal articulation, an invaluable source of inspiration.[33]

1.3.2.3 Aquinas: A Medieval Thinker

In conclusion, it must be recalled that Aquinas, as a medieval thinker, was fully unaware of any and all post-medieval developments. Nothing like a re-pristinization of his thinking, no matter how understood or reconstructed in light of succeeding intellectual developments, should be undertaken. In considering him philosophically, however, one can and indeed must, *from today's perspective*, note the *comprehensive systematic* weakness of the conception articulated in his works. What does that mean here? Briefly: he does not attend to the dimension of subjectivity (in the modern sense), to language, or to theoreticity (along with all that belongs to it). Given this, he could not possibly articulate *esse* adequately: basically, he understands it as an objective pole in the sense that human beings (human subjects), language, etc., are not effectively included within its articulation. This makes his thinking of Being external, merely cobbled together; the conception itself has the character of a medieval summa.

These widely consequential and to some degree historically conditioned weaknesses aside, Aquinas's original insight concerning *esse* has had a peculiar historical fate. Not only has it not been deepened and made more explicit (yet less corrected), but it has been essentially distorted, with the consequence that if it continues to play a role at all, it is only an unexplicated *verbal* one. After Aquinas, metaphysics is understood exclusively as the science of beings as beings (*ens inquantum ens*). The two main representatives of this scholastic position are Duns Scotus and Francisco Suárez. On them there is already a nearly unmanageable amount of literature that need not and should not be considered here. By the middle of the eighteenth century, there had emerged the stereotypical metaphysics that Kant of course had in mind as he composed his putatively annihilating critique of "metaphysics." Christian Wolff (1679–1754) and Alexander Baumgarten (1714–1762) are the ones who established that stereotypical form, which has been generally presupposed and accepted ever since, according to which "metaphysics" is a collection of four disciplines: ontology, universal cosmology, rational psychology, and natural or rational theology. Ontology is general metaphysics (*meta-*

---

[33] On Jean-Luc Marion's (mis)interpretation of Aquinas, see the "retractions" in his essay "Saint Thomas d'Aquin et l'onto-théo-logie" (1995), 33n2, and the extensive critique of this *new* (mis)interpretation in chapter 4 (4.2.1[2]), below.

physica generalis), and the three other disciplines constitute special metaphysics (*metaphysica specialis*). This ontology is the science of the most universal predicates of things/beings.

The rediscovery and reevaluation of Aquinian *esse* that occurred in the 1930s is noted above (see 1.3.2.2[1]); there, the author's evaluation of that development is also noted.

1.3.3 Transcendental Thomism

Given the purposes of this book, neither is it possible nor would it be illuminating to consider the long history of Christian metaphysics of Being in the wake of Aquinas. It suffices briefly to mention the form of Christian metaphysics that emerges from encounters with Kant and Heidegger (and in a certain respect with Hegel) and that is known as transcendental Thomism. Its most important representatives are Joseph Maréchal, Karl Rahner, Emerich Coreth, Johannes B. Lotz, Johann B. Metz, and Bernhard Lonergan. To be sure, these authors share only certain central aspects. What they have in common is the project of combining pre-Kantian Christian metaphysics (especially that of Aquinas) with Kant's transcendental philosophy.

Central for these authors is the thought of transcendence, which is understood and articulated in two different versions. The first is defended by Maréchal, the initiator of this project.[34] Maréchal understands transcendence as a dynamic teleological process that characterizes the human mind and leads it into contact with the entire dimension of actuality. More precisely, Maréchal understands the dynamism of mind as striving for the absolute, which he identifies with God. He finds support for this in one of Aquinas's central concepts: in *naturale desiderium,* natural desire,[35] which Maréchal reinterprets and attempts to situate within the framework of transcendental thinking.

The second version also develops under Kant's influence, but in this case it is Heidegger rather than Kant who is (re)interpreted. Decisive here is the Being-question as reformulated and reconsidered by Heidegger. Emerich Coreth presents a completely transcendentally reformulated version of the Christian metaphysics of Being in his book *Metaphysik.*[36] Karl Rahner develops a non-systematic but significant the-

---

[34] See his book *Le point de départ de la métaphysique,* vol. 5: *Le Thomisme devant la philosophie critique* (1949).

[35] *ScG* book 2, p. 55; book 3, p. 48.

[36] Emerich Coreth, *Metaphysik* (1964).

ology on the basis of the transcendentally reinterpreted idea of Being. Rahner's is the only one of these approaches that, because of its originality, is relevant to this book; it is therefore considered in greater detail.

The concept *transcendence* is central to Rahner's project. He rethinks this concept on the basis of a philosophical and theological conception of subjectivity that his student Johannes B. Metz terms "Christian anthropocentrics."[37] As shown below, however, this term is not fully accurate. In fact, Rahner's conception has a threefold origin: in the old metaphysical idea of excess, the Kantian idea of the transcendental conditions of the possibility of experience, and Heidegger's concept of Dasein[b] as transcendence. Rahner's own conception of transcendence is articulated in the following thesis: "The human being is that being that is essentially characterized by its capacity to transcend, insofar as all his knowledge and knowing acts are grounded in the *preconception* [*Vorgriff*] of 'Being' in general [*überhaupt*], in a nonthematic but unavoidable awareness of the infinitude of actuality."[38]

It must be added that in an analogy to Heidegger's "turn" [*Kehre*] that is important in a methodical rather than contentual respect, Rahner overcomes a purely transcendental-anthropological standpoint in that although he initially understands the human being as subjectivity and as Dasein, he ultimately understands the human being "as the event [*Ereignis*] of the free, forgiving, self-communication of God."[39]

Rahner recognizes that the designations "(pre-understanding of) Being (*esse*)" and "God" present a problem. He comments as follows: "The philosopher should above all consider how the transcendental reference to what he calls Being and the transcendental reference to God belong together and how they are distinct."[40]

Rahner never questions the requirement that he thematize the dimension of Being in order to develop an adequate articulation of his theological notion of God's self-communication, but nowhere does he undertake a systematic consideration of this dimension.

Hans Urs von Balthasar has been and still is considered by many Christian authors to be a radical opponent of transcendental Thomism,

---

[37] See his book *Christliche Anthropozentrik: Über die Denkform des Thomas von Aquin* (1962).

[b] As is widely known, "Dasein" is an ordinary-language German term usually translated by "existence," but one that Heidegger uses to designate the mode of Being specifically of *human* beings. In English translations and treatments of Heidegger, it is often—as here—left untranslated.

[38] Karl Rahner, *Grundkurs des Glaubens: Einführung in den Begriff des Christentums* (1976), 44.

[39] Ibid., 122.

[40] Ibid., 69.

and especially of the Christian anthropocentrics defended by Rahner, but that is a fully one-sided view. Rahner never championed what could be called a pure or radical transcendental, Christian anthropocentrism. He did not, however, adequately clarify his position.

Von Balthasar himself develops a significant "theological aesthetics,"[41] although he never rejects theoretical or speculative theology. The fourth and fifth volumes of his aesthetics have titles beginning with the revealing phrase "the realm of metaphysics." The last part of the fifth volume contains some deep and beautiful comments on the topic Being and God, although they are not explicitly theoretical. There and elsewhere he presents a noteworthy critique of Heidegger's interpretation of Christian metaphysics as onto-theo-logy and of the assimilation of that critique by postmodern theologians and philosophers including Jean-Luc Marion.[42]

1.3.4 Two Contemporary Examples of Semi-Systematic Indirect Approaches: Robert Spaemann, Richard Swinburne

A great variety of "proofs of God's existence" that are currently being discussed could be classified as developing from semi-systematic, indirect approaches to the question of God, but unlike the approaches of the classical metaphysical tradition that are presented above, the examples considered in this subsection do not fully merit this classification. That classification is nevertheless adequate as a general schema that provides an initial, still abstract classification.

Here, only two examples from the contemporary literature are considered, and only briefly. All that need be shown is that such approaches cannot contribute to a philosophically tenable clarification of the question of God.

[1] The first example is a "proof" presented under the unusual title "the last proof of God."[43] It is not clear whether this means "the ultimate, definitive proof of God" or "the most recent proof of God." The second interpretation appears unlikely to be correct, because if it were correct one would expect to find in the book that presents it a consideration of the current discussions of this topic, and none is to be found.

---

[41] Hans Urs von Balthasar, *The Glory of the Lord: A Theological Aesthetics* (1965/1982–1991). See also Philippe Capelle's illuminating essay "Hans Urs von Balthasar: Phénoménologie et théologie," now contained in his *Finitude et mystère* (2005), 209–26.

[42] See 4.2.2.1[3], below.

[43] Robert Spaemann, *Der letzte Gottesbeweis* (2007). Spaemann himself describes his proof as "somewhat pretentious" (7).

The "proof" is as follows:

I. All factual truths are eternal truths.
II. Every present is the past of a future present.
III. The ontological status of eternal truths is neither that of being effects nor that of being remembered, but that of being known. An absolute consciousness, God, is therefore present.[44]

Additional passages from Spaemann provide adequate clarification. Of I, he writes the following:

> There appears to be surprisingly little to be said about this. That facts are eternal (in the sense of being always valid) is undeniable.[45]

II, he writes, is "not a second premise, but instead an elaboration of the first sentence," noting that "the truth even of the most fleeting and most trivial factual assertions . . . cannot be revised by anything and therefore is never revised."[46] The last step (III) is the one "most worthy of discussion."[47] Decisive to it is the introduction of *consciousness* in connection with truth. About this he speaks succinctly and not fully clearly. He assumes in any case that truth is necessarily connected to something or other that is conscious, knowing, and known. Because even factual truths are eternal, Spaemann reasons, this something-or-other cannot be any human being. It can therefore be only an absolute consciousness that Spaemann immediately names "God."

This "proof," which of course is not a proof in the strict sense,[48] depends upon a great many intuitions and assertions that raise many serious and fundamental philosophical questions. It is based on modest, indeed everyday "understandings" of truth, consciousness, time, validity, etc. For this reason alone it could be taken seriously philosophically only if all these understandings were thoroughly articulated and examined. It is for this reason that the status of this "proof" is at best that of being semi-systematic and indirect. Systematic clarification of all the factors that play significant roles in the proof would require an immense amount of work.

---

[44] Ibid., 117.
[45] Ibid., 118.
[46] Ibid., 120.
[47] Ibid., 122.
[48] Ibid., 125.

Most important is the following point: even if the requisite clarity could be provided, what would be proved would be *at most* that there is an absolute consciousness. No matter how well explained, the "proof" would not include the additional assumptions or theses that would be required to support naming that absolute consciousness "God." This "proof" is thus yet another of those that move from some phenomenon or other to a putative conclusion that introduces something or other that is then simply designated "God." The preceding sections of this chapter clearly show just how problematic procedures of this sort are. This example shows yet again that only within the framework of a systematic conception of Being as such and as a whole is it possible to develop a thoroughly intelligible and thought-through conception of God.

[2] The second example is the conception of the philosopher who at present, more than any other, focuses on "God": Richard Swinburne. His voluminous work can only be minimally considered here.

At first glance, it appears that Swinburne's approach is semi-systematic but not indirect. And indeed, diverging from other authors whose approaches are clearly indirect, he presents a proof that includes the word "God" in its conclusion. But the procedure that he follows in reaching this conclusion is complex and multi-staged in such a manner that it in fact does qualify not only as semi-systematic but also as indirect (in the sense articulated above).

Before presenting his proof, Swinburne introduces what may be termed a definition of the concept *God:*

> I take the proposition "God exists" (and the equivalent proposition "There is a God") to be logically equivalent to "there exists necessarily a person without a body (i.e., a spirit) who necessarily is eternal, perfectly free, omnipotent, omniscient, perfectly good, and the creator of all things." I use "God" as the name of the person picked out by this description.[49]

This definition no doubt articulates a widespread notion of God that, although it cannot be identified as specifically Christian, is not incompatible with the Christian view as it is usually interpreted. Introducing such a definition is acceptable in terms of logic and argumentation, but considered philosophically, is its content wholly non-problematic? It is not, according to the systematic conception presented in chapter 3 of this book, because what this definition articulates is an enormously

---

[49] Richard Swinburne, *The Existence of God,* 7.

complex and problematic conceptual content that, as a whole, constitutes that X whose existence is supposed to be rationally secured by means of proof. The attempt to present such a proof requires paying too high a philosophical price: the various characteristics attributed to this X are both insufficiently clarified and simply thrown together. The definition does nothing more than count them off, without explaining how they might be connected or might fit together. Explaining how they are connected or how they fit together would require the development of a theory covering all of actuality or, in the terminology of this book, a theory of Being as such and as a whole. If such a theory were developed, however, then any "proof" of the existence of an X that was characterized so unsystematically would be superfluous and senseless.

It is no accident that Swinburne follows a quite specific path in his attempt to prove the existence of his X. This is the path that, in the final chapter of his book, he calls "the balance of probability" and that he concisely describes as follows: "Various occurrent phenomena are such that they are more to be expected, more probable, if there is a God than if there is not."[50] Among the phenomena that are more to be expected if there is a God are the following: "The existence of the universe, its conformity to order, the existence of animals and humans with moral awareness, humans having great opportunities for cooperation in acquiring knowledge and moulding the universe, the pattern of history and the existence of some evidence of miracles, and finally the occurrence of religious experiences." Such phenomena would be less to be expected, he says, if there were no God.

All these phenomena, according to Swinburne, are evidence. What he seeks to do is to answer the question of "just how probable all the evidence that I have considered makes the hypothesis of theism."[51] Relying on Bayes's Theorem, he constructs an inductive proof that the probability of the theistic hypothesis is greater than is the probability of its negation.

Such a "proof" no doubt corresponds to the way of thinking of many human beings who are guided by—usually rather vague—probabilities. But the value of any such proof depends on just how "probability" is understood. The *philosophical* question about this understanding cannot be answered via the provision of any formal-technical definition. What ultimately matters philosophically is the *intelligibility* of the phenomenon in question. When questions of intelligibility arise, recourse is often taken to (scientific) explanation or explainability, but that con-

---

[50] Ibid., 328.
[51] Ibid., 329.

cept is too narrow to be of use here (although that is not argued here). It no doubt makes good sense to ask whether one specific intelligibility is greater or lesser than another. In the case of the problematic of God, however, what matters is not the greater or lesser intelligibility of phenomena considered in isolation from one another, but instead that of the comprehensive systematic configuration of all phenomena. The task would be to make this comprehensive systematic configuration the subject matter for theorization, but if this were done, then questions of probability would become irrelevant. The question concerning a or the comprehensive configuration of all phenomena is correctly posed only as the question concerning Being as such and as a whole. Only within a framework including an answer to *this* question does the possibility arise of *adequately* clarifying the so-called question of God.

1.4 A Wholly Anti-Systematic, Anti-Theoretical, and Direct Approach: Ludwig Wittgenstein

[1] The reason that Wittgenstein is even mentioned in this chapter is not that he presents an important conception of God. To be sure, his works contain various remarks about faith and religion and, along with them, about God; but he does not present a developed and significant conception of God. He is treated in the chapter, then, because his philosophy—especially that of his later or second phase—exerts enormous influence on much of contemporary philosophical and theological thought, particularly concerning the philosophy of religion. The result is a wholly new orientation in this field, one that has among its consequences a situating of the question of God that is diametrically opposed to the situating of it argued for in this book. Wittgenstein's position is anti-systematic and anti-theoretical, and thus what this book calls a direct approach. This is particularly clear in the works of authors who not only fully accept Wittgenstein's way of dealing with this issue but also make it the foundation for all their work in this area. Following a brief presentation of Wittgenstein's position, some of those authors are briefly considered.

Wittgenstein's philosophy of religion is quite contested with respect to both its interpretation and its evaluation.[52] As is well known, the late Wittgenstein revised his earlier positions, particularly the one taken

---

[52] The following presentation for the most part follows the interpretation found in John Hyman, "Wittgensteinianism" (1997).

in the *Tractatus*. At the very least, however, concerning the domain that the *Tractatus* calls "the mystical," which includes ethics, aesthetics, and particularly religion, there is a strong continuity between the early and the late Wittgenstein. The central thought of the *Tractatus* concerning this domain is that we cannot "express" it either by raising questions or by providing answers: "For an answer which cannot be expressed the question too cannot be expressed."[53] This thesis is supplemented by the final sentence in the *Tractatus*, which reads, "Whereof one cannot speak, thereof one must be silent."[54]

The only passage in the *Tractatus* that relates relevantly to God is the following: "*How* the world is, is completely indifferent for what is higher. God does not reveal himself *in* the world."[55] Wittgenstein appears to explain what this means in another passage, in which he says more about "the mystical": "Not *how* the world is, is the mystical, but *that* it is."[56]

After the 1930s, Wittgenstein fundamentally revised the most important of the *Tractatus*'s theses particularly by introducing the central thought of the language game, which makes sense only if it is understood as a form of life. Language in general and every element of language are meaningful only within the contexts of language games; to ask about meaning is to ask how a language as a whole and every individual expression in the language is used.

The notion of the language game provides the background necessary for understanding some of Wittgenstein's famous formulations concerning religion. According to him, religious expressions are ones that are understandable and interpretable only within the contexts of religious forms of life and religious language games. The chief consequence of this is that religious sentences that express religious convictions are not descriptive, i.e., do not express states of affairs or facts. Religious sentences and convictions are therefore neither true nor false, and neither rational nor irrational.

Wittgenstein's "philosophy" of religion, which is articulated only fragmentarily in a number of sentences most of which are formulated in mutual isolation, consists—as Hyman (1997) argues—of two central points. (Hyman speaks of "two doctrines," but this formulation is problematic in the case of Wittgenstein, who holds that philosophy does not or should not present theses and hence doctrines.) The first central

---

[53] Wittgenstein, *Tractatus Logico–Philosophicus*, 6.5.
[54] Ibid., 7.
[55] Ibid., 6.432.
[56] Ibid., 6.44.

point is semantic: verbal expressions of religious convictions are not, according to Wittgenstein, expressions in the genuine sense (that is, they do not express states of affairs or facts), so they cannot be either predictions or hypotheses:

> It seems to me that a religious belief could only be something like a decision in favor of frame of reference. Thus, although it is a belief, it is a form of life, or a way of judging life. A passionate embrace of this conception.[57]

To be sure, however, Wittgenstein's position on this is not fully clear. This is shown, for example, in the text that immediately follows the one just quoted:

> And instruction in a religious faith would thus be the presentation, the description of that frame of reference and at the same time an appeal to conscience [ein in's-Gewissen-reden]. And these two would have to result in the one's being instructed passionately embracing the frame of reference, on his own. It would be as though someone led me on the one hand to see my hopeless situation, and on the other presented me with the tool for salvation until I, on my own, or at least not led by the instructor's hand, rushed toward it and embraced it.

What Wittgenstein here calls "instruction" he understands—at least in part—as "the presentation, description of that frame of reference." This appears to indicate that faith or belief also has a descriptive component or indeed, *pace* Wittgenstein, a theoretical one. At the very least, the second central point—now to be introduced—appears not fully to exclude such a descriptive-theoretical component.

The second point is epistemological: religious convictions—and consequently religious expressions—are immune to falsification and verification. Of the spirit that animates Wittgenstein's conception of religion, faith, etc., the following passages provide perhaps the best indications:

> Christianity is not grounded in a historical truth, but it gives us a (historical) report and says: now believe! But not, believe this report with the belief that belongs to a historical report—but: believe through thick and thin, and you can do that only as the result of a life. Here you have a report—don't relate to it the way you relate to any other

---

[57] Wittgenstein, *Culture and Value*, 64 (t.a.).

historical report! Let it take *a completely different place* in your life.—That involves nothing *paradoxical*!

. . . Strange though it sounds: the historical reports of the Gospels could be demonstrably false in the historical sense, and faith could thereby lose nothing: but *not* because it was related to something like "universal rational truths"!, but because historical proof (the historical proof game) has nothing to do with faith. This report (the Gospels) is embraced believingly (i.e., lovingly) by human beings. *That* is the certainty of this holding-to-be-true, not *something else.*[58]

The first paragraph in the preceding passage can be understood wholly traditionally: familiarity with a historical truth does not suffice for religious belief; it is a necessary but not a sufficient condition for religious belief. Religious belief involves more than discerning and accepting a historical truth. The Wittgenstein of the first paragraph thus could be a traditional theologian. But this impression is completely destroyed by the second paragraph, because according to it historical truth is not only not a necessary condition for religious belief, it is not a condition at all, and this in the strongest possible sense: even if the putative truth were demonstratively false (thus, even if the historical basis of Christianity were demonstrably false), this would be irrelevant to religious belief. Given this, it must be asked whether it was clear to Wittgenstein that the consequences of what he says here are, if assessed in light of criteria that must be satisfied by any sensible talk about Christian belief, simply absurd. That this is so is particularly strange given Wittgenstein's radical demands for philosophical clarity.[59]

Finally, there is Wittgenstein's ambitious, apodictic verdict: "If Christianity is the truth, then all philosophy about it is false."[60] He also writes,

Religious belief and superstition are wholly different. The one arises from *fear* and is a kind of false science. The other is a trusting [*Vertraun*].[61]

Such remarks are peculiar. Hyman summarizes Wittgenstein's error and his barely suppressed amazement at Wittgenstein's strange aphorisms as follows:

---

[58] *Culture and Value,* 32 (t.a.).

[59] E.g.: ". . . the clarity that we are aiming at is indeed *complete* clarity. But this simply means that the philosophical problems should *completely* disappear" (*Philosophical Investigations,* §133).

[60] *Culture and Value,* 83 (t.a.).

[61] Ibid., 72 (t.a.).

Since evidence and argument are not the exclusive property of science, Wittgenstein cannot be right to insist that if we try to prove or support the proposition that God exists we are already trapped in confusion, because we are treating religion as if it were science. It would, I think, be foolish to maintain that Anselm and Aquinas were peddling superstitions, or that apostasy cannot be based on reasons. It is certainly impossible to insulate religion entirely from rational criticism.[62]

Hyman's critique is on target, but it must be carried further. That Wittgenstein's is an inaccurate understanding of religion is clear from the fact that he reduces religion to things that are *done* such as *acts* of faith, praying, liturgies, etc. At least the Christian religion, however, has never had so narrow a form. The Christian religion has always *also* included a *global view of the entirety of actuality*, a view that is articulated in genuinely theoretical sentences. It is thus not only the case, as Hyman notes, that religious belief cannot be entirely insulated from rational critique. It is also—and more radically—the case that the Christian religion concerns human beings *integrally*, that is, with respect to *all* domains of and factors relevant to their lives. Among these belong the human capacity for attaining intelligibility. Wittgenstein's conception of the religious human being as a human being having religious beliefs is thus nothing other than a caricature of the genuinely religious human being.

[2] D. Z. Phillips is a well-known—perhaps the best-known—defender of a radically non-cognitivist philosophy of religion inspired by Wittgenstein.[63] He radicalizes Wittgenstein's thought that religion, like science and other forms of human activity, is a form of life and a language game; according to Phillips, this means that it establishes its own criteria for meaning and for rationality, and that these therefore cannot be criticized from the outside. Phillips demands a total revision of the relation between discursive research (both philosophical and scientific)

---

[62] Hyman, 155.

[63] It is difficult if not impossible to determine which of the relevant authors are among the most radically non-cognitivist. Many such "philosophers" (and "theologians") appear to attempt to outdo one another with respect to radicality. This is exemplarily the case with Don Cupitt, who defends a conception that is a contemporary postmodern and "post-Christian" form of Christianity, and who writes sentences like the following: "In post-Christianity there are no longer two worlds, but only one world—*this* world; and there is no longer an objective God" (*After All* [1994], 23). So fully undifferentiated an assertion is typical of this kind of "philosophical/theological" literature. What, for example, does "world" mean here? How is it that "two worlds" could be distinct from each other? How is "this world" defined? This formulation is the more noteworthy given that the same author maintains, "reality has become a mere bunch of disparate and changing interpretations" (in J. Runzo, ed., *Is God Real?* [1993], 46).

and religion, in order to do justice to religion as its own language game. According to Phillips, a language game can be understood only if the forms of practice internal to it are investigated, and this can be done only if no methods of description or of evaluation, including those in terms of grounds or reasons, arguments, etc., are applied to the language game. Because religious belief is its own fully self-sufficient language game, it requires no "proof."

As soon as one begins to consider the consequences of any such conception for human beings, it quickly becomes clear that it is wholly untenable. If religion were such a form of life with a language game of the sort described by Phillips, then human beings would be in the peculiar situation of having various forms of life and playing the relevant language games in such a way that all these forms and games would be completely separate from one another. It is far from clear how, if that were the case, there could be any unity at all in any human life. In fact, however, it is our experience at every moment that although we are manifold, all of our manifold aspects or dimensions communicate fully with one another (except of course in cases of permanent, total schizophrenia, in which the structural coherence of personality is lost).

Relying on insights of the sort indicated above, Phillips comes to utter assertions like the following: "The whole notion of a God and another world which we can infer from the world we know is discredited."[64] "To ask whether God exists is not to ask a theoretical question."[65] "'God exists,' though it appears to be in the indicative mood, is an expression of faith."[66] "The praising and the glorifying does not refer to some object called God. Rather, the expression of such praise and glory is what we call the worship of God."[67]

An atheist, John L. Mackie, provides the most accurately targeted critique of such putative insights. About the last, he writes the following:

> But now we are at a loss. How does the expression of praise and glory make sense unless there is a real object to be praised and glorified? Praise logically requires, it is true, only an intentional object. One cannot praise without praising something, but what one praises may exist only in one's own thoughts. But one could not consistently make a big thing of praising and glorifying a god that one at the same time recog-

[64] D. Z. Phillips, *God Without Explanation*, 21.

[65] Ibid., 181.

[66] Ibid., 180–81.

[67] Ibid., 149.

nized to exist only in one's mind, or even jointly in the minds of many believers like a figure in a widely current myth or legend.[68]

Mackie also comments critically on Phillips's attempt to defend himself from the charge that his views "are simply a form of disguised atheism."[69] In defending himself, Phillips appeals to "the conceptual character of the investigation," continuing, "if, *per impossibile,* there were an object corresponding to these pictures or perspectives, it could not be the God of religion . . . anything whose existence could be verified cannot be God."[70]

Mackie responds:

> But a misleading positivism underlies his conceptual investigation. The question is not whether statements about a god could be verified, but whether they are true—simply true, not "true" with some special grammar. . . . Phillips has given no grounds for denying that "the God of religion" is a possible subject of simple truth or falsehood; in consequence what he offers is either disguised atheism or unsupported theism—since he declines to support its factual claims—or else an unresolved hesitation between the two.[71]

1.5 A Characteristic Example of a Failed Critique: Thomas Nagel's Objections to God as "Last Point"

It is appropriate in this chapter to also critically analyze a *negative* philosophical approach to the question of God. The one considered—Thomas Nagel's—includes some of the central objections commonly raised against God, and is formulated in a simple and therefore extraordinarily clear fashion. Nagel's approach, and his objections, are representative of those articulated or presupposed by many philosophers who take its lines of argumentation to be sound. Responding to this objection contributes significantly to clarifying the subject matter and the purposes of this book.[72]

---

[68] J. L. Mackie, *The Miracle of Theism* (1982), 227.

[69] Phillips, 149.

[70] Ibid.

[71] Mackie, 228.

[72] What follows summarizes *Structure and Being* 4.5.3.4.2; some passages are taken verbatim from that text.

[1] In the final chapter of his *What Does It All Mean?* (*WDIAM*, chap. 10), Nagel addresses "The Meaning of Life." His starting point is the following: "The problem is that although there are justifications and explanations for most of the things, big and small, that we do *within* life, none of these explanations explain the point of your life as a whole—the whole of which all these activities, successes and failures, strivings and disappointments are parts" (*WDIAM* 96). To the objection that we must simply be satisfied with what we do "within life," he responds:

> This is a perfectly good reply. But it only works if you really can avoid setting your sights higher, and asking what the point of the whole thing is. For once you do that, you open yourself to the possibility that your life is meaningless. (97)

The problem Nagel identifies is this: being satisfied only with things "within life" leaves a *broader* question unanswered. The broader question is the following: if one considers life as embedded within a broader context, does it have a point, or not? Nagel responds with a course of argumentation that requires consideration by any philosophy that, in any way, affirms God.

Nagel maintains that "if you think about the whole thing, there seems to be no point to it at all" (96). His argument for this contention is a variant of an argument leading to an infinite regress:

> If one's life has a point as a part of something larger, it is still possible to ask about that larger thing, what is the point of *it*? Either there is an answer in terms of something still larger or there isn't. If there is, we simply repeat the question. If there isn't, then our search for a point has come to an end with something which has no point. But if that pointlessness is acceptable for the larger thing of which our life is a part, why shouldn't it be acceptable already for our life taken as a whole? Why isn't it all right for your life to be pointless? And if it isn't acceptable there, why should it be acceptable when we get to the larger context? Why don't we have to go on to ask, "But what is the point of all *that*?" (human history, the succession of the generations, or whatever). (*WDIAM* 98)

Nagel extends the argument by considering the assumption of an ultimate meaning or ultimate point. His argument continues to apply, he contends, because we can ask,

> "And what is the point of *that*?" It's supposed to be something which is its own point, and can't have a purpose outside itself. But for this very reason it has its own problems. (*WDIAM* 99)

Strangely, Nagel considers the assumption that life has an ultimate point to involve the attribution of a "religious meaning to life" (*WDIAM* 98). That it must be such is absolutely to be rejected because, from the beginnings of philosophy, questions concerning what is ultimate and absolute have *always* been included among *philosophical* questions. As shown above (1.3.2.1[2]), the rash introduction into and use in philosophical accounts of the word "God," which is originally characteristic of religion(s), is based on a widely consequential misunderstanding. The facile application of the designation "religious" to characterize questions and theses concerning what is ultimate is the more regrettable in that it tends to arouse an extensive series of negative psychological connotations and emotions that as a rule simply hinder rational discussion, or even make it impossible. The following discussion of Nagel's position does use the word "God," but only in connection with his formulations. In strict opposition to Nagel, however, the word is used here *purely philosophically.*

Against the assumption of an ultimate meaning (which he terms "God"), Nagel raises two objections. First (*WDIAM* 99), he proceeds from the assumption that the idea of (a) God "seems to be the idea of something that can explain everything else, without having to be explained itself." Nagel maintains that it is "very hard to understand how there could be such a thing," and then raises the following questions:

> If we ask the question, "Why is the world like this?" and are offered a religious answer, how can we be prevented from asking again, "And why is *that* true?" What kind of answer would bring all our "Why?" questions to a stop, once and for all? And if they can stop there, why couldn't they have stopped earlier?

The second objection is based on a fact that, according to Nagel, leads to the same problem. The fact is that God and his plans or intentions are presented as the absolutely "ultimate explanation of the value and meaning of our lives." Nagel continues as follows:

> The idea that our lives fulfill God's purpose is supposed to give them their point, in a way that doesn't require or admit of any further point. One isn't supposed to ask "What is the point of God?" any more than one is supposed to ask, "What is the explanation of God?"

> . . . Can there really be something which gives point to everything
> else by encompassing it, but which couldn't have, or need, any point
> itself? Something whose point can't be questioned from outside be-
> cause there is no outside? (*WDIAM* 99–100)

Before Nagel's line of thought is examined, it is important to note
that the systematic approach to the question of God taken in this book
(in chapter 3) is not based on why questions, and therefore does not
present answers to any why questions (of any sort whatsoever). That it
does not is neither an open nor a disguised weakness, and yet less is it
an attempt to conjure away a serious problem. To the contrary, chapter
3 makes clear that why questions, even—and indeed most especially—
when they appear to be or are presented as absolutely radical questions,
are based on presuppositions that are simply accepted without examination. The truly radical questions are simply not why questions. The truly
radical questions are questions of intelligibility, which are how questions.
Any why question about anything asks about only a specific aspect of that
anything (no matter how the anything is designated), not about the anything as a whole. As indicated, this state of affairs is examined below (in
section 3.2.3).

[2] Although, for the reason just given, the systematic approach
taken in this book is immune to Nagel's line of argument, the latter remains worthy of consideration. The following paragraphs show that Nagel's two arguments, which are the basis of all his other reflections, are
based on misunderstandings.

[i] The first argument is based on the thought that at every point
whatsoever, new why questions arise; they would thus arise also at a or
the putatively ultimate point, however that point might be termed or understood, but this shows the putatively ultimate point not to be ultimate.
This kind of argumentation—which is quite common—depends on a
simple and peculiar lack of understanding and of thematization of the
logic, semantics, and ontology of why questions. The argument depends
on the naive assumption that in every context and with respect to every
state of affairs, why questions *mechanically* appear and thus can always be
posed or repeated. To be sure, why questions *can* be generated mechanically everywhere and at all times, but closer analysis shows this to be a
senseless abuse because it is *incoherent*. It is incoherent in that it simply
ignores the presuppositions that make such questions possible and sensible. This is now briefly to be shown.

A given why question is sensible only if it has a clear target; otherwise, the question is undetermined and in fact asks nothing. Such a target
is, however, for its part possible only on the presupposition of a specific

context or framework, precisely because what the question asks for is the relation between its target (however specified: object, state of affairs, etc.) and *something else*. In brief: to ask *why* about something is to ask that that something be related *to something else,* which is a reason or ground. A why "question" that did not ask for this would not be a question but instead an undirected, objectless, and thus senseless attempt to get to something completely indeterminate and empty. Indeed, a genuine and sensible why question about something, as the attempt to discover how that something is related to something else (a reason or ground), presupposes that the questioner has raised the question within a theoretical framework that explicitly contains such a relation. In other words: the question is based on the presupposition that a theoretical framework, consisting at least of a logic, a semantics, and an ontology, is *already* in place.

From this basic fact there follows something that is extensively consequential: why questions cannot be arbitrarily repeated or iterated because if they were, they would soon escape the theoretical frameworks within which alone they could make sense; they would be undirected and thus senseless, no more than empty plays with words. This case is wholly analogous to the case where demands for grounding or self-grounding are made utterly independently of theoretical frameworks. As this book and particularly *Structure and Being* show in various contexts, sentences are meaningful only within theoretical frameworks. This holds also for interrogative sentences.

To Nagel's question, "What kind of answer would bring all our 'Why?' questions to a stop, once and for all?," the answer is the following: the answer that brings all our why questions to an end is the one that correctly understands *all why questions* and interprets them as questions that are meaningful only within specific theoretical frameworks. The case of a why question concerning an ultimate point is then to be interpreted as follows: if an X is understood as an ultimate point, then the question concerning the why of this ultimate point is utterly empty *if* it is understood as the demand for *something more,* an additional reason or ground to which the putatively ultimate point would be related. This "something more" would be something *ex hypothesi beyond* or *outside of* the presupposed theoretical framework, because there could be nothing *within* the theoretical framework beyond that ultimate point. The introduction of any such thing into the framework would be the introduction of a contradiction. Differently stated: the articulation of an ultimate point on the basis of an accepted framework stops every iterative, mechanical posing of why questions. Why questions make sense only within frameworks. If all of the potentialities of a given framework are taken into consideration, by the articulation of an ultimate point, the process of posing why questions comes to an end in the sense that *it turns on itself:* the why question concerning the ultimate point is answered by the ultimate point itself. If the why question concerning the ultimate point is not understood in this way, then it simply breaks apart, because there is nothing that could be its answer.

This state of affairs is helpfully comparable to the mathematical concept of the *fixed point,* which can, oversimplifying to the extreme, be presented (for the case of ordinal numbers) as follows: let F be an operation that maps ordinal numbers to ordinal numbers. Fixed points of F are ordinal numbers α with $F(\alpha) = \alpha$. The application to the philosophical case is then clear: the operation F corresponds to the concept "why" or "the reason for"; α corresponds to the "ultimate point." $F(\alpha) = \alpha$ is then contentually to be interpreted as: the reason for the ultimate point is the ultimate point itself.

To be noted is that *in another respect,* the ultimate point can and indeed must be put into question. The other respect is, concretely, that the question "Why this ultimate point?" is not understood as, "What is the ground or basis for this ultimate point itself?" but instead as, "Why *this* ultimate point?" The sense of this question is the following: is the point that has been determined to be ultimate actually the *adequately* understood or determined ultimate point?

This question is completely legitimate. But it then means precisely the following: the question, correctly formulated, concerns one of the following two possible problems: *either* the question concerning the ultimate point is not correctly posed and/or clarified *within* the presupposed framework, *or* the presupposed theoretical framework *itself* is inadequate and therefore must be replaced by one that is more adequate or more comprehensive. This second possibility is the one that is genuinely interesting philosophically, because the most decisive questions and the most decisive divergences arise as a rule from differences between theoretical frameworks.

For the question "Why *this* last point?" not to prove yet again to be an undirected and thus empty play with words, it must be ascertained that in this ultimate case (i.e., in the case that requires the development or the assumption of a broader, more comprehensive theoretical framework), such a broader, more comprehensive theoretical framework is *actually* presupposed *and explicated,* or at least that it *can be explicated.* Then, however, the mechanical procedure of asking why within this broader, more comprehensive theoretical framework comes to a standstill, as is shown above.

If nevertheless the question "And why *this* (additional) last point?" is posed in a *meaningful manner,* the question is actually meaningful only if *a broader, yet more comprehensive* theoretical framework is or can be envisaged *and* presupposed. But can this procedure of envisaging or discovering or projecting ever broader, more comprehensive theoretical frameworks ever be halted? Only at first glance does it appear that it cannot. In fact, we human beings cannot simply envisage or discover or project ever more—in principle, endlessly many more—theoretical frameworks *that are meaningful;* the thought that we could is an illusion, an empty notion or contention. That it is is shown by a simple argument. For an additional theoretical framework to be *meaningful,* it must in some way be *providable* or *articulable;* if this condition is not satisfied, then saying anything like, "Well, there *could* be an additional framework" is simply playing with words. And for the same reason, purely mechanically asking a why question about any given ultimate point is likewise simply playing with words. Such empty wordplays in the course of theorization and hence making-intelligible make no sense.

Nothing of course prevents us, as human beings (philosophers, theoreticians), from remaining *open* to additional theoretical frameworks, or from attempting to envisage, discover, develop, or project them. Our remaining thus open is in complete accordance with the basic theses defended in the structural-systematic philosophy. To be added is that this openness in no way entails any inconsistent relativism; that it does not is shown in *Structure and Being.*[73] To be kept in mind in this connection is that the broader, more comprehensive theoretical framework in question must prove to be *more adequate* than its predecessor. Even if it did, however, that would not entail that the new theoretical framework would have to negate, in every respect, everything characterizing the preceding framework or frameworks; instead, the relation between the frameworks would be that of relatively *greater adequacy.* This implies a thoroughgoing and fundamental commonality between the theoretical frameworks with respect to central factors. Thus, *all* theoretical frameworks, both actual and possible, are structured by means of the grand and fundamental thought of coherence, even if "coherence" is not understood in all in precisely the same way. To all belongs as well—and essentially—the perspective of an *ultimate factor* or a last point.

[ii] On the basis of what has just been said concerning Nagel's first argument or objection, Nagel's second argument or objection is easily dealt with. The objection says that an accepted ultimate point or God, as putatively ultimate explanation for anything and everything, itself requires explanation and thus the introduction of something else. The

---

[73] See 3.3.4.3.

response to this objection should be obvious: here again, the central importance of the theoretical framework is simply and wholly ignored. The operator "is an explanation for" has, methodologically, precisely the same status as the operators, thoroughly considered above, "Why . . . ?" and "The reason for . . . is . . ." *Within* a presupposed theoretical framework, the ultimate point explains itself; it is simply a (better: the) point that is systematically fixed. To be added, however, is that the fixed point explains itself precisely in that it explains anything and everything: it is the coherence that constitutes the interconnection of everything, itself included.

Nagel's above-cited question, "Can there really be something which gives point to everything else by encompassing it, but which couldn't have, or need, any point itself?" is ambiguous. As shown above, it is incoherent to say or to assume that the ultimate point within a theoretical framework T requires or is subject to explanation *outside of* the accepted or presupposed theoretical framework T, as long as T remains accepted or presupposed.

To Nagel's additional question, "[Can there really be] something whose point can't be questioned from outside because there is no outside?," the answer is the following: this is not only possible, it is necessary, *presupposing* that one understands "outside" as "outside the theoretical framework being used" *and* that one interprets "because there is no outside" as meaning: "there is nothing outside *of the accepted and presupposed theoretical framework, as long as one* accepts, uses, or presupposes *exclusively* this theoretical framework." This thesis is thoroughly explained and grounded above.

Chapter 2

Heidegger's Thinking of Being: The Flawed Development of a Significant Approach

With respect to the subject matter of this book and the theses it centrally defends, the thought of Martin Heidegger is of decisive significance. Many contemporary philosophical (and theological) discussions of God, especially concerning the relation between Being and God, are influenced by his thought in one way or another. In this book, Heidegger is introduced above in various contexts, and he remains relevant, in one way or another, throughout. This chapter critically examines the decisive aspects of his thought.

2.1 Heidegger's Failed and Distorting Interpretation and Critique of the Christian Metaphysics of Being

The first task is that of more precisely characterizing and analyzing an aspect of Heidegger's thought mentioned several times above: his misinterpretation of Christian metaphysics as onto-theo-logy. Heidegger presented this interpretation throughout his career in a manner that was often, in many respects, uniquely stereotypical and fundamentally repetitive. It provided for him the permanent and comfortable foil in contrast to which his own attempt to think Being in a radically new way was supposed to appear as absolutely original and revolutionary. As the following account shows, his path is, in the literal sense and in terminology he often uses, a forest path.[1]

---

[1] Heidegger, *Off the Beaten Track* (1950/2002). Added to *Being and God:* Heidegger explains the term "*Holzwege*" in the following passage:

"Wood" [*Holz*] is an old name for forest. In the wood there are paths [*Wege*], mostly overgrown, that come to an abrupt stop where the wood is untrodden.

Heidegger's misinterpretation is at heart extraordinarily simple or, more precisely, distortingly oversimplified. In connection with some of his assertions, particularly ones from "The Onto-theo-logical Constitution of Metaphysics" (*ID* 42–74), they can be reduced to three central points. Heidegger explicitly designates the first two of these points as "key words [*Leitworte*] of metaphysics:" the distinctions between Being and beings and between ground and grounded (71). The third point is Heidegger's most pointed characterization of the "metaphysical" (in his sense) God: God as *causa sui*.

[1] Absolutely central, according to Heidegger, is the *distinction between Being and beings*. From it he derives the charge that metaphysics has forgotten Being, in that it presents Being only as the Being-of-beings and as itself a being, but not as Being itself. In order adequately to understand the consequentiality and the precise sense of this interpretation and critique, one must consider many additional points that are treated below. Here, the unfoundedness and arbitrariness of what Heidegger says about Being and beings is shown in a general respect in conjunction with his failed interpretation of Aquinas's metaphysics of Being.

[i] Section 1.3.2's presentation of Aquinas's metaphysics of Being shows that the thesis that Aquinas forgot or ignored Being is simply false. The thesis, in its utter lack of discrimination, is wholly undermined by careful examination of Aquinas's works. Shown above is that Aquinas not only recognizes and articulates the distinction between *esse* and *ens/entia*, but also explicitly thematizes *esse ipsum*, even though the full sense of *esse ipsum* appears in his works only in the background. Also shown above is that the designation Aquinas deems most appropriate for God is nothing like "highest being," "first being," etc., but instead is *esse per se subsistens*. Only in relatively few passages does Aquinas name God *ens primum, supremum, maxime ens*, etc., and he does so then for linguistic-stylistic reasons.

In addition, various specific details make clear that Aquinas's *ultimate* position is *not* an onto-theo-logical one. Several relevant passages are introduced in what follows.

Normally, we can say of any being *x*, "The being *x* is" (in the sense of "The being *x* exists") or "The being *x* is such-and-such . . ."). But can we say of Being itself that it is—either in the sense of "exists" or in that of "is such-and-such"? In "On the Question of Being," Heidegger writes:

They are called *Holzwege*.
Each goes its separate way, though within the same forest. It often appears as if one is identical to another. But it only appears so. (v)

Within the perspective of scientific representation, which is acquainted only with beings, that which . . . is in no way a being (namely, Being) can present itself only as nothing. . . . How does it stand with this wholly other to every being, with that which is not a being? What this shows: the Dasein of the human being is "held within" "*this*" nothing, this wholly other to beings. . . . It does not give[a] [*gibt es nicht*] Being and nothing next to each other. One intercedes for the other in a relationship whose essential fullness we have still scarcely pondered. We also do not ponder it as long as we neglect to ask: . . . to what extent does whatever secretly gives [*anheimgibt*] the gift in "It gives Being and nothing" belong to this gift in that it keeps it safe? Glibly, we say: it gives. *Being no more "is" than is nothing.* But *It gives* both of them. (*PM* 316–17; t.a.; emphasis in the penultimate sentence added)

Heidegger's characteristically rhetorical and—philosophically— scarcely acceptable linguistic acrobatics need not be thoroughly criticized here. One point suffices. His linguistic virtuosity consists here in suggesting to the reader, in an extraordinarily imprecise and captious fashion, that he is dealing with a deep problem. In actuality, Heidegger's talk here about "nothing" (and as a rule also in all of the great many other passages in his works wherein he speaks of "nothing") rests on a confusion: the talk is of nothing with respect to beings, in that he says that Being is *not* (a) being. On the basis of this simple and obvious negative thesis Heidegger waxes poetic about "Being and nothing." Granted, one can use a noun to designate the negation in the formulation "Being is *not* (a) being" by making of the "not" a "nothing." But it then must of course be understood that *this* "nothing" is not the traditional so-called "absolute nothing(ness) (*nihilum absolutum*)," but instead a "relative nothing(ness) (*nihilum relativum*)." The former is the negation of every being *and of Being,* no matter how "Being" is more precisely understood. Relative nothing(ness), on the other hand, is the negation of a *specific* being and, in the case of a comprehensive generalization, of *all beings;* it is, however, not the negation of *Being (itself).*

It suffices here to more closely examine the passage with the aim

---

[a] "It gives" literally translates "*Es gibt,*" which is usually best translated as "There is" (and "It does not give" translates the negatives "*Es gibt nicht*" and "*gibt es nicht*"). In ordinary German, the "*Es*"—the counterpart to the English "it"—is impersonal (as is "It" in "It's morning" or "It's raining"). "It gives" is used in the main text because "There is being" appears to conflict with Heidegger's contention that one cannot use "is" in conjunction with "being," and because Heidegger's texts suggest that the "It" may be somehow referential.

only of understanding its penultimate sentence, "Being no more 'is'
than is nothing." Why and on what basis does Heidegger say this? How
these questions are to be answered is the less clear given the well-known
fact that Heidegger verbalizes "nothing," as in "What Is Metaphysics?"
(1929). He writes, "The nothing itself nothings" (*PM* 90), to which he
adds, in the work's fifth (1949) edition, the following: "As nothinging,
the nothing essences[b] [*west*], abides, preserves" (*PM* 90 note c; t.a.). Why
does Heidegger not correspondingly verbalize "Being"? Instead of doing
that, Heidegger uses another verb as the verbal analogue to the "nothings" he uses in conjunction with "nothing"; this is the verb "*wesen.*" Thus,
he often uses such formulations as "Being *west* . . ."[2] But what is the meaning of the verb "*wesen*"? That Heidegger plays with these words is clear.
Below, the question is posed whether—and if so, how—Heidegger here
takes an additional step. In any case, it is noteworthy that Heidegger
writes both "Being 'is' no more than is (the) nothing" and "As nothinging, the nothing *west,* abides, preserves."

Comparable to Heidegger's sentences is a passage from Aquinas
that explicitly makes an apparently similar point: ". . . we cannot say,
'Being itself is. . .' [. . . *non possumus dicere quod ipsum esse sit.* . .]." But for
this thesis Aquinas presents an explanation that is illuminating *within the
framework of his ontological conceptuality, with its Aristotelian orientation;* that
explanation also shows once again that Aquinas indeed envisages *Being
itself,* rather than having "forgotten" it. Understanding Aquinas's formulation requires consideration of its context:

> Being itself never means something [a subject] that is, just as running
> never means something that runs; just as we cannot say that running
> itself runs, *we cannot say that Being itself is.* But just as that which is means
> something that bears Being, what runs means something that bears
> running. Thus, just as we can say of the one that runs, or of the runner,
> that it runs insofar as it bears [or completes] running and participates
> in running, so can we say that the being, or what is, is, insofar as it takes
> part in the act of Being. And this is what Boethius says: *Being itself is not*

---

[b] On "essences [*west*]": the German past participle for *sein* (to be), *gewesen,* is irregular,
but it would be the regular past participle of the verb *wesen,* which did not occur in the
ordinary (colloquial) German of Heidegger's day, although it was used frequently in German poetry (especially by Goethe). As a noun, *Wesen* is also the German counterpart to "essence." Words that appear to be forms of the verb *wesen* thus suggest, to those conversant
in German, both *being* and *essence.*

[2] See, e.g., *Contributions,* 240: "Truth never 'is,' but instead *west.* For it is the truth of
Beyng [*Seyn*], which 'only' *west.*" Also passim.

yet [i.e., not something concrete], because it does not attribute Being
to itself as [it could/would if it were] a bearer of Being. But *that which
is, in that it takes on the form of Being, i.e., the act of Being itself, is and stands
in itself,* i.e., subsists in itself. Being in the genuine sense is true only of
substance; only this subsists in itself.[3]

Here, it is clear that the approaches of Heidegger and Aquinas are
in one respect quite different—in that they philosophize within different
theoretical frameworks—but also that in another—and indeed one that
is extremely important today—they are similar in a remarkable way: both
authors aim to articulate Being itself—*ipsum esse.* Clear in addition is that
Heidegger's accusing Aquinas of having forgotten Being reflects nothing
more than Heidegger's own ignorance. Heidegger has in view at most
the scholastic tradition of Christian metaphysics, not the work of Aquinas
as a whole and in its comprehensive consequentiality.

[ii] This interpretation is fully confirmed, and with it this judgment of Heidegger's treatment of Aquinas, by the two extensive texts
that Heidegger wrote about Aquinas. These are next examined in detail,
although to be noted is that for the most part they articulate matters that
are announced above as the second and third points considered in the
analysis of Heidegger's failed and distorting interpretation of the Christian metaphysics of Being presented in this section (2.1).

[a] The first text is a chapter from the posthumously (2006) published lecture course *History of Philosophy from Thomas Aquinas to Kant,*
which Heidegger presented in Marburg in 1926/27.[4] In the entire text,
he never once considers what Aquinas says about *esse.* He does quote a
few passages containing the word *esse,* but none is centrally relevant. The
only passage in which *esse* is used in connection with God (although Heidegger does not note that it is) is the following: "Everything, however,
that constitutes the essence of God is his own Being [*suum proprium esse*]."[5]

---

[3] "Ipsum esse non significatur sicut ipsum subiectum essendi, sicut nec currere significatur sicut subiectum cursus: unde, sicut non possumus dicere quod ipsum currere currat,
ita *non possumus dicere quod ipsum esse sit:* sed sicut id ipsum quod est, significatur sicut subiectum essendi, sic id quod currit significatur sicut subiectum cursui et participat ipsum;
ita possumus dicere quod ens, sive id quod est, sit, in quantum participat actum essendi; et
hoc est quod dicit [Boethius]: Ipsum esse nondum est, quia non attribuitur sibi esse sicut
subiecto essendi; sed id quod est, accepta forma essendi, scilicet suscipiendo ipsum actum
essendi, est, atque consistit, idest in seipso subsistit. Non enim ens dicitur proprie et per se,
nisi de substantia, cuius est subsistere" (*In librum Boetii De Hebdomadibus expositio, lectio* 2, 39;
emphasis in first sentence added).

[4] *GA,* vol. 23. The treatment of Aquinas encompasses pages 41–103.

[5] Ibid., 87.

Heidegger's inclusion of this text does not prevent him from introducing apodictic assertions about Aquinas on Being, although it is never clear whether by "Being" he means Aquinas's *ens* or his *esse*. In the "summary" of his scanty presentation of Aquinas's overall philosophical position, particularly "concerning the truth, *verum–ens*," he asserts:

> The question concerning the concept of Being [*Seinsbegriff*] results in: to be is to be created [*Sein besagt Geschaffensein*]. Being [*Sein*] read from the mode of Being [*Seinsart*] of things present at hand [*vorhandene Dinge*]. Fundamentally, not having moved beyond Being as presence at hand [*Vorhandenheit*].

And, summarily: "The decisive result: Being = presence at hand."[6] The same misinterpretation is found in Heidegger's most important work, *Being and Time.*[7]

On this basis, Heidegger also misinterprets creation, as shown below in chapter 3 (3.6.1[2][i]). To be noted here is that this misinterpretation appears, in one way or another, throughout Heidegger's works.

If one attends to what section 1.3.2 shows about Aquinas and his conception of *esse* (particularly in 1.3.2.2), it is clear that Heidegger's assertions about the Aquinian conception "of Being" constitute a colossal distortion. The question presses: how can a philosophy go so completely and so radically wrong?[8] That question is not, however, considered here.

[b] The second text encompasses paragraphs 12–15 of the posthumously (1983) published lecture course *Fundamental Concepts of Metaphysics: World, Finitude, Solitude,* held in Freiburg in the winter semester of 1929/30. Of these, §13 is devoted exclusively to Aquinas.[9] In this text, Heidegger attempts to show "the inherent incongruities of the traditional concept of metaphysics" (§12), first in relation to medieval metaphysics in general and then in the specific case of Aquinas's concept of metaphysics, which he interprets as "historical evidence for the three

---

[6] Ibid., 83–84.

[7] See *BT* §6, p. 46; §20, pp. 125–26.

[8] Yet more difficult is it to understand how such an author as Marion, who understands himself as an absolutely radical Christian author, can fully agree with this hermeneutical distortion of *esse* and of the thought of creation in Christian metaphysics, On this, see his *Au lieu de soi: L'approche de Saint Augustin* (2009), 315ff. See also the critique of what Marion says on this matter in chapter 4, below (4.2.1[2] and 4.2.4.4.2).

[9] *The Fundamental Concepts of Metaphysics: World, Finitude, Solitude* (1995). All page numbers in parentheses in [ii][b] of the main text refer to this volume.

features [i.e., the three incongruities] of the traditional concept of metaphysics" (§13).

He summarizes the three features he interprets as incongruities as follows: "We make three assertions concerning the traditional concept of metaphysics: [1.] it is *trivialized* [*veräusserlicht*]; [2.] it is intrinsically *confused;* [3.] it is *unconcerned* about the real problem of that which it is supposed to designate" (41). The first feature, the trivialization, consists for him in the fact that it understands "the metaphysical (God, immortal soul) as a being at hand, even if as a higher one [*ein vorhandenes, wenn auch ein höheres Seiendes*]" (41). And he elaborates:

> What is essential is that the object of *First Philosophy* (metaphysics) is now a *specific,* albeit *suprasensuous being.* In our question concerning the medieval understanding of metaphysics we are now . . . dealing with . . . the *principal fact* that the suprasensuous, the metaphysical, is *one* domain of *beings* among others. (43)

Heidegger characterizes the second feature, *confusion,* as "the combining of the two separate kinds of lying out beyond (μετά) as pertaining to *supra*sensuous beings and to the *non*sensuous characteristics of the Being of beings" (44). Thereby, Heidegger refers to the twofold question raised by Aristotle in characterizing first philosophy (πρώτη φιλοσοφία): the *theological* question concerning knowledge of the suprasensible and the question concerning ὂν ᾗ ὄν, concerning being(s) as such. He remarks:

> These *two fundamentally different kinds of lying beyond* come to be combined into *one* concept. The question is not raised at all of what the μετά means *here;* rather this is left undetermined. (44–45)

Finally, Heidegger characterizes the third feature as "the unproblematic nature of the traditional concept of metaphysics," explaining, "Because the traditional concept of metaphysics is thus trivialized and confused in itself, it simply cannot come about that metaphysics in itself or the μετά in its proper sense is made a problem" (45). As a consequence, "philosophizing proper as a completely free questioning on the part of man is not possible during the Middle Ages," so that "fundamentally there is no philosophy in the Middle Ages." Instead, Aristotelian metaphysics is taken over in such a way that "not only a dogmatics of faith, but also a dogmatics of First Philosophy itself arises." He then adds: "Kant really got a grip on the matter for the first time, and attempted in one particular direction to make *metaphysics itself a problem.*"

Aquinas is thus presented and interpreted by Heidegger as the thinker in whom these three features or "incongruities" of the traditional concept of metaphysics are perfectly developed. Concretely, Heidegger proceeds by introducing and commenting on some passages from the extremely concise introduction (*Prooemium*) to Aquinas's commentary on Aristotle's *Metaphysics*.[10] He carefully summarizes what Aquinas tersely says as follows:

> Thus we see how Aquinas, in his unified orientation toward the concept of the *maxime intelligibile* [that which is most highly or maximally intelligible or knowable] and in the skillful interpretation of a threefold meaning, attempts to bring together the traditional concepts that hold for metaphysics, so that *First Philosophy* deals with the *first causes* (*de primis causis*), *metaphysics* with *being in general* (*de ente*) and *theology* with God (*de Deo*). All three together are a unified science, the governing science [*scientia regulatrix*]. (49; t.a.)

Heidegger then maintains—quite correctly, if *only* this single text is taken into consideration—that

> the intrinsic problematic of this *scientia regulatrix* was in fact in no way taken up here or even dimly seen, but that these three quite different directions of questioning are instead systematically held together in a quite different way, one essentially determined by faith. In other words, the concept of philosophizing or of metaphysics in this manifold ambiguity is not oriented toward the intrinsic problematic itself, but instead *disparate determinations of passing over and beyond* are here joined together. (49)

Here, one must agree with Heidegger. Indeed, the conception of beings as beings (*de ente ut ente*), i.e., of what is most universal (in a specific sense of this word), and the conception of the highest being are conceptions of "determinations that both have the character of what is highest, what is ultimate, yet are completely different, so that no attempt whatsoever is made to comprehend them in their possible unity" (51). And one must add that the unitary science that Aquinas calls *scientia regulatrix*[11] remains fully undetermined.

This positive, well-directed side of Heidegger's analysis of and com-

---

[10] In *XII Libros Metaphysicorum, Prooemium S. Thomae*, 1–2.

[11] Ibid., *Prooemium*, 1.

mentary on Aquinas's text is, however, only one of two sides: the other side is the fact that Heidegger sees no problem in simply identifying what Aquinas says in the *Prooemium* with Aquinas's entire conception. This is a misinterpretation of enormous proportions. Heidegger completely ignores the character of Aquinas's thinking and of his works as a whole: Thomas's thinking is organized as a summa, thus, as a doctrinal whole whose constituents are only quite loosely interlinked. Chapter 1 describes and evaluates this character of Aquinas's thought.

It suffices here to introduce a single point. In his interpretation of the *Prooemium,* Heidegger says nothing at all about Aquinas on *esse.* Granted, that term does not appear in this text. But the presentation in chapter 1 of this book shows that Aquinas's thought as a whole cannot be adequately interpreted unless careful consideration is taken of his central theses concerning *esse.* It is, however, all too clear that these central theses have no place in the framework described in the *Prooemium* and commented on by Heidegger. Heidegger, however, commits the fateful error of interpreting and criticizing *all* of Aquinas's thought on the basis of the conception articulated in the *Prooemium.* The term that emerges from his interpretation and critique is the one that has become the proud slogan of postmodern thinking, and above all of its Jewish and Christian representatives: metaphysics is onto-theo-logy.

[2] The second aspect of Heidegger's misinterpretation of metaphysics is the following central thesis:

> Metaphysics thinks the Being of beings both in the grounding unity
> of the most universal, i.e., of what has the same value everywhere (and
> is thus indifferent) [and is therefore ontology], and in the grounding
> unity of allness, i.e., of what is highest overall [and is thus theology].
> It is thus that the Being of beings is thought in advance as the ground-
> ing ground. For this reason, all metaphysics is, at heart and from the
> ground up, the grounding that gives account of the ground, is called
> to account by the ground, and finally calls the ground to account.
> ("OTLCM" 58; t.a.)

This is a thesis that Heidegger repeats uncountably many times and in all possible variations in his works. The thinking of ground is the essence of metaphysics ("OTLCM" 60; t.a.):

> Metaphysics is not only theo-logic, but also onto-logic. Metaphysics,
> first of all, is neither the one nor the other *also.* Instead, metaphysics
> is theo-logic because it is onto-logic. It is the latter because it is the
> former.

Here, two critical remarks are needed.

[i] The first concerns the fact that Heidegger articulates his conception of *the onto-theo-logical constitution of metaphysics* most clearly and decisively in the already-cited text bearing that title. This work is an ambitious interpretation of Hegel's *Science of Logic*. This is no accident, because Heidegger sees in Hegel's thinking and particularly in his *Logic* the acme and completion of Western metaphysics: this is the thinking of ground, whereby the genitive is fundamentally to be understood as a subjective genitive, and in the more precise sense that this is a thinking that allows itself to be determined by the thought or concept or standpoint of *ground*. Heidegger states this unmistakably: "We understand . . . the name 'logic' in the essential sense that also includes the title used by Hegel and that explains it as the name for that thinking that everywhere establishes and grounds [*ergründet und begründet*] being [*das Seiende*] as such and as a whole from out of Being as ground [*Grund*] (λόγος)" ("OTLCM" 59; t.a.).

Heidegger interprets the whole of Hegel's thought, with the *Science of Logic* as its center, as one that is determined from "the perspective of the ground."[12] This is a misinterpretation that is extraordinarily consequential. He raises the question concerning the "measure of the conversation with the history of philosophy" and maintains the following: "In Spinoza, Hegel finds the completed 'standpoint of substance,' but that cannot be the highest [standpoint] because [at that standpoint] Being has not yet been thought equally and decisively, from the ground up, as thinking thinking itself" ("OTLCM" 47; t.a.). Heidegger here relies on a passage from Hegel's *Science of Logic* linking Spinoza to the standpoint of substance,[13] but the explanation of why that standpoint is not the highest—"because Being has not yet been thought equally and decisively, from the ground up, as thinking thinking itself"—is wholly incorrect, as is easily shown.

Even the most superficial interpretation of the *Science of Logic* cannot overlook a central factor determining this work, i.e., that the *logical* status (in Hegel's sense) of any "determination of thought" (or category) is determined by its location within the *Logic* as a whole. The nearer the beginning a given determination is situated, the poorer is its logical status, whereas the nearer it is to the absolute idea (with which the

---

[12] See, e.g., Puntel, *Darstellung, Methode und Struktur: Untersuchungen zur Einheit der systematischen Philosophie G. W. F. Hegels* (1981), 109–10n190 and 244–45n354.

[13] The passage reads as follows: "It is noted earlier, in the second book of the objective logic [536], that the philosophy that takes and remains at the standpoint of *substance* is the *system of Spinoza*" (580).

Logic concludes), the higher and more adequate is its status. Thus, every later determination of thought has a richer logical status (according to Hegel, a higher truth) than the earlier ones, which it succeeds dialectically. The category *substance* is located in the *Logic*'s second book, which presents the determinations of reflection. All of these determinations are suspended or superseded by all of the determinations presented in the *Logic*'s third book.

The determination of thought *ground* is indeed introduced in Hegel's *Logic* before *substance* is. For just this reason, just as it is the case that—as Heidegger asserts—the "standpoint of substance" is not "the highest," it is *also* the case that the standpoint of ground is not the highest. But Heidegger ignores this point and so does not notice the nonsensicality of his interpreting the *entire Science of Logic*, indeed the *entirety of Hegel's thought*, from a standpoint that Hegel's *Logic* itself presents as a standpoint with a low—or, better, an intermediate—logical status.

Against this interpretation one could object that the phrase "from the ground up" in the passage quoted above from Heidegger's "The Onto-theo-logical Constitution of Metaphysics" ("... because Being has not yet been thought equally and decisively, from the ground up, as thought thinking itself") is interpreted incorrectly; the objection would hold that "from the ground up" does not here refer to *ground* as one of the *Logic*'s determinations of thought, but instead would simply mean "completely, as a whole, not only in part," or something of the sort. The objection might also note that Heidegger correctly identifies "thought thinking itself" as the highest standpoint in Hegel's *Logic*. This objection, however, is easily countered by the introduction of three points. First, it is scarcely thinkable that a philosopher such as Heidegger, who is scrupulously careful in his use of central philosophical terms and concepts, would use the formulation "from the ground up" in its ordinary and indeed banal sense. Second, Heidegger's explicit mention of "thought thinking itself" in this context is indeed correct, but leaves wholly unanswered the question of which logical determination provides the basis for clarifying "thought thinking itself." The answer to this question is provided by the third point: various other passages from the same essay explicitly say that the highest standpoint, the one from which Hegel's *Logic* must be interpreted, is that of ground. Thus, for example, he writes in relation to Hegel's *Logic*:

> What must be thought [*Die Sache des Denkens*] is being(s) as such, that is, Being. This shows itself in the essential form [*Wesensart*] of ground. Thus, what must be thought is ... Being as ground [*als der Grund*]. ("OTLCM" 59; t.a.)

The importance of Heidegger's mistake is made clear by the following passage from a review written by Hegel of a book about his philosophy: "The author considers the relation of substantiality in his manner as that is done in the *Logic* [i.e., Hegel's *Science of Logic*], and indeed in its second part, the [Logic of] Essence; in the third part of the *Logic*, which treats the concept and the idea, *truer forms* take the place of the categories of substance, causality, reciprocity, *which themselves no longer have any validity*."[14]

For the category *ground* that is presented in the Logic of Essence, it therefore holds that in the *Science of Logic* there are *truer* forms or categories that take its place, with the consequence that the category *ground no longer has any validity*. It also follows that neither Hegel's entire *Logic* nor—much less—his system can be understood and interpreted from the "standpoint of (the category) *ground*." But that is precisely what Heidegger does, and indeed with a baffling putative self-evidence and self-certainty. This interpretation misses the mark totally and radically.

[ii] The second critical remark relates to the fact that Heidegger reinterprets the famous principle of sufficient reason [principle of ground—*Satz vom Grund*] in a manner that raises the question whether it can be made consistent with his interpretation and critique of metaphysics as the thinking of ground. At the end of his lengthy expositions in his book *The Principle of Reason*,[15] Heidegger takes a remarkable turn. The following takes into consideration only the end of the eponymous lecture included in that book.[16]

The articulation of the principle known to all is, according to Heidegger, "*Nothing* is *without* ground" (125; t.a.). In considering this formulation, Heidegger holds, insufficient attention is generally paid to the "is." If one does attend sufficiently to it, then—according to Heidegger—it becomes clear that the principle says that every *being* has a ground. The "is," Heidegger explains, is what gives "the pitch that tunes everything." If one attends to it, then the principle suddenly sounds different. No longer: "*Nothing* is *without* ground," but "Nothing *is* without *ground*." This brings in the relation to *Being*:

> Whereas now [i.e., given the "understanding" of the principle with the emphasis, "Nothing *is* without *ground*"] the "is" means "Being" and

---

[14] G. W. F. Hegel, *Berliner Schriften 1818–1831*, 351; emphases added.

[15] Heidegger, *The Principle of Reason* (1957/1991).

[16] Ibid., 117–31. All page numbers in the section ([ii]) to which this note is appended are from this text.

sets the pitch in the principle, the ground is taken up along with it in the attunement; nothing *is* without *ground*. Being and ground now ring in unison. In this ringing Being and ground ring out as belonging together in one. The principle of ground now has a different ring and says: ground belongs to Being. (125; t.a.)

Heidegger goes yet further in writing, "The principle of ground, understood as the grounding principle of the sufficient ground to be delivered, is thus true only because within it speaks a word of Being, which says: Being and ground: the same." It is easy (and widely common) to dismiss such formulations as purely metaphorical plays on words. And indeed, Heidegger's language does not satisfy strict criteria of clarity and precision. Heidegger is, however, fully aware of this situation, but literally makes of necessity a virtue: he does not want to speak an "exact" language, because he considers no such language to be adequate to "what must be thought [*die Sache des Denkens*]." Nevertheless, however peculiar may be Heidegger's formulations (one cannot speak of "arguments"), it can be the case that they both conceal and disclose remarkable intuitions. The systematic chapter of this book— chapter 3—articulates at the outset the structure and implications of the (i.e., every) *theoretical sentence*. There, it is both possible and necessary to explain one such Heideggerian intuition in a specific manner (see 3.2.1.1).

Heidegger continues by posing the questions what is called Being, and what is called ground? He adds the following (126; t.a.): "To these questions there are only the following answers: ground is called Being. Being is called ground—ground is called Being: here, everything turns in circles." The key that unlocks these answers, Heidegger emphasizes, is one that we lack. In his lecture he aims only "to open an outer gate." In conjunction with a passage from Goethe he then seeks to articulate the sense of "why" and comes to the following conclusion:

> The word from Being as ground says: Being—itself the ground—
> remains without ground, i.e., now, without why. When we attempt to
> think Being as ground, then we must step back from the question,
> why? But to what should we then hold?

This is an unnecessarily dramatic way of articulating a simple state of affairs. Just what state of affairs this is is shown above in the treatment in section 1.5 of Thomas Nagel; this state of affairs is treated more thoroughly and systematically in chapter 3 (see 3.1).

From "why" Heidegger proceeds to "because" (127; t.a.):

> The because points into the essence of ground. If however the word of
> Being as ground is a true word, then the because also points into the
> essence of Being.

Heidegger explains the meaning of "ground" as follows: "Ground is that
on which everything rests, that which precedes all beings as what bears
them." Characteristically, he appeals to the etymology and history of
the word "*Weil*" ("because") in order to explain it: "'*Weil*' is the short-
ened word for '*dieweilen*,' and the latter means: so long as it *weilt*, with
weilt meaning, ". . . abide, remain quiet, hold to and within itself, i.e.,
in restfulness. . . ." From the same perspective he adds (127), "*Weilen*,
abide, abide-always is however the old meaning of the word '*sein* [to be;
Being].'"

This extensive presentation of Heidegger's ruminations about the
principle of ground or of sufficient reason aims to illuminate his critique
of metaphysics as the philosophy that thinks under the determination
ground. What does the presentation reveal? If Heidegger does not reject *ground*, but instead reinterprets it, can he continue to maintain that
metaphysics is a thinking-of-ground? The lecture under consideration
contains a Heideggerian answer to this question, in a brief text that is
enclosed within square brackets; this indicates that they were not read
aloud. This answer is this (125; t.a.): "Because . . . Leibniz and all of metaphysics remain with the principle of ground as a principle of being(s),
metaphysical thinking demands, in accordance with the principle, a first
ground for Being: in a being, and indeed in the beingest [*dem Seiendsten;*
in the most-being]."

This passage makes fully clear how the aspects of Heidegger's position fit together. The fundamental point is the thesis—shown above by
the examination of Aquinas's work to be not only baseless but directly
false—that "metaphysics" (explicitly including Aquinas's metaphysics)
has forgotten Being and therefore considers only beings. The irrefutable
fact that Aquinas explicitly introduces *ipsum esse* is one that Heidegger
utterly ignores. It is now clear where this ignoring leads: in this case, to
the thesis that all metaphysics "remains with the principle of ground as a
principle of being(s)." This thesis is simply false. That Thomas gets to *esse
per se subsistens* (above all in the third way/proof) shows that he does *not*
"remain with the principle of ground as a principle of being(s)."

[3] The third point is Heidegger's most important and most genuine characterization of the "metaphysical" God. No one, to the author's
knowledge, has gone more widely astray in misinterpreting the Christian
metaphysical tradition. In his essay "The Onto-theo-logical Constitution
of Metaphysics," he writes:

> . . . cause as *causa sui.* This is the correct name for the god of phi-
> losophy. To this god the human being can neither pray nor make sacri-
> fices. Before the *causa sui* the human being neither can fall to his knees
> in awe nor can he make music and dance before him.—Consequently,
> the godless thinking that must forsake the god of philosophy, god as
> *causa sui,* is perhaps nearer to the divine God. Here, this means only
> the following: this thinking is more free with respect to God than onto-
> theo-logy would want to admit. ("OTLCM" 72; t.a.)

The first thing to note about this passage is that Heidegger simply identifies philosophy with metaphysics (he indeed does so throughout the essay). For him, "the god of philosophy" means nothing other than "the metaphysical god" or "the god of metaphysics." Much more could be said about this passage. Further below, in various contexts, additional critical remarks are directed against Heidegger's influential misrepresentation of (Christian) metaphysics as onto-theo-logy.

At this point, only one additional remark need be added; it concerns the way Aquinas identifies the end points of each of the five ways with God. Heidegger naively insinuates that the "God of metaphysics," understood in light of the five ways, is to be understood summarily as *causa sui;* Heidegger does not even mention the fact that this phrase is self-contradictory. But he goes much further: he insinuates that "metaphysicians" hold (or should, to be consequent, hold) that this God that is *causa sui* (thus, this God as first mover, first cause, necessary being . . .) is something before which they can (and should) fall to their knees in awe, dance, make music, etc. The absurdity of such a conception is in truth nothing other than a product of the absurdity of Heidegger's misrepresentation. Heidegger utterly ignores the methodic and systematic status of such arguments as the five ways, a status clarified above in chapter 1.

2.2 Heidegger's Four Approaches to "Retrieving" the "Question of Being"

How then does Heidegger think Being, whose thematization he mistakenly takes to be absent from metaphysics? That is the decisive question. His works articulate no fewer than four approaches aiming to treat Being as a subject matter in a philosophical fashion. Here they are only briefly characterized in an order that is not chronological but instead is most appropriate for this book. The first two approaches focus on the history of philosophy, whereas the third and fourth are quasi-systematic.

[1] The first historically oriented approach consists in a comprehensive interpretation of Western philosophy, which Heidegger simply identifies with metaphysics. Relevant here again is his misinterpretation of metaphysics as onto-theo-logy. Heidegger starts from the difference between Being and beings, whether one speaks, with metaphysics, of the Being of being(s) or of the being(s) of Being. "The onto-theo-logical constitution of metaphysics arises from the dominance of the difference that keeps Being as ground and being(s) as grounded and as what give account, apart from and related to each other; and by this keeping, resolution [*Austrag*] is achieved" ("OTLCM" 71). His objection is therefore, more precisely, the following: metaphysics presupposes this difference but does not think it. He then attempts, in a positive manner, to do the following: to think or ponder this difference, to take it into consideration, by attending to a fundamental thesis that he expresses in the form of a direct question (63–64): "What do you make of the difference if both Being and being(s), each in its/their own way, *appear from out of the difference* [*aus der Differenz her*]?" "Appear from out of the difference": that is Heidegger's presupposition and at the same time the decisive step. He thereby envisages a dimension or a space that is *more primordial* than metaphysical Being or being(s) (as he interprets these), and indeed such that (metaphysical) Being and beings appear as the differentia of Heideggerian difference. He names this coming "out of the difference" the resolution [*Austrag*] of the differentia" (see 63, 68). It is this primordial dimension or space, which Heidegger terms Being (in his sense, as distinct from the putatively metaphysical sense), that he writes sometimes as "*Seyn*" [in what follows, "Beyng"] and sometimes as "*Sein*." How Heidegger further develops this approach, and what results it leads him to, are analyzed in detail further below.

[2] The second approach, likewise historically oriented, concerns not the entire history of metaphysics but instead only modern philosophy (although Heidegger interprets modern philosophy as directly continuous with pre-modern metaphysics). Particularly important is the step that Heidegger takes not only beyond Husserl but directly *against* (the later) Husserl. The step involves a radical overcoming of transcendental thinking—of the transcendental philosophy of subjectivity—with the aim of developing a philosophy of Being.

In order to keep the presentation short, it suffices to cite a remarkable passage from a letter Heidegger wrote Husserl on October 22, 1927, following the publication of *Being and Time*. The letter is a response to the extremely critical remarks Husserl directed against that book. Heidegger opposes Husserl's procedure of *epoché* and thus Husserl's absolute privileging of transcendental subjectivity. The most important passage in the letter is the following:

We agree that the being that you [Husserl] call "world" cannot be clarified in its transcendental constitution by means of a recourse to a being having such a mode of Being.

This is not to say that what constitutes the locus of the transcendental is not a being at all—but that is just where the problem arises: what is the mode of Being of the being within which "world" is constituted? That is the central problem of *Being and Time*—i.e., a fundamental ontology of Dasein. What must be shown is that the mode of Being of human Dasein is totally different from those of all other beings and that Dasein's mode of Being, as the one that it is, contains precisely within itself the possibility of transcendental constitution. . . .

What does the constituting is not nothing, is thus something and a being—although not in the sense of the positive.

The question concerning the mode of Being of what does the constituting is not to be avoided.

Universally, therefore, the problem of Being relates to what does the constituting and to what is constituted.[17]

Here, *Being* is clearly understood not as the objective counterpole to subjectivity or to the theoretical dimension or anything of the sort, but instead as the comprehensive, primordial dimension. *Being* is thus the dimension that encompasses both the entire sphere of constituting subjectivity (or: the theoretical dimension) and the sphere of the constituted world. Such a dimension is unthinkable within the framework of Husserl's transcendental phenomenology.

The step Heidegger takes in this passage is one of the most important achievements in twentieth-century philosophy. Being is here understood as the all-encompassing primordial dimension that is not only or (as in Aquinas) almost only purely objective—not only the objective pole of the relationship between the knower and the "object"—but encompasses also the enormous dimension that can be termed the dimension of theoreticity. The latter, for its part, encompasses not only subjectivity in the traditional-modern sense, but also everything that belongs to the domain of the theoretical. Heidegger does not understand this step in exactly this manner, but—as chapter 3 shows—it can be expanded so as to be understood in this manner.

The question that arises with respect to Heidegger is the following: how does he thematize the "universal problem of Being," as he terms it in his letter—how does he thematize this primordial, all-encompassing

---

[17] E. Husserl, *Husserliana, Gesammelte Werke*, vol. 9 (1962), *Anlage* 1, 601–2; emphasis added.

dimension? What follows shows that he does not thematize it in a manner that approaches being adequate.

[3] The third approach—the first of the two that are quasi-systematic—is the one found in his most important work, *Being and Time*. For the purposes of this book, this approach may be characterized as follows: the starting point is, as the title of §1 indicates, the demonstration of the necessity of explicitly retrieving the question concerning Being. That there is a question concerning Being Heidegger accepts in part on the basis of history and in part on that of other substantive considerations. He sees a twofold task in the development of this question: first, to show "that it requires not only a fixation of *the* being that functions as what is primarily questioned," and second, to find the correct mode of access to being(s). The being "that functions as what is primarily questioned" is the human being *as* Dasein, and the mode of access is phenomenological. The result is "the interpretation of Dasein in terms of temporality and the explication of time as the transcendental horizon of the question of Being" (title of the first part of *Being and Time*).

It is clear that this approach basically follows that of the perspective of the transcendental philosophy of subjectivity, even if the subject is radically reinterpreted, specifically as Dasein. Nothing better characterizes the mode of access to Being than the concept *transcendence*, which plays a central role for Heidegger in the time prior to the publication of *Being and Time*, in that work itself, and finally in the time shortly following its publication. This is shown, exemplarily, in the following passage from a lecture course from 1928:

> Transcendence [is] . . . the primordial constitution of the *subjectivity* of the subject. The subject transcends qua subject, it would not be a subject if it did not transcend. Being-a-subject means transcending. I.e.: Dasein does not somehow exist and then occasionally accomplish a stepping beyond; instead, its existing primarily involves [*besagt*] stepping beyond. Dasein itself is the stepping beyond. It lies therein that transcendence is not some possible comportment (among other possible comportments) of Dasein toward other beings, but instead the grounding constitution of its Being, on the ground of which it can from the outset comport itself toward beings.[18]

A few years later Heidegger must have seen that this approach, although not wholly wrong, is nevertheless too narrow. This led him

---

[18] *Metaphysische Anfangsgründe der Logik im Ausgang von Leibniz* (1928), 211.

to undertake his famous turning [*Kehre*]: Being is not to be articulated starting from Dasein; instead, Dasein can only be interpreted starting from Being. The thinking or pondering of *Being itself*, of *Being as such* becomes the central and indeed the genuine and only task for Heidegger. (It may be said here anticipatorily that the structural-systematic approach presented in chapter 3 is in a certain respect analogous to Heidegger's thinking following his turning, but *only* in that certain respect.)

[4] Heidegger's fourth approach to the development of a conception of Being is the one that results from his turning, his *Kehre*. The turning is to Being itself. Heidegger goes so far as to precisely date the year in which his turning began, characterizing it succinctly and accurately in a passage in a footnote in his "Letter on Humanism," which was written in 1946, first published in 1947, and first appeared in a volume of its own in 1949. The passage reads as follows: "What is said here was not first thought through at the time of composition, but rests on the taking of a path that started in 1936, in the 'instant' of an attempt simply to say the truth of Being" (*PM* 239 note a; t.a.). Heidegger embarked on that path with the handwritten text *Contributions to Philosophy (From Enowning [Ereignis^c]*), which was published only posthumously (in 1989).[19] Of *Contributions* Heidegger writes the following:

> Here already, as in a preparatory exercise, we must attempt the
> thinking-saying of philosophy that comes in the other beginning. This
> saying does not describe or explain, does not proclaim or teach. This
> saying does not stand over against what is said. Rather, the saying itself
> *is* what is to be said, as the essencing of Beyng [*Wesung des Seyns*].—This
> saying gathers Beyng to a first ringing of its essencing and yet itself
> sounds only from out of this essencing. (*Cont* 4; t.a.)

---

^{c} Much is said below about the word "*Ereignis*," about how Heidegger uses this word, and about what Heidegger says about how he uses it. Heidegger himself declares that the word is "as little translatable as the . . . Greek word λόγος and the Chinese Tao . . . and is . . . a *singulare tantum*" (*ID* 36; t.a.). Because in addition no English translation appears to be particularly illuminating—those used by Anglophone Heideggerians include "concern," "Appropriation," "Event of Appropriation," "befitting," "enowning," and "disclosive opening"—the German term is used in this book. Likewise untranslated are the German terms "*ereignet*" (a verb that, in Heidegger's works, typically takes "*Ereignis*" as its subject) and "*Ereignete(n)*" (the direct object in the sentence "Das Ereignis ereignet das Ereignete [plural: die Ereigneten]"; "Appropriation appropriates the appropriated" or "Enowning enowns the enowned," in two possible English translations).

[19] *Contributions* was written between 1936 and 1938.

The text announces incorrectly that in *Contributions,* nothing is proclaimed, although that *Contributions* does not describe, explain, or teach appears to be true. But the book is full of proclamations: It will come: a new beginning, a new thinking, an essential thinking, beyond metaphysics. . . . Indeed, the entire tone of the book is prophetic and eschatological. It also ranks among the most obscure and (particularly with respect to linguistic formulations) is one of the most willful of Heidegger's works.[20]

Clearly, it is not possible here to consider the entire corpus of the late Heidegger. The following account treats two central topics, aiming to make two points: first, that Heidegger's interpretation of metaphysics is so problematic and superficial as to qualify only as a misinterpretation, which of course undermines his attempted critique; and second, the nearly total insignificance of his "thinkerish" efforts toward the development of a substantial conception of Being. Concerning the second, the examination makes clear that the decisive deficiency in Heidegger's account consists precisely in his reliance on a language that cannot express what he seeks to express. This is astonishing given Heidegger's claim to be the thinker who undertook the project of bringing to light what had remained undiscovered throughout the history of philosophy.

For what follows, one of Heidegger's marginal notes to a passage in the fourth (1949) edition of the "Letter on Humanism" is important. The passage reads, "Since 1936, '*Ereignis*' the lead word [*Leitwort*] of my thinking."[21] Indeed, "*Ereignis*" is the only positive term Heidegger uses in speaking of Being, the only "determination" he provides for Being, although he would not use any such qualifiers as "positive" or "determination" to characterize "*Ereignis*" as a term within his language. The account that follows shows why this matters. Worth noting anticipatorily is also that Heidegger's in-part poetic and in-part prophetic-eschatological formulations (e.g., "hearken unto Being") can be avoided without any cost in terms of adequately articulating the relevant subject matters; indeed, more precise, non-metaphorical, non-poetic formulations are more adequate to those subject matters.

---

[20] The same status must be accorded another extensive (thus, similarly quasi-systematic) work, i.e., the 428-page *Mindfulness* (*Besinnung*), which Heidegger wrote in 1938–39 following the completion of *Contributions* and which was not published until 1997 (as volume 66 of the *Gesamtausgabe*).

[21] *PM,* 241 note b (t.a.).

2.3 What Is Unthought in Heidegger's Thinking of Being I: Being-as-*Ereignis*

The first question to be answered is the following: what, ultimately, does Heidegger say about Being? Because *Ereignis* is his "lead word [*Leitwort*]," the question may be phrased more precisely as, how does he comprehend *Ereignis*? Heidegger clearly emphasizes that as his lead word, the term does not mean what it does in ordinary language, i.e., event, occurrence, etc. He asserts that the word originally means "*er-äugen*, i.e., to glimpse, to bring into view, to appropriate, learn, or pick up."[d] His additional clarifications make clear that he interprets "*Ereignis*" solely on the basis of the root "*eigen*," [one's] own. Finally, he understands "*Ereignis*" as a singular term that has no plural form (although it does have the verbal form "*ereignen*," which is transitive at least in the formulation "*Ereignis ereignet Ereignetes*").

[1] In an absolutely characteristic manner, Heidegger presents what might be termed a sort of poetic definition of "*Ereignis*": "*Er-eignis* is the domain that sways within itself, through which humans and Being reach one another in their essencing, attaining their essencing, in that they lose those determinations that metaphysics has given them" (*ID* 37; t.a.). This reference to metaphysics is a glib way to suggest that his own conception is absolutely new and original. The following account shows how senseless this suggestion is.

Heidegger's presumably most important remarks about *Ereignis* are found in his famous lecture "Time and Being" (1962). There, he speaks of "Being as *Ereignis*," interpreting the "as" as follows (*TB* 22): "Being, presence-allowing sent in *Ereignen*, time extended [or attained] in *Ereignen*. Time and Being *ereignet* in *Ereignis*."[e] Heidegger bases this interpretation on analyses of such sentences as "*Es gibt*—It gives [i.e., There is]—Being" and "*Es gibt*—It gives [i.e., There is]—time." He sees in the "*Es* [It]" "something extraordinary," writing (*TB* 19; t.a.) that we can

> bring the *Es* [It] into view simply by thinking the "*Es* [It]" from the mode of the giving [*schicken*] that belongs to it: giving as destiny [*Geschick*], giving as an opening up that reaches out. . . . In the sending

---

[d] The sentence is on pp. 28–29 of *Identität und Differenz*, the German text of *ID*; it is not included in Stambaugh's English translation of Heidegger's essay, but she notes Heidegger's suggested etymology in her introduction (*ID* 14n1).

[e] Stambaugh's translation reads as follows: "Being, letting-presence sent in Appropriating, time extended in Appropriating. Time and Being appropriated in Appropriating."

[*Schicken*] of the destiny [*Geschick*] of Being, in the extending of time, there becomes manifest a dedication [*Zueignen*], a delivering over into what is their own [*Übereignen*], namely of Being as presence and of time as the realm of the open in their ownness [*in ihr Eigenes*]. What determines both, time and Being, in their ownness, i.e., in their belonging together, we call *Ereignis*.

In concluding, he asks the following decisive question: "And this [*Ereignis*] itself? Can more be said of *Ereignis*?" Heidegger's answer is strikingly sparse. He maintains (21–22) that in the course of the lecture more is thought than is said, and what is thought but not said is "that to giving as sending [*Schicken*] belongs holding-to-itself [*das Ansich-halten*], namely this, that within the domain of been-ness and the coming [*Ankommen*] play the refusal [*Verweigerung*] of the present [*von Gegenwart*] and withholding [*Vorenthalten*] of the present." This Heidegger calls the "withdrawal [*Entzug*]." In concluding, Heidegger asks (24; t.a.), "What remains to be said?" and answers, "Only this: *Ereignis ereignet.* Thereby we say from the same about the same to the same [*vom Selben her auf das Selbe zu das Selbe*]."

[2] The passages just introduced require critical analysis.

[i] Such formulations are empty, consisting of capricious plays on words (*ereignen, an-eignen, zu-eignen, über-eignen, Enteignis*). If one takes one's bearings by the ordinary-language meaning of the word "*eigen* [own]," then some conclusions may be drawn concerning Heidegger's formulations, but the consequence is that what he says is, as far as a comprehensive conception of Being is concerned, extraordinarily meager, indeed little better than banal, because it agrees fundamentally with what happens or can happen in everyday human life when the word "*eigen*" is used. But Heidegger elevates this meagerness to the level of formulations that can sound deep. One might paraphrase the last passage quoted into something like, "*Ereignis*" (in the Heideggerian sense) is the event or occurrence or process (i.e., the "*Ereignis*" in the currently normal sense) of the "giving" of the "sending and delivering of Being and time" into the "(relevant?) ownness." And this "sending and delivering of . . ." proves to be the unitary occurring of "an appropriation or making one's own" within the (relevant) ownness, such that then the ownness of both Being and time—what is most their own, what most accurately characterizes them—is their belonging together. And what "determines" both in their belonging together is *Er-eignis*—the accomplishment or achievement of ownness, thus, perhaps, each of them coming into its own.

The ellipsis in the phrase "sending and delivering of . . ." could be replaced only by "Being" and "time," but making the replacement would introduce a serious coherence problem, as is explicitly noted in

the appended "Summary of a Seminar on the Lecture 'Time and Being'"
(*TB* 24–54). On the one hand, according to the "Letter on Humanism"
(*PM* 254–55; t.a.), "the *Es* [It] that gives here [in the giving articulated as
"There is"] is Being itself," and according to "Time and Being" (*TB* 21;
t.a.), "but the sole intention of the lecture is to bring into view Being
itself as *Ereignis*." On the other hand, Heidegger explicitly says (*TB* 21–
22; t.a.):

> In that we think through Being itself and what is its own, it proves to be
> the gift of the destiny [*Geschickes*] of presence granted [*gewährte*] by the
> offering [*Reichen*] of time. The gift of presence is the ownness [or pos-
> session or property] of *Ereignis*. Being disappears in *Ereignis*.

This latter passage seems to accord some kind of dominance to *Ereignis*
and thereby to articulate a subordination of Being.

The second answer provided in the "Summary" (*TB* 44; t.a.) is, in
essence, "what would matter would be to see that in that Being, by coming into view as *Ereignis,* disappears as Being." Between the two sentences,
then, there is no contradiction. This answer, however, utterly fails to solve
the problem; it is an empty assertion. To say that by coming into view as
Ereignis, Being disappears as Being is to overlook the fundamental fact
that it is supposed to be precisely *Being* that shows itself *as Ereignis;* but it
can show itself as *Ereignis* only if it does not disappear, but instead shows
itself as itself. Throughout the lecture "Time and Being" (and in other
works composed after 1936), such incoherences are to be found again
and again. The best explanation is that Heidegger has changed what he
means by "Being" without noting that he has done so. Here and in similar
passages in his late works, Being is understood simply as presence, thus
in the sense that permeates the tradition of metaphysics as Heidegger
understands it. In "Time and Being," he relies on that sense ("destiny's
gift [*Geschick*] of presence" [22]) without noting that he is doing so. This
explanation is wholly in line with the first answer given in the "Summary"
to the difficulty in question. That text notes (43; t.a.) that "in the passage
in question from the 'Letter on Humanism' and thus almost throughout, 'Being itself' already names *Ereignis*." But this answer is silent as far
as the central issue is concerned, i.e., that this change in the meaning of
"Being" is not explicitly noted. This change in meaning is visible in such
formulations as the following:

> If *Ereignis* is not a new coinage [*Prägung*] for Being in the history of
> Being, but to the contrary Being belongs within *Ereignis* and is taken
> back into it (in whatsoever fashion), then the history of Being comes to
> its end *in Ereignis,* i.e., for the thinking that turns [*einkehrt*] to *Ereignis,*

in that thereby Being, as it rests in fateful sending [*Geschick*], is no longer what is to be thought. (*TB* 40–41; t.a.)

This passage could occasion many misunderstandings that are far from minor. Heidegger terms (4, 19) "Being" (in the sense of "presence") and "time" "things [*Sachen;* (subject) matters]." He then writes (19; t.a.): "What allows the two *Sachen* to belong together, what not only brings the two into their own but preserves them and holds them in their belonging together—the *Verhalt* of the two *Sachen* [the way the two matters stand], the *Sachverhalt* [the matter at hand]—is *Ereignis*."

It could be extremely illuminating to compare a formulation from Wittgenstein's *Notebooks* that serves to make Heidegger's thesis more precise—albeit not in his sense, but in terms of what is in question. This is also the case with respect to the conception of Being presented in chapter 3. The Wittgenstein passage reads as follows:

> Whatever is the case is God.
> God is whatever is the case.[22]

In *Structure and Being*, this formulation is transformed so as to express that book's conception of Being:

> Whatever is the case is Being.
> Being is whatever is the case.

This formulation with "Being" can be termed the "primordial," the first and in that sense also the fundamental formulation, although not—with respect to the subject matter "God"—the fully determined formulation. Wittgenstein's formulation with "God" is the ultimate one in the sense that it presupposes the full determination of what "Being" means. Where does Heidegger stand with respect to this state of affairs?

On the basis of the various passages introduced just above, according to which the concept of the (*Sach-*)*Verhalt* takes the central position, it is illuminating to transform Wittgenstein's passage as follows:

> Whatever is the case is (Being as) *Ereignis*.
> (Being as) *Ereignis* is whatever is the case.

This formulation remains abstract in that it is largely undetermined. A significant step toward its concretization—toward making its content more

---

[22] *Tagebücher 1914–1916* (1961), 171.

explicit—is taken with the following formulation, which appears to express relatively precisely the sense presumably intended by Heidegger:

> How everything comes into or is brought into its own is (Being as) *Ereignis.*
> (Being as) *Ereignis* is how everything comes into or is brought into its own.

If this is indeed accurate, the question arises concerning what such a formulation articulates in terms of *content*.

[ii] The just-introduced formulation is not false, but it is in many respects preliminary at best. All depends on how "its own" is understood and explained. But—as is now to be shown—even on the best understanding and explanation, it remains totally deficient.

Das Eigene—one's own—in Heidegger's sense arises from a peculiar combination of two fully different significations of "*Ereignis*" and "*eigen*."[23] The first is the most important aspect of the (above-mentioned) etymological meaning of the word *Ereignis*, namely, the meaning ". . . *er-äugen*, i.e., glimpse, bring into view"; the second is the ordinary-language meaning of *eigen*. A passage quoted above from "Time and Being" articulates Heidegger's semantic combination (or confusion) (*TB* 19; t.a.): "In the sending [*Schicken*] of the destiny [*Geschick*] of Being, in the extending of time, there becomes manifest a dedication [*Zueignen*], a delivering over into what is their own [*Übereignen*]—namely of Being as presence and of time as the realm of the open—in their ownness [*in ihr Eigenes*]."[24] Heidegger explicitly terms the ownness of Being and of time their belonging together, and says (19) that this is "determined" by *Ereignis*. With this reference to "its/their own" Heidegger means not only what of Being and time are, respectively, their own, but also what of each being is its own, and in the first place what of Dasein is its own. Thus, he writes the following (23; t.a.):

> Insofar as it gives [as there are] Being and time only in *Ereignen*, to this belongs the peculiar ownness [or property] that it brings the human being into its own as the one who hears [*vernimmt*] Being in that the

---

[23] See the highly instructive essay by Thomas Sheehan, "A Paradigm Shift in Heidegger Research" (2001).

[24] This passage shows that Sheehan's assertion (ibid., 201n9) that after 1936 Heidegger understands *Ereignis* "as the opening [*Öffnen, das Offene*] of the *Da* rather than as 'appropriation [*Er-eignen, das Eigene*]'" (from Sheehan's abstract) is not accurate with respect to the text(s). The "domain of the opening" is only one of the two moments of *Ereignis*, the one associated with time.

> human being stands within authentic time. As suited [*geeignet*] in this
> way, the human being belongs within *Ereignis*.

These formulations make clear that the following question remains unanswered: what, really, is "its own"? To say that what of Being and of time are, respectively, their own is their belonging together leaves unanswered the question, *as what* do the two belong together? And concerning what of the human being is its own, the talk is only within the framework of a thesis about a factor that "belongs" to *Ereignis*. This factor is "the peculiar ownness [or property] that it brings the human being into its own as the one who hears Being in that the human being stands within authentic time [*das Eigentümliche, dass es den Menschen als den, der Sein vernimmt, indem er innesteht in der eigentlichen Zeit, in sein Eigenes bringt*]." But what is the *its own itself*? Heidegger's formulations turn in a circle and leave precisely the decisive point unarticulated. Yet Heidegger is the thinker who takes himself to be and ubiquitously and continuously announces himself to be the one who most radically and uncompromisingly completes *thinking* by thinking what, throughout the history of thinking that precedes him, remains unthought.

[3] The decisive critique concluding that Heidegger's thought is deficient includes a more general and more central point. More than virtually any other philosopher, Heidegger emphasizes the relation between thinking and questioning. But what questions does thinking have? Here one must ask, more precisely: what questions does Heidegger have concerning the central topic *Being-as-Ereignis*? He explicitly or implicitly poses many questions, and allows himself to be guided by them. But does he pose and respond to the most important, the most unavoidable ones? He does not. That he does not is now briefly to be shown for the case of the modalities necessity–possibility–contingency, which are of absolutely decisive importance for the systematic approach developed in chapter 3 of this book.

Heidegger takes thinking to be magnificent and overpowering. Thus, he writes in the "Letter on Humanism":

> Thinking, simply said, is the thinking of Being. The genitive is twofold.
> The thinking is of Being insofar as thinking, *ereignet* by Being, belongs
> to Being. The thinking is at the same time the thinking of Being insofar
> as the thinking, belonging to Being, listens to Being. (*PM* 241; t.a.)[25]

---

[25] According to a marginal note of Heidegger's (quoted in part above) appended to the phrase "*ereignet* by being [*vom Sein ereignet*]," "First edition, 1949: Only a hint in the language

Whether it makes sense, or how much sense it makes to use such formulations as "listens to Being" is not of central importance for present purposes; they have an unmistakably poetic or mythological or prophetic-eschatological overtone that could be avoided only if "Being" had been articulated in such a manner that it would make sense to say that it could be listened to. Be that as it may, far more important is the following: "thinking" would truly be "thinking of Being" (in the double-genitive sense) only if with respect to Being and—to use a Heideggerian mode of expression—taking a hint from Being, that thinking developed and brought into play *all of its capabilities for intelligibility,* thus *all* possible questions and all available "concepts,"[26] all theoretical instruments, etc. Only if it did so could thinking attain what it can and should attain: maximal intelligibility (here: as far as Being is concerned).

The just-mentioned modalities—necessity–possibility–contingency—are among these capabilities for intelligibility. Indeed, if Being—Being as such and Being as a whole—is indeed what must be examined (according to Heidegger, the subject matter for thinking [*die Sache des Denkens,* what must be thought]), then among the first and most fundamental questions that arise *from Being itself* is a question concerning the primordial status of Being, i.e., the question whether Being *is necessarily* or whether everything that is (i.e., Being and all beings) *are* only *contingently.* The price of avoiding this question is that this subject matter for thinking—what must be thought—remains at best incompletely thought, that it is never fully developed or determined. In that case, Being attains no ultimate intelligibility.

In Heidegger there is no trace of any such questioning. He would presumably reject the question of Being's modal status as "metaphysical."[27] But such a rejection would demonstrate two things: that he fails to do justice to what he identifies as the most important subject matter for philosophy (or, in his terminology, for "thinking"), and that his critique of metaphysics simply misses its mark. Heidegger's "thinking" remains caught in an *underdeveloped, inferior* condition.

---

of metaphysics. Because "*Ereignis*" since 1936 the lead word [*Leitwort*] of my thinking" (*PM* 241 note b).

[26] The word "concepts" appears in quotation marks because Heidegger would not use it. Nevertheless, it is virtually indispensable in philosophy. But one can use it without relying on any contentual philosophical presuppositions or connotations. In *Structure and Being,* it is reduced to "structure," and is therefore used here as a convenient abbreviation for "structure." See *Structure and Being* 3.1.2.1.

[27] The status of the modalities in Heidegger's thinking is considered below in various contexts; see especially 2.4[2][ii], 2.8.2[1], and 2.9[1].

2.4 What Is Unthought in Heidegger's "Thinking of Being" II: Being and being(s)—*Ereignis* and *Ereignete(s)*

A second central topic for this book is the question, central for Heidegger, of the difference and the relation between Being and beings, whereby Being is understood as *Ereignis*. Here, Heidegger has a weighty problem for which he offers no solution—and this reveals a second deficiency in his thinking, one that is in many respects more serious than is the first.

[1] It is easy to find this problem in Heidegger's writings. Two passages suffice for present purposes. The first is the "Afterword" to the fourth (1943) edition of the lecture "What Is Metaphysics?" whose first edition appeared in 1929. He writes:

> Without Being, whose abyssal but not yet unfolded essencing [*Wesen*] delivers [*zuschickt*] the nothing to us in essential anxiety, all beings would remain in Beinglessness [*Seinlosigkeit*]. But even this, as abandonment by Being [*Seinsverlassenheit*], is not a nihilating nothing, *if it also belongs to the truth of Being that Being certainly essences [west] without being(s), but that being(s) never are without Being. (PM* 233; t.a.; emphasis added)

In the fifth (1949) edition of the "Afterword," Heidegger corrects the final sentence by replacing the "certainly [*wohl*]" with "never [*nie*]" and the "but . . . never [*niemals aber*]" with "that . . . never [*daß niemals*]. With these changes, the relevant part of the passage reads as follows: "if it also belongs to the truth of Being that Being never essences [*west*] without being(s), that being(s) never are without Being." How is this extraordinarily consequential reversal to be explained?

The second text is in "Time and Being" (*TB* 2; t.a.):

> It is important to say something about the attempt to think Being without regard to a grounding of Being out of being(s). The attempt to think Being without being(s) is necessary because otherwise . . . there is no longer any possibility of bringing genuinely into view the Being of all that today *is* all over the earth.

And, at the end of that essay (*TB* 24; t.a.):

> It was important to think Being by looking through authentic time in its ownness [*in sein Eigenes*]—out of *Ereignis*—without regard for the relation of Being to being(s).—To think Being without being(s) is to think Being without regard to metaphysics.

In the "Summary" these formulations are made more precise (33; t.a.): "'To think Being without being(s) does not . . . mean that the relation to being(s) is inessential to Being, that this relation should be ignored; it means instead not to think Being in the style [*Art*] of metaphysics." Heidegger explains further that "grounding Being in being(s)" is thinking Being onto-theo-logically, whereby the following two aspects are involved: first, the theological aspect of metaphysics, understood such that the *ens summum*, as *causa sui*, achieves the grounding of all being(s) as such; and second, the metaphysical character of the ontological difference, understood such that Being is thought for the sake of thinking of being(s).

It is unmistakable that Heidegger is confronted here with a serious problem. His claim that the formulation "thinking Being without being(s)" means simply "thinking Being without regard to metaphysics" is scarcely intelligible. If the entire formulation is taken literally, the positive counterpart to the first, "thinking Being with being(s)," would mean "thinking Being with regard to being(s)" or, simply, "thinking Being metaphysically." Because, however, Heidegger wants to avoid thinking metaphysically, the consequence would be that he would want to (or have to) avoid thinking *at all* about the relation between Being and being(s). But that, for Heidegger, is also unacceptable. This makes clear that the fully undifferentiated, inexact formulation in the "Summary" had to be made more precise or indeed corrected; that formulation speaks of "thinking Being not in the way [*Art*] of metaphysics." Two questions or problems arise: first, *how* does Heidegger think of the relation between Being and being(s) *other than* in "the way of metaphysics," and second, does it make sense—or indeed, is it at all possible—to think "Being without being(s)," thus Being itself, as such. This second problem is made the more severe by the fact that according to a different passage, cited above, "Being *never* essences [*west*] without being(s)." This entire complex of problems is considered in what follows.

The next task is to examine carefully Heidegger's explanation of his phrase "Being without reference to metaphysics" by means of the formulation "without grounding Being in being(s)." As indicated above, the explanation has two aspects. The first is the onto-theo-logical one: the grounding of Being in beings is given when the *ens summum* as *causa sui* achieves the grounding of all being(s). The section on Aquinas's metaphysics of Being shows that save on the most superficial level, Aquinas does not accept an *ens summum* as *causa sui*. Instead, Aquinas identifies the *ipsum esse*, Being itself, as such and in its fullness, as *ipsum esse per se subsistens*, and being(s) (all of which are created!) as *modes of participation* in *esse ipsum*. For this configuration, Heidegger's term "ground" is in no way appropriate. His ceaselessly repeated claim that metaphysics is the thinking of ground(ing) is, as the account above shows in detail, one that simply misses its mark. Heidegger is the victim of his own stereotypical and carelessly repeated misinterpretations and distortions.

The second aspect is (*TB* 33; t.a.) "the metaphysical character [*Gepräge*] of the ontological difference, according to which Being is thought and conceptualized for the sake of being(s), so that Being, despite its Being-(the)-ground, stands under the dominion [*Botmäßigkeit*] of being(s)." This is yet another astonishing assertion that directly contradicts, to the highest possible degree, the explicit theses of (for example) Aquinas's metaphysics of Being. Aquinas articulates the *esse per se subsistens* more precisely as absolutely *free* Being, as Being that creates being(s) in complete *freedom*. It is nonsensical to maintain that thereby Being is thought and conceptualized "for the sake of being(s), so that Being"— absolutely free *esse per se subsistens!*—"despite its Being-(the)-ground, stands under the dominion of being(s)." Here yet again, Heidegger relies on his gross caricature of traditional metaphysics; the caricature is contradicted by the central theses of Aquinas. It is contradicted yet more radically by the systematic conception presented in chapter 3.

To be noted in addition is that Heidegger appears not to have reflected on his thesis that "to the truth of Being belongs [the fact that] Being never essences [*west*] without being(s)." To say that "Being never essences without being(s)" is to say that Being is *necessarily* bound up with being(s), a state of affairs expressible in Heideggerian language as follows: because Being never essences without being(s), it does indeed, despite being *Ereignis,* stand under the dominion [*Botmäßigkeit*] of being(s). Being's putatively standing under the dominion of being(s) is a problem not for the metaphysical tradition, but for Heidegger himself. That this is a basic and—for Heidegger—insoluble problem is shown in what follows.

[2] Heidegger recognizes both Being and being(s), and consequently both Being-as-*Ereignis* and beings-as-*Ereignete.* That he does raises three important questions. The first is explicitly articulated in the "Summary" (42; t.a.): "*Ereignis ereignet*—what? What is *das Ereignete* that *Ereignis* [*ereignet*]?" The second is this: How does Heidegger interpret the difference between Being/*Ereignis* and beings/*Ereignete?* How does he interpret the relation between the two? The third is, what are the consequences, for Heidegger's attempt to think "Being itself" or "Being as such," of the fact that the relation of Being/*Ereignis* to beings/*Ereignete* is in no way accidental or incidental, but instead necessary to Being?

[i] The "Summary" notes, concerning the first question, that "Time and Being" has nothing to say about it, but also asserts that in others of Heidegger's works, "some thought has been given to this" (42). Specifi-

cally, the "Summary" holds that the essay "The Principle of Identity" says the following:

> What *Ereignis ereignet*, i.e., brings into its own and maintains within *Ereignis*, [is] the belonging together of Being and human being. Within this belonging together what belong together are no longer Being and human being, but—as *Ereignete*—mortals within the fourfold [*Geviert*] of the world. (*TB* 42; t.a.)

In "The Principle of Identity" this belonging together is explained more precisely in that the together is determined by means of the belonging, whereby the belonging itself is not presented as an ordering or ordering together [*Zuordnung, Zusammenordnung*]; the belonging together is instead presented as a belonging-to-each-other. How the human being figures into this is explained as follows:

> What distinguishes the human being consists in this, that the human being, as thinking being [*Wesen*], is open to Being, is placed before Being, remains related to Being and thus corresponds to it. The human being genuinely *is* this relation of correspondence [*Bezug*], and is only this. "Only"—this names not a restriction, but an excess. In the human being there rules [*waltet*] a belonging to Being that harkens to Being because it is delivered over to it [*weil es diesem übereignet ist*]. (*ID* 31; t.a.)

According to the "Summary,"

> What belong together [are] no longer Being and human being, but—as *Ereignete*—: mortals within the fourfold of the world. Of the *Ereigneten*, of the fourfold, [other lectures] speak in different ways. (*TB* 42; t.a.)

This makes clear that the *Ereignete* is the fourfold and that human beings, as *Ereignete*, are "the mortals" within this fourfold. The constituents of the fourfold are mortals, divinities [*die Göttlichen*], heaven, and earth. How Heidegger's formulations concerning Being, *Ereignis, Ereignen, das Ereignete, die Ereigneten,* and the belonging together can be made to cohere with one another is anything but clear. For example, he explicitly says that what of Being and time is, for each, its own, is their belonging together, and that this belonging together is "determined" by *Ereignis.* How does this thesis cohere with those introduced above according to which *das Ereignete* of *Ereignis* is the belonging together of Being and human being such that what belong together are no longer Being and human being but instead—as *Ereignete*—mortals within the fourfold of the world? *Das Ereignete* proper appears to be the fourfold, the simplicity [*Einfalt*] of the four constituents (aspects? elements?) of the fourfold.

Here again, Heidegger proceeds in a manner that is poetic-mythological rather than philosophical. Further consideration of this would be utterly superfluous.

[ii] The second question concerns *how* Being/*Ereignis* and beings/*Ereignete* are different or distinct or, differently put, *how* the relation between the two is to be articulated. Is this something that Heidegger clarifies? The answer is clear: in the final analysis, not at all—whereby, however, the "in the final analysis" is significant. To see why, one must see that the question posed just above includes two different, more specific questions. The first is: of what sort is this difference or this relation? A generally negative-positive answer to this question can be drawn from Heidegger's works: the difference or relation is in no way external, as could be the case if Being-as-*Ereignis* somehow were on its own or could be—or "essence"—in isolation, such that beings/*Ereignete* could then enter, from the outside, into a or the relation to it (see *Cont* §135, p. 79). Instead, the difference/relation is integral to the essencing of Being itself, or to the *Ereignen of Ereignis* itself. Heidegger thus allows beings/*Ereignete* into the "essencing of Being" or the *Ereignen of Ereignis*.

This negative-positive answer is essentially—mutatis mutandis—the one Aquinas gives, in all clarity, in his metaphysics of Being: beings, as ways or modes of participation in *esse ipsum* (*per se subsistens*) have a relation to *esse ipsum* (*per se subsistens*) not somehow from outside *esse*, but—in Heidegger's terminology—in the essencing of *esse* and thus within *esse* or within the *self-communication* (*Selbstmitteilung*) of *esse*. ("Self-communication of *esse*" would—once again mutatis mutandis—correspond to Heidegger's "Being-as-*Ereignis*.") To the first question, then, Heidegger gives only a *partial* answer, and one that is *only negative-positive*, not genuinely positive.

But does Heidegger give a genuinely positive answer to the question concerning what kind or sort of inner difference or inner relation there is between Being and beings and/or *Ereignis* and *Ereignete*? At least one aspect of the question can be formulated—in Heidegger's language—as follows: *how* is it that *Ereignis ereignet* the *Ereignete*? To this question Heidegger provides at least a partial answer.

In non-Heideggerian language, the current question is the following: how is it to be understood that beings/*Ereignete* emerge or proceed from the essencing of Being or the *Ereignen* of the *Ereignis*? Presumably Heidegger would say that this is a metaphysical question, and that he has abandoned metaphysics. Even ignoring the fact that, as is shown above in various contexts, such a response is unjustified and empty, Heidegger cannot so easily evade the question. Given his weighty assertion, cited more than once above, that "it belongs to the truth of Being that Being *never essences* [west] *without* being(s)," it *can* and *must* be said that the emergence of being(s) from the essencing of Being—and hence the emergence of the *Ereignete* from the *Ereignen* of *Ereignis*—is, in modal terms, a *necessity*. Heidegger's answer to this second question would then have to be the following: that Being never essences without being(s)—or that *Ereignis* never *ereignet* without *Ereignete*—means that Being *necessarily* essences *with* being(s) or that *Ereignis* necessarily *ereignet Ereignete,*[28] because beings/*Ereignete* emerge *necessarily* from Being-as-*Ereignis*. Here, there would be nothing more to be explained. The answer would be correct (within the framework of his assumptions), but would raise new and imposing problems for Heidegger.

If fact, the implied modality is a *conditioned* one: *if* there is Being (-as-*Ereignis*), *then* Being *necessarily* essences being(s). But what of the modal status of *Being itself,* Being-*as-Ereignis*? To rely on Heidegger's treasured "*Es gibt* [It gives/There is]": does it *necessarily* give Being(-as-*Ereignis*)? Differently and more loosely phrased: is it the case that *everything is contingent*—both all beings/*Ereignete* and Being-as-*Ereignis* itself—or is it the case that there is (that it gives) something or other that is necessary in the genuine sense, thus (in Heideggerian language) Being that essences and (or such that) *it cannot not essence?*

As fundamental as this question is, it is one that Heidegger does not pose, and so of course does not respond to. He would presumably reject it as "metaphysical." But that would make clear not only that his critique of metaphysics fails, but above all that he accepts and engages in only an arbitrarily and drastically pruned and restricted form of the "thinking" that he so extravagantly values; this would be so because the modalities are among the highest capabilities of thinking that is *not* arbitrarily pruned and restricted. How different is the conception presented by Aquinas: in that Aquinas not only theoretically recognizes but also (at least basically) brings to bear *all of the capabilities of thinking,* he articulates the *esse per se subsistens* more precisely and determinately as absolutely necessary Being that creates being(s) in complete *freedom.* This is an adequate answer to the second question, that concerning the inner or internal relation between Being and (created) being(s)—and one that is indeed (in Heideggerian terms) "within the sphere of the essencing" of Being.

[iii] The third question concerns the consequences, for Heidegger's

---

[28] It is clear that for Heidegger, the verb "*ereignen*" is transitive.

attempt to think "Being/*Ereignis* itself (or as such)," of the fact that there is a relation between Being/*Ereignis* and being/*Ereignete.* Being as a whole is to be understood as Being-in-its-relation-to-being(s) or Being-together-with-being(s) or, yet more explicitly, Being-as-configuration-of- (or: among-)being(s). Heidegger pays scarcely any explicit attention to Being as a whole, hence to Being in relation to beings; to the contrary, he appears to recognize and speak of it only with the greatest reluctance. The reason for this is presumably that he is inclined to consider any talk of this relation to be "metaphysical" in his pejorative sense. But that he ignores this topic makes questionable—at best—his entire approach to the thematization of the primordial dimension of Being. Here, it suffices to introduce some problematic passages from *Contributions:*

> §135. The Essencing [*Die Wesung*] of Being as *Ereignis* (The Relation of Dasein and Being)
>
> [This relation] includes the *Er-eignung* of Dasein. Accordingly, and strictly speaking, talk of a relation of Dasein *to* Beyng is misleading, insofar as this suggests that Beyng essences "for itself" and that Dasein takes up the relating to Beyng.
>
> The relation of Dasein *to* Beyng belongs in the essencing of Beyng itself. This can also be said as follows: Beyng needs Dasein and does not essence at all without this *Ereignung.*
>
> *Er-eignis* is so strange that it seems to be complemented [*er-gänzt*] *by* this relation to the other, whereas from the ground up it does not essence in any other way.
>
> Talk of [a or the] relation of Dasein to Beyng obscures Beyng and turns Beyng into an over-against [*ein Gegenüber*]—which Beyng is not, since Beyng itself always *er-eignet* primarily as *that to which* it is to essence as over-against. For this reason, this relation is also entirely incomparable to the subject-object-relation. (179–80; t.a.)

This text shows in a characteristic manner that Heidegger himself does precisely what he constantly refuses to allow Christian metaphysics to do: to use—allowably and indeed unavoidably—formulations that are inappropriate and often easily misunderstood. He takes virtually every "metaphysical" formulation within which the term "being/*ens*" appears as evidence that metaphysics is concerned *only* with being(s), i.e., the highest being and the finite beings. When Aquinas explains the relation of created beings to Being as that of being participating modes of self-subsistent Being (of *esse per se subsistens*), why should it not hold for him as well that "talk of the relation of Da-sein to Beyng [Aquinas: the relation of created being(s) as participating modes of Being to *esse per se subsistens*] makes Beyng [Aquinas: *esse per se subsistens*] ambiguous, makes it appear as an over-against, although it is not, because it itself first *ereignet* (transitive) that to which Heidegger says it essences as over-against [Aquinas: insofar as *esse per se subsistens* lets what it essences as over-against participate in its own *esse* by creating it as a finite mode of Being within its own *esse*]"? Such a relation, too, is wholly different from the subject-object relation.

Given this state of affairs, what Heidegger says—and with him the hordes who accept and cite his assertions as dogmas—against the metaphysics of the Christian tradition is not only astonishing but also, in the highest degree, both self-contradictory and self-undermining.

2.5 The "Overcoming [*Überwinding*] of Metaphysics" as "Transformational Recovering [*Verwindung*]" of Metaphysics and "the End of the History of Being"

Following the lengthy preceding treatment of Heidegger's thinking of Being it is appropriate once again to analyze his thesis, so rich in consequences, concerning the necessity of the overcoming of metaphysics, now in conjunction both with the thesis—which he takes to follow from the former thesis—concerning the end of the metaphysics of Being, and with his emphasis on the finitude of thinking and the attempt—which guides him methodologically and programmatically—"simply to say the truth of Being." It should be clear by this point that Heidegger's thought exhibits nothing approaching thoroughgoing coherence. One reason it does not is the fact that he went through a lengthy period of development. Nevertheless, it is generally assumed that his thesis concerning the overcoming of metaphysics is one factor that is stable throughout that development. If this is true, then the stable thesis is his ceaselessly repeated objection to the forgetfulness of Being he falsely attributes to metaphysics. That objection therefore requires additional consideration, now in conjunction with critical analyses of various of Heidegger's statements that relate to it.

[1] The first text to cite is a central passage from "On the Being Question" (which first appeared in 1955 with the title "On 'The Line'"). The passage formulates the most important—although apparently not fully coherent—aspects of his central thesis concerning the (necessity of the) overcoming of metaphysics. In this text, Heidegger (re)interprets and clarifies this overcoming as a transformational recovering:

The transformational recovering [*Verwindung*] of metaphysics is the transformational recovering of the oblivion of Being. Such transformational recovering turns toward the essence of metaphysics. It entwines itself around it by way of what this essence itself demands, insofar as it calls for that realm that can raise it into the free dimension of its truth. In order to respond to a transformational recovering of metaphysics, thinking must for this reason first clarify the essence of metaphysics. To such an attempt, the transformational recovering of metaphysics initially appears to be an overcoming [*Überwindung*] that merely leaves exclusively metaphysical representation behind it, so as to lead thinking into the free realm attained by a transformational recovering of the essence of metaphysics. But in this transformational recovering, the enduring truth of the metaphysics that has seemingly been rejected returns explicitly as the now appropriated essence of metaphysics.

Here there occurs something other than a mere restoration of metaphysics. . . . Every restoration is an interpretation of metaphysics. Whoever today is of the opinion that he is able to see through and follow more clearly metaphysical inquiry as a whole in its specificity and history should, in his predilection for moving in these illuminated realms in such a superior manner, one day think carefully about where he acquired the light to see more clearly. One can scarcely exaggerate the grotesque way in which people proclaim my attempts at thinking to be a demolishing of metaphysics and at the same time, with the aid of those attempts, keep to paths of thought and ideas that have been taken from—I do not say, are thanks to—that alleged demolition. It is not thanks that is needed here, but mindfulness [*Besinnung*]. Yet the failure to be mindful [*Besinnungslosigkeit*] began already with the superficial miscontrual of the "destruction" [*Destruktion*] discussed in *Being and Time* (1927), a "destruction" that has no other intent than to win back the originary experiences of Being belonging to metaphysics by deconstructing [*Abbau*] representations that have become commonplace and empty. (*PM* 314–15; t.a.)[29]

It is unmistakable that in this passage Heidegger strives to articulate, emphasize, and preserve what is—so to speak—positive about metaphysics. That Heidegger indeed goes so far as to speak of the "enduring truth of the metaphysics that has seemingly been rejected" is remarkable, and this the more so in that, as shown above, he regularly misinterprets "metaphysics" by characterizing—indeed, caricaturing—it as

---

[29] See also the essay "The Overcoming of Metaphysics" in *The End of Philosophy*.

"onto-theo-logy." It is also remarkable—and bears emphasizing—that philosophers and theologians—above all those with Jewish and Christian orientations—always cite only Heidegger's uncompromisingly *negative* statements about metaphysics while paying no attention whatsoever to the *positive* ones.[30] Be that as it may, the question here is that of how the positive assessment articulated so clearly in the passage just quoted is to be understood. What is the "abiding truth" of metaphysics as Heidegger understands it? Heidegger provides an answer to this question, but his answer both is ambiguous and introduces new—and serious—difficulties.

Heidegger's thesis concerning the oblivion of Being has always been understood and treated as the most general and fundamental point of his critique of metaphysics, as it is in the critical discussions of Heidegger above in this book. But there is also in Heidegger another view that is to be accorded great significance. In the highly consequential "Summary" (which Heidegger himself reviewed and in some places expanded), there is the following passage (*TB* 29; t.a.):

> The oblivion of Being that is manifest as not thinking about the truth of Being can easily be interpreted and misunderstood as an omission of previous thinking, in any case as something that would be terminated by the question about the meaning, that is, the truth of Being when that question is explicitly adopted and followed through. Heidegger's thinking could be understood . . . as the preparation and beginning of a foundation upon which all metaphysics rests as its inaccessible ground, in such a way that the preceding oblivion of Being would thus be suspended [*aufgehoben*] and destroyed.

The "Summary" then, however, emphatically rejects this interpretation, as follows:

> This previous non-thinking is not an omission, but is to be thought as the consequence of the self-concealment of Being. As the privation of Being, the concealment of Being belongs to the opening up of Being. The oblivion of Being that constitutes the essence of metaphysics and became the stimulus for *Being and Time* belongs to the essence of Being itself. Thus there is put to the thinking of Being the task of thinking Being in such a way that oblivion belongs to it essentially. (29; t.a.)

---

[30] See section 4.2.1, below.

These are remarkable assertions; the crucial question is that of whether they are coherent. Their interpretation is facilitated by the clarification of the following distinction:

(1) Thinking-of-Being-*in*-its-self-oblivion (or: *in*-its-self-concealment), or simply: thinking-of-self-obliviation (or self-concealing) Being; and

(2) Thinking-of-Being-*qua*-Being-*with*-its-explicitly-experienced-self-obliviation (or: *with*-the-self-obliviation-that-belongs-essentially-to-it).

According to Heidegger, metaphysics is to be interpreted as the articulation of Being according to (1) and his intended "originary thinking" as the articulation of Being according to (2). But is this distinction sensible—can it be maintained? Heidegger assumes that it can in making the following two statements: "For a thinking of Being there is the task of thinking Being in such a way that oblivion belongs essentially to it," and "In thinking of Being itself, of *Ereignis,* the oblivion of Being can be experienced for the first time" (30; t.a.). But these statements are at best seriously problematic. If a thinking thinks Being in such a way "that Being's self-oblivion is essential to it," does it think (1) or (2) or both (1) and (2) (and if the last, then simultaneously, or in which order)? The self-oblivion of Being would appear to preclude the possibility of that self-oblivion Being thought. The same holds if Heidegger's language of "experience" is used: to experience whatever has putatively been in oblivion (or: been forgotten) is to negate or overcome its being in oblivion (its forgottenness). Here again, what is evident is Heidegger's all too facile skill in playing with portentous words.

That (1) is intelligible and coherent is clear. But (2), the Heideggerian alternative, presents an enormous problem that becomes manifest in light of Heidegger's thesis concerning the end of the history of Being.

[2] The "Summary" reports that in the lecture "Time and Being," the question was posed concerning the "possible end of the history of Being":

> If *Ereignis* is not a new coinage [*Prägung*] for Being in the history of Being, but to the contrary Being belongs within *Ereignis* and is taken back into it (in whatsoever fashion), then the history of Being comes to its end *in Ereignis*, i.e., for the thinking that turns [*einkehrt*] to *Ereignis*, in that thereby Being, as it rests in fateful sending [*Geschick*], is no longer what is to be thought. Thinking then stands in and in front of That which has sent [*zugeschickt*] the various forms [*Gestalten*] of epochal Being. This, however—what sends, as *Ereignis*—is itself unhistorical, or better, fateless [*geschicklos*]. (40–41; t.a.)

Understanding and assessing these largely cryptic assertions requires that additional passages be taken into consideration. Heidegger's formulations are so unusual that they must be introduced in forms as close to literal as translation allows if any sense at all is to be made of them.

> Metaphysics is the oblivion of Being, and that means the history of the concealment and withdrawal of what gives Being. Thinking's arriving at *Ereignis* is thus equivalent to the end of the history of this withdrawal. Being's oblivion thus "suspends" [*hebt . . . auf*] itself with the awakening [of thinking] into *Ereignis*. (41; t.a.)

Is the withdrawal, the concealment of Being then "suspended" once and for all? That would seem to cohere with the other passages introduced shortly above. But it is therefore surprising next to encounter the following:

> But the concealment that belongs to metaphysics as its limit must belong to [*zueigen sein*] *Ereignis* itself. That means that the withdrawal that characterized metaphysics in the form of the oblivion of Being now shows itself as the dimension of concealment itself. But now this concealment does not conceal itself; instead, it attracts the attention of thinking.—When thinking reaches its destination with *Ereignis* [*Die Einkehr des Denkens in das Ereignis*], *Ereignis*'s own way of concealment also arrives. *Ereignis* is, within itself, *Enteignis*.[f] (41; t.a.)

Here again are extremely daring and portentous statements. The oblivion of Being that characterizes metaphysics and the history of Being that is the history of metaphysics itself are suspended. The oblivion of Being is the concealment and the withdrawal of Being. But withdrawal and concealment do not end; instead, withdrawal now appears as the dimension of concealment, whereby this must be "*Ereignis*'s own." But why and how? According to Heidegger, this is distinct from metaphysics and the concealment characteristic of it: the concealment that is *Ereignis*'s own does not conceal itself (any longer), it shows itself as *Ereignis*'s own way of concealing. It is *Ereignis*'s own *Enteignis*. Is it the case that there is one and the same concealment in metaphysics and in *Ereignis*? According to Heidegger, the former does not reveal itself, but it holds of the latter "that now this concealment does not conceal itself." The concealment that is *Ereignis*'s own is characterized as a concealment that "attracts

---

[f] The prefix "*Ent-*" is presumably privative; Stambaugh translates: "Appropriation is in itself *expropriation*." Another possibility would be: "*Ereignis* is, within itself, non-*Ereignis*."

the attention of thinking." If thinking is attentive to this concealment, then the concealment reveals itself precisely *as a concealment*. How so?

Heidegger seems here somehow to hypostasize certain concepts (or, as he would say, "subject matters" [*Sachen*] or "phenomena") and thereby, in something closer to his language, to objectify them. Presumably the situation is more or less as follows: what he sees as his task is that of thinking Being-as-*Ereignis itself, as itself,* and thinking does this only when it thinks *Ereignis* as *Ereignis* shows itself. Heidegger appears to think or to presuppose that this showing itself as itself includes some sort of withdrawal: it somehow holds itself back, withdraws itself from thinking, *precisely in showing itself as itself and indeed in order to show itself as itself.* This seems to be what is always behind Heidegger's thoughts of withdrawal and concealment.

However, this analysis of the self-showing is defective because (in this case) Being-as-*Ereignis* shows itself *as itself;* the self-showing is *of* Being-as-*Ereignis* precisely *as itself.* Where then can there be any withdrawal or concealment? It cannot defensibly be said that the "it itself" that is here in question can *be itself only* if it contains or implies a withdrawal or a concealment. Instead, the "it itself" seems to be objectified as something somehow tantalizing, allowing itself to be glimpsed and then suddenly withdrawing.

What appears to be the best explanation of this state of affairs is an astonishing one: Heidegger, who criticized and fundamentally overcame the philosophy of subjectivity more fully than has virtually any other thinker (or philosopher), nevertheless, at the decisive juncture, thinks within the framework of just such a philosophy. This is supported by a reference to Kant.[31] In arguing for his transcendental idealism, Kant introduces the following premise: if x is an appearance, then x is not (simultaneously also) thing in itself. In support of this premise he presents a *modus tollens* argument: if x as appearance were simultaneously also thing in itself, then "its properties [would have to] migrate over into my power of representation";[32] this, however, is impossible and/or absurd, so. . . . Here it is clear what "appearance" ultimately means for Kant: appearances conceal the in itself, they do not reveal it; the only way this concealment could be overcome would be for the properties of what had been concealed to "migrate over into my power of representation." As a consequence, the concealment would vanish only if the appearance vanished.

Analogously, Heidegger assumes that what shows itself as such

---

[31] On what follows, see Puntel, "Transzendentaler und absoluter Idealismus," now in *SGTh.*

[32] *Proleg.* §9.

(which, in this context, corresponds to what Kant calls "appearance") does not preserve [*bewahren*] but instead suspends the *it itself* of what shows itself (the analogue, in this context, of Kant's thing in itself). But instead of concluding, as Kant does, that the it itself remains unrecognizable by us, Heidegger concludes that what shows itself *does* show itself as it is itself, but under the presupposition that it is not (so to speak) delivered to thinking, because that would require that it cease to withdraw or conceal itself. Briefly: the self-showing of something as itself is possible or given only by means of its simultaneous self-withdrawal or self-concealment. This, however, is a premise that is characteristic of the philosophy of subjectivity, as is shown by the passage from Kant. Moreover, this premise is arbitrary: the *self*-showing of *x* is the self-showing of *x itself*—nothing more and nothing less.

[3] The question now arises of what, ultimately, is or could be meant by the end of the history of Being. The end of the history of Being is not, according to Heidegger, the utter end of withdrawal or concealment, it is only the end of that form of withdrawal or concealment that "characterized metaphysics in the form of the oblivion of Being" (41; t.a.). But how to understand its replacement—the "other" concealment of which Heidegger says that it "does not conceal itself." What form does it take? Heidegger interprets metaphysics as "oblivion of Being and [thus] as the history of the concealment and withdrawal of that which gives Being" (41; t.a.). But if concealment here is understood as *Ereignis*'s own mode of concealment, must that not mean that the oblivion of Being would continue? Perhaps a different form of oblivion of Being? Perhaps a new form of metaphysics? To show that Heidegger's portentous words are not empty, one would have to show what is meant by "*Ereignis*'s own mode of concealment." What this could mean is certainly not articulated by Heidegger. To the contrary, this state of affairs reveals Heidegger's "conception" to be fatally flawed.

2.6 The Status of Heideggerian Thinking I: Thinking of Being as Thinking Within *Ereignis*, Thinking That Reaches Its Destination with *Ereignis* (*Denken, das in das Ereignis einkehrt*)

The thesis of the end of the history of Being brings with it an additional fundamental problem: what, ultimately, is the status of Heideggerian "thinking"?

[1] With respect to clarifying the status of Heideggerian thinking,

the following passage from the "Summary"—cited twice above—is revealing, indeed decisive:

> If *Ereignis* is not a new coinage [*Prägung*] for Being in the history of Being, but to the contrary Being belongs within *Ereignis* and is taken back into it (in whatsoever fashion), then the history of Being comes to its end *in Ereignis*, i.e., for the thinking that turns [*einkehrt*] to *Ereignis*, in that thereby Being, as it rests in fateful sending [*Geschick*], is no longer what is to be thought. Thinking then stands in and in front of that which has sent [*zugeschickt*] the various forms [*Gestalten*] of epochal Being. This, however—what sends, as *Ereignis*—is itself unhistorical, or better, fateless [*geschicklos*]. (40–41; t.a.)

This passage is among the best of Heidegger's characterizations of his "other beginning of thinking" (*Cont* 3). It raises many questions.

In this passage, Heidegger articulates the dimension that he views as the ultimately primordial one, the one to which he takes himself to gain access by taking what he calls his "step back." He emphasizes that the step back from Being-as-presence to *Ereignen* "must not be misinterpreted as the preparation of a yet more primordial ground" (*TB* 45, t.a.; see also 29); he must, however, be understood as claiming to have reached the ultimately most primordial dimension of thinking and for thinking. But how does he defend any such claim? In his works, he offers none. This might perhaps be explained by saying that he wants to and perhaps in fact does think phenomenologically, and that this is a form of thought that has no room for the likes of defending and justifying, but is concerned only with "showing" and "seeing." But this would raise a yet more serious problem: what is the status of his thinking if it *is* understood as phenomenological? This issue is considered below.

Something else, also highly problematic, comes into view in the passage quoted just above. Heidegger *distinguishes* "that which has sent the different forms of epochal Being"—what does the sending—from the forms, thus, from what is sent. This distinction or difference is simply central to this thinking. But it is also the case that his chief objection to the metaphysics of Being is that it does not think the difference between Being and being(s). According to Heidegger, however, the difference between the two reveals a dimension more primordial than they are (as understood metaphysically), such that "both Being and being(s) appear, each in its own way, *from out of the difference*" (*ID* 63–64; t.a.), thus, from out of the primordial dimension.

The question then presses: must not the analogous question be raised about the Heideggerian difference between what does the sending (*Ereignis*) and what is sent (the *Ereignete*)? Because Heidegger says nothing at all about this, mustn't one raise against him the objection of oblivion, of failing to think this crucial difference? Heidegger can respond that the *Ereignete* are *ereignet in Ereignis,* that what is sent is sent *in* the sending. That is correct, in his sense, but, as shown above, Aquinas's metaphysics of Being says and indeed emphasizes that beings, as created, participate *in Being itself* as participating modes *of Being itself.* Despite this fact, Heidegger raises against Aquinas the charge of not thinking the difference. If Aquinas's having failed to think his difference would have been a serious or even fatal failure, then so too must be Heidegger's failure to think his difference.

In addition, it is insufficient simply to point in some vaguely phenomenological fashion to the dimension of *Ereignis* as the putatively most primordial dimension.

[2] Here the central question is to be posed once again: how does Heidegger understand "that which has sent the various forms of epochal Being" as *Ereignis?* According to Heidegger, it is "itself non-historical or, better, fateless [*geschicklos*]." Although this non-historicality might be taken to indicate that *Ereignis*/the sender is somehow static, Heidegger asserts "that the way of movedness [*Bewegtheit*] that, for thinking, is what is ownmost to *Ereignis* is the turning-toward in the withdrawal, which reveals itself as what is to be thought" (*TB* 41; t.a.). These formulations are abstract, general, and contentless. And when Heidegger uses terms such as "*eigen* [own]," "*Eigentüm* [property]," "*schicken* [to send]," which are drawn from ordinary German—where they have specific meanings—it is not clear how these terms, in the absence of explicit articulations of *non*-ordinary meanings, can possibly provide more precise determination of the most primordial dimension. Heidegger's works provide no defense against the charge that he *totally anthropomorphizes* the primordial dimension.

2.7 The Status of Heideggerian Thinking II: Absolute Claim, Provisionality, the Poverty of Language, the Language of Thinking, the Finitude of Thinking

The analyses and considerations presented above lead directly to yet another fundamental question: what, according to Heidegger, *characterizes his own thinking?*[33] The answer involves a peculiar paradox in Heidegger's thinking, consisting chiefly of four factors.

---

[33] Heidegger speaks explicitly of the "characteristics of [his] thinking" in *TB,* e.g., 30.

[1] Heidegger makes an extremely comprehensive and uncompromising claim that *condemns* the entirety of philosophy throughout its history and in every one of its concrete forms. *His* thinking claims to be absolutely superior to all other forms of thinking in that it understands and presents itself as more primordial, more originary. Presumably, no pre-Heideggerian thinker (one might say, no "philosopher," were it not for Heidegger's ambiguous attitude toward philosophy) has turned in so radical and condemnatory manner against the entire tradition of philosophy. The radicality of his claim should be neither ignored nor minimized. Heidegger's absolute claim is the more radical—and has often been the more effective—because on the explicit level of his work this claim is usually concealed, so it is easily missed by readers or hearers. What he does is to speak and write about the *provisionality* of thinking, the *language of thinking,* the *poverty of language,* and—on the whole—the *finitude of thinking.* These are considered in what follows.

[2] Heidegger regularly notes the provisional character of his own "thinkerish" efforts, as for example in the following passage: "Above and beyond the most obvious meaning that this thinking is always merely preparatory, its being anticipatory has the deeper meaning that this thinking always runs ahead—and this in the mode of the step back" (*TB* 35; t.a.). This self-description is precisely on target. On its basis, Heidegger can always respond to revelations of the deficiencies, the inaccessibility, and the obvious mistakes and errors of and in his "originary" thinking with a kind of self-immunization strategy. Just what is the other side of this coin is shown below.

[3] One finds in Heidegger's works constantly repeated complaints about *language.* His objection is summarily indicated by the phrase "Language fails [*versagt;* stops working, breaks down]," or by reference to the ineliminable "poverty of language" (in the domain of his "originary thinking"). To be sure, one finds similar complaints in the works of other philosophers, but never to any comparable degree. Characteristic are the final four sentences of "Time and Being." The first of these identifies what needs to be said—the opening hypothetic being clearly rhetorical—and the following two suggest that language is inadequate to the saying:

> If overcoming remains necessary, it concerns that thinking that explicitly enters *Ereignis* in order to say It in terms of It about It.
>
> Our task is unceasingly to overcome the obstacles that render such saying inadequate.
>
> The saying of *Ereignis* in the form of a lecture remains itself an obstacle of this kind. (24; t.a.)

One might suspect that the "form of a lecture" is an obstacle because of limitations on time, but the final sentence makes clear that Heidegger has something wholly different in mind: "[The lecture] has spoken merely in indicative sentences [*Aussagesätzen*]." This appears to mean that the lecture has—unfortunately—had no alternative to speaking in indicative sentences.

One finds in Heidegger not only complaints about language, but also interesting and consequential reflections on this topic. For example, he makes a distinction between the language of thinking and ordinary language and makes two important points about that distinction: first, that the language of thinking must start from ordinary language, and second, that ordinary language is not to be viewed simply as "metaphysical language": "instead, *our interpretation* of ordinary language is metaphysical; it is bound up with Greek ontology" (*TB* 51; t.a., emphasis added). Heidegger concludes with the programmatic thesis, "The relation of humans to language could, however, change in a manner analogous to the change in the relation to Being."

It is both characteristic of Heidegger and significant that he never went to the trouble of investigating the structures or the possibilities for interpretation and transformation of ordinary languages and other languages (no matter how developed). Of course, he lacked even the simplest acquaintance with modern logic, semantics, etc. Instead of studying these disciplines, he came back again and again to the etymologies and histories of central words from the philosophical tradition, interpreted those words on the basis of those etymologies and histories, and at times created, on the same basis, new words, word forms, and semantic values; an example is "*Ereignis.*" How differently Heidegger could have proceeded (and would have to have proceeded) had he had the requisite knowledge of logic, semantics, etc., is shown by the introduction of an interesting point that is directly related to theses introduced in chapter 3 that are central to the structural-systematic philosophy.

According to Heidegger, ordinary language consists of "indicative sentences," which he takes to be sentences having subjects and predicates. His critique—often repeated, in various forms—of the ontology (substance ontology) most closely associated with such sentences is essentially on target. The qualifier "essentially" is included because his critique is embedded in a way of thinking that is highly problematic; its problematicity does not, however, make the core of his critique undetectable.

It is characteristic that Heidegger never attempted to project even the basic structure(s) of—in his term—a language of thinking (in a non-Heideggerian term, a philosophical language). This would be a language that would not be associated with substance ontology (called "Greek ontology" by Heidegger). Without rejecting subject-predicate sentences from the purely syntactic level of this language (which in fact would simply not be possible), it is possible to interpret the *semantic, ontological,* and on the whole the *philosophical* levels of the language in such a way that on those levels, there are no counterparts to subjects and predicates. The semantic and ontological components of such a philosophical language correspond most closely to the syntax of sentences that do not have the subject-predicate structure, such as "It's raining" and "It's morning." Similar sentences from Heidegger begin "It's essencing" and "It gives [There is; *Es gibt*]"; had Heidegger explicitly recognized the availability of this alternative sentence structure, he could also have written, for example, "It's nothinging" instead of "The nothing nothings."

This is precisely the option taken by the structural-systematic philosophy sketched in chapter 3. Within the theoretical framework of that philosophy, sentences lacking the subject-predicate structure are termed prime sentences.[34] As indicated above, presentations of the structural-systematic philosophy can (as they must) include sentences that include subjects and predicates on the syntactic level, but such sentences are reinterpreted on the semantic and ontological levels. Hence, the subject of the subject-predicate sentence is not understood, semantically and ontologically, to refer to a substance; it is instead understood on the syntactic level as an abbreviation of a complex configuration of prime sentences. Thus, for example, the term "Socrates" in the sentence "Socrates is a philosopher" is understood as a convenient abbreviation for the complex configuration including, among enormously many others, "It's being-Greek," "It's being-a-teacher-of-It's-Platoing," etc.

If one relies on such a philosophical language, the fundamental problem Heidegger takes himself to detect in language as such—i.e., the reliance of "language" on subject-predicate sentences—simply disappears. Given this, it is important to note that there is nothing in Heidegger's works that in principle rules out or even opposes such a reinterpretation even of ordinary language, although there is likewise nothing that indicates that he envisaged such a reinterpretation as possible. He does, however, ask the following:

> whether there could not be a language of thinking that would talk in
> so *simple* [originary] a way that the language of thinking would make

---

[34] See *Structure and Being*, chapter 3, which thoroughly presents a semantics and an ontology based on a philosophical language that rigorously excludes subjects and predicates, instead relying only on the structure of prime sentences (which it, however, terms "primary sentences").

visible the limitation of metaphysical language. But one cannot speak of this. The issue is decided by whether or not such a talking effectively works. (*TB* 51; t.a.)

Heidegger does not indicate what criterion would determine "whether or not such a talking effectively works." But he then adds: "Ultimately, as far as natural language is concerned, it is not at the outset metaphysical. Instead, our interpretation of ordinary language is metaphysical: it is tied to Greek ontology." If only "our" interpretation of ordinary language is "metaphysical," then there is no obstacle to our changing that interpretation—and much less is there any reason we "cannot speak of this." To the contrary, perhaps the central philosophical task emerging from the problem Heidegger identifies with ordinary language is that of speaking of this reinterpretation, and then *explicitly* and *systematically* accomplishing it. It must, however, be added that the claim that only "our" interpretation of ordinary language is "metaphysical" is inaccurate; instead, it is the case that this interpretation is the most natural in the sense that it is the one that fits most smoothly with the subject-predicate sentence structure on which ordinary English relies (as does German, among many other ordinary languages). This interpretation corresponds to what the modern literature in semantics terms the standard interpretation of first-order predicate logic.[35]

[4] In Heidegger's writings one encounters again and again references to the *finitude* of thought. The way in which Heidegger understands and introduces this putative finitude reveals the genuine form of his own thinking as a form that is impoverished in the sense that it fails to make use of all available resources. The two characteristics of his thinking considered just above—its provisionality and its assumption that language is inadequate for "thinking"—contribute to this impoverishment, in a manner comparable to two rays of light converging on the focal point that is the finitude of (Heideggerian) thinking. Viewed in another way, they emerge as consequences from that point. But what happens if—to put an accusation somewhat loosely and perhaps polemically—one contends that if one paints oneself into a philosophical corner, then one will have access only to whatever of the world or of actuality is accessible from that corner? By insisting on the finitude of thought, Heidegger paints himself into such a corner. He begins to do so in *Being and Time,* the work of which Heidegger later says that it is "the attempt to interpret Being in terms of the transcendental horizon of time," and then adds, "In the lecture 'Time and Being,' the meaning of time, as yet unthought, which

---

[35] See *Structure and Being* 3.2.2.

lies in Being as presencing, is anchored in a still more original relation" (*TB* 27–28; t.a.). As shown above, Heidegger asserts that Being and time are anchored in *Ereignis*. One place this path of thinking leads is to the theses of the *finitude* of thinking *and* the *finitude* of Being; that it does so is clearly expressed in the penultimate paragraph of the "Summary":

> The finitude of Being was first spoken of in the book on Kant. The finitude of *Ereignis*, of Being, of the fourfold hinted at during the seminar is nevertheless different from the finitude spoken of in that book in that it is no longer thought in terms of the relation to infinity, but rather as finitude in itself: finitude, end, limit, the own [*das Eigene*]— to be secure in the own [*ins Eigene Geborgensein*]. The new concept of finitude is thought of in this manner—that is, in terms of *Ereignis* itself, in terms of the concept of the own [*Eigentum*]. (*TB* 54; t.a.)

Presumably, Heidegger is referring to the following passage from *Kant and the Problem of Metaphysics:*

> As a mode of Being, existence is in itself finitude, and as such it is possible only on the basis of the understanding of Being. *There is and must be something like Being* [*Dergleichen wie Sein*] *only where finitude has become existent.* The understanding of Being—which thoroughly dominates human existence, although unfamiliar in its breadth, constancy, indeterminacy and indisputability—thus manifests itself as the innermost ground of [human] finitude.[36]

The first thing to be noted about this passage is that the sentence "*There is and must be something like Being* [*Dergleichen wie Sein*] *only where finitude has become existent*" is completely arbitrary. What reason is there to accept it as true? And even if the understanding of Being reveals Being to be "the innermost ground of [human] finitude," it in no way follows that *Being itself* is likewise finite. The passage from the "Summary" cited above suggests that the finitude of thinking and the finitude of Being are simply correlative. Heidegger attempts to undermine all objections that could be made against the contention that they are correlative by making the last-ditch claim that "the finitude of *Ereignis*, of Being, of the fourfold . . . is no longer thought in terms of the relation to infinity, but rather as finitude in itself."

There are presumably few other formulations in Heidegger's works that are as revelatory of his form of thinking as are these. It appears to

---

[36] *Kant and the Problem of Metaphysics,* 160; t.a.

be simple for Heidegger to speak of "thinking finitude in itself," and to go no further. Heidegger assumes—apparently seeing no problems with the assumption—that finitude can and indeed must be *adequately* considered, *as finitude,* on its own, in isolation. But if—to rely again on the metaphor introduced above—one can see only what is visible from the corner into which one has painted oneself, can one see that one is in a corner? Heidegger ignores the simple fact that with the particle "as" in the formulation "finitude as finitude," "thinking" articulates a limitation by determining it on the basis of a dimension lying beyond the limitation. The notion that one could think of the limitation that is Heideggerian finitude "no longer in relation" to anything beyond that limitation (for Heidegger: the infinite), but instead as limitation "in itself," is simply "thinkerish" nonsense. Such a position can be termed a variant of a purely, dogmatically positivistic attempt to condemn philosophy as a whole: it is simply *posited* that it is so, with no articulation or investigation of the conditions, presuppositions, and implications bound up with the posited thesis.

The endless ruminations of the later Heidegger (especially in the numerous works not published during his lifetime), which basically repeat the same thing over and over again, cannot conceal the fact that he remains permanently within a purely *finite* dimension of thinking and Being, and that the basis for his doing so is ultimately arbitrary.

2.8 Heidegger's Thinking and the Topic "God"

In Heidegger's thinking, the question of God has a place that is significant but far from clear. It is therefore not surprising that this topic has often attracted—and continues to attract—the particular attention of many interpreters and critics of Heidegger (above all those with Jewish or Christian orientations). Yet Heidegger never treats the question of God in a manner that is sufficiently direct or thorough; instead, his works contain many remarks in dispersed locations, remarks that cannot be combined into a clear and unified conception. In fact, they express a tension that pervades his thought. Illuminating in this respect is the following remark on Christian theology: "Without this theological legacy I would never have made my way onto the path of thinking. But legacy always remains the future."[37] The question is of course that of where his

---

[37] *Poetry, Language, Thought,* 10.

path of thinking takes him. Answering that question in detail is not a task for this book. Why doing so is neither possible nor sensible is made clear by what follows.[38]

The problematic identified in the title of this section is thematized in Heidegger's works in three forms. In what follows, these are briefly characterized and criticized without concern for their chronological ordering.

The first form, also presumably the most striking and most influential, is Heidegger's misinterpretation of Christian-oriented metaphysics as onto-theo-logy, and the critique based on that misinterpretation. The second form is thematized in Heidegger's assertions about the relation of philosophy to theology with a biblical or Christian orientation (2.8.1). The third form is the most important: it explicitly thematizes the relation of Being/*Ereignis* to "God" (2.8.2). Because the first of these forms is treated thoroughly above, in section 2.1, it need not be reconsidered here.

2.8.1 The Relation Between Philosophy and (Christian) Theology

Heidegger's statements about the relation of philosophy to theology with a Christian or biblical orientation are found in a few brief lecture texts and in many letters.

[1] From Heidegger's early period, his lecture "Phenomenology and Theology" (1927) is particularly relevant.[39] Here, he writes (*PM* 43; t.a.): "Theology is a conceptual knowledge of what initially allowed Christianity to become an originary historical event—a knowledge of what we simply call Christianness [*Christlichkeit*]." "Christianness" is, he says, something posited by theology; this positedness gives theology its positivity, its character as a positive science. By Christianness Heidegger understands faith, which he characterizes as follows: faith is

> a mode of existence of human Dasein that, according to its own testimony—itself belonging essentially to this mode of existence—does *not* emerge *from out of* Dasein, and *not by means of* Dasein, of its own free will, but instead from that which is manifest in and with this mode of existence, that is, from what the faith is in. (*PM* 43–44; t.a.)

---

[38] Philippe Capelle, *Philosophie et théologie dans la pensée de Martin Heidegger* (1998), is a thorough and insightful treatment of this topic.

[39] The text is a revised version of the second half of the lecture, which was titled "The Positivity of Theology and Its Relation to Phenomenology" (see *PM* 39).

What there is faith in, according to Heidegger, is Christ, the crucified God.

[i] To be noted is that Heidegger thereby already introduces a distinction between theology and philosophy, one according to which philosophy, unlike theology, is a mode of existence that *does* emerge from out of Dasein, and by means of Dasein, from its own free will. And Heidegger then goes so far as to say that (53) "*faith,* as a specific possibility of existence, is in its innermost core the mortal enemy of the *form of existence* that is an essential part of philosophy." Surprisingly, however, this mortal enmity is not one that Heidegger describes—at least not in the published lecture—as having what would be the expected consequence of triggering mortal combat. To the contrary, he says that "philosophy does not even begin to want in any way to do battle with it." To be sure, Heidegger here speaks of his own philosophy. He then explains this state of affairs as follows:

> This *existentiell opposition* between faithfulness and the free self-overtaking of the whole of [one's] Dasein—which arises already *before* theology and philosophy and thus does not arise with them as sciences—must bear precisely the *possible commonality* of theology and philosophy *as sciences.*

Heidegger suggests a complete separation between theology and philosophy when he says that a "Christian philosophy" would be a "square circle." How is all of this to be understood? To be distinguished are the existentiell opposition, on the one hand, and the relation between the two sciences, on the other. Even so, Heidegger's distinction is not as clear and non-problematic as it might appear at first glance. The existentiell opposition is supposed to precede the opposition between the two sciences. But what opposition is this? According to Heidegger, the opposition is between "faithfulness" and "free self-overtaking of the whole of [one's] Dasein." That the existentiell status of faithfulness has theology as its scientific or theoretical counterpart is perhaps not surprising. But what would be the theoretical or scientific counterpart to the "free self-overtaking" of one's own Dasein? Heidegger's answer appears to be clear: it is philosophy. But this answer is based on a complete idealization of the "free self-overtaking of the whole of [one's] Dasein." Does the human being who freely takes over the whole of his Dasein thereby become a philosopher? The free overtaking of the entirety of Dasein can be nothing other than a decision about the total *determinacy* of Dasein, thus about all concrete aspects of Dasein. Is this determinacy philosophical, or indeed philosophy itself? It cannot be, because the totality of Dasein can be determined in all sorts of ways—including ones involving faith (whether religious or non-religious). There is no reason to say that such determinacies cannot be "free self-overtakings of the whole of [one's] Dasein."

Here, Heidegger has committed a significant error, and one that is richly consequential. He assumes that faithful existence is not free, but instead emerges from whatever the faith is in. In Kantian terms, he assumes that faith must be heteronomous rather than autonomous. It may be that he has in mind the Christian theological doctrine of grace, particularly in its Lutheran form, which includes the axioms *sola fides* and *sola gratia*. But that would be a caricature both of Christian doctrine generally and of Lutheran doctrine specifically. Grace and faith do not preclude one's acceptance of them of one's own free will; instead, grace and faith are meaningful only on the assumption that they can be freely accepted. It is astonishing that Heidegger was unable to see any relation between philosophical and faithful modes of existence other than the one he articulates.

An additional and far more important point concerning this matter also triggers astonishment. Heidegger speaks of the philosophical mode of existence as resulting from a decision or a self-overtaking (in that it emerges "*from out of* Dasein, and . . . *by means of* Dasein"), but of the faithful mode of existence as emerging "from that which is manifest in and with this mode of existence, that is, from what the faith is in." To this point, three critical questions should be raised.

First: if one considers Heidegger's development as it is thoroughly presented and critically assessed in the preceding sections, the question presses as to what remains of the philosophical mode of existence, which is said to "emerge *from out of* Dasein and *by means of* it, by its own free will," i.e., of the mode of existence he describes as a "self-overtaking." In Heidegger's later thought there is talk only of *Ereignis* as what sends, such that Being (and with it human being, Da-sein) and time are understood only as among what is sent or as the *Ereigneten*. The philosophical mode of existence is understood not on the basis of Dasein, but on the basis of some sort of receptivity: of what is sent or of what *Ereignis ereignet*. Where is the "self-overtaking" that Dasein was supposed to be able to accomplish "of its own free will"? What remains of the difference, so emphasized in the 1927 lecture, between the philosophical and the faithful modes of existence? It is clear that in the thinking of the later Heidegger, *that* difference—the one introduced in 1927—cannot be the one Heidegger defends, but it is also the case that he does not introduce any replacement that plays a central role in his further reflections. In what follows, the new difference that he does introduce is considered only in relation to the next question to be considered.

Second: why did Heidegger not develop a fully different and more consequential conception concerning the philosophical and theological modes of existence? That he did not is typical of his entire way of thinking, throughout his entire oeuvre. The difference that replaces the one made in 1927 is now to be briefly articulated, but is treated more fully below in a different context (3.7.4.2.2[3]).

Starting from the assumption that Heidegger always concentrates exclusively on the primordial dimension for thinking—which he first calls "Being," then "Being-as-*Ereignis*" or, more simply, "*Ereignis*"—one may ask whether the "philosophical mode of existence" and the "theological mode of existence" could or should adequately be understood as follows: the philosopher (in Heidegger's sense; the "thinker") considers the primordial dimension only generally, as largely undetermined, as one that still awaits its self-determination and the corresponding articulation; in opposition, (Christian) theology begins with the fully developed, fully determined form of the primordial dimension. Or, more concretely: the Heideggerian philosopher speaks of the primordial dimension *only* as Being-as-*Ereignis* and interprets it as what sends . . . , as shown in detail above. Theology, on the other hand, articulates the primordial dimension at the outset as *God,* and indeed as the God that has revealed and communicated himself, who has initiated a history of self-communication and of salvation. The difference between philosophy (in this possibly Heideggerian sense) and (Christian) theology would then be the difference between the primordial dimension as only generally, abstractly, and largely emptily explained and that dimension as fully explained, fully determined, fully disclosed. That Heidegger never considers such a path of thinking, even experimentally, poses an enigma. More is to be said about this after the introduction of passages (under [ii], below) that seem to suggest an openness on Heidegger's part to such a position.

Third: the fact that Heidegger speaks of two different modes of existence of Dasein and thereby considers philosophy and theology from an *existentiell* perspective motivates the question whether he does full justice to the specifically *theoretical* (or, as he said at the time, *scientific*) status of philosophy and theology. The answer is that he does not. Not only Heidegger, but many philosophers and the vast majority of theologians have viewed both philosophical and theological activity as resulting from foundational decisions understood as factors that determine the entire courses of the lives of those who make them. Heidegger characterizes the "thinkerish" (he scarcely uses the term "theoretical") activity of the philosopher with designations indicating an attitude that is practical in the sense of being based on a decision. Evidence that he does so includes

his countlessly repeated references to the necessity of "listening or heark-
ening (to Being)," to the "appeal (of Being)," to Being's "call," etc. The
following is typical: "Thinking, obedient to the voice of Being, seeks from
Being the word through which the truth of Being comes to language."[40]
The terms that Heidegger uses here are *directly reminiscent* of central biblical formulations. "Thinking," both for and according to Heidegger, is
not theoretical in the sense of "theoretical" articulated below in chapter 3. No more so is the activity of the theologian: the theologian is the
"thinker" who must respond to the call of what is believed. According to
Heidegger, the theologian is above all one who has faith.

The Heideggerian view presented in the preceding paragraph ignores what is specific to the activity that is the genuine activity of *thinking:*
theoretical activity. This activity is as independent as possible from specific
existentiell attitudes and modes of behavior. The only decision on which
thinking as *theoretical* activity is based is the decision *to be theoretically active.*
And this means: to behave in such a way that the activity produces theoretical sentences, thus sentences governable by the operator "It is the
case that." This is thoroughly considered in chapter 3.

Theoretical activity is the human capability that is furthest removed
from and furthest above the other factors that determine human lives.
The "faithfulness" that Heidegger speaks of in the case of theology involves much more than a theoretical attitude; it is an *affirmation,* an *acceptance* of what the theologian articulates theoretically. Heidegger ascribes
something analogous to the philosopher: the Heideggerian philosopher
listens to the call of Being, is obedient to the voice of Being, etc. In the
first place, however, and in every case the philosopher (and indeed the
theologian as well, with the addition of details not considered here) is
a theoretician. His theoretical activity is of course based on his free decision to engage in theoretical activity, but once this decision is made,
his theoretical activity develops exclusively in accordance with the criteria of theoretical discourse and not, in any way whatsoever, under the
determination of "existentiell" factors of any sort. Heidegger's mistake
here—and one that is made by many who call themselves philosophers
or theologians—is that of not attending strictly and consequently to *what
is specific to theoretical activity.*

[ii] According to Heidegger, as noted above, there is (or can be)
a total opposition—indeed, a mortal enmity—between philosophy and
theology, but there is also "a *possible commonality* of theology and philosophy *as sciences*" (*PM* 53). One way to reconcile these two would be to

---

[40] *PM* 237.

say that there is an *existentiell* opposition and indeed enmity, one concerning the *modes of existence* of Dasein, and one that includes a wholly free self-positioning on the part of Dasein, but also a commonality (of a specific sort) on the scientific—thus, the theoretical—level. That Heidegger does not articulate a reconciliation of this sort shows that he has not adequately thought through the relevant factors and their implications.

The commonality of theology and philosophy posited by Heidegger is, as noted above, of a peculiar sort. Heidegger starts from the assumption that theology is concerned with a specific being, i.e., God. He then says the following:

> But every being discloses itself only on the ground of a preceding, although not known, preconceptual understanding of what the being in question is. All ontic interpretation moves on the ground, at first and for the most part concealed, of an ontology. (*PM* 50; t.a.)

The explication of fundamental concepts—and thus also of concepts fundamental to theology—can occur only if one "brings into view and maintains constantly in view, in its primordial wholeness, the primarily disclosed configuration of Being [*Seinszusammenhang*] toward which all fundamental concepts point back" (51; t.a.). Heidegger's comments on this read *at first* almost like explanations of one of the most fundamental axioms from the tradition of Christian theology, i.e., the axiom expressed by Aquinas as "*Gratia no tollit naturam, sed perficit*—Grace does not replace nature, but completes it."[41] And indeed, Heidegger clarifies his thesis as follows:

> The Christian occurrence as rebirth is that Dasein's prefaithful, i.e., unbelieving existence is suspended [*aufgehoben*] therein. To be suspended is not to be set aside or replaced, but to be taken up into the new creation, retained and preserved in it. In faith, pre-Christian existence is existentielly-ontically overcome. But this existentiell overcoming of pre-Christian existence, which belongs to faith as rebirth, means precisely that pre-Christian existence is existentially-ontologically included within faithful existence. To overcome is not to shove aside, but to take into a new configuration. It hence results: all fundamental theological concepts always have . . . within them some pre-Christian and therefore fully rationally graspable content that is existentielly impotent, i.e., *ontically* suspended, but that is for just that reason *ontologically* deter-

---

[41] *STh.* I q. 1 a. 8 ad 2.

mining. All theological concepts necessarily harbor within themselves *the* understanding of Being that human Dasein always has from itself, insofar as it exists at all. (*PM* 51; t.a.)

Remarkable though these assertions are, it is important to note that they were written in 1927. They contain an explosive force in that they present theology as an *ontic* theoretical affair that, according to Heidegger's understanding at that time of the fundamental difference between the ontic and the ontological, stands under what may be termed an ontological restriction. What happens with theology when the understanding of Being presupposed by it is explained in such a way as to place theological sentences radically into question? Is that not precisely what happens as Heidegger's thought develops?

This development is visible already in the 1927 lecture. In formulating the lecture's central thesis, Heidegger uses the phrase "(philosophy as ontological) *corrective* [of theology]":

> *Philosophy is the possible, formally indicative ontological corrective to the ontic and indeed pre-Christian content of the fundamental theological concepts. Philosophy can, however, be what it is without actually functioning as this corrective.* (*PM* 53; t.a.)

Shown below is how this thought of the "corrective" fares in the course of Heidegger's development, particularly in its final phase. At this point, comment need be made only on the second sentence in the passage. That philosophy can be what it is without functioning as a corrective to theology is only at first glance obvious and illuminating; only at first glance because a number of problems emerge from it. First: it assumes that what philosophy is, and what it can achieve, is clear in every respect. Particularly important is the question of its scope: does philosophy encompass what theology, according to Heidegger's characterization of it, examines as its proper subject matter? In certain respects, both philosophy and theology raise claims to universality. But how can that be? Chapter 3 shows that philosophy, understood as absolutely universal science, must also encompass the domain that theology investigates, although not in the same manner. What follows shows that Heidegger vacillates between understanding philosophy as the absolutely universal and radical science that would also have the last word to say about the theological dimension, and as restricted such that it would exist alongside theology, but would not extend into theology's domain.

[2] The just-introduced position, according to which philosophy is the "*possible, formally indicative ontological corrective to the ontic and indeed pre-Christian content of the fundamental theological concepts,*" is one that Hei-

degger appears not to have held for very long. Already two years after the composition of the lecture in which that position is presented, he writes the following in a letter of April 9, 1929, to Rudolf Bultmann:

> The more often I consider things—and that is not rarely—the more it appears to me as though all philosophical discussion must disappear from theology, and as though all the force of thinking must be transferred to historical confrontation with the [New Testament]— "historical" taken in an essential sense.[42]

The many things Heidegger has to say on this topic over the years cannot be considered here. The only text that need be added for present purposes is a letter from March 11, 1964, that is printed in the *Gesamtausgabe* as an appendix to the text of a lecture Heidegger wrote for a theological discussion at Drew University in Madison, Wisconsin. The title of the letter is "The Theological Discussion of 'The Problem of a Nonobjectifying Thinking and Speaking in Today's Theology'—Some Pointers to Its Major Aspects" (*PM* 54–62). The issue central to this text is the question of what "objectifying thinking" is. In response to this question, Heidegger says little that is informative. He repeats his prepackaged critique of metaphysics and introduces as an example of objectifying thinking "thinking and speaking . . . in the field of natural-scientific and technical representation" (60). He thereby overlooks the fundamental fact that scientific theories, *as* scientific, have *no relation* to anything like thinkers, speakers, subjects, etc. Scientific theories consist of sentences governable by the operator "It is the case that"; for the "representation," presumably someone's representation, there is no place. For this reason among others, Heidegger's remarks on "objectification" are utterly empty. Among his positive theses is the following: "There is . . . a thinking and saying that in no way objectifies" (58). He bases this thesis on a conception of language according to which (57) "language speaks [*Sprache spricht*]. The human being speaks only in that he agrees with [*entspricht*] language." Heidegger then explains these unusual formulations in an extremely interesting manner (60): "Language's saying is not necessarily an uttering of sentences *about* objects. In what is its ownmost, it is a saying *of* that which manifests itself to and addresses human beings in manifold ways." Heidegger does not understand this explanation in the sense articulated in chapter 3 of this book, according to which theoretical sentences, as governable by the operator "It is the case that," do not relate to subjects or to representations (or ideas, etc.) or objectifications or the

---

[42] Rudolf Bultmann and Martin Heidegger, *Briefwechsel 1925–1975* (2009), 108.

like, and are not sentences about objects. "Objectification" and the like are operations that are performed by subjects: "uttering sentences *about* objects" presupposes a language consisting of sentences of the subject-predicate form, and having a semantics that leads directly to an ontology of objects (and thus substances).

For present purposes, only the following point is important: Heidegger ultimately characterizes "the positive task of theology" as follows (61; t.a.):

> within its own domain of the Christian faith and out of that faith's own essence, to explain what it must think and what it must say. This task also includes the question whether theology can still be a science, because it presumably ought not to be a science at all.

Does Heidegger hereby mean to accord to Christian faith a complete self-sufficiency in the sense that its "own essence" is articulable only through its own thinking and saying? Does this mean that philosophy no longer can or must function as "the possible, formally indicative ontological corrective of the ontic and, in particular, pre-Christian content of the fundamental concepts of theology"? If so, what precisely would this total self-sufficiency and total isolation mean? Would "(the Christian) God" be a subject matter off-limits to philosophy? What follows may provide an answer to this question.

2.8.2 The Relation Between Being/*Ereignis* and "God"

The third form in which Heidegger thematizes the relation or non-relation between Being/*Ereignis* and God is the most important because it directly treats this question *as such*. In a fully non-Heideggerian terminology, he could be said to address the question *systematically*. Historically and concretely, this third form is found in Heidegger's thinking *following* his famous *Kehre*. In that phase of his thinking, Heidegger addresses this question again and again, and indeed to such an extent that it is the central focus of his post-*Kehre* thinking. As in so many cases, this book cannot consider this issue in detail; indeed, not even all of Heidegger's most important comments on this topic can be treated here. For one thing, an exhaustive treatment of the topic presumably must await the publication of all of Heidegger's works. It suffices in what follows briefly to present the basic direction of his thinking on this topic, and with it the problematic it brings into view.

The great majority of Heidegger's comments on the topic in question share no common denominator. The comments are, as is typical for him and as he himself says, those of a thinker who is under way. The following account introduces examples of such comments and critically illuminates them, aiming to attain an interpretation and a general evaluation.

[1] A passage in the "Letter on Humanism" appears, at first glance, to articulate a maximally tight relation between Being and God, explaining the conjunction "Being *and* God" as indicating the *way from Being to God:*

> The thinking that thinks out of the truth of Being questions more primordially than metaphysics can. Only out of the truth of Being can the essence of the holy be thought. Only out of the essence of the holy can the essence of the divine be thought. Only in light of the essence of divinity can it be thought and said what the word "God" ought to name. (*PM* 267; t.a.)

Being—the holy—divinity—God: that the way to God leads through the holy and divinity is to some degree familiar from the history of religions, but philosophically, it is far from obvious. Clearly, Heidegger is willing to pay any price to avoid any direct connection between metaphysics and God (i.e., to his caricature of metaphysics); this is presumably why "the holy" is included as an intermediate stage. The philosopher, however, may and perhaps must reasonably wonder whether other concepts are not available as stages, above all the modals *necessity–possibility–contingency.* Heidegger, however, rejects such concepts as metaphysical, as shown in two passages to be considered here.

Many interpreters have relied on the just-quoted passage as evidence that there is in Heidegger's thinking if not an explicit or at least an implicit theological element, nevertheless a thinking that understands itself as being "on the way from Being to God." The following account shows, however, that Heidegger's position is far more complicated and ambiguous than it might appear at first glance, and that ultimately, his answer to the question under consideration appears to be quite different from the one apparently articulated in the passage from the "Letter on Humanism."

[2] In the *Contributions,* identified above as the most obscure and arbitrary of Heidegger's works, there are formulations that express—in some respects, if not in every respect—the opposite to what appears to be expressed in the text quoted just above. In the final part (which has the title "VIII. Beyng"), there are some typical comments about "Gods" and "God." Heidegger explains "Gods"—extremely arbitrarily and misleadingly—as follows (308): "The undecidedness concerning which God

and whether a God can, in utmost distress, once again arise, from which essence of the human and in what way—this is what is named with the name 'the Gods.'" And then, the following :

> Insofar as in such fore-thinking Beyng is de-nied [*ab-gesagt*] to "Gods," it is said that all assertions about "Being" and "essence" of the Gods not only does not say anything about them—and that means about that which is to be decided—but also simulates something objective, against which all thinking comes to nought because it is immediately forced to go astray.

Heidegger does not raise the questions of how he himself can speak of the Gods, what he can say of them, of how he relates to them linguistically, or of how his thinking avoids going astray when "all thinking . . . is immediately forced to go astray." Instead, he proceeds with supreme self-confidence (308–9; t.a., emphasis added):

> Denying Being to "the Gods" initially means only that Being does not stand "over" the Gods; but the Gods also do not stand "over" Being. But the Gods *do need* Beyng; and with this motto is thought the essencing "of" Beyng. "The Gods" do not *need* Beyng as their *ownhood* [*Eigentum;* property], wherein they themselves take a stand. "The Gods" *need* Beyng in order through Beyng—which does not belong to them—nevertheless to belong to themselves. Beyng is *what is used* by the Gods: it is what is *needed by* them. And their needfulness of Beyng names its essencing— what is needed by "the Gods" but is never causable and conditionable. That "the Gods" need Beyng moves them into the abyss (into freedom) and expresses the refusal of any grounding and proving of any and every sort.

It is scarcely possible to understand such formulations other than as quasi-mythological linguistic fantasies. Heidegger fails even to note the striking incoherence of what he says. According to the passage quoted just earlier, the ascription of Being to the Gods "simulates something objective, against which all thinking comes to nought because it is immediately forced to go astray." What is then to be said about the ascriptions of categories such as "need," "ownhood," etc.? With their use, the dimension that Heidegger calls "the Gods" is demoted to a level on which they are a paradigmatic example of "the objective." In Heidegger's terms, has not "thinking come to nought" not because it has been "forced to go astray," but because it was astray from the very beginning? Heidegger no doubt would claim that he thereby thinks more "originarily," but what the passages reveal is that he speaks a naive and primitive language that under no circumstances can qualify as an articulation of thinking. If there is a place in literature for it, it is in poetic-mythological literature.

In any case, it becomes clear here that Heidegger *denies* Being to the dimension of the Gods and of God. If one avoids poetic and mythological language and instead speaks philosophically, the question arises concerning what status Being ultimately has, in Heidegger's thinking, with respect to the dimension of Gods/God, after it has been denied to Gods/God.

[3] In 1951 Heidegger held a seminar in Zürich. Its protocol contains some of his most radical formulations, ones that speak of a total dissociation between Being and God—but simultaneously offer some sort of corrective to such formulations:

> God and Being are not identical, and I would never attempt to think the essence of God by means of Being. Some perhaps know that I come [to philosophy] from theology, that I retain my old love of it and understand something about it. If I were to write a theology, as I am often tempted to do, the word "Being" would not be included in it.—Faith does not need the thinking of Being. If it needs that, it is no longer faith. Luther understood this. That seems to have been forgotten even in his own church. I think of Being, with respect to its suitability [*Eignung*] to think the essence of God theologically, quite modestly. Being has nothing to say here.[43]

A more radical dissociation between Being and God could scarcely be articulated. That philosophy could be a corrective to theology, as Heidegger took it to be in 1927, is something he appears to deem an impossibility here. Yet the passage just quoted is not the protocol's final word on this matter. To the contrary, the text continues by presenting what appear to be clear and direct corrections of what it says earlier. The correction is suggested most clearly by the word "nevertheless" in the following:

> I believe that Being can never be thought as the ground and essence of God, but that *nevertheless* the experience of God and of his revelation (to the degree that humans encounter it) *ereignet itself in the dimension of Being,* which never means that Being could serve as a possible predicate for God. Here, wholly new distinctions and delimitations are needed.[44]

---

[43] *GA* 15:436–37.
[44] Ibid., 437; emphasis added.

In this important passage, two points are remarkable. First, Heidegger clearly indicates how he takes the "representational" or "metaphysical" thinking that he rejects to relate Being to God: that thinking, he indicates, presents Being (1) as predicable of God and/or (2) as "ground and essence" of God. Heidegger denies both that Being is predicable of God and that it is the ground and essence of God. The question is, how radical is Heidegger in these denials?

First, concerning (1): Aquinas, in presenting God as *ipsum esse* (*per se subsistens*) does not predicate *esse* of God. If he did, then in so doing he would presuppose God to be determined independently of *esse*, and then more fully determined when *esse* was predicated of him. Aquinas, however, presents God as the fully determined or fulfilled *ipsum esse* (*per se subsistens*). *Esse* is therefore in no way a predicate (or attribute) of God.

Concerning (2): the phrase "(Being thought) as ground and essence of God" is fully unclear: what, for example, does "ground" mean here? In Aquinas's metaphysics of Being, *esse* is not the "ground" of God in any way, shape, or form. And what about "the essence of God"? Heidegger usually understands "essence" verbally, but what could it mean to say that Being is the essencing of God? Neither Aquinas nor any other major metaphysician of Being has ever maintained anything of the sort. When Aquinas says that *esse* and *essentia* (essence, but *not* understood verbally) are the same in God, that does not mean that *esse* is God's essence.

When Heidegger maintains that he has great reservations about Being's "suitability to think the essence of God theologically," he speaks both unclearly and ambiguously. If Being/*esse* is interpreted as by Aquinas, then it cannot be said that it is anything like a means whose suitability or lack of suitability for thinking God's essence theologically could even be discussed; instead, Being/*esse* is the designation for the initially not (yet) more fully explained or determined primordial dimension that, when fully explicated or determined, is given the name "God." Here again, Heidegger's caricature of the "metaphysical God," which stems from insufficient awareness of the tradition, leads to serious distortions and misunderstandings, to targetless questions, and to the putative necessity for new paths of thinking.

Second, Heidegger explicitly acknowledges that to the dimension of Being is—despite the apodictically asserted total dissociation of Being and God—"*nevertheless*" to be ascribed a simply central role with respect to God: for the experience of God and his revelation to reach human beings, or for human beings to encounter them, the dimension of Being must be presupposed, because only within it do the experiences of God and of his revelation *ereignen* themselves. This is an important self-correction, but it is one that requires clarification.

[4] The passage from *Contributions* quoted above in [2] includes the following assertion: "the Gods do need Beyng; and with this motto is thought the essencing 'of' Beyng." This asserting appears to accord to Beyng a certain intermediate position between God (or Gods) and human beings. In order to clarify this state of affairs as comprehensively and accurately as possible, it is necessary to introduce another important passage from *Contributions*, one that characterizes Being as "between" God (or Gods) and human beings (26; t.a.):

> The awakening of this distress [i.e., forsakenness by Being, *Seinsverlassenheit*] is the first displacing [i.e., altering of standpoint] of man into that *between* where chaos threatens while at the same time the God remains in flight. This "between" is, however, not a "transcendence" in relation to man. Rather, it is the opposite: that open to which man belongs as the founder and preserver wherein as Da-sein he is *er-eignet* by Beyng itself—Beyng that essences as nothing other than as *Ereignis.*
>
> If thanks to this displacing man comes to stand in *Ereignis* and has his abode in the truth of Beyng, then he is primarily still only ready for the leap into the deciding experience whether, within *Ereignis*, it is the God's staying away or the God's onset that decides for or against God.
>
> Only when we estimate how singularly necessary Beyng is and how it nevertheless does not hold sway as God itself, only when we have tuned what is our ownmost to the abysses [*Abgründe*] between man and Beyng and Beyng and Gods—only then do "presuppositions" for a "history" again begin to be real. Thus only mindfulness of "*Ereignis*" is appropriate for thinking.
>
> Finally and above all "*Ereignis*" can only be en-thought [*er-dacht*] (forced in front of originary thinking) if Beyng itself is grasped as the "between" for the passing of the last God and for Da-sein.
>
> *Ereignis* owns the God over [*übereignet*] to man in that *Ereignis* owns man to [*zueignet*] the God. This owning-to [*Zueignung*] that owns-over [*übereignet*] is *Ereignis*, wherein the *truth* of Beyng as Da-sein is grounded (as transformed, man is shifted into the decision to be-there and to be-away [*Da-sein und Weg-sein*]) and wherein history takes its other beginning from Beyng. (19–20)

Here, Heidegger appears to articulate his understanding of Being/*Ereignis* and God more or less as clearly as the framework of the options to which he restricts himself allows. Being/*Ereignis* is the "between," the dimension that is between God and human beings (and thus presumably all being[s]). Among the many questions that press here, one is of particular importance: that of the coherence of the entire conception. On the one hand, Being is denied of the dimension of the divine (whatever that may be: God, divinity, the Gods. . .), so the two dimensions are absolutely separated or dissociated. On the other hand, the dimension of Being is said to be the "between" that the dimension of the divine requires in order to be able to reveal itself to human beings.

How can this be? On the one hand, there is the radical rejection of any and every relation between the dimension of Being and the dimension of the divine; on the other hand, there is what appear to be from both sides massive relations to Being. As the passage from the seminar in Zürich indicates, it appears that the relation emerges (so to speak) from the dimension of the divine, in that "the experience of God and his revelation (insofar as it is encountered by human beings) *sich ereignet* in the dimension of Being"; but on the other hand, it appears to be the dimension of Being/*Ereignis* that (so to speak) initiates the relation: "*Ereignis* [i.e., Being, now thought as *Ereignis*] owns god over to man in that enowning owns man to god. This 'owning-to' that 'owns-over' is *Ereignis*, wherein the *truth* of Beyng as Da-sein is grounded." Worth noting in passing is that Heidegger's characterization of what Being/*Ereignis* is said here to accomplish is unintelligible; beyond that, the talk of "owning," "owning-to," "and "owning-over," if it is anything more than empty wordplay, is nothing more than a description of a banal exchange between two human beings. Ironically, this makes clear that Heidegger's incessant critique of the putatively onto-theo-logical character of metaphysics—thus, according to Heidegger, its being a mode of thinking that articulates only relations between *beings*—in fact finds a proper target in his own talk about Being/*Ereignis* as the event of owning, owning-over, owning-to, etc.

How can there be both a radical separation between God and Being and a relation between the two that is essential to God's revelation (such that, apparently, God *could not* reveal himself *without relying on—and thus relating to*—Being)? There appears simply to be no way for Heidegger to avoid the following dilemma:

Either one holds firm (as Heidegger does in the letter from 1964 cited above) to the thesis that (Christian) theology is a *positive task* that is understood as that of "explaining Christian faith in its own domain out of its own essence—how it is to be thought and articulated" (*GA* 9:77), which presupposes a total dissociation, in every respect, between God and Being, such that "thinking Beyng-as-historical stands *outside of every theology* and also knows no atheism, in the sense of a worldview or a doctrine structured in some other way" (*Cont* 309; t.a., emphasis added). It would correspondingly hold that theology would stand *outside* any and every thinking of Beyng-as-historical.

Or one holds firmly to the thesis that the dimension (of) *God* (or of divinity, Gods, etc.) "needs Beyng," such that Beyng is what is needed by or necessary to this divine dimension, with the following consequence: "if Beyng is what is needed by God, if Beyng itself finds its truth only in an en-thinking [*Er-denken*], and if this thinking is philosophy (in the other beginning), then 'Gods' need the thinking of Beyng-as-historical" (309). In this case, the thinking of Beyng-as-historical does *not* stand *outside of every theology*, and theological thinking does *not* stand outside of the thinking of Beyng-as-historical.

In the majority of the relevant passages, Heidegger appears at least at first glance to accept the latter horn of the dilemma. Nevertheless—or indeed for just that reason—the question must be raised whether Heidegger would acknowledge that there is a dilemma here at all. Only if there is not can there be a coherent interpretation of what Heidegger says on this matter. And there does appear to be a way to deny that there is a dilemma, but it comes with a high cost, namely, that of acknowledging that there must be a *more fundamental* (or *more primordial*) *level* of thinking on which the apparent dilemma would be shown to be merely apparent. This option is considered in the following subsection.

[5] Heidegger's final words on the problems bound up with the relation (or non-relation) between Being and God are presumably those found in some peculiar formulations—some of which are cited above—from *Contributions* and *Mindfulness*. Thus, from the *Contributions* (309; t.a.):

> That "Gods" need Beyng moves them into the abyss [*Ab-grund*] (into freedom) and expresses the breakdown of any proving and demonstrating of every sort. And as impenetrable as the needfulness of Beyng must remain for thinking, it still offers a fresh hold for thinking "Gods" as those who need Beyng.

Further along in the same paragraph one reads:

> "Gods" need philosophy, not as if *they themselves* must philosophize for the sake of their godding, but rather philosophy must be if "Gods" are again to come into decision and if history is to obtain its ownmost ground. From the perspective of the Gods, thinking-Beyng-as-historical is determined as that thinking of Beyng that understands as primary the abyss [*Abgrund*] of needfulness of and by Beyng and never seeks the essencing of Beyng in the divine itself as what is supposedly the beingest [*Seiendsten*]. Thinking Beyng-as-historical is outside any theology.

How is this to be understood? For the following interpretation and reflections concerning it, it is important to take note of a central assertion that Heidegger often makes to "explain" how he proceeds with respect to metaphysics: he says that he poses no *metaphysical* questions, and that the question that he does pose is "a question wholly different from the *metaphysical* question. That is: I ask, 'What *is* metaphysics?' I do not ask a *metaphysical* question, but ask about the *essence* of metaphysics."[45]

One could use an analogous formulation in interpreting the just-quoted passage from *Contributions:* in that passage, Heidegger presents no theses *within the framework of the thinking of Being*, none that are of "Beyng-as-historical"; instead, he proceeds—his thinking proceeds—on a higher level, on the level of a thinking-of-the-thinking-of-Being, in order (to adapt his other term) to present meta-theses about the thinking of Beyng-as-historical. This would be the level or dimension that would encompass both the dimension of Being and the dimension of God/Gods. Here Heidegger does nothing more and nothing less than, as he himself says, "think 'the Gods' as Those who need Beyng." The "meta-thinking-of-Being" that he engages in is precisely the thinking articulated in passages including the following one (already cited above), which is a statement that is not on the level of thinking-Beyng-as-historical, but instead is on the level of meta-thinking-Beyng-as-historical: "From the perspective of the Gods, thinking Beyng-as-historical is determined as that thinking of Beyng that understands the abyss of needfulness of and by Beyng as primary and never seeks the essencing of Beyng in the divine itself as what is supposedly the most-being. Thinking Beyng-as-historical is outside any theology." On the meta-level where this sentence is situated, it is true: "thinking Beyng-as-historical is outside any theology." But is *meta*-thinking-Beyng-as-historical also outside any theology? It is not, in that meta-thinking-of-Being is also meta-theological thinking: it *encompasses* both dimensions, both thinking of Being and theology, and hence both Being and God. Heidegger seems to be unaware of what is happening here, i.e., unaware both of *what* he is thinking and especially of *how* he is thinking.

How is this encompassing to be understood? It cannot be understood as anything like the "encompassing" of a universal concept that has multiple instantiations that it somehow encompasses or contains. But what is Heidegger's alternative? Of course, he does not use the word "encompass," and nothing depends on that word specifically. What is important is that Heidegger speaks both of Being and of God/Gods, and that he writes that Beyng's needfulness offers the first clue

---

[45] R. Wisser, ed., *Martin Heidegger im Gespräch* (1970), 75–76.

about "thinking 'the Gods' as Those who need Beyng." Here, Gods and Beyng are both thought and linguistically articulated together, hence somehow encompassed within that thinking and articulation, although what this encompassing is remains unclear. That is precisely the problem.

In any case Being and God are *distinct* or, in Heidegger's language, *different*. Worth recalling here is Heidegger's critique of metaphysics, which is decisively based on the concept of difference (as applied in the case of Being and beings) in that Heidegger objects that metaphysics thinks within the framework or domain of this difference, but does not think the difference itself. Ultimately, this dimension proves to be, for Heidegger, the primordial dimension that (in some sense) delivers both (metaphysical) Being and beings: this "difference" is itself "the resolution [*der Austrag*]" ("OTLCM" 68; t.a.). So: if Heidegger then distinguishes— as he does—between Being and God/Gods, this introduces a difference. Does he meet the demand that he faults metaphysics for failing to meet— that is, the demand that every difference that is *posited* be a difference that is also *thought* (or thematized)? He does not, and that he does not is yet another instance of the central aporia that characterizes all of his attempts to think, versions of which are revealed at various junctures throughout this chapter.

[6] How is this meta-dimension-of-the-thinking-of-Beyng-as-historical or this meta-thinking-of-thinking-Beyng-as-historical more precisely to be understood? Does Heidegger think this dimension, or does it remain unthought by him? It appears that one can find in Heidegger *two fully different alternative interpretations* of this level or dimension of thinking, neither of which is better supported by the relevant texts. The reason for the unclarity may well be that Heidegger was simply unaware of this problem of levels. Sections [i] and [ii] present, respectively, the two options; then, [iii] presents a significant point common to the two.

[i] The first available interpretation is suggested by the following passage (already introduced above):

> From the perspective of the Gods, thinking-Beyng-as-historical is deter-
> mined as that thinking of Beyng that understands [*begreift*] as primary
> the abyss of needfulness of and by Beyng and never seeks the essencing
> of Beyng in the divine itself as what is supposedly the beingest. Think-
> ing Beyng-as-historical is outside any theology.[46]

---

[46] It is curious that Heidegger here uses the word "*begreift*," which he usually carefully avoids. This supports what is said above in note 26: in philosophy, use of this term and its conjugates—especially *Begriff,* "concept"—is practically unavoidable.

Confronted with the difference he himself articulates between God/ Gods and Being, Heidegger here takes a remarkable turn: he places himself in effect at the standpoint of God/Gods and thinks, as it were, in the name of God/Gods in that he indicates how meta-thinking-Beyng-as-historical (and thus *his own philosophical thinking*) appears from that standpoint. From the perspective of God/Gods—which is the perspective taken here by Heidegger's own thinking—two statements are articulated. First: "thinking-Beyng-as-historical is determined as that thinking of Beyng that understands as primary the abyss of needfulness of and by Beyng," and second, that thinking "never seeks the essencing of Beyng in the divine itself as what is supposedly the beingest." The second statement, the one directed against metaphysics, is purely negative and in addition wholly unsupported and empty. The first statement, however, is significant. If thinking-Beyng-as-historical understands not only Beyng, but also the needfulness of Beyng (i.e., the fact that Beyng is what the Gods need), then this thinking *encompasses* God/Gods.

The thinking presumed (by Heidegger) to be ongoing here is no longer simple thinking-Beyng-as-historical; it is instead, as indicated above, thinking on a higher level, a meta-level. But this level is not situated *over* both Being and God; instead, this thinking is said to understand both Being and God, the two differentia, and their difference, from the perspective of one of them, i.e., that of God/Gods. Although it could be misleading to say so, the standpoint could be termed a theo-logical one; the term would mislead if it were taken to be a counterpart to the onto-logical standpoint, but somehow on the same level (such that each would be inaccessible to the other, as per Heidegger's dissociation thesis). It is instead the most comprehensive (and hence, in Heideggerian terms, the most primordial).

From *this* standpoint Heidegger addresses the meta-dimension that is *more primordial* than is the dimension of Beyng, *in his sense.* If this meta-dimension is termed *the most primordial dimension,* then Heidegger thinks this higher dimension in part in asserting, "Within the perspective of gods, thinking-Beyng-as-historical is determined as that thinking of Beyng that understands [*begreift*] as primary the abyss of needfulness of and by Beyng." This is, as emphasized above, a meta-statement about thinking-Beyng-as-historical (hence, according to the interpretation introduced above, a *theo*-logical statement)—a self-articulation of the most primordial dimension, but from the *theo-logical standpoint.*

Precise analysis of Heidegger's formulations shows that they are insufficiently clear. He would need to say: "From the perspective of gods, *meta*-thinking-Beyng-as-historical . . . etc." It is *not* (so to speak) *simple* thinking of Beyng that *understands* "the abyss of the needfulness of

Beyng," because simple thinking of Beyng is *not* thinking "from the per-spective of the Gods." Simple thinking of Beyng, in Heidegger's sense, is from the perspective of Beyng—and nothing more. For that reason, it cannot *on its own* attain to the dimension that is the dimension of God/Gods. Simple thinking of Being is precisely this: thinking-of-Being; nothing more and nothing less. But how then can one gain access to something (let us say: to a "dimension") of which Being is absolutely *denied*—as Heidegger explicitly maintains?

Heidegger famously posed the question, "How does God come into philosophy?" (*ID* 55), but he did not pose the question, "How does God come into my thinking of Being?" With respect to the issues under con-sideration here, that would have been the most important question for him to raise. His only answer would be: by means of a *leap*. The philoso-pher Heidegger happens to encounter the phenomenon of the dimen-sion of the divine—and begins to be concerned with it. In doing so, he leaps to a higher or more primordial dimension or level or stand-point. From this higher level or standpoint, he can say, "Thinking-Beyng-as-historical stands outside any theology." But *this* more primordial di-mension itself, and the meta-thinking-Beyng-as-historical that occurs on it, itself no longer stands "outside any theology," but instead *encompasses* the theological dimension.

This makes clear the more precise sense of the relevant encom-passing. In that the most primordial dimension is itself *thought* from the perspective of one of its own differentia, i.e., God/Gods/the divine, the encompassing must be a meta-thinking-Beyng-as-historical one *as* a meta-theological thinking. "Meta-theological" here means that the two differentia or conjuncta, Being and God, are conceived of and explained *from the perspective of God*. As shown, Heidegger thinks this dimension *from the perspective of God* in that he uses such formulations as, "God (or the Gods) need/require Beyng. . . ."

The only really important question here is the following: how does Heidegger think this dimension from the perspective of God or Gods? On this, one finds pompous rhetoric that is, however, either more or less banal or empty or has a prophetic-eschatological character. Of this more is said below.

[ii] The second available interpretation of the most primor-dial dimension is presented by means of sentences that do not accord God/Gods absolute priority with respect to the thinking of that dimen-sion, ones that therefore are not articulated from the perspective of God/Gods, but instead accord the dimension of God/Gods/the divine a purely *derivative* status. This interpretation is found chiefly in passages from "The Onto-theo-logical Constitution of Metaphysics," as shown in

detail above particularly in subsections 2.2[1] and 2.4. The following is a characteristic passage from the voluminous *Mindfulness* that makes somewhat clearer what Heidegger's alternative interpretation is (208–9; t.a.):

> Neither is it the case that the Gods create human beings nor that human beings invent the Gods. *The truth of Beyng decides "over" both,* not by ruling over them but in that, *between them,* it *ereignet* itself and therewith them too to a confrontation [*zwischen ihnen sich und damit erst sie selbst zur Ent-gegnung ereignet*]. . . . The God is never a being of which human beings can know now this and now that, one that human beings can approach to varying degrees; instead, *the Gods and their divinity arise from the truth of Beyng;* i.e., the representation of the God as a thing, and explanatory calculation about him, e.g., as creator, has its ground in the interpretation of beingness [*Seiendheit*] as produced and producible presence.

According to this text, the most primordial dimension is the truth of Being, and this is what "decides over" both differentia, i.e., Gods and human beings (and other beings); the Gods, as "emerging from the truth of Beyng," are derivative. These are meta-thinking-Beyng-historical statements, thus ones that cannot emerge within the framework of the most primordial dimension, but that articulate this most primordial dimension itself. This is the standpoint from which the most primordial dimension articulates itself—the dimension not of God/Gods, but of Being itself in its truth. It can be said, although only with extreme caution, that *this* interpretation more closely fits the trajectory of Heidegger's thinking as a whole.

[iii] Concerning this ultimately decisive problem of interpretation, there are again unexpected factors to be dealt with. One is a point that appears to be common to the two possible interpretations introduced in the preceding subsections. Whether this commonality is such that they cease to be alternatives is difficult to determine. From both perspectives previously identified, i.e., that of God/Gods and that of the truth of Being, Heidegger attains access to a point for which he uses the nearly magical designation "abyss [*Ab-grund*]." Two passages—both cited in part above—aid in clarifying this state of affairs.

The abyss, from the perspective of the Gods, is attained or explained as follows:

> That "Gods" need Beyng moves them *into the abyss (into freedom)* and expresses the breakdown of any proving and demonstrating of every sort. . . . From the perspective of the Gods, thinking-Beyng-as-historical

is determined as that thinking of Beyng that understands as primary the *abyss* of needfulness of and by Beyng and never seeks the essencing of Beyng in the divine itself as what is supposedly the beingest. . . .

To conceive of the abyss of needfulness for Beyng means being transferred into the necessity of grounding the truth for Beyng and not resisting the essential consequences of this necessity but rather thinking unto them and thus knowing that, without succumbing to the claim of "absoluteness," all thinking of Beyng is by that necessity withdrawn from any merely human contrivance. (*Cont* 309; emphases added)

From the perspective of the truth of Beyng, the abyss [*Ab-grund*] is articulated as follows:

> How . . . Beyng always *ereignet* for itself its truth or however it holds itself to it . . . , the human being can neither guide/steer nor force, because he himself, in accordance with the belongingness to Beyng essential to him, is attuned to the determinacy of his essence by Beyng, within gauging or having an inkling of this history.—It does, however, lie within *the freedom of the human being* how and to what extent he trans-forms and grounds that attunement that strikes him out of Beyng, thus stamping his own essencing into a particular form. *Indeed, freedom is nothing other than this abyss* [*Ab-grund*] *that accosts Beyng,* [the abyss] that determines itself to the grounding of the truth of Beyng in the sense of preserving [*Verwahrung*] it within being(s). (236; t.a., emphases added)

From both perspectives, Heidegger attains the abyss or *Ab-grund* and interprets it as freedom. Just what his obscure pronouncements might mean, the texts do not make clear. If one nevertheless attempts to make the most of them, the following interpretation emerges at least as a possi-bility: concerning the two relevant perspectives or standpoints—that of Beyng or of the truth of Beyng and that of God/Gods/the divine—the passages just introduced add nothing new. There is talk only of a level to which each of the two perspectives or standpoints appeals in its own way, i.e., the level of the freedom of human beings. The passages introduced above are among the extraordinarily rare ones in which Heidegger says anything even apparently contentual or concrete about so familiar a phe-nomenon as human freedom. "It [lies] within *the freedom of the human being* how and to what he extent he transforms and grounds that attune-ment that strikes him out of Beyng, thus stamping his own essencing into a particular form." Beyng does not determine human beings. On the other hand, however, Heidegger emphasizes what can be termed the self-sufficiency of the essencing of Beyng: "How . . . Beyng always *ereignet*

for itself its truth or however holds itself to it . . . , the human being can
neither guide/steer nor force." But Heidegger then uses formulations
that, philosophically considered, must be assessed as empty, as meaningless, or at best as poetic. Thus, he says that the human being is "*attuned*
to the determinacy of his essencing" by Beyng. That opens for him the
entire domain of "attunements" or moods. The only philosophical content one can take from what Heidegger says about this is the thesis that
being-attuned by Beyng is not a being-determined by Beyng. In relevant passages, Heidegger again and again uses the phrase "groundless-
ness [*Grundlosigkeit*] of the truth of Beyng." The term "abyss [*Ab-grund*],"
which he uses here to characterize freedom, appears to designate the
level on which the human being finds himself "in accordance with the
belongingness to Beyng essential to him," and indeed in the situation
wherein he must decide whether to "transform that attunement that
strikes him from Beyng into his determination."

If one can understand to some degree what Heidegger envisages
when he speaks of the abyss from the perspective of the truth of Beyng, the same cannot be said of what he says about the perspective of
God/Gods. What could a sentence such as the following possibly mean:
"That 'gods' need Beyng moves them into the abyss (into freedom) . . ."?
Or "Philosophy must be *if* 'the Gods' are again to come into decision
and if history is to obtain its essential ground"? If abyss and decision do
not relate somehow to human freedom, then there is not the slightest
indication of what they could mean or involve. To say that "the Gods'"
"need[ing] Beyng or hav[ing] need of Beyng" jolts [*rückt*] them into the
sphere of human freedom is to speak quasi-mythologically, at best.

In any case, the common point, the talk of the abyss, is not a factor
that illuminates the relationship between the two standpoints or perspectives in any manner worth mentioning. The attempt to take Heidegger's endless ruminations on Beyng, the truth of Beyng, "the Gods," "the
God," etc., as serious engagements in philosophical thinking can lead
only to confusion.

A final comment: in many passages Heidegger speaks of the "final
God" and the like.[47] His presumably most famous statement appears as
the title of an interview that he gave for the newsmagazine *Der Spiegel*
on September 23, 1966, but that was not published until May 31, 1976,
following his death. That statement is, "Only a God can save us now."
Such statements are not considered here. The reason is their prophetic-

---

[47] See *Contributions*, 285–93.

eschatological character. Once again, it must be emphasized that they are not subject to serious philosophical consideration or critique.

2.9 Heidegger's "Thinking": A Fundamentally Deficient and Confused Form of Thinking

This subsection makes no attempt at anything even vaguely approaching a comprehensive summary of what this chapter says about Heidegger's thinking. Instead, it treats only one aspect—albeit an absolutely central one—and that only briefly and summarily; this aspect is the *status* of Heideggerian thinking.

Among Heidegger's favorite and most-used terms is the word "thinking." In the course of his development, Heidegger speaks ever more rarely of philosophy and ever more frequently—indeed, toward the end of his life, exclusively—of thinking. One of his last essays (1964) has the revealing title, "The End of Philosophy and the Task of Thinking."[48] This subsection analyzes the three aspects of what Heidegger calls his thinking: first, Heidegger's thinking, in the sense of what Heidegger thought or, in non-Heideggerian terms, his position or conception; second, how Heidegger thinks, in the sense of what he does when he thinks; and third, thinking *according to* Heidegger, in the sense of how Heidegger conceives of thinking. The three aspects are treated together, and only briefly.

Heidegger's thinking, in all three aspects, is a fundamentally deficient and confused form of thinking.

[1] What makes Heidegger's form of thinking fundamentally deficient is that it does not rely either on all or even on all of the most important *capabilities* of thinking. Here, this is supported and illustrated only with respect to the one point that is absolutely central for the subject matter central to this book.

The peculiarity of Heideggerian thinking in all its aspects comes most clearly and most characteristically into view in his interpretation and critique of Western metaphysics. This interpretation and critique are based decisively on the thesis that metaphysics thematizes only being(s)

---

[48] First published in a French translation in 1966. The German original first appeared in *Zur Sache des Denkens* (1969). An English translation is contained in *TB* (55–73) and reprinted in *Basic Writings* (428–49).

individually and as a whole, and thereby has "forgotten" Being. This thesis is extensively examined and criticized above in section 2.1 and in various other places. These examinations and criticisms show that Heidegger's interpretation and critique are both failures. Heidegger articulates his misinterpretation in the famous formula "Metaphysics is onto-theology," and uses that formula as a kind of magic spell to be trotted out and simply repeated again and again, in a variety of contexts, as a basis for simple rejections of concepts, conceptions, ways of questioning, arguments, viewpoints, objections, etc.; they are rejected simply by being tagged "metaphysical." When Heidegger adds more detail, it is only to say, in agreement with the magic spell, that theoretical elements are exclusively elements of a thinking that thematizes *only* being(s), as individuals and as a whole. When he then makes Being, putatively forgotten by metaphysics, his own central focus, he is unable to use all those theoretical elements he has rejected as "metaphysical."

This strategy—implacably employed in all of Heidegger's important works—had a fateful consequence for his way of thinking: it led to a radical ignoring and amputation of many of the most powerful tools or potentialities of human thinking. This is why his thinking is *fundamentally deficient*, why it is an *impoverished* form of thinking. This state of affairs, which is not correctly and appropriately understood or assessed throughout the boundless literature on Heidegger, is explained in somewhat more detail in what follows, and the critique based on it further developed.

Examination of central examples of the theoretical elements in question easily shows that Heidegger's powerfully consequential tactic of assigning them to the metaphysical tradition functions to make the thinking that *excludes* them a thinking-of-being(s) rather than a thinking-of-Being. Sufficient examples are found in the *Contributions*, beginning with the following:

> Considered according to *metaphysics,* God must be represented as the beingest [*der Seiendste*], as the first ground and cause of beings, as the un-conditioned, in-finite, absolute. None of these determinations arises from the Godness of the God; they arise instead from the essence of being(s) as such, insofar as this is thought as what is constantly present, as what is objective and simply in itself and thus, in re-presenting explaining, as what is most clearly attributed to the God as ob-ject. (308; t.a.)

Here, Heidegger could and should particularly have introduced the modalities necessity–possibility–contingency. His assertion that "all these determinations . . . [arise from] the essence *of being(s)* as such" is wholly arbitrary; nothing can support it. The simplest analysis shows that what Heidegger here calls "determinations" are *capabilities* of thinking that, first and most fundamentally, belong to the *thinking of Being* and not or not only to the thinking of being(s). To clarify this state of affairs, it suffices to introduce two kinds of "determinations" or concepts.

[i] Determinations/concepts like *ground-grounded, cause-effect,* etc., are dual (or binary): they articulate distinctions between poles. As shown above in detail, Heidegger makes the difference between Being and being(s), which he claims appears in metaphysics as the difference between ground and grounded, cause and effect, etc., the heart of his critique of metaphysics. What he maintains is that metaphysics does not thematize (or, as he would put it, think) this difference. That this thesis is false is shown above in the presentation of Aquinas's thought in 1.3.2 and then, extensively, in 2.1.

Here again an astonishing result—formulated above in a different form—must be explicitly noted. If against the metaphysics of Being of (say) Thomas Aquinas it would be appropriate to object—if the objection were on target—that he thematized Being not *as itself,* but only *in relation to being(s)* (and that he had thereby forgotten Being as such), then an analogous objection would be appropriately raisable against Heidegger. This is shown in what follows in two ways.

First: Heidegger holds that "*Being never essences [west] without being(s)*" (*PM* 233), from which it immediately follows that explaining Heideggerian Being as such is impossible in the absence of an explaining of the relation of Being to being(s). This constitutes a fundamental way in which Heideggerian thinking differs from Aquinas's metaphysics of Being, because according to the latter, it is wholly possible for *esse per se subsistens,* i.e., *esse as such, as itself,* to (in Heidegger's terms) *essence [wesen] without being(s).* For that reason, *esse* as such can—at least in a certain way, or in principle—be articulated *prior* to the articulation of its relation to being(s).[49] This means that Heidegger cannot think his *primordial dimension* (Being-as-*Ereignis*) without the aid of dual categories; this is shown in what follows.

Second: if one examines Heidegger's assertions about *Being as such,* one finds that they are of two sorts. First, there are those that are more or less purely tautological, negative, or general, as in the following passage from the "Letter on Humanism":

---

[49] This is precisely the conception developed in *Structure and Being* (see section 5.2).

> But Being—what is Being? It "is" Itself. Futural thinking must learn
> to experience this and to say it. "Being"—that is not God, and not a
> ground for the world. Being is essentially broader than every being
> and at the same time nearer to human beings than is any being, be it
> a rock, an animal, an artwork, a machine, be it an angel or God. Being
> is the nearest. But the near remains furthest from human beings. (*PM*
> 252; t.a.)

Later, Being is thought as *Ereignis*. This motivates the question of how *Ereignis* is understood. Does Heidegger think it in or as itself, or only in its relation to *Ereignete(s)*? Astonishingly, given how critical of metaphysics his late works are, he thinks it *only* by means of dual categories, such as sending–sent and *Ereignis–Ereignete(s)*. He then discovers the sentence "It gives [There is] Being," and interprets the "It" as *Ereignis* and the "gives" as "gives = sends = bestows." What results is the following: It = *Ereignis* is understood only as the relation of the *Ereignen*–giving–sending–bestowing to what is *Ereignet*–given–sent–bestowed. The *terms* are different, and according to Heidegger are not metaphysical (in his sense); there is (for example) no ground–grounded or cause–effect. But the dyadic structure remains. If, then, Heidegger is correct in asserting that the dyadic determinations he classifies as metaphysical "emerge from the essence of being(s) as such," then it must also be the case that the dyadic determinations *he* relies on arise *from the essence of being(s)* qua *Ereigneten*–sent, etc. What then is the difference between metaphysics and Heidegger's "originary thinking"?

[ii] Heidegger also maintains that absolute determinations/concepts like *absolute, unconditioned, infinite* (and, in other passages, the modalities *necessity–possibility–contingency*) are metaphysical because they emerge "from the essence of being(s) as such." It is easily shown that this claim is false. If questioning is an essential characteristic of thinking, as Heidegger maintains, and if every questioning is directed in some way or other and therefore involves what in ordinary philosophical language are called concepts, then it is obvious that questions concerning Being (and not only questions also or even chiefly concerning being[s]) can and must use the absolute determinations rejected by Heidegger as "metaphysical." These include such questions as the following: Is Being itself necessary or contingent? Is it absolute? Is it infinite? Also among the potentialities of thinking that proceeds unrestrictedly, aiming at completion, are questions such as whether Heidegger's *Ereignis* is necessary, contingent, absolute, infinite, etc. Heidegger's refusal to pose these and similar questions prunes the potentialities of thinking.

[2] What Heidegger thinks, how he thinks, and what he says about

thinking reveal that his form of thinking, in all these aspects, is not only fundamentally deficient, indeed impoverished, but also confused. Heidegger, who more than any other seeks to make thinking central to all his efforts, who constantly repeats the likes of, "Most thought-provoking is that we are still not thinking—not even yet, although the state of the world is becoming constantly more thought-provoking,"[50] hides the weakness of his own thinking behind the rhetorical flashiness of his talk about it. This final section of chapter 2 shows in yet another way that this is so, i.e., by identifying and briefly characterizing the *three* chief components of Heideggerian thinking.

These three components that—in accordance with the original etymological meaning of "confused"—are "poured together" are the *theoretical* component, the *poetic* component, and the *prophetic-eschatological* component.

[i] For the most part, the sentences in Heidegger's writings are, syntactically considered, theoretical sentences. Semantically considered, however, this is not the case. At least many are instead poetic or prophetic-eschatological. As far as the qualification "theoretical" is used, Heidegger would certainly object to this term being used in any way to characterize his writings. He would, as he so often did, speak immediately of the etymology and original meaning of the word θεωρία and then make various remarks having virtually nothing to do with what the word means at present.[51]

As indicated above, the most general characterization of theoretical sentences is the following: a theoretical sentence is an *indicative sentence* whose structure is made explicit by the prefixing of a theoretical operator. In his *Tractatus*, Wittgenstein presents a theoretical operator, thereby clarifying that status of theoretical sentences, as follows (4.5): "The general form of the [indicative] sentence is: It is the case that such-and-such."[52] Chapter 3 shows in extensive detail the immense importance of this simple state of affairs. The fact that Heidegger pays no attention to questions about the structure of the sentences he himself formulates *as a philosopher* is in one respect a cause and in another a consequence of the immense confusion that suffuses his works. Worth repeating is that if the prefixability of the theoretical operator is used as a criterion, then most of the sentences contained in Heidegger's works are *theoretical sentences*.

[ii] That Heidegger takes *Denken* and *Dichten*—thinking and "poet-

---

[50] "What Calls for Thinking?" in *Basic Writings*, 370.

[51] See, e.g., "Science and Reflection," in *The Question Concerning Technology*, 155–82.

[52] Ludwig Wittgenstein, *Tractatus Logico–Philosophicus*, 4.5.

izing"—to be somehow inseparable, indeed some sort of unity, is beyond question. But what is the precise sense of their inseparability and/or unity? Two passages clearly show that his answer to this question is not as clear as most interpreters appear to assume; in addition, how Heidegger actually deals with thinking and poetizing must be distinguished from his explicitly articulated conceptions of them.

A first passage articulates a strict unity of thinking and poetizing:

> Thinking is poetizing, and not only a kind of poetizing in the sense of poesy and song. Thinking of Being is the primordial way of poetizing. In it, language first comes to language, i.e., into its essence. Thinking says what the truth of Being dictates; it is the original *dictare*. Thinking is primordial poetry, prior to all poesy, but also prior to the poetics of art, since art shapes its work within the realm of language. All poetizing, in this broader sense, and also in the narrower sense of the poetic, is in its ground a thinking. The poetizing essence of thinking preserves the reign of the truth of Being.[53]

There are also, however, many passages wherein Heidegger distinguishes between thinking and poetizing, including the following:

> Yet thinking is brought into nearness with poetizing and set off against science. But nearness is something essentially other than the insipid overcoming of a distinction. The essential nearness between poetizing and thinking so little excludes their distinction that it instead allows it to arise in an abyssal [*abgründigen*] manner.[54]

Not to be considered here is whether passages of these different kinds can be combined coherently. More important than Heidegger's explicit characterizations of the relation between thinking and poetizing is the question of how the two actually relate to each other in his works. On this question, there can be no doubt that Heidegger's thinking contains many poetic elements. His predilection for interpreting poets, above all Hölderlin, is all too clear and well documented. The extensive poetic elements in his own thinking bring with them significant problems.

The concrete problems that arise here, above all with respect to the

---

[53] *Early Greek Thinking*, 19; a different translation is included in *Off the Beaten Track;* its version of the quoted passage is on pp. 247–48.

[54] *What Is Called Thinking?* 134 (t.a.).

interpretation and philosophical evaluation of individual texts, can be reduced to one basic problem expressible via the following question: does Heidegger clearly and consequently preserve the distinction—which he himself acknowledges—between theoretical discourse and poetic language? He does not. But because he does not, the question presses whether Heidegger's own writings qualify completely as theoretical rather than as poetic. Again, the answer is no. That, however, makes philosophical engagement with and opposition to Heidegger's writings extraordinarily difficult, if not indeed impossible. To say, for example, that philosophical language "breaks down," and then to rely on various forms of poetic language is, for a philosopher, a lame way of avoiding the strictly philosophical task. Philosophy is a strictly theoretical undertaking. It is nonsensical to disfigure it or to demand of it something that it cannot achieve and should not try to achieve. This "cannot achieve" does not point to any weakness; it is instead a consequence of the specific character of theoreticity.

It must be added that a significant part of the enormous success that Heidegger has enjoyed over the years and continues to enjoy is based on a misunderstanding and a confusion. Many readers of his works have failed and still fail to notice that what the "thinker of Being" calls (his) "thinking" is in truth the result of a mixture of genuinely philosophical, poetic, and (as is shown more fully below) prophetic-eschatological elements. So confused a discourse exerts a peculiar fascination on readers who are not particularly careful and do not attend precisely to what is being offered to them: they have the impression that they are being confronted by something overpowering.

[iii] The third component in the confused jumble that is Heideggerian thinking is the prophetic-eschatological component. From the Bible it is well known that "prophetic" and "eschatological" are two characteristics of discourses that appear in various forms and variations. This is also the case with Heidegger, in whose works—and indeed in central locations—one often finds passages that sound like secularized biblical, prophetic-eschatological formulations. "Prophetic" is not defined here, but only generally characterized. The word is used today in many in-part mutually incoherent ways. Here, the word is understood on the basis of the Bible, but in a neutral manner. It unifies three factors: a condemnation or critique of the current situation, a visionary announcement—rather than any sort of scientific prediction—of a different situation that is said to be coming, and an admonishment to preparedness, to being open for what is to come. Many of the passages introduced above exhibit these characteristics.

As far as the words "eschatological" and "eschatology" are concerned, Heidegger speaks explicitly of the "eschatology of Being."[55] How he understands the word is shown by the following passage from his treatise "The Anaximander Fragment":

> The antiquity pervading the Anaximander fragment[56] belongs to the dawn of early times in the West. But what if that which is early outdistanced everything late; if the very earliest far surpassed the very latest? What once occurred in the dawn of our destiny would then come, as what once occurred, at the last (ἔσχατον), that is, at the departure of the long-hidden destiny of Being. The Being of beings is gathered (λέγεσθαι, λόγος) in the ultimacy of its destiny. The essence of Being hitherto disappears, its truth still veiled. The history of Being is gathered in this departure. The gathering in this departure, as the gathering (λόγος) at the outermost point (ἔσχατον) of its essence hitherto, is the eschatology of Being. As fateful, Being itself is inherently eschatological.[57]

This passage is a perfect example of the *poetic* character of Heideggerian thinking. But at least the text makes clear that the designation "eschatological" is, according to his own self-understanding, accurate to his thinking.

---

[55] *Early Greek Thinking*, 18.

[56] The Greek text reads: "ἐξ ὧν δὲ ἡ γένεσίς ἐστι τοῖς οὖσι καὶ τὴν φθορὰν εἰς ταῦτα γίνεσθαι κατὰ τὸ χρεών. διδόναι γὰρ αὐτὰ δίκην καὶ τίσιν ἀλλήλοις τῆς ἀδικίας κατὰ τὴν τοῦ χρόνου τάξιν" (H. Diels, *Die Fragmente der Vorsokratiker* [1903/1966], vol. 1, p. 89). A reasonable English version of Heidegger's (idiosyncratic) translation is the following: "Whence things have their origin, there they must also pass away according to necessity; for they must pay penalty and be judged for their injustice, according to the ordinance of time" (*Early Greek Thinking*, 13).

[57] *Early Greek Thinking*, 18.

Chapter 3

The Structural-Systematic Approach to a Theory of Being and God

As its title indicates, this chapter articulates a systematic conception of this book's subject matter: Being and God. The chapter shows that only within the framework of a coherent and comprehensive theory of Being as such and as a whole is it possible to develop an adequate conception of God. Chapters 1 and 2 provide the background requisite to situate the project this chapter undertakes in relation to both the metaphysical tradition and Heidegger's thought. Chapter 2's critique reveals that on the basis of his understanding of how the problem of Being is addressed throughout the history of philosophy, Heidegger addresses that problem originally and forcefully, but also unsuccessfully. The shortcomings of the tradition and of Heidegger reveal the need for the development of a new approach to the problem.

The conception presented in this chapter is a part of the structural-systematic philosophy (SSP), which is articulated in far more extensive detail in *Structure and Being: A Theoretical Framework for a Systematic Philosophy*. This chapter's subject matter is situated within the structural-systematic philosophy's comprehensive systematics, which is treated in chapter 5 of *Structure and Being*. In terms introduced and clarified above (chapter 1), this chapter ultimately presents central features of this philosophy's version of deep metaphysics. Worth reemphasizing is that deep metaphysics is importantly distinct from what, since the time of Christian Wolff and Immanuel Kant, has been termed *metaphysica generalis*. This *metaphysica generalis* is the philosophical discipline concerned with the most universal predicates (or characteristics) of all *beings*. Rather than being any form of *metaphysica generalis*, the deep metaphysics presented below is a theory of Being as such and as a whole.

This chapter contains seven sections, each of which presents a step toward the development of the structural-systematic philosophy's deep metaphysics. Section 3.1 articulates the systematic context—technically, the theoretical framework—within which this philosophy develops. Section 3.2 takes the step that is decisive for the subject matter of comprehensive systematics (and thus of deep metaphysics): the introduction of the unrestricted universe of discourse as the universal dimension of primordial Being. Section 3.3 presents the first part of the structural-systematic philosophy's theory of Being, its theory of Being as such, and section 3.4, the second part, its theory of Being as a whole; the latter includes a decisive proof concluding that the universal dimension of Being is more precisely determined as two-dimensional, including a dimension of absolutely necessary Being as well as a dimension of contingent beings. Section 3.5 explicates the relation of absolutely necessary Being to the dimension of contingent beings in a manner that shows absolutely necessary Being to be determinable more precisely as minded Being, and hence as person. Section 3.6 shows that absolutely necessary personal Being is the creator of the world. Section 3.7 shows how the move is made from the absolute creator to an adequate conception of God, and then indicates what an integral theory of God would have to include.[1]

3.1 The Systematic Context: The Theoretical Framework of the Structural-Systematic Philosophy

In this book, as in *Structure and Being*, philosophy is understood uncompromisingly and consequently as *theory*. For this reason, wholly excluded are conceptions of philosophy as therapy or therapeutics (particularly as therapeutic critique of language), all forms of philosophy that have practical aims (philosophy as wisdom, as practical reflection, as educational technique, as a way of life, as a way of shaping one's life or orienting oneself with respect to life, as education, etc.), as diagnostic activity, etc. Detailed clarification of the dimension of theoreticity in general and of philosophy as a specific mode of theorization is provided in *Structure and Being*, and need not be repeated here.

3.1.1 General Methodological Aspects of the Theoretical Framework of the Structural-Systematic Philosophy

[1] The concept of the *theoretical framework*, which is related to but an extensive modification of the concept, introduced by Rudolf Carnap, of the linguistic framework, is of central importance within the structural-

---

[1] Some of the passages in what follows in this chapter are taken from *Structure and Being*.

systematic philosophy. Its centrality is clarified by the thesis that every theoretical questioning, every theoretical sentence, argument, every theory, etc., is intelligible and evaluable only if situated within an adequately determined or determinable theoretical framework. If this condition is not satisfied, then everything remains undetermined: the meaning of any given sentence, its evaluation, etc. To every theoretical framework belong, among other things, the following constituents: a language (with its syntax and its semantics), a logic, and a conceptuality, along with all of the components that constitute a theoretical apparatus. Failure to attend to this fundamental fact—or, as is most common, failure even to recognize it—is the source of countless catastrophic mistakes from which philosophy has suffered throughout its history and into the present.

It suffices here to introduce a single example: the question raised in modernity and particularly in classical German philosophy concerning the grounding or self-grounding, and indeed the ultimate grounding of philosophy, is one that for the most part has floated in empty space, that is, in utter independence of any adequately determinable theoretical framework. Without the explication of a language, a logic, a conceptuality, fundamental assumptions, etc., the procedure has been one of immediately requesting and indeed demanding that any contention or thesis put forth immediately be grounded (or, often, "justified"). The conditions that must be satisfied if questions concerning grounding are to be meaningful are not clarified to the slightest degree. In opposition to this way of proceeding, the structural-systematic philosophy treats philosophical grounding in a manner that stringently attends to the central importance of the theoretical framework.

The task in *Structure and Being* and in this book is to develop the theoretical framework that is currently the best available *for systematic philosophy*. The central thesis that theories require theoretical frameworks, which first indicates what the architectonic of the structural-systematic philosophy requires, is made more precise by the additional thesis that a *plurality* of theoretical frameworks is potentially and indeed even actually available.

This second thesis brings with it a cluster of serious problems, including the following: How are these various theoretical frameworks to be evaluated? Can philosophical sentences be true only in *one* theoretical framework, the "absolute" one? Are all theoretical sentences that do not arise within this absolute theoretical framework false? But is there such an absolute theoretical framework, and if so, is it at all accessible to us human beings? According to the structural-systematic philosophy, true sentences emerge within every theoretical framework, but not all the true sentences are on the same level. Sentences are true only relative to (that is, within) their own theoretical frameworks. This relativity is a specific form of a moderate, non-contradictory relativism.[2]

Any theoretical framework for systematic philosophy is highly complex; that of the structural-systematic philosophy, as a whole, consists of numerous particular theoretical frameworks that are steps in the process of the development of the complete theoretical framework. At the outset, the theoretical framework is only quite globally determined, as including quite general elements (concepts, etc.). In the course of the systematic determination and concretization of the theoretical framework, new elements are added in such a way that, step-by-step, broader, more determinate, more powerful subframeworks emerge as more concrete forms of the general theoretical framework. The comprehensive presentation in *Structure and Being* traces this process of the increasingly precise determination and concretization of the (general) systematic-theoretical framework; chapter 1 of that book explains the process more precisely and in greater detail.

On the basis of the concept of the theoretical framework, the structural-systematic philosophy is characterized, with the aid of an anticipatory quasi-definition, as *a theory of the universal structures of the unrestricted universe of discourse.* This is an ambitious formulation whose worth is determined by the degree of success achieved in clarifying the concepts on which it relies and in demonstrating its importance for philosophy.

The two most important concepts in the quasi-definition of the SSP are *structure* and *unrestricted universe of discourse.* Methodically, the latter term/concept is utterly neutral in that it contains no more precise contentual determinations; it designates that dimension (this too an intentionally chosen neutral term/concept) of the subject matter of systematic philosophy (Heidegger speaks, famously, of the "subject matter [*Sache*] of thinking"). The dimension of the universe of discourse is the *comprehensive datum* in the following sense: it is what is *given to systematic philosophy to be understood and/or explained,* and is thus everything with which systematic philosophical theorization can and must be concerned. The term "datum" here is thus a technical term whose sense must be strictly distinguished from the various alternative notions of data to be found in philosophy, including sense data, what is given by the senses, etc. In addition, the topic much discussed at present of the "myth of the given"[3] is related only indirectly to the datum in the sense that is relevant here.

---

[2] For detail, see *Structure and Being* 3.3.4.3.

[3] The term is used by Wilfrid Sellars (1956) to designate a philosophical error he criticizes. See his essay "Empiricism and the Philosophy of Mind" (1956).

"Datum" in this sense can designate any linguistically articulated *candidate* for inclusion in the structural-systematic philosophy. As having counterparts potentially incorporable into the SSP, these candidates are propositions expressed by sentences. Many such candidates are available as articulated in ordinary languages. These include the wide variety of sentences that provide theoretical articulations of things, of the world, of the universe, etc. Additional candidates are or become available at higher levels of theory-formation: these include responses to questions that arise as theories are developed, and as additional topics and interconnections emerge in that process. The task is to determine which of these truth candidates are to be incorporated into the structural-systematic philosophy. This incorporation does not involve accepting such data in the forms in which they are initially found; instead, the data are candidates for restructuration within the theory, whereby their restructuration involves corrections and transformations that can be quite radical.

This state of affairs is visible in the relation between ordinary language and the philosophical language relied on by the structural-systematic philosophy. The latter connects to ordinary language and indeed begins from it, but then fundamentally corrects it, semantically although not necessarily syntactically. On the basis of the criterion of intelligibility, the structural-systematic philosophy develops an alternative semantics that has, as an implication, an alternative ontology.

In the course of the presentation, the dimension termed the *universe of discourse* is determined more precisely in a series of steps, such that additional designations are introduced: "world," "universe," and finally "Being," first in the sense of the objective counterpole to "structure," but ultimately, as explained below, as the term/concept most adequate to the unrestricted universe of discourse as a whole.

The other central concept in the quasi-definition introduced above is *structure*. In brief, this concept designates everything any theory explains. Conceptualizing and explaining are characterized most concisely as the discovery and presentation of the structure(s) of what is conceptualized or explained (i.e., of the data). The term "structure" is attached to a concept central to the SSP not because of but despite the fact that the term has become popular. Its use in the SSP is justified by the fact that in it, "structure" is scrupulously introduced, defined, and applied. For this, the mathematical signification of the term is centrally important. It is of course because of the centrality of this concept that the systematic philosophy to which both *Structure and Being* and *Being and God* contribute is termed the *structural-systematic philosophy*. Explaining how the dimension of structure and the dimension of the universe of discourse or of Being fit together is the most central task of the SSP, which is nothing other than the progressively unfolding thematization of this fitting together.

[2] The thesis most central to the structural-systematic philosophy is the following: its theorization consists in the articulation of the connection between the dimension of data (in the sense explained above) and the dimension of structure(s) or (equivalently) the structural dimension. As clarified below, the structural dimension includes *three* kinds of structures: logical, semantic, and ontological ones. These structures are concretized when data are interpreted (restructured) in accordance with them; they are then visible as the structures of the data themselves. Or, from the other direction: the data are incorporated into the structural dimension. As indicated above, the data are thereby transformed; the result is their elevation to the highest available level of intelligibility.

Every item thematized by the structural-systematic philosophy is initially and by definition a datum (in the technical sense). Because the infinitely many data are all included within the unrestricted universe of discourse, the latter can be termed the comprehensive datum. As indicated above, the integration of data and structure(s) is the most central task of the structural-systematic philosophy. The distinction between the dimensions of structure(s) and datum/data is, however, easily misunderstood. It has virtually nothing in common with the transcendentally understood distinction between a priori concepts or ideas and what is provided by the senses. Instead, the structures as such are abstract structures in the sense that they are not yet concretized as structuring data.

Initially, then, the focus is on the structures as abstract and universal, not yet as concretized. The dimension of these structures is the architectonic of actuality, of Being as a whole. The concrete status of individual items, domains, and all of the ways these interrelate—in short, the concrete structuration of the unrestricted universe of discourse—is made clear by the explication of the data as they are restructured and thereby situated systematically within this dimension.

The thesis that the structures required for the theorization of the data are, in the final analysis, structures of the data themselves—albeit generally on a level different from the levels on which the data are initially available—makes irrelevant to the structural-systematic philosophy all the problems that, in the tradition and into the present, plague discussions about realism and anti-realism, realism and idealism, etc. This is one way in which the structural-systematic philosophy is a theory superior to ones that are plagued by those problems.

The following subsections clarify the structural-systematic philosophy's restructuration of its data to the extent required by this book; a thorough, systematic treatment is provided in chapters 1–3 of *Structure and Being*.

[3] The restructuration of the data follows a specific method.
That method provides the answer to the question of *how* the reconstruction of the data is accomplished. The answer articulates a four-staged
procedure.

The SSP's four-staged method is an *idealized* method for philosophy.
The reason is that it is generally impossible, for pragmatic reasons, for
what is required by each stage to be fully accomplished. The method is
nevertheless extremely important as a regulative idea for philosophical
theorization. Philosophers who keep this method in view in developing
theories in any domains remain aware of the limitations of what they are
accomplishing, and thus of how much more would have to be done to
accomplish the philosophical task *completely*. Under the regulative idea
of the four-step (or four-stage) method, then, philosophical work can
be evaluated accurately by being situated within the broad field of philosophical possibilities in accordance with the highest philosophical criteria and requirements.

The four stages of the comprehensive method can be described concisely. The method's first or assembling stage restructures the available
datum or data—whether individual phenomenon or event, an intermediate domain, or the comprehensive datum (the unrestricted universe of
discourse)—such that what emerges is an initial, informal articulation of
a theory. The second or theory-constitutive stage puts the informal theories produced at the first stage into strictly theoretical form: it formulates
theories in the strict or genuine sense. The third or system-constituting
stage integrates the theories produced at the second stage into a network
of theories, thus a systematic whole. Finally, the fourth stage—the truth-
testing or evaluative stage—determines whether the systematic theory
and its constituent theories are theoretically adequate, i.e., ultimately,
whether they are true.

In normal philosophical practice, these steps are scarcely ever even
recognized, much less taken in order. The second and third steps or
stages are usually wholly ignored. Typically, only incidental aspects of the
first and fourth stages are applied, and the fourth stage is usually taken
to involve "justification" of an only vaguely determinate sort. More ambitious philosophical presentations ignore only the second step. In any
such case, the informal or minimal theories that result from the application of the first stage of the method are directly—in this book's terms,
without reliance upon the second stage of the method—integrated into
a network theory that is itself only informally articulated.

Concerning the second or theory-constituting stage, it is important
to note that the two most important forms for theories in the strict or
genuine sense are the axiomatic form and the network or coherentist

form. The method's second stage can, in principle, produce theories having either of these forms.

The axiomatic form differs from the network form in a number of ways, but those do not include suitability for formalization; hence, theories with the network form can (but need not) rely on formal languages, develop models, etc. The centrally important difference between the two is that theories with the axiomatic form are strictly linear and hierarchical whereas those with the network form are not. This leaves open the possibility that theories with the network form include subtheories having the axiomatic form.

The deductive structure that characterizes strictly axiomatic theories is in one respect the consequence, result, or expression of the hierarchical-linear character of those theories, whereas in another respect it is the basis of this hierarchical-linear character. Thus, the axiomatic method is characterized precisely by its moving from a (finite) series of basal theses (the axioms) to additional theses (the theorems). Coherentist or network method theories are structured wholly differently: they are structured as totalities of inferential interrelations of the theories that are made explicit by the method's second stage.

What does all of this yield with respect to the second methodic stage of the structural-systematic philosophy? The adequate answer to this question includes the following two theses: (i) the axiomatic form is the most logically exact; it is therefore the most demanding and appropriate theory-form, logically and mathematically. The network form, in contrast, is far from having a comparably unambiguous logical-mathematical status. (ii) It cannot be assumed that the relations among the elements of a theory qua form of presentation *and* among the objective (ontological) elements thereby articulated always simply have a linear-hierarchical structure. Therefore, one must assume that there is *at least in the cases of many, if not indeed in the cases of most subject matters,* a web (a network) of relations that therefore cannot be understood and articulated in a linear-hierarchical manner. The more comprehensive a theory is, the less probable is it that it can be articulated in accordance with the axiomatic theory-form.

To be sure, one could consider expanding the number of axioms, potentially infinitely, in order to articulate axiomatically the entire complexity of the web of relations to be thematized by the theory. However, there are at least two reasons for not doing this. First, articulating a number of axioms extending to infinity would be impracticable with respect to the development of theories. Second, even an arbitrarily large number of axioms could not articulate the entire web of relations, because many relations have a cyclical character in that they are between entities whose involvement is reciprocal.

Theses (i) and (ii), introduced above, support several important conclusions about the philosophical method described here. In cases in which what is to be articulated by a specific theory has a linear-hierarchical structuration, the axiomatic theory-form is the suitable one; in all other cases, the coherentist or network theory-form is appropriate. For systematic philosophy as a whole (i.e., as a comprehensive theory), only the coherentist or network theory-form can be used. With those subtheories that can, as explained above, take the axiomatic theory-form, an *informal* axiomatic theory-form is as a rule fully sufficient.

[4] A simply indispensable component of the theoretical framework of the structural-systematic philosophy is its *language*. It is, in every respect, the core of the theoretical framework. This language develops as a consequence of a radically interpreted linguistic turn. "Radically interpreted" here means that the language is not directly continuous with that of what may be termed classical analytic philosophy. Instead, it depends on an extensively redetermined conception of language. The first central aspect of the radical redetermination is the rejection of the thesis that natural or ordinary language is in any way authoritative or definitive for philosophy. The alternative language of the structural-systematic philosophy is a *philosophical language* that is connected in certain ways with ordinary language, but that both corrects ordinary language and radically transforms it with respect to semantics and ontology. The immense significance of these differences becomes clear only by way of detailed consideration.

At this point, it is important to introduce one aspect of philosophical language. As indicated above, the structural-systematic philosophy is a *theory* in the strongest sense of that term; as such, it excludes a great many undertakings that have been accepted as "philosophical" in the course of the history of philosophy and into the present. To be sure, what theories *are* is a central topic for philosophy; that topic is considered below. It suffices at this point to introduce a universal criterion for theoreticity, the *linguistic* criterion. Every philosophical theory both presupposes sentences and consists of sentences. The sentences of which philosophical theories consist are theoretical sentences. But what are those? They are indicative (or declarative) sentences, which are distinct both from practical sentences (e.g., "Tell the truth!") and aesthetic sentences (e.g., "How beautiful!"). Theoretical sentences articulate what is the case; they do not, for example, make demands.[4] In his *Tractatus,* Wittgenstein charac-

---

[4] As shown in *Structure and Being* 2.2.3.1 and 4.3.2.5, practical (deontic) sentences, like theoretical ones, can articulate semantic contents, but the *mode* of articulation is *completely different* from the theoretical mode.

terizes the structure of such sentences as follows: "That there is a general form for the [indicative] sentence is proved by the fact that there can be no sentence whose form one could not have foreseen (i.e., constructed). The general form of the [indicative] sentence is: It is the case that such and such."[a, 5]

There is no question that Wittgenstein is here concerned with *indicative* sentences. What he says of them is made more precise by the introduction of a *theoretical operator*. Every sentence that is indicative and theoretical has the following structure: it is—either explicitly or (as is usual) implicitly preceded by the operator "It is the case that." "(T)" can symbolize this operator. Adding the Greek letter "φ" as a sentence-constant or -variable, the form or structure of the theoretical sentence is "(T)φ." An example of an instantiation of this form or structure is the sentence "[It is the case that] the Earth revolves around the sun."[6]

As indicated above, the extraordinary significance of the theoretical operator is shown at various stages in the following presentation. To be noted at this point is the absolute and radical character of the articulation it makes possible. This character is such that in so-interpreted theoretical sentences there is no reference or relation to subject(s), speaker(s), situation(s), or any other factor external to theorization. This

---

[a] Wittgenstein's original phrase, of course quoted in *Sein und Gott*, is "Es verhält sich so und so." There is no English rendering that adequately captures and articulates the peculiar sense and force of the German wording, which is reflexive as well as impersonal, but the syntactic differences between "Es verhält sich so und so" and "It is the case that such and such" are irrelevant to their functioning, in their respective languages, as linguistic criteria for theoreticity. Syntactic and semantic differences between "Es verhält sich so dass" and "It is the case that" *do* become relevant at a later stage of the development of the structural-systematic philosophy; for details, see *Structure and Being*, note a to chapter 5 (p. 404).

[5] *Tractatus* 4.5, t.a. The introduction of this formulation does not imply that Wittgenstein himself intends it as a criterion for theoreticity. His intention is presumably quite different. Here relevant is what he later writes, in his *Philosophical Investigations*, concerning the cited passage from the *Tractatus:*

(*Tractatus Logico–Philosophicus*, 4.5): "The general form of the sentence is: It is the case that such and such."—That is the kind of sentence that one repeats to oneself countless times. One thinks that one is tracing the outline of the thing's nature over and over again, and one is merely tracing round the frame through which we look at it. (t.a.)

[6] To be noted is that in pragmatic contexts wherein ordinary languages are used, the syntactic-grammatical form of the indicative sentence is not a criterion satisfied only by theoretical sentences. For example, "I'll have a pound of apples," uttered by a shopper to a vendor, has the syntactic-grammatical form of an indicative sentence, but in this context serves as a polite way to make the request or demand, "Give me a pound of apples."

makes unmistakably clear an absolutely decisive point: theories *as such* are fully independent of any attitude connecting any subject to them. For an appropriate conception of philosophy, this point is of a significance that can scarcely be overestimated.

One of the most important consequences of the point just introduced concerns the entire epistemic dimension. The radical epistemological turn of all modern philosophy places the subject at the center of the entire theoretical undertaking and thus also at the center of philosophy. Here, the structural-systematic philosophy takes another radical turn in that it situates at the center of theory-formation not the subject (whether as thinking or as acting), but instead language, with all that it involves (semantics, logic, etc.). The subject is thereby radically disempowered. This disempowerment is made clear by means of considerations of two issues central to modern and contemporary philosophy: that of "justification" and that of the definition and status of knowledge.

Adequate consideration of what is generally called the issue of justification requires the introduction of a distinction between justification as a specifically pragmatic matter and grounding,[b] which is objective rather than pragmatic. As pragmatic, justification involves seeking and presenting accounts aiming to lead those who hear or read them to accept whatever it is that is being justified. Grounding, in contrast, involves only objective factors considered independently of attitudes that subjects may have toward them; the factors are exclusively ones concerning the inner coherence and the truth of what is being grounded. The consequence of the disempowering of the subject in this area is thus that ultimately, only grounding is relevant to the assessment of theories.

Thereby, the absolutely opaque and inestimable domain of all the factors that could come into question as motivating subjects to acceptance or rejection becomes one that is simply to be ignored. This remains true if pragmatic grounding is limited to appeals to the subject *as rational*, because the subject as rational ultimately proves to be the subject whose assessments of theories are determined by objective factors, so again it is those factors alone, and not the subject, that matter.

That philosophical assessments of theories must be objective rather than pragmatic is also clear from the brief account presented above of the philosophical method. Another consequence clear from that ac-

---

[b] As indicated above, the structural-systematic philosophy as a whole has a network rather than an axiomatic form. The more strongly any theoretical item (thesis, subtheory, etc.) is linked to other theses (and subtheories, etc.), the more securely is that item grounded.

count is that the task of assessment can be undertaken only at the end of the process of theory-formation, not at the beginning. The structural-systematic philosophy is thus radically anti-foundationalist.

The second issue to be considered here that clarifies the importance of the disempowerment of the subject is that of how *knowledge* is understood. Here again, the structural-systematic philosophy diverges radically from the most widely accepted notion. As is well known, Edmund Gettier provides a precise definition for that notion, which appears repeatedly in the history of philosophy. This notion is that knowledge is justified true belief (JTB). Gettier's precise definition (K_G) is as follows:

(K_G) S knows that p iff
       (i) p is true
       (ii) S believes that p,
       (iii) S is justified in believing that p.[7]

This definition is generally accepted as defining knowledge as it is understood in ordinary language and in philosophy. It is, however, highly problematic. To begin with, one must assume that knowledge is normally understood to be a *mental* state. Knowledge is a belief or conviction that has determinate conditions: it is of something that is true (condition i); this truth lies within the scope of a belief or conviction (condition ii); S is justified in having that belief.

The countless counterexamples—starting with the ones Gettier himself introduces—make the status of this definition problematic at best. In opposition to the mainstream of contemporary philosophy, the structural-systematic philosophy classifies it as radically deficient. It differs from most critiques of the definition by locating its deficiency not in condition (iii), but in condition (i). This condition is the one requiring that the (proposition) p be true, and that it be so in utter independence of the subject. It must, however, be possible to determine whether or not a condition in a definition has been satisfied. If condition (i) is determined to be satisfied, then any subject who is aware of this is aware that p is true, without any questions of justification or belief having arisen. But—in natural English as in ordinary philosophical English—any *awareness* that p is true would qualify as *knowledge* that p is true.

The error fatal to the JTB definition can be briefly characterized as follows. If knowledge is a condition or attitude of a subject, then the relation of the subject to whatever is known must be included in all of

---

[7] E. Gettier, "Is Justified True Belief Knowledge?" (1963), 121.

the conditions that must be satisfied if knowledge is to obtain; what is known cannot be placed outside of any and every relation to the subject. More precisely: in the definition, what is known can appear *only* within the scope of the operator that includes "knows that." In the Gettier formulation of condition (i), however, p is outside of the scope of the operator. Particularly (although not exclusively) for this reason, the definition must be altered to yield (in one version) the following:

(K) S knows that p iff
        (i) S believes that p is true and
        (ii) S believes that S's belief that p is true is justified.

This alteration is immensely consequential. If the attitude of the subject is something that must be considered, then one must consider it: one cannot introduce factors said to lie beyond the reach of the subject's attitudes. As indicated above and explained more fully below, theories are completely objective in that they are articulated in total independence of subjective attitudes. Theoretical sentences are therefore governed not by the operator "Subject S knows that. . . ," but by "It is the case that. . . ."

[5] It must now be explained what, more precisely, philosophical theories are. Relevant to this issue is that at present, there are ongoing discussions—ones that are intense and involve significant disagreements—concerning what scientific theories are. The structural-systematic philosophy does not accept, unmodified, any of the currently available accounts. The account that comes closest to articulating what the structural-systematic philosophy identifies as the specific status of philosophical theories is the structuralist theory-concept presented by J. D. Sneed and Wolfgang Stegmüller, but even that one requires essential corrections.[8] The following account briefly presents the structural-systematic theory-concept without significant consideration of how that concept relates to any others.

Central to the structural-systematic theory-concept is *structure*. Although this exhibits a kinship with what is termed the semantic approach to the issue—and particularly to its structuralist variant—it differs from all variants of that approach in three essential respects. First, it does not simply provide an abstract definition of this concept; instead, it articulates in detail both the *definiens* and the kinds of structures that are essential to the determination of its theory-concept. Second, the variants of

---

[8] See *Structure and Being* 2.4.

the semantic approach do no more than (marginally) recognize the relation between structure(s) and language, but for the structural-systematic theory-concept, that relation is essential. Third, the structural-systematic approach deems the explication of the relation between structure(s) and the ontological domain (the universe of discourse, the world) to be both indispensable and utterly central.

The elementary structural-systematic theory-concept has three basic components that are defined as the triple $\langle L, S, U \rangle$, where L = language, S = structure, and U = universe of discourse. To be sure, these three components must be determined, i.e., explicated, accurately and in detail. The components L (language) and S (structure) can, however, also be treated as one because the dimension of language proves to be included within that of structure: the latter dimension cannot be adequately defined if its relation to language is ignored. The theory-concept is then dyadic: the ordered pair $\langle S, U \rangle$. This ordered pair articulates, as an elementary philosophical theory-concept, the thesis most central to the structural-systematic philosophy.

In this dyadic theory-concept, the component U (universe of discourse) is the *ontological level*. The central task posed by the theory-concept is that of precisely explicating the relation between the dimension of structure S and the dimension of the universe of discourse U. This is indeed the central task of systematic philosophy. Given, however, that this relation *is* central, it makes sense to ask whether *it* should be included in the theory-concept. If it were included, the theory-concept would contain the relation as a third component. If the symbol "$\rightleftharpoons$" were used for the relation, the result would be the triple $\langle S, \rightleftharpoons, U \rangle$.

What is essential is that this relation—and thereby the ontological level—be explicitly thematized. Whether it should be included as a component of the theory-concept is another question. On the one hand, it could be included, but on the other, it need not be included. One reason not to include it is that just as language is within the dimension of structure, the ontological dimension includes its relation to the dimension of structure, and vice versa: the relation of the universe of discourse to the dimension of structure belongs essentially to the universe of discourse.

3.1.2 The Dimension of Structure as the Core of the Theoretical Framework: The Three Levels of Pervasive Structures

The concept *structure,* identified above as central to the structural-systematic theory-concept, is consequently likewise central to its theoretical framework. The initially mathematical concept *structure* is presupposed and in certain respects retained, but expanded in its concrete application and adjusted to fit different subject matters.

One peculiarity of the structural-systematic philosophy merits mention at this point. As is well known, both in the history of philosophy and at present there is an arsenal of theoretical elements or factors whose precise meanings are generally left unexplained. Among these elements or factors are *concept, category, reference, sense, meaning, semantic value, proposition, thought, state of affairs, fact,* and *object.* Within the structural-systematic philosophy, *all* of these are *structures,* although not all are the same kind of structures. Instead, each is one of the three kinds of pervasive structures or, in an alternative terminology, a specification of one of these kinds of structures. The three kinds are the comprehensive formal (logical/mathematical), semantic, and ontological structures. In what follows, each of these kinds of comprehensive structure is considered in detail.

From the fact that the structural-systematic philosophy interprets the factors mentioned in the preceding paragraph as structures, it does not follow that it cannot use the terms generally used to name those factors; avoiding their use would result in extreme linguistic awkwardness. In addition, the term "concept" is so widely used that it is currently indispensable. The continued use of the terms brings with it, however, no significant problems because those terms are used simply as convenient abbreviations for structures.

That there are three kinds or levels of structures cannot be derived a priori. Instead, this thesis emerges from consideration of all the elements that must be included in philosophical theories. The formal (logical/mathematical) structures are the most universally comprehensive ones, the ones that are unrestrictedly universal, because they provide the most general internal structuration for the semantic *and the ontological* structures. There must be semantic structures because language is the means indispensable to the articulation of theories and to the development of theories: without language, theories would be unable to express or articulate anything. There must be ontological structures because the ontological domain provides the ultimate subject matter for philosophical theories.

[1] Concerning the comprehensive *formal* structures, to be emphasized at the outset is that both mathematics and modern formal logic are disciplines that are radically different from philosophy. How logic and mathematics are related—whether they are fully distinct disciplines or ultimately constitute a single formal discipline—is a controversial issue that need not be considered here. It suffices for the purposes of this book to consider logic and mathematics to treat a single formal dimension.[9] Philosophy relies on logic and mathematics, but the *inner structura-*

---

[9] See *Structure and Being* 3.2.1.

tion of the formal dimension they investigate is not a subject matter for philosophy.

That logic and mathematics are independent of philosophy does not have as a consequence that philosophy has nothing to say about them. Instead, logic and mathematics, like every other science and domain, are both subject matters and sources of means of presentation for philosophy. Among the philosophical tasks concerning the formal dimension, two merit mention here. The first is that of interpreting or explaining the logical/mathematical dimension. An essential aspect of this task is saying what items in the logical and mathematical domain *are*. This task is undertaken in contemporary philosophies of mathematics. According to the structural-systematic philosophy of mathematics, the items within this domain do have an ontological status, i.e., they are full-fledged constituents of Being. They constitute the most comprehensive, the most universal stratum of the unrestricted universe of discourse and thus of what may also be termed the world, reality, or Being. On this stratum are all the *modes of configuration* of everything within the unrestricted universe of discourse.

The second task, which can be confronted fundamentally only following the accomplishment of the first, consists in showing to what extent and in what manner philosophical theories can or perhaps must make use of or indeed rely on logic and mathematics. The purposes of this book do not require that this task be undertaken;[10] sufficient for its purposes is the introduction, here, of the thesis that logical and mathematical structures are the comprehensive formal structures that (must) play a central and therefore indispensable role in the structural-systematic philosophy.

[2] *Semantic* structures are those that configure the language–world relation. As such, they are the axis around which turns all other aspects of philosophical theorization. To reject or fail to rely on the level of semantic structures is to be left either with a subject matter that would be somehow extralinguistic—thus, no longer the unrestricted universe of discourse or anything within it—or with a language that did not express or articulate anything. The history of philosophy includes positions tending toward—although never fully reaching—each of these extremes. Wholly extralinguistic "stuff" and utterly unexpressive languages are absolute abstracta.

[i] The semantic structures of the structural-systematic philosophy are those of its own philosophical language, not those of ordinary language. As noted above, this does not require rejection or radical altera-

---

[10] See *Structure and Being*, pp. 233ff.

tion of the *syntactic* structures of ordinary language; it requires instead that when those structures are used, they are radically reinterpreted. Because philosophical languages are purely theoretical languages, their semantics must satisfy theoretical criteria. The first and most essential criterion is negative: the semantics cannot be pragmatic in any significant sense, thus not in any sense suggested by the slogan, stemming from the later Wittgenstein, "*meaning is use.*" Instead, the sentences included in the semantics must be theoretical and so must *express* semantic contents, however the latter may be designated (for example, as "information" or "propositions"). This semantic content is simply what theoretical sentences express.

The level of semantic structures is unique in that in one respect it is intermediate, and in another respect it requires additional determination. The semantic structures constituting the semantic level are indeed the *expressa* of theoretical sentences, but this characterizes them only in terms of how they function in presentations of theories. They also, however, have the absolutely essential function of mediating by, so to speak, reaching another level—specifically, the ontological level. The structural-systematic philosophy explains this mediating function by means of the thesis that *fully determined* semantic structures are *identical with* ontological structures. In what follows, this central thesis is explained and grounded.

A central thesis of structural-systematic semantics is loosely formulable as follows: semantics and ontology are two sides of one and the same coin. Or: between the two there is a perfect conformity. Initial grounding for this thesis is provided by the observation that if there were no conformity between semantically structured language and the ontological level there could be no explanation of how language could articulate the ontological level at all. The articulation in question is indeed such that sentences literally express or articulate reality (what is, Being); but if no version of this thesis is accepted, then the relation of language to reality is made into some kind of unintelligible miracle.

[ii] But how is this conformity more precisely to be determined? Answering this question requires first briefly describing the semantics that has been dominant throughout the history of philosophy and that still today is accepted by virtually all analytic philosophers. It is termed compositional semantics, because it is based on the principle of compositionality (CPP). Restricted to sentences (CPP_S), the principle is the following:

(CPP_S)   The meaning (or the semantic value) of the sentence is a function of the meanings (or semantic values) of its sub-sentential components.

As is obvious, this principle is based on the assumption that sentences have subject-predicate structures. Each of the two sub-sentential components, the subject of the sentence (generally a singular term) and the predicate, is said to have its own semantic value. The composition of these two values is said to yield the semantic value of the sentence as a whole. The semantic value of the subject or singular term is usually designated as the denotation of the term and called a (real) object. Two opposed positions are commonly taken concerning the semantic value of the predicate: one is purely extensional and the other is often, although misleadingly, termed intensional. According to the extensional position, the semantic value of a one-place predicate is the set of objects to which the predicate applies (in the case of many-place predicates, the semantic value is identified with the tuple of objects to which the predicate applies). The "intensional" position identifies the semantic value of an expression with a specific entity, a property (in the case of one-place predicates) or a relation (in the case of many-place predicates); often, both properties and relations are called attributes. Concerning just what attributes are, opinions diverge widely. Neither that issue nor the conflict between extensionalists and "intensionalists" requires further consideration here.

If semantics and ontology are two sides of the same coin, then compositional semantics, which is precisely articulated in first-order predicate logic (or language), proves to presuppose or imply substance ontology. The reason is that what is usually called "object"—particularly in analytic philosophy—is simply what is called "substance" throughout most of the history of philosophy. A substance is supposed to be an X that can have properties and stand in relations to other substances, and that can be involved in states of affairs. But how is this X to be understood—what is it supposed to be? The following account reveals that this X is unintelligible, and therefore must be rejected.

The heart of the problem comes into view through consideration of predication on the level of the language of first-order predicate logic. The simplest and most basic form of predication of this sort is "Fa," i.e., the ascription of the predicate "F" to the constant (and thus to the object or substance) "a" (quantified: $(\exists x)Fx$). An entity (the subject or substance) that corresponds to "a" or is the value of the bound variable "x" is simply and absolutely *presupposed*. The problem is the following: this presupposed entity is unintelligible, because it must, *ex hypothesi* or by presupposition, be what first makes possible the ascription or predication of universals and hence determinations of all sorts (attributes, i.e., properties and/or relations). But then the question presses, what can this presupposed something be? If one abstracts from all *determinations*, i.e., all attributes (all properties and all relations) that are or indeed could be predicated of it, as well as from all entities with which it is involved in any manner whatsoever (and one must be able to do this, because the entity in question must exist on its own as distinct), what is left? Nothing determinate: the putative entity is not determined in any way, so is completely empty. Such an "entity" is unintelligible and therefore cannot be included in any tenable semantics (or ontology).

[iii] If no compositional semantics is acceptable for scientific/philosophical purposes, and if this is the case because of the implication of substance ontology, then a different semantics must be relied on, one that does not have this defect. The alternative semantics must be one that neither entails nor presupposes substances (no matter how they may be termed). Such a semantics, however, must not rely on the subject-predicate sentence form, because it is that form that entails or presupposes substance ontology. Avoiding this form requires that a different semantic principle be introduced and exclusively relied upon. There is such a principle; it is the context principle.

The term "context principle" (henceforth, often, CTP) appears to have been introduced by Michael Dummett to designate a principle that Frege formulates as follows in *The Foundations of Arithmetic:*

(CTP$_F$) "Only in the context of a sentence do words mean something."[11]

The structural-systematic philosophy formulates the principle as follows:

(CTP) Only within the context of sentences do linguistic terms have semantic values.

There is no consensus among Frege scholars concerning either the precise meaning of his principle in *The Foundations of Arithmetic* or its fate in Frege's later works. Currently, the CTP—often linked with the phrase "the semantic primacy of the sentence"—is defended by such philosophers as Quine and Davidson, and generally also linked to the thesis that questions of truth have semantic primacy over questions of sense and reference. So understood, the CTP is opposed to the "analytic conception of language,"[12] whose most important element is Tarski's truth theory.

Many take the two principles not only to be compatible, but to com-

---

[11] Gottlob Frege, *The Foundations of Arithmetic*, §62. There are similar formulations in the introduction and in §60 and §106.

[12] This term is used by George Romanos on p. 165 of his *Quine and Analytic Philosophy* (1983).

plete and explain each other. The two are compatible, however, only if what can be termed a weak version of the CTP is accepted. That form, however, does not exclude the ontological implications of the CPP, which are shown above to be unacceptable. What must be rejected is the factor that links to substance ontology—and that factor is the subject-predicate sentence form. One must therefore allow into philosophical languages only semantic forms that do not have the subject-predicate structure. Ordinary English has sentences that do not have the subject-predicate form, although they are relatively rare. Examples include "It's raining" and "It's morning." This book terms such sentences "prime sentences."[13]

According to the structural-systematic philosophy, every sentence semantically determined as theoretical expresses a prime proposition—that is, a semantic content that is, in the case of non-compound prime sentences, what is expressed by the verb of the prime sentence. Prime propositions are not, as in the case of compositional semantics, combinations of objects with properties/relations. Instead, a prime proposition is what is expressed by the entire prime sentence; concretely, it is what is expressed by the prime sentence's verb. This does not, however, prevent the philosopher from using sentences having the subject-predicate structure. What is different is that these sentences are convenient (and, pragmatically, scarcely avoidable) abbreviations of complex configurations of many—generally, a great many—prime sentences. The subject term is itself just such a complex configuration.

This state of affairs is clarified by consideration of the subject-predicate sentence "Socrates is a philosopher." Following Quine, one could verbalize the name "Socrates" and formulate the prime sentence "It's Socratesing." Among the prime sentences included within the complex configuration "It's Socratesing" are "It's Being-Greek" and "It's Being-born-in-469-BC." What the subject-predicate sentence "Socrates is a philosopher" abbreviates can thus be formulated as follows: There is a configuration "It's Socratesing" consisting of the prime sentences . . . , such that among these prime sentences is "It's Being-a-philosopher" (or: "It's philosophering").

This semantics could be termed "contextual," although that could also lead to misunderstandings. Misunderstanding is avoided if the context principle is understood as the factor that makes the designation appropriate.

[3] It is now both possible and easy to explain the structural-

---

[13] *Structure and Being* uses "primary sentence" for what this book terms "prime sentence."

systematic philosophy's ontological structures. Semantic structures mediate, in a way, between (philosophical) language and the ontological level. Their status as mediating is explained in section 3.1.3. It suffices here to restate the thesis that ontological structures and semantic structures are two sides of the same coin. Ontological structures are nothing other than semantic structures whose status is determined definitively. Differently stated: ontological structures are *realized* prime propositions. More precisely: to any (semantic) prime proposition that has a definitive status (i.e., as explained below, when it has a truth-status), there corresponds an ontological structure: a *prime fact*. More precise explanation of this quite complex state of affairs cannot be provided here, but is provided in *Structure and Being*.

3.1.3 The Fully Determined Status of the Theoretical Framework: The Semantic-Ontological Truth Theory

The preceding sections of this chapter concisely present the most important aspects and components of the theoretical framework of the structural-systematic philosophy. So presented, the framework has a status that remains indeterminate in that questions such as the following remain unanswered: How are these aspects and components interconnected? What can or do they accomplish? Need there not be some sort of capstone that provides all the elements of the theoretical framework with definitive determinacy?

The positive answer to these reasonable questions, and the ultimate clarification of the status of the theoretical framework, is provided by the development of the framework's truth theory. As is well known, the task of developing an adequate truth theory is one that is central to analytic philosophy. Considering the literature devoted to this task would require a book-length study. In other works, the author has considered much of this literature in detail.[14] The following sections are primarily systematic: they present the semantic-ontological truth theory that explains the tight coherence of—the tight interlinkings among—the structural-systematic philosophy's pervasive structures.[15]

---

[14] See Puntel, *Wahrheitstheorien in der neueren Philosophie* (1978); *Grundlagen einer Theorie der Wahrheit* (1990); *Structure and Being* 2.5 and 3.3.

[15] Parts of the German version of the following account of truth are taken from Puntel, "Der Wahrheitsbegriff: Ansatz zu einer semantisch-ontologischen Theorie" (2002).

3.1.3.1 "Truth" as Predicate and as Operator

A first task is determining which of the syntactic roles that a or the truth-term can play is the one that the structural-systematic philosophy's theory of truth should rely on. As is well known, the logician and semanticist Alfred Tarski, who opens the path that must be followed if any defensible theory of truth is to be developed, argues that there can be no adequate theory of truth for ordinary languages, because such languages are "semantically closed," which has as a result that paradoxes can and indeed do arise within them. By now, much work has been devoted to this issue; this book's purposes do not require that that work be considered here. Those purposes do, however, require the treatment of one issue that arises with ordinary languages. As indicated above, ordinary languages do not qualify as adequate theoretical languages; they serve for communication in the lifeworld, and are structured so as to do that. They are only minimally usable by theoreticians.

A theory of truth for ordinary language(s) would be, if not wholly impossible, extraordinarily complex and widely indeterminate because of the boundless range of contingencies that can and do occur in actual and possible occurrences in the lifeworld. The truth theory presented in what follows makes no attempt to bring order to the chaos of what can be said in ordinary language(s); for those languages, it is only quite restrictedly applicable. The languages for which it is fully appropriate are theoretical, hence scientific languages.

Because the truth theory in question here is not fully applicable to ordinary language(s), it need not explain all of the ways truth-terms are used in such language(s), and—most importantly—need not even consider whether all of those ways might be somehow reducible to one central or definitive way. It is, however, important to introduce the one reduction that is the most fundamental with respect to developing a coherent and comprehensive truth theory. In works on truth theory, there is usually talk of a or the truth predicate, in one or the other of two versions. In the first version, "true" is predicated of sentences, as in the example, "[The sentence] 'Snow is white' is true." Semi-formalized with Quine corners, this version is T $\ulcorner p \urcorner$. In the second version, a sentence is preceded by the particle "that," with the result that "true" is predicated of a nominalized sentence that denotes a proposition: "[The proposition] That snow is white is true." Semi-formalized (following Horwich),[16] this version is written either as "$\langle p \rangle$ is true" or as "T$\langle p \rangle$," whereby $\langle p \rangle$ is read as "That p" or, more exactly, as "The proposition that p."

---

[16] See Horwich, *Truth* (1998), 10.

Although the focus in the literature is on "is true" as predicate, ordinary language also includes "true" in the phrase "It is true that," which
has the syntactic-grammatical form of an operator rather than that of a
predicate. The essential syntactic distinction between the "true" of "is
true" and the "true" of "It is true that" concerns what it is that is said to
be true. When "true" appears in the predicate "is true," it is predicated
of a grammatical subject, that is, a name or singular term formed either
by the enclosure of a sentence within quotation marks ("'Snow is white'
is true") or by the prefixing of "that" to a sentence ("That snow is white
is true"). When, however, "true" appears in the operator "It is true that,"
what is said to be true is the sentence itself that is the argument of the
operator ("It-is-true-that snow is white").

At first glance, the distinction just introduced may appear to be of
no more than minor relevance. In fact, however, it is immensely consequential, as the following account shows in detail. Even independently
of details, however, the potential importance of the distinction begins
to become evident if it is considered in light of the conflict, introduced
above, between compositional and contextual semantics (and the ontologies that accompany them). Truth theories that focus on the predicate
"is true" entail compositional semantics and hence substance ontologies;
shown above is that because *substance* is unintelligible, such ontologies
and hence such semantics are inadequate. Truth theories that explain
the operator "It is true that," on the other hand, are fully harmonious
with contextual semantics and ontologies, including of course the semantics and ontology of the structural-systematic philosophy, briefly introduced above.

A second issue treated in the literature on truth that requires clarification here is that of so-called truth bearers. As is indicated by the word
"bearer," talk of truth bearers, if strictly understood, presupposes first-
order predicate language: "is true" is understood as a predicate, and what
it is predicated of is the x that is its bearer. If, however—as in this book—
what is relevant to truth theory is not "true" as appearing in the predicate
"is true" but instead "true" as appearing in the operator "It is true that,"
then there is no truth bearer, because truth is not borne. Nevertheless,
the book can use the term in a broad and unspecific sense.

The three kinds of truth bearers—that is, the three kinds of items
that can be arguments of the truth operator—are prime propositions,
sentences (including prime sentences), and sentence tokenings (utterances or inscriptions). Prime propositions are the primary truth
candidates; sentences are the first kind of derivative truth candidates;
and sentence tokenings are the second kind of derivative truth candidates.

3.1.3.2 The Central Idea of Truth I: The Semantic Dimension

3.1.3.2.1 The Central Fact About Language: Linguistic Items Require Determination

Attempts to clarify truth, no matter how, cannot avoid considering language, because true/truth is the central issue in semantics, which is the discipline that has language as its subject matter. As indicated by its title, this subsection begins to relate truth to language by considering the central fact that there is indeterminate as well as determinate language. In its most general or abstract form, language is a system of uninterpreted signs or symbols (these are generally inscriptions or sounds; for the sake of simplicity, the following account largely ignores languages as systems of sounds). In this form, language is undetermined (or underdetermined, in that the sole determination is that the signs form a system, and languages are systems of signs; the sign themselves are undetermined in every respect). Language as we know and use it, however, is a system of signs that is highly determined, indeed in many respects fully determined. A language is determined to the degree that we know how to use it, and understand one another when we do use it. Degrees of determination depend on degrees of syntactic correctness and semantic significance, whereby "significance" includes what are commonly termed sense, reference, meaning, and—in cases of full determination—truth. Of central importance here is semantic determination, so syntactic determination is considered only occasionally.

According to the structural-systematic philosophy, clarifying the truth concept requires clarifying how language can attain increasing and indeed full determination, and how that attainment is to be understood. The clarification shows that items within the indicative segment of language are fully determined when they are determined as true. Showing this requires the articulation of a sequence of steps.

How is the process of the determination of language to be explained? How is language determined? By means of determiners, of course. But what are these determiners?

One step toward clarification of linguistic determination is taken by indicating how such determination is accomplished in formal languages, in logic and formal semantics. A language that is a purely formal system can be determined by means of the introduction of either a valuational semantics or an interpretational semantics. Valuational semantics assign truth values to the sentences (or formulas) of the language. Interpretational semantics (in the tradition of Tarski) introduce models that are ordered pairs, each of which consists of a domain and an interpretation function, so that to the non-logical expressions in the language are assigned semantic-ontological values.

Valuational semantics presuppose one or another truth concept in that they take truth values simply to be available, but interpretational semantics likewise fail to provide precise determinations of a or the truth concept.

3.1.3.2.2 The Three Levels of Determination of Language

This account proceeds differently in that it approaches the question in a philosophically more primordial manner. Oversimplifying somewhat, the determination of language occurs fundamentally on three levels or in three forms.

[1] The first level—or first form—of determination of language is the *lifeworldly* or *contextual* level or form. As language is ordinarily used—when sentences are uttered in everyday life—it is usually semantically determined in that, as a rule, it enables us to communicate successfully with one another. On this level, semantic determination is accomplished without the aid of pragmatic or semantic vocabulary items (thus, without such terms as, respectively, "assert" and "is true"). Language on this level can be symbolized as L_0.

It is important to note that sentences in L_0 can be and indeed generally are fully determined—to deny this would be absurd. What is reasonable to ask is what exactly this means or how exactly it is to be understood. Sentences used purely contextually can express, determinately and indeed fully determinately, what those who utter them aim to communicate. The factor responsible for this determination is one that is *external* to language: it is the context within which the utterance occurs. The determination thus does not require any linguistically articulated reflection on what is said, how the utterance or the language itself is to be understood, or anything of the sort. Here, language is simply used, and its semantic status is determined by the lifeworldly context, which is not linguistically articulated.

Because lifeworldly-contextual semantic determinacy is not explicitly articulated, it does not qualify as theoretical, philosophical, or scientific; it is instead *simply* lifeworldly-contextual. Much more could of course be said about it, but for present purposes, the following suffices: this determinacy is neither evaluated nor explicated. This can be clarified by the introduction of a context operator implicitly governing sentences uttered on the level of L_0; an example would be "[It-is-contextually-presented-that] Snow is white." This implicitly presupposed operator is what determines the language of contextual communication.

[2] The situation changes abruptly when (for example) questions arise concerning sentences uttered on the level of L_0. Such questions break the flow of ordinary lifeworldly communication; the breaks involve moves to higher levels. Any such move to a higher level brings into ques-

tion an instance of lifeworldly-contextual determination; the instance ceases to be determined. Which higher level emerges depends upon how the break is made, but one that often emerges, and that is both familiar and reliable, is a level having one aspect internal to language and one external to language; it is thus a mixed level. On this level, semantic determination is accomplished as follows: an act is accomplished by one or more speakers, and this act is simultaneously articulated, linguistically, as being the act that it is; the linguistically articulated act determines the uttered sentence.

This mixed level is that on which *pragmatic vocabulary* is applied. Whereas "Snow is white," an L_0 sentence representable by p, is contextually determinable, it is pragmatically determinable if contained within a sentence containing pragmatic vocabulary; an example is "I *assert* that snow is white" ("I *assert* that p"), which is not an L_0 sentence. In this case, the operator—pragmatic rather than contextual—is *explicitly* articulated. A general form of the operator is, "It-is-linguistically-pragmatically-posited that (e.g., 'snow is white')." On this level, the individual sentence p attains its linguistic-semantic determination by means of a factor external to language (in the example, the act of asserting) and a factor internal to language (i.e., the linguistic articulation of that act). Because p can represent language as a whole, on the mixed level language is determined language-externally and language-internally: by means of the application of pragmatic vocabulary. Utterances become semantically determined by means of acts that are explicitly articulated by sentences including pragmatic operators. This is the basis for currently popular pragmatically oriented semantic theories.[17]

[3] There is a third level on which semantic determination takes place, and it is the most important because it is the ultimately fundamental level. This is the level on which items of semantic vocabulary—most importantly, truth-terms—are located. It is presumably obvious that the operator "It-is-true-that" also has a determinative or determining effect on language—one analogous to that of the pragmatic operator "It is asserted that." These two operators are, however, radically distinct in a way that, as shown in what follows, is of decisive significance. Unlike the pragmatic operator, the truth operator articulates no relation to any factors external to language: not to lifeworldly context, to subjects, to speakers, to agents, to acts, etc. The truth operator—like other items of semantic

---

[17] The best example of a pragmatic approach, so understood, is the large-scale semantics developed by Robert Brandom, which takes its bearings from the programmatic slogan, "Semantics must answer to pragmatics"; see his book *Making It Explicit* (1994), e.g., 83.

vocabulary—is a purely *intra*linguistic determiner of language, indeed *the* genuinely intralinguistic determiner. By means of semantic vocabulary items, language determines itself. The level that includes semantic vocabulary is thus the level on which language is self-determinative.

This linguistic self-determination is recognized as obvious by Alfred Tarski, the founder of strict (formal) semantics, as is clear from various remarks in his works, including the oft-cited following one: "*A true sentence is one which says that the state of affairs is so and so, and the state of affairs indeed is so and so.*"[18] Of the sentence—and one can then say, generalizing, of language as a whole—Tarski writes, *it says that. . . .* This is the *self-determination* of language.

3.1.3.2.3 The Relations Among the Three Levels and the Role Played by the Semantic Dimension

The preceding section distinguishes the three levels of semantic determination largely separately. It is, however, important to ask whether they are interrelated. The answer is that they are; moreover, showing how they are contributes importantly to the clarification of the truth concept.

[1] Before the interrelationships among the levels are considered, an important implication of what is said in the preceding section deserves introduction. No deflationistic truth theories can avoid introducing the self-standing sentence[19] p (the usual example is "Snow is white") on the right-hand side of the equivalence operator in the famous formula "'p' is true if and only if p." But how is this self-standing sentence to be understood—what is its status? It is said to be a sentence in a metalanguage into which the sentence on the left-hand side of the equivalence operator, and enclosed within quotation marks, has been translated. But that does not clarify its status, because there is no indication of the status of the metalanguage. Is p a sentence that is perhaps an example—as "Snow is white" often is in this book—or one used in a pronunciation exercise? As shown above, uttered sentences lacking determiners, thus also the p in the famous formula, are undetermined. Three determiners are introduced above: the lifeworldly-contextual, the pragmatic, and the semantic ones. The last is the truth operator. Each of these determiners fixes the status of the sentence in question with respect to determinacy or indeterminacy. When deflationists simply introduce the self-standing sentence p, *without in any way characterizing or qualifying its*

---

[18] Tarski, "The Concept of Truth in Formalized Languages" (1933/1983), 155.

[19] In *Sein und Gott*, note 19 explains its use of "*selbst-ständige*" to qualify *Satz* by noting that the term "self-standing sentence" is commonly used in English.

status, their procedure in so doing is literally meaningless. More is said of this below.

[2] What follows shows, concisely, that linguistic determination on the lifeworldly-contextual level presupposes or is made explicit by linguistic determination on the pragmatic level, and the latter presupposes or is made explicit by linguistic determination on the purely linguistic or explicitly semantic level. Linguistic determination at the purely linguistic or explicitly semantic level, however, neither presupposes nor is made explicit by such determination on either of the other two levels, and linguistic determination on the pragmatic level neither presupposes nor is made explicit by such determination on the lifeworldly-contextual level.

To be at all intelligible, lifeworldly-contextual linguistic determination must be such that the spontaneously uttered sentence *p* has a semantic status that is articulable linguistically-pragmatically. How else could the determination of language on the lifeworldly-contextual level be explained or made explicit? A given spontaneously uttered sentence can be understood only if it is (implicitly) identified as an assertion rather than, say, as a quotation or a pronunciation exercise. This shows that the lifeworldly-contextual level of semantic determination presupposes the linguistically pragmatic level. Briefly, to say that an uttered sentence *p* has lifeworldly-contextual determination is (in the strongest case) to say that *p* has the status of having been asserted.[20]

The next question to arise is analogous to the one considered in the preceding paragraph concerning lifeworldly-contextual linguistic determination: What does it mean to say that a sentence has the semantic status of an assertion? What indeed *is* an assertion? Crispin Wright champions the view that clarification of the truth predicate requires recognition of a series of "platitudes," of which one of the most important is "To assert is to present as true."[21] This formulation stems from Frege, who writes, for example, "In order to put something forward as true, we do not need a special predicate: we only need the assertoric force with which the sentence is uttered."[22] To be sure, this formulation does not contain a direct characterization—much less a definition—of "assertion," but it indirectly articulates how "assertion" is to be understood. And it thereby shows that to assert something is to do something with respect to truth (i.e., to put something forth as true). "Asserted" is thus not equivalent to

---

[20] For the sake of simplicity, only the mode or status of the assertion is considered here.
[21] *Truth and Objectivity* (1992), 34.
[22] Gottlob Frege, "Logic in Mathematics," 233.

"true," or, differently stated, the operators "It is asserted that . . ." and "It
is true that . . ." are neither equivalent nor synonymous.

From this it follows that linguistically pragmatic determination of
language is possible (i.e., here, intelligible) only under the presupposition of the language of truth. Thus, the linguistically pragmatic level of
linguistic determination presupposes or is made explicit by the semantic
level. And this reveals the explicitly semantic level to be fundamental.
The uniquely specific character of explicitly semantic vocabulary is again
to be emphasized: this vocabulary is absolute in the sense that it has no
relation, no relativity (no matter how conceived) to any factors of any
sort that are external to language. By means of semantic vocabulary, language speaks about itself: it qualifies or determines its own items.

3.1.3.2.4 Informal-Intuitive Formulation of the Central Idea of Truth

[1] It is now possible to present a first—still general and informal—formulation of the central idea of truth. *The word "true," understood by way of
its appearance in the operator "It is true that . . . ," accomplishes both the transition of language from an un- or underdetermined status to a fully determined
status and the result of that transition: fully determined language.* This formulation speaks of "language" quite generally; this is not wrong, because
language is ultimately to be understood as a system of sentences, however
this may be understood more precisely. Nevertheless, it is advisable to
opt for a more specific formulation and, instead of speaking so generally of "language," to speak of the so-called truth bearers (proposition,
sentence, utterance). One would then say, for example, that the proposition expressed by a sentence from the chosen language qualifies as true
means that the proposition has accomplished a transition from an un- or
underdetermined status to a fully determined status. The truth-term designates both this process of transition and its result (the latter is considered in greater detail below).

[2] That the truth operator "It is true that" is applied to sentences/
propositions has both a presupposition and a consequence. The presupposition is that arguments of the operator, which is a determiner, are
determinable by it, and thus—as arguments—are less than fully determined. Specifically, the sentence or proposition that is the argument has
an incompletely determined semantic status. The effect of the operator
is that the argument attains a fully determined semantic status.

In several preceding sections, this book uses the concept of the
fully determined status of sentences and propositions (and, generalizing, of language). But how is this central concept to be understood? Responding clearly to this question is a task that is decisive for the project
undertaken here. At this point, it can be said programmatically that the

full determination of a language is the complete articulation of its ontological dimension. Section 3.1.3.3 examines this central topic.

Preliminary clarification is provided by a brief reconsideration of the "disquotation theory" championed by Quine. The thesis that "true/ truth" is a function of disquotation[23] corresponds to the Tarskian truth-schema:

(T)   'p' is true $\leftrightarrow p$.

Despite his general acceptance of this schema, Quine—at least in some of his writings—fully recognizes the ontological dimension of truth. His remarks on this topic are unique in analytic philosophy in that they— possibly despite his own intentions—show with crystal clarity just wherein lies the basic error common to all deflationistically oriented theories of truth. One of the most interesting passages is from his *Philosophy of Logic:*

> Truth hinges on reality; but to object, on this score, to calling sentences true, is a confusion. Where the truth predicate has its utility is in just those places where, though still concerned with reality, we are impelled by certain technical complications to mention sentences. Here the truth predicate serves, as it were, to point through the sentence to the reality; it serves as a reminder that though sentences are mentioned, *reality is still the whole point.*[24]

This highly interesting text contains a magnificent and deeply correct insight and at the same time a fateful error. The correct insight is the thesis, which Quine explicitly formulates and defends, that in the case of the predicate "true," "*reality is still the whole point*"; a few lines before the passage quoted just above the thesis is formulated yet more sharply: "The sentence 'Snow is white' is true, as Tarski has taught us, if and only if *real* snow is *really* white."[25] More generally, truth involves a relation of language to the world, to the ontological dimension.

The error consists in Quine's maintaining that this understanding of truth is the genuinely correct interpretation of Tarski's truth-schema. The understanding of truth that Quine articulates for Tarski's truth-schema is accurate with respect to the issue at hand only if it meets the

---

[23] E.g., "Ascription of truth just cancels the quotation marks. Truth is disquotation" (*Pursuit of Truth* [1990], 80).

[24] W. V. O. Quine, *Philosophy of Logic* (1970), 11.

[25] Ibid.; emphases added.

following condition: this understanding of truth itself must also be articulated or made explicit in the formulation of the Tarskian truth-schema
(such a *minimal* condition must be satisfied by any interpretation that
claims to be genuinely correct). Tarski and Quine, however, fail to satisfy
this condition. The sentence on the right-hand side of the equivalence
symbol meaning "if and only if" (thus, "Snow is white," or "*p*"), without
further qualification (i.e., determination), cannot be taken as a sentence
that says anything about the world. That should be fully clear from what
is said above. But Quine—and with him all truth-deflationists—simply
assumes that this sentence is fully determined in the sense of speaking
fully determinately about the world. It does not do so unless the schema
is altered so as to include the Quinean insight introduced above.

One way this condition can be satisfied is by introducing, on the
right-hand side of the equivalence sign, the operator that Quine, in his
"interpretation," makes explicit: "really." The result would be as follows:

(T′)   It is true that snow is white ↔ **really**: snow is white.
(T″)   "*p*" is true ↔ **really**: *p*.

Another possibility would be the introduction of a special notation on
the basis of a specific convention. Thus, for example, in some of his earlier works the author has printed the sentence on the right-hand side of
the corrected or reinterpreted Tarski-equivalence in boldfaced type to
indicate the *fully determined status* of that sentence and of the proposition
it expresses:

(T‴)   It is true that snow is white ↔ **Snow is white**.
(T⁗)   "*p*" is true ↔ **p**.

Quine's "really" corresponds exactly to the factor that this book terms
fully determined status.

[3] An additional point is important to understanding the historical
context. The error just pointed out in Quine—one often identified in
this book—stems from Tarski himself. His informal characterization of
the intuitive understanding of truth, cited above, is the following: "A true
sentence is one which says that the state of affairs is so and so, and the
state of affairs is *indeed* so and so."[26] The little word "indeed" is the decisive factor in this characterization, because without the "indeed," what
the true sentence is supposed to "say" would be a senseless tautology or

---

[26] Tarski, 155; emphasis added.

repetition of the same formulation (i.e., ". . . says that the state of affairs is so and so, and the state of affairs is so and so"). Tarski's "indeed" articulates the decisive difference between the two sentences and thereby the transition from the unqualified/undetermined sentence "The state of affairs is so and so" to the qualified/determined sentence "The state of affairs is *indeed* so and so." Tarski's "indeed" is the counterpart to Quine's "really." But in his semi-formalized truth-schema, Tarski in no way articulates this decisive factor; he does not make it explicit, despite his claim that the truth-schema articulates correctly and clearly his accurate formulation of the intuitive understanding of truth.[27] This omission by Tarski is the source of the basic error made in all deflationistically oriented truth theories.

3.1.3.3 The Central Idea of Truth II: The Ontological Import of Truth as Identity of Proposition and Fact (Identity Thesis)

It is incontestable that, in the entire history of philosophy, the relation to actuality—to the ontological dimension—has been considered to be an essential constituent of what is true. Throughout that history, the utterly natural articulation of this insight is the correspondence theory of truth (which is still accepted in many philosophical circles). With few exceptions, even the authors who reject this theory do not reject the relation to reality; they see it, if not as intrinsic to truth, at least as an indispensable constituent of talk about truth.

[1] How is the ontological import of truth to be explained precisely? To explain it by means of the traditional correspondence theory of truth is to encounter enormous problems: this theory involves obscurities and difficulties that appear to be insuperable. Here the correspondence theory is not defended, although its basic idea is in a certain respect retained. Considerations of space preclude complete presentation and grounding of the structural-systematic philosophy's conception of truth.

The primary and essential arguments for the operator "It is true that" are propositions expressed by indicative sentences. Thus, the definitions of the truth of the sentence and of the utterance are dependent on the definition of truth of the proposition expressed by the sentence or intended by the utterance. A given sentence is true just when it expresses a true proposition (the true utterance would be explained in comparable fashion, in relation to the true sentence, but that is not con-

---

[27] For additional detail, see Puntel, *GThW* 41ff.

sidered here). But what is a true proposition? The ontological perspective is central to answering this question.

The idea of an "identity" of thinking and Being (reality) has an age-old tradition in philosophy. But this idea has always been rather vague. In 1989 Stewart Candlish used the expression "Identity Theory of Truth" to designate F. H. Bradley's thesis that truth is identical with reality.[28] There ensued an intensive discussion about this expression. It has been asked whether such authors as Hegel, Bradley, Moore, Russell, and Frege, among others, held identity theories of truth.

In 1990 the author of this book introduced an identity *thesis:* a true proposition "*is* nothing other, nothing less and nothing more, than a constituent of the actual world."[29] If one calls the constituents of the world articulated by true propositions "facts," then the true proposition and the fact are one and the same entity. That is an identity thesis with a precise content.

The structural-systematic conception cannot be designated simply an *identity theory of truth,* because the identity (between true proposition and fact) is only one of its aspects. The truth concept therefore cannot simply be identified with this identity thesis. The various identity theories ignore the other aspects, which are, however, essential ingredients of the truth concept.

[2] The identity of true proposition and fact (as worldly entity) can be related to the thought of correspondence. Throughout the history of the correspondence theory, the concept of correspondence has always been understood as a relation between two *non-identical relata;* the structural-systematic theory's identity thesis is *not* a correspondence theory in *this* sense. Instead, the identity thesis completely preserves the indispensable core of the correspondence theory, but without inheriting its problems. This core is the relation to the world as an absolutely essential ingredient of truth. This core is preserved in that identity can be understood as a *limiting case*—one might also say highest or perfect case—of correspondence. That this core is preserved is an invaluable advantage of the structural-systematic truth theory.

[3] Talk of an identity between a true prime proposition and a prime fact (in the sense of a worldly entity) is in one respect quite strange and in another quite illuminating. It is strange because it seems to contradict many ideas often held dear. These are the ideas according to which propositions are strictly mental or ideal entities and facts are worldly enti-

---

[28] The Truth About F. H. Bradley" (1989), 331–38; see especially 338.
[29] Puntel, *GThW* 325.

ties, such that the two belong to two utterly different domains. The identity talk is nonetheless illuminating in that it provides the most precise articulation of truth's relation to the world. The genuine philosophical problems come into view only if one looks more closely. They arise with the question, how is the identity of true proposition and fact-in-the-world to be thought *coherently?*

Authors who defend identity *theories* of truth presuppose the traditional ontology—substance ontology—according to which the world consists of objects, properties, relations, *and* facts. Facts are understood vaguely as states of affairs involving objects, properties, and relations. How these facts are more precisely to be understood is left unexplained. As a rule, "facts" are spoken of in a purely intuitive sense. The presupposed ontology remains utterly opaque. It is thus wholly understandable that within such a framework the question arises whether facts can possibly be entities in the world. Only in quite recent years has analytic philosophy begun to seek an adequate ontology. The search has brought the concepts "state of affairs" and "fact," *within the framework of substance ontology,* radically into question.[30] But the new ontological initiatives have so far had few if any effects on work on theories of truth.

This book cannot consider this issue in detail, but one essential consequence of what is said above requires explicit formulation. *Any truth theory that includes an ontological import remains vague and ultimately incomplete until the ontology on which it relies, or which it presupposes, is made explicit.* The ontology that coheres perfectly with the structural-systematic philosophy's semantic-ontological truth theory is sketched above (3.1.2[3]). That comprehensive ontology is well formulated in the second sentence of Wittgenstein's *Tractatus:* "The world is the totality of facts, not of things."[31] To be sure, the *Tractatus* does not adequately clarify this sentence, whose status is made problematic particularly by Wittgenstein's inclusion, in his ontology, not only of "objects" but of a "substance of the world" formed from these objects.[32] He also writes, "What is the case—a fact—is the subsistence of states of affairs," and "A state of affairs (a state of things) is a combination of objects (things)."[33] Wittgenstein's world as totality of facts is thus a world of objects, properties, and relations that is

---

[30] See, e.g., Dodd, "Farewell to States of Affairs" (1999); and Vallicella, "Three Conceptions of States of Affairs" (2000). For a brief critique of Dodd's position and argumentation, see Puntel, "Truth, Sentential Non-Compositionality, and Ontology" (2001), 253n7; and *Structure and Being,* 233n44.

[31] *Tractatus Logico–Philosophicus,* 1.1.

[32] Ibid., 3.021.

[33] Ibid., 2.01.

expanded to include facts or states of affairs. What Wittgenstein calls "objects" are what, in the tradition, fall under the category *substance* in the sense of *substratum*. The unacceptability of ontologies including this category is shown above. Nevertheless, Wittgenstein's famous sentence—if understood differently from the way he understood it—serves as a good formulation of the ontology that coheres most tightly with the structural-systematic philosophy's theory of truth.

3.1.3.3a Excursus 1: A Sketch of a Semi-Formalized Presentation of the Central Idea of Truth

[1] The structural-systematic account has in one respect a certain similarity to the *prosentential theory of truth* initially developed by Dorothy Grover, J. I. Camp, Jr., and Nuel Belnap[34] (1975), and modified by Robert Brandom (1994). The central idea of this theory is that "true" is not a predicate, but a fragment of a prosentence. The prosentence is analogous to the pronoun—to a term that has an *anaphoric* relation to another (already used) term, its antecedent. Those who hold this theory rely on what they call the deep structure of language. Sentences containing the truth-term (in any of its various forms) are interpreted as sentences referring back to sentences that have already appeared (generally without the truth-term). Linguistically viewed, these authors contend, every occurrence of the truth-term has the form "That is true," i.e., the form of a prosentence whose sole meaning and function are to refer to a sentence that has already appeared. According to this anaphoric conception, the famous example "'Snow is white' is true" is analyzed as "Consider: snow is white. That is true."[35]

Robert Brandom has made this conception significantly simpler and more intelligible by interpreting ". . . is true" not as a syncategorematic fragment of a semantically atomic sentence, but instead as a prosentence-forming operator:

> [This operator] applies to a term that is a sentence nominalization or that refers to or picks out a sentence tokening. It yields a prosentence that has that tokening as its anaphoric antecedent.[36]

The prosentence generated by the operator has an *anaphoric character:* it points back to or retrieves the sentence that is the argument of the

---

[34] "A Prosentential Theory of Truth."
[35] Ibid., 100.
[36] Robert Brandom, *Making It Explicit* (1994), 305.

operator. It thus holds that "It is true that snow is white" is a prosentence whose status consists in its retrieving the sentence—presupposed already to have appeared—"Snow is white." In addition to being anaphoric, Brandom's theory is deflationary: "'It is true that snow is white' expresses just the same fact that 'snow is white' expresses."[37]

In opposition to Brandom, the structural-systematic theory of truth is *cataphoric*. Καταφορά is the conceptual counterpart to ἀναφορά, but the two conceptions share one fundamental element, which makes the difference the more apparent. Common to the two is the assumption that the truth-term is not a predicate but an operator. According to the structural-systematic conception, however, what this operator initially forms are not *pro*sentences, but what may be termed *per*sentences. The artificial term "persentence" is formed from the Latin "*perficere*" (to finish, to accomplish, to perfect, to determine fully). The "per" in "persentence" is to be understood as abbreviating the gerundive form; "persentence" is then "*sententia perficienda*," "sentence to be completed or perfected."

[2] When all the points made thus far are taken into consideration, the truth operator—T—appears as a *composite* (three-step) function. Symbols for the three functions are, respectively, T^*, T^+, and $T^\times$. The truth concept is then formalized as follows:

(TC) $T = T^\times \circ T^+ \circ T^*$

The function T^* is precisely defined as follows:

(T_1) $T^* : X \longrightarrow Y$
$T^* : p \mapsto p_{PER} \in Y$

(where "X" is the set of unqualified/undetermined sentences or propositions "p" to which the operator "it is true that" is applied, and "Y," the set of persentences or perpropositions "p_{PER}" resulting from the application of the operator).

The function T^+ is precisely defined as follows:

(T_2) $T^+ : Y \longrightarrow \mathbf{Z}$
$T^+ : p_{PER} \mapsto \mathbf{p} \in \mathbf{Z}$

(where "Y" is the set of persentences or perpropositions "p_{PER}" and "$\mathbf{Z}$" the set, which results *cataphorically* from the persentences or perpropositions, of fully semantically determined sentences or propositions "$\mathbf{p}$").

---

[37] Ibid., 328.

As shown above, the functions T* and T+ do not accomplish the full explanation of the truth concept. To them must be added the identity thesis as a third function, indeed the most important and decisive one. It is as follows:

(T_3) $\quad$ $T^{\times} : \mathbf{Z} \longrightarrow \mathbf{F}$
$\qquad$ $T^{\times} : \mathbf{p} \mapsto \mathbf{f} \in \mathbf{F}$

Here, "$\mathbf{Z}$" is the set of fully semantically determined sentences or propositions and "$\mathbf{F}$" the set of facts, such that

$$\forall \mathbf{p} \in \mathbf{Z}, \forall \mathbf{f} \in \mathbf{F}(\mathbf{f} = T^{\times}(\mathbf{p}) \leftrightarrow \mathbf{p} = \mathbf{f})$$

3.2 The Unrestricted Universe of Discourse as the Universal Dimension of Primordial Being

With the fully determined structural-systematic theoretical framework in place, the tasks can be undertaken of developing philosophical theories not only about every single entity, every single domain of entities, about anything and everything in the unrestricted universe of discourse,[c] but also about the unrestricted universe of discourse as such and as a whole. This book undertakes only the last of these tasks, and develops no more than an outline. The theoretical framework within which these tasks are undertaken is nothing like a restrictive theoretical corset; instead, it allows methodological and systematic access to the immense domain of all of the human capabilities for theorization.

3.2.1 Three Ways of Disclosing the Universal Dimension of Being

This section first clarifies the task of developing a theory of the unrestricted universe of discourse as such and as a whole. The more precise—the more determinate—designation for this theory is *theory of Being as such and as a whole*. The first step consists in more precisely determining

---

[c] As indicated by the quasi-definition introduced above (3.1.1[1]), the structural-systematic philosophy is a theory of the universal structures of the unrestricted universe of discourse; it therefore develops theories "about every single entity, every single domain of entities, about anything and everything" only in that its theories of the universal structures explain the structures of all entities, domains, etc. Concerning how this theory relates to the natural sciences, see *Structure and Being* 4.2.1–4.2.2.

the subject matter of this theory. This is the task of disclosing the universal dimension of Being. This task is accomplished by means of the provision of descriptions of three ways that are three aspects of a single, comprehensive state of affairs.

3.2.1.1 The First Way: The Universal Dimension of Being as the "It" of the Theoretical Operator or as the Dimension Presupposed and Articulated by Every Theoretical Sentence

The way that in a certain manner is the most immediate and elegant consists of a deeper analysis of the structure of the theoretical sentence, a structure introduced above in section 3.1.1[4]. Every theoretical sentence has the structure "$\mathbb{T}\phi$: It is the case that ϕ." The task here is to interpret the "It" of this operator.

[1] The operator "It is the case that" is the absolutely universal theoretical operator; it is subjected to no restriction of any sort. Its significance for philosophy extends far beyond its function of making explicit the theoretical status of sentences. More precisely, its genuine significance consists precisely in the following: it indicates the entire scope or range of sentences whose status is theoretical. And this scope or range is absolutely comprehensive. Showing that this is so requires moving beyond purely grammatical analyses, but such analyses are where this showing must start.

This "It" in such formulations as "It is the case that . . ." is classified as a pronoun and more precisely as an expletive, that is, as a pronoun with either an unclear semantic role or no semantic role at all. The standard reference book *Duden: Die Grammatik* clarifies the role of the "it" as the subject of impersonal verbs as follows:

> "Impersonal" is a traditional designation for verbs (verb variants) that require either no subject or, as subject, the pronoun "it," but that ascribe to that subject no clear semantic role. Only the third-person singular pronoun satisfies the latter requirement. Because the pronoun *it,* as subject of impersonal verbs, has no indicative function, it is also called a pseudo-argument [of a verb] (a formal subject).[38]

The most common examples for such impersonal verbs are ones relating to weather, in such forms as "raining" and "snowing." In German,

---

[38] *Duden: Die Grammatik* (2005), no. 560, p. 413. [Added to *Being and God:* the *Oxford English Dictionary* includes the following in its entry for "it": "As the subject of an impersonal verb or impersonal statement, expressing action or a condition of things simply, without reference to any agent."]

impersonal verbs requiring the pseudo-argument (or pseudo-subject) "it" include "in the nominative, also some abstract, commonly used verbs that require at least some further supplementation."[39] Among the examples *Duden* introduces are "*Jetzt* gilt es [*schnell zu handeln*]" ["Now *it comes* (to acting quickly)," or "Now *it takes* (acting quickly)"]; "[*Um deinen Führerschein*] geht es *hoffentlich nicht*" ["Hopefully *it won't mean* (that you lose your driver's license)"]; "*Hier* handelt/dreht es *sich* [*um einen Serienmörder*]" ["Here *it's a matter* (of a serial killer)"]. The last example is the one most similar to the formulation of the theoretical operator "it is the case that," but even it remains importantly distinct. The theoretical operator is an absolutely singular case whose grammar can be explained in various ways, but whose full explanation is philosophical rather than grammatical. Providing the philosophical explanation is the task undertaken in what follows.

The second passage cited above from the *Duden* grammar book speaks of verbs that "in the nominative . . . require at least some further supplementation." The theoretical operator, *as* an operator, also requires supplementation, but of a specific sort. The required supplement is simply the argument (in the sense of the formal sciences) that falls within the scope of the operator and is determined or qualified by it. This argument is a *sentence* and, within the structural-systematic philosophy, a *prime sentence,* whether simple or complex (complex prime sentences are configurations of simple or complex prime sentences). Because prime sentences are defined—negatively—as not being of the subject-predicate form, in the prime sentence (for example) "it's redding," "it" cannot be a subject, and "is redding" cannot be a predicate.

To bring into view the entire problematic of cases where the theoretical operator governs prime sentences, it is vital to note that the *complete* sentences constituting such cases always contain *two* instances of "it": one in the prime sentence that is the argument, and the other in the operator. This is evident in the example, "*It* is the case that *it*'s redding." Neither "it" functions as a genuine subject.[d] The two appearances of "it" are alike in one way but different in another, as formalization easily shows. How they are alike is in one respect negative and in another positive. The negative commonality is that neither can be formalized by means of predicate logic. The prime sentence "It's redding" cannot be symbolized as "Fx"; instead, because it is a prime sentence, its formaliza-

---

[39] Ibid., no. 562, p. 413. [Added to *Being and God:* from the *Oxford English Dictionary* entry for "it": "In statements of condition, welfare, course of life, and the like; as *It has fared badly with the soldiers; How is it in the city? It will soon come to a rupture between them; It is all over with poor Jack; It is very pleasant here.*"]

[d] There is no antecedent for either "it"; this shows that neither is a genuine pronoun.

tion requires a sentence variable or constant, such as ϕ. The positive commonality is that "It is the case that," like any prime sentence "It's F-ing," can be formalized only by a single symbol—above, $\textcircled{T}$ for the operator and ϕ for a prime sentence—hence not by multiple symbols that would have distinct interpretations.[e] Grammatically, each of these components is a clause, one being independent and the other dependent, but grammar does not determine which of the two is of which sort.[40,41] This point alone suffices to show the insufficiency of grammatical analysis; it therefore requires philosophical elaboration.

[2] Following the preceding excursus concerning grammatical aspects and problems relating to the formulation of the theoretical operator "It is the case that," it is possible and appropriate, on the basis of the now-clarified linguistic situation, to develop a genuinely philosophical interpretation of the "it" that is included in the operator. The thesis at the core of this interpretation is the following: the operator's "it" is not a subject of the sort found in sentences with the subject-predicate structure, but it is nevertheless a general indication of a dimension indirectly articulated in *all* theoretical sentences; this dimension is the unrestricted universe of discourse that, more precisely determined, is the primordial dimension of Being.

The grounding of this thesis consists in a simple analysis of the structure of theoretical sentences with respect to their presuppositions and implications. The simple prime sentence "It's redding" serves as an example. It is evident that the "it" does not indicate an object or anything similar; it does, however, indicate something generally determinate, that is, the spatiotemporal location wherein it says that redding is ongoing. The meaning of the prime sentence, so interpreted, is: redding is happening here and now.[42] Once this is articulated, however, the prime sen-

---

[e] That prime sentences can be formalized only by single symbols is one reason for terming them *prime* sentences, although the sense of the qualifier is more evident in the German "*Primsatz*" than in the English "prime sentence." The reason is that whereas the English adjective "prime" has a wide variety of uses, the German prefix "*prim-*" appears predominantly in "*Primzahl*," "prime number." Prime sentences are comparable to prime numbers in the following respect: just as prime sentences can be formalized only by means of single symbols (as indicated in the main text), prime numbers can be written as products of no integers other than themselves and one (e.g., "$7 = 7 \times 1$")—so that writing a prime number as a product does not analyze the number into distinct integral components (as is the case, e.g., in "$6 = 2 \times 3$"), but instead only makes explicit that it is itself, as a unit.

[40, 41] Notes 40 and 41 in *Sein und Gott* are about German usage and are not relevant to *Being and God*.

[42] Here, it would be wrong to say: (something) is redding (here and now), if the (something redding) were understood in the sense of an object that would have the property "is

tence is linked to other—and in principle all (actual and possible)—
spatiotemporal locations wherein it's redding. Generalizing: the prime
sentence is indirectly linked to the entire dimension of reddings.

Philosophically, one can and indeed must take an additional step
by noting that the prime sentence "It's redding" is linked to every other
dimension—again, both actual and possible—in that those other dimensions are *not* dimensions of reddings. How far does this extend? In principle, and on the basis of a scrupulous and detailed analysis, it extends
to the absolutely universal dimension. An interesting variant of this procedure is introduced below as the third way to the disclosure of the dimension of Being.

At this point, the further analysis of the simple prime sentence "It's
redding" can be undertaken in a different manner, one that is concise
and is not complicated. This manner analyzes and fully explains the example prime sentence—which is a stand-in for every simple prime sentence—as a theoretical sentence. The explicit form of the example is
then "It_1-is-the-case-that it_2's redding." The two appearances of "it" are
indexed. "It_2" clearly indicates a specific spatiotemporal location: the one
wherein it's redding. But "it_1" is an indication of a fully different sort: it
indicates the absolutely universal dimension of the unrestricted universe
of discourse. This is briefly shown as follows: in contrast to it_2, which immediately indicates a specific spatiotemporal location, it_1, the meta-it,
does not relate to anything determinate, specific, or restricted, because
it is open to every prime sentence that can be governed by the theoretical
operator, and that is of course every prime sentence. It_1 thus discloses the
unrestricted space of theoretical articulation *simpliciter.* It_1 indicates the
absolutely universal dimension.

How can or must this dimension be designated? According to the
structural-systematic philosophy, the absolutely universal dimension of
theoretical articulation is the *dimension of primordial Being.* "Primordial"
qualifies "Being" here because the "Being" in question is not the "objective Being" that, at the beginning of the presentation of the structural-
systematic philosophy, is the counterpole to the dimension of structure
(see 3.2.1.3, below). This thesis is grounded by the following analysis: the
absolutely universal dimension that is indicated by the "it_1" of the theoretical operator that can precede every indicative sentence encompasses
all particular and individual cases within the unrestricted universe of discourse. For this reason, the following question presses: how are these

---

redding." Neither the prime sentence "it's redding" nor the prime proposition it expresses
in any way includes or implies any substance ontology.

cases interrelated? As the following section shows, they are interrelated in infinitely many ways of infinitely many kinds.

Is there, however, one factor that is shared not only by some or all of these cases, but instead is common to absolutely all? There must be one, for otherwise one could not speak of these cases—and thus of all cases—within the unrestricted universe of discourse. What then is this ultimate commonality, the one shared by all cases? There are various factors that are common to all cases of the articulable, for example, universal expressibility. But these factors depend on a deeper, more primordial commonality. This consists in the following: all of these cases *are*, and are thus modes of the commonality on which all other commonalities depend, that is, all are modes *of Being*. To oppose this thesis, one would have to identify a deeper or more primordial commonality. But given that Being here includes possible as well as actual Being, no such identification appears to be possible.

What this simple analysis yields is that the simple use of the theoretical operator in the case even of the simplest and most modest indicative sentence discloses and explicates the universal dimension, the dimension of primordial Being.

3.2.1.2 The Second Way: The Intentional Coextensionality of the Human Mind with the Unrestricted Universe of Discourse ("Anima Quodammodo Omnia")

The second way is inspired by a traditional thought that it thoroughly rethinks, thereby both in part correcting it and more adequately articulating it. This way is direct in that it consists in the recognition and description of one of the most central structural aspects of the human mind. This structural aspect is the intentional coextensionality of the human mind with the unrestricted universe of discourse.

Aristotle formulated this thought as the thesis, ἡ ψυχή τὰ ὄντα πώς ἐστι πάντα (literal translation: "The soul [the mind] is in a certain way all [beings]").[43] In the Latin-speaking metaphysical tradition the thesis became a kind of axiom: *anima (est) quodammodo omnia*. The immense consequentiality of this often-used thesis has in no way been adequately understood or appreciated. The phrase "in a certain way" can be interpreted to mean "intentionally." The meaning of the Aristotelian thesis could then be expressed as follows: "The mind is intentionally coextensive with the totality of beings." Aristotle speaks only of beings, not of Being. Because he does so, his version of the thesis could be introduced

---

[43] *De anima* Γ431b21.

as evidence in support of the correctness of Heidegger's interpretation and critique of metaphysics, according to which metaphysics considers only beings, and not Being. But one can go beyond Aristotle and also beyond talk of "all beings" or "the totality of beings." One does so by speaking instead of Being, and indeed of Being as such and as a whole.

The intentional coextensivity of the mind with Being as such and as a whole is a central aspect of the human mind. It is not the case that the human mind is this or that and that it then somehow transcends the this or that and thereby reaches Being itself. If it makes sense to speak of transcendence in this case, one would have to say that the human mind *is* this transcendence *itself*. Heidegger grasped and articulated this state of affairs wholly correctly and adequately, as shown in chapter 2 (see 2.2[3]) and more fully explained below. One can nevertheless speak of a transcendence here, but only in a relative sense, insofar as one attends to the fact that the human mind can start by considering individual beings, gradually expand its scope by considering additional beings in increasingly complex configurations, and ultimately thematize the configuration of all configurations, i.e., the dimension of Being itself. The third way to the disclosure of the dimension of Being involves such a process. That this process can take place at all, however, presupposes that the human mind is always already at its end point.

Aquinas treats this topic in a way that is at best partially adequate in that he explicitly speaks of a primordial relation of the human mind (or, as he says, the human intellect) to the entire domain of beings (*ens*). This is shown by his thesis, constantly repeated with only insignificant variations, that "what first falls into the intellect is being (*ens*),"[44] or that "being [*ens*] . . . is what the intellect first conceives of as what it knows best and into which it resolves all that it conceives of, as Avicenna says at the beginning of his *Metaphysics*."[45] Chapter 1 shows, however, that Aquinas nonetheless does reach Being/*esse*, as he understands it. This makes it clear that one must be cautious in speaking about Aquinas on this topic.

A wholly different but likewise famous version of this thesis, one that also serves as epigraph to this book, is provided by Pascal. It articulates what comes down to the same basic thought, but in a wholly different manner that is, for just that reason, particularly illuminating. In his *Pensées*, he writes, "Know . . . , proud man, what a paradox you are

---

[44] "Primum . . . quod in intellectum cadit, est ens." *De pot.* q. 9 a. 7 ad decimumquintum.

[45] "Illud . . . quod primo intellectus concipit quasi notissimum, et in quo omnes conceptiones resolvit, est ens, ut Avicenna dicit in principio Metaphysicae suae" (*De ver.* bk. I c. ix).

to yourself. Be humble, impotent reason! Be silent, feeble nature! *Learn that man infinitely transcends man.*"[46]

It is highly noteworthy that Pascal turns to human beings in calling their reason impotent and their nature feeble, but at the same time ascribes to them the most beautiful and deepest accomplishment that can be ascribed to them, that is, that they infinitely transcend themselves. It is wholly clear that the two appearances of "man" in the sentence "man infinitely transcends man" are not synonymous. That this is so can be indicated by the addition of indices, substituting "man_1" for the first appearance and "man_2" for the second. With the aid of these terms, the following thesis, important at this point in the presentation, can be introduced: there is meaningful transcendence only concerning man_2; it is senseless to speak of any sort of transcendence concerning man_1. Transcendence thus has only a relative meaning, not an absolute one; it is meaningful in some respects but not in all.

Superficially understood, the thesis just introduced might appear to have the highly consequential implication perhaps best known through the famous *homo-mensura* dictum ascribed to Protagoras. "He [Protagoras] says somewhere that man is the measure of all things."[47] But Pascal's thesis does not have this implication, as shown in what follows. That it does not becomes clear with the formulation of a second thesis, one that *is* implied by the first. What it articulates is diametrically opposed to what the *homo-mensura* dictum does: the dimension of man_1 that cannot be transcended is the dimension of the intentional coextensivity of the human mind and thus of human thought with the unrestricted universe of discourse, whereby the latter is the universal dimension of Being *simpliciter.* This non-transcendable coextensivity does not exclude a relation to human beings, but does show that the concrete human being—specifically, man_2—must be considered from the perspective of the universal dimension of Being. Differently stated: it implies a radical change of perspective. It is not the case that the universal dimension of Being is considered from or determined by the human perspective; instead, only from the universal perspective are human beings determined as what they truly are.

Another philosopher—and in a certain respect the most important—who traverses the second way to the disclosure of the dimension of Being was Heidegger, in *Being and Time.* Chapter 2 (section 2.2) describes the four approaches he undertook in attempting to retrieve and

---

[46] Blaise Pascal, *Pensées,* trans. A. J. Krailsheimer (New York: Penguin Books, 1995), 35 (emphasis added).

[47] Φησὶ [Πρωταγόρος] γὰρ του "πάντων χρημάτων μέτρον" ἄνθρωπον εἶναι, "τῶν μὲν ὄντων ὡς ἔστι, τῶν δὲ μὴ ὄντων ὡς οὐκ ἔστιν." Plato, *Theaetetus* 152a.

clarify the question of Being. Relevant in the current context is the third approach, which he presented chiefly in *Being and Time*. There, the understanding of Being appears as a central constituent of Dasein (hence, of human Being), as the following passage makes explicit:

> Dasein is a being that does not just appear among other beings. Rather, it is ontically distinguished by the fact that, in its very Being, that Being is an *issue* for it. But in that case, this is a constitutive state of Dasein's Being, and this implies that Dasein, in its Being, has a relationship to that Being—a relationship that itself is one of Being. And this means further that there is some way in which Dasein understands itself in its Being, and that to some degree it does so explicitly. It is peculiar to this being that with and through its Being, this Being is disclosed to it. *Understanding of Being is itself a definite characteristic of* Dasein's *Being*. Dasein is ontically distinctive in that it *is* ontologically. (*BT* §4, p. 32)

To the penultimate sentence in this passage Heidegger added, in the copy of *Being and Time* he himself used, the following richly consequential marginal note:

> Here, however, Being not as Being of humans (existence). That is clear from what follows. Being-in-the-world includes *within itself* the relation of existence to Being as a whole: the understanding of Being." (*SZ* §4, note a to page 16)

3.2.1.3 The Third Way: The Configuration of Configurations or the Most Comprehensive Configuration as the Absolutely Universal Dimension of Primordial Being

The third way to the disclosure of the dimension of Being is, unlike the first two, emphatically *contentually* determined. It is an ascent, a move from below to above. It does not begin with the famous question of Being; it neither presupposes nor investigates nor analyzes any specific meaning of the word "being." Instead, that term is introduced at a specific point in the course of the contentually analytical and ascending procedure as appropriately designating the state of affairs the procedure has disclosed.

The procedure ascends from simple beings (simple prime facts, thus simple ontological structures) through levels of increasingly complex prime facts—increasingly complex structures, thus increasingly complex configurations—until it reaches the most comprehensive structure or the most comprehensive configuration.

The following diagram serves as outline of this ascent as well as for the additional steps taken by the structural-systematic theory of Being.

The Architectonic of the Structural-Systematic Theory of Being

Absolutely Universal Configuration:
Primordial Dimension of Being

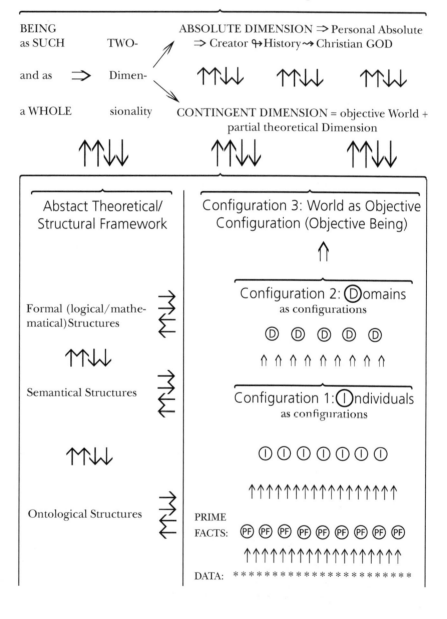

BEING
as SUCH

and as

a WHOLE

TWO-

Dimen-

sionality

ABSOLUTE DIMENSION ⇒ Personal Absolute
⇒ Creator ↬ History ↝ Christian GOD

CONTINGENT DIMENSION = objective World +
partial theoretical Dimension

Abstact Theoretical/
Structural Framework

Formal (logical/mathe-
matical) Structures

Semantical Structures

Ontological Structures

Configuration 3: World as Objective
Configuration (Objective Being)

Configuration 2: Ⓓomains
as configurations

Ⓓ Ⓓ Ⓓ Ⓓ Ⓓ

Configuration 1: Ⓘndividuals
as configurations

Ⓘ Ⓘ Ⓘ Ⓘ Ⓘ Ⓘ Ⓘ

PRIME
FACTS: ⒫Ⓕ ⒫Ⓕ ⒫Ⓕ ⒫Ⓕ ⒫Ⓕ ⒫Ⓕ ⒫Ⓕ ⒫Ⓕ ⒫Ⓕ

DATA: *

In order to disclose the dimension of primordial Being, no more is required than a concise characterization of the ontological macrostructure of the actual world—the pole that is objective in the relation between the abstract theoretical framework or dimension of abstract structures and the universe of discourse.[f]

The starting point is provided by the *data* in the technical sense explained above. In a first step, these data are prime sentences expressing prime propositions that, if true, are prime facts in the actual world. Prime facts, including simple ones, are ontological structures.[48] The simplest ontological structures are the prime facts that are not configurations. As such, taken in isolation, they are abstractions. Complex prime facts—complex ontological structures—are configurations of prime facts. For purposes of the ascent that is under way, sufficient as the next step is the step to robust individuals such as animals and human beings. Such individuals are highly complex configurations of prime facts. This step is to the level identified on the diagram as that of configuration 1.

Individuals are embedded in more comprehensive configurations. They are embedded within nature and hence related to all its phenomena, but they are also embedded within configurations including other members of their species. Together with those other members, they constitute domains. The level where configurations that constitute and define domains are located is identified on the diagram as that of configuration 2.

There are a great many domains. All of these domains relate to one another; as a consequence, together they constitute a domain that constitutes and defines the actual world. The world is the comprehensive *objective configuration* of *everything* included at any level traversed in the ascent to it. On the diagram, its level is identified as that of configuration 3.

The level of configuration 3 is a point that, for the purposes of this book, is both simply central and decisive, because this is the point at which the following question arises: what is the relation between the two dimensions—the dimension of the (abstract) theoretical framework, and the dimension of the world? To say that theoreticians apply the structures to the world (to its domains, individuals, etc.) in order to understand it is not to provide an adequate answer, because it begs a new question: how

---

[f] One aspect of the structural-systematic theory of being not shown on the diagram is its inclusion of merely possible worlds, false prime propositions being identical to prime facts in such worlds. See *Structure and Being,* chapter 3 (section 3.3.4.1) and chapter 5 (section 5.2.3).

[48] For detailed explanation, see *Structure and Being,* chapter 3 (especially section 3.2.3.2).

is this "application" itself possible, and how is it to be understood? It is clear that it is possible only if there is a tight connection between the two, indeed a unity of the two. But how is this connection, this unity of the abstract theoretical framework or dimension of abstract structures and the dimension of the world, to be understood?

It is revealing to note that this question is never raised in analytic philosophy; indeed, analytic philosophy develops all its theories on the basis of the *distinction* between the two dimensions, without considering the distinction or difference itself. It is therefore puzzling that most analytic philosophers hold that the human mind is reducible to the physical, because such reductions make of what this book designates the theoretical dimension—which is often called the mental or ideal dimension, the dimension of thinking, etc.—simply a physical piece of the world. Such reductions do relate and indeed unify mind and world, but they do so in a way that both ignores and cannot explain or even articulate the fact that the mind intentionally *encompasses* the entire world, that it is intentionally coextensive with the entire world. But this matter is not further considered here.

At this point it is important to recall Heidegger's second approach to or way of disclosing the dimension of Being, presented above in chapter 2. Criticizing Husserl's transcendental-phenomenological position, Heidegger shows that there is a dimension encompassing both *constituting* transcendental-phenomenological subjectivity and the *constituted* dimension of the datum or of data; he calls the encompassing dimension *Being*. "The problem of Being relates universally to what constitutes and what is constituted."[49] This book usually calls the first of the dimensions in question that of abstract theoretical structures and the second—initially but not ultimately—that of the unrestricted universe of discourse. The two are interrelated within a meta-dimension that encompasses both and makes possible their interrelation.

This meta-dimension is designated *the dimension of Being*. "Being" here—as in the Heidegger passage quoted just above—is not objective Being, but instead primordial Being, Being that encompasses both of the two subdimensions. Introduction of the term "Being" thus does not introduce any new meaning; the term is used only to designate what has emerged from the ascent undertaken in this section. What has emerged is *the absolutely universal configuration*, or *the most comprehensive configuration*. Yet differently put: this absolutely universal or primordial dimension is the unity of the theoretical dimension and the objective world.

---

[49] *Husserliana*, vol. 9 (1962), *Anlage* 1, 601–2 (emphasis added).

Everything that is imaginable, conceivable, that can be thematized, etc., is within this comprehensive dimension.

To make clear how richly consequential this thesis is, it is particularly important to clarify the relation between Being and existence. As is well known, in the history of philosophy, above all in the metaphysical tradition, the terms/concepts Being and existence are sometimes used interchangeably, but sometimes not. This issue is not further considered here.[50] In the structural-systematic philosophy, there is a strict distinction between the two. "Existence" is incomparably narrower than is "Being." "Existence" always designates something in the world, in the objective dimension; "existence" is thus synonymous with "objective Being." To exist is to be a constituent of the world, the objective dimension. In the metaphysical tradition "existence" is often and indeed usually used to designate the status of things insofar as they are independent of mind or intellect, hence as mind-independent. In contrast—as indicated above— "Being" here designates the universal dimension that encompasses both the dimension of objective Being, hence the world, and the dimension of intellect/mind (along with all that belongs to that dimension). It would therefore be absolutely senseless and absurd to ask whether this universal dimension exists. From this it also becomes clear that the question so often posed and considered of whether God exists is extremely unclear and misleading.

3.2.2 The Most Comprehensive Subject Matter for Philosophy: The Absolutely Universal Dimension of Being as the Dimension of Being as Such and as a Whole

With the disclosure of the universal dimension of primordial Being a decisive step is taken, but not one with which philosophizing reaches its end, because with that step emerges a new task: developing a theory whose subject matter is this universal dimension itself. This is a task often tackled throughout the history of philosophy, and one that requires tackling at present. As shown in chapter 2, Heidegger recognized—unlike his contemporaries and more recent predecessors—both that there is such a task and that philosophy must undertake it, but in his own undertaking of it he relied on wholly inadequate means of theorization and did not manage to produce any acceptable results. The account that follows summarizes the systematic presentation available in *Structure and Being* (section 5.2).

---

[50] See, e.g., A. Keller, *Sein oder Existenz? Die Auslegung des Seins bei Thomas von Aquin und in der heutigen Scholastik* (1968).

The task of this section is to show that the absolutely universal dimension is more precisely designated the dimension of Being as such *and as a whole*. Worth noting is that "dimension" is used as an initial rather than a final way of clarifying Being. It is not used as a clearly defined technical term.

[1] The next question to answer is whether the primordial, comprehensive unity or dimension qualifies as an explicit subject matter for philosophical theorization. The structural-systematic philosophy answers that its theorization is not only possible, it is indispensable. The reason is that theorizing it is among the capabilities of the human mind. To declare in advance that such theorization is futile would be a dogmatic abdication. Determining how successful its theorization can be requires that its theorization be undertaken.

In the history of philosophy, the universal dimension, the dimension of Being, has been designated in various ways, but the dimension has not been clarified in exactly the way it is clarified above. For the most part, the dimension has been understood to be objective in some significant sense; the approach taken here is more radical and comprehensive, in that it understands and *explicitly* thematizes the dimension of primordial Being as the primordial and absolutely comprehensive unity of the mental dimension—the linguistic-logical-conceptual-semantic or theoretical/structural dimension—and the dimension of the world as that of *objective* Being.

[i] This book cannot consider in detail the extraordinarily long and complex history of treatments of the dimension of Being. For present purposes, a brief remark about the current situation suffices. At present, two ways of thinking about this dimension are in evidence. One attends to the metaphysical tradition, but takes its bearings by situating itself—negatively or positively—in relation to Heidegger's thinking of Being. Chapter 2 characterizes this way of thinking thoroughly, so it need not be considered here.

[ii] The other way of treating the dimension of Being is that of analytic philosophy. Analytic ontology as it is done today cannot be designated a philosophy of Being; it is a philosophy of beings or of *domains* of beings. It treats specific topics, but does not pose the question of Being as that question is understood in this book. The following account shows that this is so in two exemplary cases.

[a] Quine, whose influence on analytic philosophy is immense, writes the following:

> It has been fairly common in philosophy early and late to distinguish between being, as the broadest concept, and existence, as narrower.

> This is no distinction of mine; I mean "exists" to cover all there is, and
> such of course is the force of the quantifier.[51]

Having thus identified existence and being, he writes the following about
existence (and hence about being as well):

> Existence is what existential quantification expresses. There are things
> of kind F if and only if $(\exists x)Fx$. This is as unhelpful as it is undebatable,
> since it is how one explains the symbolic notation of quantification to
> begin with. *The fact is that it is unreasonable to ask for an explication of exis-*
> *tence in simpler terms.* We found an explanation of singular existence,
> "a exists," as "$(\exists x)(x=a)$"; but explication in turn of the existential
> quantifier itself, "there is," "there are," explication of general existence,
> *is a forlorn cause.*[52]

Quine's "explication" is clearly circular: "existence" is explained by means
of the existential quantifier, but the quantifier is itself understood or
interpreted by means of "existence." Moreover, Quine simply maintains
that it is a *fact* (!) that it would be "unreasonable to ask for an explication of existence in simpler terms." This may be the case, but even if it is,
it is also the case that explications need not involve simpler terms; they
can instead involve situating terms or concepts to be explicated within
one or more of the broader semantic-ontological fields within which
they belong. Quine fails even to consider such fields. The claim that asking about "general existence" is a "forlorn cause" is thus arbitrary and
dogmatic.

The second position to be considered here is that of one of the
best-known analytic ontologists: Peter van Inwagen. In a review of the
book *The Four-Category Ontology: A Metaphysical Foundation for Natural
Science* (2006) by E. J. Lowe, another analytic ontologist, van Inwagen
writes the following:

> He [Lowe] has nothing to say about what being is, about what it is for
> something to be or exist. . . . (. . . I would insist that the question "What
> is being" has to come into philosophy somewhere, and ontology looks
> like a good home for it).[53]

---

[51] W. V. O. Quine, *Ontological Relativity and Other Essays* (1980), 139.
[52] Ibid., 135 (emphasis added).
[53] *Times Literary Supplement*, January 12, 2007, p. 22.

This appears at first glance to be a promising and programmatic step to suggest, but it appears quite otherwise when one discovers the kind of answer van Inwagen himself provides for it. If the approach to the question taken in this book is meaningful, then van Inwagen's answer to his question has nothing to contribute to it, because he reduces the question to other, incomparably less ambitious questions that arise when one asks about how the terms "existence" and "being" are used. This is clear from analysis of the central theses in his article "Being, Existence, and Ontological Commitment,"[54] published in 2009. This article is a kind of summary of the conception van Inwagen presents in many ways in many other articles. He explains:

> The meta-ontology presented in this essay is essentially Quine's. I present it as a series of five theses. . . .
> *Thesis 1. Being is not an activity.*[55]

It is not clear just what this thesis is supposed to say. If being were an "activity," it appears, it would be "the most general activity [any being] engages in." The thesis appears to be that being cannot be identified with such an activity. Van Inwagen appears to reject any distinction between the being of a thing and its nature; he follows J. L. Austin in asserting, "One cannot, of course, engage in this most general activity (supposing there to be such a thing) unless one *is*."[56] This clarifies nothing, because it leaves open the question of what "is" means.

"*Thesis 2. Being is the same as existence.*"[g] This is indeed one of Quine's central theses.

"*Thesis 3. Existence is univocal.*"[h] The word "existence" always and everywhere has the same meaning.

"*Thesis 4. The single sense of being or existence is adequately captured by the quantifier of formal logic.*"[i] This is the most central thesis of Quine's ontology.

Van Inwagen's fifth thesis is a global one he describes as "a set of interrelated theses—all pertaining to what Quine has called 'ontological commitment'—about how one should settle philosophical disputes

---

[54] In D. J. Chalmers, D. Manley, and R. Wasserman, eds., *Metametaphysics: New Essays on the Foundations of Ontology* (2009), 472–506.

[55] Ibid., 475.

[56] Ibid., 476.

[g] Ibid., 480.

[h] Ibid., 482.

[i] Ibid., 492.

about what there is."[j] One should, according to van Inwagen, follow rules derived from the ontological implications of the quantified sentences found in a given theory; these, for their part, are the ones that satisfy the following ontological criterion:

> To be assumed as an entity is, purely and simply, to be reckoned as the value of a variable. . . . We now have a more explicit standard whereby to decide what ontology a given theory or form of discourse is committed to: a theory is committed to those and only those entities to which the bound variables of the theory must be capable of referring in order that the affirmations made in the theory be true.[57]

Quine later abbreviated this criterion, producing the famous slogan "To be is to be the value of a bound variable."

To the question of how van Inwagen's "answer" to the question "What is being?"—an answer borrowed from Quine—should be evaluated philosophically, the answer must be that it contributes nothing significant because it avoids the question rather than responding to it. In this respect Quine is straightforward. Having introduced his thesis about the relation between existence and the existential quantifier, which van Inwagen accepts as adequately capturing "the single sense of being" (thesis 4, quoted above), Quine himself writes, in a passage quoted above, "explication of general existence is a forlorn cause."

What holds for Lowe and van Inwagen holds generally for analytic philosophy and ontology as a whole. More evidence of this is provided in the following section by way of consideration of a second point.

[b] The second point is a discussion that is extremely interesting as far as the subject matter of this book is concerned; it concerns absolute generality or universality,[58] or absolutely everything there is. These phrases are highly indeterminate, but in analytic philosophy they are immediately subjected to formalizations that rely on what analytic philosophers accept as the absolutely indispensable means for articulating everything: predicate logic (above all first-order) together with set theory. These means provide these philosophers with the universal quantifier. This quantifier is articulable as "for all x: . . . x . . ." or "for every x: . . . x . . ."

---

[j] Ibid., 500.

[57] W. V. O. Quine, "On What There Is," in *From a Logical Point of View* (1979), 13.

[58] *Absolute Generality* (2006/2009), edited by Agustín Rayo and Gabriel Uzquiano, contains thirteen essays by the most important logicians and philosophers taking part in this discussion.

or, symbolically, as "$\forall x(\ldots x \ldots)$." An example: every being is identical with itself: $\forall x(x = x)$ (this example uses the two-place predicate constant "identity," which is usually considered to expand predicate logic; hence, the expression "first-order predicate logic with identity").

The quantifier is an operator that binds variables. Bound variables have values. In the case of first-order predicate logic, the values of a given bound variable constitute the variable's *domain*. Universal quantifiers can have limited domains or the absolutely universal domain, the totality of values. "All humans are mortal" is a sentence governed by a restricted universal quantifier. Formalized (with "H" for "human" and "M" for mortal), the sentence is $\forall x(Hx \rightarrow Mx)$. In the example introduced above, $\forall x(x = x)$, the universal quantifier is absolutely unrestricted. To be noted is that in the precise articulation, by means of formalization, of restricted universal quantifiers, there is always a conditional that specifies the restriction: (for all x), *if* x is human, then . . . (i.e., if x is contained in the domain "human," then . . .).

The question under current discussion that is significant to this book is the following: what is the domain of the absolutely unrestricted universal quantifier? The question is answered in a wide variety of ways both by logicians and by philosophers. As the introduction to *Absolute Generality* shows, there are in fact two relevant questions:

> *The Metaphysical Question*
> Is there an all-inclusive domain of discourse?
> *The Availability Question*
> Could an all-inclusive domain be available to us as a domain of inquiry?[59]

The following account focuses on the first of these questions.

An assumption or presupposition shared by most analytic philosophers is the following: in order to understand quantification, we must understand the domain of the quantified variable to be an object that in some way or another encompasses all of the objects contained within it. Richard Cartwright terms this "the All-in-One Principle," and characterizes it as follows: "The general principle appears to be that to quantify over certain objects is to presuppose that those objects constitute a 'collection,' or a 'completed collection'—some one thing of which those objects are the members."[60] This "thing" would be nothing other than a set fully according with the famous characterization (or informal definition)

---

[59] Ibid., 2.
[60] Richard Cartwright, "Speaking of Everything" (1994), 7.

provided by Georg Cantor: "By a set we understand every collection into a whole M of determinate, well-distinguished objects m (termed the 'elements' of M) of our intuition or our thought."[61]

This assumption, however, generates what is known as Russell's antinomy (or paradox). Presented maximally simply and minimally formally, the antinomy is the following: the postulated universal set would be the set that does not contain itself as an element, thus (with "R" for this universal set): $R: = \{x \mid x \notin x\}$, or, briefly, $R \notin R$. If the assumption is made that R does not contain itself as an element, then R satisfies the requirement for inclusion in R and therefore must be included, but this contradicts the assumption from which it derives. If instead the assumption is made that R does contain itself as an element, then it does not satisfy the requirement for inclusion in R and therefore must be excluded, but this likewise contradicts the assumption from which it derives. There is thus the antinomy $R \in R \leftrightarrow R \notin R$. To be noted is that the derivation of this contradiction relies solely on logical means—not on anything drawn from set theory. The contradiction does assume or apply the so-called naive comprehension principle $\exists y \forall x ((x \in y) \leftrightarrow \phi(x))$, whereby the formula $\phi(x)$ does not include "y" as a free variable.

There have been many attempts to solve this problem, some purely logical and some relying also on semantic and pragmatic factors. None are considered here for a simple reason, which is that even if the problem were solved, making possible articulation of how the universal domain is to be understood, that would be of scarcely any relevance to the subject matter of this book. This is of course not to deny that solving the problem would be centrally relevant to other subject matters.

Before the irrelevance of the problem to this book is explained, it is worth noting that a similar antinomy arises if set-theoretical axioms are used in addition to purely logical means. The relevant axiom is the axiom of the power set, which is as follows: for every set M there is a set P whose elements are the subsets of M. Cantor's famous procedure of diagonalization shows that the power set of every set is larger than is the set itself; in other words, the cardinality of the power set is greater than the cardinality of the set itself. As a consequence, it is not possible to determine the universal totality itself. Patrick Grim shows the consequences for philosophy of this state of affairs in his book *The Incomplete Universe*.[62] This issue is not considered here, but it is considered in *Structure and Being*.[63]

---

[61] Cantor, "Beiträge zur Begründung der transfiniten Mengenlehre" (1932), 282.

[62] Grim, *The Incomplete Universe* (1991).

[63] See *Structure and Being*, section 5.2.2, pp. 421–31.

The primordial, universal dimension of Being considered in this book can in no way be considered to be an object or anything at all similar. Neither predicate logic nor set theory aids in the explanation of this dimension. It suffices to introduce two reasons why this is so. First, both predicate logic and set theory presuppose an ontology of objects (substances) and properties/relations. (This is also true of contemporary mereology, which is not considered here.) No such ontology is tenable, as shown above. But even if some such ontology were tenable, the primordial dimension of Being could not be included within it because it would include only beings, and the primordial dimension of Being is not a being.

Second, analytic philosophy articulates the entire problematic involving the universal domain with purely extensional concepts. According to the standard interpretation of predicate logic, predicates are sets; more precisely, one-place predicates designate properties, determined as the sets of things to which the predicates apply, whereas many-place predicates designate relations, determined as the sets of tuples of objects to which the predicates apply. Predicates (both one- and many-place) do not designate genuine entities (not what, if the predicates are interpreted intensionally, are attributes); instead, they have only extensions. But here serious philosophical questions arise. What *is* an extension? Purely mathematical or numeric determination does not answer the question of how the different "objects" fit into the configurations called extensions. And absolute universality, interpreted purely by means of predicate logic as the most universal configuration, likewise remains wholly unthought and unarticulated.

[2] In opposition to the analytic undertaking(s) just described, the structural-systematic philosophy identifies as one of its tasks that of developing a theory of Being. This theory is determined more precisely as a theory of Being as such and as a whole. Given what is said above, particularly in chapter 2, concerning Heidegger, this twofold designation should be intelligible at least programmatically. Being must be understood both in its uniqueness and in its totality, i.e., as encompassing or pervading anything and everything, thus all beings, of any and every sort. This latter topic is presumably generally intuitively intelligible. The former, however, is not, despite the fact that it emerges in various forms in the history of metaphysics. It is considered in the following section.

To be adequate, a theory of Being must treat Being both as such and as a whole. That it must is one of the most important lessons to be learned from Heidegger's lifelong grappling with the question of Being.

[3] What kind(s) of questions can sensibly be posed concerning

Being as such? The natural tendency both in everyday life and in philosophy is to ask, *what is* Being as such? The question appears to be clear and meaningful, but one central task of philosophy is to ask whether questions that initially appear to be clear and meaningful indeed are so. "What is" questions are among those about which this should be asked. To be sure, some of these prove to be fully appropriate, for example, What are atoms? and What is knowledge? More generally, any such question is reasonable only if its answer distinguishes, concerning what it asks about, what it *is* from what it *is not*, such that the latter can be explicitly articulated. But what would it be that Being is not? The only possible answer appears to be "Nothing is what Being is not," but *nothing* is a purely limiting concept or, better, a pseudo-concept. Because it is, the question "What is Being (i.e., the dimension of Being)" is not a sensible one.

What then are the alternative questions to be posed? These are such questions as the following: *How* is Being best understood, how is it best explained? But one can also ask, *As what* is Being best understood? In this case the "what" does not have the same denotation or connotations of the "what" in "What is" questions.[64] Instead, it motivates a search for an *explicans* for Being. And that search is the procedure appropriate to the development of a theory of Being: *explication*. *Explication* itself must, however, be scrupulously explained.

3.2.2a Excursus 2: The Inconclusive "Ontological Proof of God's Existence" and Its Implicit Presuppositions: A Failed Attempt to Articulate the Primordial, Universal Dimension of Being

At this point, a comparison between the disclosing (unfolding) of the primordial, universal dimension of Being (initially) articulated above and the famous so-called ontological proof of God's existence may be illuminating. The comparison can contribute significantly to clarifying both the status of that disclosing and the status of the traditional "proof." The clarification of the latter also reveals that *in a certain sense* it is based on a version of an interesting and significant thesis, although a version whose articulation in the proof is wholly inadequate. The following account identifies that version of the thesis, and then introduces a second version that overcomes the inadequacies of the first. As for the proof itself, the account reveals that it relies on presuppositions it does not explicate and that their explication shows the proof to be non-conclusive

---

[64] See Heidegger's idiosyncratic but remarkable comments in his small monograph *What Is Philosophy?* (1956/1958).

in the following sense: both the premises and the putative conclusion involve misunderstandings and confusions, and the conclusion does not follow from the premises.

[1] The following account is not a thorough analysis of the argument, and considers neither its complicated history nor the immense and growing body of literature devoted to it, which—it is perhaps worth noting in passing—contains numerous and often astute formalizations of it. The purposes both of this book and of this section are better served by a critical interpretation limited to the central theses of the proof *and of what the proof presupposes.*

The first of the argument's presuppositions that requires clarification is one that chapter 1's critique of other traditional so-called proofs of God's existence shows to be of great significance, but that in the current context requires only brief mention and commentary. Both Anselm of Canterbury, the source of the first version of the argument (and the one that has become authoritative), and all of the later reconstructions and variants of the argument, speak of it as proving *God*'s existence without recognizing such speaking as in any way problematic. Reasons given above to which others are added below make clear, however, that this characterization is inaccurate. The characterization of any putative proof should articulate what is formulated in its conclusion, so the ontological proof is accurately characterized as a proof not that *God* exists, but instead that there exists "something greater than which nothing can be thought [*aliquid quo nihil maius cogitari possit*]." Despite this, it is fully understandable that the proof has always been called a proof of God's existence because at the beginning of his famous text, *before* presenting his argument, Anselm identifies God as "something greater than which nothing can be thought."

In so identifying God at the outset, Anselm differs from Aquinas, who introduces the term "God" only after completing each of his five ways: he speaks of the first mover, the first cause, etc., and then says of each, "And all call that God."[65] As chapter 1 shows, Aquinas thereby commits a methodological error. So, too, does Anselm. Concretely: that the predicate "something greater than which nothing can be thought" can be applied to God says only that the property articulated by this predicate is among God's attributes. Because, however, God—according to both Anselm and Aquinas—has many attributes, God cannot simply be identified with any one of those attributes. This need not be further con-

---

[65] *STh* I q. 2 a. 3.

sidered here; of importance for present purposes is the proof itself, i.e., its premises and conclusion.

[2] Because this book does not require a detailed reconstruction or commentary, but instead only thematization of the argument's central theses, it suffices to introduce Anselm's formulation of it and then to analyze its central premises and its conclusion.

In chapter 2 of the *Proslogion*, Anselm writes as follows:

> Truly there is a God. . . .
> [God is] something than which nothing greater can be thought.
> . . .
> Even the fool . . . , when he hears of this being of which I speak—a being than which nothing greater can be thought—understands what he hears, and what he understands is in his understanding, even if he does not understand it to exist.
> . . .
> Hence, even the fool is convinced that something exists in the understanding, at least, than which nothing greater can be thought. For, when he hears of this, he understands it. And whatever is understood, exists in the understanding.
> Assuredly that, than which nothing greater can be thought, cannot exist in the understanding alone. For, suppose it exists in the understanding alone: then it can be thought to exist in reality; which is greater.
> Therefore, if that, than which nothing greater can be thought, exists in the understanding alone, the very being, than which nothing greater can be thought, is one than which a greater can be thought.
> But obviously this is impossible.
> Hence, there is no doubt that there exists a being than which nothing greater can be thought, and it exists both in the understanding and in reality.[66]

---

[66] Capitulum II. Quod vere sit Deus. . . .

[Deus est] aliquid quo nihil maius cogitari possit.

. . . sed certe ipse . . . insipiens, cum audit hoc ipsum quod dico: "aliquid quo maius nihil cogitari potest," intelligit quod audit; et quod intelligit in intellectu eius est, etiam si non intelligat illud esse. Aliud en im est rem esse in intellectu, aliud intelligere rem esse. . . .

Convincitur . . . etiam insipiens esse vel in intellectu aliquid quo nihil maius cogitari potest, quia hoc cum audit intelligit, et quidquid intelligitur in intellectu est. Et certe id quo maius cogitari nequit, non potest esse in solo intellectu. Si enim vel in solo intellectu est, potest cogitari esse et in re quod maius est. Si ergo id, quo maius cogitari non

In chapter 3, Anselm develops a more detailed argument under the title, "God's not being cannot be thought." He formulates its essential steps as follows:

> [The being than which nothing greater can be thought] assuredly exists so truly, that its not being cannot be thought. For, it is possible to think of a being whose not being cannot be thought; and this is greater than one whose not being can be thought. Hence, if that than which nothing greater can be thought can be thought not to be, it is not that than which nothing greater can be thought. But this is an irreconcilable contradiction. There is, then, so truly a being than which nothing greater can be thought to be/exist, that it cannot even be thought not to be/exist.

The decisive premises and their support are articulated, in the first passage (the one from chapter 2), in the following sentences:

> Assuredly that, than which nothing greater can be thought, cannot exist in the understanding alone. For, suppose it exists in the understanding alone: then it can be thought to exist in reality; which is greater.[67]

The decisive premise in the second text (the one from chapter 3) is, "it is possible to think of a being whose not being cannot be thought; and this is greater than one whose not being can be thought." The conclusion Anselm draws from these premises is that contradiction is avoided only if "there exists a being than which nothing greater can be thought, and it exists both in the understanding and in reality" (chapter 2), or "There is, then, so truly a being than which nothing greater can be thought to be/exist, that it cannot even be thought not to be/exist" (chapter 3).

[3] The decisive error in both versions of the proof is the follow-

---

potest, est in solo intellectu: id ipsum quo maius cogitari non potest, est quo maius cogitari potest. Sed certe hoc esse non potest. Existit ergo procul dubio aliquid quo maius cogitari non valet, et in intellectu et in re. (From the edition of F. S. Schmitt, S. Anselmi Cantuariensis, *Opera omnia* (1946ff.), tome 1, vol. 1, 101–2)

[67] Capitulum III. Quod non possit cogitari non esse.

Quod utique sic vere est, ut nec cogitari possit non esse. Nam potest cogitari esse aliquid, quod non possit cogitari non esse; quod maius est quam quod non esse cogitari potest. Quare si id quo maius nequit cogitari, potest cogitari non esse: id ipsum quo maius cogitari nequit, non est id quo maius cogitari nequit; quod convenire non potest. Sic ergo vere est aliquid quo maius cogitari non potest, ut nec cogitari possit non esse. (Ibid., 102–3)

ing: from "It can be thought that there is/exists, not only in the understanding but also in reality, something greater than which nothing can be thought," Anselm moves to "Therefore, something is/exists, in reality, greater than which nothing can be thought." The move requires a transition from the level or dimension articulated by "It can be thought that . . ." to that articulated by "There is/exists (in reality). . . ." Because Anselm strictly distinguishes between the two levels or dimensions *and* because his argumentation explicitly moves on the level or dimension articulated by "It can be thought that . . . ," he cannot simply step to the other level or dimension. To say, "It can be thought that there is, not only in thought but also in reality, something than which nothing greater can be thought" is only to say that this state of affairs is or can be *thought.*

It is now possible to indicate concisely how the ontological proof proceeds. Anselm compares two thoughts, as is made explicit by the addition of the operator "It can be thought that":

(1) It can be thought that something greater than which nothing can be thought is/exists in the understanding.
(2) It can be thought that something greater than which nothing can be thought is/exists not only in the understanding but also in reality.

Included in both (1) and (2) is the following thought:

(0) Something than which nothing greater can be thought.

Anselm then compares (1) and (2) aiming to determine which better qualifies as the thought of (0), concludes that what is articulated (following the operator) in (2) is greater than that articulated (following the operator) in (1), and then assumes that only the one articulated in (2) can qualify as the entity characterized in (0). He then moves to

(3) Something than which nothing greater can be thought is/exists.

Anselm goes wrong here in simply omitting the operator "It can be thought that. . . ." What is lacking is an explanation of the legitimacy of this omission.

If one understands the hopelessly indeterminate and vague word "greater" to mean "more encompassing," then one can concede to Anselm that what (2) articulates (ignoring the operator) is more encompassing than is its counterpart in (1). But what Anselm overlooks is the fact that both states of affairs are *thoughts,* in the following precise sense: they are both governed by the operator, "It can be thought that. . . ." Moving from

(2) to (3) requires replacing that operator with the operator "It is true that." But how could such a replacement be explained and grounded as *logical?* Because Anselm offers no such explanation or grounding, (2) and (3) are simply distinct sentences, lacking the connection they would have to have in order to function, respectively, as premise and conclusion. Anselm's argumentation is astute—but not astute enough.

[4] Asserted above is that Anselm's proof is based *in a certain sense* on a version of an interesting and significant thesis, although a version that the proof articulates wholly inadequately. This thesis can now be clarified by means of a comparison with the structural-systematic conception.

The basis of Anselm's line of thought is an unquestioned, unrestrictedly accepted, and radical distinction that he formulates as follows: "It is one thing for something to be in the understanding, and another to understand that it exists [*Aliud est . . . rem esse in intellectu aliud intelligere rem esse*]." This duality is presupposed throughout the proof. The entire course of argumentation consists in the attempt to escape the former side of this duality in order to reach the other side.

It cannot be contested that at first glance this distinction is not only sensible but indeed unavoidable, because one cannot simply assume that each of one's thoughts is of something that is or exists independently of its being thought. But this incontestable distinction must be made adequately precise, particularly because in analytic philosophy it is misunderstood virtually completely. It holds unrestrictedly only with respect to the relation between the dimension of thinking and the dimension that constitutes the objective counterpole to thinking, which is often termed "the world." The dimension of thinking is strictly distinguished from the world (in this sense) in that the dimension of thinking *is not* the dimension of the world, and is not even a part or a segment or a dimension of it.

The question that arises is the following: how is this relation possible? Most philosophers—above all analytic ones—assume the distinction and the relation based on it as non-problematic and unquestionable bases for anything and everything one can do philosophically. Any such assumption is, however, unacceptable, as can relatively easily (if somewhat polemically) be shown. A great many analytic philosophers simply reduce the dimension named above the dimension of thinking to the physical world. The physical dimension is thereby considered to be the whole that contains or encompasses within itself the distinction and the relation between the dimension of thinking and the dimension of the world. When this is done, however, what is called "the physical world" is no longer the-world-as-counterpole-to-the-dimension-of-thinking; instead, it is understood or presupposed to be the *comprehensive whole* that *encompasses* both the dimension of thinking and the dimension of thinking's objective counterpole.

This physicalistic/materialistic conception of the comprehensive whole is radically rejected by the structural-systematic philosophy because it fails to be adequate both to the dimension of thinking and to the dimension of thinking's counterpole. It is, however, highly interesting and revealing to discern that analytic philosophers always assume such a comprehensive whole, either explicitly or (far more often) implicitly. In fact, the distinction and relation between the two subdimensions are intelligible only if situated within an all-encompassing whole. But these philosophers assume a comprehensive whole only in an absolutely *restrictive* sense, i.e., in the sense that the dimension of thinking/mind is simply identified with elements of the physical world. Any such position, however, results from a failure to recognize the specific and thus irreducible character of this dimension; in various contexts, this book reveals that irreducible character.

With respect to this book's subject matter, the following thesis is of the greatest significance: it would be senseless and absurd to ask whether the comprehensive dimension that encompasses both the dimension of thinking and the dimension of the world (termed in the metaphysical tradition "*rerum natura*") is (on the one hand) only a concept or thought or some such or (on the other) is or exists. If one speaks of a thought or concept of this comprehensive dimension, then the talk cannot be understood as introducing or presupposing that the thought or concept could be of something that could (in Anselm's terms) be *only* in thought while failing to be (again in Anselm's terms) in reality, because *both* thought and reality *are in it*. In this book, this comprehensive whole is termed the primordial, universal dimension of Being.

The task that emerges from recognition of the primordial, universal dimension of Being is that of *explicating* it. As the following subsections of this chapter show, the question of God arises and is clarified within this explication. This procedure of explication is far removed from anything like the ontological proof and its unclarified, unexplicated, and above all unacceptable presuppositions. Nevertheless, one can see in the ontological proof—if one looks somewhat daringly—the expression of a thesis and a questioning that point in the direction of what this book articulates as a theory of Being as such and as a whole.

As far as Anselm's version goes, one can legitimately assume that in formulating it he had some inkling of the comprehensive dimension in that he conceives of the dimension of thinking (here, concretely, the dimension including the thought of that greater than which nothing can be thought) and the dimension of the world as an inseparable unity. It must, however, immediately be added that his proof is wholly inadequate to this comprehensive dimension. The proof articulates something that is the greatest, but not what is comprehensive. What is greatest cannot be comprehensive because it excludes whatever is of lesser greatness. It is a variant of the *ens supremum,* the *maxime ens,* etc. Thought of it thematizes only the dimension of beings, not the dimension of Being. In opposition to such thought, the structural-systematic philosophy decisively undertakes the thematization of the dimension of Being. But this involves nothing like vacuous reflections on or analyses of the word "being"; it involves instead scrupulous analyses such as those articulated above in sections 3.2.1–3.2.2.

Given what is said above in analysis and criticism of the ontological proof, it might appear that one could object to what is said in this book about the primordial, universal dimension of Being that it articulates only *thoughts* about the primordial, universal dimension of Being, and that whether these thoughts were accurate would have to be proved somehow or other. Showing why this interesting objection fails provides ultimate clarity for this centrally important topic.

Assume that there was *only* the *thought*-of-the-primordial-universal-dimension-of-Being, such that the Being of the primordial, universal dimension would be exhausted by (or would consist exclusively in) its being thought. (To be noted is that the structural-systematic philosophy cannot use such phrases as "the primordial, universal dimension *exists*" or "*there is* a primordial, universal dimension of Being, etc., in a naive manner because such phrases are meaningful exclusively *within the framework* of the distinction and relation between the dimension of thinking and its counterpole, i.e., the dimension of [objective] Being.) That would mean that one had remained *enclosed within* the dimension of pure thinking. But that would mean that one had remained enclosed within one of the two poles identified above, thus that one had *not* had any thought of the primordial, universal dimension of Being. If one *does* think such that what is thought is the primordial, universal dimension of Being, then what one has are indeed thoughts, but what one's thoughts are of is that dimension itself.

The primordial, universal, maximal dimension of Being is of course *thought,* but it is thought *as* encompassing both the dimension of thinking and that dimension's objective counterpole. This can also be put as follows: thinking *does* have access not only to entities whose Being is independent of thinkings of them—hence, entities within its objective counterpole—but also to a dimension that, although accessible *only* via thinking (thus, not via sight, touch, etc.), is such that the fact of its being thought establishes that its Being is not exhausted by its being thought (that it is not merely posited, imagined, hallucinated, merely dreamed of, or anything of the sort).

3.2.3 On the Concept *Explication*

Cognates of "explication," from the Latin *explicatio,* are found in all Western languages, but not used in a single way. In German, *Explikation* cannot simply be identified with *Erklärung* (explanation). The latter term can designate both semantic clarification or analysis of meanings of words or concepts and the scientific undertaking that involves empirical research and laws. The word "explication" is not used for scientific explanation. The situation is similar with the English words "explication" and "explanation."[68] In the Romance languages the cognates of "explication" do the work done in German and English, respectively, by *Erklärung* and "explanation," with the scientific use generally indicated by the addition of modifiers that are counterparts to "scientific."

[1] It is appropriate to begin by explaining the concept *scientific explanation* to the extent to which this is reasonable and helpful with respect to clarifying the concept *explication.* As indicated above, scientific explanations involve empirical research and laws. This is particularly the case when, as is usually the case, such explanations are responses to why questions. One begins with a specific phenomenon—the one to be explained—in order to relate this phenomenon to another (as a rule, a greater or more comprehensive) phenomenon or domain, etc. This is done by means of laws that articulate relations that hold universally between phenomena, domains, etc. Always presupposed thereby is a *background* dimension (a domain or domains of nature or the world, nature or the world as a whole, the cosmos . . .) as the dimension *within* which the phenomenon to be explained, the factors constituting the explanation, and the relations between the two are situated. This background dimension itself is not, however, thematized.

With the term "explanation," however, a somewhat different meaning can be associated, such that explanations answer how questions. One then explains *how* hurricanes arise, *how* the ecosystem has developed, *how* evolution unfolded, *how* the cosmos expands, etc. In many technical domains (although generally not in ontological ones), the verb "work" is used: one explains *how* a machine works, etc.

Unlike explanations *why,* explanations *how* situate what is explained within a larger whole whose inner constitution or structuration one ana-

---

[68] See, e.g., Peter Achinstein, *The Nature of Explanation* (1983).

lyzes; the analysis makes clear how the constituents of this whole are interrelated such that they constitute the whole. The whole can be relatively small, as in the case of machines, specific physical phenomena, the emergence of a given species within a specific ecosystem, etc., or much larger, as in the case of an entire domain—the domain of life, of human beings, etc., inorganic nature, organic nature, nature as a whole, the cosmos. In addition, explanations of the two sorts can be combined. How explanations are more similar to explications than are why explanations, but cannot be identified with them.

[2] To make clear how the term/concept *explication* is used in the structural-systematic philosophy's theory of Being, it is helpful to introduce some aspects of the history of the term *explicatio.* To be sure, this term has been used to designate interpretations and explanations of words, texts, concepts, etc. But in the Neoplatonic tradition its use is eminently *metaphysical:* the world is interpreted as the *unfolding (ex-plicatio)* of the essence of God.

A remarkable revaluation and novel interpretation of this term that was decisive for its later history was introduced by Nicholas of Cusa. He used the pair of terms/concepts *complicatio/explicatio*[69] to articulate the relation between one and many. Already in *De docta ignorantia,* which appeared in 1440, the two concepts play an important role. There, Nicholas describes the infinite God who allows the world to participate in him as the unfolding one that allows the many to emerge from itself:

> Thus the infinite unity is the unfolding of everything. This is precisely what "the unity that unites everything" means. . . . God is therefore the One that enfolds [*complicans*] everything, in that everything is in him. And he is the One that unfolds [*explicans*] everything, in that he himself is in everything.[70]

In *De coniecturis,* which appeared in 1442, there is a new development: there, for the first time, *complicatio/explicatio* are used for the human mind and its activities.

In Nicholas's later works, the two concepts play a central role in his

---

[69] Nicholas probably took the concepts *complicatio/explicatio,* which became central to his thought, from the school of Chartres (Thierry of Chartres). In the discussion of sources in his critical edition of *De docta ignorantia* (*Opera omnia,* vol. 1), R. Klibansky shows how Nicholas relied on Thierry of Chartres.

[70] "Unitas igitur infinita est omnium complicatio. Hoc quidem dicit unitas, quae omnia unit. . . . Deus ergo est omnia complicans in hoc, quod omnia in eo. Est omnia explicans in hoc, quod ipse in omnibus" (*De docta ignorantia,* 1, vol. 1, 2–3).

treatments of knowledge. Enfolding characterizes the essence of mind and unfolding, the manifestation of its activities. But the two terms/concepts retain their metaphysical uses in the treatments of the relation of participation that links the world to God. Human knowledge is thereby placed in a perspective such that it itself has divine creation as its background. Nicholas articulates the correspondence between human knowledge and God's creative act in numerous passages. According to these passages, human knowledge can be understood only in relation to God's creative power: it is the reflection of that power within finite actuality.[71]

This connection of the two perspectives, the metaphysical and the epistemic (or purely conceptual), is decisive for the later use of *explicatio/* explication, although the second perspective comes to play a dominant and at times the only role. Kant provides the transcendental variant of the second perspective, writing, "The German language has for the [Latinate] expressions *exposition, explication, declaration,* and *definition* nothing more than the one word 'explanation' [*Erklärung*]" (*CPuR* A730/ B758). Long after Kant, the linguistic turn took place and semantics and logic became central subject matters for philosophy. At present, as noted above, the word "explication" is no longer generally used in its earlier metaphysical sense.

Despite the development just described, this book uses the word "explication" not only and in a certain respect not chiefly as relevant to knowledge, language (semantics), and logic, but above all as relevant to metaphysics (better: to comprehensive systematics). So used, it articulates the disclosure of the dimension of primordial Being. This explication or disclosure cannot of course be accomplished (so to speak) directly, that is, without the aid of theoretical elements; instead, the dimension of Being is articulated *together with* all the requisite theoretical elements. This does not mean that there are here two different or indeed separate dimensions (that of the theoretical elements and that of Being); instead, justice must be done to the *primordial unity* of the two. In abstraction from all theoretical elements, the dimension of Being would be an absolute abstraction; likewise, in abstraction from subject matters—which include, as the ultimate subject matter, the dimension of Being—the abstract structures remain abstract, that is, without content.

Explication, as understood in this book, can now be more precisely characterized. In the structural-systematic philosophy, explication is an analytic/argumentative/disclosive procedure. As the procedure progresses,

---

[71] See T. van Velthoven, *Gottesschau und menschliche Kreativität: Studien zur Erkenntnislehre des Nikolaus von Kues* (1977), 94–95.

all three of these factors are at work, but different ones come to the fore at different stages. Sometimes the analysis of terms or of concepts predominates, sometimes argumentation, and finally the disclosive articulation of the subject matter.

3.3 Explication of the Dimension of Being I: Theory of Being as Such

What could or should an explication or self-explication of the dimension of Being include? First, it should include the immanent structural characteristics of Being or of the dimension of Being. But can such characteristics be identified? Indeed they can, as the following account shows. They are better designated as immanent characteristics of Being as such (and indeed as the most central immanent characteristics of the dimension of Being), as distinguished from the characteristics of Being within domains of Being.

What follows is only a brief analysis and explanation of the most central immanent characteristics. To develop a genuine and complete theory of the dimension of Being it would be necessary to articulate these characteristics by means of universal, comprehensively systematic sentences whose status was strictly theoretical. Such articulation is not a difficult task, but is not undertaken in this book.

[1] It is illuminating initially to consider two somewhat similar, albeit wholly unsuccessful, attempts to accomplish what this section aims to accomplish.

[i] The first is the attempt, made throughout the metaphysical tradition but particularly by Thomas Aquinas, to identify transcendentals. The complex history of this attempt is not considered here.[72] For present purposes, it suffices to consider the so-called simple (or primordial) transcendentals (*unum, verum, bonum* [and *pulchrum*]). The classical formulation is, *Quodlibet ens est unum, verum, bonum[, pulchrum]*; every being is one, true, good[, beautiful]. As the brackets suggest, beauty/beautiful is not always included among the simple, primordial transcendentals.

Two points need making here. First, at present true/truth is no lon-

---

[72] See the comprehensive M. Pickavé, ed., *Die Logik des Transzendentalen* (2003); see also Jan A. Aertsen, "Die Transzendentalienlehre bei Thomas von Aquin in ihren historischen Hintergründen und philosophischen Motiven" (1988); and K. Bärthlein, *Die Transzendentalienlehre der alten Ontologie* (1973).

ger considered to be a characteristic of every being. In the metaphysical tradition, the truth in question is ontological truth (*veritas ontologica*). But what is this truth? Thomas Aquinas, clear-eyed as ever, perhaps provides the best answer to this question, although his is one that raises many new questions. He writes:

> Truth or the true is defined [in the philosophical community] in three ways. First of all, it is defined according to that which precedes truth and is the basis of truth. This is why Augustine writes: "True is that which is," and Avicenna: "The truth of each thing is the property of the act of Being which has been established for it."
>
> Truth is also defined in another way—according to which its intelligible determination is formally completed. Thus, Isaac writes: "Truth is the conformity of thing and intellect." . . .
>
> The third way of defining truth is according to the effect following upon it. Thus, Hilary [of Poitiers] says that the true is that which explicates and manifests Being. And Augustine says: "Truth is that according to which is shown what is."[73]

It is apparent that Thomas does not accept these three determinations as three distinct definitions; instead, he reports that at the time of his writing the three definitions were available. He himself attempts to wrest a meaning from each of the three by identifying the central point that each articulates. The definition that he accepts is the second—and that is the one at the heart of the famous correspondence theory of truth. Thomas's text is extraordinarily informative when considered in conjunction with the discussions of truth that are now ongoing, and with Heidegger's lifelong grappling with the topic of truth.

As far as the transcendentals are concerned, what the passage quoted above shows is that according to Thomas the thesis "*omne ens est verum*—Every being is true" must be understood in accordance with the first of the three definitions, which to be sure is not a definition in any

---

[73] Veritas sive verum tripliciter invenitur diffiniri. Uno modo secundum illud quod praecedit rationem veritatis et in quo verum fundatur, et sic Augustinus diffinit in libro Soliloquiorum "veritas cuiusque rei est proprietas sui esse quod stabilitum est ei. . . . Alio modo diffinitur secundum id in quo formaliter ratio veri perficitur, et sic dicit Ysaac quod "Veritas est adaequatio rei et intellectus. . . . Tertio modo diffinutur verum secundum effectum consequentem, et sic dicit Hilarius quod "Verum est declarativum et manifestativum esse," et Augustinus in libro De vera religione "Veritas est qua ostenditur id quod est." (Thomas Aquinas, *Von der Wahrheit* [1986], 8–11; English translation from the modified German translation)

strict sense, but instead articulates what the genuine definition of truth presupposes.

The second point that needs to be made here concerning Aquinas on the transcendentals is made in criticism. The doctrine of transcendentals speaks exclusively of beings (*omne ens . . .*), not of Being. Heidegger's charge of forgetfulness of Being therefore is accurate of it directly and radically. The doctrine of transcendentals is not false, but it is superficial in that it does not thematize the dimension wherein all beings are situated: it does not thematize Being.

Kant's illuminating reinterpretation of the doctrine of transcendentals also merits brief mention. He touches on the doctrine of transcendentals when he writes:

> There is also yet another chapter in the transcendental philosophy of the ancients that contains pure concepts of the understanding that, although they are not reckoned among the categories, nevertheless according to them should also count as *a priori* concepts of objects, in which case, however, they would increase the number of the categories, which cannot be. These are expounded in the proposition, so famous among the scholastics: *quodlibet ens est unum, verum, bonum.* (*CPuR* B113)

He then remarks that although "the use of this principle for inferences has turned out to be very meager," the thought behind them deserves consideration. His consideration leads him to conclude that the following "conjecture" about the principle is justified:

> It must have its ground in some rule of the understanding, which, as so often happens, has merely been falsely interpreted. These supposedly transcendental predicates of *things* are nothing other than logical requisites and criteria of all *cognition of things* in general, and ground it in the categories of quantity, namely, the categories of *unity, plurality,* and *totality;* yet these categories must really have been taken as material, as belonging to the possibility of things itself, when in fact they should have been used in a merely formal sense, as belonging to the logical requirements for every cognition; thus these criteria of thinking were carelessly made into properties of things in themselves. (*CPuR* B113–14)

This reinterpretation makes the genuine status of transcendental philosophies of subjectivity strikingly clear: all concepts, thoughts, etc., are wholly restricted to the measure of transcendental subjectivity. Kant therefore cannot envisage thematizing the dimension that encompasses

both transcendental subjectivity and its counterpole. This is precisely the
dimension that the structural-systematic philosophy terms the comprehensive dimension of primordial Being.

[ii] The second attempt to identify the central immanent characteristics of Being as such is Heidegger's attempt to "think" Being as such;
chapter 2 provides both a thorough presentation of and a critical commentary on this attempt. As that chapter shows, Heidegger's attempt
yields no more than virtually empty assertions. It remains remarkable,
however, that Heidegger posed the question in a decisive manner, and
devoted virtually his entire attention to it.

[2] The pervasive immanent structural characteristics of Being
emerge from the (self-)explication of the dimension of Being. Three
ways in which the dimension of Being is disclosed are described above.
By the third way, the dimension of Being is disclosed by means of explaining the relation between the dimension of thinking/mind/language and
that of world/universe/Being-in-the-objective-sense; this relation binds
the two dimensions together such that both become visible as subdimensions of a single, primordial dimension, the dimension of Being.

Further disclosure of the dimension of Being is its detailed explication; this makes explicit the (better: some of the) pervasive, immanent
characteristics of the dimension of Being. Always to be kept in mind is
that the dimension of Being is nothing like a Platonic form or domain
of forms from which certain immanent characteristics could somehow
be derived. Instead, the dimension of Being is the configuration that
includes the dimensions of thinking/mind/language and of word/uni-
verse/Being as interrelated. This configuration is what the explication of
the dimension of Being explicates.

The explication of the dimension of Being begins with the explication of Being as such.

[i] The first pervasive, immanent characteristic of Being as such
is the absolutely universal *intelligibility* of the dimension of Being and
hence of Being as such—thus, intelligibility coextensional with the dimension of Being itself. The dimension of Being and therefore Being as
such is the absolutely comprehensive configuration that includes the entire dimension of thinking/mind/spirit; it therefore cannot be outside
the sphere of thinking/mind/spirit. Because this sphere is coextensive
with this dimension, this dimension is accessible to it; this accessibility
is precisely what constitutes the intelligibility of the dimension of Being
and hence of Being as such. It *is* understandable, knowable, articulable,
etc. This is not to say that we, as finite, can fully articulate it; it is accessible to us in its entirety—we can indeed think and know the dimension
itself, and thus Being as such—but not in all of its specificity, that is, not

in anything approaching complete detail. We can, however, grasp segments of its comprehensive intelligibility.

In the history of philosophy, this pervasive, immanent structural moment has been recognized and explicitly articulated again and again, in many ways. The first and perhaps most famous is that of Parmenides: "τὸ γὰρ αὐτὸ νοεῖν ἐστίν τε καὶ εἶναι [for thinking and Being are the same]."[74] Other formulations include that of the metaphysical tradition, "*Ens et verum convertuntur* [being (entity) and truth are interchangeable]," Hegel's equation of the idea (in his sense) and actuality, and Heidegger's equation of Being and truth (in his sense). Throughout, there is a central intuition that is, however, often expressed by means of exaggerated and/or cryptic formulations.

This history is particularly instructive because it makes clear how differently the same terms are used by different philosophers. This holds especially for "thinking/idea" in Hegel and "truth" in Heidegger. Highly revealing is the way Heidegger conceives of "truth" as a more precise explication of "Being." He interprets "truth" on the basis of what he understands to be the ancient or original sense of the Greek word ἀλήθεια as "unconcealment," or the manifestness of Being.[75]

There is a philosophical tradition that uses the term "ontological truth," but this tradition differs from Heidegger in not simply equating "truth" with "ontological truth"; it relies instead on the thesis that truth in the genuine sense is in judgment (*veritas est in iudicio*). Heidegger misses the phenomenon of truth precisely because he does not directly consider the relation of language and Being. The theory of truth sketched above clearly shows that there can be adequate consideration of truth only if the entire dimension of language enters explicitly and radically into the determination of the truth concept. The widely held traditional thesis that truth is situated primarily in judgment misses this decisive point.

[ii] The preceding analysis of intelligibility makes possible the identification of two additional immanent, pervasive characteristics of Being. The first of these is the *universal coherence* of the dimension of Being. In the structural-systematic philosophy, coherence is not simply identical with consistency; in addition to avoidance of contradiction, it requires positive interlinkings, thus configurations. The genitive in the

---

[74] Heidegger, characteristically, provides an idiosyncratic translation: "For the same perceiving (thinking) as well as being" (*TB* 18).

[75] Late in his career, Heidegger revised his understanding of "truth" (both the word and what he took the word to mean). See his lecture "The End of Philosophy and the Task of Thinking" (*TB* 76).

phrase "universal coherence *of* the dimension of Being" is thus a subjective genitive: the coherence is intrinsic to the dimension of Being rather than somehow added to it by its being thought.

The universal coherence of the dimension of Being is derivable from its universal intelligibility in that to understand, explain, etc., anything whatsoever is to articulate the configuration and thus the coherent structure within which it is situated. In a word, coherence is *systematicity*. More detailed argumentation within the structural-systematic philosophy shows that this characteristic of Being is more precisely articulable as *universal structuration,* because Being itself is the primordial and comprehensive structure.

[iii] From Being's universal intelligibility can also be derived the immanent, pervasive characteristic of the *universal expressibility* of the dimension of Being and hence of Being as such. "Expressibility" is here a technical term designating all modes of access to actuality or to Being as such or as a whole, and all modes of articulation (understanding, explaining, etc.) of actuality or Being as such or as a whole. It would make no sense to present any scientific or philosophical (linguistic) articulation of anything or of everything (the dimension of Being as a whole) if what the articulation articulated was intrinsically unarticulated and hence intrinsically inexpressible.[76]

[iv] A fourth most pervasive and immanent structural characteristic differs significantly from the first three. Those three emerge from the explication of the dimension of Being *with respect to the intellect;* in the terminology common since Aristotle (although problematic within the structural-systematic philosophy), they would be termed theoretical characteristics. This designation can be used if it is correctly understood. Given this condition, one could say that the fourth immanent characteristic is practical, in that it characterizes the dimension of Being *with respect to the will, a human capacity equiprimordial with the intellect.* Both the intellect and the will have the dimension of Being as their definitively absolute point of reference (i.e., it is that within which both thinking and willing are definitively situated, that by which both take their bearings), but *not in the same respect.* The dimension of Being is the absolutely unrestricted and complete point of reference for the intellect with respect to its first three immanent characteristics, termed above the theoretical ones. Now to be explained is the immanent structural characteristic of the dimen-

---

[76] For a more detailed treatment of this topic, see *Structure and Being,* especially chapter 5, section 5.1.

sion of Being that makes that dimension the absolutely unrestricted and complete point of reference for the will.

Within the metaphysical tradition, this fourth characteristic is termed *the good*. For this reason, an axiom of this metaphysics is *omne ens est bonum* (every being is good), or *ens et bonum convertuntur* (being and good are interchangeable). But how is "the good" to be specified? In traditional metaphysics, attempts to determine the good are made in two ways. The first begins with the will and treats the good as its "formal object," as that which guides the will in its relating to any "material object" ("*sub ratione boni*," "from the perspective of the good"). The second traditional metaphysical determination of the good is based on Being: the good is the immanent characteristic of Being that the will appeals or corresponds to: whatever the will does in any specific case, it always does with a view to the good, because that is the defining characteristic of the will. This fourth (the "practical") pervasive, immanent characteristic of Being itself is therefore the characteristic of *universal or pervasive goodness*.

[v] Sometimes, in the metaphysical tradition, *beauty* is also presented as an immanent structural characteristic of Being. It is determined by means of the thought of the harmony or consonance (*consonantia*) of the previously introduced immanent structural moments of Being. It is indeed a determination that emerges consequently from the question of how the unity or interconnection of these immanent structural moments is to be understood. The essential clarifications are provided in *Structure and Being* (chapter 4, in conjunction with the presentation of the *aesthetic world* [see section 4.4.2[2][i], pp. 315–16]).

3.4 Explication of the Dimension of Being II: Theory of Being as a Whole

The preceding section (3.3) introduces structural characteristics of *Being as such*, not of Being as a whole, that is, not of Being as the Being of any and every being. To be sure, beings are not completely absent from that analysis, because what discloses the first three structural characteristics is the relation between Being and the intellect of human beings (between Being and human thinking), and what discloses the fourth is that between Being and the will of human beings (between Being and human willing). These are genuine relations, but what they disclose in the preceding analysis are structural characteristics *immanent* to Being, characteristics that are thus independent of any actual or possible relations to any beings, thus including human beings. In other words: even if there were no beings, Being itself would have these characteristics. Human beings, via their thinking and their willing, enter the analysis only as disclosing the characteristics, not as in any way responsible for them or as constituting them.

Wholly different questions arise when the task is undertaken of directly and explicitly thematizing the relation between Being and beings. This thematization is of *Being as a whole*.

3.4.1 Being and beings: A Difference That Is Unavoidable but Misunderstood and Misused

Here again the task is one that is undertaken again and again throughout the history of philosophy; the task is that of solving the problem of unity and multiplicity, or of the one and the many. The latter formulations are, however, quite abstract, whereas "Being and beings" is incomparably more richly contentual. Given that, how is this problem to be addressed?

Heidegger's charge of forgetfulness of Being, leveled against the entire history of metaphysics, made it extraordinarily difficult for him to, in his terms, think Being itself. Chapter 2 treats Heidegger's self-imposed predicament in detail. That predicament can be briefly explained as follows: if Being is *not* to be forgotten, it appears that Being itself must be thought, and that appears to require the reliance on a form of thinking that is not determined by any consideration of beings. But how could such a form be discovered or used? Heidegger encounters his extraordinary difficulties in responding to this question because of one of his own theses: "It belongs to the truth of Being that Being never essences [*west*] without beings, that there are never beings without Being [*Zur Wahrheit des Seins gehört, daß das Sein nie west ohne das Seiende, daß niemals ein Seiendes ist ohne das Sein*]" (*PM* 306). If that is so, then Being cannot be thought unless beings are also thought. Heidegger never presented a coherent clarification of this state of affairs. The conception developed here avoids Heidegger's predicament, and with it his difficulties. That it does is made clear by what is said above and yet clearer by what is said below.

3.4.2 Modalities as Key to the Explication of Being as a Whole

The preceding sections disclose the absolutely universal dimension, the dimension of primordial Being, in three ways. Those are followed by sections identifying the most important immanent structural characteristics of Being as such. The question now to be addressed is the following: how is Being as a whole, Being in its relation to all beings, structured (or configured)?

"As a whole" does not here mean "as a totality" according to the sense attached to the term and concept "totality" in some areas of contemporary philosophy, where it is often used and discussed in such ways that it brings with it significant semantic, logical, and mathematical problems (see *Structure and Being* 5.3.3). The sense of "as a whole" is made clear in what follows.

[1] Chapter 2 shows that, confronted with the question of how Being itself is to be thought, Heidegger came to rely on the term *Ereignis,* interpreting the term in a manner relying in part on purely etymological and in part on banal ordinary-language aspects. Chapter 2 also shows that Heidegger failed to take advantage of all of the theoretical resources available to the human mind, for example—and above all—the modalities. Given Heidegger's failure, the following question presses: where should one seek an indication of how to proceed? Should one attempt to begin with Being, seeking to answer questions that arise or emerge from Being itself, or should one attempt to begin with the human mind and its resources, examining those in order to determine what questions we can or perhaps must raise about Being? This apparent duality is, however, an abstraction. The mind's questions are Being's questions—and vice versa. There is no possibility here for anything like a transcendental standpoint, that is, one that would be able to see everything absolutely one-sidedly only from the perspective of the subject and its conceptual apparatus.

Once the universal dimension of primordial Being is disclosed, one of the most radical questions that arises—that is, that is both posed by Being and to be addressed to Being—concerns the *modalities:* possibility, necessity, and contingency. Is primordial Being (only) possible, is it necessary, is it (only) contingent? Given the significance of questions of this sort throughout the history of philosophy, and given the ultimately indisputable immense intelligibility that the modalities make possible, it is incomprehensible that many (not to say most) philosophers are not willing to pose them, much less attempt to answer them, and it is even more incomprehensible that many—usually implicitly but in some cases even explicitly—attempt to disqualify them by declaring them to be simply senseless or to result from thinking that has gone far astray. Such declarations violently suppress the human mind's potential for attaining intelligibility.

[2] Modal lines of questioning like the one pursued below are at present either wholly rejected and indeed disqualified—or, if not wholly

rejected then either viewed with extreme skepticism or passed over in silence—by two radically opposed ways of philosophizing. One of these ways is that of Heidegger and postmodernists. As far as Heidegger is concerned, chapter 2 shows that he rejects the modalities by classifying them as elements of metaphysical thinking that is forgetful of Being (see 2.4[2][ii], 2.8.2[1], and 2.9[1]). Chapter 4 thoroughly treats two of the most important postmodernists, especially subjecting to penetrating critique Jean-Luc Marion's idiosyncratic "phenomenological"—which for Marion means above all anti-metaphysical—reinterpretation and application of the modalities (see especially 4.2.4.3[1]).

Many and perhaps most analytic philosophers engage in the other way of philosophizing that refuses to draw on the modalities. Here, the modalities are usually either interpreted non-ontologically or left ontologically indeterminate. Decisive for these philosophers is the modal logic developed in the twentieth century. Concerning that logic, two aspects must be distinguished and kept separate. Modal logic is a formal science that, as such, can have many applications and interpretations. A first aspect is the dimension of its application (or concretization, or of the development of models) or expansion. Because of this aspect, there are epistemic logics, deontic logics, temporal logics, conditional logics, and so forth.

The second aspect concerns the semantics of modal logic. Here, there is a strict distinction between purely logical or formal semantics on the one hand, and philosophical semantics on the other. The purely logical/formal semantics that is usually designated *semantics for modal logic* consists essentially in clarifying—i.e., defining—the truth values of modal-logical sentences. In non-modal sentential (or propositional) logic, truth values of sentences are defined most simply by means of truth tables. Such tables cannot be used in modal logic, because modal logic is not truth-functional. For this reason, so-called Kripke semantics introduces *possible worlds*. Every sentence variable is then given a truth value for every possible world. For example, a necessary sentence is one that is true in all possible worlds, and therefore is ascribed the truth value "true" in every possible world.

Philosophical semantics goes much further than does purely logical or formal semantics. This point can, in a significant manner, be made clear with the specific example of possible worlds. In Kripke semantics the concept of possible worlds is a purely logical convenience, a means of making intuitive assignments of truth values to modal sentences. The literature on Kripke semantics and on possible worlds shows that some take philosophical semantics to involve just this sort of possible worlds, whereas others take it to involve ontological interpretations of possible worlds. David Lewis's modal realism is a well-known and much-discussed example of an ontological interpretation.[77]

[3] In close connection with modal logic, philosophy is concerned with modalities. Unlike traditional philosophy, analytic philosophy understands the modalities as *modes of truth*. This means that they are interpreted as qualifying sentences and propositions. The correct logical manner of presenting them consists in articulating them as operators taking sentences/propositions as arguments. What results is the following:

It is possible that P: $\Diamond P = \neg \Box \neg P$
It is necessary that P: $\Box P = \neg \Diamond \neg P$
It is contingent that P: $\triangledown P = \Diamond P \wedge \Diamond \neg P$ or $\neg \Box P \wedge \neg \Box \neg P$

The so-defined modalities are generally designated alethic or metaphysical modalities. They are distinguished from the epistemic modalities—that is, sentences/propositions being known either a priori or a posteriori—and from the semantic modalities—that is, sentences/propositions being true either analytically or synthetically. There are similar distinctions in the cases of the other modalities—deontic modalities, temporal modalities, and so forth.

For the purposes of this book only the alethic or metaphysical modalities are relevant. Here there is a problem, or at least a situation that, as is typical in analytic philosophy, is insufficiently clear. On the one hand, authors who accept the metaphysical modalities speak *informally* in ways that suggest that these modalities are accorded genuine ontological status. For example, Timothy Williamson—who both accepts and works intensively on the metaphysical modalities—writes the following:

> Philosophers characteristically ask not just whether things are some way but whether they could have been otherwise. What could have been otherwise is *metaphysically contingent*, what could not is *metaphysically necessary*. We have some knowledge of such matters. We know that Henry VIII could have had more than six wives, but that three plus three could not have been more than six.[78]

---

[77] *Structure and Being* subjects Lewis's modal realism to a penetrating critical analysis (see section 5.2.3).

[78] Timothy Williamson, *The Philosophy of Philosophy* (2008), 134 (from chapter 5: "Knowledge of Metaphysical Modality").

Here the modalities are clearly ascribed to *things*, such that any-thing that could have been otherwise is contingent. Williamson, however, is concerned only with the problem of *knowing* metaphysical modalities. The distinction—which dates from the Middle Ages but remains in use today—between *de dicto* and *de re* is also generally understood such that *de re* modalities are modalities indeed of the *res*, the thing or object. Ex-amples: $\Diamond Fa$ is a modality *de re* when it is read as "Object a is possibly F," as is $\forall x \Box Fx$, when read as "For all (objects, things, beings . . .) x, x neces-sarily has the property F."

On the other hand, the metaphysical modalities are designated and understood as alethic modalities, which means that they are quali-fications not of things but of sentences/propositions. In terms of the *de dicto/ de re* distinction, *de dicto* modalities are explained such that the mo-dalities are ascribed not to things but to sentences and/or propositions. Alethic/metaphysical modalities are then *de dicto* modalities. One might try to clarify this state of affairs by saying that ascription of modalities is accomplished by means of sentences or propositions, so that between sentence/proposition on the one hand and thing/object/state of af-fairs on the other there would be an inseparable unity, but the objection would be that nothing would thereby be explained, because if the true sentence $\forall xFx$ means "It is true that all (objects) x have the property F," then there is an unbridgeable gap between two ways of modalizing the sentence (by means of the introduction of the operator "It is necessarily the case that"), namely, the following:

$\forall x \Box Fx$ (= "It is true that for all [objects] x it is necessarily the case that they have the property F") (= *de re*)

$\Box \forall xFx$ (= "The sentence 'All objects have the property F' is necessarily true," and/or "The proposition that all objects have the property F is necessarily true"—or, reading the modality symbol explicitly as an operator, "It is necessarily the case that the sentence 'All objects have the property F' is true," and/or "It is necessarily the case that the proposition that all objects have the property F is true) (= *de dicto*)

This shows that a consequence of the interpretation of the puta-tively *metaphysical* modalities as *alethic* modalities is that these modalities are ascribed *only* to sentences or propositions; this reduces them to *de dicto* modalities that are thus not taken to articulate the status of things or ob-jects or beings. When this step is taken, the first formulation introduced above, which articulates the modalities as qualifications not of sentences or propositions but instead of things/objects/beings, is wholly ignored. But it then makes no sense to speak of the modalities as *metaphysical.*

[4] The modalities are among the most powerful resources human thinking has for attaining intelligibility. They are absolutely indispensable theoretical components of philosophical conceptions. As briefly shown above, this does *not* mean that they are concepts or structures of the mind or of thinking, ones that thinking or the mind would, from the outside (so to speak) apply to or project onto actuality or the dimension of Being.[79] The structural-systematic philosophy radically rejects philosophies of subjectivity that so understand the mind-world relation. As shown in the following section, it understands the capabilities of the mind and of thinking instead as ways in which the dimension of Being manifests itself.

---

[79] Kant uses the term "*hineinlegen* [to put into]" in a central clarification of his transcendental conception: "Thus even physics owes the so advantageous revolution in its way of thinking solely to the inspiration that what reason would not be able to know of itself and has to learn from nature, it has to seek in the latter (not impute to it) in accordance with what reason itself *puts into nature* [*in die Natur hineinlegt*]" (*CPuR* Bxiii–xiv; t.a.; emphasis added). This text shows particularly clearly the tension and incoherence at the heart of the position of transcendental philosophy. In the passage just quoted, Kant presents the thesis that reason seeks to learn from nature what it can learn only from nature (thus, something that it would not learn by considering only itself), and it does so in accordance with what it itself puts into nature. Yet equally central to Kant's transcendental philosophy is the thesis that things in themselves—what nature is in itself—nevertheless remains unknown. The first of these theses is intricately formulated, but can in principle be understood as articulating a magnificent and correct insight—*if* it did not have to be understood as consistent with the second thesis. The incoherence lies in the following: if reason does not "impute" (*andichten*) anything to nature, but instead seeks *in* nature only "what it must learn from nature," then it is *nature itself, nature in itself*—what else?—that is grasped/articulated/understood and thereby *known*. How then can this be made to cohere with the thesis that *nature itself, nature in itself* remains *unknown*? Nevertheless, it makes sense to speak—indeed, it is ultimately necessary to speak—of reason "imputing" something to nature, presupposing that this "imputing" is correctly interpreted. And it can be correctly understood, because it is not only plausible but—as the structural-systematic philosophy shows—necessary to introduce a distinction between—in Kant's terminology—reason/thinking and nature. In order, however, not to misunderstand the distinction, one must learn a highly important lesson from the passage from Kant quoted above: in order to maintain this distinction *coherently*, one must see that (again in Kant's terms) thinking/reason and nature are two dimensions that can be put into relation to each other only because they presuppose a more comprehensive dimension containing them both. If one attempts to clarify this state of affairs adequately, it quickly becomes clear that the distinction can be articulated more adequately and appropriately in terms different from Kant's. In the structural-systematic philosophy it is articulated as the distinction between the structural (or theoretical) dimension and the universe of discourse (ultimately: the dimension of Being).

3.4.3 The Universal Dimension of Being as Two-Dimensional: The Dimension of Absolutely Necessary Being and the Dimension of Contingent Beings

[1] What must now be shown is that the subterranean problem exposed in the preceding section cannot arise within the structural-systematic philosophy. This opens the way for presenting the structural-systematic conception.

The explanation of why the problem cannot arise is quite simple: the semantics, ontology, and truth theory of the structural-systematic philosophy leave no room for it. The essential elements relevant to this problem are the following: only prime sentences—sentences that do not have the subject-predicate structure—are semantically acceptable in the conception's philosophical language. Such sentences express prime propositions. Prime propositions are, when true, simply identical with facts (prime facts or prime ontological structures). Any duality of true proposition and prime fact is thereby excluded by definition. But it is precisely the duality of true proposition and corresponding ontological state of affairs that results in the unclarity and incoherence, shown above, of the analytic conception.

If one were to develop and use a philosophical variant of German in which, syntactically, the universal dimension of Being could be articulated in strict accordance with the structural-systematic philosophy, one would be forced to introduce many strange-sounding neologisms. In this respect, English is significantly more accommodating, because it, unlike German, provides forms for both theoretical operators and prime sentences that include the verb "is," and allows "Being" to follow either is. Hence, "It's-Being-the-case-that" and "It's-Being-such-that it's redding" are both relatively easily intelligible. But because such formulations are unnecessary, the account that follows does not rely on them.

For the same reason, the following account does not rely on formalizations, even though a modal-logical formalization would be relatively straightforward. One would rely on modal sentential logic (or, as it is also called, modal propositional logic); the sentences and propositions to be formalized would be prime sentences and prime propositions. An example: the sentence "It's necessarily-Being" would be formalized, with "B" for "Being," as: $\Box B$. Read as a theoretical sentence, $\Box B$ would be, "It is the case that it's necessarily-Being."

The course of argumentation provided in the following sections proving that the self-explication of the universal dimension of Being reveals it to be two-dimensional is presented informally and—syntactically, although not semantically—in relatively ordinary language (that is: not by way of syntactically structured prime sentences).

[2] The goal of the proof now to be presented is not of the existence of God. As is emphasized in many places above, the notion *God's existence* is fully confused and therefore one that philosophical theorization should avoid using. It would be premature at this point to ask any questions about God. Moreover, what "exists" means in conjunction with God is problematic at best. This shows that at least many of the discussions concerning the question "Does God exist?" are senseless.

The next step to be taken here is one demonstrating that not everything—not Being itself and as a whole, thus as including all beings—is simply contingent, and therefore that there is *necessary Being*. This demonstration relies on the following largely neutral formulation that is sufficient for present purposes: Being includes an absolutely necessary dimension as well as a contingent dimension. A second formulation, perhaps more easily misunderstood but also more helpful intuitively, is the following: the absolutely universal dimension of Being is two-dimensional.

Many people, including many philosophers and scientists, simply assume that everything is contingent, "everything" here meaning what this book terms Being as such and as a whole. The demonstration that follows refutes this assumption by means of an indirect, *modus tollens* proof.

Before this argument is presented and explained in detail, two of its characteristics are noted. The first is that the argument articulates an extremely abstract and maximally universal state of affairs. In traditional terminology, the state of affairs argumentatively explained is a metaphysical one. No matter what terminology is used to describe it, however, what is important is that the argument involves no presuppositions concerning any specific domain or concerning time and space or anything of the sort. Its focal point is an absolutely fundamental and comprehensive consequence of the acceptance of the thesis that everything is contingent; that consequence is the possibility of absolute nothingness.

The abstractness of the proof is more clearly revealed if the proof is compared to the *tertia via* of Thomas Aquinas—his so-called third proof of the existence of God.[80] There is only a *specific* similarity, because there

---

[80] *Structure and Being* (449–51) provides an account of Aquinas's third way more detailed than the one that follows in the main text. Aquinas presents his third way in the *Summa Theologiae* (I q. 2 a. 3; the following translation is from *Structure and Being*):

The third way is taken from possibility and necessity, and runs thus: we find in nature things that have the possibility of being and of not being, because they are found to be generated and to pass away, and consequently have the possibility of being and of not

are centrally important differences between the two. The similarity is that both arguments rely on the modalities possible–necessary–contingent. There are five centrally important differences. First, Aquinas considers only beings, whereas the proof presented below thematizes Being as such and as a whole. Second, Aquinas begins from a concrete phenomenon, i.e., that there are contingent beings. This book's proof makes no reference to concrete phenomena. Third, Thomas includes time as a relevant factor, which indeed it is for him, given his exclusive concentration on beings. He writes, "If everything has the possibility of not being, then at one time there was nothing." This inclusion of time brings with it insoluble problems. The proof presented below does not include time or anything similar. Fourth, Aquinas also includes causality as a relevant factor: "Everything necessary either has its necessity caused from elsewhere, or not." There is no mention of causality in the proof presented below.

---

being. It is, however, impossible for these always to be [textual variant: . . . that all that is of this sort], for that which has the possibility of not being at some time is not. Therefore, if everything has the possibility of not being, then at one time there was nothing. Now if this is true, even now there would be nothing, because that which is not begins to be only by means of something that already is. Therefore, if (at one time) there was nothing, then it was impossible for anything to have begun to be; and thus even now nothing would be—which is manifestly false. Therefore, not all beings are merely possible, but there must be something the being of which is necessary.

[But everything necessary either has its necessity caused from elsewhere, or not. It is, however, impossible to go on to infinity in necessary (things) that have causes of their necessity, just as this is not possible in the case of efficient causes (as is shown above, in the second proof). It is therefore necessary to assume something that is necessary by itself and that does not have the cause of its necessity elsewhere, but that instead is the cause of the necessity of the other (things). This all call God.]

The original Latin is the following:

Tertia via est sumpta ex possibili et necessario: quae talis est. Invenimus enim in rebus quaedam quae sunt possibilia esse et non esse; cum quaedam inveniantur generari et corrumpi, et per consequens possibilia esse et non esse. Impossibile est autem omnia quae sunt talia, semper esse [variant text: . . . omnia quae sunt talia esse]: quia quod possibile est non esse, quandoque non est. Si igitur omnia sunt possibilia non esse, aliquando nihil fuit in rebus. Sed si hoc est verum, etiam nunc nihil esset: quia quod non est, non incipit esse nisi per aliquid quod est; si igitur nihil fuit ens, impossibile fuit quod aliquid inciperet esse, et sic modo nihil esset: quod patet esse falsum. Non ergo omnia entia sunt possibilia: sed oportet aliquid esse necessarium in rebus.

[Omne autem necessarium vel habet causam suae necessitatis aliunde, vel non habet. Non est autem possibile quod procedatur in infinitum in ncessariis, quae habent causam suae necessitatis sicut nec in causis efficientibus. . . . Ergo necesse est ponere aliquid quod sit per se necessarium, non habens causam suae necessitatis aliunde, sed quod est causa necessitatis aliis: quod omnes dicunt Deum.]

Fifth, Aquinas identifies the being to whom his way leads with God. Chapter 1 shows why this is a mistake.

[3] The proof is now to be presented in its simplest possible form, one that is informal and easily intelligible. It is in *modus tollens:* if *p*, then *q*, but not *q*, therefore not *p*. It is as follows:

If everything—that is, Being as such and as a whole—were contingent,
      then absolute nothingness would be possible;
but absolute nothingness is impossible;
therefore, not everything is contingent.

Because contingency and necessity are mutually exclusive and jointly exhaustive, it follows that there must be—in this book's preferred formulation—a necessary dimension of Being. This conclusion is of course extremely abstract and general, but the account that follows shows that its explication leads to quite concrete results.

[i] The proof is now to be explained in detail. Its first premise is an implication. Although its truth might appear obvious, analysis of it is in order. If absolutely everything, Being as such and as a whole, were contingent, *then it could have been the case* that there were neither Being itself nor any beings. This might sound like a fantastically abstract fiction, but it is not. To the contrary, careful consideration of it reveals what is at the core of all of our thinking, talking, knowing, etc. Nevertheless, the all-is-contingent thesis is generally not understood as having the implication the proof's first premise articulates. The usual understanding involves a notion of Being as a process without beginning or end, such that items in the process continually disappear but are simultaneously replaced by new items, so that Being is something like an immense, self-developing mass. To those having this notion, the thesis that, if this mass were contingent, it *could* simply vanish, is unimaginable. This reveals the utter superficiality of the notion, which can in no way withstand strict philosophical analysis. The immense systematic power of the analytically available clause "it could have been the case" cannot be seen by those who have no more than this superficial understanding of the everything-is-contingent thesis.

This state of affairs can be articulated at all only via the introduction of the pseudo-concept *absolute nothingness*. Why, and in what sense, this is a pseudo-concept is explained below, in the consideration of the second premise. What is important at this point is to emphasize that the all-is-contingent thesis cannot avoid the implication articulated in the first premise. This is important because attempts to avoid it are sometimes made, although formulations of the attempts are diffuse at best. The gist of such attempts is the following: it is indeed correct that the all-is-contingent thesis entails the possibility of everything's not having been and of everything's disappearing, but this "everything" must be correctly understood, as follows: indeed, every single thing (every being) is merely possible, thus need not have been and need not continue to be, but if any one had not been or ceased to be, then there would have been or would be some other thing (entity), because the endless process of Being must go on. The process of Being itself, as the self-developing mass, would thus not disappear.

The diffuse attempt just sketched cannot be made adequate because it leaves the process of Being wholly unclarified. Is that process contingent? If so, then it itself—the comprehensive process itself—need not have been and need not continue to be; there must be some alternative. The question is not whether the process *will* cease to be, but of whether it *could* cease to be—or instead it *cannot* cease to be. Only if it could cease to be is it contingent; otherwise, it is necessary.

The implication articulated in the first premise thus stands. To be noted is that it does not say that then absolute nothingness *would be* or *would exist*. Adding either of these phrases would make the premise obscure and problematic. The premise concerns only the modality *possibility:* absolute nothingness would be *possible*. This formulation is fully sufficient for the rejection of the all-is-contingent thesis, because if absolute nothingness is said even to be possible, contradiction ensues. Rejection of the all-is-contingent thesis also makes possible the avoidance of additional problems.

[ii] The heart of the argument is the second premise. It articulates the negation of the consequent of the first premise. Absolute nothingness is *not* possible. This is so for at least three reasons.

[a] *Absolute nothingness* is a non-concept; it is not thinkable because it is self-contradictory and is therefore a pseudo-concept. To think it at all, one would have to determine it, but one would thereby ascribe to it something or other that it excludes: one could determine it only by naming something or other, but that something or other would be a determinate way of Being—it would be something that *was*, in one way or another. One can only speak *about* absolute nothingness in a paradoxical manner, and the only reason to do so is to articulate its absurdity.

[b] The concept *possibility of absolute nothingness* is radically self-contradictory, because *possibility* is *possibility of Being;* it is contradictory to say that absolute nothingness could possibly *be*.

[c] The all-is-contingent thesis entails not only the *possibility of abso-*

lute nothingness, but also the *additional* assumption that the dimension of Being, and with it beings, could have posited by some sort of spontaneous generation so as to have replaced absolute nothingness. The thought of such a spontaneous generation even as possible is not more than a senseless pseudo-thought. There would be nothing in absolute nothingness to explain any such event and, by the pseudo-hypothesis, absolute nothingness would have been [!] all that there was [!]. No dimension of Being is in any way compatible with absolute nothingness, so there can be no sensible talk of any transition from the latter to the former.

Because the thesis that everything is contingent entails absurdities, it is not the case that everything is contingent; that is, there is necessary Being, which can be designated neutrally and generally, at this point, as a *necessary dimension of Being.* Q.E.D.

[4] The result of the preceding proof can be expressed briefly as follows: the universal dimension of Being is, more precisely, two-dimensional, consisting of a necessary dimension and a contingent dimension. To be sure, this two-dimensionality must be correctly understood. The two dimensions do not have the same status; instead, because one of the dimensions is necessary, the other—the contingent—is subordinate to it. Section 3.5 explains this fully.

Before further steps are taken in the explication of Being as two-dimensional, it is appropriate to introduce the term/concept *absolutely necessary,* because it plays an important role in what follows. *Absolute* is not synonymous with *necessary.* Necessary Being out of itself cannot not be in any respect and thus is fully independent of anything other; everything other is totally dependent on necessary Being. From this it follows that necessary Being is not conditioned in any way by anything other and is therefore absolute, because what necessarily *is* is in no way relative to and is not conditioned in any manner by anything other. This is made explicit by the formulation "absolutely necessary Being." For the sake of clarity and brevity, the following account relies primarily on the concept *absolutely necessary Being* or, for short, *the absolute.*[81]

---

[81] The Christian metaphysics of the Middle Ages (Thomas Aquinas) does not use the term/concept *the absolute.* Likewise, Kant relies instead on the concepts the necessary and (above all) *the unconditioned.* The post-Kantian German idealists were the first to use "the absolute" in a comprehensive manner to designate the necessary and unconditioned being (God). Since then, it has remained common practice to use this concept in talk about God.

3.5 Explication of the Relation Between Absolutely Necessary Being and the Contingent Dimension of Being as Key to a Conception of Absolutely Necessary Being as Minded (as Personal)

At this point begins a new phase of the systematic presentation, one that is of central importance to the subject matter and hence to the purposes of this book. Because of its novelty, some remarks on methodology are in order.

3.5.1 Methodological Considerations

The two-dimensionality of the universal dimension of Being is a topic that, even considered and adequately treated in itself, opens the way for radically new treatments of the most central metaphysical questions, particularly those that arise about the relation between Being and God. This subsection examines one central aspect of this newly opened way.

The way that is taken in traditional metaphysical considerations of the relation between Being and God, in one appropriate description, starts from the bottom and works up. Two of its most central aspects require identification. The first is that this way starts with a specific worldly phenomenon and aims to transcend that phenomenon by reaching some highest point. This way is epitomized by the classical proofs of God's existence.[82] The second aspect is one that is required by the first, but concerns the status of sentences used to articulate the ascent and transcendence essential to this way. The terms on which those sentences rely are first acquired in the worldly or finite domain but then used in the metaphysical dimension as well. This procedure is termed that of *analogy*. According to this analogical procedure, the *primary* or *genuine* semantic or conceptual content associated with a given term is attained through consideration of the worldly phenomenon that is the starting point for the ascent being articulated; its application to God is subsequent, and its semantic or conceptual content in that application is *analogical* rather than identical to its worldly application. Both aspects of this ascent show that the God that the ascent claims to reach is literally a *meta-physical X:* an *X* whose defining characteristic is that of being *meta* in the sense of beyond. This introduces a problem of coherence for the entire conception; chapter 1 considers various forms this problem has taken, and ad-

---

[82] The peculiar status of the ontological proof is considered above; see 3.2.2a Excursus 2.

ditional forms are considered both in what follows in this chapter and in chapter 4.

In complete distinction from the traditional ascent described in the preceding paragraph, the way taken in the structural-systematic philosophy does not begin with any worldly or finite phenomenon or state of affairs of any sort whatsoever. But it also does not attempt to do anything like derive determinations from the absolutely universal dimension of Being, considered abstractly. It does indeed start from the universal dimension of Being, but only as more precisely determined as two-dimensional. This determination provides the next task—that of *explicating this two-dimensionality*. More precisely: the task is that of explicating the *relation* between the two dimensions. The explication determines each of the relata more precisely. Because the contingent dimension is familiar in advance, it might appear that it requires no further determination. But that is mere appearance. Our familiarity with the contingent dimension (the dimension of the world or universe and the beings within it) does not provide us with anything approaching an adequate understanding of its philosophically systematic (traditionally: metaphysical) status. Determining that status requires explicating its relation to the absolutely necessary dimension of Being.

3.5.2 The Absolutely Necessary Dimension of Being as Absolutely Necessary Minded (Personal) Being

[1] In distinction from the contingent dimension, with which we are extensively familiar before we begin to develop scientific theories about it, the absolutely necessary dimension is initially unfamiliar and thus relatively undetermined, despite various ordinary-language formulations that vaguely articulate God(s) or heavenly dimensions taken to be beyond or outside of the physical universe. Such formulations and what they attempt to articulate are not only of no use to philosophy, they are in addition obstacles that increase the difficulty of the task of adequately articulating the absolutely necessary dimension. As indicated above, undertaking that task requires explication of the relation between the contingent dimension and the absolutely necessary dimension.

The theoretical level on which this relation can be thematized is the one introduced in section 3.2.1.2 as that of the intentional coextensionality of the human mind with Being as such and as a whole, and thus with the absolutely universal dimension of Being. It thus includes both itself and its relation to the absolutely necessary dimension of Being.

What follows shows that the absolutely necessary dimension of Being is absolutely necessary *minded* Being, whereby being minded involves intelligence, will, and freedom. (For this reason, one can also rely on currently widely used terms and say, *absolutely necessary personal Being*, although the word "person(al)" is easily misunderstood if or when so used.) It is clear that this requires the taking of a significant step; determining the absolutely necessary dimension of Being as absolutely necessary minded Being opens the way to infinitely many fully new avenues for theorization.[83]

[2] There are many arguments in favor of this thesis. The following subsections present two of them.

[i] The first argument links decisively to a central aspect of the relation between the contingent dimension of Being and the absolutely necessary dimension of Being. There can be no doubt that it would be fully unsatisfactory, indeed unacceptable, for theorization to determine this relation only negatively, that is, by saying no more than that there is a distinction between the two dimensions. This would be to say only that the one dimension was not the other. To deny that there is a positive relation between the two would be fully arbitrary, because the human intellect has the unconditional need *and* the capacity to ask and to determine

---

[83] Logical/mathematical structures (beings) are often situated within the non-contingent dimension of Being. Authors who accept the existence of only a "submaximal world" (see *Structure and Being* 5.3.2[5]) term that world "contingent." According to those authors, any submaximal world is contingent because it is a submathematical domain.

There might be several ways of making more precise the notion of the submathematical realm. Take something to be submathematical just in case its existence is contingent. Then consider this proposal: that "the world" could be taken to be the aggregate of all contingent beings. Suppose, that is, that there is such a thing as the aggregate of all contingent beings, and define "the world" to be that thing. All the mathematical entities like sets—the things which are too numerous to aggregate into any single entity—will then lie outside "the world," in this more restricted sense of the term (John Bigelow, "God and the New Math" [1996], 148).

Does this mean that the mathematical beings, in that they "lie outside" the submaximal—and thus the contingent—world, are non-contingent, and therefore necessary? But there is—in some sense—a necessary dimension of Being. Bigelow and those who proceed similarly do not consider such matters. Even aside from that, however, clarification of the *ontological* status of necessity is needed. If one were to say that what is (ontologically) necessary exists in all possible worlds, then a problem arises: what is the ontological status of these worlds themselves? Are they contingent, as they are generally assumed to be? If so, the concept of (ontological) necessity would be peculiar: the necessary would be what existed in all possible *contingent* worlds.

This cluster of problems cannot be more closely considered at this point in this book. In order for the explication of the absolutely necessary dimension of Being to proceed, it suffices to say that logical/mathematical beings (structures) have a *derivative* non-contingent status *within* the absolutely necessary dimension of Being. For additional details, see *Structure and Being*, 452n54.

what this *positive* relation is. Not to actualize this capacity would be to fail to undertake a task *central* to philosophy.

The human mind is characterized above as being *intentionally co-extensive with Being as a whole*. This characterization serves in an indirect proof in favor of the thesis formulated in the title of this section.

If one assumed that the absolutely necessary dimension were not minded but instead somehow other, perhaps a purely abstract principle (however that might be conceived of) or perhaps in some way primordially non-minded, then one would have a bizarre juxtaposition; on one side minded contingent beings that were intentionally coextensive with Being as a whole and thus with the absolutely necessary dimension of Being, and on the other a purely abstract or simply non-minded absolutely necessary dimension of Being. The absolutely necessary dimension of Being, so determined, would then fail to be intentionally coextensive either with itself or with Being as a whole. Is this a coherent conception?

Answering this question requires identifying the criteria or conditions that the relation between the two dimensions, so understood, would have to satisfy. For this, two principles can be introduced, although not simply presented; instead, the principles must be presented *simultaneously* with what reveals them to be principles. As shown in detail in *Structure and Being*,[84] in such an undertaking central argumentative considerations are those of (greater) intelligibility and—as a consequence—(greater) coherence. Intelligibility has an ontological as well as an epistemic status. On the one hand, it is the articulation of the ontological structuration of whatever is being theorized, and on the other, it articulates the intellect as it relates to that subject matter. When the intellect apprehends a specific ontological structuration, intelligibility (with respect to this structuration) is attained, although it can be attained to various degrees. If a conception or theory attains a higher intelligibility in this sense, the result is a specific form of inference to the best explanation.[85]

The decisive thesis may now be presented: the thesis that the absolutely necessary dimension of Being is minded provides *incomparably greater intelligibility* than does the thesis that this dimension is not minded.

Various considerations ground the thesis just introduced; two are briefly developed here. First, the relation between the contingent dimension of Being and the absolutely necessary dimension is one of *total* de-

---

[84] See especially chapter 6.
[85] See the excellent accounts in Peter Forrest, *God Without the Supernatural: A Defense of Scientific Theism* (1996), especially 26–35, 41–42, 117–21.

pendence. This dependence is fully ontological, such that *the entire Being* of contingent human minds is *fully dependent, in every respect,* on the absolutely necessary dimension of Being. This dependence can be explained in various ways, but the core of any explanation is the thesis that *without* the absolutely necessary dimension of Being, no human minds could actually be.

The reason for this lies in the core thought of the argument introduced above concluding that the dimension of Being is two-dimensional. In the present context, this reason can be articulated via the following question: can it be made intelligible that contingent minded beings are or could be *totally dependent*—in the manner just characterized—on a non-minded absolutely necessary dimension of Being? It cannot. To put the matter loosely: the non-minded absolutely necessary dimension of Being would have to be so constituted that the total dependence on it of the minded contingent beings would be explainable. But there is nothing in any non-minded absolutely necessary dimension that could serve in any explanation of this dependence. The contingent human mind includes capabilities that the non-minded absolutely necessary dimension could not have. Because the relation between the two must be a *positive* one, denial that the absolutely necessary dimension of Being is minded results in a simply inexplicable metaphysical gap. No attempt to explain the positive relation between the dimensions on this basis could do justice to the specific character of minded human Being.

The second consideration presented here to ground the thesis of the mindedness of absolutely necessary Being relies on the thesis, introduced above (3.3[2][iii]), that Being as a whole is *universally expressible.* The non-minded absolutely necessary dimension of Being would thus be universally expressible, and thus structured in one way or another. It would not, however, be able to express or articulate itself. The human mind has the incomparably higher status of being both expressible *and* *expressing.* This opens to the human mind capabilities of acting, and of theorizing and producing, that the non-minded absolutely necessary dimension of Being would not have. Here again, that contingent human minds were or could be totally ontologically dependent on a non-minded absolutely necessary dimension of Being cannot be made intelligible—cannot be explained.

[ii] A second argument relying on the same central thought is distinct from the first chiefly in form. It articulates the central thesis concerning the human mind in a more generalized form, that of a principle.

Every ontology that is to do justice to the specific character of different beings or different domains of Being must accept as central the following ontological principle, the *principle of ontological rank* (POR):[86]

(POR)   Something of a higher ontological rank cannot arise exclusively from or be explained exclusively by anything of a lower ontological rank.

The application of the POR to the problem of the determination of the relation between the absolutely necessary and the contingent dimensions of Being leads to an unambiguous conclusion: the ontological rank of a non-minded dimension of Being would be lower than that of contingent human minds. The latter therefore cannot be explained by a non-minded absolutely necessary dimension of Being. The absolutely necessary dimension of Being must be such as to be able to fully explain the contingent dimension of Being. It can do this only if its ontological rank is—at least—no lower than that of the most highly ontologically ranked contingent beings, including of course minded contingent beings. It follows that the absolutely necessary dimension of Being is minded.

Worth emphasizing is that the POR does not conflict with specific phenomena or natural-scientific theories, e.g., ones concerning evolution, although it can conflict with unwarranted extrapolations from those theories. That issue cannot be more closely considered here.[87]

3.6 Absolutely Necessary Minded (Personal) Being as Creator of the World (as Absolute Creating)

At this point in the explication of the universal dimension of Being it is appropriate to recall that this dimension is more precisely determined as minded, and yet more precisely determined as absolutely necessary minded, personal *Being*. It is *Being*, not *a being*, because its status is absolutely unique. It is not an additional being, not even a (or the) first or highest being. Because it is not, its explication is immune to the critiques made by Heidegger and postmodernists of onto-theo-logy, regardless of the possible effectiveness of such critiques when they are directed else-

---

[86] For explanation and grounding of this principle, the most important case of ontological rank, that of human beings as minded, is of decisive significance.

[87] See *Structure and Being*, 455ff.

where. It remains the case, however, that the approach taken here is in a specific respect continuous with one suggested—although not consequently developed—by Thomas Aquinas. The continuity is with what Aquinas says about the absolute (God) as *ipsum esse per se subsistens*.[88]

Emphasized above is that the contingent dimension of Being is *totally* dependent on the absolutely necessary dimension of Being and hence on absolutely necessary personal Being. This dependence is now to be considered in greater detail. As absolutely minded, absolute Being is characterized by absolute intelligence and absolutely free will. From this it follows that the total dependency of the contingent dimension of Being on absolute Being results from a free decision of absolute Being to originate the *contingent* dimension of Being out of its non-Being. This means that the total dependency of contingent beings on absolute Being is the dependency articulable as Being-created.

In classical Christian metaphysics, this free act of absolute Being is called creation, and the latter is characterized as bringing forth out of nothingness. It is obvious that this "nothingness" cannot mean "absolute nothingness," because absolute Being is always presupposed. The Christian metaphysical tradition more precisely characterizes creation as "the bringing forth (of a being) out of the non-Being (or nonexistence) of that being and without any presupposed or underlying subject (in the sense of any sort of underlying stuff)."[89]

3.6.1 Misinterpretations of the Idea of Creation

The idea of creation can be correctly understood and evaluated only within the framework of a conception of Being as such and as a whole. This is one of the deepest and indeed most grandiose thoughts that the

---

[88] See, e.g., *STh* I q. 4 a. 2 c; I q. 44 a 2 c; *De pot.* q. 7 a. 2 ad 5. On Aquinas's position as a whole, see Puntel, *SGTh*, chapter 3.

[89] The Christian metaphysical tradition provides the following concise and accurate formulation: "Creatio est productio entis ex sui nihilo et subiecti." A characteristic formulation by Thomas Aquinas is the following: "Creation . . . is the bringing forth of a thing [being] with respect to its entire (substantial) being, without the presupposition of any sort of substratum [*Creatio . . . est productio alicuius rei secundum suam totam substantiam, nullo praesupposito*]" (*STh* I q. 65 a. 4 c.). [Added to *Being and God:* The Latin term "*productio*," used in the metaphysical tradition, cannot be equated with "production" in the usual current sense, so "production" should not be used to translate it. "Bringing forth," as in the text to which this note is appended, is one option. Just below ([2][i]), it is shown that Heidegger makes a serious mistake in interpretation when he translates "*productio*" with *Herstellung,* the German counterpart to "production." This leads him to reduce the grand idea of creation to the level of what is done by craftsmen or machines.]

human mind can have. Precisely because of its unique status, however, it is—at least for many—not easy to grasp or articulate it adequately. It is therefore not surprising that—especially at present—it is rarely at best so grasped and articulated. Much could be said about this. What follows in this section briefly considers and corrects only two characteristically distorting misinterpretations and crass misunderstandings.

[1] The first misunderstanding is so widespread as to qualify at present as the *forma mentis* of most human beings in the contemporary lifeworld that is decisively influenced by science and technology. For those relying on this *forma mentis,* such phenomena as arising, novelty, coming into Being, etc., can be imagined or conceived of only within the contexts of more comprehensive phenomena such as processes or, especially, evolution. What characterizes everything that takes place *within* any such context is that some basis or raw material is always presupposed. That there should be matter available for reconfiguration is simply taken for granted by this way of thinking. Everything that happens is then understood as modifying or transforming something that was available for such alteration. Ultimately, all of actuality is identified with the evolving cosmos.

The way of thinking described in the preceding paragraph leaves no room for creation in the genuine metaphysical sense, i.e., creation as absolute origination, such that absolute origination in no way involves the alteration or reconfiguration of anything that the origination would presuppose. The ever-available matter (or energy, or whatever) presupposed by the technical-scientific way of thinking is in no way presupposed by creation as absolute origination. When various scientists and philosophers extrapolate wildly from scientific theories in order to raise questions about the *beginning* of the evolving cosmos—the entire physical universe—they utterly ignore creation as origination and thereby arbitrarily restrict what can be meant by *beginning.* To object to such extrapolations is in no way to object to natural-scientific theories, including those of physical cosmology; the objection is only to the extrapolations that range far beyond those theories themselves.[90]

[2] The second misunderstanding is found in the works of philosophers who consider themselves to be critics of metaphysics whose ways of thinking they present as being more radical than metaphysical thinking is. Of decisive importance to evaluating their projects is determining what they recognize as metaphysical. This book contains thorough consideration of the thought of three of these critics, i.e., Heidegger,

---

[90] For detailed treatment, see *Structure and Being* (especially 4.5.1).

Levinas, and Marion. The following subsection considers an aspect of Heidegger's critique not treated above in chapter 2. Chapter 4 is devoted to the thought of Levinas and Marion.

[i] As shown in chapter 1, in his posthumously published lecture course *History of Philosophy from Thomas Aquinas to Kant*, Heidegger attributes to Aquinas the view that "Being = presence-at-hand [*Vorhandenheit*]" (see 1.3.1[1]). He then writes as follows:

> The basis of the proof [i.e., Aquinas's proofs of the existence of God]: *videmus* [we see], *sensu constat* [our senses clearly show], *inveniuntur* [there are found] beings that are here, i.e., that were pro-duced [*hergestellt wurde*]. What is produced requires a producer. Horizon of the understanding of Being on which the proofs are based: producing and produced, as present-at-hand [*Vorhandenes*]. Producer that itself must be present-at-hand. *That this [producer] is creator, i.e., creates out of nothing, does not undermine the thesis that producing and thus Being-present-at-hand determine the idea of Being; instead, they only confirm it.*[91]

This text expresses in full clarity the radical distortion to which Heidegger subjects the idea of creation articulated in the Christian metaphysics of Being. Heidegger misinterprets Being as Being-present-at-hand, and then presents it, as present-at-hand, as produced. Both the postulated producer and the product are likewise taken to be present-at-hand. "This presence-at-hand, this product, requires a producer who was present-at-hand before the production but only as such, not as produced, but as always present-at-hand."[92] And then the creator is said to "produce from nothing." Yet this putative fact, Heidegger maintains apodictically, "does not undermine the thesis that producing and thus Being-present-at-hand determine the idea of Being; instead, they only confirm it."

Heidegger here not only presents a wholly indefensible misinterpretation, but also makes a simple and elementary mistake that he attempts to conceal behind a dogmatic assertion ("does not undermine . . ."). Chapter 1 reveals in detail that Heidegger fully misinterprets Aquinas's concept *Being*. In the passage under current consideration, he presents production [*Herstellung*] as a relation between two beings both of which are present-at-hand; this is correct, because something is produced only if it is produced *from something else*. "Produce" here has its ordinary-language

---

[91] *GA*, volume 23, p. 94 (emphasis added). Similar passages are contained in *Being and Time* (see §6, p. 33; §20, p. 123ff.). These passages are often cited and commented on.
[92] *GA* 23:95.

meaning: one takes something that is available and transforms it (transforms the material) such that something different becomes available, thanks to its having been produced. Produce "out of nothing" is therefore nonsensical. What Heidegger says is incoherent, because on the one hand he characterizes production as a relation between two beings, both present-at-hand, and on the other he presents creation as a "production out of nothing." "Nothing" is of course not present-at-hand, not available. The incoherence is clear, but Heidegger appears not to notice it.

The only way Heidegger could avoid the incoherence would be to say that the metaphysical God cannot produce anything out of nothing. The argument would have to be that the metaphysical God is also a present-at-hand being, so each of its acts would be an act of one present-at-hand being on another present-at-hand being. But no such act is a production out of nothing. If, however, Heidegger had made this move, then he would have opened himself to the objection that his incapacity correctly to understand and correctly to evaluate the thought of a radical production out of nothing shows that his premises—i.e., everything he says about Aquinas and Being-as-presence-at-hand—is false.

It is remarkable that Heidegger explicitly maintains, ". . . the cause as *causa sui.* This is the accurate name for God in philosophy" (*ID* 70–71). It is clear that Heidegger simply presupposes a simplistic concept of cause as a relation between beings present-at-hand and thoughtlessly applies it to God, such that for him God as present-at-hand has a causal *self*-relation, as *causa sui.*

Another remark is in order here. If one considers Heidegger's distorting assertions that make of creation a relation of production involving only beings present-at-hand, one does well thereby to keep in mind what chapter 2 shows about his treatments of Being-as-*Ereignis.* As noted there, in the "Summary" of the seminar on the lecture "Time and Being," the following question is posed: "What is the *Ereignete* that *Ereignis* [*ereignet*]?" (*TB* 42; t.a.). According to the "Summary," the essay "The Principle of Identity" says the following:

> What *Ereignis ereignet,* i.e., brings into its own and maintains within *Ereignis,* [is] the belonging together of Being and human being. Within this belonging together what belong together are no longer Being and human being, but—as *Ereignete*—mortals within the fourfold of the world. (*TB* 42; t.a.)

Here Heidegger speaks not of the relation between Being and beings, but of that between *Ereignis* and *Ereignete.* But how does he articulate this relation that he now names *Ereignis*? The second passage contains the answer to this question, although not obviously: "what *Ereignis ereignet,* i.e., *brings* into its own and *maintains* within *Ereignis*" (emphasis added). So: *Ereignen* involves both a *bringing* and a *maintaining,* thus an *acting* of some sort. But what of this bringing/maintaining/acting? Heidegger articulates only its *result,* that is, "the belonging together of Being and human being," such that "what belong together are no longer Being and human being, but—as *Ereignete*—mortals within the fourfold of the world." What is *Ereignen* itself as a bringing/maintaining/doing? Of this, Heidegger says nothing.

Heidegger thereby makes an extensively consequential presupposition that he never even begins to think through. The presupposition becomes clear with the posing of the following simple question: if *Ereignen brings* what it *ereignet* into its own (*in das Eigene*) and *maintains* it within (*im*) *Ereignis,* is this "what" that is *ereignet* by *Ereignen* given or available and thus presupposed? If not, does that mean that this "what" is *produced*? And if it is produced, is it produced out of nothing or out of something somehow other that, for its part, is presupposed as somehow given or available? It is intelligible that something is *brought into its own* and *maintained within Ereignis* only if whatever is brought into its own is presupposed, that it is somehow present-at-hand so that it can be brought into and maintained within. Heidegger cannot clarify this opacity, which is central to his thought. Had he tried to do so, he would have encountered the following dilemma: *either* he presupposes that *what* is *ereignet* is presupposed by *Ereignis, or* he holds that what is *ereignet* originates from the *Ereignen.* If he took the former option, he would have to accept what is *ereignet* in a basically trivial manner as available, and would have to admit that the passage said nothing more about it. This would also have as a consequence that essentially his entire conception of Being, *Ereignis,* etc., would fail to be even minimally coherent. It would also show that his conception had the same structure that his radically distorted interpretation of the metaphysical thought of creation ascribes to that thought. Creation, he says, is a relation of production between God as present-at-hand and beings as present-at hand; *Ereignen* would be just such a relation if it were interpreted as production out of something. If, however, Heidegger accepted the second horn of the dilemma, then what *Ereignis ereignet* would have been produced out of nothing, and thus created. Explicit acceptance of this consequence would shatter Heidegger's thinking in its entirety.

Heidegger cannot avoid the dilemma. There is nothing in his thinking that would enable him to sail between the Scylla of the reduction of *Ereignis* to a relation between two present-at-hand beings and the Charybdis of interpreting *Ereignis* as creation ex nihilo. That he cannot avoid the dilemma reveals the utter superficiality of his thinking.

[ii] Both Levinas and Marion deal with the thought of creation.

Marion, particularly, is decisively influenced by Heidegger in that he simply appropriates Heidegger's misinterpretation of metaphysical Being (*esse*) as presence-at-hand and the resultant misinterpretation of creation as a relation of production between two beings that are present-at-hand. Chapter 4 shows in detail how Marion understands or misunderstands this thought in light of passages from the Bible, but it first presents and analyzes the basic features of his comprehensive conception (see section 4.2.4.4). Chapter 4 also critically analyzes Levinas's wholly inadequate interpretation of creation (see section 4.1.3.2.3).

3.6.2 Creation as Positing-into-Being of the Contingent Dimension of Being

Traditionally, the attempt is made to clarify the creation of the world by God with the aid of a metaphysically understood principle of causality. The concept of causality is acquired via explanations of innerworldly phenomena and then applied to God by means of analogy. This is a decisive point of attack for postmodern critics of this concept and of creation as understood by means of it. It cannot be denied that the point is one that is vulnerable to attack. Instead of considering this issue, however, the account that follows articulates creation without explicit initial reliance on causation. What emerges is a concept of creation to which the Aristotelian concept of causation is not easily applied.

First, the question to be addressed must be formulated precisely. The question arises here within the context of an ongoing explication of the primordial, universal dimension of Being; it can therefore rely on theses introduced in earlier stages of that explication. The most central of those theses is that Being is two-dimensional, that there is both an absolutely necessary dimension of Being and a contingent dimension of Being. The former of these dimensions is further explicated as absolutely necessary minded or personal Being, and is more precisely determined as absolutely free. The task at hand is that of explicating the relation between absolutely necessary, free Being and the contingent dimension of Being.

Shown above is that the contingent dimension of Being is *totally dependent* on the absolutely necessary dimension of Being, i.e., more determinately, on absolutely necessary Being. Now to be shown is what this means. By definition, contingent beings are, but might not be, that is, that consideration of them alone can yield no explanation of the fact that they are. Because beings might not have been, the following question presses unavoidably: how did they come into Being? If they did not come into Being on their own, because they cannot have brought themselves into Being by their own means, they can have come into Being only from elsewhere, i.e., thanks to a dimension or domain other than the dimension or domain that they constitute. But what can "from elsewhere" mean here—what other dimension or domain could this be? Because it cannot be in any way contingent, the only candidate that provides an answer to the question is absolutely necessary Being, and absolutely necessary Being answers the question definitively. Because, however, this is absolutely necessary *free* Being, freedom is also a part of the answer to the question. The contingent dimension of Being came into Being by means of the absolute freedom of absolutely necessary Being.

This state of affairs is accurately expressed as follows: free, absolutely necessary Being *posits* the contingent dimension of Being *into Being*, and does so *absolutely* in the sense that the positing does not presuppose anything prior or anything underlying or anything of the sort. This is creation.

What "absolute positing into Being" means and entails and what it does not mean and does not entail require emphasis. Creation (in the active sense), as a so-conceived positing, relates to the contingent dimension of Being as a whole, that is, to the totality of beings. (To be kept in mind here is that, according to the structural-systematic philosophy, absolutely necessary, free Being is *not a being*.) This means that absolutely necessary, free Being does not posit into Being any specific or isolated being; it instead posits the contingent dimension of Being as a whole. What emerges or develops *within* the contingent dimension of Being is not *created*, in the technical sense of "created" articulated above. The reason for this is that *everything* that emerges *within* the contingent dimension of Being (the world, the universe) emerges *from* something, however this "something" may be designated (another being, matter, energy, etc.). Attaining full clarity on this point is at present a highly pressing task because of the in some cases crass and extraordinarily widespread misunderstandings of creation.

As noted above, the metaphysical tradition attempts to explicate creation by means of the concept of causality. This is problematic. To see why, one must strictly distinguish between (a) the traditional metaphysical characterization (or, one could say, definition) of creation— the bringing forth (of a being) out of the non-Being (or nonexistence) of that being and without any presupposed or underlying subject (in the sense of any sort of underlying stuff) (*productio entis ex nihilo sui et subiecti*)—and (b) the subsumption of this creation under the category of causality. Only (a) is relevant to the understanding and evaluation of metaphysical creation. Whether creation, as articulated in (a), is subsumed under any more universal concept is a distinct question.

Thomas Aquinas often explicitly characterizes *causa/cause*, but introduces four formulations that, at least at first glance, are not synonymous. These are:

(a) "The cause of something, in the genuine sense, is that without which that something cannot be, because every effect depends on its cause."[93]

(b) "What is called cause in the genuine sense is that from which something necessarily follows."[94] Thomas then clarifies this sense as follows: "Sometimes, to be sure, cause is said to be that which brings about, and that is what cause is in the genuine sense and in truth; because cause is that from which an effect follows."[95]

(c) "Cause [is] that from which the Being of another follows."[96]

(d) "This term 'cause' designates a kind of influence on the Being of what is caused."[97]

As is easily seen, these formulations are not synonymous, but neither are they mutually exclusive. Instead, they articulate determinate aspects of an envisaged concept in distinct ways. The most important aspect is the one articulated in (d): influence on the Being of what is caused. But none of the four formulations indicates how either this influence or the Being of what is caused is more precisely to be understood. It does, however, appear incontestable that all of the formulations characterize a relation (or relations) between beings, and thus between constituents of a world that is presupposed.

Aquinas, and with him most metaphysicians in the Christian tradition, subsume creation under the category of causality articulated in the four preceding formulations. This is not surprising and indeed is presumably unavoidable given the focus of these authors on beings rather than on Being. One considers a specific concept as it is realized in the domain of finite, contingent beings and then transfers it, via a daring and

---

[93] "Illud est proprie causa alicuius, sine quo esse non potest: omnis enim effectus dependet a sua causa" (*STh* III q. 86 a. 6, sed contra).

[94] "Proprie causa dicitur ad quam ex necessitate sequitur aliquid" (*De pot.*: De malo, q. 3 a. 3 ad 3).

[95] "Quandoque vero dicitur causa id quod est perficiens; et haec vere et proprie causa dicitur, quia causa est ad quam sequitur effectus" (ibid., c).

[96] "Causa [est] ad quam sequitur esse alterius" (*In octo libros Physicorum Aristotelis expositio*, L. II, 1. x, no. 240).

[97] "Hoc . . . nomen causa importat influxum quemdam ad esse causati" (*In duodecim libros Metaphysicorum Aristotelis expositio*, L. V, 1. 1, no. 750.

powerful leap, to God. If this is done with causality, then creation can appear only as an extreme case of causality so understood. This, however, is extremely problematic because all of the connotations the concept has in the finite domain remain in play, even if as negated.

Given this problematicity, one cannot simply subsume creation under the concept *causality*. Any and every such subsumption is avoided by the systematic explanation of creation introduced above, according to which creation is the positing-into-within-Being of a contingent dimension of Being, without the presupposition of any being(s) of any sort whatsoever. This is in the literal and strictest sense a *singulare tantum*—an absolute singularity, such that the plural "creations" is utterly senseless. It is an explication exclusively of the relation between absolutely necessary Being, as creating, and the contingent dimension of Being.

3.6.3 An Objection

In a consideration of all of the relevant aspects of the treatment of the creation issue within the framework of the structural-systematic philosophy, it makes sense to raise the question of what objections could be raised against that treatment. Many objections could be imagined, but most would be based on either misunderstandings or unexamined assumptions. The structural-systematic philosophy must respond to such objections, but responding to them is not required by the purposes of this book. Those purposes are, however, served by the introduction of one specific objection that, if it were on target, would make all talk of creation a waste of time. The following subsections consider a general formulation of the objection, and then one that is specifically natural-scientific.

[1] The general version of the objection can take both a quite simple form and an argumentative one. The simple version arises from noting what appears to be a widespread general—as opposed to philosophical or scientific—tendency simply to accept things as given, as some kind of brute fact requiring no explanation. If it indeed requires no explanation, then what reason could there be for even considering the issue of creation? That this question requires no answer is presumably obvious; sufficient response to it is provided by simply noting that the assumption on which it is based is at best highly problematic, because throughout history, human beings have sought and provided explanations for the givenness of what is given.

The argumentative form of the general objection requires more careful consideration. This form takes science and technology into account, and argues on that basis that it is sensible to seek explanations only for phenomena, events, or occurrences that are within a dimension that is simply presupposed (and that can be termed nature, the world, the cosmos, etc.); it thus makes no sense to seek to explain *that dimension itself.*

Responding to this argument requires clarification of *explanation.* As shown above in 3.2.3, there are on the one hand explanations of semantic values—loosely, of meanings of words and concepts—but also scientific explanations that involve laws and empirical research. Also shown above is that scientific explanations include both explanations *why* and explanations *how.* When specific philosophical questions are discussed, including the question concerning creation, the word "explanation" is generally used in a wholly indeterminate and unclarified manner. This makes no sense. Similarly, it is incontestable that many presentations, including the thesis that the world is God's creation, are themselves hopelessly indeterminate and thus likewise senseless. If the question about creation is understood as a why question in the sense explained above (in 3.2.3), it is misunderstood, because in that case the background dimension presupposed both by the phenomenon to be explained and by what is introduced to explain it is left unthematized, although its thematization is absolutely indispensable to the adequately understood concept of creation. The reason is that why questions are indeed sensible only when they concern relations *within* some presupposed dimension. Creation, however, answers a question relating to that dimension itself (the entire contingent dimension of Being).

The objection under consideration articulates an insight that, made precise, proves to be correct, but then draws from that insight a conclusion that is false. The correct insight is that when "explanation" means "explanation why," questions asking for explanations can be posed only concerning elements within a dimension that is presupposed (whatever it is called: nature, the world, the cosmos, etc.), thus not concerning that dimension itself. The argument fails, however, in assuming that the question answered by creation is or aspires to be a why question of this sort. It is not, although it often has been and still is so treated even by metaphysicians.

The question answered by creation is a question concerning the dimension itself; in the terminology of the structural-systematic philosophy, it is a question concerning the *contingent dimension of Being itself and as a whole,* not concerning anything *within* this dimension.

One can thus continue to speak of the creation question as asking for an explanation, but "explanation" must be correctly understood as an explanation of *how,* and that itself must be made adequately precise. It must be indicated what the whole is whose how—whose internal configuration or structuration—is to be explained or articulated. This is done in preceding sections: the whole in question is the primordial, universal dimension of Being, which is explicated via responses to a series of how questions. Having been explicated as a two-dimensionality of Being, it comes to be explicated as including the relation between absolutely necessary, free Being and the contingent dimension of Being. The question answered by creation is then the following how question: *how* is this relation itself most accurately articulated?

In order to avoid misunderstandings that easily arise, for the most part this book designates creation as answering this how question, not as an explanation how but instead as an explication, in the sense of explication articulated above in 3.2.3.

For the purposes of this book it is relevant to note that postmodern authors generally misinterpret metaphysically articulated creation as the answer to a why question. Chapter 4 shows this to be the case with two authors central to postmodernist thinking; it thoroughly considers the relevant texts, subjecting what they say about creation to exhaustive critical analysis.

[2] The objection to creation has an incomparably more powerful argumentative status when it is presented as a natural-scientific objection. As is well known, the question concerning the origin or beginning of the universe is addressed in natural-scientific cosmology. On the basis of theorems that he and Roger Penrose have proved, Stephen Hawking maintains "that the universe must have had a beginning," but adds that these theorems "didn't give much information about the nature of that beginning."[98] It must be asked, however, what "beginning" means here. With respect to this term, there is a deplorable unclarity and confusion that is responsible for the formulation of questions based on false presuppositions, for the presentation of utterly unfounded contentions, for the construction of nonsensical oppositions, etc., by both theistic and atheistic scientists and philosophers.

According to the standard natural-scientific physical-cosmological theory, the universe began with a big bang. This theory identifies a point at which both the density of the universe and the curvature of space-time are calculated to have been infinite. Such a point would be a case of what mathematicians term a *singularity*. Decisive here is the following consequence: because all scientific theories presuppose that "space-time is smooth and nearly flat,"[99] at the point of singularity all the laws of nature cease to hold. It therefore makes no sense to ask what there was

---

[98] Stephen Hawking, *The Universe in a Nutshell* (2001), 79.

[99] Stephen Hawking, *A Brief History of Time: From the Big Bang to Black Holes* (1988), 40.

before the singularity, because time itself begins only with the big-bang singularity. From this it appears to follow that the question concerning the origin or beginning of the universe receives a univocal natural-scientific answer: the universe begins with the big bang, and there is no basis for introducing anything like a creator.

For decades, there has been a heated controversy among natural scientists, philosophers, and theologians concerning the status of the physical-cosmological theory or theories. Many theologians and philosophers interpret big-bang theory *creationistically*. In direct opposition, other philosophers maintain that the natural-scientifically proven beginning of the universe provides an explanation that makes every other explanation superfluous, and one that is irreconcilable even with the assumption of the existence of a creator God; according to them, the origin of the universe is uncaused, the universe arises *spontaneously*.[100]

All these positions or interpretations rest on *misunderstandings;* the reason is that they do not recognize a fundamental factor, i.e., the *specific status* of the natural-scientific physical-cosmological sentences and theories. When *within the framework* within which these sentences/theories arise there is talk of an origin or beginning of the universe, the talk is— as noted above—deeply misleading and ambiguous. The meanings of the terms used by the cosmological physicists and ambiguously speaking philosophers are determined by the status of the natural-scientific *model* that is relied upon by the physical cosmologies. *Within* this model, as the Hawking-Penrose theorems show, it can be proved that the universe has its origin or beginning at a point in the past, the singularity. But this can only mean that, in any such account, the universe as a structured whole can be explained in terms of the familiar laws of nature only following this point. In this sense—which is an extremely restricted sense—physical cosmology explains the beginning or origin of the universe.

There can be no natural-scientific talk of an origin or creation ex nihilo, out of nothing, because the entire model presupposes precisely the singularity—and *it is of course not nothing*. The singularity is only something that is not structured by the familiar laws of nature. The physical-cosmological big-bang theory consists *only* in this: it shows how *one* state of the physical universe—the big bang—leads to *other* states of

---

[100] For an atheistic interpretation of big-bang theory, see Quentin Smith, "The Uncaused Beginning of the Universe" (1988) and "Atheism, Theism and Big Bang Cosmology" (1991). Particularly important is Adolf Grünbaum, "A New Critique of Theological Interpretations of Physical Cosmology" (2000).

the physical universe (including the current one). In the strict sense, one cannot even say that it shows the current state of the universe to have developed from an *earliest state* of the *same* universe, because the singularity itself cannot be situated in space-time; according to the model, time first begins with the big bang.

Within the physical-cosmological model, one can neither raise nor respond to any question like, how did the singularity itself arise? Hawking puts this point as follows:

> In fact, all our theories of science are formulated on the assumption that space-time is smooth and nearly flat, so they break down at the big bang singularity, where the curvature of space-time is infinite. This means that even if there were events before the big bang, one could not use them to determine what would happen afterward, because predictability would break down at the big bang.
>
> Correspondingly, if, as is the case, we know only what has happened since the big bang, *we could not determine what happened beforehand.* As far as we are concerned, events before the big bang can have no consequences, so *they should not form part of a scientific model of the universe. We should therefore cut them out of the model and say that time had a beginning at the big bang.*[101]

As this passage clearly shows, in the physical-cosmological model, the philosophical-metaphysical question concerning the origin or beginning of the universe is not posed—*and indeed cannot be posed,* because that question does not concern simply the relating of one state of the universe to another state of the universe; it concerns instead what this book terms the contingent dimension of Being. The question concerns the metaphysical status of Being, of necessity/absoluteness and of contingency.

Big-bang theory is not Hawking's final theory. He has come to maintain that the universe did not arise from a singularity,[102] that instead "the universe has no limits in space and time."[103] Together with Jim Hartle, he accepts Richard Feynmann's thesis that there are "multiple histories" of the universe, which are to be thought of as limitless, closed, curved surfaces comparable to the surface of the earth. According to this view,

---

[101] Stephen Hawking, *A Brief History of Time,* 49 (emphasis added).
[102] Ibid., 53.
[103] Stephen Hawking, *The Universe in a Nutshell,* 83.

the universe can have neither a beginning nor an end in imaginary time. This position cannot be treated in detail here, but worth noting is that its implications for philosophy can appear to be enormous. Hawking asserts that they are the following:

> If the histories of the universe in imaginary time are indeed closed surfaces, as Hartle and I proposed, it would have fundamental implications for philosophy and our picture of where we come from. The universe would be entirely self-contained; it wouldn't need anything outside to wind up the clockwork and set it going. Instead, everything in the universe would be determined by the laws of science and by rolls of the dice within the universe.[104]

In his earlier work, *A Brief History of Time*, Hawking writes:

> So long as the universe had a beginning, we could suppose it had a creator. But if the universe is really completely self-contained, having no boundary or edge, it would have neither beginning nor end; it would simply be. What place, then, for a creator?[105]

This passage reveals that Hawking knows nothing about the history of the thought of creation and that he misunderstands the genuine concept of creation. The philosopher and theologian Thomas Aquinas clearly and directly defends the possibility of a creation of an—in the terminology of his time—eternal world (*aeternitas mundi*), i.e., a world without beginning or end. According to Aquinas, this involves no contradiction, because creation means only this: dependence of all contingent Being on an absolutely necessary Being (or, more precisely, on *the* absolutely necessary Being).[106]

Correctly understood, the creation thesis does not contradict the in-part ambiguous sentences of Hawking cited above:

> The universe would be entirely self-contained; it wouldn't need anything outside to wind up the clockwork and set it going. Instead, everything in the universe would be determined by the laws of science and by rolls of the dice within the universe.

---

[104] Ibid., 85.
[105] *A Brief History of Time*, 146.
[106] See Thomas Aquinas, "On the Eternity of the World," 19–23.

According to the creation thesis, the *entire* Being of the contingent
universe, *and thus* also the *clockwork itself* and the entire course of its running (or of the development of the universe) is created. In this sense,
there is indeed *no outside* influence that would have to set the clockwork in motion. The creation of the contingent universe could not be
anything like the winding up of a somehow—but how?—*already present*
clockwork. If it were, then it could not explain the Being of the clockwork. If one remains with this terminology, one should say instead that if
the entire Being of the contingent universe, understood as a clockwork
and the course of its running, is created, then the following holds unrestrictedly: the clockwork is always already wound, the universe is fully
enclosed within itself, it is subject to no outside influence (creation is *not
an outside influence,* because it does not concern anything *in* the universe,
but instead the universe itself or as such).

Hawking's final sentence, in particular, shows just how ambiguous
his formulations are: "Instead, everything *in the universe* would be determined by the laws of science and by rolls of the dice *within the universe*"
(emphasis added). Hawking's theory concerns everything—but *only* everything—that happens *within* the universe; it does not concern the universe *as such.* Differently put: it does not concern the status of the Being
of the universe.

Hawking's *additional* clarification (or contention), also cited above—
i.e., "if the universe is really completely self-contained, having no bound-
ary or edge, it would have neither beginning nor end; it would simply
be"—brings to succinct expression a quite widespread way of thinking
from which arise notions that obstinately oppose the idea of the creation of the world. But this way of thinking simply fails to recognize that
the closedness here in question is determined by the framework of a
physical-cosmological model. *Within the framework of this model,* it is completely accurate to say that the universe "would simply be," and in addition that everything in the so-determined universe would be determined
"by the laws of science and by rolls of the dice within the universe." But
this natural-scientific, physical model in no way exhausts the capacities
of questioning and of intelligibility that characterize human understanding. We can—and because we can, we must—ask how, or in what sense,
can we groundedly or justifiedly say that the universe simply *is,* that it
is enclosed within itself? We have access to concepts that reveal what is
maintained and understood within the framework of this model to be
fully insufficient; these include above all *modal* concepts, which allow us
to ask whether the Being of this universe is *contingent* or instead *necessary*
(or *absolute*).

3.7 The Clarified Relation Between Being and God and the Task of Developing an Integral Theory About God

3.7.1 Absolutely Necessary Being as Creative Absolute and Therefore as God

Excepting sporadic remarks concerning methodology and the history of philosophy, the word "God" does not appear in the preceding sections of this book. In this respect, the book directly opposes the entire metaphysical tradition, which has always immediately introduced the word "God" to characterize the first mover, the first cause, etc., whose existence is taken to have been proved. The tradition recognizes no problem with this characterization despite the fact that a or the first mover, first cause, etc., cannot simply be identified with the (Christian) God. That in the preceding sections this book does not use the word "God" within any thesis belonging to the structural-systematic philosophy is not a terminological lapse or a lapse of any other sort; it is instead a consequence of a thesis central to that philosophy. The thesis is that only after the primordial, universal dimension of Being has been explicated as including the absolutely necessary dimension of Being, and the latter as absolutely necessary free or personal Being and then as absolute creating, is the point reached at which it is appropriate to introduce the word "God."

The word "God" initially appeared in the languages and traditions of religions but was taken into philosophy quite early on. In order to do full justice to the absolutely specific signification that has been connected to this word throughout its history and still today, albeit in a wide variety of forms, and in order to preclude incoherences of various sorts, the word is introduced into this book's account only at this point of the presentation of the structural-systematic philosophy's theory of Being as such and as a whole. To be sure, the word "God" has been and continues to be connected with a great many different conceptual contents. At least for the most part, however, it has been and continues to be used to designate a person, no matter how that person is more precisely understood or articulated.

To be emphasized in addition is that in this book, the task undertaken following the introduction of the term "God" is that of determining whether or to what extent absolute creating can be identified with the Christian God. The book makes no attempt explicitly to consider either all religions or the three so-called monotheistic religions. Instead, it has a clearly restricted and circumscribed goal: it aims to clarify the relation between Being and the biblical-Christian God or, more precisely,

the relation between the structural-systematic philosophy's theory of
Being and the adequately articulated biblical-Christian God. When in
what follows there is talk of God, then the talk is always of the biblical-
Christian God.

Of the three authors named in this book's subtitle, only Jean-Luc
Marion explicitly identifies himself as a Christian author. When Heidegger speaks of God, he usually speaks of the biblical-Christian God,
above all as this God is theoretically interpreted in the metaphysical tradition. To be sure, particularly after the mid-1930s Heidegger sometimes
uses the term "God" to mean something at least not directly identifiable with the biblical-Christian God, but those uses are not central to his
thinking concerning the relation between Being and God. Of yet lesser
relevance to that thinking is his occasional talk of "the Gods."

The situation with Levinas is more complicated. Levinas identifies
himself as a Jewish author in a strict sense, i.e., such that the entire Jewish
tradition plays a central role in his thinking. For sake of concision, this
book takes into clear and sufficient account the specific character of his
conception of God by designating it as biblical.

The senses of the term "God" relevant to this book are exclusively
those articulated in this subsection.

3.7.2 The Broad Expanse of the Subject Matter for a Theory of God

[1] It must first be explained why this book uses the unusual formulation "theorization of God." The formulation is essentially equivalent to
"theology," but the latter word, unless qualified, is ambiguous: on the
one hand, it can designate a subdiscipline of philosophy, as it does in
the metaphysical tradition when it is qualified as *natural* or *rational* theology, and as it does, at present, when it is qualified as *philosophical* theology. On the other hand, "theology" can be understood not to name a
subdiscipline of philosophy, but instead as connected to the Bible and
the Christian religion; it is then qualified as *Christian* theology and, more
precisely, as some variant of the latter: Catholic theology, Protestant theology, orthodox theology, etc.

As explained below, this book does not accept the traditionally defended strict distinction between philosophy and Christian theology as
that distinction is generally understood by Christian thinkers. Because
of this in-part terminological and in-part substantive situation, it uses the
term "theorization of God" rather than the term "theology." Important
at this point is that it does not take its bearings by the strict, traditional
distinction between philosophy and non-philosophical theology.

Once absolutely free Being is explicated as absolute creating, the question arises of how absolute creating may be more precisely articulated. Traditional metaphysics raises questions about God's attributes, distinguishing between entitative attributes (God's perfection, infinity, omnipotence, simplicity, inalterability, eternity, omnipresence . . .) and operative attributes (God's knowing, willing, Being free). It also considers God's "external" effects (creating and sustaining the world, prescience . . .). The restricted purposes of this book preclude its considering this expansive subject matter. It considers only creation, albeit within a quite different framework and only minimally, i.e., only as it relates to the subject matter central to this book: the relation between Being and God.[107]

The treatment of this traditional subject matter by the structural-systematic philosophy would diverge decisively from the traditional conception. The structural-systematic treatment would first clarify which of the traditional topics can sensibly be investigated, and above all how it is that they are sensible. It would also take its bearings strictly by the conception of God sketched just above. The result would exhibit a certain continuity with the traditional metaphysical view, but also a decisively different approach.

[2] Two additional topics require brief treatment at this point. The first is one from traditional metaphysics; it is the question concerning God's transcendence. It is touched on above in that it concerns a central aspect of God's relation to the world. The following subsection (3.7.3) presents the structural-systematic philosophy's response to the question concerning God's transcendence.

The second topic is completely new. It concerns the question whether it is possible and, if so, necessary for the explication of absolutely necessary Being to proceed beyond its identification as absolutely necessary, free, absolute creating. According to the structural-systematic philosophy, further explication is both possible and necessary, and that explication requires consideration of the subject matter that both traditionally and at present is that of Christian theology. Subsection 3.7.4.1 is devoted to this topic, but the purposes of this book allow and thus require only the presentation of a programmatic approach to the further development of the explication. Subsection 3.7.4.2 treats a central difficulty for the structural-systematic philosophy's theory of God that emerges *from the immanent perspective of Christian theology;* it concludes by considering the question concerning the status of the genuine philosopher in relation to the Christian faith.

---

[107] Walter Brugger's monumental *Summe einer philosophischen Gotteslehre* (1979) is a recent examination of this extensive subject matter from the traditional perspective.

3.7.3 On the Question of Transcendence

Transcendence has always been a central topic for metaphysical philosophy, particularly in its Christian variants. God is often characterized as simply transcendent and inconceivable. But this characterization is understood and interpreted in a variety of ways.

3.7.3.1 Negative Theology and the Doctrine of Analogy

Two major positions have developed in the history of the Western (Latin) tradition, one that is extreme and one that is moderate.

[1] The extreme position is *negative* (or *aphophatic*) theology. This position understands God's transcendence as something wholly other, with the consequence that in talk of God only negative assertions are considered to be meaningful. This position takes various radically different concrete forms, which this book cannot consider in detail. The currently most radical forms are those of Emmanuel Levinas and especially Jean-Luc Marion, whose positions are subjected to radical critique in chapter 4.

The moderate position rejects the restriction to exclusively negative determination of God. For God's positive determination, it relies on the doctrine of analogy. This section considers the classic form provided by Thomas Aquinas.[108]

To be emphasized at the outset is that Aquinas also introduces purely negative assertions about God, ones satisfying the requirements of negative theology; an example is, "Of God we cannot know what he is, but only what he is not."[109] Or:

> What genuinely constitutes God's essence transcends our understanding, and thus remains unknown to us. For this reason the highest knowledge of God that the human intellect attains is that it does not know God, in that it knows that what God genuinely is transcends everything that we can know of him.[110]

---

[108] For a thorough critical reconstruction of Aquinas's conception, its presuppositions, and its implications, see Puntel, "Das Denken des Thomas von Aquin as summarisch-unreflektiertes Seins- und Analogiedenken," in *SGTh* 35–176, especially section 3: "Die Analogie und die Gottesfrage," 114ff.

[109] "De Deo scire non pussumus quid sit, sed quid non sit" (*STh* I q. 3 Prol.).

[110] "Hoc ipsum quod est Dei substantia remanet, nostrum intellectum excedens, et ita a nobis ignoratur: et propter hoc illud est ultimum cognitionis humanae de Deo quod sciat se Deum nescire, in quantum cognoscit, illud quod Deus est, omne ipsum quod de eo intelligimus, excedere" (*De pot.* q. 7 a. 5 ad 14).

In addition, however, Aquinas introduces other assertions that correct or make more precise the negative character of the passages just quoted. To take this step, he relies decisively on a logical-semantic-ontological axiom that he formulates as follows: "Understanding negation is always grounded in an affirmation; therefore, if the human intellect could not know anything positive about God, it could not deny anything of God."[111] His understanding of this affirmation is based on a highly consequential distinction relating to God's transcendence, one that he introduces for this reason and formulates as follows: "Although the names that the understanding ascribes to God on the basis of such concepts designate what the divine substance is, they do not designate it completely with respect to what it genuinely is, but only in the way in which we know it."[112]

This distinction is the basis of the following dyadic schema: *modus significandi* (mode of designation)—*res* (or *ratio*) *significata* (what is designated). But what is truly remarkable in the passage just quoted is that Aquinas clearly *subjectivizes* the *res significata* (what is designated). He thus articulates a dualism (*res secundum quod est*—*res secundum quod a nobis intelligitur*) that shows a kinship to Kant. Generalizing, Aquinas's entire conception contains all of the aspects that have been identified here—but thus also all of the real or perhaps only apparent incoherences pointed out above.

The procedure that relies on analogy develops on three levels or stages or, as it is put in the metaphysical tradition, in three ways (*in triplex via*). These are:

(1) the way of affirmation (*via affirmationis*), whereby to God are ascribed the perfections that he has as the cause of his effects, i.e., the things in the world;

(2) the way of negation (*via negationis*) that consists in denying of God what the positive assertions affirm of him;

(3) the way of excellence or of eminence (*via excellentiae vel eminentiae*), whereby what is affirmed of God in the first way and denied of God in the second way is ascribed to him in an "outstanding" manner.

---

[111] "Intellectus negationis semper fundatur in aliqua affirmatione . . . unde nisi intellectus humanus aliquid de Deo affirmative cognosceret, nihil de Deo posset negare" (*De pot.* q. 7 a. 5).

[112] "Licet nomina, quae intellectus ex talibus conceptionibus Deo attribuit, significent id quod est divina substantia, non tamen perfecte ipsam significant secundum quod est, sed secundum quod a nobis intelligitur" (*De pot.* q. 7 a. 5 c.).

[2] Analogy is the semantic and epistemic articulation of the ontological structure of Being as a whole. It is clear that this structure is characterized by the distinction between finite beings and the transcendent God. It is also clear *how* this comprehensive structure is understood. What characterizes it is that it takes its bearings by beings, by the finite; this fundamentally conditions Aquinas's entire concrete way of thinking, which, to put it figuratively, moves from below to above. This is clear in the case of the proofs of God's existence, as shown in chapter 1. It is also clear if one considers Aquinas's central concept *perfection(s)*. According to Aquinas, the names applied to God designate perfections, but Aquinas distinguishes between two types of perfections. For those of the first type, the imperfection of the mode in which a creature participates in a perfection belongs to what is designated by means of the name of the perfection (*in ipso nominis significatio includitur*): such cases are, in the terminology of late scholasticism, mixed (*mixta*) perfections, ones that therefore apply to God not in the genuine sense (*proprie*), but only metaphorically. Perfections of the second type, on the other hand, are such that what is designated by their names includes no imperfection, so that the names express the perfections *purely as such,* or *absolutely;* these are the pure or absolute perfections such as Being, good, living, etc. These perfections are thus pure or absolute with respect to what is designated (*significatum, perfectio significata, res significata*), but insofar as they are used by human beings, they *also* involve a mode of imperfection, but one that remains external to the perfections as such (as absolute), because the imperfection, as a *modus significandi,* is situated solely in the activity of designating because that is an activity of the human mind (see *ScG* 1.30).

It is clear that the entire procedure is fundamentally oriented around beings, around finite perfections; they are the starting points for the movement of ascent to the transcendent perfections, those that are pure or absolute. The movement is from the bottom up, from the finite to the infinite, from the immanent to the transcendent. This is also the *only* way Thomas moves to Being as "the perfection of all perfections."[113]

As should be clear but merits emphasis, Aquinas's way to *esse* is decisively different from the third way to the disclosure of the universal dimension of Being described above in section 3.2.1.3. Analyzing (finite) beings, Aquinas discovers that the act of Being is among those that they actualize. He then transcends the level of finite beings by thinking Being, understood as the act of Being, in abstraction or isolation from its finite

---

[113] "Hoc quod dico esse est actualitas omnium actium, et propter hoc est perfectio omnium perfectionum" (*De pot.* q. 7 a. 2 ad 9).

form—hence, as absolute—then identifying it as the *pure perfection of all perfections.*

The structural-systematic philosophy's third way proceeds otherwise. To be sure, there is a specific similarity in that it too leads from below to above, but the decisive difference is that it does not focus on beings and then separate the act of Being in an attempt to gain access to the perfection of perfections. Instead, this way discloses *configurations,* identifying increasingly comprehensive configurations up to the point of the disclosure of the absolutely comprehensive configuration. It designates the latter the absolutely universal dimension of Being or the dimension of primordial Being. The dimension of Being or primordial Being is *not* identical with Aquinas's Being as act of Being (*esse = actus essendi*). Chapter 1, however, shows that Aquinas at times uses the term *esse* to mean *more* than *actus essendi* (see 1.3.2.2). In an implicit and undeveloped manner, Aquinas appears to have had an inkling of a conception of Being at least similar to that disclosed by the structural-systematic philosophy.

[3] Both traditional positions—negative theology and the more moderate stance that relies on the doctrine of analogy—thus gain access to God as the transcendent X by starting with the finite—with beings—and remaining oriented throughout to beings. Negative theology makes no positive assertions about this X; that it does not raises serious problems. One is identified by Aquinas in a passage quoted above: "Understanding negation is always grounded in an affirmation." On this topic, the purposes of this book are sufficiently served by the introduction of the following on-target remark made by Martin Luther King, Jr., concerning Karl Barth's conception of God as the wholly other:

> It must also be noted . . . that Barth speaks of the generally accepted metaphysical and ethical attributes of God, sovereignty, majesty, holiness, etc., with a degree of certainty. It was once said of Herbert Spencer that he knew a great deal about the "Unknowable," so of Barth, one wonders how he came to know so much of the "Unknown God."[114]

In opposition to negative theology, Aquinas articulates a positive relation between God as Being subsisting of itself (*esse per se subsistens*) and the things in the world, contingent beings. The finite and contingent

---

[114] Clayborn Carson and Peter Halloran, eds., *The Papers of Martin Luther King, Jr.,* vol. 2: *Rediscovering Precious Values, July 1951–November 1955* (1994), 106. King draws this passage from a work of A. S. Zerbe, without indicating that he has done so. See the editors' comments on p. 95 and in footnote 22 to page 106.

beings are modes of Being (*esse*), in that they participate or take part in Being (*esse*) and thereby in Being subsisting of itself (*esse per se subsistens*). The doctrine of participation is an essential constituent of Aquinas's metaphysical conception. As chapter 1 shows, however, Aquinas articulated his conception of *esse* only minimally; it does not take the position it merits within his comprehensive conception. For the most part, Aquinas's conception is embedded in a conceptuality inherited chiefly from Aristotle and the Neoplatonic tradition, although it never entirely disappears. As noted above, what leads Aquinas to rely on this highly problematic conceptuality is that his thinking takes its bearings from beings, not from Being—from *ens*, not from *esse*.

On the whole, Aquinas's conception of God's transcendence differs markedly from the absolute separation of God from the world and from human beings that characterizes negative theology in all its forms. It articulates a *positive* relation between the transcendent God and finite beings. But the question arises—particularly in light of Heidegger's thinking—whether Aquinas *adequately* articulates this relation. The preceding account makes clear that he does not. Two final considerations make this yet clearer.

The first consideration is a brief analysis of one of the most important and most richly consequential of Aquinas's treatments of God's transcendence as not making God wholly separate or distinct; the passage in question concerns the immanence of God within things or beings. In the passage, Aquinas addresses the question whether "God is in all things" (*utrum Deus sit in omnibus rebus*). To support his affirmative answer to the question, Aquinas argues as follows: because God is subsisting Being itself, created Being (*esse*) is God's most genuine effect, because God posits this effect in things not only when they first begin to be, but also as long as he sustains or maintains them in Being. He extends his line of argument as follows:

> Therefore as long as a thing has Being, God must be present within it, according to its mode of Being. *But Being is innermost in each thing and most deeply inherent in all things.*[115]

These are doubtless weighty and well-considered theses, but they articulate the relation between God as Being subsisting of itself or even

---

[115] "*Quandiu igitur res habet esse, tandiu oportet quod Deus adsit ei, secundum modum quo esse habet. Esse autem est illud quod est magis intimum cuilibet, et quod profundius omnibus inest*" (*STh* I q. 8 a. 1 c.; emphasis added).

as Being itself and finite beings only externally and thereby wholly insufficiently, in that they thematize only a *presence* or a *Being-within* of Being
itself within finite beings. The relations of presence and Being-within,
however, leave Being itself and beings distinct from each other in such
a way as to be other to each other. For this reason, the passage fails to
clarify how, relying on a Heideggerian term, the two *ultimately* belong
together (*zusammengehören*).

The second consideration that makes clearer the inadequacy of
Aquinas's conception concerns the thought of creation as positing-into-
Being without there being any pre-givenness. This might appear adequately to articulate the belonging-together of Being itself and beings,
because it appears to overcome the relation of otherness left by the passages considered just above. Creation, after all, means that beings are
posited in Being by Being itself (in its fullness as Being itself subsisting
of itself), so that Being itself is distinct from beings, but such that the beings contain Being within themselves. This is of course correct. But this
is only (to put it one way) a coarse-grained clarification; detailed elaboration that would make the grain finer is wholly absent. This is clear from
the fact that Aquinas's thought of creation is only one thought among
many. It is explicitly articulated, but it is not thought through and articulated in its depth and breadth and with recognition of its immense
implications.

The task of thinking Aquinas's thought of creation fully through
remains outstanding. What must be emphasized about it is that it cannot
be accomplished within the framework of Aquinas's conception of *esse*
as it stands. One would have to develop a different conception of Being,
one that was broader and more comprehensive, in order to adequately
articulate the relation between Being and beings and—more determinately—the relation between absolutely free Being as creating and the
created, contingent world. Aquinas's conception of transcendence remains external.

3.7.3.2 Starting Points for a Structural-Systematic Conception of God's Transcendence

The thesis explicated and systematically situated in this section is the following: *There is no absolute transcendence of absolutely necessary, personal Being
as absolute creating in relation to the contingent dimension of Being, in the following sense: God's transcendence in relation to the contingent dimension of Being
occurs completely within the total self-immanence of absolutely necessary personal
Being as absolute creating.*

[1] God's transcendence would be absolute only if it were a pure
negation, a pure distinctness or indeed separateness, a beyond-the-

contingent-dimension-of-Being, hence only an other-Being or Being-other. Negatively, "relative transcendence" is a transcendence that is not absolute in this sense. Positively, "relative transcendence" is a transcendence that occurs only within the comprehensive dimension that contains the contingent dimension of Being but that *itself is God*. This requires clarification.

The primordial, universal dimension of Being is not—as postmodernist authors would immediately say (see chapter 4)—a dimension that would somehow precede absolutely necessary personal Being and absolute creating as some sort of yet more comprehensive dimension that encompassed the absolutely necessary dimension of Being and the contingent dimension of Being and that would itself not be God. It is also not a background horizon that would somehow be a condition for God—of any kind whatsoever—or anything of the sort. In a word: the absolutely necessary dimension of Being and the contingent dimension of Being are not (in the ordinary sense) two subdimensions of a yet more primordial dimension. Instead, they are the *explicated* primordial dimension of Being itself; this dimension discloses itself first as two-dimensional, and then as the absolute, necessary, free (personal) dimension of Being that creates the contingent dimension of Being and thereby contains it. The stages in the (self-)explication of the primordial dimension of Being are precisely that: stages in its (self-)explication. The primordial, universal dimension of Being is the *explicandum*, and the absolutely necessary dimension of Being as creating-absolute-that-has-created-the-contingent-world is the *explicans/explicatum* of the primordial, universal dimension of Being.

"Auto-immanence" is a term appropriately introduced at this point, despite its being unusual and potentially misleading. It is appropriate in the phrase "total auto-immanence of absolutely necessary personal Being as absolute creating." "Immanence" connotes a correlativity to something outer or other, but the prefix "auto-" denies anything outer or other; the prefix could, however, be taken to suggest that there must be something outer or other to be denied. Yet in the case of the primordial, universal dimension of Being, explicated as the-absolutely-necessary-dimension-of-Being-as-creating-the-contingent-dimension-of-Being, there simply is no outer or other to which that dimension could relate even by negation. If this is not kept in mind, the term "auto-immanence" will be misunderstood.

The decisive point concerning God's transcendence can now be articulated: the transcendence of God in relation to contingent beings occurs *within God* as the consequence of God's own free act. In that God, by creating, posits contingent beings within Being, God creates within God the internal distinction by means of which God transcends contingent beings. Sticking with this thought and thinking it through is a difficult task that has seldom if indeed ever been undertaken even in the metaphysical tradition.

In the tradition of biblical-Christian thinking, the fear has often been expressed that conceptions like the one articulated in the preceding paragraph are pantheistic in the sense of denying any relevant distinction between God and the world or God and human beings. So classifying the structural-systematic conception, however, would be a mistake. That a decisive distinction remains is clear particularly from the fact that God, as free creator, creates human beings *as minded and thereby as free beings*. Just as human beings differ decisively from one another fundamentally because they are free, so too do human beings differ decisively from God because both are free.

The highest restraint and care are in order when biblical texts are introduced into philosophical works, but it appears appropriate at this point to introduce—for the sake of readers who take the Bible seriously—a passage that shows—at least when it is read philosophically—that creation and transcendence, as articulated above in a strictly philosophical language—are not utterly alien to the Bible. Speaking in Athens, Paul says,

> They [human beings] should seek God, if they could touch him and find him; for He is not distant from any of us. *For within him we live, we move and we are,* as even some of your poets have said: we are of His kind.[116]

God's comprehensiveness, God's containing everything within God, does not exclude God's transcendence in relation to the contingent dimension of Being. Quite to the contrary, God's comprehensiveness is what makes God's transcendence possible and—presupposing creation—necessary, because it is a consequence of creation. The biblical passage cited just above expresses this clearly.

To designate this conception, the term "panentheism" could be used if it were freed from the various misunderstandings that have arisen since its introduction into philosophy by Karl Christian Friedrich Krause in 1828.[117] Krause uses the term to designate the immanence of

---

[116] ζητεῖν τὸν θεόν . . . καὶ γε οὐ μακρὰν ἀπὸ ἑνὸς ἑκάστου ἡμῶν ὑπάρχοντα. ἐν αὐτῷ [τῷ θεῷ] γὰρ ζῶμεν καὶ κινούμεθα καὶ ἐσμέν, ὡς καὶ τινες τῶν καθ' ὑμᾶς ποιητῶν εἰρήκασιν: τοῦ γὰρ καὶ γένος ἐσμέν (Acts 17:27).

[117] Karl Christian Friedrich Krause, *Vorlesungen über das System der Philosophie.*

the world within God; it is synonymous with the all-within-God-doctrine [*Allingottlehre*] that—in opposition to pantheism—affirms both the dependence of the world on God and God's transcendence. The question, of course, is how this "all-within-God" is clarified. The "all" can mean only the world, the dimension of contingent things. But the meaning of the "within" remains wholly obscure. Only within the framework of a conception of Being as such and as a whole can the "within" be clarified. But whatever the history of the term "panentheism" may be, its etymology makes it eminently appropriate as a designation for the thesis that God's transcendence of the contingent dimension of Being is one that is only *relative* in the sense explained above.

[2] In concluding this book's consideration of transcendence, a point centrally important to the subject matter and for the purposes of this book requires introduction. It has become nearly a trend for Jewish and Christian authors not only to emphasize God's transcendence but to radicalize it such that it is absolute in the sense considered above. With this trend comes the danger that God becomes some kind of phantom whose only characteristic is this absolute beyondness. The heart of any such conception can be roughly characterized, relying on the concepts *God's transcendence* and *God's immanence,* as follows: God's transcendence and God's immanence are inversely proportional, i.e., the greater is God's transcendence, the lesser is God's immanence. The limiting case is this: if God's transcendence is absolute (in the sense explained above), then God's immanence is zero. Because the (postmodern) authors take God's transcendence to be absolute (in this sense), they cannot avoid reducing God's immanence to zero. God is then only the absolutely other. Because these authors do not draw this conclusion, what they say is incoherent.

The conception sketched here of the absolutely necessary, free, creating dimension of Being and its relation to the contingent dimension of Being, in terms of the relation between transcendence and immanence, can be put into the following formula: God's transcendence and God's immanence are *directly proportional:* the greater or more radical is God's transcendence, the greater or more radical is God's immanence.

3.7.4 The Transition from Absolute Creating to God of Revelation as the Final Topic for the Theory of Being as Such and as a Whole

At this point, the structural-systematic philosophy is confronted with two tasks. The first is that of deepening the conception that has now been sketched and of articulating its many facts in detail; accomplishing this task requires confronting and solving a great many difficult problems. One of these is the terrible problem of explaining the evil in the world.

Pressing as this task may be, it cannot be undertaken in this book, whose aim is to articulate an *approach* to a conception in opposition to the most important counterpositions. It may be noted that the accomplishment of this first task would certainly lead to results wholly different from those defended by most authors who write at present about God. But this must be left here as a purely programmatic thesis.

The second task is that of pressing further. It consists *not* in adding or clarifying details, but in taking an additional step. This task is the topic of the subsections with which chapter 3 concludes.

3.7.4.1 A Methodological Watershed: The Transition to a Philosophical Theory of World History and of Religion(s)

When the structural-systematic philosophy has reached the point at which it has explicated the absolutely necessary dimension of Being as absolute creating, the question arises of whether seeking further determinations of absolute creating is possible and, if so, indispensable. At this point, the investigation encounters a methodological watershed. Additional determinations of absolute creating beyond absolute intelligence, absolute (and absolutely free) will, and personhood are not explicable or derivable within the theoretical framework within which the just-named determinations emerge. But are additional determinations explicable within a new or expanded theoretical framework, one including both a clearly different form of explication and data of a fully different sort? Indeed they are. The decisive point, on which everything concerning this positive answer to the question depends, is the following: the explication of additional determinations of absolutely necessary, minded, free Being is possible only as the further explication of one of the already explicated determinations, i.e., the *absolute freedom* of necessary Being as absolute creating. The specific questions that arise include the likes of the following: Is it possible to understand or to characterize this absolute freedom more precisely? If so, how does the further explication develop?

The importance of the freedom of absolute creating becomes clear through consideration of human freedom. There is only one way further to determine, *as free*, the free human being: one must investigate the history of the human being's free decisions and acts. The situation with absolute creating is no different: its further determinations can be discovered only through investigation of the history of its freedom. Determining whether or not there *is* such a history requires investigating world history and, within it, the history of the major religions.

This step, which consists in bringing the freedom of absolute creating into consideration, may appear as venturesome or indeed as unintelligible, or as capable of yielding nothing more than fabrications. Every such appearance is false. The step is absolutely consequent, as is made clear by two brief considerations.

If, as in the structural-systematic philosophy, one concludes from arguments that *free* (personal) absolutely necessary Being has created the world—the contingent dimension of Being—*absolutely freely,* that is, has posited it within Being, then the world must be seen in light of this absolute freedom. If it is so seen, the first question that arises is whether or not absolute freedom stops with the creation of the world. Whether or not it does depends of course only on itself: as absolutely free, it is free to stop or not to stop. There cannot be anything like an a priori derivation of what it does or must do, precisely because it is absolutely free. What, if anything, it does can be discerned only from the history of this freedom itself. It is therefore necessary, at this point in the explication of the primordial, universal dimension of Being, to bring divine freedom into play.

Second, an additional question presses: if there is a history of absolute freedom, where could it manifest itself or—more concretely—where might it possibly have manifested itself? This question has no a priori answer: it is not a priori the case that absolute freedom could manifest itself only in one way or another. But there is at least a general answer that can and must be given: whether, and if so how, absolute freedom is manifest can be discovered only through investigation of world history. World history includes the history of religion(s). In addition, it is a matter of historical fact that there are religions that accept as bases for their doctrines and practices what they accept as histories of divine freedom. This is the case primarily, even if perhaps not exclusively, for Judaism and Christianity.

At this point, then, the philosopher who seeks further determination of absolute creating must turn to the study of world history and may turn to that of the history of religion(s). This turning is the crossing of a methodological and substantive watershed, a decisive break: it requires the interpretation of historical phenomena. Initially and predominantly, although not exclusively, the method must be hermeneutical.[k] To be sure, however, the philosopher who works further to develop the structural-systematic philosophy will rely on the resources and conclu-

---

[k] There is a break as far as subject matter is concerned, because the data are of a new sort. The methodological break comes with the application of the philosophical method to this data.

sions of that philosophy in interpreting the history of the world and/or of religion(s).

In pursuing this investigation, the philosopher cannot acknowledge or respect any restrictions of any sort, particularly those imposed by religious communities and above all those imposed by Christian churches. The following subsection considers this issue. The interpretation of world religions is a task that is fully open to philosophy, in every respect, and that cannot be ignored by philosophy.

Central to Judaism and Christianity is the concept of God's revelation or manifestation. This is *the phenomenon, the appearance par excellence* of God's freedom. Thus, this revelation or manifestation is the revelation or manifestation of additional determinations of God. According to the long Christian tradition, what is interpreted as God's manifestation is the exclusive domain of what that tradition calls Christian theology; that tradition radically insists that philosophy is not and cannot be competent to examine the phenomenon of God's manifestation. The structural-systematic philosophy does not accept this limitation placed on philosophy. The following subsection fully considers this issue.

3.7.4.2 On the Relation Between "Philosophy" and "Theology"

The just-sketched conception has profound implications for the relation between "philosophy" and "theology." These two terms appear here within quotation marks because that conception brings into question just what they should mean. To the end of determining what they should mean, 3.7.4.2.1 considers an objection that arises from the perspective of Christian theology; 3.7.4.2.2 then reconsiders the entire problematic.

3.7.4.2.1 Clarification of an Objection Arising from the Perspective of Christian Theology

Now to be considered is an objection to the conception of philosophy defended above and to philosophy's taking the step from absolute creating to the God of revelation. This subsection shows that the objection is inconsistent with Christian theology's own most central assumptions. This subsection is, then, an internal critique of Christian theology on this point.

[1] The thesis, formulated within the intellectual framework of traditional Christianity, that God is the creator of the world is and has always been, within this framework, the thesis with which philosophical treatment of "God" must end. Philosophy can do no more and say no more. According to this intellectual framework, however, this final point for philosophy is not a final point for thought; it is assumed instead that this thesis opens a new dimension, one that is inaccessible to philosophy

but not to thought. This is the dimension of revelation or, more precisely in this context, that of revealed contents or truths and thus of their theoretical articulation. Providing that articulation is the task of a different discipline, *Christian theology* in the genuine sense, a discipline with a theoretical apparatus *and a subject matter* wholly distinct from those of philosophy.

Both of these distinguishing characteristics result from the fundamental distinction between the natural and the supernatural levels or dimensions; in Christian theology, this is also termed the distinction between nature and grace. With respect to theoretical apparatus, supernatural light or the light of faith or of divine revelation (*lumen supernaturale* or *lumen fidei seu divinae relationis*) is the central element, whereas with respect to subject matter what is central are the truths revealed in salvation history, which has its peak and its culmination in Jesus Christ.

According to this tradition, philosophy is the articulation of the natural order and (Christian) theology that of the so-understood supernatural order (*ordo naturalis—ordo supernaturalis*). The "Christian" God in the genuine sense appears only and exclusively in the supernatural order. That God is the genuine subject matter of *sacra theologia*, of sacred theology.

This conception is often termed two-story thinking. For centuries it proceeded virtually unopposed, and it provides a clear and comfortable intellectual framework within which one can easily and clearly distinguish between philosophy and (Christian) theology. That, however, this clarity and comfort are not decisive positive elements comes to be seen in the twentieth century by Christian theologians themselves. Indeed, it is criticized and abandoned by such theologians as Henri de Lubac[118] and Karl Rahner.[119]

[2] The chief point of dispute in this discussion appears to be a presupposition that provides the basis for the distinction between "philosophy" and "theology" described above; what is presupposed is that the human being has a *pure nature* (*natura pura*) in the theological sense. De Lubac radically rejects this thesis, whereas Rahner accepts pure nature, but only as a limiting concept, not as a reality. Only Rahner, however, has

---

[118] See especially *Surnaturel: Études historiques* (1946). Lubac makes his conception more precise in additional works, especially in the essay "Le mystère du surnaturel," in *Recherches de Science Religieuse* (1949). His works on the supernatural are also found in vol. 12 of his *Oeuvres complètes* (2006), which shares the title of the just-named essay.

[119] Thomas Fössel's *Gott—Begriff und Geheimnis: Hansjürgen Verweyens Fundamentaltheologie und die ihr inhärente Kritik an der Philosophie und Theologie Karl Rahners* (2004) includes an exhaustive presentation of Rahner's conception of the supernatural.

presented a conception that is coherent within the frameworks both of Christian theology and of philosophy; he achieves this coherence by introducing what he calls a supernatural existential. He borrows the term/ concept *existential* from Heidegger's *Being and Time* (see §9), wherein the term designates characteristics of *human* Being (Dasein). Existentials are distinct from categories, which are of non-human Being.

What, then, is Rahner's supernatural existential, and how does it shed light on the problem of the supernatural? Rahner never attained ultimate clarity concerning either this existential itself or its value in explanations, but the intuition that led him to introduce it can be identified and determined to be correct. This identification and clarification require articulation of two decisive factors.

[i] Rahner holds first that God's universal willing of self-communication has an ontological effect on *all* human beings. This willing is not something purely abstract such that it would be only a divine intention; instead, this willing is *real* in the sense that—in traditional theological terminology—it has the effect of elevating all human beings to a supernatural status or condition. With this willing, then, God introduces an *additional ontological determination* into *all* human beings, or grants to all human beings an ontological status that they would not otherwise have. Specifically, this is the ontological determination or ontological status that consists in their all being addressed by God's self-communication. This has the significant ontological consequence that no human being has ever existed in the condition or with the status of pure nature (in the theological sense). This is expressed, in language typical of Rahner and in two of his works, as follows:

> This "situation" [characterized by the supernatural existential], which is comprehensively and irrevocably pre-given to and conditioning of the free acts of human beings, does not consist only in thoughts and intentions of God, but is a real ontological determination of human beings themselves that, as objectification of the universal divine willing of salvation, does indeed—thanks to grace—enter human-Being-as-"nature," but is never absent from human-Being-as-"nature."[120]

> Factical nature is *never* "pure" nature, but a nature in a supernatural order, out of which the human being (even as unbeliever and sinner) can never step, and a nature that is continually transformed (which

---

[120] "Existenzial, übernatürliches," in *Lexikon für Theologie und Kirche* (1959), vol. 3, column 1301.

does not mean: justified) by the offer of salvational supernatural grace. And these "existential" [i.e., ontological] determinations of the human being's concrete nature (the human being's "historical" nature) are not pure conditions of Being that are beyond consciousness; instead, they are effective in the experience of human beings.[121]

[ii] The second point that characterizes Rahner's concept of the supernatural existential arises from philosophical considerations. As chapter 1 shows, Rahner was heavily influenced by the transcendental approach; indeed, he counts (with some restrictions) as a defender of transcendental Thomism. This led him to understand the ontological existential as an ontological determination, but to interpret this in the sense of a transcendentally understood a priori of the human mind. This caused great obscurity and indeed confusion. The purposes of this book do not require additional consideration of this second point.

[3] Rahner appears not to have recognized the revolutionary consequences of his magnificent thought. To the author's knowledge, it is also the case that no philosopher or theologian after Rahner has taken the trouble—or perhaps had the courage—to make these consequences explicit. They concern essential issues.

For the subject matter and purposes of this book, of particular significance is the consequence that concerns the relation between philosophy and (Christian) theology. It is presumably incontestable that the traditional conception cannot be retained, because according to it philosophy is a product of pure nature (in the theological sense); philosophy is an activity only of natural reason, and is consequently guided only by the light of natural reason. From the Christian perspective, however, this is a pure abstraction and indeed more precisely a fiction, because that perspective recognizes nothing in humanity that would be purely natural (in the theological sense). Human nature as such and as a whole and therewith everything that belongs to it is—in the traditional terminology—elevated to the supernatural order, because according to Christian teachings *all* human beings are addressees of God's self-communication. Thus, everything that constitutes human beings—thus, the human essence (whatever that may be), all human capacities, etc.—is situated within the space that is opened by God's self-communication.

From this thesis there follow at least two consequences that will presumably be sharply rejected by the majority of Christian theologians. The first is that, from the Christian perspective, as it is understood here,

---

[121] "Natur und Gnade," in *Schriften zur Theologie,* vol. 4, p. 230.

the theoretician who engages in philosophy cannot be viewed and understood as one who relies solely and exclusively on the capabilities of pure human reason because that theoretician is allegedly guided only by the light of (theologically understood) purely natural reason. The second consequence is that the subject matter that the tradition identifies as a domain that can be investigated only by Christian theology is *not in principle inaccessible* to the theoretician who philosophizes *as a theoretician who philosophizes.*

The only factor to which the theoretician who philosophizes must attend unconditionally is—formulated negatively—that it is impermissible to make the claim or even the attempt to derive a priori the characteristically Christian characteristics of God (trinity, incarnation, etc.) purely from theses introduced *without recourse to history* (concretely: without consideration of an interpretation of religions, thus, in the case of the Christian God, without interpretations of the Old and New Testaments). Formulated within the framework of the structural-systematic philosophy, the situation is as follows: explication of the primordial, universal dimension of Being leads the philosopher to introduce the thesis that the absolutely necessary dimension of Being is absolute creating. Further explication is reasonable and possible only if an extensively consequential methodological break is recognized. Further determination of absolute creating as explicated at this point is possible only if the philosopher considers history, in the manner indicated above. Such determinations as trinity and incarnation are discoverable and articulable only through such consideration.[122]

---

[122] Postmodern Christian authors appear to see no problems with their manner of "interpreting" the history of religion(s) and especially Christianity. They pay no attention to the enormous methodological problems such an undertaking brings with it. For example, Marion *as a philosopher* maintains the following about his own assertions, apparently untroubled by any methodological concerns:

> I attempt a pure and simple description of two emblematic figures of the gift, which Christian theology offers without being able or having to justify them—the Eucharist and the confession of faith. We describe these as two facts that are absolutely irreducible to Being and to its logic, facts that are only intelligible in terms of the gift. In conclusion, *agape* appears only as a pure given, with neither deduction nor legitimation. But in this way the given appears all the more as a given. (*GWB* xxiv)

What can it mean that something (for Marion: the Eucharist and the confession of faith) is "absolutely irreducible to Being and to its logic"? Chapter 4 considers this issue in great detail. Here it need only be noted that it is scarcely comprehensible for a philosopher to introduce wholly unqualified assertions that have an explicitly Christian-theological character and that are therefore intelligible and open to philosophical evaluation only if clarity concerning the Christian-theological framework has first been attained.

3.7.4.2.2 Some Central Aspects of a Redetermination of the Relation of
"Philosophy" and "Theology": On the Status of Genuine Philosophy in Relation
to the Christian Faith and to Christian Theology

The preceding considerations make clear that the traditional relation
between philosophy and (Christian) theology is untenable, and therefore that the relation requires redetermination. Philosophy and theology
together constitute a *single universal science,* not in the sense of a simple
identification, but in the sense that the *thematic domain* that is the traditional concern of Christian theology is also the domain that philosophy
investigates following the methodological break described above and
when that break is effectively respected and the philosopher proceeds in
accordance with it. To be emphasized is that this thesis, although central,
is only generally formulated, and requires many explanations, specifica-
tions, and additional considerations if it is to become adequately clear
and adequately situated theoretically. This book cannot move beyond the
general formulation. What its purposes require is, to avoid certain potential misunderstandings, the consideration of two relevant issues ([1]
and [2]), and a concluding clarification of the status of the philosopher,
given the redetermined relation between philosophy and theology.

[1] The first issue is mainly terminological. What should the suggested *unified universal science* be called? It should be clear from the outset that neither "philosophy" nor "theology," without further qualification, would be appropriate. History suggests "Christian philosophy" as a
possibility, but this book rejects it, for two reasons. First, in the course of
history it has had so many and such divergent and indeed contradictory
interpretations that its history alone recommends against its adoption.
In addition, the qualifier "Christian," independently of its historical uses
qualifying "philosophy," can designate all sorts of quite different things:
doctrines, attitudes, a specific accomplishment, and various other things
that are clearly not subject matters for philosophy. Usually, the word is
understood as involving the Christian faith, and indeed the terms are
sometimes used interchangeably. The word "faith," however, which has
an extraordinarily complex and ambiguous history dating from the Bible,
is, despite the frequency of its use in such phrases as "faith and reason"
and "philosophy and faith," one that is so indeterminate, ambiguous,
and confused as to be simply unusable.

If one designated the structural-systematic philosophy as *Christian*
philosophy, what precisely would thereby be meant? In the least dubious
case, it would mean that the structural-systematic philosophy included
as a hypothesis the thesis that *if* this philosophy were to take the step into
the historical domain, as described above, the result would be that the
domain of Christian theology would prove to be the historical domain

that this philosophy would rely on in furthering its explanation of the primordial, universal dimension of Being. Given, however, that this is only one of many possible results of the taking of that step, qualifying the structural-systematic philosophy at *this* point as Christian would clearly be premature.

The designation "Christian philosophy" would be emphatically to be rejected if it were taken to indicate any presupposition that philosophers working within the structural-systematic framework would be inspired or motivated by the Christian faith (in any sense), or that they were Christians (in any sense). Yet more emphatically would it be to be rejected if it were taken as indicating that this philosophy developed in light of the Christian faith (in any sense) or on the basis of realized Christian faith (in any sense) or anything of that sort.

Because none of the available senses of "Christian" is appropriate to the structural-systematic philosophy, that qualifier is rejected.[123]

Second, there are contentual concerns. As indicated above, it is possible in principle that the extension of the structural-systematic philosophy into the domain of history, in seeking further to explicate the primordial, universal dimension of Being, would lead to an interpretation of the history of the world and/or of religion(s) that would not be a Christian interpretation. The Christian extension envisaged by this book as resulting from the completion of the structural-systematic philosophy's theory of Being is only *one* possibility. For this reason, it would be inaccurate at this point to qualify this philosophy as Christian.

[2] The second issue does not emerge—at least not directly—from the traditional distinction—criticized and rejected above—between natural truths as the domain of philosophy and revealed truths as the domain of (Christian) theology; the second issue is not essentially related to that distinction. The source of the new issue is that Christian theology has always been tightly bound to one or another Christian denomination and decisively to the doctrinal positions of authorities within those denominations (as is clearly although not exclusively the case for Catholic theology). This suggests the question: if philosophy and (Christian) theology were to constitute a single, universal science, would that have as a consequence that the theoretician working to develop that science would be a servant of one or another Christian denomination and bound to doctrinal authorities of that denomination?

The answer to this question is clear: the structural-systematic philosopher is in no way bound to any Christian or any other denomination.

---

[123] On this problematic, see the instructive book by Philippe Capelle, *Finitude et mystère* (2005).

This philosophy must develop independently of any and every external factor of any sort whatsoever. The philosopher, as philosopher, must be free from constraints of any sort. Constraints would include authorities of any kind, situations, needs, psychological or social or other coercions, etc., as well as obligations to persons or institutions, etc. Philosophy's only obligation is to its subject matter, no matter how that may be designated. As this is often put, wholly appropriately: philosophy's sole commitment is to truth.

From the thesis introduced above according to which philosophy and (Christian) theology are fundamentally a single universal science, in conjunction with what is said in the preceding paragraph, it should be clear that the philosopher working to contribute to this science *cannot*, as philosopher, be a servant of one or another Christian denomination or be bound to doctrinal authorities of that denomination. The oneness of philosophy and theology defended here is a *thematic oneness*. There is a strict distinction between the *oneness or unity of this thematic domain* and *the concrete forms of articulation* of this single domain. What is most important in the current context about the concrete forms of articulation is the question of whether or not *external factors* play a constitutive role.

The structural-systematic philosophy is influenced by *no external factors of any sort*, including service to some religious denomination, to some doctrinal authority, etc. This is in stark contrast to the form of articulation allowed (for example) to members of departments of Catholic theology, whose works are decisively guided by such factors.

What the preceding considerations show is that despite the *hypothetically* defended thesis that there is a *thematic unity of philosophy and Christian theology*, there remains a deep and consequential difference between the two endeavors that should not be ignored or underestimated. Here, the significant difference in *forms of articulation* plays a simply decisive role.

[3] Given the preceding considerations, the current status of Christian thinking, particularly in higher education, clearly deserves examination. That is not, however, a task for this book. Here, only one point requires further attention: it is important to clarify the status of the philosopher in relation to Christianity.

[i] Clarifying the status of philosopher in relation to Christianity is immensely complex. Analyzing it in detail would require an entire book, but some central aspects can be clarified by way of critical consideration of a passage from Heidegger. The passage is from his 1929/30 lecture course *The Fundamental Concepts of Metaphysics*,[124] in which he introduces as one of three "inherent incongruities [*Unzuträglichkeiten*]" in the traditional con-

---

[124] *GA*, vol. 29/30.

cept of metaphysics" the "unproblematic nature of the traditional concept of metaphysics." His treatment of this "incongruity" begins as follows:

> Because the traditional concept of metaphysics is . . . superficial and confused in itself, it simply cannot come about that metaphysics in itself or the μετά in its proper sense is made a problem. To put it the other way around: because *philosophizing proper as a completely free questioning on the part of man* is not possible during the Middle Ages, since completely different positionings are essential during that period; because fundamentally there is no philosophy in the Middle Ages: for this reason the taking over of Aristotelian metaphysics . . . is structured from the outset in such a way that not only a dogmatics of faith, but also a dogmatics of First Philosophy itself arises.[125]

In saying that the traditional concept of metaphysics has been "trivialized" Heidegger means that the μετά "*no longer* indicates a particular *orientation* of thinking and knowing, a peculiar *turnaround* in the face of everyday thinking and inquiry, but is merely a sign for the *place* and the *order of those beings* which lie *behind* and *above* other beings." He explains:

> Here the fact that philosophizing is a *fundamental orientation* [*Grundhaltung*] *that stands on its own* completely disappears. Metaphysics is leveled down and trivialized into everyday knowledge.[126]

Because Heidegger's interpretation of medieval philosophy is thoroughly considered in chapters 1 and 2, it is not reconsidered here. Important at this point is what Heidegger says about philosophy as "a *fundamental orientation that stands on its own*," and of "*philosophizing proper as a completely free questioning on the part of man*." He denies that medieval philosophers such as Thomas Aquinas have this orientation and thus that they are philosophers, contending that "fundamentally there is no philosophy in the Middle Ages." Heidegger's claim is that the thinking of these authors is guided and hence determined by the goal of making the Christian faith intelligible. This goal was so fixed and so beyond question that "*a completely free questioning on the part of man*" was no longer possible.

At first glance, Heidegger's characterization of the thinking of medieval authors appears to be on target. This characterization says more

[125] *The Fundamental Concepts of Metaphysics* (1929/1995), 45 (emphasis added).
[126] Ibid., 44.

than does the famous dictum of Petrus Damiani, according to which "philosophy is the handmaiden of theology [*philosophia ancilla theologiae*]."[127] Closer analysis, however, reveals Heidegger's claim to be too unspecific. The problem is far more complex.

This becomes clear if one attempts to determine what is meant by the phrase "*a completely free questioning on the part of man,*" by which Heidegger characterizes philosophizing. In what sense is the questioning completely free? Or, more precisely: what is this questioning free *from,* and what is it free *for*? That it is free *from* external factors is presumably incontestable, and is explained above. But Heidegger appears to want to say much more. His emphasis appears to be on what thinking is completely free *for.* But what does this mean?

Heidegger appears to understand the free questioning of human beings in an absolutely unrestricted sense in that he wants to exclude from free thinking any and every conception or conviction that precedes—and is therefore not dependent on—that thinking. In fact, however, such conceptions and convictions are not external factors; they are always already present whenever any human being begins to philosophize. What must be clarified is how their being present relates to philosophical thinking as free.

[ii] It is the case that in a certain respect philosophical questioning is never completely open because the human mind and hence human thinking relate in one way or another to absolutely everything, however this "everything" is designated. The relevant factor is the *intentional coextensionality of the human mind and of human thinking with Being as such and as a whole,* a factor examined above in section 3.2.1.2. The concrete manner in which the human mind is intentionally coextensive with the whole, *prior to its engaging in explicitly theoretical thinking,* is by way of ideas, conceptions, convictions, etc., concerning specific parts or elements of the whole but also concerning the whole itself.

From this it immediately follows that whether or not human questioning wants or aims to be "completely free," it simply cannot become a tabula rasa; instead, even "completely free" questioning is questioning accomplished by minds already containing all sorts of ideas, conceptions, convictions, and so forth. To think that any human questioning could be "completely free" of factors of this sort is to fall victim to a complete illusion, an empty abstraction. Every questioning, no matter how radical, no matter how "completely free," is a questioning by a mind that contains contents of a wide variety of sorts.

---

[127] See B. Baudoux, "*Philosophia 'Ancilla Theologiae'*" (1937).

Additional factors become evident if one considers the context within which questioning takes place. This context includes the location within the history of philosophy at which a given philosophical questioning is situated. That location is a factor that is intrinsic rather than external to philosophical questioning. And Heidegger is a philosopher who—far more than most philosophers—not only recognizes this fact, but considers it to be essential to his thinking. This context, too, is something from which philosophical questioning can never be "completely free." In Heidegger's case, and in his own view, of decisive importance is his location within the history of metaphysical thinking; that location is among his central concerns.

This general thesis must be made more specific. The decisive factor is that the mind of the human being who begins to philosophize is neither empty nor chaotically organized; instead, it contains many wholly determinate and indeed firmly and decisively accepted and rejected conceptions, ideas, etc. That is of course also the situation of one who, prior to engaging in radically philosophical questioning, embraces the Christian (or any religious) faith. Can a person of the Christian faith be a philosopher who engages in "completely free questioning"? It appears that Heidegger would deny this possibility; Heidegger's position is reconsidered below.

Whatever Heidegger may have thought, it is neither illuminating nor necessary to answer the just-posed question in the negative; quite to the contrary, the negative answer is the result of a strikingly superficial consideration of the state of affairs under consideration. That it is is now to be shown.

[iii] Concerning the problem of determining the sense in which philosophical questioning can be "completely free," in the concrete case of the relation between a person of the Christian faith who engages in theorization and philosophy, there are *three* possible positions: two extreme ones that are diametrically opposed, and one that is moderate and more differentiated. These are now briefly to be characterized and evaluated.

[a] The *first* extreme position is that of the person of the Christian faith who is wholly guided, as a theoretician, by the axiom "faith seeking understanding [*fides quaerens intellectum*]."[128] For this person, the Christian faith is the absolute premise for all theorization, a premise not subject to any questioning whatsoever. For this person, philosophy is merely an instrument: a conceptual, argumentative, etc., means to the end of

---

[128] Anselm, *Proslogion, Prooemium,* xx.

intelligibly articulating the Christian faith. Such a person *is not a philosopher in the genuine sense;* this person is instead a Christian theologian, in the classical sense. For this person, "philosophy" plays exclusively the role of *ancilla theologiae*—handmaiden of theology.

[b] The second extreme position, diametrically opposed to the first, is the position of the philosopher who understands "completely free questioning" in a manner that *fundamentally excludes any compatibility between philosophical theorization and the Christian faith.* "Completely free thinking" is so radically understood and carried out that it could never have the result of entailing or even making possible any connection to the Christian faith. For this person, the Christian faith is at most only one phenomenon among many others that can be a subject matter for philosophical theorization. This appears to be Heidegger's position (see the lengthy consideration in section 2.8, above). Four considerations reveal, however, that Heidegger's position is not sufficiently clear.

First, in the lecture course he gave at Freiburg in the summer semester of 1935, *Introduction to Metaphysics,* Heidegger made some particularly important and—at least at first glance—unambiguous assertions about this topic. In his own way, he treated a question—which he presents as the fundamental question of metaphysics—raised by Leibniz: "Why is there anything [Heidegger says: being (*Seiendes*)] at all rather than nothing?"[129] He says, among other things, that this question "loses its rank at once in the sphere of a human-historical Dasein to whom *questioning* as an originary power remains foreign."[130] In conclusion, he introduces the example of the person who believes in the Bible, writing,

> Anyone for whom the Bible is divine revelation and truth already has the answer to the question "Why are there beings at all instead of nothing?" before it is even asked: beings, with the exception of God Himself, are created by Him. God Himself "is" as the uncreated Creator.[131]

Here, Heidegger overlooks the fact that creation is the answer not to a why question but to a how question: *how* is it to be explained that there are contingent beings? A genuinely reasonable why question would be, Why did God create the world?[132] That question cannot be considered here.

---

[129] "Pourquoy il y a plustôt quelque chose que rien?" (G. W. Leibniz, *Principes de la nature et de la grâce, fondés en raison,* 6:602).

[130] *Introduction to Metaphysics* (1935/2000), 7.

[131] Ibid.

[132] On the immense importance and the precise sense of the fundamental distinction between why questions and how questions, see section 3.2.3, above.

Concerning the issue currently in question in this book, the following passage is of great significance:

> One who holds on to such a faith as a basis can, perhaps, emulate and participate in the asking of our question in a certain way, but *he cannot authentically question without giving himself up as a believer, with all the consequences of this step.* He can act only "as if—."[133]

This passage expresses a mistake because it is the result of an obvious and simple confusion. Heidegger jumbles two matters that are strictly distinct, namely, a theoretical activity (philosophical questioning) and an existential decision (i.e., a decision that binds the will and hence practical activity, but not necessarily theoretical activity).

The mistake is expressed in the sentence, "he [the believer] cannot authentically question without giving himself up as a believer." The phrase "giving himself up as a believer" is ambiguous. It can mean to give himself up as a believer *either* existentielly/practically *or* insofar as he engages in theorization. If it is understood in the first sense, then Heidegger's contention is simply false, but the contention is correct if the phrase is understood in the second sense. The person of faith who does *not* give up that faith, with all that belongs to it, including its theoretical aspects, in the sense of *retaining* that faith as an unquestioned and unquestionable premise for *all* of the person's questioning and thinking, *does not philosophize* because, in Heidegger's accurate phrase, that person cannot *genuinely* question (i.e., for Heidegger, that person cannot genuinely pose the fundamental question of metaphysics).

The distinction between the *existentiell* and *practical* on the one hand and the *theoretical* on the other is of elementary significance. Genuinely theoretical activity is—must be—absolutely free from any and every practical factor, including—above all—every existential decision. This is precisely what constitutes the unique status of theorization, although that it does is rarely seen and yet more rarely correctly explained. The examination of the structure of theoretical sentences presented above (see especially 3.2.1.1) shows how fundamental this state of affairs is. To fail to make the distinction or to fail to recognize the richness of its consequentiality—worse yet, to deny this distinction and its consequentiality—is to repeat a mistake made throughout history and still today by many philosophers, theologians, ideologues, etc. The error is codified in the thesis of the unity of theory and practice; as so codified it is a virtual

---

[133] *Introduction to Metaphysics*, 8 (emphasis added).

dogma in the Marxist tradition, in so-called critical theory, and in various other schools of thought. What results from its acceptance is that neither genuine theory nor genuine practice is realized, in any domain whatsoever; instead, there is only rhetoric, and confusion between the two.

Heidegger is thus wrong in maintaining, completely generally and without qualification, that the person of faith "cannot authentically question without giving himself up as a believer." It is, however, noteworthy that in concluding the passage within which this phrase appears, Heidegger appears to correct himself, but without explicitly acknowledging that he is doing so. He writes:

> *On the other hand,* if such faith does not continually expose itself to the possibility of unfaith, it is not faith but a convenience. It becomes an agreement with oneself to adhere in the future to a doctrine as something that has somehow been handed down. This is neither having faith nor questioning, but indifference—which can then, perhaps even with keen interest, busy itself with everything, with faith as well as with questioning.[134]

Reading these sentences, one wonders what remains from the undifferentiated and apodictic assertion that "he [the believer] cannot authentically question without giving himself up as a believer." According to the second passage, the person whose faith "does not continually expose itself to the possibility of unfaith" is for precisely that reason "not faith but a convenience"; but what then is the "faith" that the person of faith must give up in order to be able genuinely to question? If the person of faith "cannot authentically question without giving himself up as a believer"—without giving up his faith—and if as long as *this faith* is retained the person can neither have faith nor question, then the following question presses: what is Heidegger trying to say? It is all too clear that what he says, as it stands, makes no sense.

If Heidegger were to hold firm to the position articulated in the second passage, he would have to correct the first passage, transforming it into something like the following: the person of faith "cannot authentically question without exposing himself constantly to the possibility of unfaith," because otherwise the person's faith would be "not faith but a convenience." And that is not only a remarkable statement, it is also one that is completely accurate.

---

[134] Ibid., 8 (emphasis added).

The next two considerations need be formulated only briefly here, because both are examined thoroughly in section 2.8, above.

Second, Heidegger attempted again and again to establish the dimension of Christian faith (and of Christian theology) as of ultimately secondary status, as something that, according to his "essential thinking," is purely "ontic."[135]

Third, Heidegger's treatments of the relation between Being and God are discordant; at times he radically dissociates Being and God, but at others he designates Being as (necessary?) access to God.

Fourth—and this is the most essential point—Heidegger's thinking led him wholly away from the Christian God. His catchword became "*Ereignis*," and he interpreted this word—bizarrely, and with the aid of his linguistic virtuosity—as the occurring of the following "eleven ways of essencing [*Wesungsweisen*] of *Ereignis*": "*Ereignis—Er-eignen—Ver-eignung—Übereignung—Zueignung—An-eignung—Eigentlichkeit—Eignung—Geeignetheit—Ent-eignung—Eigentum.*"[136] Heidegger's presentation of this strange list provides yet another basis, in addition to those presented above in 2.6, for criticism of his reliance on this catchword.

Subsection [3][i] of this section introduces and critically comments on several passages from Heidegger concerning "incongruities in the traditional concept of metaphysics" that he takes himself to find particularly in the works of Thomas Aquinas. Among those passages is the central one about the "trivialization [*Veräußerlichung*]" of this concept, which Heidegger understands as follows: "Metaphysics is leveled down and trivialized into everyday knowledge"; it "*no longer* indicates a particular *orientation* of thinking and knowing, a peculiar *turnaround* in the face of everyday thinking and inquiry, but is merely a sign for the *place* and the *order of those beings* which lie *behind* and *above* other beings."[137]

If one notes that all of Heidegger's eleven "ways of essencing of *Ereignis*" draw whatever conceptual content they have—or, in more Hei-

---

[135] On this point, see Philippe Capelle, *Philosophie et théologie dans la pensée de Martin Heidegger* (1998).

[136] This cascade of words rooted in "*eigen*" is from chapter 5 (titled "*Ereignis:* The Vocabulary of Its Essence") of *Das Ereignis,* which was published after *Sein und Gott* had been completed. Chapter 5 is the textual core of the treatise, which articulates the relations among the eleven vocabulary items constituting Heidegger's cascade. The treatise is the sixth of seven that are devoted to "the history of Beyng [*Seyn*]"; the first is *Contributions to Philosophy (From Enowning).* (The information provided in this note about the contents of *Das Ereignis* was drawn from pre-publication documents produced by Klostermann Verlag, the publisher of Heidegger's *Gesamtausgabe.*) See also chapter 2, note 20.

[137] *The Fundamental Concepts of Metaphysics,* 66.

deggerian terms, whatever they provide to thinking—from the term
"*eigen*," one ubiquitously used in everyday German, so that what it provides to thinking has its genuine and indeed sole basis in everyday language and everyday situations, and if one notes in addition that the word
"*Ereignis*," too, is intelligible only on the basis of its use in everyday German, then one can only be astonished that Heidegger makes of just this
word his most central catchword, and takes himself to have no other
option, in articulating his magnificent, decisive, and putatively here-
tofore unthought thought, than to rely on words sharing that same
everyday root. One cannot see how Heidegger could respond to the
powerful objection that the charge he levels against the "traditional
concept of metaphysics"—the charge that it "trivialized into everyday
knowledge"[138]—strikes at the heart of his own thinking. All his machina-
tions with the word *Ereignis* show all too clearly that *he* has no "*orientation
of thinking and knowing*" that could accomplish "a peculiar *turnaround*
in the face of everyday thinking and inquiry"[139] of the sort that, he insists,
genuine philosophizing requires.

[c] The third position is a moderate position that does not consider the relata in question—philosophy, understood as radical and completely free questioning, and the Christian faith as articulable theoretically—as absolutely rigid, as fixed once and for all such that there is no
possibility of theoretical compromise. The two central aspects that make
it possible both for each of the two poles unrestrictedly to retain its specific character and for there to be theoretical compromise are articulated
in what follows.

Starting with philosophy, the possibility *cannot be excluded* that a
radical and completely free questioning would lead to the development
of a theory that would serve as the basis for an *existential affirmation* of
the Christian faith. In the optimal actualization of this possibility, the
extension of philosophical thinking into the domain of subject matter
studied by Christian theology would yield the best available comprehensively systematic theory.

Starting with so-called Christian faith, the possibility cannot be excluded that a person of this faith engages in radical and completely free
questioning. A person of faith can engage in such questioning while retaining that faith, but not while drawing inspiration, motivation, or—
especially—premises from it. That this is completely coherent is a consequence of the fact that the *effective consummation* of the Christian faith

---

[138] Ibid.
[139] Ibid.

involves an *existential decision* on the level of individuality, whereas radical and completely free questioning takes place on the theoretical level, the level of rationality and hence of universality. That the two levels can be dissociated, at least at times, is here presupposed. Only in the course of further development of theoretical thinking does the dissociation of levels become a problem, and when it does the problem is one of coherence: in the end, the two levels must be able to correlate. Just when "in the end" comes is, however, an open question. In fact, this situation, characterized by the simultaneous givenness of uncompromising commitment to philosophy as completely free theorization and the existential decision to embrace the Christian faith, is one that is never left by any person of the Christian faith who is also, at the same time and in the full sense, a philosopher.

As is presumably evident, this third position is the one that is defended in this book and presented in this systematic chapter.

Chapter 4

Critical Examination of Two Counterpositions: Emmanuel Levinas and Jean-Luc Marion

This chapter deals with the most radical counterpositions to the conception presented in chapter 3: contemporary versions of so-called postmodernist Judeo-Christian philosophy and theology. The chapter raises two central objections to these counterpositions.

First, by radically rejecting even the project of developing a comprehensive conception of reality or of Being, advocates of the counterpositions deprive themselves of any adequate basis for addressing the question of God. A "God" not situated within a philosophical theory of everything—a conception of Being as such and as a whole—would ultimately be some sort of curious, mysterious "superthing," even if it were embellished with designations like "love."

Second, in spite of all their protests and counter-assertions, these authors develop conceptions—ones that are usually completely unsystematic and that are never sufficiently systematic—on the basis of what Heidegger calls the philosophy of subjectivity, even—and especially—when they attempt to articulate an "extroversion" or a "reversal" of subjectivity. As a consequence, the God they in one way or another arrive at—if the X they arrive at deserves the name "God" at all—is the Other, the absolute Other, the absolutely Distant, or the like. But this "God" proves in the last analysis to be nothing other than a *function* of human subjectivity. If the author decided to use the language most postmodernist philosophers and theologians employ when they criticize metaphysically oriented philosophies and theologies, he would have to say that their God is an *idol*. But the author opts not to employ such language, so says instead that no postmodern "God" is the *genuine, divine God*.

This chapter's critique does not consider the immense variety of postmodernist philosophical and theological positions. To be effective, such a critique would have to be too extensive to be contained even in a voluminous book. For this reason, only two authors, whom the author considers to be the most radical opponents to the kind of conception propounded in chapter 3, are treated; these are Emmanuel Levinas and Jean-Luc Marion. Moreover, even the extraordinarily extensive oeuvres of these two thinkers cannot be fully considered in all their details. Nevertheless, the account that follows does aim to identify the decisive coordinates of their conceptions, and to subject those coordinates to meticulous critique.

4.1 Levinas's Misguided Conception of Transcendence "Beyond B/being"

4.1.1 General Characterization

Levinas states: "It is not by accident that the history of Western philosophy has been a destruction of transcendence."[1] The reason he provides is that Western philosophy has been mainly, if not exclusively, a philosophy of B/being. But, he asserts,

> the intelligibility of transcendence is not ontological. The transcendence of God can neither be said nor thought in terms of B/being, the element of philosophy behind which philosophy sees only night. But the rupture between philosophical intelligibility and what is beyond B/being, or the contradiction there would be in com-prehending the infinite, does not exclude God from the significance that, although not ontological, does not amount to simple thoughts bearing on a being in decline, nor to views without necessity, nor to words that play.[2]

How does Levinas arrive at such an extreme conception? To give an adequate answer to this question, a very long story would have to be told—a story that would include the most important stages in the history of modern philosophy, especially in Europe from the end of the nineteenth century to the mid-1960s. Because that story cannot be told here, a few elucidatory and critical remarks must suffice.

In what follows, the main points of what could be called, with Kant, the architectonic (or, mathematically, the coordinate system) of Levinas's thinking are sketched and critically examined—although it is debatable

---

[1] Emmanuel Levinas, "God and Philosophy," in E. Levinas, *Of God Who Comes to Mind*, trans. Bettina Bergo (Stanford, Calif.: Stanford University Press, 1998), 57.

[2] Ibid., 77.

whether it makes sense to speak of an architectonic of the thinking of a postmodernist philosopher. There are three fundamental assumptions (or theses)—three main coordinates or key elements—at the core of Levinas's philosophy.

4.1.2 Three Highly Problematic Fundamental Assumptions in Levinas's Philosophy

4.1.2.1 Levinas's Misguided Conceptions of Knowledge and Theory
[1] Levinas's first highly problematic assumption is visible in his conceptions of knowledge (*connaissance*) and theory. First of all, one can easily identify an inconsistency in Levinas's understanding and usage of these terms. On the one hand, he writes:

> Knowledge or theory designates first a relation with B/being such that the knowing being lets the known being manifest itself while respecting its alterity and without marking it in any way whatever by this cognitive relation. In this sense metaphysical desire would be the essence of theory. (*TI* 42)

On the other hand, he asserts: "But theory also designates comprehension [*intelligence*]—the logos of B/being—that is, a way of approaching the known being such that its alterity with regard to the knowing being vanishes" (ibid.).

According to Levinas, knowledge/theory in the first sense "is concerned with critique," whereas knowledge/theory in the second sense is a kind of "dogmatism" (*TI* 43). Interestingly, Levinas later almost always understands "knowledge/theory" in this second sense. And this is the sense he always presupposes when he develops his central conception about transcendence. In what follows only this second sense is taken into account.

Levinas writes:

> In what concerns knowledge: it is by essence a relation with what one equals and includes, with that whose alterity one suspends, with what becomes immanent, because it is to my measure and to my scale. . . .
> There is in knowledge, in the final account, an impossibility of escaping the self; consequently, sociality [*socialité*] cannot have the same structure as knowledge.[3]

---

[3] E. Levinas, *Ethics and Infinity: Dialogues with Philippe Nemo* (1982/1985), 60.

Significantly, Levinas seems to presuppose that some philosopher has held that sociality *does* have the same structure as knowledge. He emphasizes, in a radical and undifferentiated manner, that the Other is what cannot be submitted to any kind of *reduction*. But reduction is precisely what he attributes to knowledge:

> Knowledge has been always interpreted as assimilation. Even the most surprising discoveries end up being absorbed, comprehended, with all that there is of "prehending" in "comprehending." The most audacious and remote knowledge does not put us in communion with the truly other; it does not take the place of sociality; it is still and always a solitude.[4]

This strange (mis)conception of knowledge leads Levinas to introduce his no less peculiar (mis)conception of *ontology*. One of his concise characterizations is the following: "The social is beyond ontology,"[5] which he interprets in the following way:

> To theory as comprehension of beings the general title ontology is appropriate. Ontology, which reduces the other to the same, promotes freedom—the freedom that is the identification of the same, not allowing itself to be alienated by the other. Here theory enters upon a course that renounces metaphysical Desire, renounces the marvel of exteriority from which that Desire lives. (*TI* 42)

If knowledge and ontology are understood in this way, then the relationship to the other, which is constitutive of sociality, does not belong to the order of knowledge in any sense whatsoever. Therefore ontology—that is, knowledge of being(s)—must give place to *ethics,* because the ethical dimension is the one in which the other is fully recognized as other.

[2] Of this conception it must emphatically be said that it constitutes a distortion, a mistake, an error of enormous proportions, as becomes clear when the concepts used are carefully examined and the results to which it leads are critically considered. This is a case in point of the profound truth of the adage *Parvus error in initio magnus in fine—A small error at the beginning leads to a great error in the end.* It is easy to show where Levinas's initial error lies.

---

[4] Ibid.
[5] Ibid., 58.

[i] In all at least in principle clear and accurate definitions of knowledge, the first condition to be fulfilled is the following: if subject S knows (that) p, then (S believes that) p.[6] Now, in some sense or other truth has always been understood as articulating a relation of the knowing subject to the ontological dimension, a relation to some item in the world (fact, state of affairs, situation, etc.). Most generally, this relation is called the correspondence relation. How this relation has been and is still understood is clearly articulated by Thomas Aquinas: "True expresses the correspondence between being and the knowing power, for all knowing comes about through the assimilation of the knower to the thing known."[7]

Because knowledge has to do with truth, its essential point is precisely not the assimilation of things, of "the other," *to the subject;* rather, it is the diametrically opposite: the assimilation of the knower to what is known.

[ii] Knowledge makes manifest what the item known is *as such,* that is, *as it is.* Something that is an *other* as regards a or the subject is known if and only if it is made manifest that it is *an other as an other,* otherwise it would not itself be known as what it is. How then can Levinas contend that knowledge/theory involves the "vanishing" of the other?

Levinas falls victim to an absolutely elementary confusion—one between knowledge and a practical attitude or practical act. He fails to find in knowledge something that belongs not there, but instead in the domain of practical behavior and action. When he maintains, "The most audacious and remote knowledge does not put us in communion with the truly other; it does not take the place of sociality," he reveals his deep confusion. It is of course the case that "the most audacious and remote knowledge does not put us in communion with the truly other," *if* the sense of communion in question is one that belongs in the domain of practical action. Knowledge is not practical action, is not (practical) recognition of the other, is not (practical) respect of the other, is not real love of the other, or anything of the sort. But *on the theoretical level* the other is *known,* is *articulated,* precisely *as* the other. It is of course the case that sociality does not have the same structure that knowledge has. That Levinas does not see this as obvious reveals the depth of his confusion.

---

[6] See *Structure and Being,* section 2.4.2.2, pp. 102ff., where the usual definition of knowledge as justified true belief is corrected; the correction is added above by the parenthetical phrase "S believes that" (see 106).

[7] "Convenientiam . . . entis ad intellectus exprimit hoc nomen verum. Omnis cognitio perficitur per assimilationem cognoscentis ad rem cognitam" (*De ver.* q. 1. a. 1.).

[iii] Knowledge is a certain kind of attitude of subjects toward reality: this attitude is often called veritative (related to truth) or factive (related to fact).[8] What this means can be explained as follows: The first condition in the definition of knowledge, the truth condition, is articulated by a sentence preceded (usually implicitly) by the theoretical operator "It is the case that. . . ." This condition then has the form: "It is truly the case that p." What is highly significant about this articulation is that it contains no reference whatsoever to any subject or to any subjective factor. Consequently, there is not anything like a relation with what a subject renders equal to itself, with what the subject includes, with that whose otherness the subject suspends, with what becomes immanent to the subject.

[iv] A quite different but equally fundamental criticism of Levinas's statements about knowledge and theory points to a blatant self-contradiction contained in them. Levinas presents a conception that aims thoroughly to elucidate this entire topic (i.e., to explain what knowledge, theory, etc., are). His conception is articulated in theoretical sentences that express the connections among the various relevant items. But the conception, in that it is one developed and defended by a concrete subject, is itself a specific kind of knowledge—what else could it be? Levinas unmistakably wants to be considered to be a philosopher. But then he has a problem: if knowledge and theory are what he characterizes them as being, then of course the knowledge that his own conception claims to articulate must be so understood. That is: Levinas understands and characterizes knowledge and theory as "by essence a relation with what one equals and includes, with that whose alterity one suspends, with what becomes immanent, because it is to my measure and to my scale." He thereby claims to know and to say what knowledge and theory *themselves, in themselves,* are. But then the knowledge and understanding he claims to have of what knowledge and theory themselves are contradict what he says when he characterizes knowledge/theory. He commits a performative self-contradiction. His *active* knowledge/theorization falsifies his *characterized* knowledge/theorization. His conception is thus self-defeating.

4.1.2.2 Levinas's Incoherent Conception of Metaphysics

[1] Levinas's second core assumption or coordinate or key element is his understanding and characterization of *metaphysics.* Surprisingly, he introduces an unusual distinction between ontology and metaphysics: for

---

[8] See, e.g., Timothy Williamson, *Knowledge and Its Limits* (Oxford: Oxford University Press, 2000), 34ff.; see also *Structure and Being,* 106ff.

him, ontology is the philosophy of being(s) and of Being as such and as a whole. Given this, it would be nonsense to speak of a Levinasian metaphysics of B/being. If this were merely a terminological point, it would be of little significance, but it is neither exclusively nor even primarily merely terminological.

Levinas's consideration of metaphysics and ontology begins with a historical and contentual statement:

> Metaphysics . . . is turned toward the "elsewhere" and the "otherwise" and the "other." For in the most general form it has assumed in the history of thought it appears as a movement going forth from a world that is familiar to us, whatever be the yet unknown lands that bound it or that it hides from view, from the "at home" ["*chez soi*"] that we inhabit toward an alien outside-of-oneself [*hors-de-soi*], toward a yonder.
>
> . . . The metaphysical desire tends toward *something else entirely*, toward the *absolutely other*. (*TI* 33)

The central concepts in Levinas's characterization of metaphysics are the concepts *exteriority, alterity,* and *the other/Other* (*l'autre/Autrui*). The relationship to the other he calls a "metaphysical relation" (*TI* 42), and it turns out to be—in his use of the term "metaphysical"—*the metaphysical relation tout court*. The metaphysical movement of transcendence is then a *"transascendence"* (*TI* 35): "Thus the metaphysician and the other cannot be *totalized*." Metaphysics in Levinas's sense is "the breach of totality." The metaphysical relation is the relation between the I and the other. Levinas call the I the Same and the other the Other.

According to Levinas, *ethics* is genuine metaphysics (in his sense); it deserves to be granted absolute primacy and to be recognized as the genuine *prima philosophia*. "Metaphysics [as ethics] precedes ontology" (*TI* 42).[9]

[2] Levinas has an idiosyncratic understanding of ethics; he articulates it as follows:

> A calling into question of the same—which cannot occur within the egoist spontaneity of the same—is brought about by the other. We

---

[9] In his later works, Levinas does not always use the term "metaphysics" in this unusual sense. In a preliminary note to his book *Otherwise Than Being*, for example, he writes: "to hear a God not contaminated by B/being is a human possibility no less important and no less precarious than to bring Being out of the oblivion in which it is said to have fallen in metaphysics and in onto-theology" (xlii).

> name this calling into question of my spontaneity by the presence of
> the Other ethics. The strangeness of the Other, his irreducibility to
> the I, to my thought and my possessions, is precisely accomplished as
> a calling into question of my spontaneity, as ethics. (*TI* 43)

The French term *"l'éthique"* is ambiguous: it can name the philosophical discipline *ethics*, but also the domain of the ethical. Levinas at
least generally does not use it to name the discipline; he uses it instead
to designate the deepest or most fundamental dimension of human life.
Knowledge and the ethical—in this sense—are thus two different dimensions, neither of which is reducible to the other.

Knowledge and the ethical, even in Levinas's sense of the latter
term, cannot be utterly separate because the metaphysician (in Levinas's
sense) is a *philosophical theoretician* who, like Levinas himself, articulates
the relation between the I (and thus the metaphysician) and the other.
How could the metaphysician, as theoretician, be completely separated
from the other? If he were, then he would not be able to articulate the
relation. This is a point that reappears in various forms in different and
central places in Levinas's philosophy, and one about which more is said
below.

[3] There is in principle no incoherence in asserting that the ethical dimension is the dimension of *prima philosophia;* this depends on how
one understands "the ethical (dimension)" and *"prima philosophia."* But
for Levinas there is a coherence problem that arises from how he understands the ethical. He repeatedly says that the ethical is not within
the domain of knowledge. In one respect this is an almost trivial claim,
because the dimension of knowledge and the dimension of the ethical
are distinct dimensions: the one is not the other. But Levinas seems to
understand his claim in a very different way when he says that the ethical
is not within the domain of knowledge. By this he also—and mainly—
seems to mean that the ethical cannot be grasped by anything like knowledge, because knowledge "is by essence a relation with what one equals
and includes, with that whose alterity one suspends, with what becomes
immanent, because it is to my measure and to my scale."[10]

Levinas thus confronts a dilemma: either he means to be correctly
articulating the ethical relationship, and in this case he has to presuppose that the ethical in his sense can be grasped and articulated such
that there is knowledge of it, that is, that the dimension of the ethical
and the dimension of knowledge are not separated as they would be if

---

[10] *Ethics and Infinity,* 60.

they belonged to two absolutely incompatible orders; or he maintains a thorough and completely exclusive separation and incompatibility of the two orders—and in this case he would not be able to articulate the ethical dimension, because by even attempting to do that, he would contradict himself.

4.1.2.3 Levinas's Fatal Misconception of "B/being"

Levinas's third core assumption or coordinate or key element—undoubtedly the most important with respect to the topic of this book—concerns the *dimension of B/being*. According to Levinas, the dimension of "the other" must be conceived of as *otherwise than being* or as *beyond essence* (= *Being*). This is the central thesis to which points the title of his important book *Otherwise Than Being or Beyond Essence/Being*, in French, *Autrement qu'être ou au-delà de l'essence*. Here, Levinas understands the title of his second major work as follows: "*being/être*" corresponds to the Latin "*ens*" and the German "*Seiendes*," whereas "essence" corresponds to the Latin "*esse*" and the German "*Sein*."[11]

Levinas's central thesis that the other is *otherwise than being* or *beyond essence/Being* has far-reaching consequences. How does he arrive at such a conception? From the historical point of view he was inspired especially by Plato's claim that the idea of the good is "beyond Being [οὐσία]"[12] and by Descartes's idea of the infinite;[13] but the general philosophical basis is decisively influenced by Husserl and Heidegger. Despite its immense importance in explaining Levinas's thesis, this historical matter cannot be treated here. In what follows some of Levinas's central intuitions and insights (one can hardly speak of arguments) concerning Being/being(s) are critically analyzed.

[1] The first point to which the attention of the perspicuous reader is drawn is the thorough ambiguity pervading Levinas's usage of the terms "Being/being(s)—*être*" and "existence/to exist—*existence, exister*." In many passages he seems to understand the terms as synonyms, as in the following passage: "To be is to be isolated by existing."[14] In such passages as the following, however, he distinguishes existence from Being:

> Already the I exists in an eminent sense: for one cannot imagine it as first existing and in addition endowed with happiness as an attribute

---

[11] In French, "*être*" can mean either "*esse/Sein*" or "*ens/Seiendes*."

[12] Plato, *Republic* 6.509b9: ἐπέκεινα τῆς οὐσίας.

[13] See Descartes, *Meditations on First Philosophy*, "Third Meditation."

[14] Levinas, *Time and the Other* (1979/1987), 42.

added to this existence. The I exists as separated in its enjoyment, that
is, as happy; and it can sacrifice its pure and simple being to happi-
ness. It *exists* in an eminent sense; it exists above B/being. (*TI* 62–63;
emphasis added)

"Existence in an eminent sense" is "above B/being." What does this
mean? Levinas never explains this; he concentrates almost exclusively on
B/being and he explicitly identifies "existence/to exist" and "B/being" in
all the most important passages of his writings. This creates an immense
confusion. Be that as it may, the important question in this context is
this: how does Levinas understand being/being(s)—*être*? (The usage of
"existence/to exist," in cases when these terms are not synonymous with
être, is not further considered here, because that usage is not of major
importance.)[15]

[2] Levinas explicitly articulates his understanding of *être*, as in the
following two passages:

My effort consists in showing that knowledge is in reality an immanence, and that there is no rupture of the isolation of B/being in
knowledge; and on the other hand, that in communication of knowledge one is found beside the Other, not confronted with him, not in
the rectitude of the in-front-of-him. But B/being in direct relation with
the Other is not to thematize the Other and consider him in the same
manner as one considers a known object, nor to communicate a knowledge to him. In reality, the fact of B/being is what is most private; existence is the sole thing I cannot communicate; I can tell about it, but I
cannot share my existence. Solitude thus appears as the isolation which
marks the very event of B/being. The social is beyond ontology.[16]

Through sight, touch, sympathy, and cooperative work, we are with
others. All these relationships are transitive. I touch the other, I see
the other. But I am not the other. I am all alone. It is thus the B/being
in me, the fact that I exist, my existing, that constitutes the absolutely
intransitive element, something without intentionality or relations. One

---

[15] In a passage from *Time and the Other* concerning Heidegger, he writes: "His distinction between *Sein* and *Seiendes,* Being and being(s) . . . I prefer, for reasons of euphony,
to render as *existing* and *existent,* without ascribing a specifically existentialist meaning to
these terms" (44; t.a.). This passage does not make clear whether Levinas uses "Being" and
"existing" synonymously only when speaking about Heidegger or also when speaking for
himself.

[16] *Ethics and Infinity,* 57–58.

can exchange everything between beings except existing in this sense, to be is to be isolated by existing. Insofar as I am, I am a monad. By existing, and not because of any content that would be immediately within me, I am without a door and without windows.[17]

It is not an exaggeration and is in no way unfair to maintain that Levinas's "understanding" of *être* is a consequential misunderstanding and a fatal error. The following account shows that it is not difficult to counter his position.

Even brief mention of one phenomenon suffices to show that the following Levinasian assertions must be directly and utterly denied: "Solitude thus appears as the isolation which marks the very event of B/being"—"It is thus the B/being in me, the fact that I exist, my existing, that constitutes the absolutely intransitive element, something without intentionality or relations." *Utterly to the contrary:* the most radical and fundamental "element" that I *share* with others is precisely *my Being/existence*. To show this—in one among many possible ways—it suffices carefully to examine the phenomenon of our belonging to a community of human beings. What does our presence, our being present, among human beings reveal? What happens here?

Even simply Being present means that we are sharing our Being/existence with other Being/existing human beings who in their turn share with us their own existence/Being. A community of human beings is a wonderful expression and realization of what existence or Being means in the last analysis. Whatever the differences among the members of a community may be, the simplest fact is that every member in the community *nevertheless* shares at least *one thing*, namely his own existence/Being, with the other human beings. This means that all participate in this immense and fundamental dimension or space, which one can adequately call the space of Being or, more exactly: the dimension of Being as the universal space that makes it possible for human beings to communicate with one another. This phenomenon cannot be further considered here, although it is elaborated above in chapter 3.

From what is shown above, a far-reaching consequence concerning Levinas's entire philosophy follows: if Being/existence is precisely not what Levinas takes it/them to be, if, on the contrary, Being is exactly the completely diametrical opposite of the Levinasian "B/being/existence as isolation," then the immense conception he develops on the basis of the latter completely and uncompromisingly collapses. His claim that the

---

[17] *Time and the Other,* 42.

other, the transcendent, God must be conceived of *otherwise than Being,*
beyond Being, is based on a fundamental mistake and fatal error, as the
following section shows.

4.1.3 Levinas's Misguided Conceptions of Transcendence and God as Resulting from His Philosophy of Subjectivity

What do the preceding analyses yield that is of relevance to the topics
transcendence and *God?* Concerning them, one finds in his writings two
attitudes, one positive and one negative. The negative one is expressed
in a thesis that totally determines his entire philosophy, one that provides
the dark foil in contrast to which all his statements emerge. The positive
one is articulated in three ideas that could be revelatory but that Levinas
fundamentally misinterprets.

4.1.3.1 Total Negativity: The Dimension of Being
Levinas expresses the *negative idea* as follows:

> The difficulties of the climb, as well as its failures and renewed at-
> tempts, are marked in the writing, which no doubt also shows the
> breathlessness of the author. But to hear a God not contaminated by
> B/being is a human possibility no less important and no less precarious
> than to bring Being out of the oblivion in which it is said to have fallen
> in metaphysics and in onto-theology. (*OTB* xliii)

It is clear that Levinas is reacting here to Heidegger. The extensive consideration of Heidegger in chapter 2 shows how undifferentiated
and superficial is his appeal to onto-theology. The formulation "a God
contaminated by B/being" is absolutely typical: it impressively articulates
Levinas's catastrophic misunderstanding of Being and God. To be sure,
the misunderstanding grows from Heideggerian soil, but it also has specific and centrally important aspects that depend wholly on Levinas and
on his Jewish background. Among these is the central thought of *the other.*
Because that thought is considered above, particularly in 4.1.2.3, it need
only be mentioned here.

4.1.3.2 Three Positive Features of Transcendence and God Misinterpreted by Levinas

4.1.3.2.1 The Idea of the Other as the Other or of the Face to Face
The first positive idea is the idea of the Other or of the face to face.
[1] Levinas emphasizes that already the other human being is transcendent with respect to me, to my I. God is the absolute, the infinite

Other. Levinas's statements about God as the absolute, infinite Other are mostly purely negative. The reason is that his constant concern is "to hear a God not contaminated by B/being" (*OTB* xlviii). This leads him strictly to reject any conception of God's transcendence that could develop within the framework of a conception of Being. According to him, such a conception subjects God to the constraints of a totality or a system. He explains this as follows:

> The Same and the Other cannot enter into a cognition that would encompass them; the relations that the separated B/being maintains with what transcends it are not produced on the ground of totality, do not crystallize into a system. Yet do we not name them together? The *formal* synthesis of the word that names them together is already part of a discourse, that is, of a conjuncture of transcendence, that breaks the totality. The conjuncture of the Same and the Other, in which even their verbal proximity is maintained, is the *direct* and *full face* welcome of the Other by me. This conjuncture is irreducible to totality; the "face to face" position is not a modification of the "along side of. . . ." Even when I shall have linked the Other to myself with the conjunction "and" the Other continues to face me, to reveal himself in his face. (*TI* 80–81)

Shown above is that such statements do not constitute arguments. What does it mean to say "The Same and the Other cannot enter into a cognition that would encompass them; the relations that the separated B/being maintains with what transcends it are not produced on the ground of totality, do not crystallize into a system"? Levinas overlooks the following: the relation between a subject (which Levinas call "the Same") and an Other presupposes a *space*, a *dimension* wherein the two are related, a dimension that makes the relation possible in the first place. We see and say that we have a cognition precisely of the space/dimension that makes the relation possible and, thus, *encompasses* both the subject (the Same) and the Other. To say, "The Same and the Other cannot enter into a *cognition* that would encompass them" is to make a simple mistake, because what encompasses the subject (Levinas's "the Same") and the Other is not the cognition, but what the cognition knows.

Levinas always presupposes exactly this: he claims to *know* what the relation between the subject and the Other is, so he speaks continuously precisely of the conjoining *space/dimension* encompassing the two; but he characterizes this space/dimension (and, thus, the relation) in absolutely negative terms: as separation. He ignores the fact that there is no separation without a conjoining space/dimension. Levinas appears to presuppose that the only positive way this space/dimension could be thought would be as totality and/or as system, and without considering alternatives he understands those two expressions as meaning: absolutely closed big things. But this is arbitrary. If one wants to use the terms "totality" and/or "system," why exclude *a limine* the idea of an *open* totality or of an *open* system? If the encompassing space is called *the primordial dimension of Being*, then it is clear that this dimension is nothing like an enormous thing that contains everything by somehow suffocating or isolating anything or everything. Quite to the contrary, it is the *opening space*, the one that makes it possible for all of the items within the dimension to relate to one another in accordance with their own structurations.

What Levinas wholly ignores—and this is a decisive point—is that God himself is the absolute Other but *not* an *other finite* being that we would somehow be outside of. If He were an absolute Other in this sense, then He would be an other finite being, because He would have some sort of border or limit, as shown below in 4.2.4.4.2. Instead, He is the Absolute Other *in the sense* that He absolutely encompasses us and the entire (finite) world. God's otherness is God's transcendence, but God's transcendence and God's immanence are directly proportional: the greater is God's transcendence, the greater is God's immanence (that is, his encompassing of anything and everything). In that God is the absolutely unrestricted itself, God makes possible and meaningful our relation to Him as the absolute Other. This central idea, which Levinas virtually entirely misses, becomes clearer with the analysis of the two other positive ideas in Levinas: the ideas of infinity and of creation.

[2] The idea of the Other as Other is more determinately for Levinas the *idea of the face to face:*

> The dimension of the divine opens forth from the human face. A
> relation with the Transcendent free from all captivation by the Tran-
> scendent is a social relation. It is here that the Transcendent, infinitely
> Other, solicits us and appeals to us. The proximity of the Other, the
> proximity of the neighbor, is in being an ineluctable moment of the
> revelation of an absolute presence (that is, disengaged from every rela-
> tion), which expresses itself. His very epiphany consists in soliciting us
> by his destitution [*misère*] in the face of the Stranger, the widow, and
> the orphan. (*TI* 78)

No doubt, these are formulations inspired by the biblical language of the Hebrew Bible (the Old Testament). If they are understood only in a positive, not in an exclusive, sense, there is no problem with them from a philosophical and theological perspective. But Levinas clearly understands them in a radically exclusive sense: they are meant to exclude every kind of consideration and of statement that belongs to the tradition of philosophies of Being and hence even to what this book terms *deep metaphysics* (this is utterly different from the sense in which Levinas uses the term "metaphysics"!). This poses a serious problem for Levinas, as the continuation of his text makes manifest:

> The atheism of the metaphysician means, positively, that our relation with the Metaphysical is an ethical behavior and not theology, not a thematization, be it a knowledge by analogy, of the attributes of God. God rises to his supreme and ultimate presence as correlative to the justice rendered unto men. The direct comprehension of God is impossible for a look directed upon him, not because our intelligence is limited, but because the relation with infinity respects the total Transcendence of the Other without being bewitched by it, and because our possibility of welcoming him in man goes further than the comprehension that thematizes and encompasses its object. (*TI* 78)

What Levinas here calls "the Metaphysical" is the absolutely Other, in the last analysis God. But Levinas succumbs to a serious confusion: because even for Levinas metaphysics is a philosophical discipline, the formulation "our relation with the Metaphysical" (in Levinas's sense) can only mean: the relation of the metaphysical philosopher, *who is a theoretician,* to what the philosopher articulates—namely, to "the Metaphysical" (in Levinas's sense)—is *a relation to the ethical domain* (and thus to ethical behavior or to the ethical relation itself) and thus ultimately (again in the sense of Levinas) to God. The relation of the metaphysical philosopher to the dimension of the ethical is, however, *not an ethical relation, but a theoretical one.* What Levinas confusedly calls ethical behavior or the ethical relation is a *subject matter* for the theoretician who is a metaphysical philosopher; it is *not* an articulation of how the metaphysical philosopher relates to the domain that Levinas calls the Metaphysical and that he identifies with the ethical. Levinas confuses the theoretical relation with what the theoretical relation thematizes.

This confusion leads to another performative self-contradiction in Levinas's writings: as a metaphysical (in his sense) philosopher he is a theoretician, since he has a *theoretical* relation to whatever he speaks about: to the other, to the ethical (in his sense), to God, to absolutely everything. He articulates what he takes to be true about every subject matter, be it the most simple or the most sublime and "distant" item whatsoever. In doing this he is not negating what he calls the Metaphysical, ethical behavior, or the ethical relation; instead, acting as a metaphysical philosopher in the manner just described, he is doing exactly what he explicitly rejects, namely: in behaving theoretically, he is *thematizing* his subject matter, including "our ethical relation to God," but in doing so he stands in a *theoretical* relation to God, not an *ethical* one.

And Levinas does something else that he explicitly rejects: he relies at least implicitly on a thematization of God's that is made by way of *analogy*. He attributes to the Transcendent God what terms like "presence," "the other," "face," "infinity," etc., mean or designate. Levinas must presuppose that he is applying such "attributes" to God in senses that are not exactly the same as those they have when they are applied to us humans. That is: he must presuppose that these concepts/attributes apply to God *analogically*. The traditional doctrine of analogy is a formidable attempt within a philosophy of Being or being to take this fundamental point into account and to get clear about it. No such attempt is to be found in Levinas. In Levinas one finds only and always strict rejections of such "metaphysical" (not in his sense of "metaphysical") doctrines. What he says about God must therefore be rejected as empty.

4.1.3.2.2 The Idea of Infinity

The second positive theme in Levinas is the *idea of infinity*. He got his inspiration for this idea from Descartes's "Third Meditation," which he interprets in a highly arbitrary and controversial way. Be that as it may, here only the main point can be addressed. He writes:

> My analyses are guided by a formal structure: the idea of Infinity in us. To have the idea of Infinity it is necessary to exist as separated. This separation cannot be produced as only echoing the transcendence of Infinity, for then the separation would be maintained within a correlation that would restore totality and render transcendence illusory. But the idea of Infinity is transcendence itself, the overflowing of an adequate idea. If totality cannot be constituted it is because Infinity does not permit itself to be integrated. It is not the insufficiency of the I that prevents totalization, but the Infinity of the other. (*TI* 79–80)

This text is highly significant because it reveals the untenability of Levinas's philosophical position. He is exclusively preoccupied with saving or securing the absolute transcendence of the (absolute) Other, of God. And he thinks this requires him to claim that the (human) being who has the idea of Infinity must be radically separated from Infinity. He calls the relation between the "being here below and the transcendent being, which results in no community of concept and in no totality," "a relation without relation" (*TI* 80).

Levinas appears not to notice that his statements have an implica-tion that negates and thus excludes what he so radically tries to secure: the transcendence of the Infinite. He posits the "being here below" as *separated* from the Infinite. The fatal implication lies in the fact that a God, understood not as the infinite *in the absolutely encompassing sense,* is nothing more than a lesser God, not a or the true God. Indeed, if there is something (a finite "being here below") *separated* from the infinite and thus *outside* the infinite or *apart* from the infinite, then this infinite is only a *relative* infinite. But an only relative infinite is a finitized infinite, an infinite that is such only in one respect or in some respects, as is for instance the set of uncountable real numbers; on the whole such an in-finite is limited (and thus finitized) simply by the fact that *it is limited to numbers;* every entity that is not a real number is therefore *separated from it,* apart from it, and not encompassed by it. But this is incompatible with the infinite in the absolutely encompassing sense.

Levinas insists again and again that we should not try to "absorb . . . [or] . . . (in the etymological sense of the term) com-prehend" the In-finite, "because Infinity does not permit itself to be integrated" (*TI* 80). But he stops with that separation. He completely forgets or neglects to say and to show that the relation between the "being here below and the transcendent being," the latter understood as the *absolute Infinity,* requires that the "being here below" be absorbed or comprehended by or integrated into the absolute Infinite. Levinas thinks only of a putative encompassing *of* the infinite by a *finite* being; he utterly forgets to think about the encompassing *of* finite beings *by* the absolutely infinite.

Real, genuine transcendence is *within the sphere of* (subjective geni-tive!) *absolute infinity,* not outside of it. God as the absolutely transcen-dent, as the "absolute Other" in Levinas's sense, is a relativized God, a God who stands in a negative relation to an X, i.e., finite being(s). This is the most central error in Levinas's conception of God as absolutely transcendent. The consequence of this is that in order to articulate the really *divine God* it is indispensably necessary to develop a comprehensive conception of reality as a whole or, more precisely, of Being as such and as a whole. God is *not* something *within this whole;* rather, *God is the whole, is Being itself fully explicated or determined.*

4.1.3.2.3 The Idea of Creation

The just-articulated fundamental flaw in Levinas's conception of God also appears and becomes even more evident when one contemplates what he has to say about his third positive idea, that of creation. Levinas accepts creation, but what he says about it does not differ fundamentally from what he says about infinity. He thus deprives the Judeo-Christian

idea of creation of its immensely fundamental and absolutely indispensable weight and force. He writes:

> Creation *ex nihilo* breaks with system, posits a being outside of every
> system, that is, there where its freedom is possible. Creation leaves to
> the creature a trace of dependence, but it is an unparalleled depen-
> dence: the dependent being draws from this exceptional dependence,
> from its relationship, its very independence, its exteriority to the sys-
> tem. What is essential to created existence is not the limited character
> of its being, and the concrete structure of the creature is not deduc-
> ible from this finitude. What is essential to created existence is its
> separation from the Infinite. This separation is not simply a negation.
> Accomplished as psychism, it precisely opens up the idea of Infinity.
> (*TI* 104–5)

In this text there are accurate and appropriate formulations. But
the general tenor is typical of Levinas: he is preoccupied with affirming
separation. To be sure, he does not deny the dependence of the creature
on the creator, but he does not in the least think through what this really
means. To put it briefly: he does not even recognize that the creature—
in the case of human beings: the creature endowed with freedom—*in its
entirety* is what it is (free creature) only within the sphere of creation, of
absolute, creative Being. There is no separation, of the sort articulated
by Levinas, of the created existence from the creator. Instead of thinking
creation through, he has recourse to slogans and stereotypes, especially
the naively understood concepts of "system" and "totality." This failure
directly ensues from the "forgetfulness of Being" that lies at the heart of
Levinas's conception or, more precisely, of the rejection of Being that
pervades his thought.

To conclude this critical assessment of Levinas's position, it is appropriate to mention a point clearly showing that he *perhaps* in some
sense was aware of the tremendous deficiencies, limitations, and distortions of that position. The point is made in a passage in his book *Of God
Who Comes to Mind* (*De Dieu qui vient à l'idée*). In the chapter titled "Questions and Answers" Levinas explains, in response to a question, what he
calls the "anteriority" or "precedence" of ethics with respect to ontology
and the philosophy of B/being. He concedes that this can be understood
as transcendental if "transcendental means a certain anteriority" and then
he continues:

> For me the ethical is not at all a blanket that covers ontology; rather it is
> that which in a certain manner is *more ontological than ontology, an empha-*

sis of ontology. . . . The ethical precedes ontology. It is *more ontological than ontology, more sublime than ontology.*[18]

The introduction of subscripts facilitates examination of this text. If the ethical (in Levinas's sense) is "more ontological$_1$ than ontology$_2$," then it is clear that ontology$_2$, which is the ontology he criticizes and rejects in all of his writings, is not identical with ontology$_1$: ontology$_2$ is a completely deficient, ill-understood, and ill-characterized form of genuine ontology, i.e., ontology$_1$. The just-quoted concession, which amounts to a confession, comes too late to make possible any adequate correction of the disastrous consequences his lifelong rejection of ontology has for his entire oeuvre. But be that as it may, the remarkable formulation just quoted clearly shows that Levinas finally (even if inadvertently) became aware that he never had been really clear about what he had spoken of, throughout his life, as "ontology."

That said, it remains the case that Levinas never took even a first step toward developing a genuine ontology (his ontology$_1$). That he did not suggests a question with which this critical examination of Levinas's conception appropriately concludes: what would his entire conception have been if he had developed the doctrine he called "more ontological$_1$ than ontology$_2$," that is, ontology$_1$, the ontology deeper and more original than that ontology he so often characterized and criticized on the basis of a far-reaching misrepresentation? This question can be answered only with a distinction that reveals the question's ambiguity: if one understands by "Levinas's philosophical position" the one that he articulates in his writings, then the answer is that what he would have developed *as a philosopher would not have been* his real philosophical position, i.e., the position actually presented in his published writings. It is possible that, *as a philosopher,* he would have developed a completely different position, although this would not exclude the possibility that certain thoughts contained in that position could also be found in a fully different position. But as a matter of fact, Levinas never ceased to reject every form of philosophy of Being.

---

[18] *Of God Who Comes to Mind,* 89–90 (emphases added). Original French: "L'éthique n'est pas du tout une couche qui vient recouvrir l'ontologie, mais ce qui est, en quelque façon, plus ontologique que l'ontologie, une emphase de l'ontologie. . . . L'éthique est avant l'ontologie. Elle est plus ontologique que l'ontologie, plus sublime que l'ontologie" (Levinas, *De Dieu qui vient à l'idée* [Paris: Vrin, 1982], 143).

4.1.3.3 Levinas's Specific Form of Philosophy of Subjectivity: Extroverted Subjectivity

The mostly critical considerations in this section (4.1) show that Levinas develops a specific and original philosophy of subjectivity: he transforms modern subjectivity by elaborating an *extroverted form* of subjectivity: his subject is confronted—"face to face"—with the (absolute) Other. But an extroverted form of subjectivity is still a form of subjectivity. Levinas fails to overcome the radical limitations and internal incoherences that plague all forms of the philosophy of subjectivity. His conception of transcendence and God is a mere function of *extroverted* subjectivity.

4.2 Jean-Luc Marion's Failed Conceptions of "Radical and Non-Metaphysical Transcendence" and of "God Without Being"[19]

The topics *metaphysics, transcendence,* and *God* are at the core of Jean-Luc Marion's philosophical-theological conception. Thorough treatment of these topics would therefore require adequate consideration of his entire corpus, but no such treatment is undertaken in this book. The following account focuses on the inner logic or architectonic of his thought—or indeed on the absence from his thought of an inner logic or architectonic.

Marion aims to transcend (in an active sense) all known forms of transcendence. He mentions especially the following: Husserl's transcendence of consciousness toward the transcendental ego, Heidegger's transcendence of Dasein toward Being, the metaphysical transcendence of all things or beings toward (the universal concept of) being(s) (*ens*) and toward Being (*esse*) and, within this framework, toward God as *ens primum/ supremum* or as *esse per se subsistens*. This last transcendence is, according to Marion, the one that characterizes Christian metaphysics, and this metaphysical transcendence constitutes for him the central target of as well as the most important background foil for his incessant and harsh criticisms of all conceptions of God that he denigrates as "metaphysical."

---

[19] The first quotation in this section title is from the last paragraph of the essay "IM–G" (38); the second is the title of *GWB*.

Marion aims to go decisively beyond metaphysics, which he identifies with the philosophy of Being in the sense of *ens* as well as in the sense of *esse*. The result of his own transcendence, which he calls "radical and non-metaphysical," is the allegedly "divine God," conceived of negatively as *God without Being* and positively as God as *caritas/love*.

The following analysis proceeds in four stages. The first stage (4.2.1) presents general remarks on Marion's radical anti-metaphysical and post-metaphysical stance and on his misrepresentation of Heidegger's "overcoming of metaphysics"; thereafter, critical comments are made on Marion's noteworthy retractions relating to Thomas Aquinas. The second stage (4.2.2) identifies a first fundamental contradiction and a strange incoherence in Marion's conception of the relation between Being and God and adds, in an "Excursus" (4.2.2.4a), a critique of the rhetorical-polemical style Marion uses in treating the problem of this relation. The third stage (4.2.3) gets to the root problem underlying Marion's comprehensive conception; it shows that the root problem and, thus, Marion's fundamental failure are located in his idiosyncratic appropriation and transformation of Husserl's phenomenological approach. Central to Marion's version of phenomenology is his attempted reversal of the subject-object relation, which he takes to result in pure phenomenality. Finally, the fourth stage (4.2.4) subjects to a penetrating critical analysis the arbitrariness of Marion's shifting to "the point of view of God" and the incoherence of his usage of negative and positive concepts in his talk of God.

4.2.1 Preliminary Remarks on Marion's Anti-Metaphysical Stance, on His Misrepresentation of Heidegger's "Overcoming of Metaphysics," and on His Retractions Concerning Thomas Aquinas

[1] As chapter 1 shows, there is at present a fundamental *dogma fidei postmodernisticum:* the anti-metaphysical credo, whereby "metaphysics" is identified with "onto-theology." Most postmodernist Christian thinkers take themselves to need only to label something (a concept, a view, a question, an argument, a doctrine, etc.) as *metaphysical* in order to be justified in radically rejecting it. Marion himself not only indulges in this practice and style of thinking, but increases the radicalization of this anti-metaphysical attitude, writing, for example:

> We should, I think, keep in mind one of the final statements by Heidegger at the end of *Zeit und Sein* [*Time and Being*]: that we should let

metaphysics die itself [*sic*]. In other words, let metaphysics bury metaphysics, and don't use metaphysics as metaphor.[20]

This passage is highly significant because it clearly articulates what
is going on in postmodernist (anti-metaphysical) "Christian thinking."
As noted in chapter 2, postmodernist authors tend to quote only those
passages from Heidegger's writings in which he speaks of the necessity
of overcoming metaphysics. This leads to crass misinterpretations of Heidegger's thought. In typically postmodernist fashion, Marion misinterprets the passage from the end of "Time and Being" to which he refers.
The passage reads:

> To think Being without beings means: to think Being without regard
> to metaphysics. Yet a regard for metaphysics still prevails even in the
> intention to overcome metaphysics. Therefore, our task is to cease all
> overcoming, and leave metaphysics to itself. If overcoming remains nec-
> essary, it concerns that thinking that explicitly enters *Ereignis* in order
> to say It in terms of It about It. (*TB* 24; t.a.)

Unless one is prepared to attribute to Heidegger a patent self-
contradiction, one has to interpret the expression "metaphysics" in this
quotation in light of his explanations of transformational recovering [*Verwindung*], as in chapter 2, above. That many interpreters do not do this
is something of which Heidegger himself was fully aware. This is clear,
for example, from a passage quoted above in chapter 2, which includes
the following: "The failure to be mindful [*Besinnungslosigkeit*] began already with the superficial miscontrual of the 'destruction' [*Destruktion*]
discussed in *Being and Time* (1927), a 'destruction' that has no other intent than to win back the originary experiences of Being belonging to
metaphysics by deconstructing [*Abbau*] representations that have become commonplace and empty [*geläufig und leer gewordene Vorstellungen*]"
(*PM* 315; t.a.)[21]

When in "Time and Being" Heidegger says that "our task is to cease
all overcoming, and leave metaphysics to itself," he clearly means that our
task now is not to continue dealing with "representations that have become commonplace and empty," representations of "the originary expe-

---

[20] Ian Leask and Eoin Cassidy, eds., *Givenness and God: Questions of Jean-Luc Marion* (New
York: Fordham University Press, 2005), chap. 13: "Giving More: Jean-Luc Marion and Richard Kearney in Dialogue," 243–57; at 245.

[21] See also Heidegger, "The Overcoming of Metaphysics" (in *The End of Philosophy*).

riences of Being belonging to metaphysics" or, for short, of "the essence [*Wesen*] of metaphysics"; rather, the task is to tackle directly the question posed by "the essence of metaphysics," leaving aside endeavors that aim at showing that those "representations" must be overcome. This is a completely different sense that directly and radically contradicts Marion's misrepresentation of the passage. In this passage Heidegger *does not* make the statements Marion attributes to him, namely, "that we should let metaphysics *die itself* [*sic*]. In other words, let metaphysics bury metaphysics, and don't use metaphysics as metaphor." This is utterly different from what Heidegger says about "the essence of metaphysics."

In his book *God Without Being*, Marion has two epigraphs, one from Pascal, the other from Heidegger. The latter reads,

> If I were still going to write a theology, as I am often tempted to do, then it would not include the word "Being."—Faith does not need the thinking of Being.[22]

The use of these lines as an epigraph cannot, of course, explain what they mean in the context of the seminar from which they are drawn. But passages that, taken out of context, are unavoidably misinterpreted should not be used as epigraphs. The passage Marion uses is just such a passage. Chapter 2 (2.8[3], especially [iii]) comments extensively on Heidegger's numerous assertions concerning the relation of Being to God. That account shows that Heidegger even makes assertions that directly contradict the passage Marion quotes out of context. For example, he writes the following in the "Letter on Humanism":

> The thinking that thinks from the question of the truth of Being questions more primordially than metaphysics can. *Only from the truth of Being can the essence of the holy be thought. Only from the essence of the holy is the essence of divinity to be thought. Only in the light of the essence of divinity can it be thought or said what the word "God" is to signify.* (*PM* 267; emphasis added)

Here, the conjunction *Being and God* is understood as the *way from Being to God*. Moreover, even in the immediate context within which Marion's epigraph is found Heidegger says something that contradicts what that epigraph, taken out of context, appears to say. He writes, in the following paragraph, "I believe that Being cannot be thought as the ground

---

[22] "Zürcher Seminar" (1986), 436–37.

and essence of God, but that *nevertheless* the experience of God and his revelation (as far as this is open to human beings) *ereignet itself within the dimension of Being,* which in no way means that Being could be a possible predicate for God." Decisive here is the word "nevertheless," which clearly must be understood as a clarification and indeed as a correction of the passage Marion uses as an epigraph. As for what Heidegger says negatively about Being as "the ground and essence of God" and "predicate for God," section 2.8 provides thorough critical commentary. All this shows how superficial Marion's reliance on Heidegger is.

[2] Marion uses the term "metaphysics" in a wholly undifferentiated manner; he uses it as a comfortable and glibly applicable designation for everything he rejects in considering the question of God. This procedure both creates enormous confusion and misleads Marion into introducing pseudo-problems and pseudo-solutions and various senseless assertions. His interpretation of metaphysics as onto-theo-logy, thoughtlessly taken over from Heidegger, could be accepted as a characterization of the mainstream of so-called scholasticism after the time of Thomas Aquinas, a characterization that is, if not accurate in every respect, nonetheless not fundamentally distorting. Aquinas's original intuition about *esse* was not only not further deepened and explained (yet less corrected), it was indeed fundamentally misunderstood; as a consequence, if *esse* continued to play a role at all, it was only a *verbal* one that was not understood. Metaphysics was understood exclusively as the science of being(s) as being(s) (*ens inquantum ens*). As noted in chapter 1 (1.3.2.2[1] and 1.3.2.3), the chief representatives of this scholasticism were Duns Scotus and Francisco Suárez.

Given this background, it is particularly revealing to briefly consider Marion's treatment of Thomas Aquinas. His interpretation of Aquinas's *esse* in his book *God Without Being* (1982/1991) triggered much discussion. Concerning central points of that (mis)interpretation, Marion published retractions, particularly in "Saint Thomas d'Aquin et l'onto-théo-logie" ("ThA-OT"), which appeared in 1995.[23] That essay is considered below. Surprisingly, Marion defends Aquinas against the charge of being an onto-theo-logist, and does so in ways that are in many respects quite interesting, but he goes far beyond that in that he aims to show that his treasured phrase "God without Being" "can be understood in a fundamentally Aquinian way" (63).

[i] Marion simply appropriates Heidegger's characterization of meta-

---

[23] In *Revue Thomiste* 95 (1995): 31–66. Marion himself uses the formulation "partial retractions [*rétractations partielles*]" (33n2).

physics as onto-theo-logy. How superficial such a procedure is should be clear from chapter 2 and from earlier sections in this chapter. Marion introduces three "extremely precise characteristics" as "defining" onto-theo-logy: 1. "God [*Le Dieu*]" must belong explicitly to the domain of meta-physics, i.e., "He must be determinable by one of the historical determina-tions of Being as [a] being [*l'être en tant qu'étant*], perhaps by the concept *being* [*étant*]"; 2. In this domain, God must provide "a causal foundation" for all of the ordinary beings; 3. In order to do the latter, God "must always assume the function and perhaps the name *causa sui*," and thus qualify as "the being who is the supreme founder because he is supremely founded by himself." In elaborations that are in part noteworthy—ones that to a certain degree resemble ones made in chapters 1 and 2 of this book—Marion shows that Aquinas's philosophy is not an ontotheology in the defined sense. In doing so, however, he distorts some of the Aquin-ian texts, above all because he does not take into account the fact that Aquinas relies on a categorical-ontological conceptuality inherited from Aristotle. Marion's specific remarks are not considered here.

Concerning the systematic conception defended in this book and this book's critiques of the three presumably most important opponents of conceptions of that sort, the only points from Marion's essay that are important are ones found in its last two sections (7 and 8); these treat the Aquinian understanding of the relation between *esse* and God. Marion's interpretation is highly idiosyncratic and clearly guided by an attempt that his own conception makes highly problematic, i.e., that of present-ing Aquinas as a great Christian thinker. Marion can so present Aquinas only by foisting onto him his own position concerning the relation of Being to God. He considers an objection that arises immediately from that; he presents it as the objection that Thomas subjected himself to the "a priori of Being" in that he "proceeded on the presupposition that God, in general and in principle, has to do with Being—so that the hori-zon of Being for him (God) can be fit to be the adequate horizon of his manifestation" (55). In presenting the objection, Marion relies on some strikingly strong although typically postmodernist formulations. Thus, for example, that Aquinas speaks not only of *ens/entia* but also of *esse* does not provide a response to the objection because, according to Marion's Aquinas, "not only is God inscribed in beingness [*étantité*], but he stands out, he singularizes himself, in brief: he accomplishes his divinity by mak-ing beingness possible" (56).

This last formulation shows how peculiarly Marion—like other post-modernists—deals with Heidegger: he appeals (typically, they appeal) to some things that Heidegger says while ignoring (or suppressing) others. That happens here: Marion forgets (as others forget) the famous passage, thoroughly considered in chapter 2, announcing that "it also belongs to the truth of Being that Being never essences [*west*] without being(s), that being(s) never are without Being" (*PM* 233; t.a.). And when Heidegger later spoke of *Ereignis* rather than of Being, he *never* understood *Ereignis* without *Ereignen* and *Ereigneten* (see 2.4, above). Marion's objection to Aquinas's treating *esse* in connection with God thus cannot be raised on the basis of Heidegger's authority. If one were to use the same superficial talk about Being and beings in relation to Heidegger, one would object that he thought Being only as the Being-of-being(s), as responsible for beingness. As chapter 2 shows, Aquinas is radically distinct from Heidegger in this respect, because Aquinas never defended and indeed could not defend the thesis that *esse* never "essences" without *ens* or *entia*.

[ii] From his objection, Marion does not draw the conclusion that one should "first break off with Aquinas" if one wants to avoid onto-theology. He recommends instead "a completely different way of proceeding," one that consists essentially of two steps and a "methodological-programmatic" principle that supports the entire conception.

[a] Marion's first step consists in articulating the specific character of God's *esse*. Marion's preferred term for this character is "excess" (*excès—excessus*), which has a long history in the *metaphysical* (!) tradition that Marion, who ceaselessly polemicizes against metaphysics in a fully undifferentiated manner, appears to have forgotten. According to Marion, God is, on the basis of his *esse*, simply elevated above being and all beings in the sense of onto-theo-logy, and above Heidegger's *Ereignis*. What results is the following:

> To say it clearly: Aquinian *esse* [Marion always says: *l'esse thomiste*] cannot be understood on the basis of ontological determinations of any sort whatsoever, but only on the basis of his distance from every possible ontology, and indeed such that in opposition thereto there is full compliance with the exigencies that God's transcendence imposes on beings and on his Being. (58)

This is not problematic, at least not if one follows chapter 1's procedure in not according to every single passage from Aquinas exactly the same weight, but instead attending to what is essential in his corpus as a whole. But Marion quickly articulates just what his retraction is about when he adds, "The Being of beings endures its distance from *esse*, because this *esse* first and above all identifies itself as possessing the characteristics of the *mysterium tremendum et fascinosum* of a God that manifests itself conceptually" (58). According to Marion, "the divine *esse* remains just as unknown as does God himself" (61)—and not only unknown, but unknowable.

[b] Marion next attempts to take a decisive—and quite problematic—step toward the reduction of *esse* to the point that it is excluded
from any relation to God. He refers to *STh* I q. 13 a. 11, where Aquinas
defends the thesis that the name *Qui est*[24] is "the maximally appropriate
name of God." In responding to the first objection to this thesis, according to which the name "God" is more appropriate, Aquinas introduces
three distinctions:

> The name "He who is" is the name of God more properly than the
> name "God," as regards its source, *esse;* and as regards the mode of
> signification and consignification. . . . But as regards what the name
> designates, the name "God" is more proper, as it is imposed to signify
> the divine nature; and still more proper is the name "Tetragrammaton,"
> which is introduced to signify the substance of God itself, incommuni-
> cable and, if one may so speak, singular.[25]

Marion maintains that this text shows that

> the *esse* that Aquinas recognizes in God opens no metaphysical horizon,
> belongs to no onto-theo-logy, and is so distantly analogous to what we
> call "B/being" that God is not to be thought of from Being [*Dieu n'en est
> pas*], that God is not in Being [*n'y est pas*], indeed—paradoxical though
> this may sound—that God *is* not [*n'est pas*]. The *esse* designates God
> only to the degree that he is said without Being [*L'esse ne désigne Dieu que
> dans la juste mesure où il se dit sans l'être*]. . . . The phrase "God without
> Being" could be understood as fundamentally Aquinian. (63)

Marion's entire line of argumentation is based on his failure to attend to the facts that Aquinas's second and third distinctions deal with
pure (and obscure) concepts that are metaphysical in the traditional
sense: *nature* (often understood to be synonymous with *essentia*, although
that is problematic) and above all *substantia*. Such concepts belong to the

---

[24] Exodus 3:14. Translations of this passage differ significantly. The Latin Vulgate, which
Aquinas cites, is translated literally as "(the one) who is." This text provides the basis for
what has been known in France since the 1930s as "the Exodus metaphysics."

[25] Hoc nomen Qui est est magis proprium nomen Dei quam hoc nomen Deus, quantum
ad id a quo imponitur, scilicet ab esse, et quantum ad modum significandi et consignifi-
candi. . . . Sed quantum ad id quod imponitur nomen ad significandum, est magis proprium nomen Deus, quid imponitur ad significandum [*sic!*] naturam divinam. Et adhuc
magis proprium nomen est Tetragrammaton, quod es impositum ad significandam
ipsam Dei substantiam incommunicabilem, et, ut sic liceat loqui, singularem. (*STh* I
q. 13 a. 11 ad 1)

categorial conceptuality that is questioned historically in chapter 1 and systematically in chapter 3. It is paradoxical that Marion relies precisely on such extremely problematic metaphysical concepts to disempower *esse*. What is said in chapter 1 makes clear that the weakness of Aquinas's conception lies precisely in his articulating his deep intuition concerning *esse* by means of an arsenal of concepts (chiefly Aristotelian) that ultimately hinder his attempts *adequately to articulate that intuition*.

As chapter 1 also shows, another way the Aquinian *esse* is deeply deficient is that it designates only the *act* of Being, the *actus essendi*. The path this book follows concerning Aquinas's position is that of overcoming its weaknesses by developing a fully adequate theory of Being. Marion takes a quite different path: he aims single-mindedly to disempower *esse* so radically that it ultimately disappears from talk about God. Where this path leads and whether it can be traversed coherently are thoroughly considered in what follows.

[c] Marion's analyses of Aquinas's position are, as he explicitly says at the end of his essay, attempts to expose a fundamental principle or axiom; to be added, however, is that in another respect all that he says in the essay depends on and is guided by this principle. The principle is first introduced by means of a question:

> What is it to take Aquinas seriously? Is it to think God starting from
> Being, or Being starting from God? (65)

Marion hereby articulates the basic framework for his thought as a whole: when God is in question, he subordinates everything—every question, every assertion, every conception—to the following basic principle or axiom: *God can be adequately understood, articulated, bespoken only if one starts absolutely with God.* This means, negatively, that any access to God, any articulation or understanding or bespeaking of God, starting from any dimension that is not God himself—no matter how that dimension may be designated, as Being, as world, as any phenomenon of any sort, or as anything else—is absolutely to be excluded. The main dimension against which Marion directs his unrelenting critique is the dimension of Being (as he understands or misunderstands it).

[c'] This chapter's particularly long section 4.2 concentrates exclusively on subjecting Marion's position and its most striking theses to thorough critiques. Here, it is appropriate to introduce—purely programmatically, anticipatorily, and thetically—the two most important points.

The first is the principle or axiom introduced just above. Marion simply asserts, as though it were obvious beyond question, that any adequate account of God must start from God. In other writings, he calls this starting point "God's point of view." All of section 4.2.4.2, below, is devoted to discussion of this principle. At this point, the following suffices: How does Marion come to speak of God: from where, and in what sense? In the essay on Aquinas, there is a slight, scarcely noticeable answer to this question, but one that is comprehensively consequential and immensely problematic. The answer is the following:

> What matters now is not so much deciding whether or not God should be named *esse* as deciding whether we have access to an understanding of *esse* that could claim, not to attain God, but to envisage whatever it *may be that we call God*. What matters is not deciding whether *we* should say God in the name of Being [*dire Dieu au nom de l'être*], but deciding whether Being (taken as *esse* or however one wants) still has the quality and dignity to express anything that *may be* about God [*quoi que ce* soit *sur Dieu*] that is worth more than straw. (65; first emphasis added)

These are powerful formulations that speak volumes. Relying in part on Marion's own words, the following is the case: until Marion explains *of what and in what sense* he is talking when he talks of "God"— whether of God/*Caritas*/Love *as* (or *in the sense of*) a pure fiction or a pure dream or a pure idea or . . . whatever else—then what he says in his voluminous discourse about God is not "worth more than straw." Much of the detailed critique of Marion presented in this section (4.2) boils down to what this admittedly polemical formulation says. Put in different terms: until Marion provides an adequate answer to the question, he has no response to the objection that everything he says about God constitutes a novel, in the strict sense: a fictional account produced by an artist. If he were to respond to the question, however, what could he say other than that he speaks of the God who *is* or *exists*? Given the countless things he says about this, however, it is presumably the case that he would attempt at all costs to avoid every form of the word "Being" and would attempt instead to rely on something like the New Testament formulation "living and true God."[26] But then he would either have to explain or have to presuppose as explained the terms "living" and "true"—but how could he do that without relying, one way or another, on *Being*?

The passage introduced just above includes the phrase "*that we call God*." This transforms a phrase from Jules Renard, whom Marion cites in other works.[27] It articulates the crux of Marion's position. But here press weighty questions: Who is this "we"? Is it Christians, and if so, which ones:

---

[26] See 1 Thessalonians 1:9: "δουλεύειν θεῷ ζῶντι καὶ ἀληθινῷ [to serve the living and true God]."

[27] ". . . celui que tout le monde connaît, de nom [the one whom everyone knows, by name]." Jules Renard, *Journal 1887–1910* (1960), 227. See "IM–G" 20 and note 76, below.

Catholics, Protestants, Orthodox Christians, or yet other Christians? Is it Muslims, Jews, adherents of other religions? To appeal to "we/us" in talking about God, and particularly to make such an appeal the absolutely decisive support for the claim that one is articulating the actually divine God rather than engaging in some form of idolatry, reflects nothing other than immense theoretical naïveté.[28] What would it then mean to understand or to articulate God starting from God? Utterly thoughtlessly, Marion asserts that "the task is . . . to pass over to God's point of view [*passer au point de vue de Dieu*]" ("IM–G" 34). This too clearly reflects theoretical naïveté, in simply assuming that we can abandon ourselves, leave ourselves behind, in order somehow—but how?—to take "God's point of view." And when Marion subjects the I-we to a reversal—a move discussed below (see 4.2.3.3)—subjectivity does not disappear, but instead remains the all-determining central point. Of the fundamental clarifications that are unconditionally required here and that are thoroughly presented below in 4.2.4.2, there is in Marion's work utterly no trace.

Also to be noted is that Marion himself does not take a coherent position when he attempts to think God starting from God. As is shown particularly in 4.2.4.3, he attempts in some works to get to God in order then to be able to talk of God starting from God. His most revealing piece on this topic is "The Impossible for Man—God," which is thoroughly analyzed below (again, 4.2.4.3). Only by means of a phenomenological consideration of the phenomenon of the impossible does he arrive at the statement that what is genuinely impossible is God. Marion's access to God is radically phenomenological, as shown in detail below.

[c″] Already the way Marion formulates the question concerning the relation between Being and God reveals the erroneous presupposition on which his entire critique of the metaphysics of Being is based: he asks whether God is to be thought starting from Being or Being is to be thought starting from God. Such a question, as he understands and treats it, makes sense only if Being and God are somehow fully different and separate, such that they could or perhaps must be brought into relation. The following sections thoroughly analyze both the radical manner in which Marion understands this presupposition and how it provides the basis for his obstinate rejection of all talk of Being in connection with God.

---

[28] Because—as is shown below—Marion relies fundamentally on Husserl in developing the transcendental-phenomenological approach to his entire conception, it is appropriate to use the word "naïveté" because Husserl often relies on it. To be sure, neither in Husserl's works nor in this book is the word used in its psychological-sociological sense and yet less in its moral sense: here, as with Husserl, it means simple lack of reflection—thoughtlessness. That is why the qualifier "theoretical" is used.

This book shows that talk of a so-called relation between God and Being is misleading, because God is the fully explicated meaning of Being or, more simply put, is fully explicated Being itself. Being is nothing like a or the horizon, nothing like a dimension that would somehow encompass God or be presupposed as lying somehow behind God; that it is not must be emphasized in all clarity in radical opposition to all of Marion's endlessly repeated assertions on this topic. Ironically, the interpretation and critique of Marion's position presented in this lengthy section (4.2) ultimately shows that he is the one who attempts one way or another to articulate God starting from a *horizon in the genuine sense*[29] or from a grounding condition. *His* horizon or grounding condition is what he calls "an essential law of phenomenality [*une loi d'essence de la phénoménalité*]" that has the "figure of the paradox of paradoxes" (*BG* 235).

It is now clear that given his own position, Marion could recognize Thomas Aquinas, the *doctor communis* of the Catholic Church, at all positively only by making of him a maximally negative (apophatic) theologian and then introducing an unbelievably venturesome hypothesis ("our hypothesis [*notre hypothèse*]") about him:

> Why not assume that Thomas Aquinas retained this *esse* only because he intended *for tactical reasons* [*tactiquement*] to rely on the term preferred by his philosophical interlocutors, without ever accepting it [i.e., *esse*]

---

[29] The term/concept *horizon* is essential to both Husserl's and Heidegger's phenomenologies. For both thinkers, it is fundamentally based in a mode of thinking stamped by the philosophy of subjectivity. There is presumably no question that this is so for Husserl (see, e.g., *Crisis*, §37). It could, however, appear that it is problematic or indeed false in the case of Heidegger. But the genuinely phenomenological Heidegger is the Heidegger of (the time of) *Being and Time*, even though he himself considered his later thinking to be largely phenomenologically oriented (according to a fundamentally transformed understanding of "phenomenology"). Characteristic in this respect is the title of the whole first part of *Being and Time*: "The Interpretation of Dasein in Terms of Temporality, and the Explication of Time as the Transcendental Horizon for the Question of Being." Here, subjectivity is called Dasein, which indicates that the subjectivity in question is wholly transformed or reinterpreted. Here, Being provides (so to speak) the horizon for time/temporality, which provides the horizon for Dasein. Heidegger's later turn (*Kehre*) consists essentially in his explicating Being itself (later: as *Ereignis*) instead of envisaging Being/*Ereignis* only as the ultimate horizon for temporality and the latter as the horizon for Dasein and its interpretation.

The dimension of primordial Being presented in chapter 3 of this book—more simply, Being in the primordial sense—is not a "horizon" in any phenomenological sense, and it is certainly nothing like a horizon that would be in any way requisite for discerning the meaning of "God." According to the structural-systematic philosophy, primordial Being is not in any sense a horizon for God, because God is precisely Being itself, fully explicated.

affirmatively [*sans cependant jamais l'assumer affirmativement*] and without elevating it to eminence [*ni l'ériger par éminence*], instead discharging it as apophatic [i.e., as negative]? ("ThA-OT" 64)

Such a "hypothesis" is an extreme disparagement that would make of the philosopher Thomas Aquinas a mere tactician. This "hypothesis" cannot belong in any philosophical or scientific text. It is simply undiscussable and is therefore not discussed here.

4.2.2 Incoherences, Contradictions, and Topics Unthought in Marion's Conception of the Relation Between Being and God

Marion attempts to articulate a God free of all categories of Being and of Being itself. Taking a characteristically postmodernist stance, he challenges a fundamental premise of both metaphysics and neo-Thomistic theology: that God, before all else, must be. In diametrical opposition, Marion presents a "God without Being" situated in the realm of agape, of Christian *caritas* or love.

4.2.2.1 The Contradiction Between "God Is, Exists" and "God Loves Before Being"

Since the publication of *God Without Being* (1982), critics have accused Marion of atheism precisely because he speaks of God without Being. In the "Preface" to the English edition of that book, he defends himself as follows:

> The whole book suffered from the inevitable and assumed equivocation of its title: was it insinuating that the God "without Being" is not, or does not exist? Let me repeat the answer I gave then: *no, definitely not. God is, exists,* and that is the least of things. (*GWB* xix; emphasis added)

[1] Marion's statement seems to be fully clear. It is not. If a philosopher *declares*—even if this happens solemnly—that he accepts or does not accept something—a thesis, a statement, etc.—as belonging to his conception, it does not follow that such acceptance or nonacceptance makes sense, that it is consistent, that it is clear, etc. The author of this book decisively denies all of the following: that the declaration just introduced is consistent with other aspects of Marion's comprehensive conception, that it is unambiguous, that it is self-consistent, and that it is clear. He holds instead that it is a purely *verbal concession.* Indeed, at the end of the same paragraph Marion writes: "If . . . 'God is love,' then God loves *before being*" (*GWB* xx; emphasis added). Has Marion committed a blatant

contradiction? Presumably, he would deny that. He seems to be right, *if* one considers the fact that—as far as this book's author can see—after the publication of the "Preface" the objection of atheism has not been raised again, or at least not vehemently. The (former) critics seemed (and seem) to be satisfied with Marion's declaration. If they were and are, then they were and are wrong. The account that follows shows why.

The structural-systematic philosophy sketched in chapter 3 of this book introduces and explains a distinction between Being and existence; Marion does not, as the passage quoted just above clearly shows. So, to say "God loves before being" amounts (for Marion) to saying, "God loves before he exists." Hence, the loving God is a non-being/non-existing God. This is undoubtedly a blatant contradiction to the statement "God is, exists." Playing with words, a practice common in postmodernist circles, does not solve philosophical problems.

[2] Marion seems to see no contradiction between the two statements. Indeed, immediately after the first passage quoted above comes the following:

> At issue here is not the possibility of God's attaining Being, but, quite the opposite, the possibility of Being's attaining to God. With respect to God, is it self-evident that the first question comes down to asking, before anything else, whether he is? Does Being define the first and the highest of the divine names? When God offers himself to be contemplated and gives himself to be prayed to, is he concerned primarily with Being? (*GWB* xx)

What kind of questions are being asked here? What does it mean to talk of "the possibility of God's attaining Being" and of "the possibility of Being's attaining to God"? Such questions presuppose that Being and God are two completely different, distinct, heterogeneous dimensions (or some such). This book's author knows of no metaphysical thinker who has ever imagined such a thing, much less stated such a thing. Why does Marion not contemplate the idea, presented in chapter 3 of this book, that God understood *as love* is the *full explicatum* of the term "Being" as the *explicandum*? Were he to do so, then the peculiar radical separation of Being from God, which Marion makes the center of his philosophy and theology, would disappear, and all the questions and problems triggered by that separation would be visible as pseudo-questions and pseudo-problems.

[3] At this point it is illuminating to speak briefly of Hans Urs von Balthasar, whom Marion admires and praises. As noted in chapter 1, von Balthasar strongly criticizes Marion's statements about Being and God.

In the context of a consideration of the Trinitarian God, he writes the following: "The unprethinkability of the self-giving or self-emptying [*kenosis*] that above all makes the Father the Father [cannot] be ascribed to knowledge, but only to the groundless love that identifies Him as what is 'simply transcendent.'" To this he appends the following footnote:

> What this sentence states is already seen in Plato's "*epekeina tēs ousias* [beyond Being/essence]" (*Republic* VI, 509c), but *this should not lead astray toward moving God away from Being* (Jean-Luc Marion, *God Without Being*, Fayard, Paris, 1982). *Groundless love is not before Being; it is Being's highest act*—that upon which His intelligibility founders: "*gnōnai tēn hyperballousan tēs gnoseos agapēn* [to know the love that surpasses knowledge]" (Ephesians 3:19, New International Version).[30]

---

[30] Hans Urs von Balthasar, *Theologik*, volume 2: *Wahrheit Gottes* (Einsiedeln: Johannes Verlag, 1985), 163, footnote 9; see also 125–26, footnote 10. An impressive global presentation is to be found in his monumental work *The Realm of Metaphysics*, volume 5 of *The Glory of the Lord: A Theological Aesthetics*. See especially 614ff.

Another philosopher, the hermeneuticist Jean Grondin, introduces a commentary similar to von Balthasar's in his review of Marion's *Au lieu de soi: L'approche de Saint Augustin* (2009), where he writes the following:

> Marion pays too little attention to the fact that his beautiful and beloved thought of donation is and remains the articulation of an understanding of Being, indeed of Being as gift. . . . Marion is not wrong when he maintains that the encomium that he [Augustine's] *Confessions* is less a discourse about God (in the sense of what he [Marion] calls "metaphysics") than it is a discourse that turns to God; but if "praising God means that I climb to my highest elevation, that I elevate myself to the point from whence I am, and turn myself toward what I come from" [from *Au lieu de soi*, 37], then one would have the greatest difficulty in making it credible to the reader that this thought is in no way metaphysical. Instead of interpreting the *Confessions* as a work "in place" of metaphysics, it is preferable to see in that work one of its [metaphysics's] high points. Perhaps against its explicitly declared intention, Marion's work makes to that [view] an effective and lovingly presented contribution. (Jean Grondin, "Au lieu de la métaphysique? Les méditations augustieniennes de Jean-Luc Marion"; http://www.laviedesidees.fr/Au-lieu-de-la -metaphysique.html [accessed December 27, 2009])

These are well-balanced words—with the exception of the final sentence, which to the author of this book appears unfounded. Marion's undifferentiated critiques of metaphysics and of every form of philosophy of Being—unparalleled and, in their sharpness and radicality, unsurpassable—are in no way "an effective and lovingly presented contribution" to the recognition of any high point in metaphysics (either that made by Augustine's *Confessions* or that made by any other text from the history of philosophy).

In her recently published book *Reading Jean-Luc Marion: Exceeding Metaphysics* (Bloomington: Indiana University Press, 2007), Christina M. Gschwandtner writes: "This new dimension [the 'fourth dimension' that Marion introduces in the final chapter of his book *Idol and Distance* and that he describes as the dimension of charity] actually has been sug-

According to von Balthasar, love is *the highest act of Being*. That means: love is fully explicated Being: *esse plenum*, *fulfilled Being, Being in its fullness*. Von Balthasar's are among the most beautiful and profound texts about Being, about "the wonder at Being [*die Verwunderung über das Sein*]," which he describes in highly elegant and expressive terms, although not ones that are theoretically refined.[31] Von Balthasar is far from Marion's immoderate assertions and objections according to which as far as God is concerned, Being is not even insignificant, but is instead an *idolatry*, indeed *the chief idolatry* (of this, see 4.2.5).

[4] When Marion asks: "With respect to God, is it self-evident that the first question comes down to asking, before anything else, whether he is?" he is asking a fallacious question, a question that arises out of a completely equivocal situation. It presupposes that it is already clear what he is speaking—and, thus, asking—about, when he uses the word "God." But this is by no means clear. Indeed, the extremely general formulation "with respect to God" can mean several very different things: it can mean (among other things) "with respect to the abstract idea of God," "with respect to the concept of God," "with respect to the problem of God," "with respect to what a determinate religion means when it speaks of 'God,'" or, finally, "with respect to the living and true God" (see note 26, above). If this equivocal situation is not clarified at the outset, it is nonsensical to ask whether "it is self-evident that the first question comes down to asking, before anything else, whether he is." If a question is asked "with

---

gested already by Hans Urs von Balthasar, by whom Marion is deeply influenced, who distinguishes between four orders or differences of the 'miracle of Being' (referring, among others, to Heidegger)" (282, endnote 26). But then Gschwandtner surprisingly adds: "Marion seems to follow him [von Balthasar] repeatedly in these distinctions." And she refers to von Balthasar's book *The Realm of Metaphysics*, volume 5 of *The Glory of the Lord*.

Gschwandtner's statement is not only astonishing, it is plainly false. She completely ignores von Balthasar's powerful criticism of Marion's treatment of Being and God. Moreover, she pays no attention to the far-reaching significance of the fact that von Balthasar decidedly uses the language of Being, in absolute contrast to Marion's no less decided rejection of such language. Finally, she forgets what she herself has written precisely about this point in her book, for example on page 142, where she interprets Marion—correctly, in the author's opinion—in the following terms:

> Love overcomes Being and renders it insignificant. It thus gets outside of metaphysics, distorts its boundaries, becomes limitless. Love overcomes all the metaphysical idols of God and thinks of God most authentically.

This is in marked contrast to what von Balthasar says in his critique of Marion's treatment of Being and God: "Groundless love is not before Being; it is Being's highest act."

[31] *The Realm of Metaphysics*, quoted in the preceding footnote.

respect to God" in general terms, then a meaningful answer can be given only in the conditional form: *If* by "God" is meant—for instance—"the concept of God,"or "living God, the God that is or exists," then . . . , etc.

Apparently without noting how obviously problematic his question is, Marion next asks, "Does Being define the first and the highest of the divine names?" There is no point in asking such a question, because "Being" is not a "name" in the genuine sense, and therefore is not comparable to other names potentially ascribable to God. A *name* in the genuine sense always presupposes the Being of that to which it is ascribed. Being is thus the absolute *presupposition* for any sensible talk of names and of ascribing names. Being is thus also the absolute presupposition for the meaningful ascription of any name to God. Differently stated: if God is not a *being/existing God,* there is no point in attributing to him any names whatsoever. Doing so would be merely playing with words. Being is the opening space for the self-manifestation and self-communication of the X that is designated with the word "God." It is impossible to conceive of Being thus understood as something different or separate from God, as something to which God would be subjected, such as a "horizon" that would condition the appearance of God.

In Marion's writings one constantly encounters—sometimes as explicitly formulated but sometimes as implicitly presupposed—the following assumption concerning the relation between Being and God: if one were to ascribe to Being any positive role relating to God, this would be to introduce a *condition* to which God would be subjected. This—as shown below—is how Marion interprets talk of *Being as horizon* for every statement and therefore for statements about God. Marion vehemently opposes this, maintaining that God cannot be subjected to any condition, to any horizon, or to anything of the sort (or, as he tends to put it, *God* cannot *subject himself* to any condition, any horizon, or anything of the sort).

In the philosophical and theological literature on the topic Being and God, particularly in connection with Heidegger, there is often talk of Being-as-horizon. Many formulations in this literature are misleading and indeed deeply problematic, and thus can motivate questions and assertions like Marion's. But the statement that Being is the horizon for talk about God must be correctly and precisely understood. This requires taking into consideration that there is an important weakness and deficiency in the attempt to articulate a *positive* relation between Being and God. The decisive point is the following simple one: *if Being* is designated "horizon," then the only way an appropriately positive relation between Being and God can be articulated requires that Being-*itself*-as-horizon be thematized. "God" then appears not as somehow subordinated to Being, as would be the case if Being were an external condition; instead, God appears as fully explicated or as fulfilled Being-*itself*-as-horizon. Briefly: God is the full *explicatum/explicans* of the *explicandum* Being. Neverthe-less, because of the historically conditioned connotations of the term "horizon," it is avoided in this book.

What sense could be made of Marion's second question, i.e., "When God offers himself to be contemplated and gives himself to be prayed to, is he concerned primarily with Being?" Assuming *that* God offers or manifests himself, does it make sense to ask about what he is primarily concerned with? It certainly makes no sense to ask whether he is primar-ily concerned with (his) Being, because his Being is presupposed by his self-manifestation. A God who was not, who did not exist, could neither manifest himself nor not manifest himself. It is clear that Marion has a peculiar and wholly distorting understanding of Being.

4.2.2.2 Marion's Failed Conception of the Relation Between Being and Absolute Freedom

Marion's strange questions continue in a kind of rhetorical crescendo. He asks: "No doubt, God can and must in the end also be; but does his relation to Being determine him as radically as the relation to his Being defines all other things?" How strange a concession—that "God can and must *in the end* also be." Here it becomes clear how Marion understands Being: as a kind of property or feature that "can/must" be given "in the end." Can? Must? In the end? What happens *before* "the end"? How is this "end" to be understood? The only way a philosopher seeking a serious un-derstanding of Marion's texts can come to grips with their manifest incon-cinnities is to seek to explain how Marion could have come to so strange a conception. This is the task of this section and of section 4.2.3.

In the "Preface" to *God Without Being*, Marion introduces the topic of this subsection when he attempts to explain "the radical reversal of the relation between Being and loving" (*GWB* xx):

> Under the title *God Without Being*, I am attempting to bring out the absolute freedom of God with regard to all determinations, including, first of all, the basic condition that renders all other conditions possible and even necessary—for us, humans—the fact of Being. Because, *for us*, as for all the beings of the world, it is first necessary "to be," in order, indissolubly, "to live and to move" (Acts, 17:28), and thus eventually also to love. But *for God*, if at least we resist the temptation to reduce him immediately to our own measure, does the same still apply? Or, on the contrary, are not all the determinations that are necessary for the finite reversed for Him, and for Him alone? (Ibid.)

This passage seems to contain the most fundamental motive behind Marion's *forma mentis,* but this manner of thinking runs aground already at the beginning of the first sentence: "Under the title *God Without Being,* I am attempting to bring out the absolute freedom of God with regard to all determinations." The most fundamental "content" Marion attributes to God in this context is his "absolute freedom," which, according to Marion, applies rigorously to "all determinations" (of God). If one wanted to express this state of affairs logically/mathematically, one would say: (God's) absolute freedom is the absolute and highest operator that has as its arguments (in the logical-mathematical sense) all determinations (of whatever sort, including all other operators): this absolute or maximal operator would determine simply everything.

The self-destructive consequences of such a conception are easily seen. One need only apply this principle. Its application shows that Marion should also "bring out the absolute freedom of God" in the case of precisely *that determination of God Marion calls God's absolute freedom. God should or indeed must be absolutely free with respect to Being absolutely free.* Obviously, this generates an infinite regress: in order to be absolutely free with respect to his own absolute freedom, God would have to exercise absolute freedom at a superior (meta-)level; and in order to be absolutely free with respect to his freedom at this meta-level, he would have to exercise absolute freedom at a yet higher (meta-meta-)level—and so on . . . *in infinitum.* This absurdity—that God could and indeed must be absolutely free with respect to Being—brings to light that Marion's concept of absolute freedom is self-contradictory: it is a *contradictio exercita,* a performative self-contradiction. What is more, it proves to be the exact opposite of what it claims to be. Absolute freedom in Marion's sense is absolute unfreedom, in the sense that it is not free with respect to itself. To follow Marion's strange logic (or, more precisely, non-logic), one would have to characterize God's condition in something like the way his countryman Sartre characterizes the human condition when he says, "Man is condemned to be free [*L'homme est condamné à être libre*]."[32] This may not be nonsensical for human beings, because they are finite and have no absolute status: their freedom is not absolute because they do not somehow give it to themselves, but instead receive it from an X (no matter how that X is designated in this context) with which they are not identical. The case of God, however, is wholly different: his freedom is absolute, and it is absolute *as freedom that is;* conversely, God's Being is precisely this: absolute freedom. To say that God's absolute freedom

---

[32] Jean-Paul Sartre, *Existentialism Is a Humanism* (1965/2007), 29.

is free in relation to his own Being is to engage in a naive thinking that envisions absolute freedom and Being as two separate dimensions such that the second (Being) is an object for the first ([absolute] freedom). Marion's "understanding" of absolute freedom is a contradictory and therefore senseless construct.

The same consequence results from consideration of another of Marion's points. As indicated above and considered in more detail below, according to Marion the deepest or most primordial determination of God is love/*caritas*. If, however, God's freedom is indeed absolute in Marion's sense—that is, such that God is free with respect to *all* his determinations—then God is also free with respect to his putatively deepest and most primordial determination, namely, love/*caritas*. If this is accepted, however, then it becomes questionable whether what results is coherent. Be that as it may, God as absolutely free in Marion's sense is empty, self-contradictory, and incoherent.

4.2.2.2a Excursus 3: The Historical Source of Marion's Conception of Absolute Freedom: Schelling's Conception of the Relation Between God's Freedom and His Existence

In order to give historical support to his questions and statements, Marion refers to F. W. J. Schelling: "Under the title *God Without Being* we do not mean to insinuate that God is not, or that God is not truly God. We attempt to meditate on what F. W. Schelling called 'the freedom of God with regard to his own existence'" (*GWB* 2).[33]

Marion wholly disregards the complex context in which this statement is made. Schelling presents some independent considerations relating to Descartes's ontological argument, of which he provides an idiosyncratic and problematic interpretation. Finally, he arrives at the concept of "the necessarily existing being [*Wesen*]"[34] and then raises the question whether the concept of "the necessarily existing being" is identical with the concept of God. He denies the identity, arguing in a way that only superficially appears to be original. In fact, he draws some of the most radical consequences of the philosophy of transcendental subjectivity.

He interprets "the necessarily existing being" as "the being that cannot not be" and therefore as "the blind being," arguing that a blind being is "that for which no possibility of itself preceded it." And then he states:

---

[33] This quotation is a passage from Schelling's writing *Zur Geschichte der neueren Philosophie—Münchner Vorlesungen* (1827) (in *Schellings Werke,* edited by Manfred Schröter [Munich: Beck'sche Verlagsbuchhandlung, 1965], vol. 5, 71–270; at 92).

[34] Ibid., 89.

"That for which it is impossible not to be (*quod non potest non-existere*) also never has any possibility to be—for every possibility to be includes also the possibility not to be—therefore, that for which it is impossible not to be does not have any possibility to be, and Being, reality, precedes possibility."[35] He then reasons: "If, then, God were the necessarily existing being, he could only be determined as rigid, immobile, simply unfree, not capable of free action, of progress, or of going beyond itself."[36] This line of thinking leads "not to the living God, but to the dead God."[37] But the Christian God, Schelling affirms, is a living God.

The decisive step in the line of thought that leads Schelling to the passage Marion cites is taken from this point. He says that "animation [*Lebendigkeit*] consists in the freedom to suspend [*aufheben*] one's own Being, posited as immediate, as independent of it, and in the ability to transform it into a self-posited Being."[38] Schelling emphasizes that "what is not free against its own Being has no freedom—is absolutely unfree."[39] This Schelling calls "the freedom of God with respect to his own existence, the freedom to suspend this existence as absolutely posited."[40]

Schelling's statements are among the most striking consequences of taking the philosophy of transcendental subjectivity to extremes with respect to the topic "God." According to the Kant of *Critique of Pure Reason*, "*Being* is obviously not a real predicate, i.e., a concept of something that could add to the concept of a thing. It is merely the position [*Position*] of a thing or of certain determinations in themselves" (*CPuR* B626).

Kant's "*Position*" (like Schelling's "*Setzung*") must be understood mainly (not exclusively) not in the active sense of "positing," but rather in the passive or resultative sense of "(Being) posited." To be sure, according to the fundamental assumptions of transcendental philosophy, positing (in both senses) presupposes a positing subject. Assuming with Schelling that God as subject is absolute freedom and attributing Kant's concept of "being" (as just explained) to God's *own being* directly yields the consequence that God's own being is not "absolutely posited," whereby "absolutely posited" is understood as "posited independently of a positing subject," in this case God himself. Instead, God's own Being is God's *self-posited Being*. But because Schelling also assumes that God is *absolute freedom*, God's freedom is to be thought as "the freedom of God with

---

[35] Ibid.
[36] Ibid., 90–91.
[37] Ibid., 92.
[38] Ibid.
[39] Ibid., 90.
[40] Ibid., 92.

respect to his own existence [his own being], the freedom to suspend this existence [this being] as absolutely posited [in the sense just explained]."[41] In the last analysis, there is nothing here to wonder about— except why one would accept the philosophical framework within which such a consequence or thesis is not only possible and understandable, but also compelling. What must be called into question is the *transcendental-subjective theoretical framework* that Schelling relies on.

It is no accident that Marion refers to Schelling's passage. There is, indeed, a striking agreement between his conception of Being and Kant's and Schelling's view. This makes all too clear that Marion's philosophical stance is basically and through and through a specific philosophy of subjectivity (on this, see also 4.2.3.3, below).

Against Schelling's thesis, one of the many objections that can and must be raised is the one raised in the preceding subsection against Marion's position: that it leads to an infinite regress and, thus, includes a performative contradiction.

4.2.2.3 Marion's Reversal Principle and the Relation Between God and Human Beings

[1] Marion's conception is grounded in what may be termed his reversal principle. He formulates this principle in connection with a passage cited above:

> Because, *for us,* as for all the beings of the world, it is first necessary "to be" in order, indissolubly, "to live and to move" (Acts, 17:28), and thus eventually also to love. But *for God,* if at least we resist the temptation to reduce him immediately to our own measure, does the same still apply? Or, on the contrary, are not all the determinations that are necessary for the finite reversed for Him, and for Him alone? If, to begin with, "God is love," then God loves before Being, He only is as He embodies himself—in order to love more closely that which and those who, themselves, have first to be. This radical reversal of the relations between Being and loving, between the name revealed by the Old Testament (Exodus, 3:14) and the name revealed, more profoundly though not inconsistently, by the New (First Letter of John, 4:8), presupposes taking a stand that is at once theological and philosophical. (*GWB* xx)

As becomes clear, this reversal principle plays a fundamental role in Marion's thinking; it takes a number of concrete forms. The current

---

[41] Ibid.

concern is chiefly with the determinations that characterize finite beings. A simple question suffices to unmask as internally contradictory formulations of Marion's concerning this topic that at first sight can appear to be impressively profound and even evident. The question is this: is this reversal principle itself one that we human beings introduce?

That the principle *is* one that we introduce cannot be contested. But from the fact that it is, it immediately follows that what the principle says is the case *is* the case *only for us,* and the principle is a principle only thanks to and only within the scope of *our human measure.* But if that is its status, then how can it be applied to God? Its application to God would have to be based in a reversal. Given, however, that the principle says that all determinations of finite beings are reversed in the case of God, the principle itself must be reversed when applied to God. Because the principle contains a *negation* (the determinations can*not* be *directly* applied to God), its application to God is a negation of negation. The principle is, "All determinations of the finite are *reversed* in their application to God." Because, however, this is a human principle, one that applies to the finite, it itself must be reversed when it is applied to God. What results is the following: all determinations of the finite that are reversed in their application to God are reversed. Or: the reversal principle that holds concerning the relation between human beings and God is reversed when applied to the relation between human beings and God. As is easily seen, here again there is an infinite regress.

Among other things, from this it follows that this principle can be presented as a principle only by those who have not reflected on what its presentation presupposes; the lack of reflection is at the heart of the naïveté of postmodernist thinking. In fact, this principle articulates a superficial, an all-too-human way of thinking about the relation between human beings and God. With respect to God, the all-too-human attitude is to project onto Him exactly the reversal of things human. Like other postmodernist authors, Marion fails to subject his *own discourse* to critical examination: he *deconstructs* all discourses about God except his own.

This point is made clear and precise in a famous dictum of Heidegger's. Of metaphysical sentences (or principles), he writes, "The reversal of a metaphysical statement remains a metaphysical statement" (*PM* 251). In the case under consideration, the counterpart to Heidegger's dictum is the following: the reversal of the human condition remains a human condition, or: the reversal of a principle introduced by human theoreticians remains a principle introduced by human theoreticians. The task is not that of naively reversing the human condition; rather, the task is—as shown in chapter 3—to articulate the *entire, unlimited space or scope* that characterizes the human mind. Within this space or scope it is possible and necessary to articulate God—or, more precisely: God *is* this infinite space or scope.

[2] There is in Marion's thought a still more profound and disturbing incoherence. In his attempt to reverse the relations between Being and God, he asserts the following: "All the determinations that are necessary for the finite [are] reversed for Him [God], and for Him alone" (quoted above). But Marion's most central statements about God blatantly violate this principle. The most important violation is his transposition of the relation of human love directly, and indeed literally, to God. As shown below, he describes as an example of a saturated phenomenon the following "love situation": "a particular face that I love, which has become invisible not only because it dazzles me, but above all because in it I want to look and can look only at its invisible gaze weighing on mine" ("SP" 121).

This is, almost verbatim, the way Marion conceives of God. But he appears not to notice in the least what he himself says in articulating his conception of God. Is he really exempt from "the temptation to reduce him [God] immediately to our own measure" (*GWB* xx)? That the metaphysical treatment of the topic "God" succumbs to this temptation is *the fundamental objection* Marion raises against that treatment. Now, it becomes clear that his objection, which he globally raises against the entire Christian metaphysical tradition, is not only untenable when so raised, but is also one that applies directly to his own position. Indeed, no Christian metaphysical philosopher or theologian—at least none among the truly great thinkers—has ever transposed directly to God the model of any human phenomenon (including the phenomenon of love) as thoughtlessly and directly as has Marion. What then is left of his reversal principle?[42]

[3] The lesson to be drawn from Marion's statements is clear: in spite—more exactly, because—of the manner in which he attempts to think God (putatively) "not reduced to our measure," he in reality of-

---

[42] Interestingly, in his own postmodernist language and from a very different perspective, the philosopher-theologian John D. Caputo articulates a similar criticism:

> *God Without Being* confirms Derrida's suspicion that it is just when someone purports to speak or to teach without mediation that we are visited by the most massive mediations. It is precisely when someone claims to have reached, or been granted, God's point of view that things start getting very ungodly. It is just when someone thinks to have laid hold of the Wholly Other that we are visited by the human, all-too-human." ("God Is Wholly Other—Almost: *Différance* and the Hyperbolic Alterity of God," in *The Otherness of God*, ed. Orrin F. Summerell [Charlottesville: University Press of Virginia, 1998], 190–205; at 195)

fers a vision of God resulting from a patent *anthropomorphism*—when he speaks of "us, humans," he does not take into consideration the unlimited space that characterizes human beings/minds; instead, he presupposes a diminutive caricature of human beings/minds. He identifies the human being/mind with Pascal's "man$_2$"—that man of whom Pascal says that he is transcended infinitely by *man$_1$*.[43] Marion simply identifies the human being with Pascal's man$_2$ and does not—or does not adequately—consider and thematize man$_1$.

4.2.2.4 The Incoherence of "God Loves Before He Is" in Conjunction with God's "Being-Given"[44]

In what Marion says of Being and God there is an additional contradiction, one whose clarification is of great significance with respect to the evaluation of his philosophical position. This contradiction is not so easily exposed as those identified above, because it is indirect. For this reason, it is here termed not a contradiction, but an incoherence.[45]

[1] Marion himself is the best—although unwilling and unconscious—critic of his own statements on this matter. One of his most important books has the title *Étant donné: Essai d'une phénoménologie de la donation*. The title of the English translation is *Being Given: Toward a Phenomenology of Givenness*. The main title *Étant donné—Being Given*, especially in its French version, is an extraordinarily good one, because according to Marion's own explanation, it articulates a coherent conception of the given, which is the central concept of his philosophy and theology. But this coherent conception, although technically coherent, directly contradicts other central statements of Marion's—especially the statements about Being and God that pervade his entire oeuvre. This is shown in what follows.

Precisely understanding Marion's title requires consideration of its French version. Marion does not understand "*étant*" ("Being" in the clause "*étant donné*") as the substantive "*l'étant*"—"the being"; if he did, then the phrase would be read as "*l'étant est donné*—the being is given" (or "the being is what is given"). Significantly—but erroneously—Mar-

---

[43] See section 3.2.1.2, above.

[44] *BG* xx, 1ff.

[45] In accordance with the usage widely accepted or presupposed in contemporary philosophical literature, coherence is here understood as positive compatibility or positive interconnection—thus, as requiring more than consistency in the strictly logical sense, which requires only negative compatibility (i.e., lack of contradiction). Coherence thus entails consistency, but not vice versa.

ion adds that this would be a "metaphysical" reading or understanding. He explains his alternative reading as follows:

> Without added article, "Being" must be taken for a verb, and a verb that works for another (an *auxiliary* verb), since it puts into operation that which now proves itself ultimately "given." . . . Here "Being" is preparation for "given," which completes it and confers on it the force of a fait accompli. (*BG* 2; t.a.)

These formulations are highly significant; they are a highly appropriate analysis, at least in that they provide a partial characterization of what Marion means by *Being*, of how that term should be understood. Instead of saying that Being puts into operation that which now proves itself ultimately given, one could use the more adequate formulation: *Being articulates* that which proves itself ultimately given. The latter formulation corresponds—at least fundamentally—to what is elaborated and shown in chapter 3: love/given/giving is the full *explicatum* of Being. This proves, however, not to be at all what Marion intends.

Why did Marion choose this title? Was he not aware that it directly contradicts everything he says in many, many writings about Being and beings? To avoid incoherence with what this title expresses and implies, Marion should have said "*Being [existing] love*," "*Being [existing] God*," and the like. But that would have put into question the basic coordinates of his entire position.

This becomes clear from the fact that the in-part positive evaluation of Marion's formulations must be accompanied by an important restriction. In the same passage from which the just-quoted statements are taken, Marion adds some further statements that, although they do not directly contradict the statements quoted and interpreted above, do clearly intimate that he still had/has the tendency to, as he puts it, "deposit" [*dé-poser*] Being. The following passage reveals something like a struggle between two tendencies in Marion's conception: to clarify the "being" used in the phrase "being given" *and* to de-pose or de-posit Being by making it disappear and/or by reducing it to an independent and subordinate dimension:

> Considered only as an auxiliary, "Being," as a verb, topples and *disappears in the "given"* because it intends only to reinforce it: "Being" posits the fact of the "given" and is *entirely de-posited therein.* . . . "Being given" does not reconduct the given to the status of a being [*un étant*] not yet adequately named, nor does it inscribe it in supposedly normative beingness [*étantité*]. Rather, "Being given" discloses it as a given, owing

nothing to anybody, given inasmuch as given, organized in terms of givenness [*qui s'ordonne à la donation*][46] and even employing "Being" therein. In one and the same move, the given earns its givenness, and Being (verbal being) disappears in its enactment therein [*en s'y accomplissant*]. (*BG* 2; emphasis added)

It is clear that Marion has the tendency—in opposition to his own explicit explanation—to reduce "Being" (taken as verb) to "a being [*étant, Seiendes*]," and thus to consider "given" and "Being" as two distinct dimensions such that the dimension of Being has to disappear in order to let the given appear *as the* given—thus contradicting what he himself had said, namely that Being must be taken "for a verb, and a verb that works for another (*auxiliary* verb), *since it puts into operation that which proves itself ultimately 'given.'*" According to this formulation, it would be a fatal mistake to understand "Being" and "given/love" as two different dimensions, because according to this formulation, "Being" is the still indeterminate and thus not yet unfolded given. But this "Being" cannot disappear; it has to unfold until it reaches its plenitude, at which point it deserves the name "love/gift." It makes sense to speak of love/gift and God only if one understands them as *Being.*

This is, moreover, exactly von Balthasar's understanding of "Being" (see 4.2.2.1[iii], above). And it corresponds, even quite precisely, to central statements in the passage from Marion quoted above, e.g., "It [*étant*-being] puts into operation that which now proves itself ultimately 'given.' . . . Here 'being' is a preparation for 'given,' which completes [*étant*-being], confers on [*étant*-being] the force of a fait accompli."

---

[46] The French text contains subtleties and connotations involving plays on words. The French word for "given" is "*donné.*" From this Marion develops verbal associations that, as far as the subject matter is concerned, are problematic and indeed arbitrary. This procedure of developing conceptions from usually contingent verbal associations is typical of postmodernist authors. Marion links "*donné*" to words meaning "what is given" and "gift." "Givenness" is linked to "donation." Husserl's key terms "given," "what is given," and "givenness" undergo magical changes in signification. It is not surprising that serious interpreters of Husserl object strenuously to these purely verbally supported "reinterpretations." To be sure, it is the case that the word "*donné*" (from the Latin *dare*) *can* have the meaning "to give (a gift)." But that is not its only meaning and in any case is not the meaning it has in Husserl's works. The passage cited above includes the formulation, ". . . donné en tant que donné, qui s'ordonne à la donation. . ." It is clear that Marion here relies on an imagined (better: a purely phonetic) association between "*ordonner*" and "*donation.*" "*Ordonner*" comes from the Latin "*ordo/ordinare,*" whereas "*donation*" comes from the Latin "*donatio/donare.*" The purely phonetic/graphic similarity does not reveal any similarity—much less identity—in meaning.

According to this passage, the given is precisely the completion of the *étant*–being. This corresponds essentially to the conception presented in chapter 3: God, as the full *explicatum/explicans* of Being, is *fulfilled Being*. But how can Marion then say that the *étant*–being (and therewith being) *disappears,* that it *de-posits* itself in the given? It is nonsensical to say that *completion* entails or even is *disappearance.*

What explains Marion's statements is, as noted above, that he considers the dimension of Being/being(s) and the dimension he calls givenness in the sense of bestowing, the gift, love, etc., as fixed and separate. This is an error that is richly consequential, and one that also, as just shown, contradicts other statements that are central to his works.

[2] It must also be noted that in the just-quoted text Marion commits a fallacy that is evident as well in various other passages in his works, as shown below. One could call this fallacy the *throwing-away-the-ladder fallacy.* This wording is of course reminiscent of the penultimate paragraph of Wittgenstein's *Tractatus,* which reads:

> 6.54 My sentences are elucidatory in this way: he who understands me finally recognizes them as senseless, when he has climbed out through them, on them, over them. (*He must so to speak throw away the ladder, after he has climbed up on it.*) He must surmount these sentences; then he sees the world rightly.

Despite the numerous attempts undertaken by Wittgenstein's keenest supporters to interpret this passage in such a way that it does not have absurd consequences, it is undeniable that here Wittgenstein commits a crude fallacy.

If one considers, on the one hand, Marion's apodictic statements about God without Being, about God loving before Being, and the like, and, on the other hand, his partly clear and partly ambiguous explanations of "being given," it is apparent that he commits the fallacy of throwing away the ladder he himself has used to get to what is his central idea and aspiration: *the pure phenomenon* (*phenomenality*), *nothing other than the pure phenomenon,* the *pure given,* or, as he puts it in the "Preliminary Answers " at the beginning of *Being Given,* "'being given' discloses it as a given, owing nothing to anybody, given inasmuch as given, organized in terms of givenness and even employing 'being' [*étant*] therein" (*BG* 2). But Marion also insists that "'being,' as a verb, topples and disappears in the 'given' because it intends only to reinforce it; 'being' posits the fact of the 'given' and is entirely de-posited therein." The "disappearance" and "de-positing" of Being: these are the terms/concepts with which Marion characterizes his throwing away of his ladder. This is a fallacy: how can

Being/being(s) disappear given that it is Being/being(s) that "put into operation that which now proves itself ultimately 'given,' and that at the end attains its own completion"?

4.2.2.4a Excursus 4: Remarks on the Rhetorical-Polemical Style Marion Uses in Considering the Problem of the Relation Between Being and God

Marion's questions about the relation between God and Being that have been commented on to this point are for the most part, even if not fully meaningful, at least—to some extent—relevant to the matter at hand. In other passages, however, Marion relies on a rhetorical-polemical style that is manifestly inappropriate for dealing with such a difficult issue philosophically and theologically. For example, in the already quoted "Preface" to *God Without Being*, he asks, "To be or not to be—that is indeed the first and indispensable question for everything and everyone, and for man in particular. But with respect to Being does God have to behave like Hamlet?" (*GWB* xx).

In an essay from February 2002 entitled "Does God Have to Exist?" ("Dieu a-t-il à exister?"),[47] he asks: "Why would God have to exist? [*Pourquoi Dieu aurait-il à exister?*]." What a strange question! The reply to Marion is simply the answer already given above to another similar question of his: what is he talking about when he uses the word "God" in this question? He adds:

> Perhaps God does not have to exist, if it is by loving that He reveals Himself. If it is in order to love that He gives Himself. If God is love.
> [*Dieu n'a peut-être pas à exister, si c'est en aimant qu'il se révèle. Si c'est à aimer qu'il se donne. Si Dieu est amour.*]

So, a loving God, a God as love does not—"perhaps"—have to exist, to be. Should we conclude that Marion's loving God is a fiction or—to use a term he likes to use when he addresses what he calls the God of metaphysics—an idol, a beautiful idol, perhaps, but an idol nonetheless?

In another passage he asks even stranger questions: "Why would He [God] exist like us? [*Pourquoi existerait-il comme nous?*]." Answer: no metaphysician has ever stated or assumed that God exists "like us." But Marion continues: "By what right do we take ourselves to impose our diktat on

---

[47] *Conférences-débats* 2002 Association Saint-Etienne, February 7, 2002, in the French town of Caen. See http://abbaye-aux-hommes.cef.fr/activites/conf06.htm (accessed December 29, 2009). The following quotations without indication of pages are to the document on this Internet site.

Him and to demand from Him that He should prove His existence? Or that he subject Himself to our rationality? [*De quel droit prétendons-nous lui imposer notre diktat et exiger de lui qu'il prouve son existence? Ou qu'il se soumette à notre rationalité?*]." Questions such as these cannot be answered because they are simply meaningless. One reason that they are is that they are based on a *hysteron-proteron fallacy:* they presuppose what is at stake, namely that God exists/is. One can attempt to impose a diktat only on someone who exists/is, not on a fiction, not on an idol. No X could subject itself to our rationality or be subjected to our rationality if it were not, if it did not exist.

But Marion takes a step further—and this is an extremely problematic step. He asks: "Doesn't God have better things to do than to exist? [*Dieu n'a-t-il pas mieux à faire qu'à exister?*]." To this one should unhesitatingly respond: this is not only a meaningless question because of the wholly unacceptable assumptions on which it is based, it is in addition a fallacious, populist rhetorical question to which one can only say: it is not a serious philosophical question. Once again: the *hysteron-proteron fallacy.* And finally, Marion asks: "And we, don't we have better things to do than to prove that He exists—or that He doesn't exist? [*Et nous, n'avons-nous pas mieux à faire qu'à démontrer qu'il existe—ou qu'il n'existe pas?*]." And once again the non-recognizing and even the denying of our human condition. What Marion ignores is that *we* are confronted with the question of God, and—especially from a Christian perspective—*we* have not only the right, we have above all the *duty* to attempt to get clear about this question. Whether—and if so, in what sense—one could or should not speak of "proving the existence of God" constitutes one aspect of the complex question of God. This is shown in chapter 3.

4.2.3 The Fundamental Failure or *Proton Pseudos:* Marion's Attempted Transformation of Husserl's Phenomenological Approach by Means of the Reversal of the Subject-Object Distinction, Resulting in Pure Phenomenality

Identifying the contradictions, incoherences, arbitrary assumptions, and the like in Marion's philosophical and theological work is a meaningful and indeed indispensable task. But it is neither the only task nor the most important task posed by that work. After it has been accomplished, a final fundamental question arises, namely: why and how does Marion arrive at his strange position as regards transcendence and God? There is an answer to this question—and it is provided, in detail, in this section. To state it briefly: what explains Marion's having taken so strange a position is what can be called a *magnus error in initio,* a fundamental failure at the beginning, or a *proton pseudos*. This is Marion's attempted transformation of Husserl's phenomenological approach by means of the reversal of the subject-object distinction, which has as its result, according to Marion, the appearance of the genuine, original idea of pure phenomenality.

4.2.3.1 Problems with Husserl's Phenomenological Approach and with Marion's Attempt to Transform and Complete Husserl's Project

[1] Marion is driven by the project of developing Husserlian phenomenology in a radical sense, with the aim of developing its full potential, but also of correcting errors and, thus, of profoundly transforming it. He tries to achieve this by performing what he calls a *third* (*phenomenological*) *reduction*. He overcomes a first reduction, Husserl's transcendental-phenomenological reduction, which he interprets as a reduction of the given to the transcendental ego (*Ich*): the object is understood as constituted by the transcendental ego. Marion aims to also overcome a second reduction, namely, Heidegger's reduction of the given to Dasein and of Dasein to the world and then to Being. He envisages a third reduction: the reduction of the given (in a non-specific sense) to *pure phenomenality*, which he interprets first as *pure givenness* and then as *donation*. He attributes to this third reduction "an incontestable priority."[48]

According to Marion, phenomenology—as he understands it—diverges both from transcendental philosophy and from metaphysics by the doubly negative manner in which it conceives of the phenomenon. First, it does not interpret it as *an object*—that is to say, for Marion, "not within the horizon of objectity [*objectité*]," not as something constituted by the subject. Second, it does not understand the phenomenon *as a being* [*étant*]—that is to say, again for Marion, "not within the horizon of Being [*être*]" (*BG* 320).

[2] To understand what this means, one has to go back to *the central idea* of Husserl's phenomenology, to what Husserl calls "the principle of all principles." Husserl characterizes that idea—a metaprinciple—as follows:

> No conceivable theory can make us err with respect to the *principle of all principles: that every originary presentative intuition* [*Anschauung*] *is a legitimizing source of cognition,* that *everything originarily* (so to speak, in its "personal" actuality) *offered* to us *in "intuition* [*Intuition*] " *is to be accepted*

---

[48] Marion, "L'autre philosophie première et la question de la donation," in *Le statut contemporain de la philosophie première*, ed. Philippe Capelle, Centenaire de la Faculté de Philosophie, Institut Catholique de Paris (Paris: Beauchesne, 1996), 29–50; at 45.

simply as what gives/presents itself, but also *only within the limits in which it is presented there.* We see indeed that every [theory] can only again draw its truth itself from originary data. Every statement that does no more than confer expression on such data by simple explication and by means of significations precisely conforming to them is . . . actually an *absolute beginning* called upon to serve as a foundation, a *principium* in the genuine sense of the word. But this holds especially for this kind of generic cognition of essences to which the word "principle" is commonly limited.[49]

What is given in originary intuition, the phenomenon: this is Husserl's central idea and also Marion's central idea. What must be determined is how Marion himself understands and in a profound sense transforms Husserl's conception. Two aspects of Husserl's understanding of the phenomenon are particularly important.

[i] The first is indicated by Husserl's famous phrases: "Bracketing of existence/Being [*Existenz-, Seinseinklammerung*]" and "switching off existence/Being [*Ausschaltung der Existenz, des Seins*]."[50] In the first place, these phrases indicate a methodological principle according to which the "natural attitude" toward the world and all things has to be ignored or dismissed by the phenomenologist. The natural attitude presupposes what Husserl calls "the general thesis [*Generalthesis*]," according to which there is an existing world and there are existing things whose existence or Being is wholly independent of us, our consciousness, and our intentional acts. Husserl's bracketing of existence/Being is not a denial or negation of the independent existence/Being of the world or of things. Instead, it removes the question of that existence/Being from the phenomenologist's consideration: the task of the phenomenologist is to perform a reduction from the natural attitude, one that leads him to investigate the intentional acts that constitute the objects. The idea of reduction has many stages, including what Husserl calls the phenomenological, the transcendental, and the eidetic reductions. This topic cannot be pursued here in more detail.

What is important in this context is that Husserl later (unquestionably by 1913, the time of the publication of the *Ideas I*) transformed the *methodological principle* of bracketing existence/Being into a strictly *systematic principle* in the following sense: existence/Being is no longer "brack-

---

[49] *Ideas I: Ideas Pertaining to a Pure Phenomenology and to a Phenomenological Philosophy: First Book* (1913/1983), §24, p. 44 (t.a.).

[50] E.g., ibid., §31.

eted" in the sense of not being considered or thematized; instead, it is rejected outright as a dimension independent of intentional acts. Existence/Being is reduced to *Being for consciousness,* to pure appearance/ phenomenon. This is the famous transcendental-idealistic turn of Husserl's phenomenology that split the phenomenological school into two currents: the idealistic and the realistic. Husserl continued to employ the terms "Being" and "being(s)," but he clearly stated that he understood Being exclusively in the sense of a reduction of Being to phenomenon/ appearance. The following passage from his *Ideas I* clearly articulates this central point:

> Thus the sense commonly expressed in speaking of Being is reversed. The Being that is first for us is second in itself; i.e., it is what it is, only in "relation" to the first. [But it is] not as though there were a blind regularity such that the *ordo et connexio rerum* necessarily conformed to the *ordo et connexio idearum.* Reality [*Realität*], the reality of the physical thing taken singly and the reality of the whole world, lacks self-sufficiency in virtue of its essence (in our strict sense of the word). Reality is not in itself something absolute which becomes tied secondarily to something else; rather, in the absolute sense, it is nothing at all; it has no "absolute essence" whatever; it has the essentiality [*Wesenheit*] of something which, of necessity, is *only* intentional, *only* an object of consciousness, something presented [*Vorstelliges*] in the manner peculiar to consciousness, something apparent [as apparent].[51]

On this basis, Husserl radically reinterprets his phenomenological reduction, as follows:

> Instead . . . of living naively in experience and theoretically exploring what is experienced, transcendent Nature, we effect the "phenomenological reduction." In other words, instead of naively *effecting* the acts pertaining to our Nature—constituting consciousness with their positings of something transcendent, and letting ourselves be induced, by motives implicit in them, to effect ever new positings of something transcendent—instead of that, we put all those positings "out of action," we do not "participate in them"; we direct our seizing and theoretically inquiring regard to *pure consciousness in its own absolute Being.* That, then, is what is left as the sought-for "*phenomenological residuum,*" though we have "excluded" the whole world with all physical things, living beings,

---

[51] Ibid., §50, pp. 112–13; t.a.

and humans, ourselves included. Strictly speaking, we have not lost any-thing but rather have gained the whole of absolute Being which, rightly understood, contains within itself, "constitutes" within itself, all worldly transcendencies.[52]

It is important that Husserl now speaks of "*pure consciousness in its own absolute Being.*" What does "Being," what does "absolute," and what does "own" mean here? These terms are at the heart of the tremendous ambiguity of the last stage of Husserl's phenomenological development. Some phrases in the last two passages quoted above, if taken literally, could suggest that Husserl was advocating an absolute idealism; these include, "The Being that is first for us is second in itself; i.e., it is what it is, only in 'relation' to the first." In this case, phenomenological "consti-tution" would be creation. Shown below ([3][i]) is that this is not Hus-serl's position. That it is not is suggested by the following line from the first passage: "the sense commonly expressed in speaking of Being is reversed." The question, then, is of the *sense* of "Being." The question whose asking reveals the ambiguity of phenomenology is that of how its "sense" or "meaning" is to be understood. In Heideggerian terminology: Husserl thematized only sense/meaning (whatever he meant by sense/ meaning), but not *Being itself.*

[ii] The *second* particularly important aspect of Husserl's central idea of the phenomenon is that Husserl finally understood the phenom-enological reduction as leading to the transcendental dimension, to the transcendental subject or ego. In the final analysis, this ego is what con-stitutes all "objects"—and hence all phenomena—however they may be designated.

[3] As for the first important aspect of Husserl's idea of the phe-nomenon, although Marion fully accepts Husserl's association of the phenomenon with the idea of originarily giving intuition, he does not follow the idealistic path Husserl embarks on in *Ideas I*. Instead, he radi-calizes the idea of originary givenness in a way that is not accepted by most other phenomenologists.

As for the second important aspect of Husserl's idea, Marion re-jects it outright, but in a way that is highly significant: he does not utterly abandon the idea of constitution; he instead reverses it, so that it is the subject that is constituted.

[i] Henceforth, this book considers mainly Marion's transformed phenomenology. As regards the immensely serious consequences of his

---

[52] Ibid., 113.

phenomenological position for the question of transcendence and God, it is no exaggeration to say that the *proton pseudos,* the fundamental failure of Marion's philosophical-theological conception, results from his assumption and radicalization of Husserl's idea of phenomenon. The account that follows explains and grounds this central thesis.

In this context it is important to indicate that there is a strange "logic" (or "pseudo-logic") in Marion's way of treating the problem of transcendence and especially the relation between Being and God. Indeed, as is shown by the exposure of the deep ambiguities of Marion's phenomenological approach, in one respect Being disappears *as Being,* whereas in another respect it is reduced to "pure consciousness in its own absolute Being," i.e., to the "phenomenological residuum."

In a fundamental respect, this explains Marion's strange statements about God and Being. The phenomenon is *what* appears. But what is this "what," what is that which appears? Is what appears the appearance of Being or of beings? If this is the case, then what the appearance is the appearance *of* should be explicitly thematized. But neither Husserl nor Marion explicitly thematizes it. If, on the other hand, what appears is not the appearance of Being or of beings, then the appearance is *not* the appearance *of* anything. In this case all of reality, all things/beings, is/are simply reduced to *pure* appearances, to *pure* phenomena. But how could *pure* appearances or *pure* phenomena be understood?

Neither Husserl nor Marion succeeds in articulating pure appearances or phenomena in isolation from factors that constitute and that are constituted: these factors always remain the absolutely fundamental basis for everything. As shown below, Marion attempts to reverse the constituting-constituted relation and the subject-object distinction. But even if one were to accept that such reversals could make sense, the reversals would remain bound to frameworks including these dualities themselves.

By introducing the concept *pure phenomenality,* Marion gives the impression that he has freed himself from the straitjacket of these dualities. He has not, however, succeeded in doing so: his *pure* phenomenality remains a phenomenality that is an appearing-to-a-consciousness-or-subject. He has no other sense of "phenomenon." The relation to subjectivity/consciousness is thus an essential factor in his determination of "phenomenon." Heidegger understands the "phenomenon" wholly differently: no longer as a relation or in relation to any other factor, no matter how that factor might be understood or articulated: not as subject(ivity), not as consciousness, not even as Dasein. Instead: "the expression '*phenomenon*' signifies *that which shows itself in* itself, the manifest" (*BT* 51). As shown in chapter 3, phenomena in this Heideggerian sense are what are articulated in theoretical sentences, whose structure is made explicit by the inclusion of the operator "It is the case that."

In any case, both Husserl's and Marion's positions are *phenomenological idealisms* that are not *absolute idealisms*. Phenomenological idealisms are ambiguous because the concept *phenomenological appearance/phenomenon* is ambiguous; this is the fundamental ambiguity in both Husserl's phenomenology and in Marion's. It consists in the two following assumptions of this idealism: everything is reduced to phenomena, which are determined as pure points of reference for subjectivity/consciousness; according to Husserl, subjectivity/consciousness does the constituting of phenomena, whereas according to Marion, the phenomena do the constituting of subjectivity/consciousness. In neither case is constituting equivalent to creating, and what is constituted is thus not created. As a consequence, the phenomenon, as understood in phenomenology, is the appearance of something that, as such and as a whole, is *not identical with* its appearance, and hence with the phenomenon: the reality or Being of the something that *appears* as phenomenon is not exhausted by its Being-for-consciousness/subjectivity. Likewise, subjectivity understood as phenomenologically constituting is *not the entire reality or Being of subjectivity*. From both directions, the relation of constitution presupposes a twofold dimension that remains unthematized: an unthematized dimension of subjectivity and an unthematized dimension of subjectivity's "other." This twofold dimension that evades the relation of constitution is here termed the U-dimension ("U" for Unconstituting/Unconstituted, Unthematized, Unthought . . .).[53]

---

[53] As is well known, Husserl's concept *constitution* is quite unclear. Its interpretation cannot be considered extensively here, but two points are worth making. The first is both positive and negative: constitution has to do with sense or meaning, not with the reality or Being of what is constituted. The second is purely negative: whatever else constitution may be, it is in any case not the creation or production of the "object/Being" that it constitutes. Husserl exegete Elisabeth Ströker makes these two points clearly and convincingly:

> [It could appear] that transcendental constitution is simply a matter of creation. But creation, even if it is understood in a strictly transcendental sense, would obviously lead to the exact opposite of what Husserl is striving after as a phenomenological basis for the grounding of knowledge; it would lead, namely, into the mysterious depths of a creation of the world through a transcendental consciousness that is no longer comprehensible. Yet Husserl never ascribed the capabilities of creating or producing Being to consciousness—not even to transcendental consciousness. Husserl made few explicit contributions to the positive determination of the concept of constitution; yet it clearly and unambiguously follows from the contexts of its utilization that the productive possibilities of consciousness are only possibilities of bestowing, and upon closer examination, of sense-bestowing. Noeses do not produce Being; they posit, in each case, Being

[ii] At this point the following question presses: what is this U-dimension (both on the side of subjectivity/consciousness [Husserl] and on the side of the other [the "object," the phenomenon; Marion]) that constitution must presuppose but that remains withdrawn from constitution? The answer: phenomenology as idealistic phenomenalism *presupposes* such a U-dimension, but in phenomenology (whether Husserl's or Marion's) this U-dimension remains fully in the dark, it remains a kind of black hole.

This state of affairs has a consequence for phenomenology that is absolutely revolutionary, because it brings into view a task that is vital for philosophical thinking: if the "achievement" of subjectivity/consciousness does not (so to speak) extend so far as to be able to thematize (or grasp, think, explain, etc.) the *presupposed* U-dimension, then the preeminent—indeed, absolutely primary and all-determining—significance and role that has been claimed for the phenomenological approach, by both Husserl and Marion (among others), can in no way, shape, or form be ascribed to that approach. Phenomenology cannot be the *prima philosophia* Marion explicitly presents it as being.[54]

How, then, can or should philosophy deal with the U-dimension? Can or indeed must it be thematized? That it can and must is a central thesis of this book and of *Structure and Being*. But if so, then how? The first point to be noted is this: the U-dimension emerges as a presupposition or implication of phenomenology. It is, so to speak, an unintended and extremely onerous by-product, ultimately simply ignored as a kind of black hole, of phenomenology's form of the philosophy of subjectivity. What this shows the philosopher who wants to get clear about the U-dimension is the following: the framework of the philosophy of subjectivity must be abandoned, and that means in addition that the subject-object distinc-

---

in some definite sense. Here it is not a question of where Being comes from, or even who created it. Such a question would have no place at all in Husserlian philosophy. Husserl's question is metaphysically more modest, but phenomenologically more penetrating: what is the sense of the diverse ways of speaking about Being, and in what terms can this sense be conceived? But if the accomplishments of consciousness were to be investigated in particular for the purpose of answering this question, it would become apparent that a Being maintained to be in itself, as it is understood in the natural attitude as a Being transcendent to consciousness, is nothing else but a Being *posited as Being in itself*. For this Being could not be understood on any other basis than that of the noetically posited sense that such an "in itself" actually has. (*Husserls transzendentale Phänomenologie*, 107–8)

[54] Marion, "L'autre philosophie première et la question de la donation" (1996), especially 43ff.

tion can no longer determine or define the framework for philosophical thinking. What this means *positively* is that what must be thought and thematized is the *comprehensive* dimension, i.e., the one containing (1) subjectivity and all that belongs to or is ascribed to it *and* (2) objectivity (as the counterpole to subjectivity, no matter how it is designated) *and*— especially—(3) what is introduced above as the U-dimension. That this is so is explained and supported in what follows.

A word on Heidegger at this point is not only helpful, but nearly inescapable, because this is the point at which his epochal step beyond Husserl is situated. The point itself is introduced in chapters 2 and 3, but his on-target remarks are well worth repeating in the present context.

In a letter to Husserl in which he responds to the latter's in-part vehement critique of *Being and Time,* Heidegger writes:

> There is agreement that being(s) in the sense of what you [Husserl] call "world" cannot be clarified, in its transcendental constitution, by any reliance on being(s) having that mode of Being.
>
> This is, however, not to say that what makes up the locus of the transcendental is not a being at all—instead, that is the source of the *problem:* what is the mode of Being of the being within which "world" is constituted? That is the central problem of *Being and Time*—i.e., a fundamental ontology of Dasein. The task is to show that the mode of Being of human Dasein is completely different from that of all other beings and that it, as the one that it is, contains within itself the possibility of transcendental constitution. . . . *What constitutes is not nothing, is thus something that is—although not in the sense of the positive. The question of the mode of Being of what constitutes cannot be avoided. Universally, the problem of Being thus involves both what constitutes and what is constituted.*[55]

Marion has never taken even this first and most fundamental step taken by Heidegger, notwithstanding his relying on so many alleged insights of the late Heidegger, particularly his interpretation and critique of metaphysics (as Marion interprets them).

Heidegger's argument is based on the accepted universality of the concept of Being: this concept is applicable to anything and everything, and thus also to subjectivity as phenomenologically constitutive. In one sentence, Heidegger totally dismantles the transcendental-phenomenological approach by clearly formulating the consequence,

---

[55] Husserl, *Husserliana, Gesammelte Werke,* vol. 9 (1950), *Anlage* 1, 601–2 (emphasis in the last three sentences added).

for that approach, of the fact that the problem of Being is universally related to what constitutes and what is constituted. The dismantling is total because it articulates a dimension that reveals the transcendental-phenomenological schema, subject-object, as fully subordinate, absolutely one-sided, and thus wholly inadequate. The dimension Heidegger articulates is that of Being; that dimension is, as chapter 2 shows, the central focus of Heidegger's thought.

The transcendental phenomenologist could attempt to counter Heidegger by denying the universality of the concept of Being. That philosopher could point out that this putative universality is in conflict with Husserl's principle of principles, which holds that *"every originary presentative intuition [Anschauung] is a legitimizing source of cognition, that everything originarily . . . offered to us in 'intuition [Intuition]' is to be accepted simply as what gives/presents itself, but also only within the limits in which it is presented there."*[56] The objection would then be that there is no "originarily giving intuition" of a phenomenologically constitutive subjectivity that *is;* moreover, the objection would add, to assume such a subjectivity would be nonsensical, because subjectivity is the *presupposition* for every such intuition, and therefore cannot be "given" (or cannot give itself) in any such intuition.

The putative objection sketched in the preceding paragraph is, however, nothing more than a repetition of the basic thesis of phenomenology as articulated in Husserl's principle of principles. This thesis, however, is precisely what is at stake in the discussion. Heidegger's development may be the best answer to the objection: instead of subjectivity, structured in terms of intuition and concept, he increasingly places *thinking* at the center of his philosophy, to such a degree that intuition and concept disappear altogether. Thinking, as he understands it, is wholly distinct from subjectivity, because it is not a dual concept requiring a counterpole. Thinking is absolutely universal: thinking can think itself.

The thesis, formulated above, relating to the "U-dimension" that is both a presupposition and an implication of phenomenology, can also be explained and grounded independently of Heidegger. The thesis in question is that a or the *comprehensive* dimension must be thought and thematized, such that it actually encompasses *constituting* subjectivity in its entirety, *constituted* objectivity—the dimension of the counterpole to subjectivity—in its entirety, and also the entire U-dimension (*non*-constituting subjectivity *and* the *non*-constituted "other").

---

[56] See footnote 49, above.

The non-Heideggerian approach relies on a systematic analysis of the theoretical state of affairs that has come into view. This state of affairs includes both intra-phenomenological and meta-phenomenological theses. The most important *negative* meta-phenomenological thesis is the following: constitution is not the creation of objects/beings. Whereas the intra-phenomenological theses articulate the "pure" relation between phenomenologically constitutive subjectivity and the object as constituted, the negative meta-phenomenological thesis articulates an *additional, comprehensive* relation, even if (at first) only negatively: the relation between the dimension of subjectivity *insofar as it presents itself as* non-*constituting* and the other/Being insofar as it appears as *non*-constituted. But this merely *negative determination of the more comprehensive* relation is only one side of the coin whose other side is the *positive* determination of this relation. Even a *negative* relation is a relation: the one (subjectivity) is *not constitutive* of the other; it thereby relates to the other in this *negative* manner; the other also relates to subjectivity in a negative manner. How is this possible? How can it be understood? The answer is evident: only such that both subjectivity and objectivity are understood as contained within a dimension that encompasses them both.

What results is the following: phenomenologically constitutive subjectivity *and* phenomenologically constituted objectivity *and* the twofold U-dimension (subjectivity that is *not* phenomenologically constitutive and objectivity [other, Being] that is *not* phenomenologically constituted) presuppose a space or domain or dimension that encompasses all of them, one within which alone they can appear as what they are. This is the dimension or space Heidegger names "Being"—as, also, does chapter 3, above.

[iii] What consequences result for Husserl and Marion? The two are confronted with different forms of a problem. For Husserl, what constitutes is subjectivity/consciousness. If he wanted to thematize the U-dimension as encompassing *both of its poles,* how could he proceed? He would have two options: the first would be to absolutize subjectivity/consciousness by radicalizing its constitutive function: constitution would be reinterpreted as creation. Then the other would no longer be a phenomenologically understood pure phenomenon-for-subjectivity/consciousness, it would be created by subjectivity/consciousness. The two poles of the dimension *encompassing* subject(ivity)-objectivity would be identical with the (reinterpreted) constitutive pole, subjectivity/consciousness. This constitutive instance would suspend the duality subject(ivity)/consciousness–objectivity within subject(ivity)/consciousness. The result would be an *absolute* idealism.

Husserl's other option would be to follow his student Heidegger in not identifying the encompassing dimension with a reinterpreted or transformed version of either pole (that would thereby have been made absolute), but instead thematizing the encompassing dimension *as such.*

If Husserl were to take either option, he would thereby abandon Husserlian phenomenology.

The situation is different for Marion. Because—as shown in detail below—he *reverses* the subject-object relation, what is constitutive for him is not subject(ivity)/consciousness, but instead the other to subject(ivity)/consciousness, which is, in Marion's terminology, the (saturated) phenomenon. Subject(ivity) is then what is constituted, the (saturated) phenomenon what constitutes. Marion's articulation of his entire philosophical-theological position remains within the framework of this *reversed* relation. And—as is now to be shown—that is the fundamental problem with his conception of transcendence and God.

One might wonder whether Marion either has overcome or could overcome the subject-other duality. That he has not and cannot is shown in detail below, but a preliminary remark on the topic is appropriate here. As indicated above, Marion *reverses* the subject-object relation: he understands the phenomenon (particularly the saturated phenomenon) as constituting the subject, which is consequently transformed from an I to a me. This relation holds particularly for the absolutely saturated phenomenon that Marion presents as God's "mode of appearance." God is absolute *caritas,* absolute giving, who shows or communicates himself, in the form of the absolute phenomenon, to the subject as the receiver, the recipient of the gift. The reversed subject-object relation then has the form of a relation of other (= phenomenon) to subject (= me/receiver/recipient); the other *constitutes* the subject such that the constitutive function is located in the other, the phenomenon. But then the question presses, what is this reversed constituting? Does the other "constitute" the subject-as-constituted/recipient with respect to the latter's *entire reality?* If so, then reversed constitution would be the creation, the positing of the subject-as-recipient.

If reversed constitution is *not* creation, then Marion faces a problem analogous to the one faced by Husserl: a U-dimension, relating to both poles, remains presupposed but unthematized. And indeed, Marion denies that "his" constitution is creation, as is clearly implied by the names given to the constituted: receiver, recipient (*attributaire, allocataire, adonné*). But for X to be a recipient, X must already *be.* The *Being* of the reversed subject is thus *not* effected by constitution. The same holds for the opposite pole: Y can give to X only if Y already *is.* The U-dimension is thus one that Marion cannot avoid.

This state of affairs confronts Marion's entire conception of God with a *fundamental* problem that does not and cannot emerge for Hus-

serl. Anticipatorily, it is the following: the reversed subject-object relation along with reversed constitution provide in a certain respect the
fundamental coordinates of the framework within which Marion develops his conception of God. God then appears as the absolute other, the
absolutely distant, etc., who relates to human beings as the *caritas* or love
that gives him- or itself. In this manner, it constitutes the human being in
the sense that the human being appears as reversed subject, as recipient
of the divine gift. Between God and the human being there holds the
relation of (self-)giver to recipient. God *constitutes* the human being as
recipient, but then the question arises of how God is to be understood:
as an absolutely other/distant self-giver, that the human being is, so to
speak, somehow outside of, such that the giver does not encompass the
recipient? Such a God, conceived of within the framework of the phenomenologically understood subject-object relation *and* of its reversed
form, would be a strange God: a God that would have something "outside
itself," something that it *did not encompass*. This would be—to say the very
least—a highly problematic God.

To be sure, as a Christian theologian Marion does introduce the
concept *creation* in some passages within his oeuvre. But—as shown in
detail below, in section 4.2.4.4—he does not recognize the depth and
breadth of this concept. Fully explicated, this concept articulates God's
absolutely unrestricted comprehensiveness. In order to be able to give
Himself to human beings, God first creates human beings; he posits
them within Being. Before being a receiver, the human being is *a created
being*. Creation cannot be articulated within the framework of either the
Husserlian or the reversed subject-object relation. If one wanted to use
the word "constitution" in conjunction with the issue of creation, one
would have to say that creation is the very first "constitution" of the entire
reality, the entire Being of human beings. Only on the basis of creation
is God a self-giver. In this case, "constitution" would be synonymous with
"creation"; but this is wholly different from the phenomenological use of
"constitution," including the use of it made by Marion when he reverses
its directionality.

4.2.3.2 The Concepts of Pure Phenomenality and of the Saturated Phenomenon

[1] Marion aims at working out what he calls genuine or pure phenomenality, thus going decisively far beyond Husserl, contradicting him with
respect to essential features of the phenomenological approach, but—
and this must especially be emphasized—maintaining the most fundamental tenets of this approach and, consequently, maintaining its *proton
pseudos*.

Marion classifies phenomena into three categories or domains, depending on their amounts of intuitive content (see *BG*, book 4, 179–247). Phenomena in the first domain either lack intuitive content or have quite little intuitive content; this is the domain of formal languages and mathematical "idealities" (*BG* 222). The second domain is the domain of "the common-law phenomena," whose "signification (aimed at by intention). . . can be adequate [although] most of the time it remains inadequate." Finally, the third domain is the domain of *saturated phenomena* (which Marion also calls "paradoxes"); these are the phenomena "in which intuition always submerges the expectation of the intention, in which givenness not only entirely invests manifestation but, surpassing it, modifies its common characteristics" (*BG* 225).

Marion initially distinguishes among four types of saturated phenomena. First, there is "the figure of the historical phenomenon, of the event carried to its apex" (*BG* 228). In the second type the saturated phenomenon "appears . . . under the aspect of the unbearable and bedazzlement." Marion calls this type "the idol" and sees the painting as its "privileged occurrence" (*BG* 229). As a third type of saturated phenomenon Marion presents the "absolute character of the flesh [*chair*], such that it is torn from the category of relation and carries the *fait accompli* to its excellence" (*BG* 231). Finally, the fourth type of saturated phenomenon occurs "in the aspect of the irregardable and irreducible, insofar as they are free from all reference to the I, therefore to the categories of modality." He calls this fourth type "the icon," "because it no longer offers any spectacle to the gaze and tolerates no gaze from any spectator, but rather exerts its own gaze over that which meets it" (*BG* 232).

Marion subsequently introduces a fifth type of saturated phenomenon, "its most complex figure, the phenomenon of revelation" (*BG* 246). This is the phenomenon with "the maximum of saturated phenomenality," and thus "an ultimate possibility of the phenomenon" (*BG* 235): "This concerns a fifth type of saturation, not that it adds a new one (arbitrarily invented in order to do right by the supposed right of the 'divine') to the first four (the sole describable ones), but because, by confounding them in it, it saturates phenomenality to the second degree, by saturation of saturation" (*BG* 235).

Marion is concerned with making clear that even in the case of such a phenomenon as Jesus Christ he proceeds "as a phenomenologist—describing a given phenomenological possibility—and as a philosopher—confronting the visible Christ with his possible conceptual role . . . with an eye toward establishing it as a paradigm" (*BG* 236). He explains:

> We are obliged *here*—in phenomenology, where possibility remains the norm, and not actuality—only to describe it in its pure possibility and

in the reduced immanence of givenness. We do not *here* have to judge its actual manifestation or its ontic status, which remains the business proper to revealed theology. (*BG* 236; t.a.)

This poses a serious coherence problem for Marion, as demonstrated below (see [3][v]).

The following account focuses almost exclusively on Marion's domain of saturated phenomena and within this domain most especially on the fifth type of such phenomena, i.e., the phenomenon of revelation.

[2] Understanding and assessing Marion's statements about pure phenomenality require examination of his way of describing it. Characteristically, he relies on Kant, following the guiding thread provided by the Kantian classification of the pure concepts of the understanding, or categories: quantity, quality, relation, and modality.[57] Pursuing his main idea on this topic, the excess of intuition over concept, Marion aims to show that the intuitional component of the saturated phenomenon exceeds the pure concepts or categories and also the principles of the understanding.

As regards *quantity,* the saturated phenomenon is invisible, incapable of being looked at (*irregardable*), incommensurable, immense, and without measure. As an example, Marion describes the phenomenon of *amazement* (see *BG* 200–201; "SP" 113–15). With respect to *quality* or intensive magnitude, the saturated phenomenon cannot be borne, that is to say, perception can no longer anticipate what it might receive from intuition; and, what is more, it can no longer bear the intense degree of intuition. "The intensive magnitude of the intuition that gives the saturated phenomenon is unbearable for the gaze" ("SP" 114). What the gaze cannot bear Marion characterizes as *bedazzlement*. As a consequence, in the case of the saturated phenomenon intuition does not give reality in degrees; to the contrary, "intuition gives reality without any limitation (or, to be sure, negation)" (ibid.).

With respect to *relation,* Marion characterizes saturated phenomena as "absolute" ("SP" 115). They

occur without being inscribed, at least at first, in the relational network that ensures experience its unity, and . . . they matter precisely because

---

[57] This is yet another revelatory indication of Marion's basic stance in philosophy: it is a philosophy of subjectivity, although in the sense of a philosophy of *reversed subjectivity*. But, as the following account reveals, the reversal of subjectivity still remains within the theoretical framework of a philosophy of subjectivity.

one cannot assign them any substratum, any cause, or any communion. . . . [They] assume the character and the dignity of an event—
that is, an event or a phenomenon that is unforeseeable . . . , not
exhaustively comprehensible . . . ; in short, absolute, unique, occurring.
("SP" 116)

At this point, Marion addresses the question of whether there is a
horizon within which the saturated phenomenon appears. His clear position is that such a horizon is neither necessary nor possible, because
saturated phenomena can exceed every horizon:

We should specify that it is not a matter of dispensing with a horizon
in general—which would undoubtedly prohibit all manifestation—but
of freeing oneself from the delimiting anteriority proper to every horizon, an anteriority that is such as to be unable not to enter into conflict
with a phenomenon's claim to absoluteness. ("SP" 117)

In giving itself absolutely, the saturated phenomenon gives itself also
as absolute—free from any analogy with the experience that is already
seen, objectivized, and comprehended. It frees itself therefrom because
it depends on no horizon. On the contrary, the saturated phenomenon
either simply saturates the horizon, or it multiplies the horizon in order
to saturate it that much more, or it exceeds the horizon and finds itself
cast out from it. But this very disfiguration remains a manifestation.
In every case, it does not depend on that condition of possibility par
excellence—a horizon, whatever it may be. We therefore call this phenomenon unconditioned. ("SP" 118)

Marion's treatment of the categories of *modality*—which he understands as Kant does—is of special interest for the purposes of this book.
The specific character of these categories in Kantian philosophy consists in making explicit the relation of objects to the cognitive apparatus.
Characteristically, Marion deals only with the category of *possibility*, ignoring completely the categories *existence* (Dasein) and *necessity*. Kant characterizes possibility as follows: "The postulate of the *possibility* of things . . .
requires that their concept agree with the formal conditions of an experience in general" (*CPuR* B267). Marion interprets this as meaning that
only what agrees with the transcendental "I" is a *possible* phenomenon.
At precisely this point he performs a typical *reversal* by saying that Kant's
condition of possibility does not hold for saturated phenomena. "In the
face of saturation, the I most certainly experiences the disagreement
between the at least potential phenomenon and the subjective condi-

tions of its experience; consequently, the I cannot constitute an object in them" ("SP" 119).

A problem arises here with Marion's assertion that the "I most certainly experiences the disagreement." This Kant would reject. Marion, however, relies on the presupposed idea that in the case of saturated phenomena, intuition exceeds every concept. This idea is intelligible only within a generally Kantian framework. As is well known, Kant holds that "thoughts without content are empty, intuitions without concepts are blind."[58] According to Marion, saturated phenomena overwhelm this strict correspondence between intuitions and concepts. It is for this reason that the subject cannot, in such cases, constitute any object. This point is central for Marion in every respect:

> The saturated phenomenon refuses to let itself be looked at as an object, precisely because it appears with a multiple and indescribable excess that suspends any effort at constitution [by the subject]. Determining the saturated phenomenon as a non-objective—more precisely, non-objectivizable—phenomenon has nothing to do with a flight into the irrational or the arbitrary. (119)

This fundamental state of affairs disempowers the subjection of the phenomenon to the I. Yet more important is that it accomplishes a reversal of this relation:

> Far from being able to constitute this phenomenon, the I experiences itself as constituted by it. It is constituted and no longer constituting because it no longer has at its disposal any dominant point of view over the intuition that overwhelms it. (Ibid.)

Thus, the subject emerges "at its last appeal: the *interloqué* [interlocuted; addressed]—as the one addressed [*interloqué*]. . . . This reversal leaves it interlocuted [*interloqué*], essentially surprised by the more original event that detaches it from itself" (ibid.). The subject is no longer an "I"; it is a "me."

The most important point in Marion's characterization of the saturated phenomenon is a further aspect: the saturated phenomenon must be understood as showing *itself*. According to Marion, this *showing itself*

---

[58] *CPuR* B75. See also B74: "Intuition and concepts . . . constitute the elements of all our cognition, so that neither concepts without intuition corresponding to them in some way nor intuition without concepts can yield a cognition."

is a *giving itself:* this *givenness* (*Gegebenheit*)—which Marion interprets as *donation*—is Marion's third phenomenological reduction. The phenomenon shows/gives/donates itself "to us." Are we then "subjects," in the genuine or active sense? Marion speaks powerfully about this:

> The phenomenology of givenness/donation has finished radically—
> in our eyes, for the first time—with the "subject" and all its recent
> avatars. . . . To have done with the "subject," it is . . . necessary not to
> destroy it, but to reverse it—to overturn it. It is posited as a center: this
> will not be contested, but we will contest its mode of occupying and
> exercising the center to which it lays claim—with the title of a (think-
> ing, constituting, resolute) I. . . . We will oppose to it the claim that it
> does not hold this center but is instead held there as a recipient where
> what gives itself shows itself, and discloses itself given to and as a pole
> of givenness/donation, where all the givens come forward incessantly.
> At the center stands no "subject," but a receiver of the gift [*adonné*], he
> whose function consists in receiving what is immeasurably given to him,
> and whose privilege is confined to the fact that he is himself received
> from what he receives. (*BG* 322; t.a.)

This is beautifully said, but not quite accurate, because it disguises the real and profound problem this conception poses. Marion decisively remains within the coordinates of his version of the philosophy of subjectivity. His description is perhaps appropriate, although only if the concept of the saturated phenomenon is intelligible and defensible and the description is only of *finite* saturated phenomena. But as regards God it poses a profound problem. Different finite subjects can be described in this way—again, if the concept of the saturated phenomenon is accepted: they are articulated as being mutually recipients/donees *and* givers/ donators. But what cannot be given by another (finite) "subject" and what a finite "subject" cannot give to the other subject is its own Being/ existence. Giving His own Being is, however, what God does in the first place when he communicates Himself. How can this be taken into account and articulated in the absence of a comprehensive, systematic conception of reality or of Being as a whole—and how much worse is the situation if one explicitly rejects any and every such conception, as Marion does?

A comprehensive, adequate critical assessment of this position would lead far beyond the limits of this book. What follows addresses only the two most fundamental points: first, the concept of the saturated phenomenon ([3]); second, Marion's attempted reversal of the subject-object relation (4.2.3.3).

[3] The concept *saturated phenomenon,* as Marion understands and describes it, is highly problematic and ultimately not acceptable. This section raises five main objections that articulate two central topics.

[i] Marion presupposes that *intuition* is a clear and unproblematic matter: it is not. He certainly cannot understand "intuition" only or chiefly as sensible intuition in the sense of Kant, the German idealists, and many other philosophers in their wake. But it is not clear what Husserl and Marion really *do* mean when they speak of intuition. What emerges from what Marion says is this: intuition is a wholly indeterminate, undifferentiated, and confused conglomerate of heterogeneous elements: modes of seeing in any and every sense and, corresponding to them, items that are seen.

When Marion, following in Husserl's footsteps, assumes that in a given phenomenon there is an excess of intuition in relation to concept(s), he moves within a phenomenological framework, even if an unusual one; for this reason, the idea of an excess of intuition is one that is *possible* as a phenomenological idea. But Marion's interpretation of the excess is not only problematic (even from the phenomenological perspective), it is not conceivable theoretically.

Marion understands "excess" in an eminently positive sense, as an excess *in content,* and this in an extreme and total sense: what gives shows itself *as* giving *itself,* that is, it shows itself *as what it actually is.* But this could *not* be done by any intuition that exceeded any and every concept. The reason is that that intuition would be an indeterminate, confused, unarticulated, undifferentiated, obscure conglomerate. If one could speak of content at all, this content could be simply chaotic, precisely in need of clarification and articulation. Since in this case what "offers itself to us originarily in 'intuition'" is an indeterminate and confused conglomerate, it cannot "be taken quite simply as what it gives itself out to be."[59] Instead, what is offered as an indeterminate and confused conglomerate is not what is *in reality;* rather, what is offered in intuition, the phenomenon, is an *explicandum* in the first place: it is what is in need of an *explication,* until the *explicans* of what is simply offered in intuition has been made manifest. Marion's *reversal* of *explicandum* and *explicans* is characteristic of his entire procedure. It is a case of the classic *hysteron-proteron fallacy.*

[ii] The second objection points to the fact that Marion's concept of saturated phenomena is the result of a conflation of the *three distinct and mutually irreducible modes of the relation of human mind to the world* or

---

[59] Husserl, *Ideas I,* 44.

to the things in their boundless variety. The three modes or dimensions are theoreticity, practicity, and aestheticity.[60] Marion conflates the three modes/dimensions and, thus, also conflates the resulting phenomena. Of these three modes much would have to be said to make fully clear what is meant in the last analysis when it is said that Marion conflates them. Here it is possible to clarify this state of affairs only minimally.

Marion typically uses *aesthetic* attitudes and phenomena as examples of what he calls saturated phenomena. In addition, he excessively privileges the *visual perspective*, often using the German term *An-schau-ung*, whose root is *schauen*, "to see." The following passage is characteristic of his predominantly visual mode of thinking:

> Confronted with the saturated phenomenon, the *I* cannot see it, but neither can it look at it as its object. It has the eye to see it, but not to look after it [*pour le garder*]. What, then, does this eye without a look [*cet oeil sans regard*] actually see? It sees the overabundance of intuitive givenness/donation, not, however, as such, but as blurred by the overly short lens, the overly restricted aperture, the overly narrow frame that receives it—or rather, that no longer accommodates it. The eye apperceives not so much the appearance of the saturated phenomenon as the blur, the fog, and the overexposure that it imposes on its normal conditions of experience. The eye sees not so much another spectacle as its own naked impotence to constitute anything at all. . . . Through sight, it receives a pure givenness/donation, precisely because it no longer discerns any objectivizable given therein. ("SP" 119; t.a.)

First of all, this passage confirms the correctness of the critical remarks just made about Marion's concepts of *intuition* and *saturated phenomenon*. He himself, indeed, declares that "it [the I] sees the overabundance of intuitive givenness/donation, not, however, as such, but as blurred by the overly short lens, the overly restricted aperture, the overly narrow frame that receives it . . . The eye apperceives not so much the appearance of the saturated phenomenon as the blur, the fog . . ." But then how can he simply affirm: "Through sight, it receives a pure givenness/donation, precisely because it no longer discerns any objectivizable given therein"? How can the I receive a "pure givenness/donation," when according to Marion (and Husserl) it accepts the saturated phenomenon "*simply as what gives/presents itself*"[61] and this is understood and explained

---

[60] See *Structure and Being*, e.g., p. 27; section 2.2.3.1.

[61] This formulation is from a passage quoted more than once above: "The *principle of all principles: that every originary presentative intuition* [*Anschauung*] *is a legitimizing source of cogni-*

thus: "the eye apperceives not so much the appearance of the saturated phenomenon as the blur, the fog"? This is wholly unintelligible.

As indicated above, Marion relies almost exclusively on *visualizations*. Now, it is perfectly permissible to use or to appeal to visualizations in philosophy, although philosophy is a theoretical enterprise, because visualizations and visual vocabulary can be taken as metaphors—and metaphors, if rightly understood, are harmless, even if not relevant to theories. But what happens in Marion's thinking is something quite different and highly problematic: he largely conflates the theoretical, the aesthetic, and (to a lesser degree) the practical dimensions. To be sure, aesthetic and practical phenomena that appear aesthetically or practically *and are perceived aesthetically or practically* (however this perception is understood or accomplished) can be subject matters for philosophical theorization. What Marion does, however, is quite different from this.

When aesthetic and practical phenomena are made subject matters for philosophical theorization, the philosopher cannot simply (and here this means: literally) accept, as appropriate for the philosophical articulation of practical or aesthetic phenomena, *immediately* practical or aesthetic language—that is, the language that someone (an artist, a mystic, a moral agent, etc.) uses when directly engaged in practical or aesthetic experience.[62]

Philosophy is *interpretation* or, more strictly, is *theorization*. This presupposes an absolutely clear *non-identification* of the theorizing philosopher with the artist *as artist*, the mystic *as mystic*, the practical agent *as practical agent*, etc. When philosophers treat aesthetic or practical subject matters, then their attitude is neither aesthetic nor practical: it is purely *theoretical*. Only the theoretical attitude is directly focused on what the aesthetically or practically perceived object *is, in truth, in itself.* This is precisely what is articulated in true sentences about (aesthetically or practically perceived) objects or phenomena.

The next task is that of explaining what happens with Marion. This

---

tion, that *everything originarily . . . offered* to us *in 'intuition [Intuition]' is to be accepted simply as what gives/presents itself"* (quoted more extensively in 4.2.3.1[2], above; see also footnote 49, above). Marion's French version is the following: "Le principe des principes pose que . . . tout ce qui s'offre originairement à nous dans l'intuition est à prendre tout simplement pour ce qu'il se donne" ("PhS" 39).

[62] To be noted is that persons calling themselves or called by others "artists," "mystics," "practical agents," etc., do not always (and perhaps even not usually) *behave as* artists, mystics, or practical agents, which means, among other things but above all, that they do not always *speak* as artists, etc. Any such person can also speak *as* philosopher, *as* e.g., critic or interpreter of literature or of art, etc. That is why the main text uses the formulation "*immediately* practical or aesthetic language—that is, the language that someone (an artist, a mystic, a moral agent, etc.) uses when directly engaged in practical or aesthetic experience."

requires the making of some distinctions. First: his treatments of what he calls saturated phenomena contain assertions of two kinds that must be strictly distinguished from each other. Terminologically, there are various options. The distinction is between *descriptive* assertions and *philosophically interpretative-commentative-conceptional* ones, or between descriptions and interpretations or commentaries or articulations of conceptions. Marion's *descriptions* are also of two sorts, ones that are *theoretical*—that aim exclusively to express the truth of the described subject matter— and ones that are *expressive of subjective experiences*—ones that concern the experiences had by the subject doing the describing. These *expressions of experiences* are also of two sorts: some are theoretical, and some are not. The former are those describing exclusively *theoretical* experiences or ways of behaving, and the latter, those describing not theoretical but instead aesthetic or practical experiences or ways of behaving.

Marion's works contain sentences of all the kinds identified in the preceding paragraph. The problem is that they are simply intermingled, with no indications that they have different statuses and hence no indications of what the statuses of any might be. They have in common only that they all relate somehow to saturated phenomena. What this leads to becomes clear only if specific examples are considered.

What is decisive is the role played by non-theoretical descriptions that are expressive of non-theoretical experiences or modes of behavior. These descriptions aim to articulate the experiences or modes of behavior of artists *as* artists, of mystics *as* mystics, of practical agents *as* practical agents, and so forth. They are, to put it another way, non-theoretically oriented self-descriptions, statements describing non-theoretical experiences of the persons making the statements.

Including statements of these various sorts is of course fully legitimate *as long as* no inadmissible, unjustified conclusions are drawn from them. But Marion draws such conclusions. The descriptions he uses in characterizing the saturated phenomenon provide the central example. These are, in the terminology introduced above, non-theoretical descriptions expressing subjective (non-theoretical) experiences or modes of behavior. When Marion says that the eye is "blinded," that its intuition is "overexposed," etc., these are descriptions expressing non-theoretical experiences. From them, Marion draws fundamental conclusions concerning what the saturated phenomenon genuinely is: it is precisely what blinds, that whose intuition is overexposed, etc. Drawing such conclusions is precisely what is problematic and unacceptable in Marion's procedure. The simple and direct transition from non-theoretical descriptions expressing non-theoretical subjective experiences to philosophical interpretations or conceptions is illegitimate.

A typical example of a saturated phenomenon, introduced above in a different context (see 4.2.2.3[2]), is one Marion describes as follows: "[A] particular face that I love, which has become invisible not only because it dazzles me, but above all because in it I want to look and can look only at its invisible gaze [*regard invisible*] weighing on mine" ("SP" 121). This is a description of a partly practically and partly aesthetically perceived phenomenon; it is not a philosophical interpretation or conception, unless one simply conflates—as Marion does—the theoretical, the practical, and the aesthetic attitudes as well as the phenomena accessible to or through them. It is highly revelatory that in Marion's thinking the philosophical analysis of *language*, that marvelous means of articulating anything and everything that philosophy is concerned with, is almost completely absent.

[iii] The third objection targets one of the most unintelligible features of the saturated phenomenon as Marion conceives it: the feature of *absoluteness:* "In giving itself absolutely, the saturated phenomenon gives itself also as absolute—free from any analogy with the experience that is already seen, objectivized, and comprehended. It frees itself therefrom because it depends on no horizon" ("SP" 118). Once again, this is at best a description of a practically and/or aesthetically perceived or experienced phenomenon. But Marion illegitimately shifts from the description to a philosophical *interpretation* of the phenomenon and takes the two to be identical. Strictly philosophically articulated, the phenomenon is by no means "absolute": it is a phenomenon distinct from other phenomena, therefore related to them. Of course it has a horizon, as is easily shown in the case of the love phenomenon just alluded to: the person having the practical-aesthetical attitude described in the example does not at all think that she/he is making presuppositions, has a horizon, etc., but this is due precisely to the fact that she/he is behaving practically-aesthetically, *and not theoretically.*

Theoretically seen, it is clear that the "particular face that I love, which has become invisible not only because it dazzles me, but above all because in it I want to look and can look only at its invisible gaze weighing on mine" is the face of a human being, which is a being among other beings in the world, but in such a way that, as Heidegger would say, what is distinctive about it is that it is the face of a human person, having a mind endowed with an infinite transcendence, etc. The "saturated phenomenon" of the "particular face that I love" is absolutely anything but an "absolute phenomenon" in Marion's sense.

It would be simply unacceptable to assert that the theoretical attitude toward the face that I love does not have such presuppositions, such as a horizon, etc. This can be shown immediately: if this loving person at the moment of her/his having the loving relation to a face were asked, "Isn't what you love wholly fictitious?" or something of the sort, this person would immediately shift to a theoretical attitude and answer with something like, "No, I love this person, who is real, and who really has this face." This means: this person, who in the act of gazing lovingly at a face is not behaving theoretically, is *of course* implicitly presupposing that in gazing, she/he is in the real world, that the beloved person is a real person, etc.

The basic error Marion makes in characterizing the saturated phenomenon can now be briefly, precisely, and illuminatingly articulated: Marion simply and literally reproduces, on the theoretical level, the intellectual situation of the person he takes to experience what he calls a saturated phenomenon. "Intellectual situation" here means the *explicit, comprehensive understanding* that the person has of what the person is experiencing. This *explicit* comprehensive understanding is, as shown above, minimal: this person is concentrated (indeed, fixated) exclusively on what she/he is experiencing. This person does not think about precisely what this means, about the presuppositions, implications, etc., of the experience. This is shown by the consideration above of the example of gazing at the face of the beloved. Marion describes the situation of the person absorbed in the experience and simply transposes or copies it to the theoretical level, making of it a philosophical thesis. This explains the philosophically peculiar fact that he describes the saturated phenomenon as he does: he presents the saturated phenomenon as an X-in-splendid-isolation, as itself, as absolute, without conditions, without presuppositions, without relations, beyond anything conceptual. His descriptions might possibly be accurate accounts of what the person experiences. But, as shown above, that person has *implicit knowledge* of the conditions, presuppositions, relations—indeed, of the *complete* concept of what is being experienced.

From these considerations follows a centrally important consequence: the phenomenon Marion calls the "saturated phenomenon" is *not* characterized by an *excess of content* in comparison with the theoretically perceived and articulated phenomenon. The exact contrary is the case: it is characterized by a profound *deficiency* of content. The putative excess of intuition (in relation to the conceptual) is in truth the result of Marion's ignoring or making implicit (or, in a Husserlian term, bracketing) all content. The excess is in reality a deficiency.

[iv] The fourth objection to Marion's understanding of *phenomenon* is an objection to the principle that is the basis of his purportedly profound transformation of the phenomenological approach: his third reduction. The principle reads as follows:

> Appearance is always aligned with donation on the basis of the prin-
> ciple "however much reduction, that much givenness" [= the more
> strictly the reduction is applied, the more does givenness increase], . . .
> nothing manifests itself that does not give itself, and nothing gives itself
> that does not manifest itself. [*L'apparaître s'ordonne toujours la donation*
> *selon le principe 'autant de réduction, autant de donation,' . . . rien ne se montre*
> *qui ne se donne et rien ne se donne qui ne se montre.*][63]

The second clause of this sentence—"nothing gives itself that does
not manifest itself"—is unproblematic. But the first clause—"nothing
manifests itself that does not give itself"—is highly problematic. Indeed,
it is rejected, so far as the author can see, by most phenomenologists.
Obviously, from the fact that something manifests itself it does not follow that it gives itself, *if* the phrase "gives itself" is understood as Marion
understands it: as a *donation*. Such a statement could only be accepted
on the presupposition that a comprehensive philosophy of reality (of
Being!) had been developed that conceived of reality/Being as something like "universal or comprehensive donation"; in this case every particular "thing" or "datum/given" (taken initially in an unspecified sense)
could and would be considered and could and would appear as a particular mode of (the universal) donation. But such a conception could in
no sense be considered a phenomenological one. And Marion is far from
having even the slightest intention of accepting or developing a comprehensive view of reality/Being. What this shows is the scarcely deniable
fact that Marion implicitly relies on a *theological view*, whereby "theological" should be understood in the sense of philosophical theology as well
as revealed theology. This matter cannot be considered further here (but
see 4.2.4.3[6][ii], below).

[v] The fifth objection consists in demonstrating that Marion's efforts to respond to objections that are or can be raised against his conception—particularly against his fifth type of saturated phenomena,
phenomena of revelation—are utter failures. One of those objections,
and Marion's response to it, are of particular significance for the subject
matter of this book and for critical evaluation of Marion's position; it is
the focus of the following account.

Marion distinguishes between the possibility and the actuality [*effectivité*] of the phenomenon of revelation, whereby he stresses that he,
as a phenomenological philosopher, is concerned only with possibility. It

---

[63] Marion, "L'autre philosophie première et la question de la donation," 50.

remains to be seen what he means by this, how he supports his position, and whether the position is coherent.

> The phenomenon of revelation remains a mere possibility. We, indeed, will be able to describe it without presupposing its actuality [*effectivité*], and yet all the while propose a precise figure for it. . . . Phenomenology cannot decide if a revelation can or should ever give itself." (*BG* 235; t.a.)

This distinction gives rise to two very different problems, both regarding the coherence of Marion's position. The first problem results from the fact that the "actuality" of the revealed phenomenon "remains the business proper to revealed theology" (*BG* 236). That problem is not considered here. The second problem arises from the status of Marion's own enterprise with respect to transcendence and God. One of his most radical postulates says that God's transcendence should be absolutely free of every kind of constraint, of every condition, horizon, limitation, etc. And this point constitutes his most radical objection against every philosophy and/or theology that articulates the dimension of Being. He repeatedly asserts that God conceived of within the horizon of Being is in reality an idol, not the divine God. But now, Marion himself becomes aware that his own procedure, though not anything like an articulation of the dimension of Being, still could be considered a kind of precondition for conceiving of transcendence and God. He writes:

> We will say only: if an actual revelation must, can, or could have been given in phenomenal apparition, it could have, can, or will be able to do so only by giving itself according to the type of paradox par excellence—such as we will describe it. Phenomenology cannot decide if a revelation can or should ever give itself, but it (and it alone) can determine that, in case it does, such a phenomenon of revelation should assume the figure of the paradox of paradoxes. If revelation there must be (and phenomenology has no authority to decide this), then it will assume, assumes, or assumed the figure of paradox of paradoxes, *according to an essential law of phenomenality*. In this sense, because revelation remains a variation of saturation, itself a variation of the phenomenality of the phenomenon inasmuch as given, it still remains inscribed within the transcendental conditions of possibility. (*BG* 235; t.a., emphasis added)

And Marion himself raises the question:

Would we have come all this way only to recover precisely what we wanted to destroy—conditions preceding possibility and delimiting it a priori? Better, wouldn't we have recovered them precisely in regard to revelation, the very type of phenomenon that neither can nor should submit to them? [*N'aurions-nous donc parcouru tout ce chemin, que pour retrouver ce que nous voulions précisément détruire—des conditions précédant la possibilité et la délimitant a priori? Mieux, ne les retrouvons-nous précisément à propos de la révélation, le type même de phénomène qui ne peut ni ne doit par principe s'y soumettre?*]. (Ibid.; t.a.; the published English translation is strikingly incorrect)

This is a good formulation of the objection that spontaneously arises at this point. But Marion's answer is not good; quite to the contrary, it avoids the problem and it has a fatal consequence for his entire position. He answers:

In fact, it's nothing like this—here . . . the condition of possibility does not consist in rendering the phenomenon possible by delimiting it a priori by means of impossibilities but in freeing its possibility by destroying all prerequisite conditions for phenomenality, therefore by suspending all alleged impossibilities, indeed by admitting the possibility of certain ones among them. (*BG* 235–36; t.a.)

Marion's answer clearly fails to address the heart of the problem. Even if one agrees—although the author of this book does not agree— that it makes sense to speak of "freeing its [the phenomenon's] possibility by destroying all prerequisite conditions for phenomenality," the most fundamental factor, which is the *fundamental prerequisite* for having an absolutely unrestricted access to transcendence and God, according to the phenomenological approach *as Marion understands it*, remains utterly unchanged: this is that prerequisite that Marion calls *phenomenality itself*. He takes himself to free the phenomenon from all prerequisites, *except for its phenomenality*. He takes his own position to be one that has freed the phenomenon from all (pre)conditions, but he thereby completely overlooks phenomenality itself, that is, the framework or the dimension within which phenomena are what they are and can be what he supposes them to be.

Transcendence and God thus remain bound to phenomenality. Indeed, Marion states explicitly: "If revelation there must be . . . , then it will assume, assumes, or assumed the figure of paradox of paradoxes, *according to an essential law of phenomenality.*" *Phenomenality* and *its essen-*

tial laws: these are the fundamental, the effectively *limiting* conditions of possibility for revelation; revelation is bound to and, thus, limited by this precondition. And there is more: the fundamental presupposition Marion makes is just the statement that revelation is "a variation on satu-ration" (*BG* 235) or, in other words: "an actual revelation must, can, or could have been given in phenomenal apparition." He cannot conceive of revelation otherwise than on the basis or within the horizon of *phe-nomenality.*

Here a critical question arises: why must revelation, the self-communication of God, be restricted to this basis (or framework or ho-rizon)? The answer, as far as Marion's position is concerned, is clear: because, as shown above, Marion's fundamental philosophical frame-work is determined by the coordinates of the philosophy of (reversed) subjectivity. The absolute reference point is the subject, and it makes no difference that according to Marion this point is the reversed subject, the subject as "me," as the "receiver," as the one addressed (*interloqué*). It is the structure of such a reversed subjectivity with its coordinates that *determines*—a priori, of course (how else?)—what and how a revelation could or should be, i.e., the conditions that a revelation does or would have to satisfy.

This shows that Marion is not successful in his attempt to dismantle the serious objection he himself formulates against his own position. In reality, he restricts revelation—and, thus, also transcendence and God—to the laws and limits of phenomenality. These laws and limits are then "conditions preceding possibility and delimiting it a priori," conditions of precisely the sort that he "wanted to destroy" (*BG* 235). This is an immensely far-reaching restriction: the restriction to the framework of (reversed) subjectivity.

This makes clear that Marion is in no way justified in radically criti-cizing the entire tradition of Christian metaphysics. At least what chapter 1 calls and chapter 3 develops as *deep metaphysics* is *incomparably* more ade-quate to the task of addressing the questions of transcendence, God, and revelation. The chief reason for this is that this deep metaphysics does not restrict transcendence, God, or revelation in any way whatsoever. Instead, it starts with the absolutely unrestricted universal dimension (termed above the dimension of Being), with which the human mind is intentionally coextensive. It then progressively explicates this dimen-sion or, better, the dimension progressively explicates itself, such that it is revealed or manifest at an early stage of its self-explication as absolutely necessary Being and at a later stage as God. God is not thereby subjected to any restrictions of any sorts, thus to nothing like phenomenality determined by laws of subjectivity. Instead: God reveals or manifests himself as fully explicated Being.

A final remark is required concerning the tactical procedure Marion applies in his attempt to evade the just-introduced objection. The tactic aims to reverse the state of affairs in question; concretely, Marion seeks to reinterpret and to characterize those factors that, according to his own formulation of the objection, are limiting preconditions of God, such that they actually "consist in . . . freeing its possibility [i.e., the possibility of the phenomenon of revelation] by destroying all prerequisite conditions for phenomenality" (BG 235–36, quoted just above). The result, according to Marion, is that "the condition of possibility does not consist in rendering the phenomenon possible by delimiting it a priori by means of impossibilities." One is thus confronted with the following: Marion affirms the thesis that there is (or must be) a condition of possibility of the phenomenon of revelation, but contests the assertion that it "consist[s] in rendering the phenomenon [of revelation] possible"; he then maintains that the condition of possibility "consist[s] in . . . freeing" the possibility of the phenomenon of revelation.

Here again there is only play with words. Is there a contentual distinction between "rendering possible" the phenomenon of revelation and "freeing" the possibility of the phenomenon of revelation? What Marion in fact attempts to do is the following: he seeks to understand the or a condition of possibility of the phenomenon of revelation exclusively in a purely *negative* manner, such that the condition "consist[s] in . . . freeing its possibility by destroying all prerequisite conditions for phenomenality, therefore by suspending all alleged impossibilities, indeed by admitting the possibility of certain ones among them."

It suffices to present two critical remarks concerning this tactical procedure Marion introduces. First: it is incontestably clear on the basis of what is said above that this putatively purely negative move is nothing other than one side of a coin whose other side is a massively positive conception of human subjectivity and of all that belongs to it. At the center of this conception is the absolute, massively positive thesis about *pure phenomenality* and what Marion calls "an essential law of phenomenality [*une loi d'essence de la phénoménalité*]" (BG 235). And this dimension of pure phenomenality is a massively limiting (pre)condition for what Marion calls the phenomenon of revelation or God. Second: it is astonishing that Marion appears not at all to notice a consequence of his tactical procedure that is simply destructive of his entire position and *forma mentis*, i.e., that *every metaphysician* could *rightfully* characterize his own theoretical work aiming at reaching God as a "destruction of all the putative impossibilities" of talk about God. Given that, does Marion's ceaseless critique of metaphysics have a leg to stand on?

4.2.3.3 Marion's Reversal of the Subject-Object Distinction and Radicalization of the Philosophy of Subjectivity

Marion's entire endeavor aims at reversing the subject-object relation that is characteristic of the philosophy of subjectivity, as it is understood particularly by Kant and Husserl. He aims to replace the constituting I with the constituted I, which he calls "me." But this reversal—assuming, hypothetically, that it can be performed—does not free Marion from the philosophy of subjectivity. As Heidegger once said, in a sentence quoted above: "The reversal of a metaphysical statement remains a metaphysical statement" (*PM* 251). It is likewise the case that the reversal of the subject-object relation that is characteristic of the philosophy of subjectivity remains a relation that is characteristic of the philosophy of subjectivity. This is a central point for the adequate assessment of Marion's entire position. Indeed, his conception of everything, most especially of transcendence and God, hinges decisively on his maintaining fundamentally the theoretical framework *of the philosophy of reversed subjectivity.* In what follows, this stance is submitted to a critical analysis.

[1] The thesis that the subject—the *reversed subject,* the subject no longer as I, but as me—is the central point of reference for all statements and conceptions in Marion's oeuvre can be clarified by a brief, mathematically oriented exposition of the subject-object relation and its reversal. In the traditional transcendental perspective—to repeat, a perspective Marion wants to overcome in the sense that he intends to reverse it—the object can be accurately characterized as being a function of the subject: that is, there is a one-to-one function, i.e., a mapping, from the subject (or from subjectivity) ($= S$) to the object (or to objectivity) ($= O$).

The function can be formalized as follows: $f : S \to O$. The *inverse* of this function is the function $f^{-1} : O \to S$, which is obtained by reversing f. Thus, for each s in S and each o in O, if $f(s) = o$, then $f^{-1}(o) = s$. The domain of f^{-1} is thus the range of f and its range is the domain of f (i.e., that class of elements of the domain of f for which f has a value). Further, if f^{-1} is one-to-one, then its inverse, $(f^{-1})^{-1}$, is equal to f. What this shows (among other things) is that the inverse function—in the example, the reversal of the subject–object relation—depends on or is determined by the starting point—and this is the subject-object relation. The subject thus remains the determining factor.

The consequences of this for Marion's position are far-reaching and extremely serious. The following account considers only those that relate to transcendence and God.

Because the permanent point of reference is the subject = I = me, transcendence and God can be conceived of only in explicit conjunction with and on the basis of this point of reference. This has the noteworthy consequence that transcendence and God are *functions of this point of reference, of subjectivity.* The subject = I = me transcends the level of the objective pole of the subject-object relation, but it is precisely this *subject itself* that accomplishes this transcending. The major stages in this transcending are, according to Marion, the transcendental subject, then the world, and then the dimension of Being. One of his most important statements on this topic is that even this last transcendence—to Being—must be transcended, such that it is requisite that the subject = I = me transcend Being. This state of affairs is considered in greater detail further below.

It is important to note at this point that these transcendings are simply *functions, projections,* or, more accurately, self-projections of the subject = I = me. What this means is that the subject = I = me pushes its own extroversion further and further, thereby producing ever greater distantiations from itself. At the point Marion takes to be the most distant point of this extroversion procedure, he thinks he reaches the absolutely distant God whom he immediately characterizes as love/*caritas.* From Marion's statements it follows that this process or procedure is simultaneously and indissolubly progressive *and* retrogressive, is transcendence *and* retroscendence. The retroscendence is the transformation of the subject from a transcendental I to a me. But it is to be emphasized that the fixed point of this inverse-directional procedure is the starting point: the subject = I = me. God as the absolute distant other, beyond Being, is the other-of-the-subject = I = me.

Clarity is increased via consideration of the status of the sentences Marion formulates. Because Marion aims to develop a philosophical conception, it must be assumed that his sentences are *theoretical* sentences. The structure and status of such sentences can be articulated in an informal language that relies on ordinary language. The resulting articulations are complicated and far from ordinary or natural, but that is unavoidable if complete clarity concerning the theoretical character of these sentences is to be attained.

Taking as an example the sentence "God is love," as a sentence appearing within Marion's philosophy, one clear formulation would be: "It is the case that (on the basis of the structure of the particular subject = I = me it is the case that) God is love." The structure is further clarified by formalization. Let ⓉⒾ = the unrestricted theoretical operator "it is the case that," $\mathbb{T}_{PS}$ = the restricted theoretical operator "it is the case on the basis of the structure of the particularistic subject = I = me that," and ϕ = the sentence "God is love." Then the sentence "It is the case that (it is the case on the basis of the structure of the particularistic subject = I = me that) God is love" is formalized as $\mathbb{T}(\mathbb{T}_{PS}(\phi))$. The sentence, taken as a whole, is an unrestrictedly theoretical sentence, not restricted to the perspective or structure of any subject; it thus presents itself as universally valid. But within the scope of the unrestricted theoretical operator there is a sentence preceded by a restricted theoretical operator—the form that restricts the theoretical operator to a merely particularistic perspective, the perspective based on the structure of subjectivity understood as subject = I = me. The sentence "God is love," which lies within the scope of this second operator—the restricted theoretical operator—is therefore not presented as unrestrictedly true. Even if Marion conceives of God as love ("before He is"), within his theoretical framework God-as-love remains a function of reversed human subjectivity. This God cannot qualify as the genuinely divine God.[64]

What this shows is that the most important requirement that must be satisfied by any fundamentally adequate articulation of the actual, divine God is the avoidance of any restricted theoretical operator, including of course Marion's, which is based on the structure of the particular perspective of reversed subjectivity. That God is love is adequately and truthfully articulated only if *every* restriction is avoided. Such avoidance is accomplished when the sentence "God is love" is read and understood in accordance with the formalization $\mathbb{T}(\phi)$ (and not in accordance with $\mathbb{T}(\mathbb{T}_{PS}(\phi))$), thus, as follows: "It is unrestrictedly and absolutely the case that God is love."

---

[64] Guillaume de Lacoste Lareymondie comes to the same conclusion—although he uses a different terminology—in his review of Marion's *Au lieu de soi: L'approche de Saint Augustin* (2009). He writes:

One finds at the end of the Conclusion the following summary of the book's argument: "Because I (me, the ego [*moi, l'ego*]) am what I seek (the place of the *self* [*le lieu de* soi], because I am what I love, it follows that I will never cease to come to the place of the self [*je ne cesserai jamais de venir au lieu de soi*], to the degree that I sink into the inconceivable, as whose image I understand myself. There where I find God, and the more so as I continue to search for him, the more do I find myself as I do not cease to investigate that whose image I bear." Although one does not know whether the relevant verb is to be [*être*] or to follow [*suivre*] (!), it is significant that the subject of the sentence is "I." God, who because of overemphasized incomprehensibility turns out to be inconsistent, is summoned only as a mirror of the self, the sole true agent [*n'est convoqué qu'en miroir du soi, seul vrai acteur*]. (www.nonfiction.fr/article-2104-portrait_de_saint_augustin_en_proto_phenomenologue.htm [accessed December 30, 2009])

[2] It is now possible to tackle the most radical objection to Marion's position as a whole: Marion has never attempted to overcome the theoretical framework characteristic of the philosophy of subjectivity. Historically, this means that he has not taken the decisive step beyond Husserl that Heidegger took. This step is articulated by Heidegger with great brevity and clarity in a passage quoted above more than once. It is now clear that Heidegger's critique of the philosophy of subjectivity remains fully applicable if the constituting-constituted relation is reversed in the way Marion attempts to reverse it. The important point here is not that Heidegger introduces a dimension he calls "Being"; instead, it is the fact that he thematizes the reciprocal relation between what constitutes and what is constituted. Adequately thematizing this relation requires not only and not primarily thematizing each of the two relata, in isolation, because if this is all that is done the *relation as such* is not thematized at all. It is thematized only when it is seen that the relation presupposes a dimension or space within which it is situated, one that encompasses the relata and makes it possible for them to *be* relata. Heidegger designates this meta-dimension, this encompassing space, as Being. Once that dimension is identified, it is clear that the task is nothing like reversing the subject-object relation; it is instead thematizing that dimension itself, the one that makes the subject-object relation possible (no matter how the subject is understood).

This is the point to start from if one is to get to the sense of God—of the *divine God*. And this is where the author definitely parts company with Heidegger. As chapter 2 shows in detail, Heidegger's attempt to "think" Being led only to empty formulations, to tautologies, and to meaningless etymological reconstructions of words, as is made clear by his only quasi-systematic book, *Contributions to Philosophy (From Enowning)*, and his essay "Time and Being."[65]

4.2.3.3a Excursus 5: Remarks on Joeri Schrijvers's Interpretation and Critique of Marion's Reversal of the Subject-Object Distinction and on His Ambiguous Treatment of Ontotheology

In his article "Ontotheological Turnings? Marion, Lacoste and Levinas on the Decentering of Modern Subjectivity,"[66] Joeri Schrijvers extensively examines Marion's attempted reversal of the subject-object distinction. He convincingly states that "a simple reversal of the subject-object distinc-

---

[65] See *Structure and Being* 5.4.1[3]. See also "Metaphysikkritik bei Carnap und Heidegger: Analyse, Vergleich, Kritik," *SGTh* 255–87.
[66] *Modern Theology* 22 (2006): 221–54.

tion is not yet a decentering of the subject."[67] Schrijvers shows both that "such a reversal cannot escape the structure and metaphors of traditional transcendental subjectivity" and "in what manner the subject-object distinction recurs in Marion's thought and what the consequences of that recurrence might be."[68] In accurate analyses, he demonstrates that to decenter modern subjectivity by reversing intentionality, as Marion does, is to "'subjectivise' reality, a reality of which I am the object and objective. . . . To be in relation to God means that (my own) visibility is weakened to such an extent that I can be transpierced with invisibility—as if human beings are as transparent as objects!"[69] And Schrijvers attempts "to show that our relation to God must not necessarily mean that God disrespects singularities and that transcendence therefore is not indifferent to ontic and immanent differences."[70] In this context he criticizes Marion's "depiction of God's indifference to Being" and especially "what Marion regards as God's indifference to ontic differences."

At this point he—surprisingly—introduces the typical postmodernist stereotype *ontotheology:* the necessity to respect the "secret of facticity— secret, of course, since we do not know *who* we are (our privacy, in that sense)" and, in general, to respect the ontic differences in our relation to God is, according to Schrijvers, "at last a means to cope with the problem of ontotheology": "Ontotheology is also to be considered an *existential* problem."[71] How so?

The understanding and treatment of ontotheology are a weak point in Schrijvers's otherwise excellent essay. The concept is simply assumed, unexamined. And Schrijvers seems to be heedless of an ambiguity and even incoherence in his handling of this concept. Indeed, he explicitly assumes the stereotyped characterization of ontotheology, which he describes in the following terms:

> Ontotheology is given when "God" is interpreted as a means to an end, that is, when the name of God appears as a necessary function of a(ny) rational system seeking to take account of the totality of beings. In the history of philosophy, this attempt to seek an ultimate foundation for contingent and finite beings has led to the thought that only an

---

[67] Ibid., 227.
[68] Ibid.
[69] Ibid., 230.
[70] Ibid.
[71] Ibid., 221.

instance that is neither contingent nor finite could serve as the ultimate ground or foundation of this contingent world.[72]

And then, in order to reject such a view, he appeals in typical post-modernist fashion to Nietzsche as if the latter were an incontestable authority in this matter. He then argues as follows:

> An attempt to think the infinite in and through the (dialectical) negation of the finite remains trapped in the logic of finitude. It is always possible to ask how the ground, be it the *Causa sui* of modern thought, or the Ideas of Platonism, is itself grounded. As such the rational attempt to look for an ultimate foundation leads unto an infinite regress. To stop such a regress, philosophy decides to let "God" enter into its discourse. But this "God," then, is the means used to the end set out by philosophy itself: the non-contingent, non-finite, "eternal" and "otherworldly" God that grounds and justifies the finite and contingent world. In this sense, Mary Jane Rubenstein's metaphor for the God of ontotheology, a "*deus ex machina* flown in to stop a conceptual gap," is very precise.[73]

This passage concisely articulates the heart of the position that postmodernist thinkers generally take on Christian metaphysics. The first thing to observe here is that it is not clear why Schrijvers considers onto-theology, as he understands it, to be "an *existential* problem" in a *positive* sense. He wants to respect "the ontic differences in our relation to God," but then asserts that *this* is "at last a means to cope with the problem of ontotheology." Why can and/or must it be that? Be that as it may, some critical remarks on Schrijvers's characterization and assessment of onto-theology are requisite.

For strictly systematic reasons articulated in chapters 1 and 3, the author of this book is radically critical of so-called proofs of the existence of God. But his rejection is based on considerations that differ completely from the superficial manner in which postmodernist authors present their rejections of these proofs. To unmask the mode of "argumentation" leading postmodernists to their rejections, it suffices to present a simple argument from retortion (a *tu quoque* argument). One need only ask the following question: what are postmodernist Christian thinkers

---

[72] Ibid., 237.
[73] Ibid.

aiming at when they develop "conceptions" or "views" of God? What are they searching for, what are they attempting to do? One way or another, they are searching for or attempting to show something *ultimate*, even if they would not use this terminology. Indeed, this remains true even if it is explicitly denied. When postmodernists speak of God in any way whatsoever, then if what they say is to be meaningful in any sense, what they are doing must make sense. The question is not what they explicitly assert or deny, the question is what they are effectively *doing*. Postmodernist anti-metaphysical, anti-ontotheological discourse turns out to be simply nonsensical if this question is not clearly answered. But the postmodernists provide no clear answer.

Schrijvers asserts that any "attempt to think the infinite in and through the (dialectical) negation of the finite remains trapped in the logic of finitude." First, his formulation misrepresents what the entire metaphysical tradition has and has not done: it has never attempted to think the infinite purely "in and through the (dialectical) negation of the finite"; this characterization is therefore a distortion. The finite dimension has always been seen in light of or within the horizon of the infinite. Pascal's famous sentence (as clarified in 3.2.1.2)—"Man$_1$ infinitely transcends man$_2$,"—articulates exactly this absolutely central state of affairs. Second, how do postmodernist rejecters of metaphysics themselves proceed? It suffices here to refer to what is said above about the positions of Levinas and Marion.

Furthermore, Schrijvers states that "it is always possible to ask how the ground, be it the *Causa sui* of modern thought, or the Ideas of Platonism, is itself grounded." Such a statement reveals a deep methodological, conceptual, and logical deficiency with respect to the meaning and the systematic status of such central concepts as *ground* and *grounded*. Schrijvers simply assumes that the absolutely *unrestricted* use or application of such concepts is completely unproblematic and even compelling. Hence, if one speaks of a last ground, the concept *ground* is applied again: What is the ground of the (allegedly last) ground? What is the X that is more ultimate than the (allegedly) ultimate X? And so forth. This could be described accurately as a wild (or blind) manner of thinking.

In reality, even a superficial analysis shows that all such concepts have meanings and appropriate, i.e., intelligible *and defensible*, applications *only within determinate theoretical frameworks*, with the consequence that every *regressus in infinitum* is radically excluded. The specter of the *regressus in infinitum* emerges only within manners of thinking that have never been subjected to careful and rigorous examination. This is shown above in the specific case of Thomas Nagel (1.5).

Contrary to Schrijvers's statement that "Mary Jane Rubenstein's metaphor for the God of ontotheology, a '*deus ex machina* flown in to stop a conceptual gap,' is very precise," it follows from the remarks made above and from the conception propounded in chapter 3 not only that this "metaphor" is not precise, but that it is worse than a caricature: it is a falsifying distortion, based on stereotyped assumptions and ideas. Even if one rejects what—ambiguously and erroneously—is called "the metaphysical God," it can in no justifiable sense be said that this "metaphysical" God is "flown in to stop a conceptual gap." Such an assertion completely ignores the fundamental fact that traditional Christian metaphysics, as exemplarily represented by Thomas Aquinas, had high theoretical standards: a proof was a proof (according to the logical rules of the accepted logic, namely Aristotelian logic). And the conclusion of a proof or demonstration can *in no way* be interpreted to have been drawn "to stop a conceptual gap" (as this is understood in Rubinstein's quotation). Instead, conclusions make explicit what premises entail—and premises do not entail anything like "a conceptual gap" that could or should be stopped.

As shown in chapters 1 and 3, the problem with these "proofs of the existence of God" lies in the fact that the starting point has always been an isolated phenomenon in the world. Moreover, as is remarked there, these proofs were/are only a superficial phenomenon within Christian metaphysics, as becomes manifest when one attends to what this book terms deep metaphysics. When one treats the so-called question of God within the scope of deep metaphysics, one must say that God is what emerges when the universal dimension of Being is thoroughly and consequently explicated. Such explication is not undertaken in order to stop a putative conceptual gap; instead, thoroughly explicating the universal dimension of Being excludes every intention or idea of stopping a conceptual gap. The explication of the universal dimension of Being is the result of the most radical and complete actualization of the intellectual capabilities of the human mind.

4.2.4 Marion's Failed "Access to Transcendence [to God] Without Condition or Measure"[74]

As shown in section 4.2.3, Marion's position and its problems derive fundamentally from the phenomenological approach as he understands and develops it. But he has another in many respects equally fundamental line of thinking, one intimately connected with but also distinct from his

---

[74] "IM–G" 20.

phenomenological approach. This subsection reconstructs and critically examines that second line of thinking.

From the feature of his concept of the saturated phenomenon Marion calls "the *absoluteness* of the phenomenon," i.e., the saturated phenomenon's independence from every horizon, from every condition whatsoever, he implicitly draws a richly consequential conclusion that he introduces by means of the following question: "Do we have access to transcendence without condition or measure?" ("IM–G" 20). To this question Marion sometimes presupposes and sometimes explicitly elaborates an answer, basing it on two procedures. The first is negative and the second is positive. The latter has two subprocedures: first, a philosophico-theological[75] subprocedure consisting in the utterly immediate introduction of God as "instaurating" himself as God ("IM–G" 20) and in the making explicit of "God's point of view"; second, a phenomenological subprocedure relying on the concept of the phenomenon, especially in the sense of the fifth type of saturated phenomenon (see 4.2.4.2[1], below, and *BG* 235). The following critical account shows that these two subprocedures or positive factors decisively condition each other.

4.2.4.1 Marion's Groundless Radical Rejection of Metaphysics (of Being) Based on a Misinterpretation

[1] Marion's negative procedure consists in radically rejecting every metaphysics. The rejection is based on the theses that every metaphysics is a thinking of Being, and that Being can be conceived of only as some kind of limiting horizon. Marion's reliance on these theses is evident in the following passages:

> When it comes to God, the relationship between assent and existence is likely to invert itself. It follows from this that Being, insofar as it claims the title of horizon or transcendental, offers no privileged access to the question of God and provides no grounds for a decision procedure. Rather it disconnects God and Being absolutely. ("IM–G" 19; t.a.)

> Transcendence that is taken according to *these* [namely, metaphysical] meanings does not open up transcendence but instead slams it shut. ("IM–G" 20)

---

[75] The terms "philosophico-theological" and "philosophical theology" are introduced in order to qualify a discourse different from the discourse of what in the tradition and today is termed "revealed theology."

Marion argues here in a curious fashion. He begins with "the model of questions concerning things of the world" (ibid., 19) and maintains that in asking such questions we are especially concerned with the Being or existence of things in that we distinguish between Being/existence and the things themselves. He then maintains that questions of this kind cannot be posed of God, explaining this as follows:

> If God by definition surpasses the regime of common experience
> and the conditions it sets on what is possible in a worldly sense (and
> God would not, otherwise, deserve the title "God" since he would be
> a worldly phenomenon among others), in what way would his exis-
> tence (which is to say his inscription among phenomena existing in
> the world) serve as the criterion for my belief or rejection? ("IM–G"
> 19–20; t.a.)

This passage makes fully clear how Marion understands (or mis-understands) Being. He simply equates Being with existence, and then interprets both on the basis of things in the world. God's existence would then be "his inscription among phenomena existing in the world." This is an astonishing assertion. In light of what chapter 1 shows about Being (*esse*) in the thought of Thomas Aquinas, and chapter 2, about Being (*Sein/Seyn*) in the thought of Heidegger, it is clear that Marion's way of proceeding is far below the level of philosophical sophistication that has been attained for a long time.

A text quoted above speaks of "assent and existence." Marion's com-ments about these are fundamentally epistemically oriented. But he him-self then criticizes "identifying the question of God with my belief [in God]" ("IM–G" 20), saying,

> This [identification] is characteristic of a very peculiar theoretical
> stance, which assumes that the question of God requires that a prelimi-
> nary question first be answered regarding his existence, and therefore
> that a proof of his existence be supplied. The underlying assumption is
> nothing less than the perfect hegemony, without exception, of the hori-
> zon of Being, such as metaphysics understands it. ("IM–G" 20)

In opposition, Marion emphasizes that God is subjected to no con-ditions, no horizon, etc. "God can only be instaurated as God on the basis of his pre-ontological condition and pre-transcendental freedom" ("IM–G" 20). But Marion's presupposed and at times articulated under-standing of Being has absolutely nothing to do with Aquinian *esse* or with primordial Being as introduced and explicated in chapter 3. Remarks made earlier in this chapter clarify other aspects of the two texts quoted above in this section. The following sections introduce other central aspects of his position in appropriate systematic contexts.

4.2.4.2 The Arbitrariness and Ambiguity of Marion's Immediate Move to "God's Point of View"

Above (see 4.2.4), in the consideration of Marion's account of our putative "access to transcendence [to God] without condition or measure" ("IM–G" xx), a negative and a positive procedure are identified. The preceding section examines the negative one; this one begins to treat the positive one by considering the first of its two subprocedures.

The first positive subprocedure consists of two steps.

[1] The first step is the introduction of what can be called, polemically but accurately, a deus ex machina. Marion describes God's sudden appearance on the world's stage as follows: "Before the world comes into Being, and thus before Being unfolds its horizon, God imposes straightaway his question—a question that no one is free to avoid since God defines himself, prior to any proof of existence, as 'the one whom everyone knows, by name'"[76] ("IM–G" 20).

How Marion speaks of God here is astonishing, precisely in light of his own other works. Apparently forgetting what he has often written about God as the "wholly other," and imitating the styles of some of the worst Christian metaphysicians, he seems to imagine God appearing in the universal theater (whatever that may be) still devoid of theatergoers ("before Being unfolds its horizon" . . .) and straightaway imposing ("*impose d'emblée*") "his question." What is meant here by "his question"? Given that nothing other than God is or exists, God's question can be addressed only to God. But then who is it that is not free to avoid the question? This simply makes no sense.

The least one can say of such a formulation is this: it reveals an immense theoretical naïveté, in Husserl's sense of "naïveté." What is it intended or supposed to prove or clarify? By saying that "God defines himself, prior to any proof of existence, as 'the one whom everyone knows, by name,'" Marion commits another *hysteron-proteron* fallacy, because it is not at all clear what the word "God" in his statement really means.

Marion wholly ignores all such objections and requirements by simply stating that God is not subjected to any questions, restrictions, requirements, demands, etc., that he is absolutely unconditioned in every

---

[76] Marion cites Jules Renard, *Journal 1887–1910* (1960), 227; see note 27, above.

sense and respect. He presents a deus ex machina by maintaining that "*God institutes himself as God* in no other way than on the basis of his pre-ontological condition and pre-transcendental freedom" ("IM–G" 20; t.a., emphasis added)."God institutes himself as God": this is the result of a colossal theoretical tour de force.

Granted, some of Marion's phrases ("God institutes himself . . .") can be given defensible meanings, but those are not the meanings they have in Marion's works. If it is clear in what sense there is talk of God and that what is meant is the God that *is,* then such phrases can serve to characterize God. Marion, however, radically vaults over the question concerning the meaning of talk about God. Following his (il)logic, he would say that the critique formulated here subjects God to a condition, namely, the following: if it is clear what "God" means, then. . . . But this counter-critique dissolves because it presupposes that it is clear what is meant when it speaks of a condition to which "God" is subjected. The putative condition (if one can even speak in this case of a condition) is nothing other than the articulation of something presupposed by all talk, i.e., that it makes sense. Moreover, what follows shows that Marion himself attempts to do what he radically rejects both in the passage cited above and often elsewhere: he attempts to clarify the meaning of talk about God.

[2] Marion's second step makes explicit a point of view on which all of his thought on the question of God relies, albeit elsewhere only implicitly: *the point of view of God himself.* Marion characterizes this second step as follows: "The task is to transcend our own finite point of view in order to pass over to God's point of view—or at least to aim for it, to admit it as an intention" ("IM–G" 34). Marion constantly proceeds on the implicit assumption that he has succeeded in taking this step. This explains his uncompromising attitude as regards all questions about God's existence or Being and the like: nothing like demands, criteria, or need of justification can be imposed on God. And Marion himself speaks as if he has constant access to God's point of view. No doubt, *if* God's point of view is not, for us humans, a chimera, is not a hubris, if it is not the result of a profound mistake and irresponsibility, if it is not an absolute impossibility, but an immediately accessible reality, then, of course, Marion is right. But is the concept *God's point of view,* as Marion understands, explains, and uses it, coherent and clear? It is not.

Marion's position on this central matter, presented and therefore to be assessed as philosophical, is an arbitrary one based on a profound confusion and mistake, as is demonstrated shortly below. First, however, it is important to note that there is precisely one situation in which it makes sense for theoreticians to speak of and from "God's point of view":

this is the wholly specific theological situation in which one takes the Bible to be God's word and the specific task to be that of interpreting it. When one quotes and interprets the Bible in the execution of this task, one can speak sensibly *of* God's point of view and to a certain extent also *from* God's point of view. To be sure, this cannot be understood in an absolute sense, namely in the sense that the theologian would speak "from God's point of view" *simpliciter,* without any restrictions, because this would mean for the theologian to put himself simply in the place of God. On the contrary, for the theologian who is at work on the task in question, "speaking of and/or from God's point of view" means that he *as-a-human-being* is considering, interpreting, and arguing in favor of what he takes to be God's point of view. This cannot be considered further here.

Things change completely if the theoretical situation is not the one described in the preceding paragraph, i.e., if the Bible is not taken to be God's word and therefore not considered as an absolute authority. If in the case of Marion it is not, then Marion's discourse is purely philosophical. It is therefore important to ask whether Marion's discourse is philosophical or instead theological. Many interpreters of his writings, including the author of this book, hold that in his discourse there is no clear distinction between philosophical and theological discourse.[77] In lieu of discussing this issue, which would lead it far afield, this book assumes that at least in his recent essay "The Impossible for Man—God," Marion intends, on the whole and particularly in the essential sections (not in the conclusion), and despite his inclusion of passages from the Bible, to proceed philosophically. Given this assumption, the task is that of assessing, *as philosophical,* the thesis that "the task is to transcend our own finite point of view in order to pass over to God's point of view."

Undoubtedly, human beings can have quite different points of view concerning all possible questions, problems, states of affairs, etc. Undoubtedly, they can transcend one determinate point of view in order to assume another; they can also assume another person's point of view, they can transcend a limited point of view in order to assume a superior point of view, they can transcend a particularistic point of view in order to assume a universal point of view, and so forth. All these changes of points of view make sense, but the reason they make sense is that *all* these points of view remain *within* the possibilities and capabilities of what generally can be called the dimension of the human mind. But what does it mean to say that we, human beings, could or should "transcend our own finite point of view"? Herein lies Marion's ambiguity or, more exactly, his mistake.

To "transcend our own finite point of view" means for Marion simply to take God's point of view. From this it follows that he understands (or must understand) "our finite point of view" simply as the point of view that characterizes us *as* human beings/minds *simpliciter,* since the result of transcending it, as he articulates that result, is taking God's point of view, thus the point of view of someone totally distinct from human beings, from the human dimension.

It is nonsensical to presuppose or to demand that we, as human beings, could or should jump out of our human dimension or human condition, but it is not nonsensical to raise the question of whether there is something *positive* in the fundamentally mistaken idea of "transcend[ing] our finite point of view." The answer to the question is that there is, and to see what it is requires attending to two things. The first is that one should not simply identify "our own *finite* point of view" with "the human being's/mind's point of view *simpliciter*"; the second is that, as a consequence, one should not simply oppose "our finite point of view" and "God's point of view" and, therefore, not simply speak of "transcend[ing] our own finite point of view in order to pass over to God's point of view." These points require elaboration.

As chapter 3 shows, a primordial characteristic of the human mind is its intentional coextensionality with the unrestricted universe of discourse, which is more determinately the universal dimension *simpliciter,* yet more determinately the primordial dimension of Being and, finally, when fully explicated, God himself. The human mind *is not* this dimension; it is only intentionally coextensive with it. There is absolutely no point in thinking of or assuming anything beyond this dimension and, therefore, in entertaining the possibility or undertaking the project of transcending it. From this it directly follows that *our so-called human point of view, when it is understood in its entire universality, is coextensive with the un-transcendable, primordial dimension of Being.* This requires further clarification.

Chapter 3 presents God as the full *explicatum* of the universal dimension of primordial Being, as fulfilled Being. Does it follow from this that our human point of view is the same as (is identical with) the point of view of the universal dimension, the dimension of primordial Being? Strictly speaking, there is only *coextensivity,* and coextensivity is not simply identity. But in the course of philosophical theorization the difference can often be neglected, so the two points of view need not always be explicitly distinguished. Chapter 3 shows that this general point of view is the one presupposed (and implicitly articulated) by *every theoretical sentence;* indeed, it is the point of view expressed by the universal theoretical operator "It is the case that. . . ."

As the universal dimension of Being is articulated with increasing adequacy, increasing care must be taken with the term "point(s) of view." The general coextensivity between the human universal theoretical point of view and the universal dimension of Being remains firm, but the more fully the universal dimension of Being is determined, the greater is the difference between the attained degrees of determination of Being itself and of human Being and, thus, of the human point of view. The maximal degree of determination of Being itself is its determination *as God,* which is, consequently, the point of maximal difference from human Being and, thus, from the human point of view. This maximal difference is what characterizes and constitutes *God's transcendence* with respect to human beings and all finite beings *within God's immanence.* At this stage of determination the difference between the universal theoretical *human* point of view and God's point of view emerges as absolutely un-transcendable, un-surmountable. It is then evident that there is no point in attempting to transcend our own human point of view *in the sense of our universal theoretical point of view* in order to pass over to God's point of view.

4.2.4.3 The Incoherence of Marion's Phenomenological Usage of Negative and Positive Concepts in Talk About God

The second positive subprocedure Marion develops in attempting to gain access to transcendence and to God is based in his idea of *phenomenality.* Here the interdependence of his two modes of procedure, the philosophico-theological and the phenomenological, is especially striking. Thoroughgoing critical analysis would require working step-by-step through Marion's essay "The Impossible for Man—God." This section presents an analysis that is thorough, but is not fully detailed and not complete in every respect.

[1] Marion motivates his phenomenological subprocedure with the following question, introduced above: "Do we have access to a transcendence without condition or measure?" ("IM–G" 20). From his phenomenological position, especially as regards the "absoluteness" of the saturated phenomenon, he develops a positive answer.

Simply presupposing "God" (as "the one whom everyone knows, by name," as he says, quoting Jules Renard),[78] Marion next formulates a the-

---

[78] See footnote 76, above.

sis that he takes to be a further consequence of the negative procedure described above, i.e., his total rejection of metaphysics. The thesis is that within the framework of any philosophy of Being, only beings can manifest themselves as phenomena. The account presented above shows that this thesis is false. Marion, however, relies on it to support the contention presented by way of the following rhetorical question: "If, on the one hand, the horizon of Being does not allow us to stage what is properly at stake in the knowledge we have of God's name; if, on the other hand, nothing appears within this horizon that is not a certificate-bearing being [*à titre d'étant*]: Must we not conclude that there is no possible phenomenalization of God and, moreover, that this very impossibility defines God?" ("IM–G" xx).

From this false thesis about the metaphysics of Being, in conjunction with his phenomenological assumptions, Marion draws the conclusion that God is "the Impossible." This conception of God is the most important philosophical thesis about God—in any case, the most original—that Marion has formulated. But what does "possible/impossible" mean in Marion's formulation(s)? He himself asks the question and gives an answer with which his entire theoretical philosophico-theological enterprise stands or falls. He says: "The terms refer to experience, namely to what experience allows and excludes—therefore to what *may* or *may not* appear and let itself be seen, the phenomenon" ("IM–G" 20–21).

This answer is Marion's version of one of the most fundamental theses of the philosophy of subjectivity, a thesis Kant formulates as follows: "The postulate of the *possibility* of things . . . requires that their concept agree with the formal conditions of an experience in general" (*CPuR* B267). Whether any item whatsoever—thus including all of reality, all beings, the world, and God—is possible *in this* (transcendental) *sense* depends *wholly* on whether it satisfies the conditions subjectivity dictates for what it can experience; whatever does *not* satisfy those conditions is *impossible*, again of course in this transcendental sense. Subjectivity remains, to repeat the famous Protagorean sentence quoted above in chapter 3, "the measure of all things, of the things that are that [or how] they are, of the things that are not that [or how] they are not."[79] This is a purely transcendental sense of possibility/impossibility, so Marion's understanding of these modalities is best characterized as a version of the *transcendental-phenomenological* concept of possibility/impossibility. It is immediately clear that this concept is quite narrowly restricted and thus impoverished. That it is requires no argument, because it is immediately evident that accepting such a concept would have the consequence

---

[79] Plato, *Theaetetus* 152a.

of arbitrarily and incoherently imposing on our intellectual capabilities extraordinarily narrow limits. But this is exactly what Marion does, as shown in what follows.

Having restricted the scope of the possible in the manner just indicated, Marion attempts to make a virtue of his poverty. In order to avoid concluding simply that God does not satisfy the conditions of subjectivity, he applies a form of his reversal principle. The result of its application is the characterization of God as "the Impossible" *simpliciter*. But, as shown above, every reversal of this sort remains within the framework from which the reversal aims to escape. In the case of possibility/impossibility understood with respect to experience/phenomenon and God, the result is that God as the Impossible is simply and exclusively viewed and determined from the perspective of subjectivity and its structure; God is simply a function of subjectivity. Marion's "God's instituting himself" is a God who is a function of and the result of the reduction to the measure of reversed phenomenological subjectivity. Not surprisingly, this powerfully reconfirms the conclusions drawn from the critical considerations presented above.

[2] Marion takes additional steps. The phenomenological approach, which in this case derives directly from Kant's transcendental position, implies as regards intuition and concept(s) what Kant famously stated: "Intuition and concepts . . . constitute the elements of all our cognition, so that neither concepts without intuition corresponding to them in some way nor intuition without concepts can yield a cognition."[80] To Marion's conception of intuition, completely inspired by Kant and Husserl, some critical remarks are presented above (see 4.2.4.1). Marion never attempts to clarify what concepts are, instead simply sticking to the purely mentalistic understanding of them that is characteristic of modern philosophy (with the possible exception of Hegel). But this understanding can no longer simply be assumed, particularly after the linguistic turn initiated by Frege. Most especially the introduction of the so-called *context principle*, which attributes semantic primacy to sentences rather than to words, could be the basis for a genuine revolution in philosophy.

The structural-systematic philosophy does not recognize concepts as, so to speak, primitive mentalistic, semantic, or theoretical items not reducible to anything else; on the contrary, it interprets and explains

---

[80] Kant, *Critique of Pure Reason*, B74. See also B75: "Thoughts without content are empty, intuitions without concepts are blind." The first clause is often rephrased as "Concepts without intuitions are empty." See Mario Caimi, "Gedanken ohne Inhalt sind leer," *Kant-Studien* 96 (2005): 135–46.

them as being colloquial and comfortable abbreviations of sentences that express propositions. This cannot be explained here.[81] It suffices to say here that reinterpretation involves not only focusing on sentences rather than on words (subjects and predicates), but also accepting as philosophical only sentences that do not have the subject-predicate structure. This does not mean that sentences having the subject-predicate *syntactic* structure cannot be used; what is required is that such sentences be reinterpreted *semantically* as convenient abbreviations of (typically great numbers of) prime sentences, that is, sentences that do not have the subject-predicate structure.[82] The shift from words (singular terms and predicates) to sentences completely overcomes the mentalistic framework or schema relying on concepts and intuitions. This requires thorough revision of traditional notions of concepts and intuition, but that cannot be further considered here.

Considerations on the basis of his transcendental-phenomenological understanding of "(im)possibility" and of his unmediated assumption of God as "the one whom everyone knows, by name"[83] lead Marion to "conclude, regarding God, that all we ever find is a triple impossibility—impossibility with regard to intuition; impossibility with regard to concept; and impossibility, therefore, with regard to experiencing the slightest phenomenon" ("IM–G" 24). But Marion fails both to clarify and to legitimate his statement that God is the impossible for man, which amounts to saying: the impossible for or according to the theoretical framework of (reversed) subjectivity. Because of this failure, the following question becomes unavoidable: why identify the unlimitedly indeterminate space of "the impossible" with God? Such an identification is unintelligible.[84]

---

[81] See *Structure and Being* 3.1.2.1.

[82] See sections 2.7[2] and 3.1.2[2][iii] above; and *Structure and Being* 3.2.2.4.

[83] See footnote 27 to chapter 1 (p. 41) and footnote 76 to this chapter (p. 370), above.

[84] Even some postmodernist philosophers and theologians strongly criticize Marion's conception. A case in point is John D. Caputo, who sees Marion's beginning directly with God beyond Being as incoherent. According to him it is "risky to begin with the Wholly Other, to insist throughout on utter alterity," because

> then things begin to slip a little and we will begin to lose our grip. We will not know what is wholly other, whether it is God or something else, or whether it even has a *what*. We will not know whether *wholly other* is a predicate of some being, however exalted, or itself a subject, or a quasi-subject, some kind of dark halo of indeterminacy and anonymity that surrounds and eventually seeps into—and saturates—our lives. (Caputo, "God Is Wholly Other," 191)

Caputo's paper appeared long before Marion published "The Impossible for Man—God." Of Marion's "the Impossible" Caputo would presumably say more or less what he says of the "Wholly Other" in the passage just quoted.

[3] On this point there is a striking analogy between Thomas Aquinas and Marion. A chapter 1 shows (see 1.3.2.1[2]), Aquinas committed a significant methodological error by adding to the conclusions of each of his five ways the phrase "and that we all call God." Marion proceeds similarly, asserting that "the Impossible, as the concept above all concepts, designates what we know only by name—God" ("IM–G" 26). But there is a significant difference: Aquinas's proceeding from each conclusion to the genuine God is more intelligible than is Marion's abrupt theoretical leap from "the Impossible" to "God" and, specifically, to "God as charity" (see "IM–G" 38). Aquinas introduces God as creator on the basis of purely philosophical arguments, and adds such additional determinations as trinity and love on the basis of clearly articulated methodological steps that rely on his acceptance of what he calls revealed truth. When Marion moves from "the Impossible" to "God as *caritas*," on the other hand, he makes no clear methodological or theoretical distinction between philosophical and (biblical-) theological steps. Nevertheless, it appears clear that his moves both to the concept *the impossible* and to the identification of the impossible with God (in general, not as *caritas*) are purely philosophical.

Interpreting Marion's procedure as philosophical also shows that both thinkers attempt to attain access to God by developing what is traditionally called *theologia naturalis,* although they profoundly diverge with respect to the methodological status and to the contents of their versions of this discipline. Consideration of the ultimate and decisive coordinates of Aquinas's thinking reveals that he gains access to God through his metaphysics of Being: in the course of the explication of *esse,* God appears as *esse,* fully explicated. In a nutshell: access to God is through *esse.* Marion, on the other hand, speaks not of Being, but of the impossible. He could not be clearer on this point: "The only possible pathway to God emerges in, and goes through, the impossible [*Le seul chemin possible vers Dieu s'ouvre dans l'impossible et passe par lui*]" ("IM–G" 26). His access to God is through the impossible.

Two points must be made about this difference between how Aquinas proceeds and how Marion proceeds. First, whereas Aquinas's rational procedure is fully coherent, that is not the case for Marion's, because Marion insists—as shown and criticized in detail above—that God cannot be subjected to any conditions, horizons, restrictions, or the like. Given, however, that Marion rejects traditional natural or rational theology, whose most important form is the Christian-oriented metaphysics of Being, on the basis of his charge that for that theology, Being is a restriction or condition placed on God, the question arises whether *his* access to God by way of the impossible itself involves a restrictive horizon.

If the two processes involve different forms of access to God, why should one introduce a restriction and the other not? Marion's uncompromising statements, quoted in various places above, exclude *every* access to God, of any and every sort. When he then claims access to God, a serious problem of coherence arises.

Also to be asked is how intelligible each of the two modes of access is, and whether either raises additional problems. The phrase "access to God by way of Being" is succinct and inadequate, so easily misunderstood. As explained thoroughly in chapter 3 and emphasized in various other passages in this book, according to deep metaphysics Being and God are nothing like the distinct dimensions Marion takes them to be. Instead—to use a drastic and unusual formulation—Being *is* God, but not yet fully unfolded (in the sense of: not yet fully explicated). God is fully explicated Being—fulfilled Being or the fullness of Being.

[4] But how is Marion's relation between the impossible and God to be understood? It appears clear that there cannot be a *positive* relation that is in any way comparable to that between Being and God within deep metaphysics. The move from the impossible to God is instead an unintelligible leap—not, as in the move from Being to God, a relation of explication. The reason for this difference is that Marion's concept *the impossible* arises within his philosophy of subjectivity; in the Kantian formulation quoted above, what is impossible (in this sense) is what "does *not* agree with the formal conditions of an experience in general." It is thus a purely relative negation, a negation relative to the structure of subjectivity. This is wholly different from the *esse* of deep metaphysics, which is not defined or determined by any kind of relation to subjectivity, but instead explicates itself *as itself*.

What the distinction just articulated reveals is that it is *not Being* that subjects God to any condition, horizon, restriction, or anything of the sort, and thereby fails adequately to articulate him (or indeed, as Marion says, makes of him an "idol"; see 4.2.5, below); it is instead *Marion's concept, the impossible,* that subordinates God to the conditions dictated by subjectivity.

[5] Of special importance for the purposes of this book is Marion's rigidly maintained *impossibility of the concept* with respect to God, which he—on the basis of his phenomenological framework—explains as follows: "[I] cannot— . . . by definition—legitimately assign any concept to God, since every concept, by implying delimitation and comprehension, would contradict God's sole possible definition, namely that God transcends all delimitation and therefore all definitions supplied by my finite mind" ("IM–G" 21–22).

This is among the statements that best characterize Marion's *forma mentis:* within a single sentence he first says that something cannot be done, and then proceeds to do it. In the sentence just quoted, Marion first says that *no concept*—by definition—can be assigned to God, but then states that there is solely one possible *definition of God,* namely that "God transcends all delimitation and therefore all definitions supplied by my finite mind." Definitions (to use Marion's language) delimit concepts, thereby making them comprehensible; Marion's "God's sole possible definition" makes explicit the concept of "God's-transcending-all-delimitation-and-therefore-all-definitions-supplied-by-our-finite-minds" (or: the concept *God is the X that transcends all delimitation and therefore all definitions supplied by my finite mind*). Marion assigns *precisely this concept* directly to God. This, however, flatly contradicts his statement that we "cannot . . . legitimately assign any concept to God."

And there is more: Marion attempts to support this last statement by saying that "every concept [implies] delimitation and comprehension." If this is so, then he must *also* say that the concept *God's-transcending-all-delimitation-and-therefore-all-definitions-supplied-by-our-finite-minds* implies delimitation and comprehension. But then how can *this* concept be assigned to God? Finally, how can Marion state that "God's sole possible definition" says "that God transcends all delimitation *and therefore all definitions* supplied by my finite mind"? Is "God's sole possible *definition*" not a *definition*? Is it not supplied by a finite human mind? By whom or by what is it then supplied? Because it is a definition presented by Marion, "God's sole possible *definition*" is, of course, supplied by his finite mind. So, according to Marion, God must transcend also what "God's sole possible definition" says or expresses. So, according to Marion, the "sole possible definition of God" says nothing about God.

Marion might attempt to respond to this objection. No response is formulated in the passage under consideration, but one could be drawn from other passages in his essay. The answer would require shifting to God's point of view. This Marion takes himself, simply and uncritically, to be able to do: he takes himself to be able to clearly distinguish between what belongs to our conceptualization and what belongs to God himself, to God's point of view. This ability provides him with a kind of magic wand whose waving he takes to enable him to get rid of all problems concerning God. For example, if problems arise because of a contradiction between concepts, he simply waves his magic wand to resolve them. As regards such concepts he asks, "How does a concept contradict itself?" And he answers:

> According, obviously, to the norms, rules and axioms of conceptualization. One cannot speak of absolute contradiction, but only always

of *contradictio in conceptu*.[85] Now what concept other than one of *our own representation* can be at stake here? . . . The representable and the non-representable come into play only within *our* conceptualization; therefore within our finite conception; therefore within our finitude. There is no contradiction other than what is conceivable, and nothing is conceivable that is not within *our own conceptualization*—and therefore *quoad nos*, for us, for our finite mind. ("IM–G" 30)

[6] Marion's magic wand applies most magically to the concepts *possibility* and *impossibility*. This can be illustrated by considering the central aspect of his radical reinterpretation of the so-called *ontological argument*. He says:

The chief difficulty, contrary to what is stubbornly claimed and repeated, does not lie in the illegitimacy of passing from a concept to existence as a position external to the concept. It lies instead, far more radically, in assuming that a concept adequately defines the divine essence in the first place. The argument inevitably results in forging an idol of "God." ("IM–G" 28)[86]

---

[85] Marion quotes Descartes, "Lettre à Arnauld," from July 29, 1648, in *Oeuvres de Descartes*, ed. Adam and Tannery, vol. 5, p. 223.

[86] Significantly, Marion completely misunderstands and misrepresents the ontological argument. He presents a reinterpretation made possible only by his basic phenomenological assumptions. Indeed, he fails to distinguish between two very different states of affairs or issues that have been confused throughout the history of this argument and also of the other (the so-called classical) arguments for the existence of God. It is one thing to prove the existence of X; it is a quite different thing to identify X with Y. If the identification of X with Y is incorrect, then the proof of the existence of X clearly is not a proof of the existence of Y.

To show that Marion's reinterpretation fails, it suffices to consider a concise and simplified version of the argument as it is presented by Anselm of Canterbury. Anselm begins with a definition: God = that thing than which nothing greater can be conceived (*id quo maius cogitari nequit*). What then happens in his argument? What the argument purports to prove is *only* the existence of "that thing than which nothing greater can be conceived." This—and only this—is the conclusion in the strict sense. But on the basis of his initial definition, he simply identifies "that thing than which nothing greater can be conceived" with "God," and concludes that the proof is of God's existence. But, of course, this identification can and must be contested and Anselm, as a great Christian theologian, evidently knew very well that "God" cannot simply and adequately be identified with "that thing than which nothing greater can be conceived," because "that thing" lacks qualifications it would require in order to deserve the name "God." Simply identifying this thing with God was and is a tremendous *methodological* error. Interestingly, as is noted above more than once, Thomas Aquinas also commits such an error, not at the beginning (as Anselm does), but at the end of each of his five ways, in addenda to the conclusions proper: having arrived at the

Marion calls this an aporia and asks how it could be overcome. His answer is a kind of summary of his entire procedure in treating the topic "God":

> [The aporia can be overcome] by renouncing all presumed concepts of God and rigorously sticking to his incomprehensibility. Yet how are we to conceive this incomprehensibility in such a way as still to be able to think at all? By conceiving it not only as the impossibility of every concept, but also as the concept of impossibility—impossibility, namely, as the distinctive hallmark of God's difference with regard to man. Concerning God, indeed, we cannot without contradiction assume any concept other than the concept of impossibility to mark his specific difference—God, or what is impossible for *us*. From the moment that we substitute, for a comprehensible concept, the incomprehensible concept of the impossible, the whole [ontological] argument is turned down: It no longer proves God's existence, but the impossibility of his impossibility, and therefore his possibility. God turns out to be the one whose possibility remains forever possible, precisely because it turns out that nothing remains impossible for him, especially not himself. The necessity of God's possibility flows from the impossibility of his impossibility. ("IM–G" 28–29)

This text is a magnificent example of an unrestrained play on words. Only a few points need be noted here.

[i] As regards the ontological argument: even if one were willing to grant—for the sake of argument—that it makes sense to "substitute, for a comprehensible concept, the incomprehensible concept of the impos-

---

conclusion that, to take one example, there is (exists) a first mover, he then adds: ". . . and that all call God." As noted above, this methodological error has had devastating effects in the history of Christian thinking.

As regards Marion's reinterpretation of the ontological argument, the fact that he fails to make the distinction just introduced and explained leads him to introduce strange and arbitrary contentions; for example, he contends that Anselm, in holding that "that thing than which nothing greater can be conceived" "adequately defines the divine essence in the first place," succeeds only in "forging an idol of 'God'" (see quotation above). But Anselm does not hold what Marion takes him to hold. Marion completely overlooks the distinction made above between proving the existence of an X and identifying that X with a Y. It is absurd to suppose that, for example, Anselm of Canterbury and Thomas Aquinas assumed they had "adequately define[d] the divine essence" when they attempted to prove the existence of "that thing than which nothing greater can be conceived" (Anselm) or of a "first mover" or a "first cause," etc. (Aquinas). This aspect of the Marion passage under consideration in the main text cannot be pursued here. As shown below, the passage is introduced for a different reason.

sible," from that it would not follow that "the whole [ontological] argument [would be] turned down: [that] [i]t [would no longer prove] God's existence, but the impossibility of his impossibility, and therefore his possibility." First, the argument would not be "turned down"; rather, the argument would have been transformed into something very different. Second, even less would it be the case that the (transformed) argument would prove "the impossibility of his [God's] impossibility, and therefore his possibility." Indeed, performing Marion's "substitution," we would have: God = the Impossible. In this case the argument, if conclusive, would—if anything—"prove" that "the Impossible = God" "is (exists)" not only in our intellect, but also in reality.

[ii] According to Marion, we have to "stick to God's incomprehensibility." But then, surprisingly, he has a great deal to say about God's incomprehensibility. We have to *conceive*—therefore, to build a concept of—this incomprehensibility. And this concept has the content: "impossibility of every concept." But must not a concept that expresses the impossibility of *every* concept express its own impossibility? Marion either does not notice or does not care about this; instead, he simply goes further in his playing with words. It is simply mysterious how he gets from "the impossibility of every concept" to "the concept of impossibility." Of course, in plays on words all associations are permitted. Having reached "the concept of impossibility," he speaks next of impossibility itself, not caring about the distinction between "concept of impossibility" and impossibility itself.

[iii] And then God appears on stage as a deus ex machina, and "impossibility" turns out to be "the distinctive hallmark of God's difference with regard to man." As shown above, Marion's unmediated admission of God or presupposition of God raises a serious problem. What is he speaking of: of God as a fiction, as a pure idea, as a dream—or as the true and living God? Marion cannot get rid of this profound ambiguity for "systematic" reasons, that is, reasons that emerge from his phenomenological approach.

Marion's plays on words may be brilliant as literary flourishes, but they are not defensible or even intelligible as formulations of philosophical theses. To show this, it suffices to analyze the following sentence (subscripts added): "The necessity of God's possibility flows from the impossibility$_1$ of his impossibility$_2$" ("IM–G" 28–29). What is said above makes clear that in this sentence, which summarily articulates Marion's entire procedure, the terms "necessity" and "possibility" are understood *not in the transcendental-phenomenological sense*—i.e., *not* as terms that "refer to experience, namely to what experience allows and excludes—therefore to what *may* or *may not* appear and let itself be seen, the phenomenon"

("IM–G" 20)—but rather in a universal sense, as these terms are explained in modal logic and in traditional metaphysics. That itself introduces ambiguity into Marion's formulations. But the term "impossibility," which appears twice in the sentence, is used equivocally: in the second occurrence, i.e., as impossibility$_2$, this term has a purely *phenomenological-transcendental* meaning (according to Marion's understanding of "phenomenological-transcendental"), whereas in the first occurrence, i.e., as impossibility$_1$, the term has a universal logical and metaphysical signification. If this were made explicit, then his talk of "paradox(es)" would be revealed to be empty.

Why does Marion not clarify this quite elementary theoretical state of affairs? The answer may be obvious: if he had, then little of his procedure or line of "argumentation" would have been left. In addition, he often uses the terms "possible" and "impossible" in their vague, ordinary-language senses, like that relied on when someone, in a concrete situation, says, "But that's impossible!" He also quotes passages from the Bible that contain these terms. He provides no analyses articulating the specific senses these terms have in these various contexts. His formulations are therefore equivocations.

[7] Despite his strict rejection of the application of *any* concepts to God, Marion appears to have no problem applying various concepts to God. The ones he uses tend to be positive characterizations of God. Among the two most important are *love* (*caritas*) and *creation*.

In the final act of Marion's phenomenologico-theological procedure, God enters yet again as deus ex machina, now as charity, as love. The last paragraph of "The Impossible for Man—God" reads:

> The radical and non-metaphysical transcendence for which we have
> been seeking reveals itself with great clarity in the impossible—but
> in the only [im-]possible [Marion's brackets] worthy of God, which is
> charity. Only with love, and therefore with "God who is love" (1 John
> 4:8, 16), is nothing impossible: God's transcendence manifests itself in
> charity, and only thus does transcendence reveal itself to be worthy of
> God. ("IM–G" 38)

What *philosophical* path could lead or could have led Marion to this point? From "the impossible" to "God as love": there are many, many stages to go through before one could be justified in making such a striking identification. In Marion there is no theoretical procedure leading to God as love, hence no philosophical justification for his introduction of God as love. Marion here suddenly shifts to a biblical-theological level without explaining, and so of course without justifying, this methodological and theoretical leap.

4.2.4.4 Marion's Failed Conception of Creation

The last topic in Marion's thinking this book considers is his concept *creation*. This concept is the *experimentum crucis* of every conception of God that deserves to be called a Christian one. If we do not conceive ourselves *and* the entire so-called world or universe as having been created by God, then all our statements about God remain statements about an X that in the last analysis is an idol, a poor pseudo-God. What, then, does Marion say about creation? The account that follows criticizes in detail two central passages from his works that deal with this topic.

4.2.4.4.1 Marion's Confused Connection of the Concept *Creation* with the Concept *Causality*

The first passage on creation to be considered here is contained in "The Impossible for Man—God." This essay contains highly consequential assertions about creation, particularly ones relating creation to the "metaphysical" concept *causality*.

[1] Marion begins by considering the phenomenon of birth, of which he writes the following:

> I emerge, or rather I *have* emerged into existence through a very different mode [one different from causality]—through the mode of an event in which I myself advene to myself. . . . Birth, *my* birth—which delivers me, bears me into the world and makes me—happens without me. . . . My birth advenes to me in the form of a directly effective impossibility. Thus I am forced to admit that the case of my birth provides me the experience of radical possibility—namely the one from which I come and which has effectively made me [*m'a rendu effectif*].
> ("IM–G" 32)

Marion then asks: "Still, based on the [im-]possible that is my birth, how is an [im-]possible for God to be imagined? Does the disproportion between the two domains (finite and infinite) not forbid transition and assimilation?" He answers as follows:

> It undoubtedly does, if we cling to the division that remains internal to the concept of Being [*étant*]. But not if we focus on the advent of the [im-]possible as such. Indeed, what birth accomplishes for each living being, creation brings about from God's point of view—as long of course as we understand creation here in the theological sense, not as a mere taking of efficient causality to the limit. The point is that *for us* creation thematizes and gathers together the totality of events that advene of themselves [*la totalité des événements qui adviennent à partir d'eux-mêmes*]—without concepts, without predictions, and therefore

without cause—radical possibles, in short, which we not only receive in it [the creation] but from which, first and foremost, we receive ourselves. Certainly, for *me*, creation starts always and only with my birth. Yet by the same token my birth exposes me to the whole of creation, giving me access to every [im-]possible in its primordial [im-]possibility. God, the master of the impossible. ("IM–G" 32–33; all instances of "[im-]" in original; t.a.)

Ignoring for the moment the fact that much of this passage merely plays with words, especially "possible" and "impossible," the passage does contain formulations that, at first glance, appear promising; closer analysis shows, however, that these passages express little or nothing that is philosophically defensible. Is the point that is decisive with respect to creation a point that is only for us? Does not Marion, in the preceding sentence, explicitly introduce God's point of view and say that he is taking the concept *creation* in the "theological sense"? Why then, and with what meaning, does he introduce the qualification "for us" in the very next sentence?

Ignoring such unclarities, some of Marion's formulations do, in certain respects, articulate some important aspects of the concept *creation*, particularly the following: "creation thematizes and gathers together the totality of events." Indeed, the *thematization* of the *totality of events* (*beings*) is the immensely important task Christian philosophy has tackled by using the term "creation" and that should be tackled by every philosophy that aims to say anything meaningful about (the Christian) God. But Marion simply throws in this phrase; he does not consider the issue. And yet worse, Marion's entire philosophical stance is one from which there is not any possibility, even the most minimal, of thinking through creation, because thinking through creation requires thinking and speaking of Being, and Marion consistently not only rejects but also derides all such thinking and speaking.

Characteristically, Marion immediately explains the promising formulation "creation thematizes and gathers together the totality of events" in a way that deprives it of its potentially far-reaching meaning and thus of the far-reaching tasks it could pose and consequences to which it could lead. He speaks of "the totality of events that advene of themselves—without concepts, without predictions, and therefore without cause—radical possibles, in short, which we not only receive in it [the creation] but from which, first and foremost, we receive ourselves."

Here, the following question presses: if the events "advene of themselves," why is there any need to introduce the idea of creation? Marion explains the sense of to "advene of themselves" by using a threefold "without": "without concepts, without predictions, . . . without cause." Concepts and predictions are theoretical items, whereas causes are onto-logical items. It makes no sense to conjoin these items in order to explain "to advene of themselves."

[2] In what sense does Marion take "cause" when he rejects it *a limine*? The Christian metaphysical tradition at least raises and addresses one of the central questions concerning creation: *how* is it that we and all finite beings "come from God"? In doing so, it relies on the concept *causality*, which it introduces and explains. In order to assess the real mean-ing, the validity, and the explanatory value of such a concept it is first of all indispensable to analyze it on the basis of the philosophical position within which it is situated systematically. Marion bypasses any such anal-ysis by simply labeling causality a "metaphysical" concept. His writings suggest that this labeling results from two considerations that appear to play decisive roles. Both are misunderstandings.

[i] The first consideration leading Marion to reject causality as metaphysical is his location of causality in the domain of beings, and indeed in the physical world. He says that this concept is, in a manner he classifies as typical of metaphysics, applied to God, and deems that application to be not only mistaken but senseless. Even if the concept of metaphysics is "taken to the limit" ("IM–G" 32), it cannot clarify the relation between God and the world. This is one of the central points in Marion's critique of metaphysics.

A first point to be emphasized is that the use of analogy in meta-physical talk about God, including Aquinas's talk about God, on the basis of the three ways of knowing God (the way of affirmation or causality, the way of negation, and the way of eminence) is extremely problematic. How can something discoverable in the finite domain be applied to God, as infinite? Even if God is understood as the highest or first being, so that the relation between God and the world is interpreted as a relation between beings—no matter how different they may be—such an appli-cation is not immediately intelligible. Such an application is yet more problematic if God is understood not as a (first or highest) being, but instead, as by Aquinas, as Being subsisting of itself, as *ipsum esse per se sub-sistens*. The problem is that of transcendence, in the active sense of that term: going beyond the finite, going beyond being(s). Chapters 1 and 3 consider this topic in various contexts. No doubt, Marion is concerned here with a fundamental problem.

The issue of transcendence is clarified by the deep metaphysics introduced in chapter 1 and systematically developed in chapter 3. Par-ticularly important is the treatment of transcendence in section 3.7.3.2. The central point can be summarized as follows: there is no real transcendence = transcending. At best, the terms "transcendence" and "transcending" are inadequate designations for the intentional coextensivity of the human mind with Being as such and as a whole. In addition, transcendence in the resultative sense, i.e., as the result of transcendence = transcending, is likewise an inadequate designation for an essential structural characteristic of the human mind. Making this characteristic explicit reveals the traditionally understood procedure of analogy to be superficial. To be sure, there are natural and pragmatic moves from the finite to the infinite along the three traditional ways, but these moves are made on the level of the outside or surface structure of the human mind, not on its deep structure. The primordial, universal dimension of Being is, as absolutely unrestricted, what the human mind must thematize; its thematization is its explication, and that does not involve anything like transcendence or transcending.

This is widely consequential for talk about God because God is, as chapter 3 shows, fully explicated primordial Being. What consequences does this have concerning causality in connection with creation? In traditional metaphysics, creation is a species of causality, albeit a unique species. This is extremely problematic; at best, it is absolutely superficial. A brief explanation suffices.

However causality is more precisely characterized within the Aristotelian tradition, in any case it means—broadly put—the production of something *out of something* that is already available. Creation, however, is not such a production. Creation is positing-within-Being *ex nihilo sui et subiecti*, out of the non-being of what is posited and of anything from which what is posited could in any way be produced. As chapter 3 shows, creation is positing-within-Being out of nothingness. It is thus radically distinct from any notion of causality within the Aristotelian tradition. There is a certain commonality: both in cases of (Aristotelian) causation and in the case of creation, there is coming-to-be. But this commonality is superficial, because it fails to articulate the fact that creation as positing-within-Being out of nothingness is utterly different from any kind of production, given that production unavoidably connotes a relation between beings.

Creation is absolutely unique, an absolute *singulare tantum*. Justice cannot be done to it, in its full scope, if it is understood as a species of causality. But this in no way means that treatments of creation in the metaphysical tradition, if carefully interpreted, are false or inadequate. What is inadequate is only the subsumption of creation under causality. But this subsumption is, strictly speaking, *external* to the concept *creation*. In thoughtlessly and undifferentiatedly maintaining this subsumption, Marion makes the error of systematically mislocating this concept *crea-*

tion, and as a consequence—shown in the following section (4.2.4.4.2)—
he empties that concept of content.

[ii] The second consideration is more specific, because it concerns
Marion's specifically transcendental-phenomenological conception. How
causality is understood within this conception is articulated in a passage
from "The Impossible for Man—God." What Marion says is based on the
concepts *possibility* and *impossibility,* concepts that, as shown in detail above,
he interprets purely phenomenologically-transcendentally: what agrees
with the conditions of subjectivity (the conditions of conceptualization)
is possible, what does not is impossible. Marion deems God impossible,
in this sense. Yet he also says that this impossible is possible. How then
can *this possibility* be thought? Marion attempts to think it by introducing
radical possibility:

> Radical possibility would, as such, transcend all limit and, being thus
> completely unconditioned, would give us access, finally, to the transcen-
> dence which we seek. Formally, such possibility would define itself as
> the transcendence of all impossibility—taking its point of departure
> not in some non-contradiction concocted within the limits of represen-
> tation and positive conceptualization, but negatively, in transgressing
> these very limits, namely within what remains impossible for conceptu-
> alization and representation. Possibility taken in the radical sense would
> take its point of departure in the impossible, by transcending it, which
> is to say by annulling it through effectively bringing it about. Radical
> possibility would start with the impossible and, without passing through
> conceptualization of a non-contradictory possible for finite representa-
> tion, would impose it within effectivity. *Radical impossibility* or *effecting the
> impossible.* ("IM–G" 31)

This passage articulates the basis on which Marion understands and misunderstands the concept *causality.* He asks:

> How can this be done [i.e., how can the concept *radical possibility* be
> related to God], if I know of no such [im-]possible? No doubt I know
> of no such [im-]possible as long as I define myself as *ego cogitans,* think-
> ing according to my own representation and concept. By adopting this
> posture, indeed, I submit everything that can advene to the screen, so
> to speak, of my own conceptualization and finitude. ("IM–G" 31; all
> instances of "[im-]" in original; t.a.)

Here Marion introduces the concept *causality.* The passage just
quoted is immediately followed thus: "Hence causality (whether it starts

with me as a causal agent or with some cause other than myself) never brings about anything, by definition, except what my concept has fore-seen for it as possible, according to what is non-contradictory for my representation" (31–32). Marion proceeds: "I do not, however, define myself always, or even primarily, according to a conceptual representa-tion" (32). This is supposed to explain how, for me, radical possibility can become actuality (*effectivité*). It is supposed thereby to explain how God is supposed to be thought as the impossible: as beyond representation and concepts and thereby—and this is peculiar—beyond the concept *causal-ity*. In other words: *causality* does not come into question as a concept that might help to determine the concept *creation* with respect to how it is supposed to occur.

Clearly, Marion's concept *causality* is situated within a purely phenomenological-transcendental framework that is concerned with the conditions of possibility of (our) experience. Because according to him God appears *within this framework* as the impossible, the concept *causality* cannot clarify his creative activity.

This shows once again how radically the transcendental-subjective framework determines everything Marion says about transcendence and God. He naively introduces the concept *causality* as though it were obvi-ous what it means. He wholly ignores the problematicity, treated just above under [1], of the subsumption of creation under causality.

[3] Marion's explicit and radical rejection of the concept *causality* is the more unintelligible given that he himself uses formulations that involve paraphrases of this concept. An example: "God, the master of the impossible, *effectuates* [*effectue*] creation by making the [im-]possibility of each birth *effective* [*en rendant effective*], starting with my own" ("IM–G" 33; "[im-]" in original; emphasis added). The word "effectuates" directly articulates the concept *causality:* a cause is an X that effectuates some-thing, that has an effect. This is explicit in the metaphysical concept *causa efficiens*, efficient cause. But Marion does not think through what he says. And not only that: he directs powerful rhetoric against the "meta-physical" concept *creation*, superficially and thoughtlessly subsuming it under a vague concept of causality. This is the more peculiar and unintel-ligible in that it is based on a crass incoherence. This way of thinking and of criticizing philosophical conceptions utterly lacks the seriousness and rigor required in this (as in every other) theoretical domain.

[4] What Marion is aiming at when he characterizes the "adve-nience" of events "of themselves" by indicating a threefold "without" seems to be clear within the context of his phenomenological approach: he conceives of the created events as phenomena in their *absoluteness* (see above 4.2.3.2[2]). He does not move beyond this phenomenological

background, and this is the real reason why he fails even to pose the essential questions about creation. This is confirmed by the last clause of his characterization of created events: they are "radical possibles, . . . which we not only receive in it [creation] but from which, first and foremost, we receive ourselves." This passage reveals Marion's continued reliance on the subject-object relation, which defines the starting point and the fundamental presupposition of the phenomenological approach. At this point it becomes clear that he conceives of creation on the basis of this distinction or duality: "*we*" receive the (totality of) events as radical possibles "*in it* [i.e., in the creation]" and from these events "*we*, first and foremost, receive ourselves."

Here, Marion totally misrepresents the idea of creation: if this idea means anything determinate, then it means this: it articulates God's absolutely *encompassing action,* an action that in no way presupposes us as receivers, but rather in the first place posits us within Being in order that we can become receivers. There are no pre-given or presupposed receivers of God's creating action. This reveals yet again that so profound an idea can be articulated only on the basis and within the framework of a comprehensive theory of everything, a comprehensive conception of the universal dimension, the dimension of Being as such and as a whole. Therein, God appears as Being in its fullness, as Being that is the creator of all finite beings.

4.2.4.4.2 Marion's Total Emptying of the Thought of Creation

The second passage wherein Marion speaks significantly and in detail about creation, one therefore requiring critical analysis here, is chapter 4 of his book *Au lieu de soi* (2009; *LS*); the chapter is titled "The Creation of the Self" ("La création du soi"). Marion describes the book as presenting a non-metaphysical (more accurately: a radically anti-metaphysical) interpretation of Augustine's *Confessions,* but in fact, the book presents an interpretation of Augustine's thinking as a whole. This interpretation is identical in every respect to Marion's own position. What holds the book together is its opposition to metaphysics. This leads to assertions and theses that, in light of the preceding treatment of Marion, appear significantly more problematic. Of course, this section cannot consider Marion's book in detail, and cannot consider its adequacy as an interpretation of Augustine. Instead, it considers only a few of the book's particularly important remarks about creation, because those are relevant to this book's purposes.

[1] According to Marion, Augustine's understanding of creation is not a conception of the world (*mundus,* κόσμος) as the totality of beings, but an absolutely non-metaphysical interpretation of the first sentence of

the Bible: "In the beginning God created heaven and earth." Marion insists that this heaven and earth cannot be identified with the metaphysically understood world. Such an identification would be characteristic of our usual "metaphysical and Greek attitude [*posture*]" (*LS* 317). According to Marion, Heidegger "opened our eyes [*nous a laissé voir*]" to this by showing what the metaphysically thought totality of beings actually is: according to Heidegger, metaphysical Being is presence-at-hand (*Vorhandenheit*) and the totality of beings is the totality of things present-at-hand (*Vorhandene*). According to Heidegger, this metaphysics presents creation as nothing other than the production of things present-at-hand by the first or highest being, which is also present-at-hand.

> All beings other than God need to be "produced" [*hergestellt*] in the widest sense and also to be sustained. "Being" [*Sein*] is to be understood within a horizon which ranges from the production of what is to be present-at-hand to something which has no need of being produced. (*BT* 125)

In the lecture course *History of Philosophy from Thomas Aquinas to Kant*, given in Winter 1926/27 (thus, during the time when Heidegger wrote *Being and Time*), he puts the point more directly as follows:

> What is produced [*Hergestelltes*] requires a producer. Horizon of understanding of Being that is the basis of the proofs [of God]: *producing* [*Herstellen*] *and what is produced as present-at-hand* [*als Vorhandenes*]. *Producer that itself must be present-at-hand.*[87]

Marion unrestrictedly adopts this "interpretation," which chapter 3 (3.6.1[2]) shows to be fundamentally misguided both for Aquinas's thought of Being/*esse* and for the metaphysical concept of creation. (That an author who explicitly writes as a Christian can fall prey to so radical an error motivates many questions, but they are not considered here.) Marion deploys Heidegger's error in a move of strategic immunization aiming to shield from any objections his full-scale, uncompromising, and wholly undifferentiated rejection of any and every "metaphysics." What he maintains is that Heidegger has allegedly shown what happens if creation is taken to be the answer to an ontological question ("Why is there anything at all rather than nothing?").

Heidegger's *only* error, according to Marion, was his having pre-

---

[87] *GA* vol. 23, p. 94 (emphasis added).

supposed "that creation claims to provide a Biblical response—no matter how inadequate [*aussi inappropriée qu'on voudra*]—to a metaphysical question, the one concerning the provenance of being(s)" (*LS* 319). Creation, Marion maintains, is not the answer to such a why question. (Worth noting is that Marion does not arrive at the thesis, defended in chapter 3 [3.6.3(1)], that, metaphysically considered, creation is the answer not to a why question, but to a how question. He hence cannot note that so-understood, metaphysical creation corresponds fully to what the Bible says, because the Bible articulates *how* heaven and earth came to be, not *why*.)

In this context Marion introduces the following passage, from Heidegger's *Introduction to Metaphysics,* which is introduced and thoroughly considered above in chapter 3 (3.7.4.2.2[2][iii][b]):

> One who holds on to such [biblical] faith as a basis can, perhaps, emulate and participate in the asking of our question [Why are there beings at all instead of nothing?] in a certain way, but *he cannot authentically question without giving himself up as a believer, with all the consequences of this step. He can only act "as if".* . . .[88]

Yet again, Marion misinterprets a Heideggerian text. He pays no attention to the context in which this sentence appears. Most importantly, he ignores the fact that immediately following the text just quoted Heidegger writes, "*On the other hand,* if such faith does not continually expose itself to the possibility of unfaith, *it is not faith* but a convenience and an agreement with oneself to adhere in the future to a doctrine as something that has somehow been handed down" (emphasis added). As is shown in this book in the section indicated above, this sentence rules out the kind of interpretation of the passage preceding it that Marion provides. But Marion neglects even to consider Heidegger's corrective and explicative sentence. Yet more fully does he neglect to clarify the issue, a task this book accomplishes in the indicated section.

Instead, Marion poses the following question: "Nevertheless, how could one avoid being astonished by the weakness of this [Heideggerian] objection?" (*LS* 318). In typically postmodernist fashion, he reverses Heidegger's objection, making of it a pillar supporting his radical rejection of any interpretation of creation that could even be suspected of being "metaphysical," accepting as sufficient reason for such suspi-

---

[88] *Introduction to Metaphysics* (1935/2000), 7–8 (emphasis added). This passage is included in a quotation in *LS* (318).

cion any thematization whatsoever of Being/being(s). This is shown in what follows.

At first he appears largely to agree with Heidegger in that he—correctly—notes that even later (1949), Heidegger continues to understand Leibniz's question as metaphysical, in the following sense:

> Why are there beings at all, and not rather nothing? Granted that we do not remain *within metaphysics* to ask metaphysically in the customary manner, but that we recall the truth of Being out of the essence and truth of metaphysics, then this might be asked as well: How does it come about that beings take precedence everywhere and lay claim to every "is," while that which is not a being—namely, the nothing thus understood as Being itself—remains forgotten?[89]

From this Marion concludes the following: the (metaphysical) question that according to Heidegger the "believer" cannot genuinely ask would not be a way to the *question of Being;* instead, it would close off and disguise the question of Being because it would consider being(s) at the expense of Being (see *LS* 319). Marion then asks, rhetorically, "Could it not then be—peculiarly—that faith would have good reasons not to consider a question that does not lead to the question of Being but instead smothers it under the noise of being(s) [*l'etouffe sous le bruit de l'étant*]?" (*LS* 319).

[2] Marion fails to consider the possibility of thematizing creation in conjunction with the question of Being; instead, he articulates only the problematic of the relation between faith and the question "Why are there beings rather than nothing?" a question that according to both Heidegger and Marion concerns only beings, and not Being. He then "argues" by introducing rhetorical questions, including the following: "Is it obvious that the one for whom 'the Bible is divine revelation and truth' 'seeks' therein first and above all 'answers' to 'questions'?";[90] "Is it obvious that the Bible at some point in time raises the why question about creation?"; "Does not the Bible offer instead the exemplary case of an absence of every why—not from deficiency but from excess?" (*LS* 319).

Shown above is that creation is not the answer to a why question, but is instead the answer to an (implicit) how question. When Marion insinuates that those with faith in the Bible do not first and foremost seek answers to questions in it, he proceeds captiously, as is easily shown. Per-

---

[89] "Introduction to 'What Is Metaphysics?'" (1949); *PM* 290 (emphasis added; t.a.).
[90] Heidegger, *Introduction to Metaphysics,* 7–8.

haps not all with faith in the Bible, perhaps indeed not most with faith in the Bible seek therein first and foremost answers to questions. But Marion's formulation does not exclude the possibility that some or many with faith in the Bible *do,* even if not first and foremost, nevertheless *also* seek in it answers to questions. The important question is, to *which* question(s) *can* the one with faith in the Bible seek answers in the Bible? And indeed Marion later says, "We will seek the question to which creation gives the answer" (*LS* 320). Can he find this question? Does he formulate it explicitly? It is shown just below ([3]) that what Marion says about this is a typical example not only of rhetorically masked unclarity and incoherence, but above all of a conjuring away of the problem in question.

First, however, Marion maintains succinctly, "Heidegger's objection to the doctrine of creation turns into its opposite and appears from now on, read against the grain, as a quite certain indication of the path to be followed" (*LS* 320). One might expect that Marion would identify as "the path to be followed" treatment of the question of Being. But Marion is far from that. Marion's treating the question of Being in consequent fashion would show that his ceaseless polemics against "metaphysics" are fully undifferentiated and, as far as metaphysics of *esse* in the sense of Thomas Aquinas is concerned, wholly untenable. In light of the approach to a systematic conception of Being developed in chapter 3 of this book, Marion's unrelenting rejection of everything that in any way points in the direction of Being is revealed to be completely untenable and arbitrary. How far he goes in his radical rejection of Being becomes clear from analysis of that to which he reduces the thought of creation.

[3] As shown above, Marion assumes that those with faith in the Bible can seek answers to questions in the Bible. But how he then proceeds is anything other than clear and coherent, as shown by the following decisive passage: "We will no longer pose the question whether creation gives an answer to the question concerning why in relation to the world; instead, we will do the reverse, seeking the question to which creation does offer an answer, because this answer in any case cannot take the form of a cause, a sufficient reason, an ontology, and yet less a cosmology" (*LS* 320).

One would expect Marion next—finally—to articulate the question that he takes what the Bible says about creation to answer. Instead of doing that, however, he gives the answer to a or the question he has repeatedly invoked but never expressed, formulating that answer—rhetorically, postmodernistically, and enigmatically—as follows: "It could be that creation brings no other answer than the answer itself—in the sense that every thing, in heaven and on earth, arises within the domain of the created only in order to *answer*" (*LS* 320).[91] To an unexpressed question about creation the answer is thus answering, or what is created as answer.

This passage—considered in its context—contains *in nuce* a significant number of the unclarities, incoherences, indeed contradictions, that, as the preceding account shows, characterize Marion's position. Detailed analysis makes this clear.

First, it is not difficult to determine from Marion's formulations—although none is explicit about the matter—what the question is (or at least what one of the questions is) that he takes what the Bible says about creation to answer. It is indicated in the explicative part of the passage introduced above, in the phrase, "brings no other answer than . . . to *answer*." Positively stated—by complete equivalence—the explication is this: "every thing in heaven and on earth, arises in the domain of the created precisely in order to *answer*." This is the answer to the following question: *to do what* does every thing, in heaven and on earth, arise in the domain of the created? The question asks for *the goal* of God's creation of the world.

That this is so is fully clear when one considers how Marion more precisely characterizes the answering done by what is created as expressing the goal of creation. He formulates this state of affairs as follows: "Between creation and the answer there is a mutual and necessary connection [*lien*] that unfolds simultaneously as praise [*louange*] and as confession" (*LS* 320). Such a formulation would be non-problematic if it were understood in a positive sense rather than in an exclusive sense. That is to say: if this formulation said that creation, when fully recognized and understood, requires and includes the practical-existential attitudes of praise and confession, then it would be accurate. If, however, as is clearly the case with Marion, it is understood in an *exclusive* sense, then it means that creation, in the resultative sense of the created, is *nothing other than pure praise and pure confession*—to the total exclusion of every other factor or aspect. Creation is then absolutely reduced to praise and confession. That is precisely what Marion says and defends when he maintains, apodictically,

> To impose on heaven, earth, and every other thing the designation "creature" literally comes back to praising in them the gift of God, to praising God in recognizing him as creator. What results from this is

---

[91] "Il se pourrait que la création n'apporte aucune autre réponse que la réponse elle-même—en ce sens que toute chose, au ciel et sur la terre, ne surgit dans le créé que précisément pour cela, répondre."

that the hermeneutics of creation consists precisely in *not* defining
things as beings . . . but in recognizing them *as* gifts received from creation and returned in praise, [as things] whose presence is maintained
only in this exchange. (*LS* 324)

Summarizing this position both negatively and positively, he writes
as follows: "'Creation' belongs to the lexicon neither of being(s) nor of
Being; instead, it belongs to liturgical vocabulary, as do the praise and the
confession that alone recognize and confirm it [i.e., creation]" (*LS* 324).

In all of his writings, and particularly in the book *Au lieu de soi*, Marion strictly avoids using the term "being(s)," both in general and especially in discussing creation; he prefers the banal term "things [*choses*]."
This only seemingly fully insignificant detail brings into view the deep
incoherence and contradictoriness that is thoroughly exposed in the preceding critique of his position (particularly in 4.2.2). The text just quoted
clearly says or implies that "the things" *are not things that are.* What then
are they? Marion would presumably reject this question as metaphysical,
as an expression of a "metaphysical and Greek attitude" (*LS* 317).

[4] Despite all his rhetorical and arbitrary slogans, however, Marion
cannot evade the incoherence and indeed contradictoriness of his assertions. Even ignoring the banality that is bound inevitably to the use
of the term "thing" in articulating central philosophical issues, Marion
owes an answer to the following philosophically unavoidable question:
what is he talking about when he speaks of "things" *as gifts:* are they
imaginary, dreamed up, fictive, etc., or are they *real* things, thus things
that are? Until he answers this question in an unobjectionable manner,
rigorously drawing and attending to the consequences of his answer, his
entire conception resembles a castle in the air that might look beautiful,
indeed magnificent, but that remains nothing more than a castle in the
air. If he were to answer the question, however, his answer would expose
his current conception precisely as a castle in the air.

The fundamental presupposition or assumption on which Marion relies is the following: creation as praise and confession absolutely
excludes anything like the positing-within-Being out of nothingness of
contingent things/beings. This, however, is a fundamental error and is
manifestly incoherent. In all brevity: in Marion's terminology, creation
(understood in the resultative sense) is the totality of things that praise
God as creator and that confess to God. It is then asked, if these things
are not things that *are*, then what are they? If they *are* things that *are*, then
they are *beings*. What then could be the objection to say that creation is the
totality of *beings* that praise God as creator and that confess to God?

To avoid Marion's one-sidednesses and artificial dichotomies, distinctions must be introduced. The state of affairs requiring clarification

at this point is most simply presented with the aid of distinctions among a reductive-exclusive sense of creation, a core sense, and a full sense. The reductive-exclusive sense corresponds to Marion's conception: Marion *reduces* creation to praise and confession by *excluding* any and every consideration of the status of the praising and confessing things or the praising and confessing beings. The core sense of creation emerges when the status of the praising and confessing things/beings is explicitly thematized. Creation is then, in the resultative sense, the totality of contingent beings posited-within-Being by God out of nothingness; creation in the resultative sense thus presupposes creation in the active sense, precisely as the positing-within-Being of contingent beings out of nothingness. This is the core sense of creation. The full sense of creation is attained when the core sense is not articulated purely abstractly and theoretically, but is also—so to speak—practically-existentially recognized, experienced, or, in whatever form, accomplished (e.g., in singing the book of praises, the Psalms). The core sense as such is a matter of theoretical consideration, of the intelligibility of things/beings or of Being as such and as a whole; as such, it entails the possibility but not the realization of the complete sense. But the full sense is never actualized without the explicit presupposition of the core sense.

Marion's far-reaching error can now be formulated precisely: he reduces creation—in an exclusive manner—to a "common and liturgical status" (*LS* 322) and considers the term "creation" to belong exclusively to "liturgical vocabulary" (*LS* 324). "Creation" in Marion's sense cannot be equated with what is identified above as the complete sense of creation, because the complete sense presupposes and recognizes the core sense, whereas Marion's sense does not recognize any core sense; according to him, creation is reduced to an answering in the sense of a *contentless praising and confessing.* Neither the central biblical-Christian thought of creation nor the philosophical thought of creation is to be found in his works.

[5] This conclusion is reconfirmed in an impressive manner by the analysis of statements of the author whose conception Marion thoroughly analyzes and, as is now to be shown, misunderstands: Augustine. It suffices to consider three contentually interrelated passages from Augustine that Marion himself introduces and comments on.

[i] The first passage is a brief excerpt from book 10 (3, 5, 14, 278) of the *Confessions;*[92] it reads, "Audiam et intelligam, quomodo 'in principio' fecisti 'caelum et terram' [(I want to) hear and understand how

---

[92] Marion cites the edition from the Bibliothèque augustinienne (Paris: Desclée de Brouwer, 1947ff.) by volume, chapter, section, book, page (see his bibliographic note, *LS* 14).

'in the beginning' you made 'heaven and earth']" (*LS* 321). In his extensive commentary on this sentence, Marion emphasizes only that understanding (*intelligere*) the creation of all things "has a common and liturgical status because it aims to invoke initial confessions, both from readers and from the author [of the *Confessions*]" (*LS* 322). Typically, Marion does not consider the enormously important terms and concepts that appear in this passage. These are the following: *Audiam*—(I want to) hear—*intelligam*—(I want to) understand—*quomodo*—how—and *fecisti*—you made.

"Hearing" is an aspect of the practical-existential attitude Augustine assumes in the *Confessions* and that characterizes the status of this work: as the title says, it is a book of *confessions*. Fundamentally, all statements in the book are implicitly preceded by a practical-existential operator that can be briefly articulated as, "I confess (in praise) that ... ϕ" (whereby "ϕ" is a variable for an indicative or theoretical sentence). Marion recognizes this status (not in accordance with this operator, of course, but that is of no importance here),[93] but his interpretation of this status is utterly one-sided and therefore misleading. The main point is the following: Marion does not consider the fact that within the framework of this status (in the semi-formal terminology: within the scope of the practical-existential operator [or "common and liturgical" operator]) sentences appear that are purely indicative and therefore purely theoretical. The most important of these is, "You (God, the creator) made heaven and earth." This point is considered further below.

It is highly interesting to note that Augustine in fact has precisely this state of affairs in mind when he conjoins "*intelligam*"—"and that I understand"—to "*audiam*." This is the most central point that Marion stubbornly and consistently ignores, with consequences that are enormous—as shown shortly below.

The third term/concept is "*quomodo*—how." It responds to a how question, not to a why question; the question is indicated by the formulation, "(so that I understand) how it is with heaven and earth." Given the detailed consideration above of what Heidegger and Marion have to say about the question "Why are there beings rather than nothing?" the significance of this fact is presumably obvious.

The fourth important term/concept, "*fecisti*—you made," articulates in an ordinary-language formulation what is termed above the core sense of "creation." Of this, more below.

Marion pays no attention to the weight of this passage. He situates

---

[93] If Marion were to use a semi-formal presentation, he would have to introduce a "common and liturgical" operator.

it from the outset on the practical-existential level of the *Confessions,* but misunderstands even this level because he ignores the significance of the four terms/concepts analyzed above.

[ii] The second passage is not a single sentence, but a small collection of interrelated sentences that need not be quoted here (see *LS* 324ff.). Marion's intention is to move from these sentences to explanations and solidifications of one of his own comprehensive theses. The thesis concerns what he calls "the place of creation" (*LS* 325). He formulates it as follows:

> Creation does not come at the beginning, but after and in the interior of praise, because it alone can and wants to interpret the visible things as gifted with a commencement, hence as created. There would not be any possibility of seeing the world as heaven and earth created by God if one did not consent at the outset to praise God as God. Praise thus displays the *liturgical* condition of possibility of the recognition of creation—even if, after the fact and as an anachronism, one can gloss over praise and present creation as an ontic commencement. But this reversal of the real and primordial liturgical order into a cosmological order reconstituted *a posteriori* remains, even if one can accept it as a commodity, an artifice of method that, as such, is deprived of even the least legitimacy with regard to *confession*. Creation does not make confession possible, as the ontic place of its exercise; it does not itself become possible except from confession, its liturgical precondition. In a word, by praising God, confession gives its first place to the creation of heaven and earth, not the reverse. (*LS* 324–25)

These striking assertions appear at first glance to be clear, but they are not. First, it is fully unclear how "creation" is to be understood here: in the resultative sense, as the totality of created things/beings, or in the active sense, as the creating act of God? Marion appears not to recognize any such distinction, at least not explicitly; instead, he constantly uses the formulation "creation of heaven and earth," explicitly adding the negative explanation, "to repeat: *not* the creation of the world or of beings" (*LS* 326). But how does he understand "the creation of heaven and earth" *positively*? That is the essential question here. To it, Marion provides only the positive answer cited above, according to which "the hermeneutics of creation consists precisely . . . in recognizing [things] *as* gifts received from creation and returned in praise, [as things] whose presence is maintained only in this exchange" (*LS* 324). But instead of more closely considering the question of what such an assertion about things as gifts from the creator presupposes and implies, Marion constantly repeats two kinds of statements: positive ones and negative ones.

Positively, Marion introduces a number of assertions like "the creation of heaven and earth intervenes only in order to answer the original question [*question originelle*] of confession" (*LS* 326). How is this absolute *priority* (Marion: *préalable* [*LS* 325]) of praise (of *confessio*) in relation to creation to be understood? There are many possibilities: the priority could be epistemological, existential, ontological, etc. At first glance the assertion gives the impression that it should be understood in an epistemological-existential sense. Concretely, this would mean the following: a normal, philosophically sophisticated reader would take Marion to mean that for a person/theoretician/philosopher to recognize and understand creation at all, that person must *first* participate actively and positively in a communal liturgical act in which God is praised as God, such that the person in question fully affirms this praising.

If this were what Marion means, that would not have as a consequence that ontological assertions about creation could not be made; it would have only the consequence that they would not have epistemological-psychological-existential priority. The two kinds of statements would not be mutually exclusive, but instead would be mutually implicative. In at least one passage, Marion appears not to reject such a view, writing, "Creation gives no answer to the ontic or ontological question, because [creation] precedes [this question] and, at best, makes [the ontic or ontological question] thinkable, although always derivatively, as a second step" (*LS* 326). This is a sentence that appears flatly to contradict many other of Marion's assertions that are thoroughly commented on and criticized above. And indeed, strictly—that is, in terms of coherence—it is indeed incompatible with Marion's quite numerous absolutely *negative* assertions about ontology, beings, Being, etc.

In the very next sentence, however, Marion writes—significantly—the following: "In fact, the metaphysical interpretation of creation presupposes that the question of the place is already resolved, and in the most brutal fashion [*de la manière la plus brutale*]: as the production of a world of beings by the exercise of an efficient causality" (*LS* 326). No comment is made here concerning the appearance of such a formulation as "in the most brutal fashion" in a book purporting to be philosophical. How one should assess Marion's characterization of the "metaphysical" thought of creation, relying as it does on fully unexplained and purely polemically-rhetorically deployed terms/concepts like "production" and "efficient causality," is made clear by what is said about this topic and this practice above in this chapter and in chapter 3 (see 3.6.1–3.6.2).

The substantive question at this point is the following: is what Marion here calls the metaphysical interpretation of creation *the* solution to the ontic or ontological question to which he refers in the preceding sentence, a question that it appears that he has not, in principle, excluded?

If so, then there is a striking contradiction between the two sentences. If not, then this can only mean that by "metaphysical interpretation" Marion means either no ontic or ontological conception at all or only a specific version of such a conception. In fact, however, Marion always means by "metaphysics" some kind of conception of Being/being(s). Given this, Marion avoids the striking contradiction only if "metaphysical interpretation" means one or more specific *forms* of ontic or ontological conceptions. But there is no evidence worth mentioning in Marion's work that he makes any such distinction among forms of ontic or ontological conceptions. To the contrary, as is shown in the final section of this book, Marion considers "the idolatry of Being itself" to be "the chief idolatry" ("IM–G" 339).

To summarize: Marion in no way takes into consideration the analysis of creation, introduced and explained above, that identifies its three senses. The senses are the reductive-exclusive sense, the core sense, and the full sense. The priority Marion so highly values could be explained in various ways in terms of this threefold distinction. If, for example, a theoretician accords unconditional *epistemological* priority to the existentially accomplished recognition of God's creation, this would mean that this theoretician would proceed methodologically, from the outset, from the full sense of creation, in order gradually to articulate the entire content of the full sense—to which, in the first place, belongs the core sense of creation. This would be different from the approach taken in this book, but the difference would be based on a methodological issue that would not be central.

[iii] The third Augustinian passage is particularly revealing. Marion comments on sentences including the following:

> And I, for what do I ask when I ask that you come to me, to me, who would not be being if you were not being in me? . . . So I would not be being if you were not being in me, or rather I would not be being if I were not being in you, in you, of whom it holds that "from him and through him and toward him is all of creation" [Romans 11:36].[94]

(To emphasize what is crucial here, Augustine's uses of "*esse*" in the subjunctive preterite ("*essem, esses*") are translated into the unusual formulations "would not be being," etc.)

---

[94] "Et ego, quid peto, ut venias in me, qui non essem, nisi esses in me? . . . non ergo essem, nisi esses in me, an potius non essem, nisi essem in te, 'ex quo omnia, per quem omnia, in quo omnia'" (*Confessiones* 1, 2, 2, 13, 276; quoted *LS* 326).

Strangely, Marion cites this text and immediately thereafter adds the above-cited negative assertions concerning the ontic or ontological question and the metaphysical interpretation of creation. It thus appears that only one thing interests him in the text just quoted: its identification of praise/confession as what Marion calls "the place of creation." In one respect this is not at all controversial, given that the text appears in the *Confessions*. This is then a matter of what can be termed a contingent-contextual priority, not a substantive priority. Augustine speaks of creation *within the framework* of a confession praising God. This is, of course, completely legitimate. But from it one cannot draw the conclusion Marion draws, namely, that statements about creation are possible and meaningful absolutely exclusively within such frameworks.

One other point is important in the current context. Marion simply pays no attention to what Augustine actually says. In articulating his confession, Augustine formulates sentences whose status is unambiguously indicative, and thus theoretical: "I would not be being if you were not being in me [*non essem nisi, esses in me*]." With such sentences, within the framework of his confession, he reflects on his relation to the creator and thereby articulates the ontological presuppositions of his confession. What he discovers to be fundamental is the following state of affairs: his own Being would not be without God as Being: his own Being-within-Being *is* such only as Being-within-God-as-Being. This is the core sense of creation. To repeat: the core sense is precisely that—the *core* sense— and is therefore not yet the *full* sense. Given this, it is clear that Marion's problems with Being and God result from his misunderstanding Being as something fixed and finished. As shown in this book, however, "Being" is a word that has an *expressum* as an *explicandum:* God then becomes visible not as something other than Being, as beyond Being, or anything similar, but instead as *fully explicated Being, esse plenum.*

It is highly typical that Marion does not consider Augustine's statements about *essem, esses,* even though he himself quotes them. In not doing so, he misinterprets and distorts Augustine's thought.

[6] The substantive conclusion to be drawn from the preceding analyses of relevant passages from Marion's book on Augustine and more generally from Marion's entire conception of creation is the following: Marion's position is both the expression and the result of an uncompromising *refusal to think.* Unlike Augustine, Marion fails to explain the genuine presuppositions of the thought of creation as recognized through praise and confession and as implemented in an existential manner of living. He thereby deprives this thought of its core sense with the result that he builds only a castle in the air. More generally formulated: Marion's ceaseless attempt to avoid at absolutely any price relying on "the

metaphysical lexicon [*lexique de la métaphysique*]" (*LS*, "Avertissement," 11), "the lexicon of being(s), . . . of Being [*le lexique de l'étant, . . . de l'être*]" leads to results that are not only unacceptable but are also destructive for what he wants to maintain.

This can be shown summarily. It turns out that by his refusal to thematize the dimension of Being, Marion foregoes the possibility of attaining to or even envisaging, in any way whatsoever, the *actually divine God.* That is, when he refuses to recognize what is presented above as the core sense of creation, instead reducing creation to gift, praise, and confession, what results is the following: created "things" are thereby viewed fundamentally only as addressees of God, so that God proves to be gift-giving love to which or to whom the created things answer. These created things thereby remain outside God: God remains the distant, fully other, inaccessible, absolutely unknowable X, furnished only with such names as "the impossible," "love/*caritas*," "the gift-giver," etc.—and the created "things" remain other to God, not beings genuinely encompassed within God. Everything that Marion says about creation, even if in beautiful, literarily brilliant, and indeed pious formulations, in no way excludes this radically ultimate otherness of God to *and separateness of God from* the "created things."

As an additional result, God is radically *relativized:* he is no longer truly infinite, because there is something outside of him. Such a God is ultimately a phantom and thus the opposite of what Marion—in absolute opposition to the entire tradition of Christian metaphysics—claims to attain or to envisage, namely, the genuinely divine God. Marion's "God" is precisely *not* the truly divine God. This confirms from a different perspective the result of the analysis provided above (in 4.2.3.3) of his attempt to subject the subject-object relation to a radical reversal: God is thereby thought as a function of (reversed) subjectivity. Such a "God" is not the truly divine God.

This radical contradiction can be overcome only if the absolute fact that "things" are completely encompassed within God is truly and radically thought through. This cannot be done if "things" are thematized in an indeterminate manner simply as "gifts" that are said not to be beings; it requires the thematization instead of all of reality—and that means being(s) and Being, all that is. One could then say that created things are *beings* that, fully explicated, prove to be *beings-as-gifts.* The fundamental giving of the creator God consists precisely in his having posited and in his sustaining contingent beings within Being. Showing this requires the development of a comprehensive conception of Being in order to fully clarify creation.

An additional consequence can be stated concisely: Marion's radical attempt to avoid even "the lexicon of beings, . . . of Being" and the refusal to think based on it prevent him from overcoming, in a superior, positive, and creative manner, the weaknesses and "incongruities" (Heidegger) of all positions in the metaphysical tradition (including Aquinas's).

[7] This section concludes with an attempt—one that is daring in a specific respect—to give a brief indication of one reason—possibly the decisive reason—from which one could develop an explanation of why and how Marion arrives at his unquestionably peculiar conception. The articulation of the reason is found in the "Avertissement" at the beginning of his book *Au lieu de soi*. The relevant passage is the following:

> [In the course of his philosophical development Marion was led] to pose the question about the limits of metaphysics and to bring into view the possibility of its transgression. This question poses itself with greater clarity within the framework of phenomenology than within the framework of the history of philosophy: if one wants to get beyond generalities, i.e., pure approximations and indeed ideological deviations [*dérives idéologiques*], one must discover phenomena, describe them, and identify and isolate those that—in part or radically—evade the objectivity and beingness [*étantité*] sought (practiced) by metaphysics. (*LS* 9)

Marion's maximally general and undifferentiated critique of "metaphysics" could not fail to be included in such a text. Enough is said about that above. The decisive point in this passage is the reference to phenomenology and the task that then emerges: to discover, to describe, and to identify phenomena that are not infected by metaphysics. This is an accurate characterization of the status of Marion's mode of thinking. The questions that press here are the following: Is the concept of the phenomenon clear and load-bearing? Is the discovery, description, and identification of phenomena tantamount to the understanding or conceiving of phenomena? Is the intelligibility of any subject matter (no matter how it is designated) thereby attained? This book answers all these questions in the negative. These negative answers are at the heart of the book's critical analysis of Marion's conception.

4.2.5 Conclusion: "The Chief Idolatry: The Idolatry of Being Itself"?

This book's lengthy consideration of Marion's philosophical-theological conception concludes by quoting and commenting on a passage from Marion's essay "The Impossible for Man—God." The passage includes some of the most astonishing and most arbitrary statements that can be encountered in philosophical (and theological) literature. Marion speaks of theism and atheism in order then to identify both of them as idolatries, the difference between them being that atheism is a negative idolatry, whereas theism is a positive idolatry. He then introduces the fiercest of his astonishing and arbitrary statements, the one quoted in part in the title to this section. The passage merits being quoted at length:

> Whenever theism tries to reach conceptual formulations that are definitive and dogmatic, it condemns itself to idolatry no less than does atheism. The two differ from one another only as a positive idolatry differs from a negative idolatry. Whether or not we decide in favor of God's existence seems at first blush to make a meaningful difference, but the difference turns out, in truth, to be indifferent, as soon as we recognize that in both cases the conclusion is reached only on the basis of defining or conceptualizing God's presumed "essence." Both conclusions thus ratify the same dogmatic *idolatry*. Both cases also assume that "Being" and "existing" signify something that is knowable to us even when applied to "God"—which is not self-evident in the least and betrays a *second idolatry*, namely the *chief idolatry, which is the idolatry of Being itself*. ("IM–G" 22–23; emphasis added)

The first of two remarks this passage requires concerns what Marion says about theism and atheism. He there commits an elementary and weighty error of interpretation. As chapter 1 shows about the traditional so-called proofs of God's existence, as chapter 3 (3.2.2a) shows about the inconclusive so-called ontological proof and its unexplained presuppositions, and as this chapter (4.2.4.3[6]) shows about Marion's attempted reinterpretation of the ontological proof, all exhibit the same confusion in simply identifying what their conclusions putatively prove to exist with God. Marion thus falls prey to the same confusion that plagued Aquinas and so many other authors. Marion distorts traditional theism and therefore fails to develop the critique that this theism deserves. No known traditional proof of God's existence presupposes even a concept, must less a definition, of God; instead, they proceed from specific principles and phenomena and develop arguments purporting to prove the existence of an X, assuming that the conclusions follow from the accepted principles in conjunction with the selected phenomena. In Aquinas's five ways, this X is the first mover, the first cause, the necessary being (*ens necessarium*), etc. The word "God" is then immediately introduced, as connected with a meaning that it derives *not* from the arguments, but from elsewhere. Aquinas, for example, means by "God" the Christian God. God, as understood independently of the proof, is then simply identified with the X whose existence is said to have been proved. This book terms that identification a methodological error.

Marion fails to notice that he applies a wholly analogous procedure, albeit one burdened with an additional error. When he proceeds philosophically, as he does—at least fundamentally (excluding the "Conclusion")—in "The Impossible for Man—God," he "argues" (in his manner) in such a way that he ends up at a or the dimension of the impossible (in the transcendental-phenomenological sense). Then, however—as shown above—he simply identifies "the impossible" with "God": "The impossible, as the concept above all concepts, designates what we know only by name—God" ("IM–G" 26; see 4.2.4.3[2]–[4], above). This is an error analogous to that made by Aquinas (and other metaphysicians), but it is a far more serious error.

There is a significant distinction between Aquinas's methodological error and Marion's error. If one situates the passages wherein Aquinas makes his error within the context of his thought as a whole, it is clear that the error is not serious; it is no more than an inexactitude. Aquinas makes the identification within a concrete process of explication. In fact, he further develops his conception in such a way that the conclusions of the five ways are increasingly further determined, such that at the philosophical end of this development the determination *creator* appears. There is then a methodological turning point—the acceptance of revealed truths—which constitutes the transition to theology and the yet further determination of what has rightly come to be named "(Christian) God."

This brief characterization of Aquinas's position makes clear that it is simply senseless to say, as Marion does in the passage quoted above, that a definition and a concept *God's essence* is presupposed. Aquinas absolutely does not presuppose a definition or a concept of God's essence; as explained above, only by taking many steps does he arrive at the articulation of what could (following scrupulous analysis of the relevant concept) be called "God's essence."

Marion's identification of "the impossible" with "God," on the other hand, is a punctual leap that is wholly unmediated in every respect: he leaps from "the impossible" to "God," who is then immediately identified with God-as-*caritas*/love. It remains wholly unclear how this leap takes place: is it (still) philosophy? Is it (already) theology? The question of the theoretical justification or at least of the theoretical explanation of what is supposed to happen here is unavoidable—but Marion does not answer it.

There is an additional problem, also serious, that arises from the assertions in the passage quoted above about atheism/theism and concepts in relation to God. The problem is with Marion's repeatedly asserted thesis that God is above all concepts. It suffices here to note that subsection 4.2.4.3[5] exposes Marion's unclarities, ambiguities, and incoherences as regards concepts and definitions, especially with respect to what he calls "God's sole possible definition."

The second remark required by the passage quoted above targets Marion's fiercest statement and accusation: "The chief idolatry, which is the idolatry of Being itself." This chapter shows at considerable length the thoroughly unfounded and nonsensical character of this statement and accusation. The two main results of this book relevant to this accusation are a positive one and a negative one. Positively, the book shows that the universal dimension of Being is the only unrestrictedly open space or dimension within which God can emerge in the course of philosophical theorization, because God is the full *explicatum/explicans* of Being itself or Being in its fullness. In radical contrast—and this is this chapter's main negative conclusion—according to Marion's conception, God reduces to a function of the framework that he calls the phenomenological approach. This God, precisely in being conceived as absolutely distant, as absolutely other, as absolutely impossible, etc., is an X whose determination is always measured by reversed subjectivity. Marion never reaches a God who really and radically *encompasses* all beings in or of the world/universe, including the subject(s), whether reversed or not. His God is always *the other* for reversed subjectivity, even if this other is suddenly given the wonderful name *love*. The most profound reason for Marion's radical failure is his misrepresentation and rejection of the universal dimension of Being, and this in its turn is due to his misconceived and unsustainable philosophical approach: his brand of phenomenology.

Given this, his talk of the "chief idolatry" and his identification of this idolatry with "the idolatry of Being itself" is wholly unfounded, incoherent, and nonsensical. This assertion of his is not philosophically tenable and indeed not even philosophically discussable. Historically considered, it is based on an ignorance and distortion of the tradition of Christian metaphysics that one might reasonably have thought to be impossible at present for any philosopher treating the issue of Being and God. Substantively or systematically considered, it collides with insoluble problems that cannot be rationally avoided by means of stereotypically repeated catchphrases and rhetorical-polemical formulations.

Works Cited

Achinstein, Peter. *The Nature of Explanation*. Oxford: Oxford University Press, 1983.

Aertsen, Jan A. "Die Transzendentalienlehre bei Thomas von Aquin in ihren historischen Hintergründen und philosophischen Motiven." In *Thomas von Aquin*, edited by A. Zimmermann and K. Kopp. Berlin: de Gruyter, 1988.

Anselm of Canterbury. *Opera omnia*. Edited by F. S. Schmitt. Unchanged photomechanical reprint of the Seckau edition, Rome. Tome 1, volumes 1–2. Stuttgart–Bad Cannstatt: Frommann Verlag (G. Holzboog), 1946ff.

———. *Proslogion*. In *Opera omnia*, tome 1, volume 1.

Bärthlein, Karl. *Die Transzendentalienlehre der alten Ontologie. Teil I: Die Transzendentalienlehre im Corpus Aristotelicum*. Berlin: de Gruyter, 1973.

Baudoux, Bernardus. "*Philosophia 'Ancilla Theologiae.'*" *Antonianum* 12 (1937): 293–326.

Bigelow, John. "God and the New Math." *Philosophical Studies* 82 (1996): 127–54.

Brandom, Robert. *Making It Explicit: Reasoning, Representing, and Discursive Commitment*. Cambridge, Mass.: Harvard University Press, 1994.

Brugger, Walter. *Summe einer philosophischen Gotteslehre*. Munich: Johannes Berchmans Verlag, 1979.

Bultmann, Rudolf, and Martin Heidegger. *Briefwechsel 1925–1975*. Edited by Andreas Grossmann and Christof Landmesser, with a foreword by Eberhard Jüngel. Frankfurt am Main: Klostermann; Tübingen: Mohr Siebeck, 2009.

Caimi, Mario. "Gedanken ohne Inhalt sind leer." *Kant-Studien* 96 (2005): 135–46.

Candlish, Stewart. "The Truth About F. H. Bradley." *Mind* 98 (1989): 331–38.

Cantor, Georg. "Beiträge zur Begründung der transfiniten Mengenlehre." In *Mathematische Annalen* 46 (1895): 481–512; 49 (1897): 207–46. Cited edition: G. Cantor. *Gesammelte Abhandlungen*. Edited by Ernst Zermelo and Adolf Fraenkel. Berlin: Springer, 1932, 282–356.

Capelle, Philippe. *Finitude et mystère*. Paris: Les Éditions du Cerf, 2005.

———. *Philosophie et théologie dans la pensée de Martin Heidegger*. Paris: Les Éditions du Cerf, 1998.

Caputo, John D. "God Is Wholly Other—Almost: *Différance* and the Hyperbolic Alterity of God." In *The Otherness of God*, edited by Orrin F. Summerell. Charlottesville: University Press of Virgina, 1998, 190–205.

Cartwright, Richard. "Speaking of Everything." *Noûs* 28 (1994): 1–20.

Chalmers, David J., David Manley, and Ryan Wasserman, eds. *Metametaphysics: New Essays on the Foundations of Ontology*. Oxford: Clarendon, 2009.

Coreth, Emerich. *Metaphysik: Eine methodisch–systematische Grundlegung.* 2nd edition. Innsbruck: Tyrolia Verlag, 1964.

Cupitt, Don. *After All.* London: SCM, 1994.

———. "Can We 'Go Beyond Language'?" In *Is God Real?* edited by Joseph Runzo. London: Macmillan, 1993.

De Lacoste Lareymondie, Guillaume. "Portrait de saint Augustin en proto–phénoménologue." www.nonfiction.fr-article–2104–p4–portrait_de_saint_augustin_en_proto_phenomenologue.htm (accessed December 30, 2009).

De Lubac, Henri. "Le mystère du surnaturel." *Recherches de Science Religieuse* 36 (1949): 80–121.

———. *Le mystère du surnaturel.* In *Oeuvres complètes,* volume 12. Paris: Les Éditions du Cerf, 2006.

———. *Surnaturel: Études historiques.* Paris: Aubier, 1946.

De Raeymaeker, Louis. "La profonde originalité de la métaphysique de S. Thomas d'Aquin." In *Miscellanea Mediaevalia,* volume 2. Berlin, 1963, 14–29.

Descartes, René. *Meditations on First Philosophy.* Translated by John Cottingham. Cambridge, Eng.: Cambridge University Press, 1986.

———. *Oeuvres de Descartes.* Edited by Charles Adam and Paul Tannery. Volume 5. Paris: Vrin, 1964.

Diels, Hermann, ed. *Die Fragmente der Vorsokratiker.* Volume 1. 12th edition. Dublin: Weidmann, 1966.

Dodd, Julian. "Farewell to States of Affairs." *Australasian Journal of Philosophy* 77 (1999): 146–60.

Duden: Die Grammatik. 7th fully newly reworked and expanded edition. Mannheim: Dudenverlag, 2005.

Fabro, Cornelio. "L'originalité de l'*esse* Thomiste." *Revue Thomiste* 64 (1956): 240–70, 480–507.

Forrest, Peter. *God Without the Supernatural: A Defense of Scientific Theism.* Ithaca, N.Y.: Cornell University Press, 1996.

Fössel, Thomas. *Gott—Begriff und Geheimnis: Hansjürgen Verweyens Fundamentaltheologie und die ihr inhärente Kritik an der Philosophie und Theologie Karl Rahners.* Innsbruck: Tyrolia Verlag, 2004.

Frege, Gottlob. *The Foundations of Arithmetic.* Selections in *The Frege Reader,* edited by Michael Beaney. Oxford: Blackwell, 1997, 84–129.

Geiger, Louis B. *La participation dans la philosophie de S. Thomas d'Aquin.* 2nd edition. Paris: Vrin, 1953.

Gettier, Edmund. "Is Justified True Belief Knowledge?" *Analysis* 23 (1963): 121–23.

Gilson, Étienne. *L'être et l'essence.* Paris: Vrin, 1948.

Grim, Patrick. *The Incomplete Universe: Totality, Knowledge, and Truth.* Cambridge, Mass.: MIT Press, 1991.

Grover, Dorothy, Joseph L. Camp, Jr., and Nuel Belnap. "A Prosentential Theory of Truth." *Philosophical Studies* 27 (1975): 73–125.

Gschwandtner, Christina M. *Reading Jean-Luc Marion: Exceeding Metaphysics.* Bloomington: Indiana University Press, 2007.

Hawking, Stephen. *A Brief History of Time: From the Big Bang to Black Holes.* New York: Bantam, 1988.

————. *The Universe in a Nutshell.* New York: Bantam 2001.

Hegel, G. W. F. *Berliner Schriften 1818–1831.* Edited by Johannes Hoffmeister. Hamburg: Meiner, 1956.

————. *Hegel's Science of Logic.* Translated by Arnold V. Miller. London: Allen & Unwin; New York: Humanities, 1969.

Heidegger, Martin. *BT. Being and Time.* Translated by John Macquarrie and Edward Robinson. 1927; New York: Harper, 1962.

————. *Cont. Contributions to Philosophy (From Enowning).* Translated by Parvis Emad and Kenneth Maly. 1936–38; Bloomington: Indiana University Press, 1999.

————. *GA. Gesamtausgabe.* Frankfurt am Main: Klostermann, 1975ff.

————. *ID. Identity and Difference.* Translated by Joan Stambaugh. 1957; New York: Harper and Row, 1969.

————. "OTLCM." "The Onto-theo-logical Constitution of Metaphysics." In *ID,* 42–74.

————. *PM. Pathmarks.* Edited by William McNeill. Cambridge, Eng.: Cambridge University Press, 1998.

————. *TB. On Time and Being.* Translated by Joan Stambaugh. 1969; New York: Harper and Row, 1972.

————. *Early Greek Thinking.* Translated by David Farrell Krell and Frank A. Capuzzi. New York: Harper and Row, 1975.

————. *The Fundamental Concepts of Metaphysics: World, Finitude, Solitude.* Translated by William McNeill and Nicholas Walker. 1929; Bloomington: Indiana University Press, 1995.

————. *Geschichte der Philosophie von Thomas von Aquin bis Kant: Marburger Vorlesung 1926/27.* Edited by H. Vetter. *GA,* volume 23, 2006.

————. *Introduction to Metaphysics.* Translated by Gregory Fried and Richard Polt. New Haven, Conn.: Yale University Press, 2000.

————. *Kant and the Problem of Metaphysics.* Translated by Richard Taft. Bloomington: Indiana University Press, 1997.

————. *The Metaphysical Foundations of Logic.* Translated by Michael Heim. 1928; Bloomington: Indiana University Press, 1984.

————. *Mindfulness.* Translated by Parvis Emad and Thomas Kalary. London, New York: Continuum, 2006.

————. *Off the Beaten Track.* Translated by Julian Young and Kenneth Haynes. 1950; Cambridge, Eng.: Cambridge University Press, 2002.

————. *Poetry, Language, Thought.* Translated by Albert Hofstadter. New York: Harper and Row, 1975.

————. *The Principle of Reason.* Translated by Reginald Lilly. 1957; Bloomington: Indiana University Press, 1991.

————. *The Question Concerning Technology.* Translated and with an introduction by William Lovitt. New York: Garland, 1977.

————. *What Is Called Thinking?* Translated by J. Glenn Gray. New York: Harper, 1976.

————. *What Is Philosophy?* Translated by William Kluback and Jean T. Wilde. 1956; New York: Twayne, 1958.

―――. "Zürcher Seminar." In *Seminare,* edited by C. Ochwaldt. *GA,* volume 15, Supplement, 1986, 423–39.

Horwich, Paul. *Truth.* 2nd edition. Oxford: Oxford University Press, 1998.

Husserl, Edmund. *The Crisis of European Sciences and Transcendental Phenomenology.* Translated by David Carr. 1937; Evanston, Ill.: Northwestern University Press, 1970.

―――. *Husserliana, Gesammelte Werke.* The Hague: M. Nijhoff, 1950ff.

―――. *Ideas I: Ideas Pertaining to a Pure Phenomenology and to a Phenomenological Philosophy: First Book.* Translated by Fred Kersten. 1913; The Hague: M. Nijhoff, 1983.

Hyman, John. "Wittgensteinianism." In *A Companion to Philosophy of Religion,* edited by Philip L. Quinn and Charles Taliaferro. Oxford: Blackwell, 1997, 150–57.

Kant, Immanuel. *CPuR. Critique of Pure Reason.* Translated by Paul Guyer and Allen Wood. Cambridge, Eng.: Cambridge University Press, 1998. Following long-standing practice, "A" indicates the first (1781) edition, "B" the second (1787).

―――. *Proleg. Prolegomena to Any Future Metaphysics That Will Be Able to Come Forward as Science.* Translated and edited by Gary Hatfield. Revised edition. Cambridge, Eng.: Cambridge University Press, 2004.

Keller, Albert. *Sein oder Existenz? Die Auslegung des Seins bei Thomas von Aquin und in der heutigen Scholastik.* Munich: Hueber, 1968.

King, Martin Luther, Jr. *The Papers of Martin Luther King, Jr.* Volume 2: *Rediscovering Precious Values, July 1951–November 1955.* Edited by Clayborne Carson and Peter Holloran. Berkeley: University of California Press, 1994.

Krause, Karl Christian Friedrich. *Vorlesungen über das System der Philosophie.* Göttingen: Dieterich, 1828.

Kreiner, Armin. *Das wahre Antlitz Gottes—oder was wir meinen, wenn wir Gott sagen.* Freiburg: Herder, 2006.

Küng, Hans. *DGE. Does God Exist?* Translated by Edward Quinn. Eugene, Ore.: Wipf and Stock, 2006.

Leask, Ian, and Eoin Cassidy, eds. *Givenness and God: Questions of Jean-Luc Marion.* New York: Fordham University Press, 2005.

Leibniz, Gottfried Wilhelm. *Principes de la nature et de la grâce, fondés en raison.* In G. W. Leibniz, *Die philosophischen Schriften,* edited by C. I. Gerhardt. Hildesheim: Olms, 1965, volume 6, 598–606.

Levinas, Emmanuel. *OTB. Otherwise Than Being: or, Beyond Essence.* Translated by Alphonso Lingis. The Hague: M. Nijhoff, 1981. Original French edition: *Autrement qu'être ou au-delà de l'essence.* The Hague: M. Nijhoff, 1974.

―――. *TI. (Totality and Infinity). Totalität und Unendlichkeit: Versuch über die Exteriorität.* Freiburg: Alber Verlag, 1987. Original French edition: *Totalité et infini: Essai sur l'exteriorité.* The Hague: M. Nijhoff, 1965.

―――. *Ethics and Infinity: Conversations with Philippe Nemo.* Translated by Richard Cohen. Pittsburgh: Duquesne University Press, 1985. Original French edition: *Éthique et infini: Dialogues avec Philippe Nemo.* Paris: Fayard, 1982.

―――. "God and Philosophy." In Levinas, *Of God Who Comes to Mind,* 55–79.

————. *Of God Who Comes to Mind.* Translated by Bettina Bergo. 2nd edition. Stanford, Calif.: Stanford University Press, 1998. Original French edition: *De Dieu qui vient à l'idée.* Paris: Vrin, 1982.

————. *Time and the Other.* Translated by Richard A. Cohen. Pittsburgh: Duquesne University Press, 1987. Original French edition: *Le temps et l'autre.* Montpellier: Fata Morgana, 1979.

Lewis, David. *On the Plurality of Worlds.* Oxford: Blackwell, 1986.

Lowe, E. J. *The Four-Category Ontology: A Metaphysical Foundation for Natural Science.* Oxford: Oxford University Press, 2006.

Mackie, John L. *The Miracle of Theism: Arguments for and Against the Existence of God.* Oxford: Clarendon, 1982.

Maréchal, Joseph. *Le point de départ de la métaphysique.* Volume 5: *Le Thomisme devant la philosophie critique.* Brussels: L'Édition Universelle, 1949.

Marion, Jean-Luc. BG. *Being Given: Toward a Phenomenology of Givenness.* Translated by Jeffrey L. Kosky. Stanford, Calif.: Stanford University Press, 2002. Original French edition: *Étant donné: Essai d'une phénoménologie de la donation.* Paris: Presses Universitaires de France, 1997.

————. GWB. *God Without Being: Hors-Texte.* Translated by Thomas A. Carlson. Chicago: University of Chicago Press, 1991. Original French edition: *Dieu sans l'être: Hors–Texte.* Paris: Fayard, 1982.

————. "IM–G." "The Impossible for Man—God." Translated by A. Davenport. In *Transcendence and Beyond: A Postmodern Inquiry,* edited by John D. Caputo and Michael J. Scanlon. Bloomington: Indiana University Press, 2007, 17–43. Original French edition: "L'impossible pour l'homme—Dieu." In *(Révue) Conférence* 18 (2004): 329–69.

————. LS. *Au lieu de soi: L'approche de Saint Augustin.* 2nd corrected edition. Colléction Épimethée. Paris: Presses Universitaires de France, 2009.

————. "PhS." "Le phénomène saturé." In Jean-Luc Marion, *Le visible et le révélé.* Paris: Éditions du Cerf, 2005, 35–74.

————. "SP." "The Saturated Phenomenon." Translated by Thomas A. Carlson. *Philosophy Today,* Spring 1996: 103–24. Original French edition: "PhS."

————. "ThA-OT." "Saint Thomas d'Aquin et l'onto-théo-logie." *Revue Thomiste* 95 (1995): 31–66.

————. "L'autre philosophie première et la question de la donation." In *Le statut contemporain de la philosophie première,* edited by Philippe Capelle. Centenaire de la Faculté de Philosophie, Institut Catholique de Paris. Paris: Beauchesne, 1996, 29–50.

Metz, Johannes Baptiste. *Christliche Anthropozentrik: Über die Denkform des Thomas von Aquin.* Munich: Kösel Verlag, 1962.

Mojsisch, Burkhard, ed. *Kann Gottes Nichtsein gedacht werden? Die Kontroverse zwischen Anselm von Canterbury und Gaunilo von Mormoutiers.* Latin and German; translated and commented on by B. Mojsisch. Mainz: Dieterich, 1989.

Mondin, Battista. *La metafisica di S. Tommaso d'Aquino e i suoi interpreti.* Bologna: Edizioni Studio Domenicano, 2002.

Montagnes, Bernard. *La doctrine de l'analogie de l'être d'après Saint Thomas d'Aquin.* Louvain Publications Universitaires. Paris: Béatrice-Nauwelaerts, 1963.

Nagel, Thomas. *The Last Word.* New York: Oxford University Press, 1997.

———. *WDIAM. What Does It All Mean? A Very Short Introduction to Philosophy.* Oxford: Oxford University Press, 1987.

Nicholas of Cusa. *De docta ignorantia.* Edited by E. Hoffmann and R. Klibansky. *Opera omnia,* volume 1, 1945.

———. *Opera omnia.* Leipzig: Meiner, 1932ff.

Pannenberg, W. *Systematische Theologie.* Volume 1. Göttingen: Vandenhoeck & Ruprecht, 1988.

Pascal, Blaise. *Oeuvres complètes.* Edited by J. Chevalier. Bibliothèque de la Pléiade. Paris: Gallimard, 1954.

———. *Pensées: The Provincial Letters.* New York: Random House, 1941.

Philipps, Dewi Zephaniah. *God Without Explanation.* Oxford: Blackwell, 1976.

Pickavé, Martin, ed. *Die Logik des Transzendentalen.* Festschrift for Jan Aertsen. Berlin: de Gruyter, 2003.

Plantinga, Alvin. *WCB. Warranted Christian Belief.* Oxford: Oxford University Press, 2000.

———. *Warrant and Proper Function.* Oxford: Oxford University Press, 1993.

———. *Warrant: The Current Debate.* Oxford: Oxford University Press, 1993.

Puntel, Lorenz Bruno. *GThW. Grundlagen einer Theorie der Wahrheit.* Berlin: de Gruyter, 1990.

———. *SGTh. Auf der Suche nach dem Gegenstand und dem Theoriestatus der Philosophie.* Tübingen: Mohr Siebeck, 2007.

———. *Analogie und Geschichtlichkeit: Philosophiegeschichtlich-kritischer Versuch über das Grundproblem der Metaphysik.* Freiburg im Breisgau: Herder, 1969.

———. *Darstellung, Methode und Struktur: Untersuchungen zur Einheit der systematischen Philosophie G. W. F. Hegels.* Bonn: Bouvier Verlag Herbert Grundmann, 1973; 2nd edition 1981.

———. "Der Wahrheitsbegriff: Ansatz zu einer semantisch-ontologischen Theorie." *Deutsche Zeitschrift für Philosophie* 50 (2002): 871–91.

———. *Structure and Being: A Theoretical Framework for a Systematic Philosophy.* Translated by and in collaboration with Alan White. University Park: Penn State University Press, 2008. German original: *Struktur und Sein: Ein Theorierahmen für eine systematische Philosophie.* Tübingen: Mohr Siebeck, 2006.

———. "Truth, Sentential Non-Compositionality, and Ontology." *Synthese* 126 (2001): 221–59.

———. *Wahrheitstheorien in der neueren Philosophie: Eine kritisch-systematische Darstellung.* Darmstadt: Wissenschaftliche Buchgesellschaft, 1978; 3rd edition, expanded by an extensive appendix, 1993; special edition 2005.

Quine, Willard Van Orman. *Ontological Relativity and Other Essays.* Revised and enlarged edition. Cambridge, Mass.: Harvard University Press, 1980.

———. *Philosophy of Logic.* Englewood Cliffs, N.J.: Prentice-Hall, 1970.

———. *Pursuit of Truth.* Cambridge, Mass.: Harvard University Press, 1990.

Quinn, Philip L., and Charles Taliaferro, eds. *A Companion to Philosophy of Religion.* Oxford: Blackwell, 1997.

Rahner, Karl. "Existenzial, übernatürliches." In *Lexikon für Theologie und Kirche.* 2nd edition, 1959. Volume 3, column 1301.

————. *Grundkurs des Glaubens: Einführung in den Begriff des Christentums.* Freiburg: Herder, 1976.

————. "Natur und Gnade." In *Schriften zur Theologie,* volume 4, 209–36. Einsiedeln: Benziger, 1960.

Rayo, Agustín, and Gabriel Uzquiano, eds. *Absolute Generality.* Oxford: Clarendon, 2006; reprint 2009.

Renard, Jules. *Journal 1887–1910.* Edited by L. Guichard and L. Sigaux. Paris: Gallimard, La Pléiade, 1960.

Romanos, George D. *Quine and Analytic Philosophy.* Cambridge, Mass.: MIT Press, 1983.

Runzo, Joseph, ed. *Is God Real?* New York: St. Martin's, 1993.

Sartre, Jean-Paul. *Existentialism Is a Humanism.* Translated by Carol Macomber. New Haven, Conn.: Yale University Press, 2007.

Schelling, F. W. J. *Zur Geschichte der neueren Philosophie—Münchner Vorlesungen* (1827). In *Schellings Werke,* edited by Manfred Schröter. Munich: Beck'sche Verlagsbuchhandlung, 1965, volume 5, 71–270.

Schrijvers, Joeri. "Ontotheological Turnings? Marion, Lacoste and Levinas on the Decentering of Modern Subjectivity." *Modern Theology* 22 (2006): 221–54.

Sellars, Wifred. "Empiricism and the Philosophy of Mind." In *Minnesota Studies in the Philosophy of Science,* volume 1, edited by Hans Feigl and Michael Scriven. Minneapolis: University of Minnesota Press, 1956, 253–329.

Sheehan, Thomas. "A Paradigm Shift in Heidegger Research." *Continental Philosophy Review* 32 (2001): 183–202.

Smith, Quentin. "Atheism, Theism and Big Bang Cosmology." *Australasian Journal of Philosophy* 69 (1991): 48–66.

————. "The Uncaused Beginning of the Universe." *Philosophy of Science* 55 (1988): 39–57.

Spaemann, Robert. *Der letzte Gottesbeweis.* Munich: Pattloch, 2007.

Ströker, Elisabeth. *Husserls transzendentale Phänomenologie.* Frankfurt am Main: Klostermann, 1987.

Swinburne, Richard. *The Existence of God.* Oxford: Clarendon, 1979.

Tarski, Alfred. "The Concept of Truth in Formalized Languages." In A. Tarski, *Logic, Semantics, Metamathematics: Papers from 1923 to 1938.* Oxford: Clarendon, 1983, 152–278.

Thomas Aquinas. *De pot. Quaestiones disputatae de potentia.* Edited by P. M. Pession. Turin: Marietti, 1953.

————. *De ver. Quaestiones disputatae de veritate.* Edited by R. Spiazzi. Turin: Marietti, 1964.

————. *ScG. Summa contra Gentiles—Summe gegen die Heiden.* Edited and translated by K. Albert and P. Engelhardt. Darmstadt: Wissenschaftliche Buchgesellschaft, 1974ff.

————. *STh. Summa Theologiae.* Edited by P. Caramello. Turin: Marietti, 1952.

————. *Die Gottesbeweise aus der "Summe gegen die Heiden" und der "Summe der Theologie."* Translated with introduction and commentary by Horst Seidl. Hamburg: Meiner, 1982.

―――. *In duodecim libros Metaphyisicorum Aristotelis expositio*. Edited by R. M. Spiazzi. Turin: Marietti, 1964.

―――. "In librum Boetii De Hebdomadibus expositio." In *S. Thomae Aquinatis Opuscula Theologica*, edited by R. M. Spiazzi. Turin: Marietti, 1954.

―――. *In octo libros Physicorum Aristotelis expositio*. Edited by P. M. Maggiòlo. Turin: Marietti, 1954.

―――. "On the Eternity of the World." In *On the Eternity of the World*. Translated and with an introduction by C. Vollert, L. H. Kendzeirski, and P. M. Byrne. Milwaukee, Wis.: Marquette University Press, 1964, 19–26.

―――. *Opuscula Philosophica*. Edited by R. M. Spiazzi. Turin: Marietti, 1954.

―――. *Von der Wahrheit: De veritate (Quaestio I)*. Latin-German. Translated and edited by Albert Zimmermann. Hamburg: Meiner, 1986.

Van Inwagen, Peter. "Being, Existence, and Ontological Commitment." In *Metametaphysics: New Essays on the Foundations of Ontology*, edited by David J. Chalmers, David Manley, and Ryan Wasserman. Oxford: Clarendon, 2009, 472–506.

Van Velthoven, Theo. *Gottesschau und menschliche Kreativität: Studien zur Erkenntnislehre des Nikolaus von Kues*. Leiden: Brill, 1977.

Von Balthasar, Hans Urs. *The Glory of the Lord: A Theological Aesthetics*. San Francisco: Ignatius, 1965/1982–1991.

―――. *Truth of God*. Volume 2 of *Theo-Logic*. Translated by Adrain J. Walker. San Francisco: Ignatius, 1985/2004.

Welte, Bernhard. "Zum Seinsbegriff des Thomas von Aquin." In B. Welte, *Auf der Spur des Ewigen: Philosophische Abhandlungen über verschiedene Gegenstände der Religion und der Theologie*. Freiburg: Herder, 1965, 185–96.

Williamson, Timothy. *Knowledge and Its Limits*. Oxford: Oxford University Press, 2000.

―――. *The Philosophy of Philosophy*. Oxford: Blackwell, 2008.

Wisser, Richard, ed. *Martin Heidegger im Gespräch*. Freiburg: Alber Verlag, 1970.

Wittgenstein, Ludwig. *Culture and Value*. Translated by Peter Winch. Chicago: University of Chicago Press, 1980.

―――. *Notebooks 1914–1916*. Edited by G. H. Von Wright and G. E. M. Anscombe, with an English translation by G. E. M. Anscombe. New York: Harper and Brothers, 1961.

―――. *Philosophical Investigations: The German Text, with a Revised English Translation*. Translated by G. E. M. Anscombe. Oxford: Blackwell, 2001.

―――. *Schriften*. Frankfurt am Main: Suhrkamp, 1969ff.

―――. *Tractatus Logico–Philosophicus*. Translated by David F. Pears and Brian F. McGuinness. New York: Routledge, 1962.

Index

absolute, the, 45, 230, 237, 342
absolute freedom, 94, 237, 242–43, 254, 260, 264–65, 319–23
absolute idea, 74
absolute idealism, 335, 337, 341
absolutely necessary Being, 4, 97, 146, 230, 231–37, 243, 260–61
absolutely necessary dimension of Being, 232–37, 243, 251, 260–61, 264, 270
absolutely universal dimension, 185, 189, 193–94, 226, 232, 391
absoluteness, 249, 353, 390
  of the phenomenon (Marion), 368
absolute nothingness, 67, 228–29, 237
Achenstein, Peter, 209
actus essendi, 41, 258, 310
Aertsen, Jan A., 212
aestheticity, 350
aesthetics, theological, 47, 316
all-is-contingent thesis, 228–29
analogy, 46, 231, 255–58, 298, 309, 353, 387–88
  doctrine of, 242, 255, 258, 298
analytic philosophy, 4, 31, 161, 165, 174, 192, 194, 197, 206, 221–24
Anaximander, 144
anima quodammodo omnia, 186
Anselm of Canterbury, 55, 201–6, 381–82
anti-realism, 150
appearance, 104–5, 266, 334, 336–68, 350–51, 355, 356, 358, 370
approaches to the issue of God, 9
  anti-metaphysical, 303–4, 391
  anti-systematic, 12, 51
  anti-theoretical, 51
  direct, 9, 11, 14–29, 49, 51, 78–79
  inadequate, 11–64
  indirect, 9, 12–13, 28, 30, 34, 47–51

  non-systematic, 14–29
  partially systematic, 9, 12–13, 30, 34
  purely systematic, 13
  semi-systematic, 47–51
Aquinas. *See* Thomas Aquinas, Saint.
Aristotle, 18, 71, 186, 217, 242, 259, 307
atheism, 16, 57, 128, 297, 406–8
attribute, 126, 162, 200, 202, 254, 259, 297
Augustine, 213, 316, 391, 398–99, 402–3
Austin, John. L., 196
Avicenna, 187, 213

Barth, Karl, 16, 258
Bärthlein, Karl, 212
Baudoux, Bernardus, 275
Baumgarten, Alexander Gottlieb, 32, 44
Bayes's theorem, 50
beauty, 36, 217
beginning, 4, 17, 74, 83–84, 106, 238, 247–50
Being
  absolutely necessary, 4, 97, 146, 230, 321–37, 243, 260–61
  absolutely necessary dimension of, 232–37, 243, 251, 260–61, 264, 270
  act of, 41, 257–58, 310
  and being(s), xxi–xxii, 66–67, 80–81, 91–99, 219
  and *Ereignete(s)*, 140, 142
  and *esse*, 126, 187, 303, 378
  and existence, 193, 194–97, 291–93, 369
  and God, 3, 7, 47, 65, 122–23, 124–29, 130–31, 145, 230, 252–54, 280, 302–3, 305–6, 307, 308–9, 316–17, 318–19, 330, 336, 369–70, 403
  and ground, 75–77

Lorenz B. Puntel is professor emeritus of philosophy at the University of Munich.

Alan White is Mark Hopkins Professor of Philosophy at Williams College.